Russian: A Linguistic Introduction

This book provides an accessible introduction to the linguistic structure of Russian in all its aspects, including its history, dialects and sociolinguistics, as well as the central issues of phonology, morphology, syntax and word formation/lexicology. It particularly emphasises the special linguistic features of Russian which are not shared with English and other non-Slavonic languages. For intermediate/advanced students of Russian, this will help to reinforce their understanding of how all levels of Russian function. Students and scholars of linguistics will find it a useful starting point for comparative work involving the structure of Russian and the Slavonic languages, or issues such as standardisation, multilingualism and the fate of former colonial languages. Each chapter begins with an introduction to the basic theoretical concepts of the area covered, presenting the linguistic facts and relationships in an easily accessible form. It will also serve as a learning aid to Cyrillic, with all examples transliterated.

PAUL CUBBERLEY is Senior Research Fellow in Russian in the School of Languages, University of Melbourne, and Former Senior Lecturer in Russian at the University. His publications include *Handbook of Russian Affixes* (1994), *The Suprasegmental Features in Slavonic Phonetic Typology* (1980) and articles in journals including *Scottish Slavonic Review, Russkii iazyk za rubezhom, Wiener Slawistischer Almanach, Russian Language Journal, Australian Slavonic and East European Studies* and *New Zealand Slavonic Journal*.

Russian: A Linguistic Introduction

Paul Cubberley

CAMBRIDGE
UNIVERSITY PRESS

PUBLISHED BY THE PRESS SYNDICATE OF THE UNIVERSITY OF CAMBRIDGE
The Pitt Building, Trumpington Street, Cambridge, United Kingdom

CAMBRIDGE UNIVERSITY PRESS
The Edinburgh Building, Cambridge CB2 2RU, UK
40 West 20th Street, New York, NY 10011-4211, USA
477 Williamstown Road, Port Melbourne, VIC 3207, Australia
Ruiz de Alarcón 13, 28014 Madrid, Spain
Dock House, The Waterfront, Cape Town 8001, South Africa

http://www.cambridge.org

First published 2002

Printed in the United Kingdom at the University Press, Cambridge

Typeface Times 10/12 pt   *System* LATEX 2$_\varepsilon$ [TB]

A catalogue record for this book is available from the British Library

ISBN 0 521 79191 X hardback
ISBN 0 521 79641 5 paperback

Dedicated to the many cohorts of students who have led
me to whatever degree of intelligibility and coherence is
now resident in this description . . .
and to my ever-patient wife, never critical of the time
I gave to them or it.

Contents

Maps

Tables

Acknowledgements

My thanks go to my former colleagues and continuing supporters Roly Sussex and Robert Lagerberg for their comments on various aspects of this work as it took shape, and to Kate Brett who set it in motion and cared for it as it gestated. The final content is of course my sole responsibility.

Abbreviations and symbols

- Case and number quoted together are reduced to initial capitals, e.g. NP = Nominative Plural; accompanying gender is indicated by a lower-case initial, e.g. NPn = Nominative Plural Neuter.
- Person and number quoted together are reduced to lower-case letters following the number, e.g. 3pp = 3rd Person Plural.

Abl	Ablative Case
Acc	Accusative Case
Act	Active voice
Adj	Adjective
Adv	Adverb
Amer Eng	American English
Anim	Animate
Aor	Aorist Tense (Old Russian)
Bg	Bulgarian
Br	Belarusian
Brit Eng	British English
BS	Balto-Slavonic
B(V)	Back (Vowel)
C	Consonant
coll.	colloquial
Cond	Conditional Mood
Conj	Conjunction
CR	Central Russian (dialect)
Cr	Croatian
CSR	Contemporary Standard Russian
Cz	Czech
Dat	Dative Case
Du	Dual
Eng	English
Fem	Feminine
Fr	French

FSU	Former Soviet Union
Fut	Future Tense
F(V)	Front (Vowel)
IE	Indo-European
Imp	Imperfect Tense (Old Russian)
Ital	Italian
Gen	Genitive Case
Germ	German
Gk	Greek
Imper	Imperative Mood
Impf	Imperfective Aspect
Inan	Inanimate
Inf	Infinitive
Instr	Instrumental Case
Intr	Intransitive
Lat	Latin
lit.	literally (word-for-word translation)
Lith	Lithuanian
Loc	Locative Case
Mac	Macedonian
Masc	Masculine
N	Nasal
Neut	Neuter
Nom	Nominative Case
NP	Noun phrase
NR	Northern Russian (dialect)
Obj	Object
OCS	Old Church Slavonic
OCz	Old Czech
OEng	Old English
OP	Old Polish
OR	Old Russian
Part	Participle
Pass	Passive Voice
Perf	Perfect Tense (Old Russian)
Pers	Person
Pf	Perfective Aspect
Plup	Pluperfect Tense (Old Russian)
Plur	Plural
Pol	Polish
PPA	Past Participle Active
PPP	Past Participle Passive

Prep	Prepositional Case
Pres	Present Tense
PresPP	Present Participle Passive
Pron	Pronoun
PS	Proto-Slavonic
RCS	Russian Church Slavonic
Refl	Reflexive Voice
RF	Russian Federation
Rus	Russian
SC	Serbian/Croatian (or former Serbo-Croatian)
Serb	Serbian
Sing	Singular
Sk	Slovak
Sn	Slovenian
Son	Sonorant
Sorb	Sorbian
SR	Southern Russian (dialect)
Subj	Subject
Subjve	Subjunctive Mood
Sup	Supine
Trans	Transitive
Ukr	Ukrainian
V	Vowel
Vb	Verb
VP	Verb phrase

Symbols

[ ]	phonetic transcription, using IPA
/ /	phonemic transcription, using ISO
{ }	morphemic transcription, using ISO

These formal symbols are used only where essential; for most purposes, italics are used for transliterated or transcribed forms, as well as for all linguistic examples; English glosses are given within quote marks.

Stress position is marked by a prime (') following the stressed vowel on the transcribed form only (not on the Cyrillic); since this is the principle for Russian words, it is retained for all other situations, including IPA (though this is not the normal IPA procedure).

For transcription and transliteration of Russian Cyrillic, see chapter 2, table 9; for IPA transcription system, see website: www2.gla.ac.uk/IPA/ipachart.html.

Note on transliteration

Details of the transliteration and transcription of Russian Cyrillic will be offered in chapter 2 (section 4.1, table 9). For the purposes of the introductory chapters, where names and words will necessarily appear in transliteration, we mention here the main features which might appear confusing through their use of unfamiliar symbols.

(1) Russian consonants appear in two varieties, most commonly referred to as hard/soft or ±Palatalised (or ±Sharp); the soft or palatalised variants are indicated in syllable-final positions variously by a following acute accent, apostrophe or prime; we will use the acute. Thus *rus'* is to be understood as ending in a soft [sʲ].

(2) The palatal consonants, like English *sh* or *ch*, are represented by a diacritic borrowed from the Czech alphabet (where it is called a 'hook') placed over the underlying sound, e.g. *š, ž, č*, for Eng *sh, zh, ch*.

(3) The symbol *j* represents the palatal fricative or glide (the *jot* or *jod* sound), that is the strong *y* of Eng *yes*.

(4) The symbol *x* represents the voiceless velar fricative, usually written *kh* in Eng.

(5) The symbol *c* represents the affricate usually written *ts* in Eng.

(6) Vowels do not present any difficulties, but note that *y* always represents roughly the first vowel in Eng *cynic, sin*.

(7) Stress position is indicated by a prime (') written *after* the stressed vowel.

Introduction

1 The Russian language in the world

Russian is currently spoken by some 150 million speakers as their first language in the FSU, by a further 100 million as a second language in the FSU, and at least a further half-million as first language in other countries (of emigration), notably the USA, Canada, Australia and Israel.

Since the break-up of the FSU in 1991 and the subsequent failure (to date) of the new Russian Federation (or simply 'Russia') to establish itself as an economic competitor on the world stage, interest in the language outside the FSU has dropped rather dramatically, to the point where large numbers of university departments of Russian have been closed or at least drastically cut; this applies even to the non-Slavonic states of the FSU and to the former satellite states of Eastern Europe, in all of which Russian was the first foreign language, compulsory in all basic schools. This means that the number of students of the language worldwide has been decimated, a situation which will not change until Russia sets its economic house in order and again takes a place in world commerce. While it seems clear that this will not happen in less than a generation, it seems equally clear that it will happen eventually, given the size and resources of the country. When it does, there will again be an external demand for those with a knowledge of Russian, and not simply for speakers of the language, but also for those with a linguistic understanding of it, who can become the next generation of teachers and language specialists.

The fact remains that Russian continues to be a language of major interest on many levels: it remains the language of a major world literature, with a still active literary culture, indeed one which is now free of the bonds of the socialist realism of the Soviet days and able to reflect in literature as honestly and freely as any western country the concerns of their society; it remains the language of a very active scientific community which, in spite of its economic restrictions, continues to produce a prodigious quantity of research in all areas; it remains the language of a vast country with great tourist potential, in many ways already functioning more easily than in the Soviet period, when all sorts of restrictions on travel clearly presented too great an obstacle for many; while

1

1 Russian Federation

travel is still more difficult at the practical level than it should be, this, too, can only improve; finally, in the, hopefully unlikely, event of a return to a cold-war situation, we would see a reinstatement of the need for specialists in the 'language of the enemy'. In other words, there is every bit as much point in non-Russians learning Russian now as there has ever been, and most would say a lot more.

2   Russia

The Russian Federation (Rossijskaja federacija) covers European Russia, the Caucasus, Siberia and Far Eastern Russia, thus from the Baltic Sea in the west to Vladivostok in the east, and from Archangel in the north to the Caucasus in the south (see map 1). In the non-European part (usually taken as east of the Ural Mountains, conventionally regarded as the dividing line between Europe and Asia, or east of the lower Volga), Russian has been imposed over the local languages in the same way as any other colonial language in the history of colonialism. The local languages have survived in similar fashion as elsewhere, possibly somewhat better during the Soviet period, when support for local ethnic groups and their languages was an official policy. For an overview of these languages and their balance with Russian, see Comrie 1981 or the websites of the University of Texas or the Library of Congress.

As for the European part of the federation (see map 2), it is essentially (except for the Caucasian republics) what is referred to simply as Russia (*Rossija*). Note that there are two Russian adjectives which are rendered 'Russian' in English: 'rossijskij' – derived from the place name *Rossija* – is the geo-political term referring loosely to the federation as a whole or, more correctly, to the Russian republic within it; and 'russkij' – derived from the old ethnonym 'rus'' – is the ethnic and linguistic term.

3   Russian

Russian is a member of the Slavonic group of Indo-European languages, which includes also European groups such as Germanic, Romance, Celtic and Baltic, Indic languages such as Sanskrit and Hindi, and Iranian languages such as Persian and Ossetic, and the isolated languages Greek, Armenian and Albanian. As a first cousin of the other European groups, it therefore does not differ greatly from them in respect of most major linguistic features: it does not have sounds which might be called alien or non-European (like pharyngeals, clicks, etc.); its grammatical system is essentially familiar, certainly if one relates it to Latin or Greek – in other words it is at most somewhat more archaic than the other main groups; and its lexical stock is essentially European, with other elements acquired from its particular location, associations and history just like all the others.

2 European Russia

It is often said that the Slavonic group has moved (physically) least of all
the European branches of IE, though this does depend on the perceived starting
point of that branch; the original homeland of IE has been taken to be either Eastern Anatolia (in Asia Minor) (or the 'Fertile Crescent' of Mesopotamia) or the
South Russian steppes (north of the Black Sea), the former being more popular;
most other aspects of its history are likewise unclear and disputed, from the time
of its expansion (anywhere between 4,000 and 8,000 years ago) to the direction
of expansion: from the Russian steppes west into Europe and east into Asia,
and south via the Caucasus into Asia Minor and India (Gimbutas); or from Asia

Minor west across the Dardanelles into the Balkans, thence north into central and eastern Europe, north via the Caucasus into Asia and south to India (Renfrew); or, in a more recent variant of the last itinerary, all future Europeans except the Greeks and Albanians went north through the Caucasus into the Russian steppes (Gamkrelidze and Ivanov). Further, this dispersal has typically been regarded as a military expansion by mounted nomads, and thus very fast; but more recently it has been seen as a slow agriculture-based expansion (Renfrew 1987). In this view it would have taken some 3,000 years for the European Indo-Europeans to reach Britain and Scandinavia. There may have been a mixture of driving forces, indeed Renfrew limits the agricultural principle to the European group, starting from Greece; and if we accept the Caucasian route for the Europeans, the agricultural view is less convincing. Assuming the Asia Minor starting point, most likely there was expansion both into the Balkans and via the Caucasus into the South Russian steppes – as well as eastwards into Asia, as evidenced by the location of some later IE Iranian groups, like the Sarmatians and Scythians, and probably including the speakers of the (extinct) language known as Tocharian, in Chinese Turkestan.

The Caucasian route would mean that the Slavs were the group which stayed in the Ukrainian steppe area while the future Germanic, Celtic and Romance groups continued westwards and the future Balts northwards; the Balkan route would mean that they, with the Balts, split off eastwards (to the same Ukrainian area) while the rest went west. The movement of the Slavs northwards and westwards (into present-day Polish and Czech regions) would have occurred later, as a more military expansion at the expense of other Europeans, as opposed to the assimilation of the previous non-Indo-European inhabitants of northern Europe. The strictly northern expansion brought the Slavs into contact – again – with the Balts. There is a possibility that the original move to the Baltic area was accomplished by a group which might be called Balto-Slavs, since the very close linguistic ties between the Slavonic and Baltic groups are often put down to a period of common heritage; more scholars, however, regard these similarities as explicable by a (relatively later) period of adjacent living (possibly 1500BC to AD 500; see Shevelov 1964).

Mention should be made of an alternative view of the Slav homeland which places it much further north and west than the Ukrainian steppe, roughly in southern Poland. This view has been put mainly by Polish archaeologists (e.g. Jażdżewski) and tends to be regarded by most others as unlikely. More popular is the view that the Slavs expanded into these areas somewhat later.

As for the Slav presence in the Balkans, that is well documented, as it dates from relatively recent times – from the early sixth century AD. It was the Slavs who took greatest advantage of the collapse of the Hun empire by promptly filling the vacuum to their south. They soon became the major population of the Balkans, having penetrated right to the southernmost parts, and even as far as Crete. From then until the late ninth century there was a north–south Slav continuum from the Baltic to the Aegean. Then the invasion of the Magyars – the future Hungarians – inserted a wedge between the northern group and the Balkan group, and this wedge was subsequently infiltrated also by Germanic peoples – the future Austrians. By then, the Balkan Slavs were established in their present lands – Bulgaria and northern Macedonia in the east, and Serbia, Croatia, etc. in the west. By that time, too, the Bulgarians, originally Turkic invaders of the Balkans from Asia via the north of the Black Sea in the late seventh century, had become completely assimilated to the Slav majority. Over the next couple of centuries the Slavs themselves were assimilated to the Greeks in Greece proper (the south of Macedonia), though there are still (or again) Slavs living on modern Greek territory in that area.

The linguistic evidence separates the Slavs into three main groups corresponding to the above movements – East, West and South (see map 3): the eastern group are those who remained in the Ukrainian steppe area and those who (later) expanded northwards to the Baltic and to a certain extent also east and northeast, into former Finnic territory, now Russia proper; the western group are those who expanded westwards into central and northern Europe, as far as the Elbe, between the second and sixth centuries; and the southern group is the Balkan one. In terms of the modern languages involved, the groups are related as follows: the eastern group includes Russian, Ukrainian and Belarusian, the last of these occupying the area between the Ukrainian and the Baltic groups; the western group includes Polish and Sorbian in the north and Czech and Slovak in the south; and the southern, Balkan, group includes Bulgarian and Macedonian in the east and Serbian, Croatian, Bosnian and Slovenian in the west.

Hence Russian is the language of the most northeasterly branch of the Slavs. In the southwest its neighbour is Belarusian (formerly called in English Belorussian – including by Comrie and Corbett 1994), the border being roughly 30° E; in the south Ukrainian (border roughly 55° N and as far as 35° E); in the southeast Russian-speaking territory runs down as far as the Caucasus area – 42° N; in the northwest the border at 30° E is with Finnic speakers, and in the east the border is roughly 60° E (the Urals), beyond which is non-Slav (mainly Altaic/Turkic) territory. (See map 2 above for European Russia; chapter 6, map 4 for language borders; and chapter 1 for historical details.)

4   Russian within linguistics

Russian was relatively slow (within the European group) to become an object of linguistic interest in its home context. The first grammars of the language appeared only in the mid-eighteenth century, the first major dictionary at the end of that century (see chapter 1). While there were practical grammars and lexicons at earlier dates (from the late sixteenth century), they were either, in

3 Modern Slavonic languages

fact, of the language known as Church Slavonic (see chapter 1) or were bilingual lexicons of limited areas. Even in the nineteenth century there was relatively little activity in this direction, and it was really only in the twentieth century that matters changed. As in most European countries, the main linguistic interest in the nineteenth century was historical, some of the main names being Vostokov, Buslaev and Sreznevskij for historical grammar; for synchronic description Aksakov and Potebnja; and for linguistic theory Boduen de Kurtene (Baudouin de Courtenay). In the early twentieth century come important synchronists like Šaxmatov and Ščerba, and the famous comparativist Fortunatov, while the early Soviet period has names like Trubeckoj (Trubetzkoy) and Jakobson, both early émigrés who settled respectively in Vienna and Brno, where they were instrumental in the foundation of the famous Prague School of Linguistics (in 1926). Jakobson's subsequent move to the USA in 1941 was to be the inspiration for a primary interest in Russian by generations of US linguists, through the contribution of Russianists to general linguistics; the most notable example is perhaps Morris Halle, who worked with Jakobson and Chomsky (of Russian descent, though not a Russianist) on general phonological matters (e.g. Jakobson, Fant and Halle 1952, Jakobson and Halle 1956, Chomsky and Halle 1968) as well as on Russian in his own right (e.g. Halle 1971). The first experiments on machine translation, conducted at Georgetown University, used Russian as their model. One of the foundation works on translation theory made great use of Russian examples (Catford 1965).

The later (postwar) Prague school continued to be influential in general linguistic theory – for example, with its development of the notion of Functional Sentence Perspective, and, unsurprisingly, being Slavs, continued to use Russian, as well as Czech, as the demonstrator of the theory.

Within the USSR there was a lively linguistic community, involved as much with linguistic theory as with the description of Russian. Only the fact that not a lot of that activity found itself translated into English prevented it from occupying a much more prominent place in mainstream linguistics than it did. Those western linguists who could read Russian, and in particular the Russianists themselves, were in a position to utilise the material. Some of those whose works have appeared in English are (with dates of English versions): A.V. Gladkij (*Formal Grammars and Languages*, 1978; *Elements of Mathematical Linguistics*, 1983 (with I. Mel'chuk)), I.I. Revzin (*Models of Language*, 1966), Iu.D. Apres'jan (*Principles and Methods of Contemporary Structural Linguistics*, 1973; *Lexical Semantics*, 1992; *Syntactic Lexicography*, 2000).

5   Readership

There exist many textbooks and descriptions of the language of all sorts which will be there for some time to come to cater for any rise in demand for practical courses (see General descriptions section of the bibliography); there do not, however, exist many books – certainly not in English – aimed at providing an overall linguistic view of the language, that is, a view of the language which will provide the understanding of its structure which is essential for potential teachers and specialist users. While it is of course possible to teach a language using a more or less direct or communicative method which avoids 'explaining' anything about its structure to students, and it is even possible for those taught in this fashion to teach it in turn, rather as an uninformed native speaker would be able to 'teach' it, I remain convinced that the most efficient and effective teachers are those who understand the linguistic structure of the language in question, even if they opt for a methodology which avoids explicitly communicating this structure to students, and be they native speakers or second-language users. Native speakers, of course, have access to similar descriptions in the first language, of which there are a great many, but, if they are teaching or using the language in an English-language context, there are some advantages in consulting a book written in English, mainly for English users, not only for the terminology, but for the whole 'way of looking at' the language as a foreign linguistic system. This, then – students and teachers of Russian – is the first group of readers to whom this book is addressed.

A second group are those who are not directly or professionally involved with Russian, but see it as a language of intrinsic linguistic interest, representing a major language, and related to a very large group of major languages, with particular features of interest at all linguistic levels, and diachronically as well as synchronically – in other words, those with a professional or amateur interest in linguistics or language studies, seeking knowledge of another important area for purposes of comparison or broadening of horizons.

Given these two groups as our central readership, it follows that our approach will not assume a professional competence in linguistics, but rather will attempt to elucidate theoretical linguistic approaches to description with a minimum of specialist terminology. Where useful, the relevant terms will of course be used and/or explained.

Similarly, in respect of recommended further reading, we will concentrate on English-language references, offering Russian or other sources only in particular cases.

6 Structure and aims

We will attempt to offer a 'story line' of the Russian language; as far as possible we will follow the pedagogical practice of proceeding from basic to complex, known to unknown, familiar to unfamiliar, using English as the given (assuming not necessarily native English, but only a knowledge of English sufficient to read such a book as this). The diachronic aspect will be ever-present, for two reasons:

first, this is a direct contribution to the story line in the temporal sense; second, it is my conviction, supported by extensive teaching experience, that a general comprehension of the historical dimension – not necessarily a detailed under-standing – contributes directly to an understanding of the synchronic structure, and indeed in some cases, for example morphophonology, is indispensable. Further, many readers may be directly interested in the diachronic view, and, while this is not a historical grammar of Russian, and its single chapter on the history of the language cannot but be very general, the interspersing of histori-cal information as appropriate throughout the synchronic description allows a much broader coverage of it without, it seems to me, departing from the central synchronic aim.

Also present at all stages of description will be comment of a contrastive na-ture, again using mainly English as the point of comparison; here, too, the thrust is pedagogically based, on the grounds that comparison allows a clearer view of the structural similarities and differences. Where appropriate, comparison with other languages, including other Slavonic languages will be offered; the latter are of interest in this respect in that their relationship to Russian allows comparison to act as an entry-point for deeper interest in the other language. In this way much of the content may also serve as (mini-)introductions to the other Slavonic languages.

In many cases the differences between languages are the areas where learners have problems, so that highlighting them may usefully lead to suggestions for handling the learning aspect of the language. As this is not in fact a textbook of Russian, this side of things will necessarily not occupy a central place in the description, but the step from description to application – in this case to learning or acquisition – is not large.

Chapter 1 covers the history in a non-linguistic as well as a very general linguistic way, covering the relevant history of the country and of the literary or standard language, including the writing system and orthography; it describes the main linguistic features retained or lost from Proto-Slavonic. Chapters 2–5 describe the standard levels of Russian – phonology, morphology, syntax and word-formation/lexicology; that order is the normal English descriptive prac-tice, and while it differs slightly from the logical 'story-line' one – which would be: sounds, formation or acquisition of words, inflecting words for syntactic purposes, and syntax proper – we find it preferable to treat the morphemic concepts common to morphology and word-formation under 'morphology'. Chapter 6 considers the Russian dialectal situation, including consideration of the dialects as alternative developments (to the standard) from the Old Russian period. Thus the story line *within* these chapters is provided by historical refer-ence, and the story line *across* them by their logical order, and also by means of interrelations between the levels, for example via morphophonological alterna-tions or inflection. Each of these sections includes some comments on stylistic factors, since stylistics as a separate section would have to cover all levels and thus be repetitive; they also include appropriate indications of the current trends (dynamics) within the given level. Chapter 7 (Sociolinguistics) concludes the story of Russian by pursuing this last topic: what is currently changing and where and how it is changing. It covers attitudes towards standardisation and variation, and questions of interference from contact languages, whether at home or abroad, in the former case with particular reference to the changing status of Russian within the FSU and the Russian Federation, and includes some basic elements of modern Russian 'pragmatics'.

1   History of the language

The transcription used in this chapter is transliteration, based on the Slavic linguistic variant of ISO R9 (see chapter 2, table 9).

1   Historical background (important dates for the language)

From the time of the Slav expansion into the Balkans (sixth century) until the mid-ninth century there were only rare instances of the Slavs setting up any sort of formal state: in the early seventh century (after the defeat of the Avars in 623) the western Slavs in the Bohemian and Moravian area set up one under Samo, which lasted thirty-five years, ending with Samo's death in 658 (Schenker 1995); in 680 was formed the Bulgarian Khanate of Asparuch, initially not Slav, but which later (early ninth century) became a Slav kingdom lasting until the early eleventh century (1014). As for the eastern Slavs, they were living generally in tribal groupings until the mid-ninth century, at which time, according to the legend of the early chronicles, those living in the area of Novgorod invited the 'Norsemen', or Vikings, also known as Varangians, to come and help them establish a state; the date given for this invitation is 860, and the first incoming Norsemen arrived in Novgorod between then and 862. The first ruler in Novgorod was allegedly Rurik (Scandinavian 'Hrørekr'), who was succeeded by his son (or possibly other kinsman) Oleg in 879. In 882 Oleg transferred his seat to Kiev (taking over by force from Varangians Askold (Hoskuldr) and Dir), and this date is taken as the start of the state known as Kievan Rus' (*Kievskaja Rus'*). An alternative view – held strongly by Soviet historians – was that the Kievan state had been formed before the arrival of the Varangians, whose initial role was that of mercenaries in the pay of particular tribes; of these Askold and Dir were the first to take political power – by force – in Kiev, followed by Oleg in Novgorod, then Kiev, as noted above; and that the whole Novgorod 'invitation' – including the person of Rurik – is no more than a legend added later to the revised chronicle. These opposing views are referred to as the 'Normanist debate' (see Stokes 1976, Rybakov 1965).

Even the origin of the name 'Rus'' is disputed: for some it was in fact the name applied to the Scandinavians, and probably indeed a Scandinavian ethnonym in origin, which then found itself attached to the inhabitants of the state, and in turn to the state itself; for others – again mainly Soviet – it reflects an old Slavic tribal name, with the variant 'Ros', from which was formed later the toponym 'Rossija' (fifteenth century), based on the European Latin-style nomenclature of states. All the early rulers (and their consorts) following Rurik have slavicised Scandinavian names, e.g. Oleg, Ol'ga, Igor', Gleb, gradually replaced by native formations, usually compounds of a high-flown sort, e.g. Vladimir 'great in power', Jaroslav 'renowned for ferocity', Jaropolk '(leader of) a fierce army', Svjatopolk '(leader of) a pious army', Mstislav 'avenger of honour'. Sometimes southern Slav names were used, e.g. Boris, and then Christian(-style) names, e.g. Jurij (George), Andrej (Andrew), Ivan (John).

Kievan Rus' was a federative state, initially very loose, made up of many principalities, all accepting the predominance of the prince of Kiev, known as the Grand Prince (*Velikij knjaz'*). Over the next 250 years the state survived with various high and low points – the principle high points being the reigns of the strong grand princes Vladimir I (the Great) (980–1015) – which saw the 'Baptism' of the state (that is, its official acceptance of Christianity), Jaroslav I (the Wise) (1036–54) – during which there was a flowering of religious culture and the first code of laws (known as *Russkaja Pravda*), and Vladimir II and his two sons Mstislav and Jaropolk (1113–39). After Jaropolk's death the squabbling over the Kievan principality – there were seventeen princes of Kiev over the next thirty years – brought the state to a very weak condition, during which many other principalities began to vie for superiority in their own right, as opposed to trying to acquire the Kievan one. This brought several northern principalities to the forefront: that of Novgorod became independent in 1136, and from the 1150s those of Vladimir and Suzdal' (north-east of Moscow) became dominant, leading via the sack of Kiev in 1169 and the dominance of Vladimir-Suzdal' from the 1170s to the acceptance of Jurij of Vladimir-Suzdal' as Grand Prince in 1218. In theory the Kievan state was still functioning, but in reality it had completely lost any unified strength.

Moscow first appears in the story in 1147, when a chronicle entry describes it as a small town with a castle on the Suzdal' border; it was then set up as a defence fortress in 1156 by Jurij Dolgorukij (or his son Andrej Bogoljubskij, the one who sacked Kiev).

In 1237 the effective death-blow was dealt to the state by the arrival of the Tatar-Mongols (commonly known in English as Tartars), who took every major town in Kievan Rus' over the next three years and were to keep the whole area under their subjugation for the next 250 years, the period known in Russian history as the 'Tatar yoke'. However, in fact the Rus' princes mostly simply paid tribute to the Tatars and were allowed to go about their business, which continued to include struggling amongst themselves for supremacy. It also included fighting other foes, like the Swedes or the Livonian knights whom

Aleksandr Nevskij (of Novgorod) defeated in 1240 and 1242. Aleksandr became Grand Prince in 1252, beginning a period of Novgorod supremacy over all the north. In 1271 his son Daniil (or Danilo) moved his court to Moscow. Meanwhile the symbolic end for Kiev came when the Metropolitan of the Church moved his seat from Kiev to Vladimir in 1299. In 1326 the seat of the Metropolitan was moved to Moscow, and in 1328 the prince in Moscow (Ivan II) declared himself 'Prince of Vladimir and all Russia' at the same time as another invader was occupying Russian territory: the Lithuanians moved into the south-west of Russia, ultimately taking Kiev in 1380. This date is also significant for the 'north', for in that year the Russians defeated the Tatars in battle for the first time, in the famous Battle of the Don, near Tula, that is, actually in the south(-east) of the still unoccupied part. However, this was a purely symbolic victory, as the Tatar yoke was to remain in place for a further century. Further, an alliance between the Lithuanians and Poles allowed the Poles to take over control of much of the south – mostly the future Ukraine, while the Lithuanians retained the west, mostly the future Belorussia (Belarus).

During that period the one development of importance was not a political one, but one which concerned the cultural life, and thus the language, of the Russians: late in the fourteenth century there began to arrive in Moscow southern Slavic churchmen from the Balkans, fleeing the invading Ottoman Turks. While we know only a few by name, they exerted an influence which was to prove most important, in that they were able to introduce into the Russian Church elements of the ascetic tradition of the Hesychastic movement of Greece (centred mainly on Mt Athos); these included an attempt to restore the purity of church books by reinstating what were perceived to be the pristine forms of their language. (See section 3.2 below for details.)

Only in the 1460s did the next important politically based development occur – the reign of Ivan III, from 1462 to 1505. This reign saw the final defeat and official renunciation of subservience to the Tatars (1480) and the taking of Novgorod (1478) and of other major northern towns, making Moscow supreme for the first time. Ivan began to refer to himself as 'Tsar' of all Russia', and to Moscow as 'the new Constantinople' or 'the third Rome', that is, as the successor to Constantinople/Byzantium as the world's centre of (Orthodox) Christianity. Ivan's son and successor, Vasilij III, completed the task of making Moscow the master of all the remaining 'free' area of 'Russia', that is, of the part not occupied by the Lithuanians and Poles. The next tsar, Ivan IV (the Terrible) was the first to retake some of the occupied territory, including the Khanate of Kazan' from the Tatars in 1552 and some of the south-east from the Poles in the 1570s (immediately following the formal union of Lithuania and Poland in 1569); the colonisation of Siberia began in 1584. In 1654 Ukraine (whose name originally meant simply 'borderland, frontier', and was applied especially to this south-western border) managed to gain independence from Poland, and the eastern part of it (known as the 'Cossack Host') became an autonomous province within Russia, to which Kiev was added via treaty in 1667.

By this time, both Ukraine and Belorussia had gone their own way linguistically, not so much at the spoken as at the literary level, as they had missed out on the neo-southern Slavonic influence that the north had received (see section 3.2 below). On the other hand, they, but especially Ukraine under Polish control, had had access to the western European culture and religion of Poland. This in turn was to contribute to the next injection into the language and culture of Moscow under Pëtr I (Peter the Great), who effectively (though not formally) incorporated the independent Ukraine in 1709, and it subsequently became an important element in his 'Europeanisation' or 'westernisation' of Russia as a linguistic conduit for much of that culture. Peter's reign also saw the start of the occupation of the Baltic coast, where he set up his new capital of St Petersburg in 1703; but, more importantly in our context, it marks the start of the separation of church and state in 'cultural' matters, including language and its writing. Peter introduced a 'civil script' (*graždanskij šrift*) to be used for non-religious publications, set up the first newspaper and laid the ground for the establishment of the Academy of Sciences, founded in the year of his death, 1725.

The story of Russia from then is one of continual expansion and political consolidation, and that of the Russian language one of the business of normativisation and standardisation, which does in theory place it ahead of the same processes in most other Slav countries, which had to wait until the national movements of the nineteenth century to work out their standards. However, it was really only in the nineteenth century that Russian itself finally established its standard forms, and the whole eighteenth century was a battleground in this respect (see below).

In summary, therefore, the following are the crucial periods in Russian history which have a bearing on the development of the standard language:
(1) sixth–ninth centuries: the eastern Slavs live separated from the western Slavs by the geographical boundaries of the Pripet marshes in the north and the Carpathian mountains in the south, and so develop certain dialectal features of their own; internally there would have been some special local features at the extremes, especially via contact with non-Slavs in the north and east.
(2) ninth–fourteenth centuries: the state of Kievan Rus' maintains the overall linguistic direction of all its constituent areas. The language of the state is known (now) as Old Russian. Nevertheless there is clearly already a south versus north dialectal division.
(3) fourteenth–sixteenth centuries: the occupation of the western and southern parts by the Lithuanians and Poles creates a political separation which puts the north-east and the south-west on different linguistic paths, at the spoken level possibly simply emphasising already existing differences, at

the written level introducing quite different ones. The rise of Moscow as a centre with a northern dialectal base, but attracting southern dialectal speakers, gives rise to a transitional dialect group, referred to as 'central'.

(4) seventeenth–eighteenth centuries: the formation of a strong Russia, open to the west and with a growing empire; the start of the standardisation process, with the freeing of the literary language from religious-based ties; the opening-up to western borrowings.

(5) nineteenth–twentieth centuries: the establishment of the modern norms.

2   Linguistic features

Note the following terms and their abbreviations.

Proto-Slavonic/Common Slavonic: usage is divided between those who distinguish between the terms 'Proto-Slavonic' and 'Common Slavonic' and those who use one or the other exclusively. For the former group the difference is one of age: Proto-Slavonic refers to the oldest situation, Common Slavonic to the latest stage before the break-up. This is most typical of Slavonic, especially Russian, usage, where the relevant terms are 'praslavjanskij' and 'obščeslavjanskij'. For our purposes a single term will suffice, as we will be setting out in this chapter the developments over the whole period, without dwelling on questions of chronology, leading us to the East Slavonic stage, which will be the basis for observations within each language level of modern Russian; we will use Proto-Slavonic (as done also by Comrie and Corbett 1993).) As necessary we will refer to (relatively) early and late Proto-Slavonic.

Balto-Slavonic: without entering the debate about whether there was ever a single Balto-Slavonic language stage or simply a period of close association and shared development of Proto-Slavonic and Proto-Baltic, we will use Balto-Slavonic to refer to the common forms which would have occurred during such an intermediate stage of common developments.

Old Russian: refers to the East Slavonic language spoken and written in Kievan Rus' in the period between the tenth and fourteenth centuries.

Old Church Slavonic: refers to the written language based on the Bulgaro-Macedonian Slavonic spoken in the late ninth and tenth centuries; it took on local features as it became used in other areas, giving Russian Church Slavonic, amongst others.

Russian Church Slavonic – the language of religious writing, then also of secular writing, in Russia.

For the sake of simplicity, the tradition of attaching asterisks to reconstructed, hypothetical linguistic forms is abandoned; it is to be assumed that all Indo-European and Proto-Slavonic forms are such.

2.1   Slavonic as an Indo-European dialect

For this earliest period we look at the phonology only.

The first major division of Indo-European languages is into what are called the *centum* and *satem* groups, that is roughly into west and east respectively, the names being based on the word for '100' in Latin and Avestic. These names represent the first major phonological split in the family, namely the different treatment of the palatalised velars, the base Indo-European form for the given word being *k'ṃtom*. The western group converted these into simple velars like [k], the eastern into sibilants like [s]. Slavonic belongs to the *satem* group, the Proto-Slavonic form being *sŭto*.

A second early dialectal feature concerned the treatment of the aspirated voiced stops, like [bʰ], which became fricative in some, plosive in others, including Slavonic, e.g. (stems only) IE *bʰrātr–* 'brother' > Lat *frat(e)r–*, PS *bratr–*. The relative chronology of these first two features is indicated by the development of the aspirated *and* palatalised [gʰ'] into [z] in Slavonic, namely, first, the loss of aspiration, then the assibilation – e.g. **gʰ'eim–* 'winter' > PS *z'eim–*.

A third feature concerns the treatment of the syllabic sonorants, like [r̥], which in Proto-Slavonic became VC (vowel + consonant) sequences, which may be regarded as falling diphthongs whose non-nuclear (semi-vowel) element is a sonorant; the vowel part was a short [i] or [u], possibly (but not clearly, see Shevelov 1964: 86) depending on a front/back quality of the original syllabic sonorant, e.g. *mr̥t–* 'dead/death', Lat *mort–*, PS *mirt–*.

A final important consonantal feature concerned the behaviour of Indo-European [s]: in the eastern group this sound underwent change in certain contexts, namely following the high vowels [i] or [u] and the consonants [r] or [k]. Possibly the context /k— (that is, after [k]) was the first to be affected, the others following through analogical forms. The simplest statement of its Slavonic result is that it became [x] in these contexts; others believe its initial result was [š], as in Balto-Slavonic (Lithuanian). (For detailed argument see Schenker 1995: 80.) For our purposes the traditional statement: s > x /i, u, r, k— will serve well, e.g. IE *ur̥s–* 'summit' > BS *virš–*, PS *virx–*, IE *rek–s–* 'say' Aorist > BS/PS *rekx– > rēx–*.

Within PS it is possible that in some areas plosive [g] early became fricative [ɣ], thus partnering the new [x] rather than the old [k] within the new three-member velar set; if it is not an early feature, it certainly occurs later in those areas, which include part of the East Slavonic region, however the early view facilitates the explanation of certain later developments (see below).

The semivowels [u̯] and [i̯] became consonantal in prevocalic position, namely [w] (immediately or later in some areas > [v]) and [j] respectively, e.g. *u̯l̥kʷ–* 'wolf' > PS *vilk–*, *trei̯e–* 'three' > PS *trej-e*.

In respect of vowels confusion between [o] and [a] was common across many areas; the Slavonic result is, again most simply put, complete fusion into a low back rounded vowel which may be designated /$_o$a/, e.g. *nŏkt–* 'night' > PS *n$_o$ăkt–*, *bʰrătr–* 'brother' > PS *br$_o$ătr–*.

It then makes sense further to describe the low (or mid-low) front vowel /e/ as /$_e$a/ (short and long); this too facilitates the explanation of later developments (as well as making for a 'tidier' phonological picture!).

At the suprasegmental level:

(a) while vocalic quantity remained distinctive in pure vowels, it probably ceased to be so in the vocalic part of diphthongs, as the latter came to be seen as the maximum length – of two morae – of a syllable nucleus;

(b) stress was free, and probably already associated with particular morphemes in a hierarchical way (see Garde 1976);

(c) pitch had first ceased to be distinctive (from having been so in late IE), but had survived at the phonetic level as a concomitant of quantity (long = rising, called 'acute', short = non-rising, called 'circumflex'). With the shortening of the diphthongs, the tonal difference was apparently retained, such that pitch again became distinctive, though only on diphthongs (until the latter became vowels; see below).

Most of the above features were in principle shared with Baltic, though the details are not always identical (e.g. s > š /i, u, r, k— works better for it, and the confusion of [o] and [a] had different results).

Thus, the probable shape of the earliest Proto-Slavonic phonological system was as shown in table 1 (bracketed forms joined by a vertical line are likely dialectal variants).

2.2   Developments within Proto-Slavonic

The following discussion is topic-based rather than chronological, though as far as possible chronological order is followed.

2.2.1   Phonology

A generalisation which may be made in respect of almost all developments – and certainly all the major ones – within Proto-Slavonic is that the syllable boundaries and relations within the syllable altered: the unit of the syllable became more discrete, the boundary was clearly marked by a drop in sonority – that is, syllables became 'open', always ending in a vowel, and the elements within the unit influenced each other directly. No doubt this came about in stages, and at any rate it is useful to describe it as though it developed in such a way.

Table 1 *Early Proto-Slavonic phonological system*

Consonants

	Labial	Dental	Palatal	Velar
Stop	p	t		k
	b	d		(g) ⎤
	m	n		⎮
Fricative		s		x ⎮
	(v) ⎤	z	j	(ɣ) ⎦
	(w) ⎦			
Affricate				
Liquid		r		
		l		

Vowels

	Front	Central	Back
High	ĭ ī		ŭ ū
Mid-high			
Mid-low			
Low	$_e$ă $_e$ā		$_o$ă $_o$ā

Diphthongs

$_o$ăĭ $_e$ăĭ $_o$ău $_e$ău

All short vowels plus r, l, m, n; e.g. ĭr $_e$ăr

Suprasegmental

Stress	Free
Quantity	All pure vowels, not diphthongs
Tone/Pitch	Automatic acute on long vowels;
	diphthongs may have acute or circumflex

2.2.1.1 Velars.

A change which seems logically to predate the syllable restructure is the fronting of the velars in the vicinity (on either side) of a front vowel, e.g. BS *kětū–r–* 'four' > PS *k′$_e$atūr–*; *–ĭkŭ* 'agent suffix' > *–ĭk′ŭ*. Within the revised (open) structure mutual effects across a sonority boundary should be minimal (and those within the unit maximal), so that the influence of a vowel on the following consonant is not expected, hence the second example above should have been in place before the restructuring. We shall see below (section 2.2.1.8) that this particular development of the velars has caused problems in respect of chronology, and the positing of an early stage of fronting across the syllable boundary while it was still weak is useful.

2.2.1.2 Effects of [j]; palatalisation.

The consonant change which was to be a major feature of Slavonic may usefully also be said to begin early, namely the production of palatal consonants (chuintantes/hushers) by fusion with a following [j]; while sequences of C+j would always have been within the new syllable unit, so that this change is not tied to the restructure, it does seem probable that it is a manifestation of an early assimilative tendency which could be the precursor of the syllable restructure.

Again, there are clearly stages in this development: while most subsequent results are common to the whole group, some are not, so we need to indicate the principle in some way, and it is useful to start from fused consonants which are simply palatalised versions of the base consonant, e.g. stops like *p'*, *t'*, *k'*, fricatives like *s'*, *x'* and sonorants like *r'*, *l'*, *n'*.

In a few cases consonant clusters were affected together: for example, it is useful to see the clusters *kt* and *gt* as jointly becoming *t'* at this first stage.

The final stage, producing genuine palatal consonants like the chuintantes, is late, and belongs after the syllable restructure. Some of the results are phonetically 'natural', and occur in many languages, if only at the level of rapid style, e.g. *s'* > *š'*, *z'* > *ž'*, common to all the group; others are less so, for example the labials become clusters of labial plus *l'* – that is, the palatal element is realised as a palatal lateral. There is no agreement about whether this *l'* element was initially common or not: the western group (e.g. Polish, Czech) does not show it except in a few odd cases, so it is possible either that they never developed it and borrowed those few cases, or that they subsequently lost it and these cases are remnants. For the sonorants *r*, *l*, *n* there is no special further development until after the break-up into East, West and South. The velars show mostly common results: all the group has *k'* > *č'* and *x'* > *š'*; the results of *g'* depend on the stop or fricative nature of this phoneme: the stop [g'] gives *dž'* (locally later simplified to *ž'*), the fricative [ɣ'] gives *ž'*. (Note that if the fricativisation of /g/ is allocated only later, it would be then accompanied by the deaffrication of *dž'* to *ž'*; thus, the positing of early local preference for fricative /ɣ/ seems useful.)

2.2.1.3 Palatalisation of velars. The above results of the effect of [j] on consonants may now be expanded to the specific context of the new syllabic structure, within which vowel articulation may (begin to) influence that of preceding consonants: at the most basic level this means simply the palatalising effect of a front vowel of the sort normally producing allophones (cf. the nature of /k/ in Eng *key*, *cut*, *caught*). This is effectively the result for dentals and labials. However, for velars the result was much more drastic, matching the effect of /j/ noted above (and similar to that which occurred in the Romance group, e.g. Lat *camp–* > Fr *champ–*, Lat *cent–* ([kɛ–]) > Fr [s–], Ital [tʃ–]): again, in Proto-Slavonic all areas have *k'* > *č'*, *x'* > *š'* and either *g'* > *dž'* or ɣ' > *ž'*. These changes are traditionally called the 'First Palatalisation of the Velars', and the context is any of the front vowels existing at that point in time, namely high /i/ and low /ₑa /, both either long or short. Further changes to the velars came later, following interim vowel developments (see section 2.2.1.8).

Table 2 *Quantity > Quality*

Old	New	Examples	(Early PS > Late PS)		Other
$_o$ă	o	n $_o$ăkt ĭ	not'ь	'night'	Lat *noct*–
$_o$ā (via oá?)	a	d$_o$ā-t ī	da-ti	'give'(Inf)	Lat *da*-/*don*–
$_e$ă	e	m$_e$ădŭ	medъ	'honey'	Gk *meth*–
$_e$ā (via eá?)	ě ([ä])	s $_e$ād–	sěd–	'sit'	Lat *sed*–
ĭ	ь ([ĭ])	vĭx'ŭ	vьx'ъ	'village'	Lat *vic*–
ī	i	g'īvŭ	živъ	'alive'	Lat *viv*–
ŭ	ъ ([ŭ] or [ə])	dŭkt(er) ĭ	dъt'i	'daughter'	Gk *thugater*–
ū (via uí?)	y ([ɨ])	dūmŭ	dymъ	'smoke'	Lat *fum*–

2.2.1.4 Opening of syllables. The syllable restructure, or the 'opening of syllables', had, not surprisingly, major consequences for all aspects of the phonological system. We have seen some of the effects on the consonants; others include the dropping of word-final consonants (probably one of the earliest) (e.g. IE *(w)ūs* 'you' > PS *vū*; IE NS endings *–us/um* etc. > PS *–ŭ/–ŏ*) and simplification or reorganisation of unacceptable clusters (usually of falling sonority), e.g. IE *wapsa* 'wasp' > PS *osa*; IE/early PS *ved–ti* 'lead' Inf > PS *vesti*.

Changes to the vowels were not actually results of the syllable restructure, but they do occur at the same time, and we shall treat them first, especially since the new vowels are easier to describe and their further developments easier to follow. Furthermore, one view actually sees the vowel changes as having predated the changes to diphthongs, which explicitly supports the following order.

2.2.1.5 Vowel quantity > quality. The system of four pure (i.e. non-diphthongal) vowels with long and short versions was replaced by a system in which quantity ceased to be distinctive and was replaced by qualitative distinctions, though the former length was preserved phonetically, that is, was automatic, or inherent, in the new vowels. It is possible that the long vowels were first converted to falling diphthongs – and this is a very common conversion for languages in general (e.g. OEng *ī* > Eng *aị* as in 'bride', *ā* > *eị* as in 'name'); however, such an unprovable hypothesis does not advance us much. We need simply state the starting and finishing points ('Old' and 'New' in table 2). In the table the 'New' column uses the transcription to be used hereafter for PS phonemes. On the quality of these new vowels, we can see that:
(a) rounding has become distinctive at the low level (assuming that we treat /o/ and /a/ as being of the same level), but for the high vowels, on the contrary, rounding was removed at least from the long /u/, and logically also from the short; however, it could be that the former long/short opposition was replaced by ±Round (short > round for the low, short remains round for the high); the subsequent development of /ə/ leaves its rounding status at this stage unclear;

(b) the short high vowels are generally assumed to have become lowered to mid-high and are less extreme, in other words their quality has been reduced – hence they are frequently referred to as 'reduced vowels' (Rus *reducirovannye*) (their symbols are the Cyrillic letters used for these vowels in Old Church Slavonic); see also point (d) below on their length;

(c) the quality of /ě/ is also a matter of disputation, again because of the variety of later reflexes: most popular is the view that at this stage it was a low front unrounded vowel ([ä]); for others it was a rising diphthong of the [ia]/[iä] type; and for still others, it had already shifted to a higher position in some areas, namely East Slavonic (this is to account for local reflexes; see chapter 2). Its symbol is the modern Czech letter representing its common reflex in Czech;

(d) The quantity of the old vowels continued to reside in the new, thus /a/, /ě/, /i/ and /y/ were inherently long, and the other four short. The subsequent developments of /ъ/ and /ь/ suggest that they were even shorter than /o/ and /e/. However this remains a hypothesis, related presumably to their higher position; the further shortening may have occurred later.

2.2.1.6 Monophthongisation. Diphthongs were prime casualties of the new syllabic structure, since in principle the semivowel second part of a falling diphthong represents a drop in sonority and hence means a closed syllable – at least when followed by a consonant or word boundary – and indeed virtually all such tautosyllabic diphthongs were 'monophthongised' in Proto-Slavonic. We say 'virtually', because it appears that the final stages of this process were overtaken by other changes which reversed the syllabic restructuring process and reinstated closed syllables within the system. The diphthongs which failed to complete the process were those in which the closing element was one of the sonorants *r*, *l*, while the rest changed consistently; the results are as described below (the vowel nucleus of the diphthong is by this stage always short, but the new, derived, pure vowel is phonetically long; other Indo-European languages are shown as evidence of the original diphthong).

(a) *Closed by semivowel (i̯, u̯).*

(Early PS)	Late PS	Examples	
(₀ai̯ > ₑa, i)	oi̯ > ě, i	berěte, beri	'take' Imper 2p, 2s (cf. Gk *feroi-te*)
(ₑai̯)	e > i	iti, id–	'go' Inf, Pres. (cf. Lith *eiti*)
(₀au̯)	ou̯ > u	turъ	'aurochs' (cf. Lat *taurus*)
(ₑau̯)	eu̯ > (j)u	l'udь	'people' (cf. Lith *liaudis*)

For the above at least, one might postulate an intermediate step of conversion to a rising diphthong, that is, the nucleus shifts to the second element; the appearance of *ě* from *oi̯* is sometimes explained by metathesis (inversion of elements), but this cannot explain the rest. For the vowel system, the new /ě/ and /i/ merge with the existing ones from long front vowels (though often they are marked for etymological purposes as /ě₂/ and /i₂/); the new /u/ replaces the /u/ lost by unrounding to /y/; the front /e/ of *eu̯* is reduced to [j], which then, as usual, fuses with the preceding consonant to make a palatal consonant.

(b) *Closed by nasal sonorant* (m, n). As expected (cf. for example French or Polish), the reflex of these is a nasal vowel (NV), with the front or back quality of the nuclear vowel retained (FNV, BNV). The traditional marker of nasality in Slavonic linguistic usage is the subscript hook, taken from the modern Polish alphabet. The underlying symbols are those of the basic (new) mid-vowels *e* and *o* (while modern Polish uses underlying *a* for the back nasal). Thus (with the new vowels inserted as base, and other Indo-European as evidence of the original nasal):

FV (e, ь) +m/n > FNV	ę pętь 'five'	(Gk *pente*)
	desętь 'ten'	(Lat *decem*)
	–męti 'mind, memory'	(Lat *ment–*)
BV (o, ъ) +m/n > BNV	ǫ pǫtь 'way'	(Lat *pont–*)
	gǫsь 'goose'	(Lat *anser*)
	dǫti 'blow' Inf	(Lith *dumti*)

The quality of the underlying vowel may be taken initially to be mid-low *e*, *o*. The former height of the nuclear vowel is irrelevant, that is, height is irrelevant for the new nasals (newly acquired nasality being complication enough). The front/back opposition is reinforced within the system, as also is ±Round.

(c) *Closed by liquid sonorant* (r, l). This set of diphthongs is reflected in various distinct ways over the whole group, indicating that it had its final realisation after the beginning of the break-up of the group, though the motive force of syllable opening belongs to the unified period (before the sixth century, since the period of break-up is roughly sixth to ninth centuries). The relative lateness in the opening of this type of diphthong may be related to the phonetic nature of the liquid sonorants, which are particularly able to function as nuclei themselves – witness the many languages, especially Slavonic ones, in which both /r/ and /l/, or at least /r/, may be nuclei, e.g. Czech, Slovak, Serbian/ Croatian, Macedonian. The proposed interim stage of a shift to rising diphthong, as suggested above (section 2.2.1.6), is most easily accepted for these. However, the fact is that these diphthongs did in principle shift in different ways to open the syllable.

In this set, the height of the nuclear vowel *is* relevant. Perhaps the lateness of the results means that the new vowel system is well in place by then, so that the different height of the former high vowels – that is, the height difference between the new /u/, /i/, on the one hand, and /ъ/, /ь/ on the other – is well established, and means that these latter vowels will not be fused with the low /e/, /o/, as happened with the nasals. Or perhaps it is simply that the combination of high(er) and/or short(er) /ъ/ and /ь/ with /r/, /l/ led more easily to a syllabic sonorant (traditionally marked ŗ, ļ).

Thus we see in principle different results for ъ/ь + r/l and o/e + r/l; but in addition we see different results for each set across the dialectal spectrum. The most common way of formulating this structure is to use 'C' (or 't') for any consonant and 'R' for r/l; thus we are tracking the late Proto-Slavonic structures *CъRC*, *CьRC*, *CoRC* and *CeRC*, and also *#oRC* (that is, where /o/ is word-initial). In some cases *r* and *l* behave differently.

(i) CъRC, CьRC. The tendency for the two *jers* (the name given to the vowels *ь* and *ъ* from the old name for these Cyrillic letters) to be reduced, and in many areas to end up as *schwa* ([ə]), would have allowed these sequences easily to become syllabic sonorants in those areas where these were developed, namely the South Slavonic and southern West Slavonic (Czech/Slovak) areas; in principle the quality of the vowel was at least initially preserved in the hard/soft varieties of the new syllabic sonorant. In some cases the syllabic sonorant later developed further (e.g. ŗ reverted to vowel + consonant in Bulgarian, ļ became a full vowel in Serbian/Croatian). In the rest of the area (that is, 'northern' Slavonic) languages remained more consonantal, and these sonorants did not become syllabic, or, if they did, it was a short-lived phenomenon. If they did not, then we have apparently evidence of the failure of these closed syllables to open. The 'syllabic' solution is thus structurally more likely.

Thus, in all the south and Czech/Slovak (that is, 'southern' Slavonic), we have initially (with further local developments as in examples):

CъrC > CŗC   CьrC > Cŗ'C
CълC > CļC   CьlC > Cļ'C

PS	South Slavonic	SC	Cz	Slk	Bg	Mac
tъrg– 'trade'	trg–	trg–	trh–	trh–	tərg–	trg–
pьrv– 'first'	pŗ'v–	prv–	prv–	prv–	pərv–	prv–
čьrn– 'black'	čŗ'n–	crn–	čern–	čiern–	čərn–	crn–
dъlg– 'debt'	dļg–	dug–	dluh–	dlh–	dəlg–	dolg–
dьlg– 'long'	dļ'g–	dug–	dlouh–	dlh–	dəlg–	dolg–
žьlt– 'yellow'	žļ't–	žut–	žlut–	žlt–	žəlt–	žolt–

In the northern half (the East and Polish/Sorbian), we have no change at this stage; the reflexes are the same as those of the *jers* in other contexts. Thus, for common East Slavonic, which we will later be calling Old Russian, the base formula shapes (CъrC etc.) remain the valid ones. Further changes within this group will be treated later (section 2.3.1.3).

(ii) CoRC, CeRC. For this structure we have three distinct groups, though initially there may only have been two types. There are really only two possibilities for resolution of the given problem where the nuclear vowel is not of the reduced sort: (1) insertion of a new vowel (epenthesis), thereby creating an extra syllable (as is typical of borrowings into open-syllable-type languages, like Japanese or Italian); or (2) metathesis (inversion) of the vowel/sonorant sequence. Solution (1) is realised in the East and solution (2) in the north-west area (Polish/Sorbian, known jointly as Lekhitic). A third type in Slavonic is a variant of metathesis, in which the vowel has additionally been lengthened (o > a, e > ě), and is found in the 'southern' area. The three types, based on the modern situation (with possible intermediate steps in brackets, where *ъ* and *ь* represent roughly phonetic [ə] and [ɪ]), are:

a. East: CoRC (via CoRъC?) > CoRoC
CeRC (via CeRьC?) > CeReC

b. Polish/Sorbian (Lekhitic): CorC (via CoRъC > CoRoC?) > CroC
CeRC (via CeRьC > CeReC?) > CreC

c. South + Czech/Slovak CoRC (via CoRъC > CoRoC?) >
('southern'):   CRōC > CraC
CeRC (via CeRьC > CeReC?) >
CRēC > CRěC

PS	OR	Rus	Pol	Cz	SC	Bg
korva 'cow'	koro'va	koro'va	krowa	kráva	krava	kra'va
bergъ 'bank'	be'regъ	be'reg	brzeg	břeh	breg	breg
zolto 'gold'	zo'loto	zo'loto	złoto	zlato	zlato	zlato'
mel-ti 'grind' Inf	molo'ti	molo't'	mleć	mlét	mleti	–
želbъ 'gutter'	že'lobъ	žo'lob	żłób	žleb	žleb	žl'ab
želza 'gland'	železa'/	železa'	zołza	žláza	žlezda	žleza'
	želoza'					

The East Slavonic result is referred to in Russian as 'polnoglasie', in English as 'pleophony' or 'full vocalisation'. As suggested in the bracketed forms, it seems likely that the Lekhitic group went through this step also, but then removed the first vowel; the point-to-point statement could equally well be simply metathesis, as is accepted to be the case for the South, which then lengthened the one vowel, possibly in compensation.

At the suprasegmental level the above picture is somewhat more complicated, since the place of stress in the East may be on either the old or the new (inserted) vowel (see chapter 2, section 3.1), and in the other languages the new vowel may be accompanied by different quantity or pitch. The cause of these variations is the nature of the pitch (rising or not) on the original diphthong.

(iii) #oRC. In theory there should be also the structure *#erC*, but there are no reliable examples for it, so it is normal to exclude consideration of it, though of course one can say what it might have done. We have here two results, both described as metathesis, one with lengthening of the vowel in some forms; while the inserted-vowel approach is in theory a possible intermediate step, as suggested for the Lekhitic group above, there is in this case no secondary evidence which might support it. Here, moreover, the isoglosses are different, in that all of the East and West have the same result – simple metathesis in some forms, metathesis plus lengthening in others, while the South has always metathesis plus lengthening. In other words, while the South is consistent in its reflexes of the initial and medial contexts, neither the East nor the West is. It is presumed that the initial position presented other factors, which caused either an earlier or later shift; the most important of these was the vulnerability of the absolute initial vowel position in a language shifting towards open syllables, since the preceding sound, that is, the end of the preceding word, would now be ending in a vowel, thus producing undesirable hiatus. In other contexts the typical solution taken by Proto-Slavonic was to insert a prothetic glide (*u̯* or *i̯*) which later became a consonant (*v* or *j*); in this particular context metathesis may have been seen as a useful alternative solution (of course, the inserted vowel remains a possibility, as indicated in brackets).

Thus, we have:

East/West: oRC (via oRъC?) > RoC/RōC > RoC/RaC
South: oRc (via oRъC?) > RōC > RaC

PS	OR	Rus	Pol	Cz	SC	Bg
orv–ьnъ 'even'	rovьn–	rov(e)n–	równ–	rovn–	rav(a)n–	rav(ə)n–
ordlo 'plough'	ralo	ralo	radło	rádlo	ralo	ralo
olkotь 'elbow'	lok(ъ)tь	lok(o)t′	łok(ie)ć	lok(e)t	lak(a)t	lak(ə)t
olk–omъ 'hungry'	lakom–	lakom–	łakom–	lakom–	lakom–	lakom–

The two results in East/West are again caused by pitch differences in the underlying diphthong: a rising pitch was responsible for the lengthened form (reflected in /a/) of the new vowel.

In all the above cases of diphthongs, where the diphthong was followed by a vowel, the solution to the open syllable impetus was simply to shift the new boundary to after the nuclear vowel, such that the former semivowel or sonorant became a syllable-initial consonant, as follows: *i̯* > *j*, *u̯* > *w* (> *v*), *m, n, r, l*. This is an important source of often quite complex morphophonological alternations, based on whether inflections began with a vowel or consonant (see chapter 2, section 3.5).

2.2.1.7 Syllabic harmony. Within the new syllabic structure (CV), therefore, the relationship between the consonant and the following vowel became very close, such that each influenced the other. This general feature is called 'syllabic harmony' (or 'synharmony'). The features affected are centred around front/ back tongue position, which for vowels means indeed front/back, for consonants the raising of the tongue at the front or back. Thus we have effects like the following.

(1) Consonant fronting. A front vowel caused raising of the tongue at the front during the consonant articulation, producing what is called a 'palatalising' effect, and so-called 'palatalised' or 'soft(ened)' (or 'sharp') consonants.

(2) Palatalisation. In the case of the furthest back consonants, the velars, the result was indeed, as we have mentioned above, their conversion to full palatal consonants, that is, articulated in the high front tongue position (a shift from soft to hard palate location).

(3) Vowel fronting. Where palatal consonants had arisen as a result of the effect of [j], and where the following vowel had been a back one (say, /o/ or /u/), this back vowel was fronted by the influence of the consonant. In the case of short /o/ and /ъ/ the fronted versions were in fact the front partners /e/ and /ь/, supporting the notion that any rounding was not strong in these short vowels, while for the long /u/ and /ǫ/ the result was at most a fronted [ü] or nasal [ö] – they did not lose their rounding and merge with their front partners (/i/, /ę/). Most interesting is the long /a/, whose formal front partner was /ě/: it seems that a fronted [ä] was the result in most areas, and since this is what we believe /ě/ itself was in most areas, this result means normal fronting (to the partner); however, the ultimate result in all areas was a reflex of /a/, and not of /ě/, and moreover, the result of /ě/ itself preceded by a palatal was also /a/ (!). But it is also clear that in those areas where /ě/ in other contexts shifted to another position (higher), it is not joined by the vowels following palatal consonants, so that the [ä] of these areas was not identical to /ě/. Incidentally, no area has retained these three fronted articulations, which were clearly only allophones, and which ceased to function after the syllable was again restructured. At this later stage the sequence Palatal C + Back V again became acceptable (see below, section 2.4.1.1).

The extent to which these shifts are reflected in the modern languages varies: for some (including Russian), the 'soft' articulation of consonants – and not just before front vowels – has become an inherent feature; the fronting of vowels is reflected everywhere in morphophonological alternations, in particular in the opposition between hard and soft declension types (e.g. Rus neuter nouns, hard *mest–o* 'place' versus soft *pol–e* 'field'; see chapter 3, section 2.1.3).

2.2.1.8 Further palatalisation of the velars. Later than the 'First Palatalisation of the Velars' described above (section 2.2.1.3), producing alveolo-palatal consonants of the chuintante/husher type (/č/, /š/, /ž/), there occurred a second fronting process affecting the velars, producing probably first (dorsal) palatal sounds (like those in modern Polish and Serbian/Croatian), which by the time of the break-up had become soft dentals (or alveolars) (which is the reverse of the Polish and Serbian/Croatian cases, where these palatals were derived from soft dentals), as follows:

$$/k/ > /c'/; /g/ > /dz'/ \text{ or } /z'/; /x/ > /s'/ \text{ or } /š'/$$

The variants for /g/ are parallel to those for the first set, that is, they probably initially related to the stop versus fricative nature of /g/; however, subsequently even areas with stop /g/ converted /dz'/ to /z'/ (including Russian). The variants for /x/, on the other hand, are geographically based, the alveolo-palatal /š/ occurring in the west only.

These velar frontings occur in two contexts. One is the expected following front vowel, specifically one of the two new front vowels, or rather new sources of existing front vowels, which had not been present at the time of the first change, namely the new /ě₂/ and /i₂/ which had arisen from the (monophthongised) diphthong /oi̯/ (see above, section 2.2.1.6). This set is referred to as the 'Second Palatalisation of the Velars'. Examples are:

PS		Rus	Bg/SC	Cz	Pol
koi̯na > kěna 'price'		cena	cena	cena	cena
goi̯lo > gělo 'very'		OR zělo		OCz zielo	
xoi̯d– > xěd– 'grey (haired)'		sed-oj	SC sed	šed–ý	szad–y

This change occurred in important inflections, like the Locative Singular and Nominative Plural of nouns, and Imperative of verbs, hence frequent alternations resulted, e.g.:

PS	(North Slavonic)	OR	Cz
rank–oi̯ > rǫkě > rǫcě 'hand' LS	(ruka)	rucě	ruce
nog–oi̯ > nogě > nodzě 'foot' LS	(noga)	nozě	noze
doux–oi̯ > duxě > dusě/dušě 'spirit' LS	(dux)	dusě	duše

The second context in which this same set of changes occurred is more puzzling: it appears to be caused by a *preceding* high front simple or nuclear vowel (that is, mainly long and short /i/). This makes it a progressive assimilation, which in itself suggests rather the period before the opening of the syllables, since after that there was a clear boundary between a vowel and a following consonant; on the other hand, the fact that only one diphthong-type with nuclear [i] *–iN* (but not *iR*) provokes the change means that it almost certainly occurred *after* the quantity changes and monophthongisation (that diphthong would first have become a nasalised /i/, then merged with the lower nasalised /e/ (/ę/)); the identical results to the Second Palatalisation also suggest a similar late period. These conflicting facts have led to a range of interpretations about this set of velar changes: traditionally this set has been called the 'Third Palatalisation of the Velars', suggesting a late chronology, but it is now more commonly called the 'Progressive Palatalisation of the Velars', and many place it as the *earliest* of the three. The compromise position, which attempts to accommodate the contradictions, sees it as having occurred in two stages, the first early and producing simply fronted velars, the second simultaneous with the Second Palatalisation and taking these sounds along with those in the new front vowel context forward to the palatal area. This is why we suggested above (section 2.2.1.1) the early appearance of fronted velars when adjacent to front vowels.

There are also other complications with this set: one is that certain following vowels (high and/or rounded) seem to have prevented it, which fits with the later syllable situation; another is that there must have been some analogical levelling, for example where the following vowel (in a paradigm) was sometimes a preventer, sometimes a supporter (the latter mainly /a/), and analogy would be particularly strong where the motive force was never an inflection, but always a stem (or root) vowel. These last facts account for the absence of alternations arising from this set. Examples are:

PS	Rus	Bg/Sn	Cz	Pol
ot-ĭkŭ > ot–bc′b 'father'	ot–(e)c	Bg ot(e)c	ot(e)c	ojc(ie)c
kŭningŭ > kъnędz′b 'prince'	knjaz′	Bg knez	OCz kněz	ksiądz
vĭxŭ > vbs′ъ 'all'	v(e)s′	Sn v(e)s	OCz v(e)š	OP wszy
suffix –īka > –ic′a Female/ Abstract (but not –īkŭ, –ĭka Diminutive, which > –ikъ, –ъka)	–ica	–ica	–ica	–ica

Those following back vowels which did not prevent the change were then fronted by the rules of syllabic harmony (section 2.2.1.7).

2.2.1.9 Suprasegmental. Two late changes affected all areas: (1) tone became restricted to stressed position (meaning that the old pure vowels – a, i_1, $ě_1$, y – could now be non-rising in unstressed position); (2) all vowels which had rising pitch (automatic on the above four, possible – thus phonemic – on the vowels derived from diphthongs: i_2, u, $ě_2$, $ę$, $ǫ$) were shortened (meaning that these vowels – that is, i, u, $ě$, $ę$, $ǫ$, since the different origins of /i/ and /ě/ were irrelevant – now had phonemic quantity under stress, since it was no longer predictable). Furthermore, inasmuch as the new short vowels retained their rising pitch, tone was no longer limited to long vowels (and diphthongs); however, there was no longer a simple tonal opposition on any vowel; pitch remained tied to quantity, the opposition on the above vowels being between 'short + rising' and 'long + non-rising', while the remaining short vowels (o, e, $ъ$, $ь$) were automatically non-rising.

2.2.1.10 Late PS phonological system. We may now consider the system which had arisen by the end of the common period of development, just before the break-up (of the sixth century), which saw different results for jointly motivated changes and the start of locally motivated changes. The following table (table 3) may be compared with that in section 2.1.1 (table 1). Brackets indicate regional or temporary variants, as follows: the combination of labial + l' (as the 'jotated' version) probably did not arise in the West; of the soft dentals (from palatals) only /c´/ (from /k/) was general; the palatal stops are conveniently described as still general in this form; /g/ and /v/ have alternative articulations by region, as stop versus fricative for the first, as labio-dental versus bilabial for the second. The apostrophe is used to distinguish palatal sounds from simply palatalised ones (marked with acute).

2.2.2   Morphology

2.2.2.1 Nominal. The following are the features and categories of the late Indo-European nominal system of relevance for us and how they were treated in Proto-Slavonic (discussion of the actual forms is taken up in other chapters and sections as appropriate, especially chapter 3, section 2.1):

> *case*: the seven cases of Indo-European – Nominative, Accusative, Genitive, Dative, Instrumental, Locative, Ablative, plus Vocative – were reduced to six plus Vocative in Proto-Slavonic (and Baltic) by the conflation of Ablative into Genitive;

> *number*: of the three numbers – Singular, Dual, Plural – the dual was already losing ground in Proto-Slavonic, having its range of cases reduced to three by the conflation (syncretisation) of the Nom+Acc, Gen+Loc and Dat+Instr. Subsequently it was completely lost except in a couple of areas (Slovenian and Sorbian), but it was still

Table 3 *Late Proto-Slavonic phonological system*

Consonants

	Labial	Dental	Palatal	Velar
Stop	p (pl')	t	t'	k
	b (bl')	d	d'	(g)
	m (ml')	n	n'	
Fricative		s (s′)	š'	x
	(v) (vl')	z (z′)	ž'	(ɣ)
	(w)		j	
Affricate		c′	č'	
		(dz′)	(dž')	
Liquid		r	r'	
		l	l'	

Vowels

	Front	Central	Back
High	i	y	u
Mid-high	ь	ъ	
Mid-low	e ę		o ǫ
Low	ě	a	

Also fronted allophones in the context /PalC—: ü, ȯ, ä

Syllabic sonorants

  r̥ , l̥ in west and south only

Suprasegmental

Stress   Free

Quantity   After shortening of acute: automatic short on /a/, /y/ and
           former short (o, e, ъ, ь); free on rest.

Tone   After shortening of acute: double opposition between new
           short acute and former long circumflex.

functioning in at least Old Church Slavonic and Russian Church
Slavonic in the Old Russian period;

gender: the three genders (Masculine, Feminine, Neuter) were retained,
inherent (syntactic) in substantives and agreeing (morphological)
in adjectives, pronouns and some numerals (1–4); Proto-Slavonic
refined the Masculine group with subcategories of ±*Personal* and
±*Animate*;

adjectives: no change in gradation – positive, comparative and superlative; an added feature of ±*definite* in most (non-possessive);

pronouns: no change to the general range and type.

2.2.2.2 Verbal. The verbal features inherited from Indo-European are:

tense: the six tenses of late Indo-European (Present, Future, Aorist, Imperfect, Perfect, Pluperfect) were all retained in Proto-Slavonic, though their formation in many cases was different, in that the Future, Perfect and Pluperfect were re-formed analytically with auxiliary verbs and either the Infinitive or past participles – as occurred elsewhere also, for example in Germanic.

mood: the four-way system of Indo-European (Indicative, Subjunctive, Optative, Imperative) became a three-way one in Proto-Slavonic, with the replacement of the Imperative forms by those of the Optative and the loss of the latter category; the Subjunctive forms became primarily Conditional, again analytical in form.

voice: Indo-European Active and Middle were redefined in Proto-Slavonic as ±*Reflexive* and a new Passive was added, a participial form like that of English *-en.*

aspect: the most important development in Proto-Slavonic was the gradual shift in the relative importance of aspect over tense; the feature ±*Complete* (Perfective/Imperfective), while already present in Indo-European's past tenses, became more important than time relations; a further development was the splitting of Imperfective motion verbs into ±*Determinate* (or ±*Continuous*).

person: no difference, the three persons – 1st, 2nd, 3rd – were retained.

Two new, non-finite, verbal categories in Proto-Slavonic were the Infinitive and the Supine, both derived from Indo-European deverbal nouns with an added *–t* suffix, in oblique case forms, frozen into indeclinable forms.

2.2.3   Syntax

Little more can be said about the details of syntax of either Indo-European or Proto-Slavonic than follows from the morphological changes noted above. Given the continued high degree of inflection in PS, little would have had to change in terms of word order, and the overall categories able to appear in a given syntactic position would likewise have been in principle the same.

2.3   Early East Slavonic developments, leading to Old Russian

Here we note changes which occurred in the east between the sixth and tenth centuries, that is, in the post-break-up, but pre-literary period. Some of these would have the same results in other areas, but these are still the basic early markers of the East as a group.

2.3.1   Phonology

2.3.1.1 Consonants. The palatal stops became affricates in natural phonetic fashion, including assimilative hushing of preceding dental fricatives:

t' > č' (cf. casual Brit Eng *tune*) (*svět'a* 'candle' > *svěč'a*)
st' > šč' (cf. casual Brit Eng *stupid*) (*pust'ǫ* 'let' 1ps > *pušč'ǫ*)
d' > dž', then mostly > ž' (cf. casual Brit Eng *duke*)
   (*xod'ǫ* 'go' 1ps > *xodž'ǫ/xož'ǫ*)
zd' > ždž' (*ězd'ǫ* 'travel' 1ps > *ěždž'ǫ*)
dz' > z' (*nodz'ě* 'foot' LS > *noz'ě*, *kɒnędz'ь* 'prince' NS > *kɒnęz'ь*)
/g/ = g (North), ɣ (South)
/v/ = v (North), β or w (South)

2.3.1.2 Vowels.

2.3.1.2 Vowels. The nasal vowels are denasalised, the front one probably becoming first [ä], whence it later merged with /a/. So long as we can still say that the vowel is 'front(ed)', we can still call any softness (palatalisation) of the consonant allophonic (contextual). If we go straight to non-front [a] we would have to say that the softness of the consonant – which is clearly there at the next stage – is already phonemic. Nonetheless, this is clearly the beginning of a situation where softness is detaching itself from the vowel context and thus becoming phonemic.

   ę > a   *pętь* 'five' > *pätь*

The back rounded nasal merges with the other strongly rounded one, /u/:

   ǫ > u   *pǫtь* 'way' > *putь*

These changes are significant for the morphophonology, since the already complex alternations between nasal vowels and nasal consonants now become even more distant, namely between oral vowels and nasal consonants.

/ě/, whose reflexes in the East are all front vowels higher than [ä], must have shifted there early, as it is never fused with [ä]; possibly it was early diphthongal, at least in some areas (see chapter 6 on dialects); the most likely position is a mid-high (close) [e].

2.3.1.3 Syllabic sonorants.

2.3.1.3 Syllabic sonorants. While it is probable that in the south-western area (future Ukrainian and Belarusian) syllabic [r̥] and [l̥] arose (from *CъRC*, etc., see section 2.2.1.6 (c)), any such development was short-lived, and certainly by the end of the period under review there were none in the system. (There is other evidence in these areas that these sounds also developed, again briefly, in the next period, from *CRъC*, etc. (e.g. to account for the placename *Pskov* from *Plьskovъ*.)

For the north-eastern area (future Russian) there is some evidence of *CъrC* having either softened the /r/, which would mean by progressive assimilation (and is therefore relatively unlikely), or added a second, reduplicated, vowel after the sonorant, parallel to the situation with *o/e* (see section 2.2.1.6 (c)). In the case of /l/ the assimilation is (as expected) regressive, the hard /l/ causing the preceding vowel to move back to /ъ/ (see section 2.2.1.7), except where the first C is palatal, when /e/ is preserved. Otherwise, there is no change. Thus, in the East we have (Š represents any palatal C):

CъRC > CъRC	CьRC > CыrC or Cыr'C or CыrьC			
CъlC > CъlC	CыlC > CыlC	ŠьlC > ŠыlC		
PS	**OR**	**Rus**	**Ukr**	**Br**
tъrgъ 'trade'	tъrgъ	torg	torg	torg
pьrvъ 'first'	pьrvъ	p'erv–	perv–	p'erv–
vьrxъ 'summit'	vьrxъ	v'erx	verx	v'erx
čьrnъ 'black'	čьrnъ	čorn–	čorn–	čorn–
dъlgъ 'debt'	dъlgъ	dolg	dovg	douǧ
dьlgъ 'long'	dьlgъ	dolg–	dovg–	douǧ–
žьltъ 'yellow'	žьltъ	žolt–	žovt–	žouṭ–

Note that while in *CъlC* the sequence of change was /ъ/ > /ʏ/ > /o/ (e.g. *dъlgᴕ*), that in *CьrC* and *ŠьlC* was /ь/ > /e/ > /o/ (sometimes) (e.g. *čьrnᴕ, žьltᴕ*). On the subsequent changes converting /ь/ to /e/ and /o/, see section 2.4.1.1.

2.3.1.4 Diphthongs. As noted above (section 2.2.1.6), the eastern solution to the problem of internal syllables closed by [r] or [l] (of the type *CoRC/CeRC*) was the insertion of an epenthetic vowel. The quality of this vowel would logically be initially that of the short /ъ/ and /ь/ (as the nearest to a back/front central vowel of the schwa type), which should then develop like any other /ъ/ and /ь/; however, the evidence is mixed and suggests different chronologies over the area. For example, most dialects treat this vowel rather as an original /o/ or /e/, meaning either that the inserted vowels were indeed those or that the shift to /o/ and /e/ occurred earlier than the development of /ъ/ and /ь/. It is possible, and is the traditional view, that the inserted vowel was from the start a reduplication of the preceding one. At any rate, this is the simplest adequate description at this stage. For examples, see section 2.2.1.6 (c).

For word-initial diphthongs of this sort (type #oRC), the solution was metathesis, shared by the whole group (see section 2.2.1.6(c)).

2.3.1.5 Contextual changes. Phonotactic changes – that is, of sounds in particular contexts, include the ones given below.

(1) tl, dl > l   vedl– 'lead' Past Part stem > *vel–*; *pletl–* 'plait' Past Part > *plel–*. This change was shared with the South, but not the West (cf. Cz *vedl–, pletl–*). Basically it is a continuation or extension of the Proto-Slavonic simplification

of clusters, these being of rising sonority and thus in principle acceptable (see section 2.2.1.4).

(2) The following three changes relate to word-initial vowels. These would have become vulnerable under the open syllable structure, since they would inevitably cause hiatus with the preceding compulsory final vowel (see section 2.2.1.4).

  (a) #a, #ę > jä   azъ 'I' > jäzъ; ęti 'take' Inf *> jäti; ęzykъ* 'tongue' *> jäzykъ.* Almost every area inserted a prothetic [j] before initial /a/, that is, the old low back unrounded vowel (the exception is Bulgarian, including Old Church Slavonic, e.g. Bg *az*, OCS *azъ*, which also treated initial /ę/ in the same way, e.g. Bg *ezik*, OCS *ęzykъ*). This would have preceded denasalisation, though for the east this is irrelevant, since /ę/ became [ä] (> /a/) anyway.

  *(b) #ě > je (*via *ie?)   ěxati* 'travel' Inf *> jěxati; ěsti* 'eat' Inf *> jěsti.* Since in Proto-Slavonic /ě/ preceded by [j] (or any palatal) merged with /a/, this development must be late in the East, and mostly elsewhere, too (probably caused by analogy with prefixed, thus non-initial, non-*j* forms; see Schenker 1995: 88); the exception again is Bulgarian (and Old Church Slavonic), where the change to /a/ did occur, e.g. Bg *jada* 'eat' Pres 3ps, OCS *jasti, jaxati* Inf. For modern Russian the reflex is *je–*, that is, the normal fusion of /ě/ and /e/ which occurred much later (Rus *jexat', jest'*), however there is not the same etymological confusion here as in other contexts, for the reason that initial /e/ did not acquire a [j], but behaved as follows.

  *(c) #e > o   ed*ъ*n-* 'one' *> od*ъ*n-; ezero* 'lake' *> ozero.* This is a specifically eastern feature not shared by either West or South (cf. Cz/SC *jedn–, jezero*; Bg *edn–, ezero*). It appears to be an alternative solution in which the feature of rounding obviates, or at least makes acceptable, the hiatus, perhaps because the rounding acts like a prothetic [w]. This is supported by the fact that initial /o/, /u/ and /ǫ/ also do *not* normally acquire prothetic consonants, where in other areas a prothetic consonant (usually /w-v/, but also /j/) is common on the last two, including in Ukrainian and Belarusian (while /o/ rarely acquires one anywhere), e.g.:

PS	OR	Rus	Ukr/Br	Bg	SC/Sn	Cz	Pol
okъno 'window'	okъno	okno'	Ukr vikno	okno	okno	okno	okno
utro 'morning'	utro	u'tro		utro	jutro	jítro	jutro
ugъ 'south'	ugъ	RCS jug		jug	jug	jíh	
ǫtroba 'womb'	utroba	utro'ba	Ukr utroba	utroba	Sn votroba	útroba	wątroba
ǫsъ 'moustache'	usъ	us	vus	vəs	Sn vos	vous	wąs

  In one fairly rare context, initial /o/ did acquire a prothetic /w-v/ in the (north-)east, namely where the /o/ carried the so-called 'neo-acute' pitch, that is, one generated from a following previously stressed *jer* (ъ/ь). The most prominent example is:

PS	OR/OCS	Rus	Ukr/Br	Bg	SC/Sn	Cz	Pol
osmь 'eight'	osmь		vo's(e)m′	Ukr vi's(i)m	o'səm	SC os(a)m	osm	os(ie)m

The most likely explanation for this is to be found in the next feature, namely the development of internal /o/ under the same suprasegmental condition, where in the dialects the reflex is either a mid-high [o] or a rising diphthong of the [u̯o] type (in other words one with strong rounding).

(3) Internal o > [o] under neo-acute   stolъ̏ 'table' > st[o]'lъ. This change was later reversed in most dialects, including the future standard (Contemporary Standard Russian), by the fusing of the mid-high and mid-low versions of /o/, so that Contemporary Standard Russian no longer has a mid-high [o] in any context. Chapter 6 describes the situation in the other dialects.

2.3.1.6 Suprasegmental. By the end of the period, the sole surviving feature is stress. Quantity has again become only phonetic, probably with only the *jers* marked as short(er); it ceased to function as stress became more important (and perhaps dynamic), such that stressed syllables tended to be longer (and louder) than unstressed. The case of the *jers* is symptomatic: as short, and perhaps previously extra short, they would come under even greater pressure in a system with strong stress. Already in the previous Proto-Slavonic stage they had ceased to be able to bear the stress and had passed it back to the preceding syllable – giving rise to the 'neo-acute' pitch mentioned above. They were also under segmental pressure in all areas, and everywhere underwent change. While this was a Proto-Slavonic phenomenon, the results were local, occurring rather late, generally between the eleventh and fourteenth centuries.

As for tone, it too ceased to operate throughout the whole area, leaving its traces mainly in either place of stress or new quantity oppositions. For the East, this meant almost exclusively in stress, the most visible case being that of the expanded *CoRC* type, in which a former rising pitch (including neo-acute) resulted in stress on the inserted vowel (*CoRo'C*), a former non-rising pitch in stress on the original vowel (*Co'RoC*); more generally the reflection of pitch is found in morphological stress patterns, though many of these date from much earlier Proto-Slavonic; and there are a few segmental reflexes, such as the closed [o] mentioned above, which mostly began as quantity reflexes (especially length from rising pitch).

Other areas developed new oppositions of quantity (especially the West) and/or pitch (especially the South) from such stimuli as contraction (after loss of intervocalic [j]), compensatory length (after the loss of the *jers*) or stress shifts (Serbian/Croatian and Slovenian). In the East there are only sporadic, and at best short-lived, effects of this sort in the Ukrainian area (possible length by compensation).

2.3.1.7 Early East Slavonic system (tenth century). As a result of the above changes, we now have a distinct East Slavonic system, which we can begin to call the Old Russian system, as in table 4.

Table 4 *Old Russian phonological system*

Consonants

	Labial	**Dental**	**Palatal**	**Velar**
Stop	p {pl'}	t		k
	b {bl'}	d		(g: N)
	m {ml'}	n n'...>[a]		
Fricative		s s'...>	š' {šč'}[b]	x
	v/ß {vl'}	z z'...>	ž' {ždž'}	(ɣ : S)
	(w)		j	
Affricate		c´...>	č'	
		(dz')...>	(dž')[c]	
Liquid		r r'...>		
		l l'...>		

[a]The soft dentals may have still been palatal at the early stage (tenth century), until the phonemicisation of positionally soft consonants (see section 2.4.1); this is the meaning of the symbol '...>'.

[b]/šč'/ and /ždž'/ are included insofar as they functioned as morphophonemes, alternating with /st/ or /sk/ and /zd/ or /zg/ respectively (hence marked in {}), while at the phonemic level they are clusters; the same goes for the four clusters of labial plus /l'/, alternating with the labials.

[c]/dz'/ and /dž'/ are early versions of (i.e. will be superseded by) /z'/ and /ž'/ (see section 2.4.1).

Vowels

	Front		**Central**		**Back**
High	i		y		u
Mid-high	e	ь		ъ	o
Mid-low	ɛ				ɔ
Low			a		

Also allophones in the context /PalC—: ü, ä

Syllabic sonorants
    Possibly ŗ, ļ in some areas

Diphthongs
    i̯e, u̯o as regional variants of high e, o

Suprasegmental
    Stress   Free

2.3.2   Morphology

Most of the Proto-Slavonic developments noted above (section 2.2.2) survived into the post-Proto-Slavonic period, only then undergoing further changes in different areas. Thus Old Russian (and Old Church Slavonic) still had the system described there: a six-case (plus Voc) nominal system, with three genders and three numbers; a verbal system with six tenses, two aspects, a three-way voice system and three moods, plus the indeclinable Infinitive and Supine.

The noun declension system was essentially the same, but phonetic adjustments had removed many of the transparent criteria for these in Indo-European; in their place was developing a system in which gender played a greater classifying role. However, for the initial period, it is still traditional to classify nouns using the old, Indo-European-based, principles, in which the important classifier was the thematic suffix joining the root to the inflectional ending. Thus, the declensions of Old Russian, Old Church Slavonic, and all the contemporary languages are traditionally classified into 'x-stems', where 'stem' actually means 'thematic suffix' and 'x' the vowel or consonant central to this suffix. There were four vowel stems – *a–*, *o–*, *u–* and *i–*, and various consonants reflecting Indo-European derivational suffixes, notably *n–*, *r–*, *s–*, *nt–* and *v–* (from *u̯*) (grouped together as 'consonant stems'); moreover, the presence of a suffixal *j–* in some classes (*a–* and *o–*) produced variants which could differ quite markedly from the non-*j* variant as a result of the major phonetic changes related to palatalisation (see above).

The classification of the conjugational system, too, centred on the thematic suffix between stems and endings. A complication is that different stems were common for Present versus Infinitive forms, and it is normal to use the former (the Present Tense suffix) as the classifier. The vowels *e–* and *i–* form the most common types; then there are two variants of the *e*-type, one with *n–e–* and one with *j–e–*; this accounted for all but a few high-frequency verbs which had no thematic suffix – and are therefore known as *athematic* – notably *be*, *give*, *have* and *eat*.

Details of forms will be given in the appropriate places (in chapter 3) as backgrounds to the modern system.

2.3.3   Syntax

For this period the most significant development is that related to Old Church Slavonic, which became the literary language of many areas, but in particular Kievan Rus', at this time. It had developed as a formal written language by translation mainly from Greek, also Latin, and so had acquired a syntax as sophisticated as theirs, presumably quite different from that of the local spoken language(s). We shall see below (section 3.2) how the two interacted, but the central point is that by the end of this period we have a language with the syntactic structures typical of both spoken and written styles, in gross terms typified as preferring respectively coordination and subordination, with all that that implies, for example, differences in the use of pronouns (especially personal and demonstrative), participles and word order.

2.4 Developments from Old Russian to Modern Russian (post-tenth century)

Here we offer only a summary of the changes which have taken place between Old and Modern Russian. Each feature will be taken up in more detail within the appropriate chapter as the background to that particular topic. 'NE' and 'SW' represent the early dialectal division of north-east (future Russian) versus south-west (future Ukrainian and Belarusian), though not all features match this division. 'S' alone implies future Ukrainian only; 'W' future Belarusian; and 'NR' non-standard northern Russian.

2.4.1 Phonology
2.4.1.1 Early changes (pre-fourteenth century)
(1) Consonants
- hard/soft (±Palatalised or ±Sharp) opposition develops in most of the area (weakly in S) after the loss of the *jers* (when consonants positionally softened by following front vowels become phonemic in new syllable-final position); henceforth we will use 'hard' and 'soft' in this sense;
- the former palatals *r' l' n' s' z'* merge with soft dentals *r' l' n' s' z'* (*mor'e* 'sea' NS > *mor'e, korol'a* 'king' GS > *korol'a, kon'a* 'horse' GS > *kon'a* – cf. *r'äd* 'row', *l'ěto* 'summer/year', *n'e* , 'not', with original positionally soft *r/l/n*); likewise *c'* (and *dz'* while it survived) became (now, if not before) dental affricates (there being no other source of these);
- dz' > z' (*nodz'e* 'foot' LS > *noz'e*);
- dž' > ž' in NE (*xodž'ü* 'go' 1ps Pres > *xož'ü*);
- some NR: confusion of c'/č'; known as *cokanje/čokanje*, usually with only one of these surviving; not a feature of Contemporary Standard Russian or the dialect at the base of the standard (see chapter 6);
- some NR: tl > kl, dl > gl (very localised).

(2) Vowels
- ъ > ɔ ~ φ (later in S);
- ь > ɛ ~ φ (later in S);
(on the context and other details of the loss of the *jers* see chapter 2, section 3.1.1)
- [o] > ɔ except in NR; some NR > u̯o;
- [e] > ɛ except in NR; some NR > i̯e.

In other words, at this stage the former three-way distinction by height was lost in the main (> standard) dialects (ɔ, o, ъ all > ɔ; ɛ, e, ь all > ɛ), with the qualification that the former *jers* were sometimes lost (became zero).

- the relationship between /i/ and /y/ changes as a result of the new hard/soft system: they become positional variants (allophones) of the same phoneme, the first following soft, the second following hard consonants (however, see chapter 5 for other views of the modern system);
- the fronted variants [ä] and [ü] cease to appear in the simple context of /Pal C—, where they fuse with the basic back versions [a] and [u]; they do, however, continue to appear in the enclosed context S—S (see chapter 2, section 3.1.3).

(3) Contextual changes
- NE+W: final devoicing and assimilation of voice in obstruents (after loss of *jers*) (including *v* > *f* in NE);
- e (from /e/ or /ь/, but *not* /ě/, which was still a different vowel) > /o/ in the following contexts:

> NE+W   /—'HC (under stress and followed by a hard consonant)
> S   /Pal— (after a palatal consonant).

Since preceding soft consonants remained soft after this change, the freeing-up of the vowels and consonants from the old syllable-based structure is continued: from now on all vowels except /e/ may follow either hard or soft consonants; further, /o/ – like /a/ and /u/ – may have a fronted variant [ö] between two soft consonants (see chapter 2, section 3.1.3).

(4) Suprasegmental
- Quantity: in S (>Ukrainian) compensatory lengthening for a lost *jer*, at least on /o/ and /e/, but these soon break down into diphthongs *ŭo/ĭe*, then > *i* (this is similar to the appearance of the 'neo-acute' pitch in the previous period, caused by a stress retraction from a *jer*).

2.4.1.2 Later changes (post-fourteenth century)
(1) Consonants
- the palatals begin to change their phonetic nature, from soft ([+Sharp], high tongue position, similar to English) to hard ([−Sharp], low position); for the Contemporary Standard Russian source dialects, only /š/ and /ž/ do this; /č/ remains phonetically soft (high);
- /c'/ also becomes hard in the standard area.

It seems likely that the phonetic proximity of /č/ and /c'/ (both in the alveolar region with raised tongue position) made their distinction difficult in the new hard/soft system; the various dialectal results can be seen as different methods of distancing them phonetically, by hardening one or the other, or even both;

some areas in fact failed to do this and fused the two (see *cokanje* above, and chapter 6).

(2) Vowels
- reduction of unstressed vowels in Central Russian (and Belarusian), leading to fusion of /a/ and /o/ and of /e/ and /i/ in this position; actual results vary greatly by dialect (see chapter 6); this did not occur in either Northern Russian or Southern Russian (or Ukrainian); the whole phenomenon is known as *akanje* '*a*-pronunciation';
- ě > ɛ   in Central Russian dialects only, and much later; hence in these areas yet another vowel joins the phoneme /e/, however, this later source of /e/ does *not* become /o/ in the contexts noted above, except by analogy.

(3) Contextual changes
- soft velars (k'/g'/x') become possible, then obligatory, before (front) /i/ and /e/, thereby allowing the replacement – adopted in the nominal system only – of a complex set of morphophonemic alternations (velar ∼ palatal) with the simpler one of hard ∼ soft; that is, in this context they behave like other paired consonants, except that before /i/ the hard partner (*ky* etc.) is impossible; also, the soft versions remain unable – in the standard area – to occur before the back vowels.

2.4.2   Morphology
As in this last case, there are many instances of phonological (including phonetic) changes which caused or made possible morphophonological changes, either the formation of new alternations or the elimination of old ones; of course, analogy is also a major force in the elimination. For example, the loss of the nasals created greater distance between the alternating forms related to them; the loss of the *jers* – in which they became by context either *o/e* or zero – produced one of the most striking alternations throughout the Slavonic group, that of the 'fleeting vowels' (also known as 'mobile vowels', 'inserted vowels' and 'fugitive vowels'); the possibility of /o/ occurring after soft consonants and under stress produced a major stress-related alternation of /e/ ∼ /o/; and the fusion of /ě/ with /e/ allowed the elimination of a large number of – mainly nominal – alternations.

At the morphological level proper, the major operative motivation for change was regularisation of pattern (by the exclusion (or conversion) of exceptional and infrequent forms), probably the most common general motivation for all languages.

Here we give an overall view of the major changes related to these stimuli (further discussion will precede relevant sections of chapter 3).

(1) Whole system
- the loss of the Dual.

(2) Nominal
- the reorganisation of the declension system on the basis of gender (which had begun much earlier), basically reducing the number of classes from five to two;
- the loss of the Vocative.

(3) Verbal
- the Supine is lost, replaced by the Infinitive;
- the reflexive pronoun in its Direct Object form (*sja*), at first a separable pronoun, becomes attached to the verb as the reflexive form becomes a multi-purpose expression of intransitive and passive, as well as reflexive;
- in the Imperative, the 1st Person Plural forms are lost, leaving only the 2nd Person command forms; also there is regularisation of the suffix vowel – which had been *ě* in several conjugations, *i* in others – to *i* throughout.

Otherwise, the conjugation system remained unchanged in principle; there were some phonetic effects, mainly the loss of unstressed *i* in several forms (giving zero in Infinitive and 2nd Person Singular Present and some Imperative endings, and /j/ in other Imperative forms).

2.4.3   Syntax

The following is a summary of the main syntactic developments, many of which are taken up again in chapter 4.

(1) Nominal
- greater use of prepositions, less use of simple cases, though no loss of cases; this mainly means greater precision of meaning, but also implies greater analyticity, and the possibility of the loss of cases, or at least fusion of forms;
- more precise use of prepositions and cases, via greater semantic restriction of both, but especially the prepositions.

   (a) Adjectives
- loss of ±Definite in adjectives and limitation of short adjectives to predicative position (in the associated meaning of 'specific/particular' versus 'general(ised)' for long forms);
- loss of gender distinctions in Plural.

   (b) Pronouns
- loss of enclitic forms for 1st/2nd Plural Direct and Indirect Object (except reflexive *sja*, see above);
- greater independence of personal pronouns with Past Tense verbs, where person ceases to be indicated in form.

(2) Verbal
- formation of adverbial participles;
- loss of Present Tense of copula.

(3) Nominal predicate
- continually increasing use of Instrumental (versus Nominative) as an indicator of non-permanence.

(4) Coordination
- greater and more precise use of conjunctions, in the direction of a discrete one for any clause type (though still with a range of stylistic variants).

There has been little other change in features like subject or predicate membership or in agreement between the two.

3 Development of the standard language

3.1 Periodisation

As signalled above in section 1, the main periods of the literary language relate to those of the major historical movements. Thus, the first period covers Kievan Rus' up to the expansion of the Lithuanians in the fourteenth century, and is referred to as the 'Old Russian' period. We know of no writing before the arrival of Christianity in the late tenth century; although there had been treaties between the Rus' and the Greeks from the early tenth century, and reports of their terms are reproduced in the Chronicles written much later, we can say little other than hypothetically about the language in which they might have been written, even if there were a Rus(s)ian version; it is entirely possible that they were written only in Greek. At any rate the documents that we have clearly correlate the appearance of writing in Kievan Rus' with the arrival of Christianity and religious texts. The earliest dated text is that called *Ostromirovo Evangelie* 'Ostromir's Gospel', dated 1056, a date which belongs to the period of great translation activity under Jaroslav the Wise. Otherwise there are documents dating from the early eleventh century, some possibly late tenth century. The content of all of these is religious. For non-religious texts we have only indirect evidence via later copies; these include chronicles, legal codes and commercial documents.

The period from the fourteenth to the sixteenth centuries is known as the 'Rise of Moscow', when the centre of activity moved to the north and when the dialectal base operating in Moscow itself began to shift from 'northern', as opposed to 'southern', to the formation of a new 'central' type, as Moscow attracted speakers from all areas – including some 'foreigners' who exerted an important influence on the literary language (see below on Kiprian).

The seventeenth century formed a sort of interim period: politically Moscow's (or Russia's) power was (re-)expanding, including, in the mid-seventeenth century, the effective reannexation of Ukraine. This period has been regarded as the start of the formation of the Russian nation, at its peak in the reign of Peter the Great, though continuing until the mid-nineteenth century. From the language point of view, it is Peter who is most significant, since his efforts at drawing Russia into Europe included the importation of western cultural and linguistic elements into Russia.

Thus, ultimately, for the language, the main pivotal points are the shift to the north in the fourteenth century, and Peter's reign in the early eighteenth century. In the next section we look more closely at these events.

3.2   Old Russian and Old Church Slavonic

On the 'origin' of Old Church Slavonic and its graphic features see section 4.1 below; on the linguistic differences between it and Old Russian (as South versus East Slavonic dialects), as reflected in Contemporary Standard Russian's morphophonology and lexicology, see mainly chapter 5, section 2.1.4.

The earliest surviving documents from the Old Russian period were essentially religious, and were translations usually from South Slavonic originals written in Old Church Slavonic – or rather simply copies in which East Slavonic linguistic features were, whether consciously or not, allowed to appear. Thus, Ostromir's Gospel is written in Old Church Slavonic, but displays Old Russian phonological features, for example the local reflexes of the nasal vowels and the *jers*. In subsequent texts we find more and more of such features, but most interestingly, there is the definite sense that there was little conscious distinction between the two sets of elements. It is now generally accepted that Old Church Slavonic, being perceived as very close to Old Russian, was regarded simply as a written (or literary, or high) variant of the same language (Uspensky, Worth, Lunt).

In the past, arguments have raged over whether the two functioned as two distinct languages, each with its own preferred area of operation, but nevertheless in theory separate languages, each with its own written and spoken variants. As a spoken language, Old Church Slavonic would certainly have been restricted to the religious sphere, and the case for written Old Russian rests on texts of the commercial and legal sort; in other words, neither 'language' was really a complete one in the normal sense of 'standard'. Defenders of the 'two languages' view were further divided in their opinion on which one formed the 'base' of the Old Russian literary language; for some Old Church Slavonic (or rather Russian Church Slavonic, that is, Old Church Slavonic with the acceptance of some East Slavonic features) was the base, and it slowly became 'Russianised', achieving the final stage of 'genuine' Russian only after Peter's period (Unbegaun,

Isačenko); for others, Old Russian was the base, and Old Church Slavonic was clearly a foreign language functioning only at the restricted level of religious writing, and 'lending' many of its features to Old Russian, which was happy to incorporate them, at first at the 'high' levels of writing, then – likewise only after Peter's period – at all levels (Obnorskij and early Soviet language historians, e.g. Černyx). In other words, for them Old Russian was the base of the literary language, and it slowly became 'Slavonicised'. Much of this latter argumentation was based on ideological viewpoints; not surprisingly, it was most staunchly proposed during Stalin's period.

Probably also ideologically inspired – though this may be unfair – was a compromise view which arose in the Soviet Union in the 1950s, its main proponent being V. Vinogradov, namely that Old Church Slavonic and Old Russian were different 'types' of the same literary language, functioning in different spheres, the former in religious writing, the latter a written variant of spoken Old Russian (Vinogradov and virtually all subsequent Soviet historians of the literary language, e.g. Efimov, Gorškov). The literary language is thus essentially a fusion of these two types. Note that this differs from the view described above as now 'generally accepted', in which the two were regarded simply as the same language in a high, or written, and a low, or spoken, variant.

The fact is that attempts to sort out the use of the two by means of labelling texts or their forms as marked linguistically – as Old Church Slavonic/Russian Church Slavonic or Old Russian on the one hand, and as religious, literary or non-literary on the other – have really failed. In the first place, in any text the proportion of linguistically marked (and thus distinguishable) forms is actually very low, and one could end up classifying a text as one or the other on the basis of a very limited set of examples. Secondly, while we can have no doubt about the Old Church Slavonic nature of religious texts, and count the odd cases of Old Russian forms as exceptions, at the 'lower' end even legal and commercial texts – and certainly any with the slightest literary pretension – have quite large numbers of Old Church Slavonic features, and, more to the point, the two are frequently mixed together in no particular pattern. Thus it seems clear that scribes or writers believed they had both forms at their disposal, and while they knew in principle that they were not interchangeable at least in 'high' texts, in practice the distinction was not maintained.

That is the situation for the Old Russian period. However, in the next period, from the fifteenth century, the picture becomes very confused by the developments in relation to the arrival in Moscow of southern Slav churchmen who wished to 'reinstate' the purity of the Church books by eliminating the Old Russian (i.e. eastern) features which had crept into them. (The name most closely associated with these 'reforms' is that of Kiprian, a Bulgarian who was Metropolitan of the Russian Church in 1381–82 and 1390–1406.) While their target might only have been the church books, the result was nevertheless that Russian Church Slavonic, in its new guise (which, incidentally, incorporated some South Slavonic features which were actually contemporary (Middle) Bulgarian and not genuine Old Church Slavonic) became regarded as the proper language of any serious writing, and not only religious writing. (This effect is referred to traditionally as the 'Second South Slav Influence', the notional first influence being the original introduction of Old Church Slavonic in the tenth century.) This produced a serious gulf between the written and spoken language, both because the new Russian Church Slavonic was a reactionary form and because the spoken language was undergoing major changes in its grammatical structure. By the seventeenth century the situation had become impossible, and many texts of the late seventeenth century indicate complete confusion and non-understanding of the relationship between the two sets of language forms, complicated further by the flood of borrowings which began to enter the language. This flood was 'aggravated' further by Peter the Great, however Peter did make a positive contribution by trying to separate out the religious, or church, sphere from the civil, with his 'civil script (or alphabet)' (*graždanskij šrift*), to be used for all non-religious publications. Moreover, Peter's reign also saw the blossoming of printing in Russia.

It had become clear to all that some order had to be brought into the written language, and this was a task undertaken by the new Academy of Sciences, founded in 1725, which adopted as its model the Académie Française, which had a well established role as arbitrator on the language. However, while the matter became a central point of debate from this time on, in reality it was by no means a simple matter to impose a set of norms: in the first place, the norms had to be worked out, and the relationship of Russian Church Slavonic and spoken Russian was not an easy matter to sort out; secondly, even if norms were 'declared', there was (for some time to come) no mechanism for imposing them on writers. All this normativising took the whole of the eighteenth century and a good part of the nineteenth, before some clear sense of order began to be observed.

The credit for producing the final state, effectively that of modern Russian, is usually given to Pushkin, and not without some justification, though the rapturous praise showered on him, especially during the Soviet period (cf. typical chapter headings like 'Progenitor/Founder of the modern Russian literary language'), is certainly rather exaggerated. His true contribution is twofold: at the *linguistic* level, his knowledge of, and feeling for, the 'true' spoken language – as opposed to the often artificial speech of the upper classes in their salons – and at the *literary* level, the breadth of literary genres in which he operated. Others before him had commanded a similar linguistic feeling, and had been able to write in unaffected Russian (e.g. Karamzin, Fonvisin, Krylov), but they had been limited in respect either of their genres – Fonvisin wrote mainly plays, and some prose, Krylov mainly fables and plays – or of their literary outlook – Karamzin wrote 'sentimental' prose, an approach which brought some literary ridicule which obscured his elegant command of the written language (apparent also in his monumental *History of Russia*). So, Pushkin in effect set the seal on the new language by his breadth of production (lyrical poetry, short and long poems, some plays, but in particular prose); without the work of the eighteenth century, both writers and grammarians, he would not have been able to do what he did, and had he not done what he did, it would have been done soon enough by someone else; his significance is that he came when he did and did what he did. So the credit is deserved.

3.3   Normativising in the eighteenth and nineteenth centuries

Prior to the eighteenth century, internal grammars (that is, produced within the broad Russian region) had been of Russian Church Slavonic, the most popular being one which had originated in Ukraine (by Smotrickij). In fact, most of the grammar and dictionary activity took place outside Russia proper, mainly in Ukraine and Belorussia, where Old Church Slavonic had not become established in what were mainly non-Orthodox areas. As soon as the Polish/Lithuanian control weakened, Moscow became regarded as a political defender of the eastern Slavs, and this implied also interest in Slavic Orthodoxy and its language, Russian Church Slavonic. Hence, all the first Slavonic grammars and dictionaries, or simply primers, were aimed at allowing these groups – and also other Orthodox Slavs, such as the Serbs – to learn Russian Church Slavonic.

There were also various non-Slavonic works which described either Russian Church Slavonic or, in some cases, spoken Russian, for the benefit of foreign learners (e.g. Ludolf, Ridley, Sauvage, James). Some of these made explicit reference to the difference between Russian Church Slavonic and local (spoken) Russian (especially Ludolf); others seem not to have been aware of it.

It was only in the 1730s, following the stimulus of the Academy, that homegrown descriptions of the local spoken language began to appear, and indeed the earliest of these actually began life as just such a Russian description, but it was published only in a German version of 1731 (Adodurov, see Uspenskij 1975). The first published grammar of Russian (and thus credit as the first writer of a grammar of Russian) is that of Lomonosov in 1755/1757; moreover, Lomonosov differentiates throughout between Russian Church Slavonic and spoken Russian, most often referring to them as 'high' and 'low' style, sometimes condemning spoken forms as 'too low', sometimes condemning Russian Church Slavonic forms as 'archaic'. The normativising thrust is clear and this grammar was to remain influential for much of the rest of the century.

Lomonosov is also well known as the producer of the theory of the 'three styles (of literary language)', that is, 'high', 'middle' and 'low'. While such a theory was not at all new (even in Russia) in respect of the classification of genres and, by extension, of their language, Lomonosov gave it a concrete form that was new in applying it to the lexicon: he classified notionally all the Russian lexicon into five groups: 'obsolete and unusable', 'familiar Russian Church Slavonic, usable in high style', 'common to Russian Church Slavonic and Russian [that is, unmarked forms], usable in any style', 'marked Russian, usable in non-high styles' and 'vulgar and unusable, except perhaps in very low style'; and the genres included in the three styles were also named, in traditional manner. This 'theory' was expounded in many of his minor works, most fully in Lomonosov 1757, and it appears to have had some considerable effect, at least on all but the major writers – but therein lies its weakness: it is in practical terms the major writers who have the real task of imposing (by accepting or rejecting) the norms which grammarians (or the writers themselves) suggest, and it would appear that the most influential of these rejected the straitjacket of Lomonosov's theory. Also, the tying of language style to genre left the language at the mercy of literary fashion or movements, and it was in fact the genres allotted to the middle style (e.g. tale, elegy, eclogue) which failed to develop (or were, rather, non-literary, e.g. journalistic or technical writing), thereby giving no momentum to the compromise mixture of linguistic forms; it thus took longer than it might have for the language to settle on a happy mixture of high and low forms – that is, a middle language style – to be the basis of the modern literary language. And it was the writers, ultimately Pushkin, who brought about this result (many, including Pushkin, by theorising as well as producing creative writing); even the first major dictionary, that of the Academy, published in the last decade of the eighteenth century, which attempted to classify words as high or low wherever possible, was criticised by the writers as being too conservative.

In the latter half of the nineteenth century and in the twentieth, the main issues for the literary language, still as hotly debated today, have been rather the extent and place of foreign borrowings and of low-style (especially slang) forms.

4   Writing (graphics)

4.1   The historical background

Traditionally the first Slavic writing is credited to Constantine (also known as (St) Cyril, the name he took on becoming a monk). He and his brother Methodius (also St), natives (and most likely Slav, though possibly Greek) of the Macedonian town of Salonica (now Thessaloniki), led a mission from Byzantium to the Moravian Slavs in the early 860s, in preparation reputedly having created an alphabet in which to write the liturgical texts in 'Slavonic'. The written language which was thus formed is that known as Old Church

Slavonic. There is no factual evidence of any writing of a Slavonic language before that time.

A major complicating factor is the existence of not one, but two alphabets both clearly 'created' to fit Slavonic needs: Glagolitic and Cyrillic. Arguments over the origin of and relationship between these have continued unabated throughout the nineteenth and twentieth centuries. In fact, Cyrillic presents little trouble: it is clearly based on uncial (capital) Greek, and its problems are reduced to determining the origin of the letters which could not have come from Greek, like those representing the sounds /š, ž, č, c, b/, which Byzantine Greek did not have. The problems centre around Glagolitic, whose formal origin is still quite unclear, and the relative chronology of the two alphabets. Here we will simply report the most popular view amongst scholars, if only because Glagolitic is of purely historical interest, all of its major documents having long since been transcribed into Cyrillic and studied in that form.

The most likely scenario is as follows: Glagolitic was formed by the adaptation of cursive Greek by some Slavs during the couple of centuries preceding the Moravian mission; it was formalised by Constantine, who also added letters for the non-Greek sounds; Constantine's disciples in Bulgaria and Macedonia (in the 890s), especially the Macedonian Ohrid group, headed by (St) Clement, perceived Glagolitic as unsuitable for Church books and made up a new Slavonic alphabet based on the 'more dignified' uncial Greek. This is the alphabet we now know as Cyrillic, formally named (much later) after St Cyril, even though it is likely that the alphabet he created was in fact Glagolitic.

Whatever the origin of the Glagolitic letters, there are probably enough similarities to allow a derivation of the Cyrillic letters for the specifically Slavonic sounds from Glagolitic, though more commonly these are said to be derived rather from other ancient alphabets, notably Hebrew and Coptic.

Table 5 gives the full set of Cyrillic characters used in Old Russian and Old Church Slavonic, with their transliteration, using the so-called 'Slavonic linguistic variant' (reflected in ISO, but with different symbols for the *jers* and nasals – referred to in the table as ISO+), which also indicates their phonemic application. These may be compared with the preceding discussion of PS phonology. Asterisks indicate characters which have been subsequently removed, over the last three centuries, starting from Peter the Great's reforms in the early eighteenth century. Line numbers are given to allow easy reference to letters discussed in the text, and the column 'Replaced by' uses these to indicate the modern character. (In the case of variants in column 1, the first is the modern one.) The column 'Numerical Value' refers to the fact that – also as in, and indeed inherited from, the Ancient Greek system – letters also served as numerals, with an assigned value related to their alphabetic position; discrepancies between position and value, or the absence of a value, are caused by the inheritance of the Greek values. Similarly, the principle of

Table 5 *The Old Cyrillic alphabet*

	Old Church Slavonic Cyrillic	Numerical value	Name (ISO+)	Transliteration /Phonological value (ISO+)	Replaced by
1.	a	1	azъ	a	
2.	б	—	buky	b	
3.	в	2	vědi/vědě	v	
4.	г	3	glagoli/glagolь	g	
5.	д	4	dobro	d	
6.	e	5	jestъ/estъ	e	
7.	ж	—	živěte	ž	
8.*	s/ꙅ	6	(d)zělo	dz′	9
9.	з	7	zemlja	z	
10.	и	8	i, izhei	i	
11.*	i/ï	10	izhe	i	10
12.*	(ħ)	—	g′ervь/d′ervь	g′	4
13.	к	20	kako	k	
14.	л	30	ljudъje/ljudije	l	
15.	м	40	myslite/myslěte	m	
16.	н	50	našь	n	
17.	o	70	onъ	o	
18.	п	80	pokoi	p	
19.	p	100	rьci	r	
20.	c	200	slovo	s	
21.	т	300	tvьrdo/tverdo	t	
22.	y/oy/ȣ/ꙋ	400	ukъ/ikъ	u	
23.	ф	500	fьrtъ	f	
24.	x	600	xěrъ/xerъ	x	
25.*	ѿ/ω	700	otъ	o	17
26.	ц	900	ci	c	
27.	ч	90	črvь	č	
28.	ш	—	ša	š	
29.	щ	—	št′a	št′	
30.	ъ	—	jerъ	ъ	
31.	ы/ъи/ъi	—	jery	y	
32.	ь	—	jerь	ь	
33.*	ѣ	—	ětь/jatь	ě	6
34.	ю	—	ju	ju	
35.	я/ꙗ	—	ja	ja	
36.*	ѥ	—	(je)	je	6
37.*	ѧ	900	jusъ malyj	ę	35
38.*	ѩ	—	jusъ malyj jotirovannyj	ję	35
39.*	ѫ	—	jusъ bolьšoj	ǫ	22
40.*	ѭ	—	jusъ bolьšoj jotirovannyj	jǫ	34
41.*	ѯ	60	ksi	ks	13 + 20
42.*	ψ	700	psi	ps	18 + 20
43.*	ѳ	9	(thita)/fita	f	23
44.*	v/r/ɣ	—	ižica	i/v	10 (or 3)

naming letters was continued on the Greek model, with the crucial difference that the traditional Slavonic names are, with a few exceptions, recognisable Slavonic words (Greek having inherited Hebrew names which were meaningless in Greek). (The modern system is given with more information in chapter 2, table 9.)

Changes in the application of letters (as opposed to purely formal changes and overall styles) are usually the result of phonological changes which cause either redundancies or inadequacies in the symbolic representation of the sounds. Three solutions are possible in these circumstances: (1) retain the old symbols as phonetically redundant, but etymologically informative, symbols; (2) delete the old symbols and replace them with the ones used for the sounds with which they have fused; or (3) apply the old symbols to some new function for which a new need has arisen (for this there will usually need to be some association between the old and new functions). All of these approaches were applied at some stage in the various reforms of Cyrillic in every area.

Another general cause of trouble was the inheritance of an alphabet that was created for another language system, as was the case for Cyrillic in general (and to a lesser extent early Glagolitic), with the rather serious problems of the multiple vowel symbols brought in from the Greek system: the three letters for /i/ (table 5: 10/11/44), the two for /o/ (table 5: 17/25), and the variants for /u/ (table 5: 22). There were similar problems with the Greek consonantal letters, with two each for /z/ (table 5: 8/9) and /f/ (table 5: 23/43). The variant values for v (table 5: 44) were inherited from Greek (the letter *upsilon*), where the consonantal value [v] occurred after vowels, in old diphthongs like [eṷ]; for Russian, this was the more common result, examples being *Evropa* 'Europe' and *avto-* 'auto-'; the vocalic value ([i]) is reflected in Greek words such as *sintaksis* 'syntax'.

In Russia the first attempt to come to grips with these problems was Peter the Great's 'civil script' of 1708/1710 – not only did this settle on simpler forms of all letters for use in administrative printing, but it also made a start on deleting redundant letters which were marked as 'church' variants, and introduced some new forms, notably э and я (see chapter 2, table 9: 31, 33). The debate about shapes and variants continued until 1918, there being until then (there as elsewhere) no mechanism for the enforcing of a norm. The 1918 reform (the last to date) saw the removal of the redundant i, v, ѣ and ѳ (table 5: 11, 44, 33, 43) in all cases, and of ъ (table 5: 30) in its redundant final position (see further chapter 2, section 4.5).

4.2   Orthographic principles

Apart from odd proposals of a phonetic principle, most Slavonic areas have always applied the 'morphological' principle in orthography, that is, to retain visible morphological relations in spite of surface phonetic facts. The exceptions are Belarusian, which has gone for a phonetic representation of the vowels, though, inconsistently, not of the consonants; and Serbian/Croatian – and to a lesser extent Ukrainian – which have simpler surface realisations of the morphology and can thus boast of having 'a(n almost) phonetic spelling system', as they simply do not have the morphophonological (or phonotactic) complications of languages like Russian. For example, apart from Serbian/Croatian and Ukrainian, all Slavonic languages devoice final obstruents, but none indicate this in the spelling, since, for example, the devoiced version typically occurs in only one out of twelve noun forms. See further discussion in chapter 2, in relation to the phonology and graphics of the modern language.

2 Phonology

In this chapter we shall introduce Cyrillic forms only after the 'Graphics' section (4), as the phonological discussion proper will be better understood without that complication. The transcription used will be ISO for phonemic, IPA for phonetic.

For the benefit of those readers who do not already have some theoretical linguistic training, we begin this chapter (sections 1 and 2) with some basic concepts and terminology. Those familiar with these may pass on to section 3.

1   The 'phoneme' and related terminology

Where the 'phonetics' of a particular language is a physical science – analysing and describing the subset of total human sounds used to communicate in that language, the 'phonemics' of a language is a purely linguistic science – describing only those sounds from within that subset which may be used to distinguish words (or linguistic elements).

For example, consider the initial sounds in the following English words: *pin*, *bin*; these words clearly mean different things, that is, they are clearly different 'words' in English, and the only sound difference between them is that of the *p/b*; hence one can say that in English /p/ and /b/ are different 'phonemes' since confusing them would confuse different words. Now consider the sound [p] in the word *spin*: speakers normally fail to notice that this sound is actually different from the [pʰ] in *pin* in that it is lacking the aspiration (puff of air) which accompanies the latter; this is because that aspiration is a feature only of initial /p/ in English. If one consciously substituted one for the other, that is, swapped the aspirated one in *spin* and the non-aspirated one in *pin*, the result in either case would not be a different word, but only a word pronounced 'incorrectly', or strangely. In other words this difference is not one which is usable in English to distinguish words, and so it is said to be (only) 'phonetic', and not 'phonemic'. The two sorts of /p/ are said to be 'phones', and not 'phonemes', and since the issue always relates to comparisons, to differences among sets, each one is normally said to be an 'allophone', or 'positional variant' of the 'phoneme' /p/.

In the description of the elements of each system, it is customary to use square brackets for phonetic elements, and oblique ones (forward slashes) for the phonemic ones. While the number of phonemes in a given language is fairly limited – typically under forty – such that the symbols of a basic alphabet like the Latin one will usually suffice, the number of phones is well above this, so it is necessary to have recourse to extra, non-alphabetic, symbols. The most widely used 'phonetic alphabet', even in languages with non-Latin-based alphabets, is the International Phonetic Association alphabet, or IPA. This is what we will use hereafter. For any formal description a desirable criterion is that of 'one symbol for one sound', and this extends also to phonemic descriptions; where there is a need for more symbols than the given (or a basic) alphabet offers, often the IPA symbols are used for phonemes, too, as in English /ŋ/ in *bang* (versus /n/ in *ban*, the rest of those words being identical; hence /n/ and /ŋ/ are separate phonemes in English), or for, say, the sounds written *sh* or *ch* in English. However, within Slavonic linguistics it has become customary to use symbols with diacritic marks for this purpose, specifically those used in the modern Czech alphabet; thus, the sounds of English *sh* and *ch* would be transcribed as *š* and *č* respectively. The only 'digraph' (two letters for one sound) which Czech has is *ch* for the final sound in *Bach*, and in the 'one-symbol' system this sound is transcribed by *x*, which is the Cyrillic symbol for this sound.

All of this relates to the writing of sounds, known as 'transcription' (further qualified as 'broad' for phonemic and 'narrow' for phonetic). A parallel science is 'transliteration', which means the writing of the *letters* or *symbols* of one system (alphabet or script) via the letters of another system, as in the transliteration of Cyrillic letters into Latin letters. This is a requirement mainly of library catalogues and the like, where pronunciation need not be, or at least is assumed not to be, relevant. However, the principle of one transliteration symbol for one graphic symbol is sometimes adhered to, in our case the example being the ISO transliteration of Cyrillic, which is also based on the same Czech alphabetic symbols (including *x* for *ch*). It is not used in older systems such as those of the Library of Congress or the British Library, which use the normal English digraphs, like *sh*, *ch*, etc.

The close similarity between the Slavists' phonemic transcription system and the ISO transliteration system provides Slavists with the very useful possibility of using effectively one system for both purposes; hence in some of our tables (e.g. table 9) one will find a column headed 'Phonemic and transliteration (ISO)', the parallel being incomplete only in a few instances (e.g. the Cyrillic symbols *ъ* and *ь* are used by linguists for these as old phonemes, while the ISO system uses " and ' respectively for the modern letters).

In this book the term 'phonology', used in the chapter heading (as well as its adjective 'phonological'), is taken to cover the whole area of the sound system, that is, including both the phonemic and the phonetic. It should be noted that some linguists use this term with the meaning we are allotting to 'phonemics', either as a synonym of this or in place of it. Given the existence of the three terms, we prefer the usage which allots a different meaning to each.

2 Description

The traditional terminology of phonological description derives from both the articulatory (or physiological) procedures involved in producing sounds and from the acoustic effects produced by them on our ears. In some cases the two sets of terms operate in parallel, that is, as synonyms, in others one or other is customary. They are usable for both phonemic and phonetic levels, and will be the basis of our descriptive approach.

However, we must first note a further set of acoustic terms which belong to a particular type of *phonemic* description. This is referred to usually as 'distinctive feature' analysis (or description), though in reality the notion of 'distinctive feature' is much more generally applicable to phonemics, where it may simply indicate which of the basic features is 'distinctive', or 'phonemic', for the given language. Thus, we may say that a given feature is phonemic or distinctive in that one may make minimal pairs of words distinguished solely by this feature. Some of the terms used in this system are the same, or almost the same, as in the traditional system, but others are distinct terms which do not easily convey the acoustic – or for that matter the articulatory – effects involved. In the actual description of the Russian system (section 3), we shall usually offer parallel versions.

2.1   Traditional (articulatory)

From articulatory anatomy (physiology), that is, what the organs of speech are doing, we derive terms based on: (1) what happens to the air as it passes through the mouth – giving various general sorts of consonant and vowel, referred to as 'mode or method of articulation'; (2) at what point it happens – giving particular types of consonant, referred to as 'place of articulation'; (3) whether the vocal cords (the glottis) are resonating or at rest – giving respectively voiced or voiceless sounds; (4) whether the nasal passage is open or not – giving respectively nasal or oral sounds; (5) whether the tongue is raised or not, and how far, and which part of it – giving particular types of vowel; and (6) whether the lips are rounded, relaxed or spread – also contributing to vowel type.

From (1) come the following terms:
(a) *stop*, or *plosive* (consonant) (e.g. [t], [p], [k]);
(b) *fricative* (consonant) (e.g. [s], [f]);
(c) *affricate* (consonant) (e.g. [t͡s] in Russian – not English, where such a sound would be made of two distinct consonants, pronounced much more slowly).

(A term which covers all of these three types is *obstruent*, since they all involve obstruction.)

(d) where the obstruction is complex – that is that more than one effect is operating – a useful term is *sonorant*, although it must be noted that not everyone uses this term thus (and some use the form *sonant*); the common sounds included here are: [r] (vibration or tapping); [l] (lateral); [m] and [n] (nasal);

(e) where the obstruction is very weak, that is, not producing any friction, sounds are called *semivowels* (e.g. Eng /w/, /j/).

Note that the term *consonant* covers at least (a) to (d), and for most linguists also (e).

(f) where sounds are not obstructed at all, except perhaps in respect of mouth shape, sounds are called *vowels*.

From (2) come the following terms:

(a) *labial* (consonant) (e.g. [p], [w]);

(b) *dental* (e.g. [t], [s]);

(c) *labio-dental* (e.g. [f], [v]);

(d) *alveolar*, produced at the teeth-ridge (alternative to *dentals* in given languages, e.g. [t] is 'alveolar' in English, but 'dental' in most European languages, including Russian);

(e) *palatal* (e.g. [ʃ], [j]);

Two other terms used by the IPA are used with considerable inconsistency: *alveolo-palatal*, produced at the very front of the hard palate, further forward than the 'palatal' proper (IPA example [ɕ], [ʑ], as in Pol *ś*, *ź*), and *palato-alveolar*, even further forward (IPA example [ʃ]); both of these are much more often called simply *palatal*, at least where a given language does not have a contrast, as is the case in Russian. Equally confusing and unnecessary are terms like *pre-palatal*, *post-palatal* and *post-alveolar*, all found in different English descriptions of Russian and other Slavonic languages. Russian-language descriptions are no more consistent: in principle they distinguish between 'front-palatal', 'mid-palatal' and 'back-palatal' (meaning *velar*), to which they add the part of the tongue involved – also 'front', 'middle' and 'back', but there is just as much variation in usage as in the English-language sources.

(f) *velar* (e.g. [k], [g]).

For Russian, we need no more than (a) to (f), and *not* the following terms: *uvular*, *pharyngeal*, *glottal* (or *laryngeal*).

From (3) come the following terms:

(a) *voiced* (e.g. [d], [b], [z], [v]);

(b) *voiceless* (e.g. [t], [p], [s], [f]).

From (4) come the following:

(a) *nasal* (e.g. [m], [n]);

(b) *oral* (nasal passage closed off).

From (5) we have: *high/mid/low* combined with *front/central/back* vowels (e.g. [i] is 'high front', [u] 'high back'), and from (6): *rounded* (e.g. [u]), *unrounded* (e.g. [a]) and *spread* (e.g. [i]) vowels.

Thus, we describe consonants such as a voiced (bi-)labial stop/plosive (= [b]), a voiceless velar fricative (= [x]), or a nasal dental stop/plosive (= [n]); and vowels such as high front stretched (= [i]), high back rounded (= [u]), mid-central unrounded (= [ə]) or mid-high rounded nasal (= [õ]).

2.2 Distinctive feature description

An alternative sort of description uses a number of abstract features based on the acoustic effect of sounds rather than the articulatory procedures involved in their production. The phonemes of a particular language are described in terms of having or not having each of the features relevant for that language. These features are usually much broader in application than the articulatory ones. Typically the overall description of a system lays out all the phonemes in a matrix table, with each slot marked as +, − or 0 (meaning irrelevant for that phoneme). For example, the summary table in Halle's *Sound Pattern of Russian* (Halle 1971: 45) gives the following features: vocalic; consonantal; diffuse; compact; low tonality; strident; nasal; continuant; voiced; sharped; accented.

The features requiring explanation, since they are unlike the traditional ones and/or not readily understandable, are as follows, explained in parallel articulatory terms:

diffuse: for vowels only, +Diffuse = 'high'; −Diffuse = 'mid' and 'low';

compact: for non-diffuse vowels, +Compact = 'low', −Compact = 'mid'; for consonants, +Compact = palatal and velar, −Compact = dental and labial;

low tonality (versus *high tonality*) (also called ±*Grave*, or *grave/acute*): for non-compact vowels, +Low Tonality = 'back', −Low Tonality = 'front'; for compact consonants, +Low Tonality = 'velar', −Low Tonality = 'palatal'; for non-compact consonants, +Low Tonality = 'labial' or 'labio-dental', −Low Tonality = 'dental';

strident (versus *mellow*): for non-compact, low-tonality consonants only, +Strident = fricative (labio-dental), −Strident (or +Mellow) = stop (labial);

continuant (versus *interrupted*): +Continuant = 'fricative' or 'lateral' ([l]-type), −Continuant = 'stop' or 'affricate', including 'vibrant' ([r]-type);

sharped (versus *plain*): for most consonants, +Sharped = 'palatalised' (also simply *Sharp*).

Of the more 'understandable' ones, note the following:

> *vocalic*: +Vocalic covers not only the vowels, but also the sonorants, /r/ and /l/;
>
> *consonantal*: −Consonantal covers not only the vowels, but also /j/;
>
> *voiced* (versus *voiceless*): for obstruents only, as for articulatory description;
>
> *accented*: for vowels only, separates out stressed and unstressed (see below).

Thus, a full distinctive feature description of some of the same sounds as above would give (excluding irrelevant features):

> /b/: {−Voc; +Cons; −Comp; +Low Ton; −Strid; −Nas; +Voiced; −Sharped}
>
> /x/: {−Voc; +Cons; +Comp; +Low Ton; +Contin}
>
> /n/: {−Voc; +Cons; −Comp; −Low Ton; −Strid; +Nas; −Sharped}
>
> /i/: {+Voc; −Cons; +Diff; −Low Ton; ±Acc}
>
> /u/: {+Voc; −Cons; +Diff; +Low Ton; ±Acc}

Of course, other than in the matrix table, it is customary to list only the features necessary to distinguish a given phoneme from its close relatives.

Some features occur in contrasting pairs of terms, where the presence of one implies the absence of the other, a system which may be simplified to a reduced number of features marked as + or −; thus, Halle offers only 'strident' or 'voiced' in the table above, but in discussion includes the opposite terms 'mellow' and 'voiceless' as the equivalent of '−strident' and '−voiced'. However, as it is often possible for both such features, or neither, to be present in one phoneme, sometimes both terms are required, as with 'vocalic' and 'consonantal' or 'compact' and 'diffuse'.

Further, Halle's is not the only such interpretation or application of these features either in general, or to Russian in particular; for example, his limiting of 'diffuse' to vowels is not the only approach: for consonants +Diffuse = 'labial', 'dental' and 'alveolar', −Diffuse = 'palatal', 'velar' (in other words articulated in the front versus back parts of the mouth).

Finally, note that the three-way system of +/−/0 is often reduced to the two-way +/− when the phonetic facts are also of interest. Thus, for example, once /n/ is described as +Nasal, the issue of ±Voiced becomes irrelevant, as it does also in the absence of a voiced phonemic partner (e.g. for Rus /č/); however, it is often considered useful nevertheless to enter the phonetic information, +Voiced for the former, −Voiced for the latter. We will use this approach in the distinctive feature tables below (section 3.2.1, table 7).

Some other features used in this system, and potentially relevant for Russian, are:

tense/lax: while this is most often the equivalent of 'voiceless/voiced', there is often a disparity, at least in some positions; see later on consonant distribution; for vowels, this feature usually means 'long/short';

flat/plain: for vowels, +Flat = 'rounded', –Flat (or Plain) = 'unrounded'; for consonants +Flat = 'labialised'.

3   The phonology of Modern Russian

3.1   Historical orientation

Over the period from Old Russian to Modern Russian we observe the changes described below (see also chapter 1, section 2.4).

3.1.1   Vowels

• The *jers* (ъ/ь) have been lost as vowels, fusing with *o/e* respectively when in a so-called 'strong' position, elsewhere becoming zero. The process was similar to that of modern French's colloquial treatment of the neutral vowel ([ə]), whereby it may be lost next to any other vowel (e.g. *j(e) t'aime* 'I love you'), and in a sequence of these alternate ones are lost, that is, one never has two consecutive ones (e.g. *je ne le vois pas* 'I can't see him' may be pronounced *j(e) ne l(e) vois pas* or *je n(e) le vois pas*). The principal phonological effects of this major change (which affected all Slavonic languages in a similar way) were: (1) the loss of all final *jers* produced new closed syllables, thus ending the 'open syllable' structure in Slavonic; (2) in the east at least, the former positional softness of consonants before front vowels became phonemicised, notably via the final position, where the palatalisation remained, unsupported by any following vowel; (3) the freeing-up of the syllabic structure, once more allowing closed syllables, meant that the basic phonological unit became the phoneme, rather than the syllable as before. Secondary effects involved the simplification of clusters which arose – or would have arisen – with the loss of a *jer*; indeed most of the apparent exceptions to the loss rules may be explained by the avoidance of potentially difficult clusters, though certainly morphological analogy played a large part also. Following from this arose certain distributional effects, the major ones being the assimilation of voice in clusters and the devoicing of word-final obstruents. Beyond this, the major effect was morphophonological, namely that typical Slavonic alternation of vowels with zero, in the Russian case of *o/e* with zero, the so-called 'fleeting [also 'mobile', 'fugitive', or 'inserted'] vowels' (see below, section 3.5.1.2 and chapter 3, section 2.1.3.2).

(In Russian, as distinct from the rest of the Eastern group, even *jers* in the so-called 'tense' position, that is, followed by [j], which were strong – which in this case means under stress – also gave *o/e*, as opposed to *y/i* in Ukrainian and Belarusian (e.g. Rus *še'ja* 'neck' < *šьja*, Ukr/Br *šy'ja*).)

- The *o/e* which resulted from this change were the lower (more open) versions of the previous system ([ɔ] and [ɛ]); while some dialects retained the higher ones ([o], [e]), the majority soon eliminated the distinction, and we are left in the modern language with only the low versions.

- On the other hand the old phoneme /ě/ was in most areas probably high [e], and many areas also kept this separate, however the majority, and the standard, ultimately (much later) eliminated this distinction, too, and merged /ě/ with /e/ in the low [ɛ] position.

- The relationship between /i/ and /y/ was changed by the phonemicisation of palatalised consonants; the phonemic status of /y/ is still debated (see below).

- The change of /e/ to /o/ in certain contexts (under stress and not followed by a soft consonant) made of /o/ a phoneme almost as free as the other vowels, able to occur after either type of consonant (previously it could only follow hard consonants); the fact that it may do so only under stress is not a feature limited to /o/, and also affects /o/ after hard consonants (see below).

- An increase in the intensity of stress, as this became fixed as the sole suprasegmental feature, led to loss of quality in non-high unstressed vowels, including loss of rounding of /o/ and fusion of the unstressed versions of /a/ and /o/ after hard consonants, and of /e/ and /o/ after soft consonants; a further result of the same phenomenon was the loss of post-tonic /i/ after soft consonants (= [i]) in several morphological contexts, leaving either zero after a consonant or [j] after a vowel; this meant an extension of /j/ to the new context of syllable- or word-final (thus to all contexts), while prior to this it could occur only in pre-vocalic position.

- The fronted variants of back vowels which had occurred after palatals were no longer necessary and fused with the non-fronted ones.

3.1.2   Consonants

- Soft (palatalised) consonants have become phonemic through the loss of the *jers* (ъ/ь) as vowels.

- Regressive assimilation of voice occurs in clusters of obstruents (only in a few common words now indicated in the orthography, e.g. *gde* 'where' < *kъde*).

- Word-final obstruents are devoiced (also not indicated in the orthography, which remains morphologically based).

- Through these last two developments there appears a native [f], as the devoiced partner of [v]; along with the large number of Greek borrowings which entered via Church Slavonic, this [f] acquired phonemic status, supported also by the occurrence of a palatalised [fʲ], the result of a devoiced final [vʲ] (e.g. *krov′* 'blood' > [krɔfʲ], alongside *krov* 'cover' > [krɔf]) (in the orthography, the letter *f* (Cyrillic ф) reflects only the foreign source).

• The unpaired palatals hardened phonetically, variously by area; for the standard, the fricatives (/š/, /ž/) did, but not the affricate /č/.

• The other unpaired reflex of the palatalised velars, the dental affricate /c/, also hardened in the standard.

• The former distinction between palatal and positionally soft /r/, /l/, /n/, /s/ and /z/ was lost, and these fused as new soft consonants.

• The velars acquired soft variants, whose phonemic status is still a matter of debate (see below).

• Other effects concern further simplification of clusters, some of which are still not indicated in the graphic system.

3.1.3   Syllable

From the Old Russian situation of a 'syllabeme' as the base unit, with consonants being positionally softened before front vowels and all syllables being open, we have changed by the Modern Russian stage to the independence of the consonant and vowel parts of the syllable; the former 'syllabic harmony' ceases to function as the bonds between 'hard consonant and back vowel' and 'soft consonant and front vowel' are removed. The Old Russian stages of syllabic development may be seen as follows (where 't' = any hard labial or dental, 'k' any velar, 't′' any positionally soft labial or dental (but including /c/), and 'š' any palatal; /r/, /l/, /n/, /s/ and /z/ may occur in any of the three forms):

1. ta/ka   to/ko   tu/ku   ty/ky   tь/kъ   tọ/kọ
   t′ě   t′e   t′i   t′ь   t′ę
            š'e   š'i   š'ь   šę   š'ä   š'ü   š'ọ
2. (after loss of nasals) add   t′ä (< t′ę) (and remove all ę and ọ)
3. (after loss of *jers*) loss of fronted variants:
   t′ä > t′a   š'ä > š'a   š'ü > š'u

Palatal l′ä/r′ä/n′ä/s′ä/z′ä fuse with old soft l′ä (<l′ę), etc. > new l′a, etc.; likewise palatal l′ь > soft l′ь, etc., giving the following possible sequences:

ta/ka	to/ko	tu/ku	ty/ky		
t′a		t′u (r/l/n/s/z only)	t′i	t′e	t′ě
š'a		š'u	š'i	š'e	

4. (after e > o) add   t′o   š'o

At this point the only limitations are the missing *te and the odd status of /ě/ – missing tě and š'ě.

5. (after appearance of soft velars) add   k′e   k′i

remove   ky

Still impossible are k′a, k′u, k′o – to this day in the standard.

6. (after changes to palatals and /c′/) the palatal group is no longer
   homogeneous;
   š' > š   ž' > ž   c' > c (but no change to č'); thus for these three:
   š'a > ša   š'u > šu   š'i > šy   š'e > še

This adds three contexts of 'hard + /e/', to this day the only ones in the native
system; it leaves /č′/ isolated.

7. (after loss of /ě/, fused with /e/)   t′ě > t′e

Removal of the odd situation of /ě/ gives the final, present-day (standard)
system:

ta/ka/ša	t′a		č′a
tu/ku/šu	t′u (extended to all labials and dentals		č′u
	by morphological analogy)		
to/ko/šo	t′o		č′o
ty/šy	ti/ki		č′i
še	t′e/k′e		č′e

On the basis of the above, we may now proceed to the synchronic description
of the contemporary language.

3.2   The phonemes of Modern Russian

3.2.1   Consonants

The two most common ways of representing phonemes in a tabular fashion
are the older 'articulatory' method and the newer 'distinctive feature' method;
examples of these for Russian are shown in tables 6 and 7.

3.2.1.1 Problems

(1) k′/g′/x′. The three soft velars are limited in their distribution as follows (see
above for reasons):
• they cannot occur in syllable-final position (/ –C,#);
• they cannot occur before back vowels (/–a, o, u) except in foreign and dialectal
  words.

Table 6 *Russian consonant phonemes (articulatory)*

	Labial	Dental	Palatal	Velar
Plosive	p p′	t t′		(k′) k
	b b′	d d′		(g′) g
Nasal	m m′	n n′		
Fricative	f f′	s s′	(š′) š	(x′) x
	v v′	z z′	(ž′) ž	
			j	
Affricate		c	č'	
Liquid		r r′		
		l l′		

Notes: (a) as an indicator of articulatory position, consonants in the palatal and velar regions have their palatalised member listed first, as having a tongue position further forward than the non-palatalised one, but see below on the actual nature of this articulation.
(b) phonemes in brackets are those requiring special comment in regard to their phonemic status (section 3.2.1.1).
(c) In the more specific, but unnecessary, terms, /s-s′/, /z-z′/ and /r-r′/ are rather *alveolar*, and /š/, /ž/ and /č′/ are *alveolo-palatal*.

The hard velars *k/g/x* are also limited in not being able to occur before /i/ (/– /i/) (though see below on /i/ itself).

This has led to distinct interpretations of the phonemic status of the soft velars, essentially as items in the different approaches taken by the so-called Moscow and Leningrad/St Petersburg schools of linguistics, but with more than these two approaches. One view (the Moscow school) sees them as variants of the hard phonemes occurring before front vowels, which relies on relegating foreign words to a subsystem, and further on ignoring one verb in the standard language (*tkat'* 'weave') in whose present tense forms there does occur the syllable [kʲɔ]; in this view, too, [i] and [ɨ] are seen as variants of /i/. The opposite view (the Leningrad school) sees them as separate phonemes, partly through recognising foreign words and dialectal forms as part of the system, partly in the interests of a 'tidy' description, in which all consonants are phonemic; and in this view /i/ and /y/ (/ɨ/) are seen as separate phonemes.

There are weaknesses in both these approaches at the theoretical level (even without considering the question of foreign and dialectal elements), in the relationship of the velars to *i/y*: making *i/y* variants of /i/ is based on the notion that all paired consonants are followed automatically by one or the other – hard + [ɨ], soft + [i] – but given that there is no question of the phonemicity of the consonants (e.g. they occur in final position), it makes a better description to say that there is only one /i/ phoneme with variants controlled by the consonant; in turn it makes a better description then to include the soft velars as phonemes, albeit of limited distribution. On the other hand, if, for other reasons (see below),

Table 7 *Russian consonant phonemes (distinctive features; two-member – ± only)*

	p	p′	b	b′	m	m′	f	f′	v	v′	t	t′	d	d′	n	n′	s	s′	z	z′	š	(š′)	ž	(ž′)	č′	c	k	k′	g	g′	x	x′	r	r′	l	l′
Vocalic	–	–	–	–	–	–	–	–	–	–	–	–	–	–	–	–	–	–	–	–	–	–	–	–	–	–	–	–	–	–	–	–	+	+	+	+
Consonantal	+	+	+	+	+	+	+	+	+	+	+	+	+	+	+	+	+	+	+	+	+	+	+	+	+	+	+	+	+	+	+	+	+	+	+	+
Diffuse	+	+	+	+	+	+	+	+	+	+	+	+	+	+	+	+	+	+	+	+	–	–	–	–	–	+	–	–	–	–	–	–	+	+	+	+
Compact	–	–	–	–	–	–	–	–	–	–	–	–	–	–	–	–	–	–	–	–	+	+	+	+	+	–	+	+	+	+	+	+	–	–	–	–
Grave	+	+	+	+	+	+	+	+	+	+	–	–	–	–	–	–	–	–	–	–	–	–	–	–	–	–	+	+	+	+	+	+	–	–	–	–
Strident	–	–	–	–	–	–	+	+	+	+	–	–	–	–	–	–	+	+	+	+	+	+	+	+	+	+	–	–	–	–	–	–	–	–	–	–
Nasal	–	–	–	–	+	+	–	–	–	–	–	–	–	–	+	+	–	–	–	–	–	–	–	–	–	–	–	–	–	–	–	–	–	–	–	–
Continuant	–	–	–	–	–	–	+	+	+	+	–	–	–	–	–	–	+	+	+	+	+	+	+	+	–	–	–	–	–	–	+	+	+	+	+	+
Voiced	–	–	+	+	+	+	–	–	+	+	–	–	+	+	+	+	–	–	+	+	–	–	+	+	–	–	–	–	+	+	–	–	+	+	+	+
Sharp	–	+	–	+	–	+	–	+	–	+	–	+	–	+	–	+	–	+	–	+	–	+	–	+	+	–	–	+	–	+	–	+	–	+	–	+

i/y are seen as separate phonemes, while (all) the soft consonants are also certainly phonemes, then the two issues are not being related in principle, and the soft velars may form a limited subset in their own right.

Between these two positions lies another view, which is simply more pragmatic, basing itself strictly on occurring forms: given the existence of the standard verb *tkat'*, containing the syllable [kʲɔ] (in the Present), it follows that at least /kʲ/ is a separate phoneme, but in the absence of similar forms for [gʲ] and [xʲ], these two are not phonemes. This is an unsatisfactory theoretical position, since the three clearly function as a group and their description should treat them as such; the absence of forms may be seen as chance, not as a prohibition on their occurrence.

There is also the question of the status of foreign forms (and also dialectal ones, though this may be seen as a separate argument): for some, such elements are indeed an integral part of the system, some of them having been around for a long time, and if speakers use them happily, that is, without feeling that they are straining their language (usage), then they should be accommodated into the description. Even if there are few actual words containing soft velars, the principle is a larger one: even now the phoneme /f/ (and the letter *ф*) occurs only in what are historically foreign words, albeit dating from the Old Church Slavonic/Greek period at least, yet no one disputes its status; the presence of soft /fʲ/, occurring notably in personal names like *Fyodor* ([fʲɔ-]), supports the nativeness of the sound, but does not change the history, and the fact that the phone [f] occurs in native words as an allophone of /v/ merely makes the *sound* more common.

(Another important question relying on the same principle will be taken up below (section 3.4.1): that of syllables with a hard consonant followed by /e/, which we noted in the historical discussion as being the only sequence still 'missing' from a complete independence of paired consonants and the five vowels; this sequence, too, is common in foreign words, and becoming increasingly common with current borrowing.)

One final issue in connection with the velars is that of the sequence [kɨ], which is excluded from the normal list. First, again this could occur in foreign words, but it appears also in two native phonetic situations, one parallel to foreign in its non-centrality, namely non-lexical interjections (*kyš* is the representation of the sound made in driving animals, like geese), but the other occurring in normal language across a proclitic boundary, as in the phrase *k Igor'u* 'to Igor', in which the independent hardness of the preposition *k* determines the pronunciation of the following /i/ as [ɨ]. (See also section 3.7.6 below.)

(2) š':, ž':. These two sounds, phonetically soft *and* long palatal fricatives, occur in the speech of some speakers only, however both are considered standard variants, though not each in the same way. We must, therefore, consider them

separately, though their history is essentially the same (namely, they are derived from *stj/skj* and *zdj/zgj* respectively, and the first also from OCS *tj*).

š': ([ʃʲː]). This is the most common pronunciation for what is written with the letter *щ*, and to a lesser extent certain other written forms, in an area centred on the Moscow region; elsewhere these forms are pronounced *š'č'* ([ʃʲtʃʲ]). While the latter is easily seen as a cluster of the existing phonemes /š/ and /č'/ – with the softness of /š/ explained by assimilation, making it allophonic – the [ʃʲː] pronunciation does not allow this, and even if seen as a geminate cluster ([ʃʲʃʲ]), still requires the extra phoneme /š'/ in the system. Written forms other than *щ* pronounced in this way are all at least historically cross-morpheme forms (e.g. *sčast'e* 'happiness', where *s-* was a prefix, though not now recognised as such); where the morpheme boundary is still explicit, for example where the first element is a preposition, as in *s čest'ju* 'with honour', even Muscovites normally pronounce [ʃʲtʃʲ]. (See chapter 7, section 3.3 on current situation.)

ž': ([ʒʲː]). The main written form here is *зж* (e.g. *pozže* 'later'), also *жж* (e.g. *vožži* 'reins'). This pronunciation is age-based, and marked as 'older', the 'younger' version being hard [ʒː]; the latter may be interpreted as a geminate sequence of hard /ž/, thus not requiring any extra phoneme, but the former still becomes [ʒʲʒʲ] or [ʒʒʲ], either requiring the addition of soft /ž'/ to our inventory.

Thus we have the situation where a local standard variant produces an extra phoneme for those speakers (the case of *š'*), and the acceptance of an older variant (the case of *ž'*) requires one for those speakers. In the latter case we expect, and are observing, the gradual removal of the 'odd' variant, but in the former case there is no evidence that the 'odd' variant is disappearing.

3.2.1.2 (Secondary) phonetic features. While the distinctive feature 'sharp/ plain' (±Sharp), or the articulatory one of hard/soft (±Palatalised) are sufficient to account for the phonemes, as sharpness/palatalisation is certainly the marked feature, in fact the unmarked, hard consonants often have a noticeable (labio-) velarisation, involving raising of the back of the tongue, with or without lip-rounding. These effects are useful to learners in the acquisition of, particularly, the palatals /š/ and /ž/, which are thereby distinguished from their English cognates; but even the other hard consonants 'sound better' when these features are emphasised. We shall see below (section 3.2.3.2) that this phonetic feature combines with vowels in a particular way, too.

Further discussion of the distributional limitations and allophones of the consonants is left until after discussion of the vowel system.

3.2.2   Suprasegmental features of the phonetic word
We deal with this here as the description of the vowel system depends on it.

3.2.2.1 The phonetic word. By 'phonetic word' is understood any sequence of morphemes clustered around one nuclear stress. The phonetic word may, therefore, consist of more than one lexical item (a 'word' in the dictionary sense); however, it will normally include only one item from a major morphological category (noun, pronoun, adjective, adverb, verb), plus one or more minor categories (preposition, particle). The latter in Russian are always 'clitic' forms, meaning that they form a single accentual group with one member of the former set. Thus, prepositions are always 'proclitic', that is, they are attached at the front of the major item; particles are 'enclitic', that is, they are attached at the end of the major item. Note that while the particle may never be accented, the preposition may be accented, that is, may bear the primary stress of the phonetic word, leaving the major item unstressed. This is relatively rare, is a remnant of accentual changes in late Proto-Slavonic, and is currently being removed as a possibility in Contemporary Standard Russian, its retention being limited to prepositional phrases which are effectively adverbs (e.g. *za' ruku* '(take someone) by the hand', where the meaning is more often metaphorical).

3.2.2.2 Stress in Contemporary Standard Russian. Stress in Contemporary Standard Russian is *free* – it may occur on any syllable of the word and is not predictable in purely phonetic terms (such as relation to the beginning or end of the word or its number of syllables); it is also *mobile* – it may shift amongst the syllables within the paradigm of a particular word (e.g. in different cases of a noun, or different persons of a verb); and it is – at least traditionally said to be – *dynamic* – its phonetic nature is primarily one of 'amplitude', or loudness (and not pitch or length). While stress is usually said to be amplitude-based, with duration a concomitant feature (e.g. Academy Grammar 1970: 424), which would match the northern type, some linguists consider duration to be primary (e.g. Bondarko 1977: 152), though mainly on the grounds that the inherent amplitude differences between vowels are so great that absolute amplitude cannot be a distinctive feature – which would seem to mean, however, that amplitude could never be distinctive in any language. We will, therefore, accept the traditional 'amplitude' base as more realistic.

To say that stress is phonemic means that words (lexical items) may be distinguished solely on the basis of the place of their stress. Strictly, even one such minimal pair is sufficient to warrant the claim of phonemicity, but preferably one wants to see a larger number and, moreover, one wants to be sure that similar morphological or syntactic items may be so distinguished (e.g. pairs of nouns, verbs, etc.). This is certainly the case for Contemporary Standard Russian, in which there are many homographs (visual homonyms) distinguished only at the spoken level by stress position (one count of the lexical pairs thus distinguished gives some 150 pairs), e.g. *замо́к/za'mok* 'castle' ~ *zamo'k* 'lock', *атла́с/a'tlas* 'atlas' ~ *atla's* 'satin', *стоит/sto'it* 'be worth' 3ps Pres ~ *stoi't* 'stand' 3ps Pres;

then there are different inflectional forms of words thus distinguished, e.g. *pyku/ru'ki* 'hand' NP ~ *ruki'* 'hand' GS; a mid-way situation distinguishes the aspectual forms of verbs by stress, e.g. *срезать/sr'e'zat'* 'cut off' Pf ~ *sr'eza't'* Impf. For these one relies on the logical context to decide which is intended, but where different syntactic forms are involved, there is much less of a problem, e.g. *уже/u'že* 'narrower' ~ *uže'* 'already', *пропасть/pro'past'* 'abyss' NS ~ *propa'st'* 'be lost' Inf. It is only where genuine confusion might arise at the visual level that the graphic system actually indicates the stress position, e.g. *большая/bo'l'šaja* 'bigger' NSf ~ *bol'ša'ja* 'big' NSf, where the stress would if necessary be marked (by an acute) on the comparative (= less frequent) form, or to distinguish the object pronoun *что/čto* 'what' from the proclitic conjunction *čto* 'that'. A related cause for visual confusion (to be taken up later under 'Graphics') is the fact that normally written Russian does not distinguish between /o/ and /e/ when stressed and preceded by a soft consonant, the letter *e* doing duty for both; the letter *ë*, available for use in pedagogical or lexicographical writing, is drafted into use occasionally to avoid confusion, e.g. *vs'e* 'all/everyone' NP ~ *vs'o* 'all/everything' NSn are both written *все*, but the latter, where necessary, may be written *всë*.

3.2.2.3 Effects of stress; word rhythm.

As mentioned above, Russian's stress is free (as in English) and of high intensity (higher than English), such that unstressed vowels undergo quality reduction, as well as being shorter than stressed. Furthermore, the rhythmic shape of the phonetic word is that of a steady rise to the stressed syllable, then a sudden drop; three levels of intensity are discerned: the highest occurs only on the stressed syllable, the second on the pre-tonic and on absolute initial vowels, and the third elsewhere (other pre-tonic and all post-tonic syllables). To each of the last two corresponds a progressively increasing degree of reduction of vowel quality, especially of the low and mid-low vowels. Secondary stress is a word-formational feature only, occurring only in the first part of compounds; its phonetic value (level) is that of stressed vowels. In the following we shall use the terms Level 1 (stressed), Level 1a (where necessary, secondary stress), Level 2 (pre-tonic and initial) and Level 3 (other). Thus we might describe the difference between English and Russian word rhythm via the example of middle-stressed five-syllable proper names common to both – *California* (for English we can use Level 2 for its 'secondary-stress' level): the English pattern is 2 – 3 – 1 – 2 – 3 (assuming for the purpose a formal disyllabic pronunciation of the ending) – for Russian 3 – 2 – 1 – 3 – 3; *Alexandria* is also 2 – 3 – 1 – 2 – 3 in English, and 2 – 2 – 1 – 3 – 3 in Russian (the absolute initial vowel being stronger).

This situation causes some problems for phonemic description, as the reduced variants of many phonemes are identical. However, they are nevertheless

Table 8 *Russian vowel phonemes*

Articulatory method			
	Front	**Central**	**Back**
High	i ([i])		u ([u])
Mid-High			
Mid-Low	e ([ɛ])		o ([ɔ])
Low		a ([a])	

Distinctive feature method (omission of 0, e.g. Sharp not relevant for vowels)

	a	e	o	i	u
Vocalic	+	+	+	+	+
Consonantal	−	−	−	−	−
Diffuse	−	−	−	+	+
Compact	+	−	−	−	−
Grave	+	−	+	−	+
Strident	−	−	−	−	−
Nasal	−	−	−	−	−
Continuant	+	+	+	+	+
Voiced	+	+	+	+	+

variants and hence must be related to their appropriate phoneme. On the other hand, this is advantageous in respect of either the graphic or morphological systems, as neither of these takes unstressed variants into account. Hence our tabular descriptions, of whatever method, will offer only five vowel phonemes.

3.2.3   Vowels

3.2.3.1 Phonemes (stressed vowels). In light of the discussion above of the status of *i/y*, we will opt for the system which regards *y* ([ɨ]) as a variant of /i/, giving a five-vowel system as in table 8.

3.2.3.2 Allophones
(1) Stressed vowels (Level 1). The quality of stressed vowels is affected by surrounding consonants. The principle involved is that neighbouring soft (palatalised/sharp) consonants cause fronting of these vowels, and within this principle the stronger effect comes from the *following* consonant, in other words, by the regressive assimilation which is usual in Slavonic. Preceding consonants produce only an additional effect. The exception in this description is /i/, for which only the *preceding* consonant's quality is relevant. For the back vowels the fronting is noticeable – that is, it produces a distinct allophone – only in the maximal context of soft consonants on both sides. The effects are as follows:

/a/ normal [a] is fronted to [æ] only when between two soft consonants: e.g. [a] in *tak* 'so', *mat'* 'mother', *da* 'yes', *m'at* 'crumpled',
ad 'hell', *aj*, 'ouch!'; but [æ] in *p'at'* 'five';

/e/ normal [ɛ] is raised and fronted to [e] before soft; the preceding
consonant is irrelevant (in native words the only hard consonants
possible are the unpaired palatals (/š/, /ž/) and /c/): e.g. [ɛ] in *ce'l-ij*
'whole', *ob'e'd* 'dinner', *stol'e'* 'table' LS, *e'to* 'this' NSn; but [e] in
e't'i 'this' NP;

/i/ normal [i] is backed to [ɨ] after hard (paired or unpaired): e.g. [i]
in *b'il* 'beat' Past Masc, *b'it'* 'beat' Inf, *I'ra* 'Ira' NS, *I'r'e* 'Ira' LS;
but [ɨ] in *bil* 'was' Past Masc, *bit'* 'be' Inf, *vi* 'you' NP.

The rather large and clearly audible difference in the articulation of these two
variants is really what makes linguists, especially native Russian ones, want
to at least use a different *symbol* for the two, even when they accept that they
are not different phonemes. In other words, using the same symbol is counter-
intuitive, hence the tradition of using *y* to represent /i/ after hard consonants even
in such systems. The pressure of tradition and visual effect is strong; however
we intend not to succumb, so from here on we shall use *i* as the transcription
of this phoneme. (Note that *y* will continue to be used as the *transliteration* of
Cyrillic ы.)

/o/ normal [ɔ] is fronted to [ö] between two soft consonants: e.g. [ɔ]
in *dom* 'house', *kon'* 'steed', *ono'* 'it' NSn, *s'ola* 'villages' NP, *vs'o*
'all' NSn, *o'sen'* 'autumn', *jo'lka* 'fir-tree'; but [ö] in *t'ot'a* 'aunt';

/u/ normal [u] is fronted to [ü] between two soft consonants: e.g. [u]
in *tut* 'here', *sut'* 'essence', *jemu'* 'he' DS, *um* 'mind', *jug* 'south';
but [ü] in *l'u'd'i* 'people'.

(2) Secondary phonetic features of stressed vowels. Secondary effects of neighbouring consonants on vowels, noticeable only at colloquial (including dialectal)
level, or sometimes in slow style, are on- and off-glides, especially where
the consonant and vowel are maximally contrasted: hard consonant and front
vowel, soft consonant and back rounded vowel. Taking into account the labio-
velarisation present in all hard consonants (see above, section 3.2.1.2), we see
effects such as the following:

- back vowels followed by soft consonants tend to have an *i*-glide *onto* the
consonant (e.g. *kon'* 'steed', *bud'* 'be' 2ps Imper, *bit'* 'be' Inf);
- back rounded vowels following a soft consonant tend to have an *i*-glide *from*
the consonant (e.g. *n'os* 'carry' Past Masc, *kr'uk* 'hook').

Note that this is why the maximum fronting effect occurs with these back vowels
when *surrounded* by soft consonants (e.g. *t'ot'a* 'aunt', *l'u'd'i* 'people').

- all vowels followed by a hard consonant tend to have an [ə]-glide *onto* the
consonant (e.g. *vot* 'see there', *n'et* 'no', *eto* 'this' NP, *b'il* 'beat' Past Masc);

- /o/ tends to have an *u*-glide *after* a hard consonant (e.g. *dom* 'house', *kon'* 'steed');
- /o/ may have an *ü*-glide *after* a soft consonant (e.g. *s'ol* 'village' GP, *n'os* 'carry' Past Masc).

Note that a soft consonant + /o/ may therefore have either an *i*-glide or an *ü*-glide; the difference lies in the timing of the lip-rounding: earlier lip-rounding will produce a rounded glide, later an unrounded one.

It must be emphasised that these are purely automatic effects which are normally not noticeable except in certain speakers, certain dialects or certain contexts. For example, the [ə] off-glide is often heard in a drawn out, emphatic *n'et* 'no', but more often in St Petersburg than in Moscow. Nonetheless, it is worth understanding the possibility.

(3) Unstressed vowels (Levels 2 and 3). One may say that the high vowels /i/ and /u/ are unaffected by stress, whether after hard or soft consonants; the only effect of absence of stress is some shortening and perhaps a slight loss of quality, but the vowels continue to be articulated and recognised as [i], [ɨ] or [u].

For the other vowels, we may generalise as follows: /a/ and /o/ after hard consonants share the same allophones, and /a/, /e/ and /o/ after soft consonants share the same. The picture is complicated by the behaviour of foreign words and the participation of morphological factors. The details are as follows, remembering that Level 2 occurs in pre-tonic and absolute initial positions, Level 3 in pre-pre-tonic and post-tonic, including absolute final. The 'word' means the 'phonetic word', that is, including clitics, the most frequent of which are the (proclitic) prepositions. The symbol # represents the word boundary, as an indicator of an absolute initial or final vowel.

Remember, too, that the unpaired consonants have the effect appropriate to their phonetic value, thus /š/, /ž/ and /c/ are hard, /č/ (and /šč/ or /šš/) soft. The latter are here marked soft (′), though this is not necessary or normal.

In the following, the unstressed vowels in question are underlined.

(i) /a/ and /o/ after hard C or # (/HC,# – or /–Sharp, # –):

    Level 2   [ʌ] (as in Eng *up*)

              pre-tonic   /a/: *s̲a̲dy'* 'garden' NP; *na̲ sto'l* 'onto the table'; /o/: *mo̲r'a'* 'sea' NP; *po̲ mo'r'u* 'over the sea';

              absolute initial even if not pre-tonic   /a/: *a̲br'iko's* 'apricot'; /o/: *o̲goro'd* 'kitchen garden'

    Level 3   [ə] (as in Eng article *a*)

              pre-pre-tonic /a/: *k̲a̲randa'š* 'pencil'; *na̲ stol'e'* 'on the table'; /o/: *go̲lova'* 'head'; *po̲ stran'e'* 'around the country';

              post-tonic, including absolute final   /a/: *ko'mna̲ta̲* 'room'; /o/: *go'ro̲do̲m* 'town' IS; *slo'vo̲* 'word'.

(ia) Special cases:

- potential [ə] > [ʌ] before another unstressed vowel: *n*a*uga'd* 'at random' ([nʌu –]); *v*oob*šč'e*' 'in general' ([vʌʌ –]);
- prepositions tend to move to Level 2 ([ʌ] rather than [ə]) (examples *na, po* above);
- many foreign words retain Level 1 [ɔ] for /o/ in all positions: *ra'di*o 'radio', *š*osse' 'highway'. These are not predictable, though the general trend is assimilation to the native pattern;
- /o/ after the unpaired hard palatals behaves like /o/ after soft consonants, a remnant of their former status (see below);
- in the so-called Old Muscovite Norm, pre-tonic /a/ after /š/, /ž/ and /c/ had [ɨ]: *ž*ara' 'heat'; see (3) below on /e/ or /o/.

(ii) /a/, /e/ and /o/ after soft C (/SC— or /+Sharp—): Note that (1) the IPA system uses only the one symbol for all positions (both levels), while the Cyrillic descriptions use different symbols for Levels 2 and 3; the fact is that we are dealing here only with a minor difference in quality and/or length, the basic articulation being the same. The Cyrillic symbols are given alongside the IPA ones. (2) For /o/ after soft consonants the assignment of sounds to /o/ rather than /e/ is based on the morphophonemics of given words: if the given vowel is [ɔ] when stressed, then it is /o/. The reason why this comment, which will seem obvious, is made is that graphically – and therefore also in transliteration – there is no indication of the difference between /o/ and /e/, so that for most native speakers (and students!) it is often surprising to have these written *e* forms assigned to /o/. See below on the graphic system.

> Level 2   [ı]/[иᵉ]
>
> > pre-tonic   /a/: *p'*at*'i*' 'five' GS; *č'*ast*'i'čno* 'partly'; /e/: *l'*esa' 'forest' GS; *n'*e *zna'ju* 'I don't know'; /o/: *s'*olo' 'village'; *v'*ola' 'lead' Past Fem (normally 'transcribed' *selo, vela*).
>
> Level 3   [ı]/[ь]
>
> > pre-pre-tonic   /a/: *j*azyka' 'language' GS; *P'*at*'igo'rsk* 'Pyatigorsk'; /e/: *n'*eb*'esa*' 'sky' NP; *n'*e *govor'i't'e* '(you) don't say'; /o/: *č'*ornov'i'k 'draft';
> >
> > post-tonic   /a/: *vi't'*anu 'stretch out' 1ps Pres; *plo'šč'*ad'i 'square' GS; /e/: *vi'l'*eč'it 'cure' 3ps Pres; /o/: *mo'r'*o 'sea'; *je'd'*ot 'travel' 3ps Pres.

(iia) Special cases:

- /a/ in case endings and absolute final usually (now) = [ə]: *bu'r'*am 'storm' DP; *mo'r'*a 'sea' GS; the latter position was [ı] in the Old Muscovite Norm, now restricted to high-style stage pronunciation;
- /e/ (or /o/) in absolute final was [ə] in the Old Muscovite Norm; this pronunciation is still the more common in the neuter adjective NS ending *–oje, –eje*.

(iii) /e/: after hard (any) or # (/HC, #— or /–Sharp, #—) and /o/ after unpaired hard (/HP (hard palatal)— or /–Grave +Strident –Sharp—):

Level 2   [ɨ]/[ɨɪᵉ]

pre-tonic   /e/: ce̱na' 'price'; še̱st'i' 'six' GS; /o/: žo̱na' 'wife'; šo̱pta't' 'whisper' Inf

absolute initial   /e/: (foreign only) e̱kza'm'en 'exam'.

Level 3   [ə]/[ъ]

pre-pre-tonic   /e/: ce̱lova't' 'kiss' Inf; še̱rst'ano'j 'woollen'; /o/: žo̱n'ixa' 'bridegroom' GS; žo̱ltova'tij 'yellowish';

post-tonic   /e/: r'e'že̱ 'more seldom'; t'i'še̱ 'more quietly'; mu'že̱stvo 'courage'; /o/: xoro'šo̱m 'good' LS; s'e'rdco̱m 'heart' IS.

(iiia) Special cases:

- in the Old Muscovite Norm, Level 3 also had [ɨ]; [ə] is newer;
- /e/ in foreign words, parallel to /o/ after hard, is frequently given Level 1 [ɛ], often as a variant (e.g. e̱kza'm'en).

3.3   Distributional limitations (phonotactics)

The consonants are limited in their freedom in respect of the features of voice and palatalisation: in general, consonant clusters tend to be homogeneous in respect of these two features, but especially voice, since the situation in respect of palatalisation is currently changing – towards greater freedom (i.e. less assimilation).

3.3.1   Limitations on voice; assimilation

The generalisations to be made are as in the following.

(1) Clusters

(a) Voiced obstruents (but not sonorants) always lose their voice when followed by voiceless obstruents. Another way of putting this is that in a cluster of obstruents the voice status of the final one determines that of the whole cluster (or in distinctive feature terms: for paired consonants only: +Voice > −Voice / — −Voice). This is the typical Slavonic regressive assimilation; it operates in essentially the same way throughout the whole group.

(b) Voiceless obstruents always become voiced when followed by voiced obstruents (but not sonorants) (−Voice > +Voice /— +Voice); /v/ behaves like a sonorant when it is in second (last) position, but like a voiced obstruent when it is first (see below).

(2) Word-final position. Voiced obstruents lose their voice except when followed by a word or enclitic beginning with a voiced obstruent. Structurally this

context behaves as though the boundary were a voiceless obstruent. This rule, too, is typical of the whole Slavonic group; however, in this case there are two exceptions: Serbian/Croatian and Ukrainian retain voice in this position.

The rules apply only to obstruents, or to consonants paired by the feature Voice. The class of 'sonorants' (/r/l/m/n/) is excluded, since they are unpaired, all being +Voice only, at least at the phonemic level. These neither become devoiced in a cluster nor cause devoicing in a preceding obstruent. The only exception is the interesting hybrid case of the pair /v/-/f/, for which the rule is: /v/ becomes devoiced to [f] before a voiceless obstruent (thus behaving like a normal obstruent), but obstruents followed by /v/ are *not* devoiced (thus /v/ here behaves like a sonorant). This is the result of the history of /v/, which was a sonorant until the above rules began to operate after the loss of the *jers*, when the frequent occurrence of foreign [f] allowed the production of a native [f] from /v/, which became regarded as a separate phoneme (see above, section 3.2.1.1); in contexts where it could not become [f], that is, other than the two under discussion, it remained perceived as a voiced-only sonorant.

The sphere of operation of Rule (2) is larger than the (phonetic) word, as even clusters with an intervening word boundary are affected. Further, the nature of the boundary is relevant, as clitic boundaries behave differently from 'independent' (non-clitic) ones. It will be of use to separate out the various boundary types to better observe the facts. We shall allot the following abbreviations:

#0 internal, or stem + ending (that is, a 'non-boundary', as inflectional endings do not involve boundaries in any phonetic sense);

#1 word + word, or word + pause (that is, a 'full' boundary);

#2 proclitic + word (such as preposition + noun/pronoun/adjective);

#3 word + enclitic (such as verb + particle);

Note that ##1–3 are written with a space, but ##2–3 form a single 'phonetic word'.

#4 prefix + stem;

#5 stem + suffix.

Note that ##4–5 are not written with a space and are normally viewed as single words.

Further, since the nature of the sound *after* the boundary is relevant, we shall allot abbreviations to these as follows:

vowel	a
sonorant (including /v/)	b
voiced obstruent (not /v/)	c
voiceless obstruent	d
silence	e

The behaviour of the feature Voice in these contexts is as follows:

Rule (1a): +Voiced (obstr) > −Voiced

	a	b	c	d	e
#1	+	+	−	+	+
#2	−	−	−	+	−
#3	+	+	−	0	−
#4	−	−	−	+	−
#5	−	−	−	+	−

(+ = operates; − = does not operate; 0 = no real examples, would be +)

Examples (in this section using transliteration only):

#1 +

    a: *ded ušël* 'grandfather went off', /d/ > [t];

    b: *ded našël* 'grandfather found', /d/ > [t];

    d: *ded sošël* 'grandfather went down', /d/ > [t];

    e: . . . *ded.* '. . . grandfather', /d/ > [t].

#1 −

    c: *ded byl* 'grandfather was', /d/ > [d].

#2 +

    d: *v škole* 'in school', /v/ > [f]; *pered tem* 'before that', /d/ > [t];

#2 −

    a: *v okno* 'through the window', /v/ > [v];

    b: *v reku* 'into the river', /v/ > [v];

    c: *v dom* 'into the house', /v/ > [v].

#3 +

    a: *ded už* 'it's grandfather!', /d/ > [t];

    b: *ded li* 'is it grandfather?'; *ded ved'* 'but grandfather', both /d/ > [t];

    d: (no such particles).

#3 −

    c: *ded že* 'but grandfather', /d/ > [d].

#4 +

    d: *raz–skaz* 'story', /z/ > [s] (also graphic); *v–xodit'* 'enter' Inf, /v/ > [f].

#5 +

    d *naxod–ka* 'a find', /d/ > [t]; *pev–cy* 'singers' NP, /v/ > [f].

Compare the sonorants, which neither change themselves (i.e. they are not devoiced, e.g. *verx* 'summit', *volk* 'wolf', *lampa* 'lamp', *bank* 'bank'), nor cause change (voicing) to preceding (e.g. *teatr* 'theatre', *smysl* 'sense', *ritm* 'rhythm', *žizn'* 'life'). In the latter case, it should be noted that there does exist a casual-style variant in which the final sonorant is devoiced after a voiceless obstruent (thus by *progressive* assimilation), as in the first three examples, most commonly in the case of /r/ and /l/ (e.g. *teatr*); however, the more frequent pronunciation of these two is now syllabic [ŗ] and [ḷ], in the case of /r/ in reality an inserted [ə] plus consonantal [r]; in other words both of these are close to the final sounds of Eng *theatre* and *people*. For /m/ and /n/, too, the more common pronunciation is syllabic, more so than Eng *rhythm*, which usually has a strong [ə], but similar to the syllabic variant of *mutton*.

Rule (1b): –Voiced (obstr) > +Voiced

	a	b	c	d	e
#0	–	–	+	–	–
#1	–	–	+	–	–
#2	–	–	+	–	–
#3			+		
#4	–	–	+	–	–
#5	–	–	+	–	–

That is, this rule operates at all boundaries, but only when followed by a voiced obstruent (not /v/). Examples:

#0 c: (now graphics reflect the change): *gd'e* 'where?' < OR *k(ъ)de*, /k/ > [g];
   b: *sneg* 'snow', /s/ > [s]; *tvoj* 'your', /t/ > [t].
#1 c: *kak dela* 'how are things?', /k/ > [g];
   b: *kak naš/vaš* 'how is our/your?', /k/ > [k].
#2 c: *ot goroda* 'from the town', /t/ > [d];
   b: *s nami/vami* 'with us/you', /s/ > [s].
#3 c: *kak že* 'what do you mean?', /k/ > [g];
   b: *brat ved'* 'but (my) brother', /t/ > [t].
#4 c: *s–bit'* 'knock off', /s/ > [z]; *ot–zyv* 'report', /t/ > [z];
   b: *ot–nesti/ot–vesti* 'carry off', /t/ > [t].
#5 c: *pros'ba* 'request', /s'/ > [z'];
   b: *mestnyj* 'local', /t/ > [t]; *listva* 'foliage' /t/ > [t].

Note that amongst the voiced allophones produced by a following voiced obstruent are three which do not exist as phonemes, viz.:

   [d͡z]   *otec byl* '(my) father was', /c/ > [d͡z];
   [d͡ʒ]   *doč' byla* '(my) daughter was', /č'/ > [d͡ʒ];
   [ɣ]   *petux byl* 'the cockerel was'; *ix doč'* 'their daughter', /x/ > [ɣ].

One final phonetic comment, in relation especially to Rule 2 on the devoicing of obstruents in word-final position (#1e): while the feature of Tense/Lax is not normally considered relevant for Russian, since for vowels length is dependent on stress and is not phonemic, and for consonants the usual association of

Tense = −Voiced and Lax = +Voiced is assumed to be valid, it is possible that the allophones produced by voice assimilation involve a change in voice, but *not* in tension, such that a devoiced allophone might still be lax, that is, might not acquire the tension of the voiceless phoneme, and the voiced allophone might remain tense. The latter is actually less likely, since it involves an assimilated sound becoming more 'strongly' articulated than its underlying phoneme, while for the former, intuition tells us that assimilation of laxness is also more natural. For the same reason, it is not difficult to accept the likelihood of an underlying lax sound remaining lax. The problem with this issue is the lack of reliable instrumental indicators of tension ∼ laxness in consonants: instruments identify the features of length, vocal cord activity and spectral frequency, but identify articulatory tension at best only by larg(er) spread of acoustic energy. At the empirical level, this may be the reason why native speakers (especially linguistically naive ones) are convinced that they are pronouncing voiced consonants in final position, claiming that, say, *rod* 'sort' and *rot* 'mouth' are *not* phonetically identical. Of course, it is equally likely that such convictions actually stem from orthographical or morphological considerations. All formal descriptions insist that such pairs are indeed homophones (in the Nominative form only).

3.3.2   *Limitations on hard/soft (in mixed clusters)*

3.3.2.1 Word-final position and clusters of soft + hard. Limitations on the occurrence of soft consonants vary somewhat within the three articulatory groups of paired consonants.

(1) The soft *velars* may never occur before a hard consonant (or in final position); this is a reflection of the (relatively) recent appearance of these sounds, limited to the pre-front-vowel position.

(2) The soft *labials*, on the other hand, have been becoming more limited throughout their recent history; in Ukrainian they are as limited as the velars, occurring only before front vowels; in Belarusian and in some Russian dialects they may occur before any vowel, but not before a consonant or finally; for Contemporary Standard Russian they are mostly still free in final position, only /m'/ having been virtually removed. Contemporary Standard Russian examples of other final soft labials are common (e.g. *st'ep'* 'steppe', *golub'* 'pigeon', *krov'* 'blood'), but /m'/ occurs in only two words: *s'em'* 'seven' and *vos'em'* 'eight'; common inflectional endings which had /m'/ in Old Russian now have /m/ (e.g. Instrumental Singular Masculine).

In clusters, soft labials have already disappeared, cf. the derived adjectives from the above: *st'epnoj* 'steppe', *krovnij* 'blood', and the diminutive *golubka* 'little pigeon' (endearment).

Given the dialectal situation overall and the Contemporary Standard Russian situation in clusters, it is likely that soft labials will sooner or later disappear from final position, too.

(3) Only the soft *dentals* remain completely free in these positions:
       final: *t'en'* 'shadow', *s'ad'* 'sit' 2ps Imper, *p'at'* 'five';
       clusters: *sud'ba* 'fate', *p'is'mo* 'letter', *St'en'ka* 'Steve' (< *St'epan*).

The hard or soft nature of the above consonants is indicated in the graphical system, the soft version being indicated by the 'soft sign' (ь), that is, the former front *jer*. This is the only function for this letter.

3.3.2.2 Clusters of hard + soft. In this case the language is currently changing in the direction of non-assimilation. The former situation, typified by the Old Muscovite Norm of a century ago, might be summed up as follows: labials and dentals followed by any soft consonant became soft; velars became soft only before other velars. The present situation is that all consonants are softened regularly only before a member of the same group (labial + labial, dental + dental, etc.); otherwise assimilative softening is more and more considered a marker of age, that is, it is becoming old-fashioned. Already gone is softening of non-velars before velars; elsewhere, as in the previous context, the labials are moving faster than the dentals, such that even before other labials they are now typically not softened; of the dentals, /r/ and /l/ are never softened. Often particular words (high-frequency) continue to show softening even though the equivalent group rules suggest this should not be the case. In this context the palatal group is relevant in respect of /č/ (and /šč/ or /šš/), since these are phonetically soft; however, the typical assimilation here is of preceding dentals, which are also assimilated in respect of *place* of articulation, that is, they become palatals, so we will deal with most of them separately in the next section.

From the point of view of hearing, or 'proving', whether softening is occurring or not, a feature which assists greatly is the above-mentioned (section 3.2.3.2) effect of soft consonants on preceding stressed vowels, e.g. if one hears a raised [e] for /e/, the reason must be that the following consonant is soft. Examples of the occurrence of softening in different contexts follow.

(1) Softening normal (recommended by pronouncing dictionaries):
       double velar: *m'agk'ij* 'soft' and *l'ogk'ij* 'easy', /g/ > [xʲ] (soft + devoiced + fricative); in these, too, we hear the fronted vowels [æ] and [ö] for /a/ and /o/; *k k'itu* 'towards the whale', /k/ > [kʲ];
       double dental (particular words): *sr'edn'ij* 'average', /d/ > [dʲ] and vowel is [e]; *jesl'i* 'if', /s/ > [sʲ] and [e]; *vm'est'e* 'together', /s/ > [sʲ] and [e].

(2) Softening acceptable (variants possible):

double dental: *d'er'evn'a* 'village', /v/ > [v]/[vʲ] and vowel correspondingly [ɛ]/[e];

dental + /j/: *sjest'* 'eat' Inf, /s/ > [s] or [sʲ]; note that this is possible
only at a prefix boundary (#4), where the 'hard sign' (ъ) (the former
back *jer*) graphically indicates the theoretical independence, and
hardness, of the prefix {s}, as well as the retention of the root-
initial /j/;

labial + /j/: *vjexat'* 'enter' Inf, /v/ > [v] or [vʲ]; see the preceding
comment on the relevance of a boundary.

(3) Softening not recommended:

double labial: *vm'est'e* 'together', /v/ > [v];

/r/ + dental: *s'erd'its'a* 'get angry' 3ps Pres, /r/ > [r] and [ɛ];

pre-velar: *kr'epk'ij* 'strong', /p/ > [p]; *r'edk'ij* 'rare', /d/ > [t]; in both
we hear the non-raised vowel [ɛ];

pre-labial: *dv'e* 'two' Fem, /d/ > [d]; *razv'e* 'really', /z/ > [z];

pre-dental: *uč'ebn' ik* 'textbook', /b/ > [b] and [ɛ];

labial + palatal: *kr'epč'e* 'stronger', /p/ > [p] and [ɛ].

(4) Softening not acceptable:

/r/ + non-dental: *t'erp'it* 'endure', 3ps Pres; *S'erb'ija* 'Serbia', both /r/
> [r], and in both we hear the vowel [ɛ], not [e];

/l/: *moln'ija* 'lightning', /l/ > [l]; even before palatal: *molč'at'* 'be
silent' Inf.

3.3.3   Limitations on place of articulation

3.3.3.1 Clusters of dental + palatal. The dental stops and fricatives (/t/, /d/,
/s/, /z/) shift into the palatal area before a palatal other than /j/. Before /j/
they are simply softened (see above). This is a phenomenon natural to many
languages, including English: cf. rapid style *Is she?*, where the /z/ becomes [ʒ]
(or devoiced to [ʃ]) before the [ʃ]. The results are as follows (remembering also
the assimilation of voice):

s, z > š /—š   *sšit'* 'sew', *iz šest'i* 'out of six'

> ž /—ž   *izžit'* 'wear out', *s ženoj* 'with (my) wife'

> š' /—č'   *sč'itat'* 'count', *izvozč'ik* 'coachman', *s č'est'ju*
'with honour'

Note that this last produces the same sound sequence ([ʃtʃʲ]) as the morphophoneme {šč'}, written with a single grapheme (щ). (See chapter 7, section 3.1
on the current pronunciation of these.)

t, d > t' / — š   *mladšij* 'younger', *pr'išedšij* 'arrived' Past Part,
ot šest'i 'from six';

Russian descriptions usually mark this as t > č/—š; this is partly to avoid introducing the 'new' allophonic sounds, palatal [c] (t') and [f] (d'), and partly to indicate the length of the combined unit: it differs from simple [t͡ʃ] (č') in having extra length of both the [c] and the [ʃ] parts. It seems sufficient to distinguish [cʃ] (t'š) from [t͡ʃ] (č') to indicate this length, and preferable to writing [t͡ʃʃ] (č'š), which leaves very unclear the actual articulation. Note also the reduction involved in the cluster čš: č' > t' /—š (e.g. lu*čš*e 'better'), leaving the same overall sound.

> t, d > d' /—ž   ot *ženi* 'from (my) wife', *Džon* 'John'

Here, too, the combined sound is clearly a sequence, to be distinguished from simple [d͡ʒ], as in Eng *John*.

> t, d > t' /—č'   l'ot*č'*ik 'pilot', p'er'evod*č'*ik 'translator'

A similar comment applies as for [cʃ] above, the Russian description here being the even more unlikely and unhelpful [t͡ʃt͡ʃ] (č'č'). The sound involved is a double-length palatal [c] plus a single soft [ʃʲ], or better, simply [c] plus [t͡ʃʲ] (see below, section 3.3.4.1 on reduction of geminates).

> n > n' /—š, ž, č'   zast'en*č'*ivij 'shy'

Here, too, a new palatal allophone is the simplest description, and not just a soft [nʲ], though there is little, if any, audible difference.

One last sequence which it is useful to include here, though it does not involve a change in place of articulation, but rather extra length, is:

> t, d + c: ot*ca* 'father' GS, p'eše*xodci* 'pedestrians' NP

Again, the Russian descriptions have for this t > c / —c, which gives the visual sequence [t͡sts], likewise unhelpful as to the pronunciation, which involves double-length [t] plus double-length [s]. We prefer to leave this in its base form, namely [t͡ts], which is effectively also the articulation, the length of the [s] being less significant and non-obligatory.

3.3.4   Simplification of clusters
Clusters of three or more consonants are frequently simplified in pronunciation by the deletion of one of them. (This rule would follow the previous ones of assimilation, as will be seen.) Some effects are unrestricted, others are lexically restricted. Clusters of two may be simplified by dissimilation or deletion.

3.3.4.1 Geminate consonants
(1)/V—V. Where a cluster of two identical (geminate) consonants is surrounded by vowels, the more common pronunciation is double or long, that is, the

pronunciation is geminate, too. In native words there is normally a morpheme boundary between the two, usually an affix boundary (#4 or #5), which no doubt is responsible for the double-length pronunciation (also, usually these clusters are historically the result of the loss of the *jers*); in foreign words the situation is fluid at present, and even the direction is unclear: some believe that these words were initially pronounced as singles, and that the double pronunciation is new and growing; others see the reverse – original double (= spelling) pronunciation giving way to single, perhaps influenced by current donor-language pronunciation, especially English. At any rate, synchronically, perhaps the most likely analysis is that the spelling tends to encourage double pronunciation, and this will be supported by the occurrence of given groups in the native system – hence dental stops and fricatives and /n/, rather than labials, velars or /l/; meanwhile the current pronouncing dictionaries seem to be moving in subsequent editions mainly from double to single pronunciation, but may simply be more accepting of variation. For example (Pron. Dict. 1960, 1983 and 1989 editions):

> *gru'ppa* 'group'   1960: [p]; 1983/1989: [pp] or [p];
> *t'el'egra'mma* 'telegram'   1960: [mm]; 1983/1989: [mm] or [m];
> *gra'mma* 'gram' GS   1960: [mm]; 1983/1989: [m];
> *ka'ssa* 'cash-desk'   1960/1983/1989: [ss];
> *kass'i'r* 'cashier'   1960: [s's']; 1983/1989: [s's'] or *acceptable* [s']
> (where *acceptable* means a less common variant).

(2) / — C, #. Where geminate consonants are adjacent to another consonant or a final boundary, they are always reduced to one; that is, one cannot normally have geminate/long consonant plus a third consonant or silence. This is a general rule, covering both native and foreign words, even where an affix boundary is involved. Here, too, however, there is uncertainty and variation, such that dictionaries now allow double even in final position. For example: *russk'ij* 'Russian' ({s–sk}) /ss/ > [s]; *rass'č'el'ina* 'crevice' ({raz–šč–}) /sš'č'/ > [ʃʃtʃ'] (š'š'č') > [ʃtʃ'] (š'č'); *rasskazat'* 'tell' ({raz–skaz–}) /ssk/ > [sk].
   The confusion in direction of foreign words may be seen by the following:

> *t'el'egra'mm* 'telegram' GP   1960/1983/1989: [m];
> *summ* 'sum' GP   1960/1983/1989: [m] or *acceptable* [mm];
> *kass* 'cash-desk' GP   1960/1989 /ss/ > [s] or [ss] (1983: no comment,
> which should imply [ss]).

Stress position is relevant also, for example (1983): *to'nna* NS: [nn]; *tonna'ž* 'tonnage': [n]; and the example above of *ka'ssa* ~ *kass'i'r*, indicating that preceding stress supports double, following stress single.
   Other examples are: *šotlandci* 'Scots' NP /ndc/ > [nt͡ts] > [nt͡s]; *istca* 'plaintiff' GS /stc/ > [st͡s]; *s'erdce* 'heart' /rdc/ > [rt͡ts] > [rt͡s], all usually treated as loss of a medial consonant.

3.3.4.2 Word-specific clusters. Here we have remnants of older simplifications which occurred as the language shifted from open- to closed-syllable structure. Currently, here as elsewhere, the language is undergoing a spelling influence which resists simplification. Some of the groups and words involved are:

(1) by dissimilation

/čt/, /čn/ > [št], [šn]   *čto* 'what, that'; *kon'e'čno* 'of course'; but: *čte'n'ij–e* 'reading' [čt]; *sro'čno* 'urgent' NSn [čn].

(2) by deletion

/vstv/ > [stv]   *ču'v–stvo* 'feeling'; *zdra'v–stvujt'e* 'hello'; but: *d'e'v–stvo* 'maidenhood' [vstv];

/stn/, /zdn/, /stl/, /zdl/   as a group, tend to lose the middle consonant: *gru'stno* 'sad' Adv [sn]; *p'ozdno* 'late' Adv [zn]; *sčastl'i'vij* 'happy' [sl]; /lnc/ > [n͡ts]   *so'lnce* 'sun';

/ndsk/ > [nsk]   *šotla'nd–sk'ij* 'Scottish';

/stsk/ > [ssk]   *marks'i'st–sk'ij* 'Marxist'; note that the morphological structure of this word excludes it from further change under the rule of geminate simplification (*> [sk]), which would lose too much structural information.

3.3.4.3 Simplification by insertion. Where loss is prevented by grammatical factors, an *inserted vowel* may appear, as an alternative solution to difficult groups. From the historical perspective, these represent the older response to the loss of the *jers* (ъ/ь), which was to retain the *jer*, that is, treat it as strong, in order to avoid the cluster which would be formed by dropping it. The contexts given below occur.

(1) Geminate consonants at proclitic and affix boundaries. Where the proclitic (preposition or prefix) ends in the same consonant as the root-initial one and there is another consonant following, we have the pattern $C_1\#C_1C_2$, which, as we saw above, led to the deletion of one C_1; here we have the insertion of /o/, the reflex of /ъ/. For example:

(a) proclitic (#2): *vo vtorn'ik* 'on Tuesday', *so stud'entom* 'with the student';

(b) prefix (#4): *so–sč'itat'* 'count', *vo–vl'eč'* 'entice'.

(2) Two consonants in final position, usually involving a suffix (#5). *p'is'em* 'letter' GP (#0) (stem: *p'is'm–*), *polok* 'shelf' GP, *marok* 'stamp' GP (stems *pol–k–, mark–*); but cf. *polk* 'regiment', *park* 'park', with no insertion.

(3) Other. *bož–e–sk'ij* 'godlike' (stem *bog–*); but cf. *praž–sk'ij* 'Prague' (stem *prag–*), Adj, *p'et'erburg–sk'ij* 'St Petersburg' Adj, with no insertion.

(4) Two lexically specific initial clusters have been generalised in respect of an insertion after all prepositions (the forms of *vs'–* 'all' and *mn–* 'me').

    so vs'em 'with all', *ko vs'emu* 'to all', *b'ezo vs'ego* 'without all';
    vo mn'e 'in me', *ko mn'e* 'to me', *podo mnoj* 'under me';
    (*vo vs'om* 'in everything', also fits the phonetic rule of (1)).

We shall see in the morphology the extent to which this 'inserted' vowel has become part of the system.

3.4   The subsystems of foreign words and abbreviations

3.4.1   Foreign borrowings

The rules of phonotactics described above may be broken or added to in the pronunciation of foreign borrowings (that is, those which have become a part of the language) as well as of foreign words (those which are used as reference to items of another language). While the latter on their own are certainly not to be considered any part of the home language's system, the former group do have such a claim, as was alluded to in the discussion of the soft velars (section 3.2.1.1). In many cases the words concerned were borrowed many centuries ago and often native speakers may not even think of them as foreign in any way. Thus it is impossible to exclude them completely from the 'system'. The most appropriate solution is to assign them to a subsystem with rules which may be alternative or additional to those of the base system. The three main features of this subsystem follow (for further discussion and examples see Cubberley 1993).

(1) Consonants before /e/. By far the most interesting and important feature of this subsystem in Russian is the possibility of having paired hard consonants before /e/. Long-established examples include: *kafe'* 'café', *šosse'* 'highway', *mode'l'* 'model'; more recent ones are *fone't'ika* 'phonetics', *pri'nter* 'printer', *komp'ju'ter* 'computer'. Against these are others in which the consonant is soft – usually, but not necessarily, old borrowings, e.g. *ko'f'e* 'coffee', *eff'e'kt* 'effect', *sportsm'e'n* 'sportsman'. The choice is therefore phonetically unpredictable; nor is there a morphological clue: both *kafe* and *kof'e* are indeclinable, a morphological feature of foreign borrowings. The unpredictability is perhaps best seen in the large set of borrowings beginning with the Latin prefix *de–/des–*, where the proportions with hard and soft /d/ are roughly equal. We are talking here, of course, of the standard language recommendations; the majority of such words are literary in the general sense, and so the majority of speakers would not have any idea which was the 'correct' pronunciation. They will tend to generalise, and here lies the crux of the matter: if they generalise 'hard', they are opting for a general 'foreign' solution; if they generalise 'soft', they are opting for a 'native' solution. Both approaches are employed, but what is interesting is that the 'foreign' solution is actually the one which would bring

about the elegant completion of the consonant–vowel relationship, by allowing all paired consonants to occur freely before all vowel phonemes, since 'hard C + /e/' is the only one not possible. The jury is still out on what will actually happen, but this juror believes that speakers are heading for the elegant phonemic solution.

(2) Unstressed /o/ and /e/. Here, too, many long-established borrowings continue to be pronounced – at least in the standard recommendation – as unreduced vowels (Level 1) [ɔ] and [ɛ], e.g. *ra'd'io* 'radio', *šosse'* 'highway'. The trend, however, seems clearer than in the preceding situation, in that subsequent editions of the recommendations tell us that speakers are tending to reduce these vowels in accordance with the native norm, for example: *šosse*: 1960 [ɔ] only, 1983 [ʌ] or [ɔ].

In the case of /e/ there is a clear correlation between this feature and the preceding one: in such words [ɛ] is normally preceded by a hard consonant, while a soft consonant normally causes reduction of the vowel, e.g. *deka'n* 'dean' may be [dɛ] or [dʲɪ], not any other combination. 'Surviving' words which remain 'foreign' do so mainly because of their high frequency, always a restrictor of analogical change. This is not a problem which affects phonemes or the system, but only their allophones in relation to stress, and so we should not be surprised at the direction of the adjustment.

(3) Geminate consonants. As indicated above (section 3.3.4.1), geminate consonants in native words arose because of lost *jers* (ъ/ь) at morpheme boundaries; as such the group continued – and still continues – to be pronounced as double (or long). It was only in borrowings that geminates could appear inside roots, and, perhaps through the influence of the foreign pronunciation, for example of English (the more and more frequent source of borrowings), the reduction to a single consonant appears to be becoming more and more common, though, as noted above, the trend is unclear. While there is no effect on the phonemic or phonetic system related to this feature, there is a problem related to the graphic system and its relation to pronunciation: generally speaking, the Russian graphic system is a good guide to, or predictor of, the pronunciation (see details below), and that system has probably been the most important motive for change this century (the 'spelling influence' factor), and this would make us expect that geminate consonants would be, or continue to be, pronounced double. If the trend towards single pronunciation is accurate, it is a move against spelling influence.

3.4.2   Abbreviations

As with most languages, abbreviations began life as written forms meant to reduce printing space, but then became spoken forms, mainly this century, as they became typical of bureaucratic language and this language became more and more commonly spoken in democratic societies. The Soviet Union was one of the most bureaucratised societies in the world, and this is reflected in the language by the huge number of abbreviations and acronyms formed during that period. One of the most typical and specific methods of formation was the building of syllables (or parts) of multiple words into single new words (the so-called 'stump compounds'), which are relatively rare in English, and are usually specifically bureaucratic, e.g. *Aussat* (Australian Satellite), *EUCOM* (European Command). Many words formed in this way in the Soviet period are familiar to English (and most other languages), e.g. *kolkhoz, politburo*. Otherwise the available forms are structured as in English: initials said as initials (e.g. Eng *BBC*, Rus *KGB*), initials said as acronyms (e.g. Eng *UNESCO*, Rus *TASS*), mixed initials (e.g. Eng *VLAN* [vi'lan], Rus *SŠA* 'USA' [sɛʃa']) and mixtures of initials and syllables (e.g. Eng *AusAID*, Rus *GULag*). We take up the question of the formation and morphology of abbreviations elsewhere (chapter 3, section 2.1.3.1; chapter 5, section 2.2.3.3), but here we offer a few relevant phonetic features.

(1) Stress and vowels. The position of stress in abbreviations is fixed on the final syllable, which follows the pattern of compound words, where the stress is always on the second, or last, part. This applies to all, including initials. Insofar as the abbreviations are native Russian, for the most part the acronyms follow the rules of normal words in respect of reduction of unstressed vowels. However, there is some variation here in the stump type, where unstressed /o/ and /e/ may retain their stressed variants [ɔ], [ɛ]; probably the explanation is the perception of them as compounds, in which secondary stress on the first part is normal. For example, in the full compound *tr'oxl'e'tn'ij* 'three-year-old' the primary stress is on the syllable *–l'et–*, yet the first vowel /o/ is pronounced [ɔ]; in the same way, in the stump compound *Mosga'z* 'Moscow Gas (Co.)' /o/ is [ɔ]. On the other hand, in *kolxo'z* 'collective farm', the first /o/ is reduced to [ʌ]. The difference is caused by the shift of words from perceived acronyms, that is, compounds, to simple words. The parallel procedure in initial acronyms is common in both Russian and English, where one observes former acronyms like *radar* or *scuba* accepted as words; Russian may accept this transition less easily than English, in that such acronyms more often continue to be written in capitals or remain indeclinable; examples of the full transition are *vuz* 'higher education institute', *bomž* 'vagrant'.

(2) Consonant assimilation. For the same reasons (the retention of the compound nature of stump compounds), while they are thus perceived the rules of voice assimilation are suspended. For example, in *Mosgaz*, the /s/ remains [s] and is not assimilated (*> [z]) to the following [g]; similarly, in *profb'il'e't* 'union card', the /f/ remains [f]. This feature and the preceding normally and logically go together, that is, one would not expect to see reduction of the vowel

but no assimilation or the reverse (i.e. assimilation without reduction); however, during the transition process this may happen: the Soviet compound *sovnarxoz* 'Soviet (national) economy' is described at different stages as [sɔvnʌrxɔs] and [səvnʌrxɔs], both of which represent the normal first and final stages; but, curiously, also as [sɔfnʌrxɔs], that is, the /v/ is treated as word-final and devoiced. This illustrates the real way in which these forms are unusual: if the forms *prof* and *bil'et* occurred as separate(d) words in a phrase (not to mention as a single word), the /f/ would become [v], yet it does not do so in the compound form. No doubt it is precisely the need to retain the separate lexical identity of the parts in spite of the apparent phonetic union which accounts for this. As the parts are subsumed into the new whole, the phonetic unity is allowed to dominate.

(3) Initials. The initial type (pronounced as such, and not as acronyms) offers one other curiosity: the name of the initial is sometimes different from its normal alphabetic name. The Russian names are styled in principle as in English, with the vowel [ɛ] normally used after the consonant sound where English uses [i] (thus [bɛ], [vɛ], etc., parallel to Eng [bi], [vi]); as in English, there are exceptions (like Eng [keɪ̯], Rus [ka]). (Incidentally, here too, in the letter-names, is a case of native paired hard plus /e/, albeit in an artificial situation.) Examples of the alteration of names in initial abbreviations are: *KGB* [kɛgɛbɛ], with [kɛ] instead of regular [ka], and *SŠA* 'USA' [sɛ ʃa], with [sɛ] instead of regular [ɛs].

3.5   Morphophonology

For the purposes of this chapter, we introduce the major alternations which will be seen to operate in both morphology and word-formation. We will not here detail their locations, but only indicate this in general terms. The intention is to identify the nature and origin of the alternations, and more detail of the latter may be found in chapter 1.

In this section we give examples in transliteration, thus with *i* and *y*, but with soft consonants marked before /e/; stress position is marked; and endings are marked off by a dash (including zero as –∅).

3.5.1   Vowels

3.5.1.1 Pre-Slavonic. The oldest set of vowel alternations date from Indo-European, and appear inside roots. They are in principle similar to the alternations we see in English, like *sing ~ sang ~ sung ~ song*. The two most frequent are *e ~ o* and *u ~ o*, also *i/y ~ e/o*. Examples are: *n'esti ~ nosit'* 'carry' Determinate/Indeterminate; *dux ~ –dox ~ –dyxat'* 'breath(e)' Nom/Nom/Verb; *–birat/ ~ ber– ~ –bor* 'take' Impf ~ Pres ~ Nom. Since these are pre-Slavonic, we cannot 'explain' them by any rules of Slavonic phonological history. In some cases, however, their use is specifically Slavonic, for example, the ±Determinate function, which replaced a pre-Slavonic ±Iterative one.

3.5.1.2 Slavonic

o ~ *ø, e* ~*ø*   very common, especially throughout the nominal system, the result of the loss of the Old Russian vowels *ъ/ь*. The most common context for the vowel alternant (*o/e*) is in roots ending in a consonant cluster followed by a zero ending (itself formerly a *jer*). Examples are: *son* ~ *sna* 'dream' NS ~ GS; *d'en'–ø* ~ *dn'–a* 'day' NS ~ GS; *okn–o'* ~ *o'kon–ø* 'window' NS ~ GP; *p'ej–ø*~*p'j–u* 'drink' 2ps Imper ~ 1ps Pres.

i ~ *e, y* ~ *o*   not common, the second a reflex of *ъ/ь*, before /j/. In verbs, Inf ~ Pres, e.g. *bri–t'* ~ *br'e'j–u* 'shave' Inf ~ 1ps Pres; *my–t'* ~ *mo'j–u* 'wash' Inf ~ 1ps Pres. An associated alternation is *i* ~ *j* (actually *i* ~ *ø*), e.g. *pi–t'* ~ *p'j–u* 'drink' Inf ~ 1ps Pres.

ov ~ *u, ev* ~ *ju*   not common, a reflex of the old diphthong *oụ /eụ* in heterosyllabic versus tautosyllabic position (at the time of the opening of the syllable). In verbs, Inf ~ Pres, e.g. *kova'–t'* ~ *kuj–u'* 'forge' Inf ~ 1ps Pres; *pl'eva'–t'* ~ *pl'uj–u'* 'spit' Inf ~ 1ps Pres.

ja ~ *n, ja* ~ *m* (where /j/ represents any palatal or soft consonant) not common, the reflex of the old nasal vowels, likewise in heterosyllabic versus tautosyllabic position. In verbs, Inf ~ Pres, e.g. *nača'–t'* ~ *načn–u'* 'begin' Inf ~ 1ps Pres; *vz'a–t'* ~ *voz'm–u'* 'take' Inf ~ 1ps Pres.

3.5.2 Consonants (all Slavonic)

3.5.2.1 Alternations involving palatals. The following are typically given in textbooks as a table of mutations, very common in the verbal system. They are the result of the Proto-Slavonic palatalisation process (caused by a following /j/ for all consonants, and by any front vowel for the velars).

(1) Velars (first Conjugation verbs)

g ~ *ž*   *mog–u'* ~ *m'ož–et* 'be able' 1ps ~ 3ps Pres; *b'eg–u'* ~ *b'ež –i't* 'run' 1ps ~ 3ps Pres;

k ~ *č*   *p'ek–u'* ~ *p'eč–ë't* 'bake' 1ps ~ 3ps Pres; *pla'ka–t'* ~ *pla'č–u* 'cry' Inf ~ 1ps Pres;

x ~ *š*   *maxa'–t'* ~ *maš–u'* 'wave' Inf ~ 1ps Pres;

sk ~ *šč*   *iska'–t'* ~ *išč–u'* ~ *i'šč–et* 'seek' Inf ~ 1ps ~ 3ps Pres;

zg ~ *zž* (phonetic [ʒʒ])   *bry'zga–t'* ~ *bry'zž–u* 'sprinkle' Inf ~ 1ps Pres.

(2) Labials (/p/b/f/v/m/). All alternate with labial + /l'/; all examples are Inf ~ 1ps ~ 3ps Pres:

kupi'–t' ~ kupl'–u' ~ ku'p–it 'buy'; ka'pa–t' ~ ka'pl'–u ~ ka'pl'–et
'drip'; l'ubi'–t' ~ l'ubl'–u' ~ l'u'b–it 'love';
grafi'–t' ~ grafl'–u' ~ gra'f–it 'draft'; lovi'–t' ~ lovl'–u' ~ lo'v–it
'catch'; dr'ema'–t' ~ dr'eml'–u' ~ dr'e'ml'–et 'doze'.

(3) Dentals. Unless marked, examples are Inf ~ 1ps Pres ~ 3ps Pres; the last
may be replaced by the Past Participle Passive (PPP) (for /t/ and /d/ there are
two sets, the first the Old Russian (East Slavonic) one, the second Old Church
Slavonic):

    t ~ č (OR)   *plati'–t' ~ plač–u' ~ pla't–it* 'pay'; *m'eta'–t' ~ m'eč–u'*
    ~ m'e'č–et 'cast';

    t ~ šč (OCS)   *pro–sv'eti'–t' ~ –sv'ešč–u' ~ –sv'et–i't* 'enlighten';
    ropta'–t' ~ ropšč–u' ~ ro'pšč–et 'grumble';

    d ~ ž (R)   *vi'd'e–t' ~ vi'ž–u ~ vi'd–it* 'see'; *gloda'–t' ~ glož–u' ~*
    glo'ž–et 'gnaw'; *po–sadi'–t' ~ –saž–u' ~ –sa'ž–en* 'set' (PPP);

    d ~ žd (OCS)   *o–sadi'–t' ~ –saž–u' ~ –sažd'–ë'n* 'beseige' (PPP);
    rodi'–t' ~ rožd'–ë'n 'give birth' (PPP) ~ *rožd'e'nij–e* 'birth' NS;

    s ~ š   *po–v'e'si–t' ~ –v'e'š–u ~ –v'e'š–en* 'hang' (PPP); *pis–a't' ~*
    piš–u' ~ pi'š–et 'write';

    z ~ ž   *u–grozi'–t' ~ –grož–u' ~ –gro'ž–en* 'threaten' (PPP); *skaza'–t'*
    ~ skaž–u' ~ ska'ž–et 'say';

    st ~ šč   *pusti'–t' ~ pušč–u' ~ pu'st–it* 'let';

    zd/zž (= [33])   *je'zdi–t' ~ je'zž–u ~ je'zd–it* 'travel'.

3.5.2.2 Other consonant alternations

(1) As a result of the very early Proto-Slavonic simplification of clusters there
occur alternations with ∅ or with /s/, the latter first a simplification (by dissimilation) of /t/, /d/, then extended by analogy in infinitives. Unless marked,
examples are 1ps Pres ~ Inf ~ Past Masc:

    t ~ s ~ ∅   *pl'et–u' ~ pl'es–ti' ~ pl'ë–l* 'plait';

    d ~ s ~ ∅   *s'a'd–u ~ s'es–t' ~ s'e–l* 'sit'; *jed–i'm* (1pp Pres) ~ *jes–t*
    (3ps Pres)~ *jes–t' ~ je–l* 'eat';

    n ~ s ~ ∅   *kl'an–u' ~ kl'a–st' ~ kl'a–l* 'swear';

    b ~ s   *gr'eb–u' ~ gr'es–ti' ~ gr'ëb–∅* 'rake';

    v ~ ∅   *živ–u' ~ ž–it' ~ ži–l* 'live'.

(2) As a result of the Proto-Slavonic clusters /kt/ and /gt/ becoming /č/:

    g ~ č   *mog–u' ~ mo–č' ~ mog–∅* 'be able';

    k ~ č   *p'ek–u' ~ p'e–č' ~ p'ëk – ∅* 'bake'.

In some derived words the Old Church Slavonic result, /šč/, occurs, but the alternation is lexical only (not inflectional), e.g. *mošč* 'power', *moščnyj* 'powerful';
p'eščera 'cave' (< *p'ek–*).

(3) Hard ~ soft: this alternation occurs automatically where a suffix or ending formerly began with a front vowel (graphic *e*, *i*; transliterated *e*, *ë*, *i*; phonemic /e/, /o/, /i/; morph(ophon)emic {e}, {′o}, {i} – see chapter 3). It is regular in one group of First Conjugation verbs (those without a /j/ suffix, that is, Class I (see chapter 3, section 2.2.5), where the root normally ends in a hard conso- nant and the majority of Pres endings begin with {′o}, e.g. *n′es–u′* ~ *n′es–ë′t* (/-s′o/)'carry' 1ps ~ 3ps, *id–u′* ~ *id–ë′t* 'go' 1ps ~ 3ps; also in hard-stem nouns with the LS ending *–e* ({′e}), e.g. *nos–ø* ~ *no′s–′e* 'nose', *go′rod – ø* ~ *go′rod–′e* 'town'. The latter case includes the velar stems, e.g. *r′ek–a′* ~ *r′ek–′e* 'river', *nog–a′* ~ *nog–′e* 'foot'. Noun endings in [i] are normally restricted to soft- stem words, the hard-stem ones normally having [ɨ]; the exceptions are again the velars, which may not have the sequence [kɨ], but have instead [kʲi], e.g. NP *r′e′k–i*, *no′g–i* (this is a result of the appearance of soft velars since the Old Russian period, now extended to obligatory status before /e/ and /i/).

(4) Any further alternations are purely phonetic, based on the positional rules noted above (fronting/raising of stressed vowels, reduction of unstressed vow- els, assimilation of consonants, simplification of clusters).

(5) Shifting stress within a paradigm may also be regarded as a case of mor- phophonological alternation; however, it is not amenable to simple description and must be related to declension and conjugation types. It will therefore be dealt with in chapter 3.

3.6   *Sentence intonation*

For the purposes of this chapter, we will describe the phonetic contours used in sentence intonation, with only a general indication of the functionality of the different types, whose details belong to chapter 4. In this section transcription is transliteration only.

  Describing intonation patterns in a clear and readily intelligible fashion is not a simple task. Approaches that have been taken include: identification of 'melodies' associated with particular sentence types (Jones and Ward 1969, and most early Russian descriptions); identification of contour types and their application to sentence types (Boyanus 1955, Odé 1989, and all recent Russian descriptions – see below). In the description of Russian, the most successful approach, it seems, and by far the most commonly used, certainly in Russian descriptions, is one developed by E.A. Bryzgunova in the 1960s, and it is the one we will use. (For a critique of this system, see Keijsper 1992.) It is based on the principle of defining the contours which may be said to be 'dis- tinctive', that is, which distinguish meaning at the sentence level in the same way as phonemes do at the word level. The formal description involves three relative levels of pitch, the mid-level being a speaker's neutral pitch against which significant rises and falls are marked; the location of these significant movements is marked, called in Bryzgunova's system the 'logical centre' (the central word) or the 'logical stress' (the stressed syllable of that word), marked in our examples by "after the vowel (the syntactic 'focus'). She identifies – in the last version, of 1977 (used also in Academy Grammar 1980) – seven contours, which are named 'IK-1', etc., where 'IK' stands for *intonacionnaja konstrukcija* 'intonational contour'; four of these (IK-1–4) serve to distinguish basic communicative functions (statement, command, etc.), and three operate purely at the expressive level (surprise, annoyance, etc.). It must be said that the last two (IK-6–7) were elevated to types only in recent versions, IK-6 having originally been seen as a variant of IK-4, and IK-7 not noted at all; neither is very frequent and each can have its typical functions fulfilled also by other types. While we will note them, we have little conviction that they are important elements in the description.

IK-1. This is the basic statement contour. It differs from English in that its pre-centre syllable is higher in pitch than that of the centre, which is actually low, while in English the central syllable is the highest of the contour. Thus, in the sentence *Èto gaze"ta* 'This is a newspaper', the syllable *ga-* is highest, followed by a drop onto the central, stressed *–ze–*.

IK-2. This pattern is actually effectively that of the English statement, with the central syllable highest (just above the mid-level), and also loudest; however, its main function is that of emphasis or contrast, which presents problems for English learners, who tend thereby to sound over-emphatic to Russians in what should be neutral statements. The same sentence *Èto gaze"ta* said with this contour means 'This is a *newspaper* (and not something else)'.

   This pattern is also used for *wh*-questions, e.g. *Kak vas zovu"t?* 'What's your name?' and for (peremptory) commands, e.g. *Zakro"jte okno!* 'Shut the window!'

IK-3. This is a peculiarly Russian contour in shape: the central syllable is marked by a sharp rise to the speaker's top level, followed by an equally sharp fall to the bottom level. The sharp rise itself is difficult to imitate, but it is its function which is the most surprising to English speakers, for whom such a rise would have to be expressive: its primary function is the expression of *yes/no* questions. Further, the segmental structure of such questions in Russian is typically identical to that of statements, such that *Èto gaze"ta?* with IK-3 means 'Is this a newspaper?', the intonation being the sole marker of the syntactic function. English learners used to a rising intonation for such questions have problems here.

This pattern is also used for (polite) requests, such that *Zakro"jte okno* with IK-3 is not an order; here too English learners tend to use IK-2 for all Imperative forms, thereby sounding over-abrupt or even rude.

IK-1–3 are the three primary contours, expressing the basic functions of statement, question and command.

IK-4. Thus far, it will be noted that no contour ends with a rise, and especially not either type of question. IK-4 does have a rising contour, and is used for a type of question; it is, however, typified by the fact that its central syllable is actually the *lowest* pitch in the sentence, followed by a rise similar to that of English *yes/no* questions. The segmental shape of this type is limited: it is used only with 'incomplete' (elliptical) sentences, much of whose syntax is carried over from the preceding utterance. Thus, they tend to be questions asking for further detail, and cannot be non-contextual. They typically begin with the conjunction *a* 'and/but', for example *A Nata"ša?* 'And what about Natasha?' The syllable *–ta–* is lowest, and *–ša–* rises; any subsequent syllables, no matter how numerous, remain on the high level.

IK-5. This is the most common of the exclamation contours, indicating most often pleasant emotions (pleasure, excitement, delight, etc.). Segmentally, it typically begins with an interrogative pronoun used as an exclamation, as in English 'What a . . . !' It may be described as having two centres (such is Bryzgunova's description): the first a rise on the first (exclamatory) word, the second a fall on the final word; in between, all words (and syllables) are at the high level. Thus *Kako"j prekrasnyj de"n'!* 'What a beautiful day!' differs from English only in the location of the rise, which in English would normally occur on 'beautiful', not on 'What'.

IK-6. In shape, this pattern is a variant of IK-4: it is also a rising contour, but the rise begins *on* the stressed syllable, not after. It is used to express mainly positive emotions, like IK-5, but may also be used for negative ones; the rising contour in an exclamation tends to indicate wonderment, secrecy or the like, e.g. *Kni"g u nego skol'ko!* 'What a lot of books he's got!', *A čto" u menja jest'!* 'Guess what I've got!'

IK-7. This is a very uncommon contour and expresses negative emotions (contempt, disgust, impatience, etc.). It is really a variant of IK-3, having the same sharp rise on the centre, but there is a slight pause or check before the sharp fall on the following syllable. Frequently the lexical content is positive, such that this contour makes the expression ironic or sarcastic. Thus, *Xoro"šij doklad!*, literally 'a good lecture', would mean sarcastically 'Great/Some lecture!'; or,

with a *wh*-word, the shape could be that of a question or a positive exclamation, but the meaning 'What a (bad)...!', e.g. *Kako"j on èkspert!* 'What do you
mean, he's an expert?/Some expert, he is!'

In addition to the simple-sentence functions of all these contours indicated
above, some may appear in the non-final clauses of complex sentences. In
principle IK-3 and IK-4 may both indicate incompletion in a subordinate clause,
the difference between them being basically stylistic: IK-3 is the normal spoken
contour in this function, paralleling English's use of the rising question contour
here (though it does strike English speakers as just as odd that a non-rising contour should indicate incompletion as that it should indicate a *yes/no* question);
IK-4, the actual rising contour, is used in artistic or dramatic reading style.
In sentences where the *final* clause is subordinate, usually meaning either that
it is an afterthought or that the inversion is stylistic, IK-1 may appear in the
non-final, but main, clause (for example in the English equivalents 'I'll do *x*, if
you (don't) do *y*').

3.7   Style in phonology

As most stylistic effects in phonology are dialectal or sociolectal (including
by age) in nature, the 'standard or not' aspect of this topic is treated further in
chapter 7. For now, we will note the phonological features involved and offer examples of only those which function as standard variants within Contemporary
Standard Russian.

3.7.1   Unstressed vowels
There are no standard variants: any alternative pronunciation is non-standard
(dialectal or archaic) (e.g. distinguishing between /o/ and /a/ after hard consonants – called *okan'je* (standard is *akan'je*) – or between /e/ and /i/ after soft
consonants – called *ekan'je* (standard is *ikan'je*)). Such pronunciations may also
appear on the stage in high classical drama, where they are nonetheless marked
as non-standard.

The reduction of the high vowels [u] and [ɨ] to [ə] (which includes unrounding
of [u]) and the loss (ellipsis) of vowels or syllables are features of casual or
rapid spoken style.

3.7.2   Consonants
The only consonant which is relevant here is /g/: while its standard pronunciation
is officially (occlusive) [g], and (fricative) [ɣ] is dialectal except in odd words,
in fact the latter pronunciation is widespread among the educated classes, where
it is treated as an 'acceptable dialectalism'.

3.7.3 Assimilation of consonants

Non-assimilation of voice or place of articulation (dental > palatal) is non-standard. Again, it may appear in formal stage speech, partly as a result of slow delivery, partly of tradition.

Assimilation of hard/soft is currently in a state of fluctuation within the standard (see above, section 3.3.2). Since the direction is towards non-assimilation, the option of assimilation is more common among older speakers and, again, on the classical stage.

3.7.4 Consonant clusters

Failure to simplify particular clusters in particular words in the recommended manner (see above, section 3.3.4) is non-standard, though in many such cases two variants are acceptable.

3.7.5 /j/ + /i/

/i/ is the only vowel phoneme before which /j/ is now impossible (having been previously possible), so that the pronunciation of stressed [ji] is now non-standard (dialectal or archaic) (e.g. *ix* 'their', *moïx* 'my' GP, *stoït* 'stand' 3ps Pres are [ix], [mʌiˈx] and [stʌiˈt]); unstressed /i/ is no different, but the sound [ɪ], which is its unstressed allophone, may be preceded by [j] when it is actually derived from the phonemes /e/ or /o/, e.g. *znaˈjet* 'know' 3ps Pres is normally [znaˈjɪt]; in casual/rapid style even this [j] may be dropped. Compare *stoˈit* 'cost' 3ps Pres = [stɔˈɪt].

3.7.6 Specific forms (morphemes)

The most frequent morpheme to vary stylistically is the reflexive suffix (formerly accusative pronoun) *–sʹa* (and its variant *–sʹ*): in the Old Muscovite Norm the /s/ in these was actually pronounced *hard*; currently the norm is to pronounce it soft except where it follows a /t/ or /tʹ/ (in 3ps/p and Inf), and the hard variant elsewhere is regarded as 'old', but acceptable, and is another feature of classical stage speech.

One other such current change concerns the suffix *–yva–* (Imperfective Aspect indicator) when it is attached to a stem in a velar, when the phonology officially requires **ky/gy/xy* to become [kʲi], etc., which is reflected in the orthography; again, the old norm made an exception of these and pronounced [kɨ], etc. (e.g. in *vskakivatʹ* 'jump up', *vzdragivatʹ* 'quiver'). The new norm is the soft (and spelling) version, the hard version 'old'.

Parallel to this is the NS Masculine adjectival ending when attached to a velar stem, e.g. *russkʹij* 'Russian': the old variant is [ruˈskəj], the new [ruˈskʲij].

3.7.7   Foreign words

Since the pronunciation of features like unstressed /o/ and /e/ or hard/soft before /e/ is quite unpredictable, yet recommendations are fairly specific, pronunciations which differ from the recommendation may be regarded as at least 'uneducated'. However, if the 'mistake' follows native rules, it may also be seen as a natural extension of the general trend, whereas the true *faux pas* will be hypercorrection, (in this case) the extension of the foreign rule in an attempt to sound correct.

3.7.8   Stress

Apart from (relatively few) cases of completely free variation in stress position (see chapter 7, section 3.3), there are some cases of stress position being marked stylistically, either as non-standard (dialectal) or as professional. For native words, one of the most common non-standard variants is the stem stress of certain verbs in the Present Tense, e.g. *zvonit* 'ring' 3ps: *zvo'nit* versus standard *zvoni't*; this is in origin a dialectal feature which has been influencing verb stress for many centuries, and continues to do so, but the recommenders continue to try to slow the process (see chapter 3, section 2.2.11 on verbal stress patterns). For foreign words stress changes are rather arbitrary, and most older versions are now regarded as substandard, e.g. *dokum'ent* 'document': old *doku'ment* versus new *dokume'nt*; *alfavit* 'alphabet': old *alfa'vit* versus new *alfavi't*. The competing positions are usually the result of multiple sources of the same word, e.g. French and Polish, French and English.

Examples of professional variants are: *kompas* 'compass': neutral *ko'mpas* versus nautical *kompa's*; *iskra* 'spark': neutral *i'skra* versus motor-mechanics *iskra'*.

Some stress variants belong to 'folk-poetry' style, where they will usually also be distinguished lexically or at least by reference, e.g. *molodec*: poetic *mo'lodec* 'young fellow' versus colloquial *molode'c* 'bravo!'; *de'vica* poetic 'young girl/maiden' versus neutral *devi'ca* 'spinster'.

3.7.9   Casual or rapid style

As is typical of all languages, rapid speech style produces ellipsis of segmental elements. Russian examples are: *govori't* 'say' 3ps Pres, reduced to [gʌʌrʲi't] or [grʲit], e.g. in joke-telling 'he says'; *bu'det* 'be' 3ps Fut, reduced to [bu'ɪt]; *Aleksa'ndr Aleksa'ndrovič* (name + patronymic), in its most extremely casual form reduced to [san sa'n(t)ʃ]; the patronymic suffixes *–ovič* Masc, *–ovna* Fem lose at least the syllable *–ov–*, e.g. *Iva'novič*, *Iva'novna* become [iva'nɨtʃ], [iva'nnə], in all but careful speech; *zdravstvujte* 'hello' loses the /v/ before /stv/ as standard, and is reduced to [zdra'stvəjtʲɪ], [zdra'sstʲɪ] and [zdra'sstʲ] at progressively casual styles.

This loss of unstressed vowels (and their syllables) has resulted in the appearance of a new vocative form for affectionate first-name forms whose nominative forms end in *–a*, regardless of gender, by the deletion of that final *–a*, e.g. *Saš!* 'Sasha!', *Nataš!* 'Natasha!'

4   Graphics

Here we describe the graphic system: the symbols of the Cyrillic alphabet, their transliteration and transcription, and the relationship between them and the phonemes.

4.1   Cyrillic and its transcription and transliteration

Table 9 gives the Cyrillic alphabet
- Col. 1: in its official order
- Cols. 2 and 3: the transliteration of the letters used in two systems: Library of Congress (as the most popular general system) without its optional ligatures for the digraphs, and ISO (R9) (as the one closest to a one-to-one correlation and effectively that used by linguists for phonemic transcription) (Col. 3 with brackets indicating the phonemic symbols used by Slavists where they differ from ISO)
- Col. 4: the phonetic transcription in IPA symbols and
- Col. 5: the names of the letters in IPA format
    Column 3 represents the basic phoneme and does not take account of context, which will be taken up in the next section.

It will be noted that there is virtual identity between lower and upper case letters of the non-italic script, 'A/a' being the only exception. In italic script, the only discrepancies are the lower case forms of *Г/г*, *Д/д*, *И/u* and *T/m*. The letters *ъ* and *ь*, that is, the old *jers*, represent no sound, but are simply written symbols either giving information about the preceding consonant's hard/soft nature or marking the presence of /j/ after a consonant. The names 'hard sign' and 'soft sign' refer to the former function, but in reality only the soft sign serves this simple function, when there is no following vowel sound, while the absence of a soft consonant (that is, the presence of a hard consonant) is the default, so is not indicated in any way; only in the second function, that of indicating the presence of a /j/, does the hard sign occur, normally between a prefix and a root beginning with /j/; the soft sign may also indicate a /j/. See further below on the writing of /j/.

4.2   Correlation of graphics and phonemes

4.2.1   Hard/soft consonants

The most striking feature of the graphic system is in the writing of the soft consonants: given that there are fifteen pairs of hard/soft consonants (including

Table 9 *The (Russian) Cyrillic alphabet and its transliteration/transcription*

Cyrillic	Library of Congress	ISO (Phonemic)	Phonetic (IPA)	Name (IPA)
А/а *A/a*	a	a	a	a
Б/б *Б/б*	b	b	b	bɛ
В/в *B/в*	v	v	v	vɛ
Г/г *Г/г*	g	g	g	gɛ
Д/д *Д/д*	d	d	d	dɛ
Е/е *E/e*	e	e	ɛ	jɛ
Ё/ё *Ё/ё*	e	e('o/ë)	(j)ɔ	jɔ
Ж/ж *Ж/ж*	zh	ž	ʒ	ʒɛ
З/з *З/з*	z	z	z	zɛ
И/и *И/и*	i	i	i	i
Й/й *Й/й*	ĭ	j	j	*i kra'tkoje* ('short' *i*)
К/к *К/к*	k	k	k	ka
Л/л *Л/л*	l	l	l	el
М/м *М/м*	m	m	m	ɛm
Н/н *Н/н*	n	n	n	ɛn
О/о *O/o*	o	o	ɔ	ɔ
П/п *П/п*	p	p	p	pɛ
Р/р *P/p*	r	r	r	ɛr
С/с *C/c*	s	s	ʒ	ɛs
Т/т *T/m*	t	t	t	tɛ
У/у *У/y*	u	u	u	u
Ф/ф *Ф/ф*	f	f	f	ɛf
Х/х *X/x*	kh	h (x)	χ	χa
Ц/ц *Ц/ц*	ts	c	ts	tsɛ
Ч/ч *Ч/ч*	ch	č	tʃʲ	tʃʲɛ
Ш/ш *Ш/ш*	sh	š	ʃ	ʃa
Щ/щ *Щ/щ*	shch	šč	ʃʲt ʃʲ/ʃʲ ʃʲ	ʃtʃʲa
(Ъ)/ъ *ъ/ъ*	"	"	(—)	jɛr ('hard sign')
Ы/ы *Ы/ы*	y	y	ɨ	jɛrɨ
(Ь)/ь *ь/ь*	'	'(')	(—)	jɛrʲ ('soft sign')
Э/э *Э/э*	è/ė	ê(ė)	ɛ	ɛ(ɛ *oboro'tnoje* 'reversed' *e*)
Ю/ю *Ю/ю*	iu	ju ('u)	(j)u	ju
Я/я *Я/я*	ia	ja('a)	(j)a	ja

the velars), a system which used different consonantal symbols would therefore require thirty symbols for these sounds, whereas the Russian system has only eighteen, this being achieved by using five extra *vowel* symbols instead of fifteen consonant ones. Thus, there are ten vowel *letters* in the system, in five pairs, one of each pair indicating that the preceding consonant is hard, the other that it is soft; the pairs are:

Phoneme	After hard	After soft
/a/	а	я
/e/	э	е
/i/	ы	и
/o/	о	ё
/u/	у	ю

By way of example, the syllable ма represents /ma/, while мя represents /m'a/.

The second, 'soft', set cause perceptual problems for learners in that they are somewhat counter-intuitive for those used to the Latin script; non-linguistically oriented textbooks refer to them most commonly as 'jotated' vowels, or even worse, 'soft' vowels, which suggests that we are dealing with different *vowels*, which is not the case – they are merely double symbols (vowel letters) for the same vowel sounds. Since a term for the 'soft' set is desirable, and since 'jotated' is acceptable so long as it is qualified as 'letter', not 'vowel', we shall hereafter refer to this set as the 'jotated' set (while acknowledging that 'jotated' should strictly be a phonetic term, and as such is potentially misleading in this usage; the less desirable alternative would be to create an entirely new term).

Given, however, that the soft consonants need not always be followed by a vowel, there is still a need for a way of marking them elsewhere, and this is the primary function of the soft sign (ь); thus, мать = /mat'/, мять = /m'at', судьба = /sud'ba/.

4.2.2   The writing of /j/

Given, in turn, the existence of the jotated set of vowel letters, the system has made further powerful use of them in the writing of /j/: where /j/ is followed by a vowel, the jotated set serve the purpose of indicating the sequence of /j/+ vowel; thus, *я* = also /ja/, *e* also /je/, *ё* also /jo/ and *ю* also /ju/. Note that the exception is *u*, which is only /i/, since the sequence /ji/ is (now) impossible (see above, section 3.7.5). This applies where there is no preceding consonant letter, that is (1) word initially, e.g. *я/ja* 'I', *ем/jem* 'eat' 1ps Pres, *ёлка/jo'lka* 'fir tree', *юг/jug* 'south'; and (2) after a vowel, e.g. *моя/moja'* 'my' NS Fem, *моё/mojo'* 'my' NS Neut, *мою/moju'* 'my' AS fem, *моему/mojemu'* 'my' DS Masc.

When /j/ is not followed by a vowel, but by a consonant or silence (word-finally), these letters cannot be used, and the system has one other symbol for this: *й*, e.g. *мой/moj* 'my' NS Masc, *мойка/mo'jka* 'washing'.

Finally, when /j/ is preceded by a consonant and followed by a vowel, there has to be a way of indicating its presence, since the simple sequence of consonant + jotated letter would signify only 'soft consonant + vowel', with no indication of /j/. This is where we again use the soft sign, and also the hard sign, in principle according to the hard/soft nature of the consonant (though see above, section 3.3.2.2), e.g. *объявить* /objavi′t′/ 'announce' (where the *ob–* is a prefix and the root is *jav–*), *статья*/stat′ja' 'article' (where the /j/ is – historically – a suffix), *пьеса*/p′jesa* '(a) play' (representing a borrowed /j/, from Fr *pièce*).

4.3   Orthographic principles

As in English, the central orthographic principle is 'morphological', that is, the retention of visible morphological and derivational relations in spite of surface phonetic facts. Allophonic variation is not indicated, thus, for example, vowels are always represented by the stressed phoneme, e.g. *voda*' 'water' NS, even though the /o/ is in fact pronounced [ʌ] – cf. the form *vo′du* AS with the /o/ stressed. Final devoicing and assimilation of voice in clusters are not indicated, e.g. *год*/god 'year' NS [gɔt], where all other case-forms have following vowels and [d]; *водка*/vo′dka 'vodka' [vɔ'tkə], even though in all forms this /d/ is devoiced before the /k/, so the derivation from *voda* is visually retained (and the voiced [d] appears in further derived forms, e.g. *водочный*/vo′dočnyj 'vodka' Adj).

This principle is common to the Slavonic group, though some languages do not have the morphophonological (or phonotactic) complications of Russian; for example, Serbo-Croatian and Ukrainian lack final devoicing, and only Russian, Belarusian and Bulgarian alter the quality of unstressed vowels; the only major concessions to phonetic spelling are Belarusian's writing of the unstressed vowels and Serbo-Croatian's spelling of voice assimilation.

4.4   How 'phonetic' is the system? (or: How far can one predict pronunciation from spelling?)

Russian's orthographic system is strong on phonemic representation; as far as the predictability of pronunciation from graphics goes, the phonological rules concerning the consonants are sufficient, certainly in the case of voice assimilation, and to a lesser, but steadily increasing, extent for hard/soft assimilation (in view of its increasing non-implementation); for the vowels all depends on a knowledge of the place of stress, which presents a major problem for learners: while many rules for stress placement exist, both inflectional and derivational, in most instances prediction is impossible. The fact that this problem is similar in English is of little help!

Only in isolated cases is there complete non-correspondence between the two; the most notable example is the GSm of the adjective declension, in whose ending *–ogo/–ego* the graphic *g* is actually pronounced [v] and must be regarded as representing the phoneme /v/ (see below, section 4.5.3).

4.5   Major steps in the history of the graphic system

4.5.1   Early system

The inherent problems in the early (Old Russian) alphabet centred around its Greek origins: first there were the multiple letters for the same sounds inherited from a spoken Byzantine Greek in which much redundancy had developed alongside the Ancient Greek writing system; for example, the Greek vowel letters *ι*, *η* and *υ* all represented [i] and were imported with that value into Old Church Slavonic (as *i/ï*, *u* and *v* respectively); likewise Greek *o* and *ω* both represented [ɔ] and were thus imported (as *o* and *ω*). Then there were Greek sounds which had no Slavonic equivalent, whose letters were nevertheless imported either with borrowed words or for their numerical value (e.g. *θ*, *ξ*, *ψ*, the first of which soon joined *ф* in the value [f]); in a similar way, *ς*, in Greek by then only a numerical symbol, originally represented [dz], but soon joined *з* as Old Russian converted /dz/ to /z/.

The various phonological changes which Russian underwent (see chapter 1, section 2.4.1) created further similar problems: the nasal vowels joined /a/ and /u/, the *jers* joined /o/ and /e/, *jat'* joined /e/, all producing multiple letters for the same sounds; the contexts in which the *jers* became zero created a problem of a different sort, namely the retention of redundant letters; the expansion of /j/ to (syllable-/word-)final contexts increased the existing problem of writing /j/, since no separate letter existed.

Up until the early eighteenth century, there was no mechanism for handling such problems, much as in other cultures, and orthography was to a large degree arbitrary. Nonetheless, also as elsewhere, the Church was able to maintain some level of consistency in such matters at an empirical level. We have mentioned (chapter 1, section 3.2) the one case of theoretical involvement in orthographical matters, that of Metropolitan Kiprian in the early fifteenth century, which, however, had if anything a negative effect on the issue, based as the revisions were on a different phonological system (Middle Bulgarian), as well as being specifically intended to be backward-looking.

4.5.2   Peter the Great and the eighteenth century

It was only with Peter the Great that conscious efforts were undertaken to normalise the orthography. Significantly, Peter was not intent on competing with the Church, but in distancing non-clerical writing from that established, and confusing, system. Apart from his major aim of opting for less complex and decorative shapes for the letters, his attempts at removing some of the anomalies met with little success: his revision of 1708 removed the Greek-only letters and some of the duplicates, but that of 1710 actually reinstated some of these; this version formally introduced two letters which had had no status until then, though they had been appearing in Ukrainian sources: я and э, the first probably formally derived from ꙗ and/or ᴀ/ꙗ, all used for [ja], the second used for /e/ and subsequently established for /e/ after hard consonants (which is still a foreign sequence) or initially, leaving *e* to indicate a preceding soft consonant.

The newly formed Academy of Sciences initially attempted similar statements about the letter inventory in the 1730s, with one important recommendation and one innovation: the two forms for /i/ (i, и) were to be kept as positional variants (the first before a vowel or final /j/), and they introduced й, clearly a formal variant of *u*, for final /j/ (while pre-vocal /j/ continued to be indicated by the vowel letter, previously a ligature of *i* plus vowel, e.g. ѥ, ꙗ). No further formal recommendations came from the Academy.

The other contributors to this matter were individuals, either language-oriented or simply writers of literature, and especially those who were both. Prominent amongst the last were Trediakovsky, Tatishchev and Lomonosov; mainly language-oriented were Adodurov and Barsov; mainly literary was Karamzin. They toiled over the questions of a phonetic versus a phonemic or morphological system (Trediakovsky and Tatishchev opting for the former, Lomonosov and Adodurov for the latter), of how to write /o/ after soft consonants (the most popular suggestion being *io*, but the first proposal of *ë* being put by Karamzin in 1797), of what to do with the former *jers* (ъ, ь) (only the 'phonetic' group being willing to remove them completely), and whether to retain ѣ (*jat'*).

4.5.3   Twentieth century

It was only in 1918, as part of the official onset of the communist state, that a decree was issued regarding the orthography. It decreed the complete removal of three letters – ѣ, θ, i – and the removal of ъ from final position. It appears to have assumed the prior loss of the other unnecessary letters, including ѵ, which is sometimes – mistakenly – said to have been included in the 1918 list. It made no mention of *ë* (or any way of writing /o/ after soft), and no subsequent statement has tackled this problem, except that *ë* has by consensus become acceptable in lexicographical or pedagogical publications.

In the end, Russian has overall an efficient graphic system which has opted for the morphophonemic principle over the phonetic, and whose only shortcomings – mainly from the learner's viewpoint – are the formally missing *ë* and the odd

case of the Genitive Singular Masculine adjectival ending –*ogo* (= /ovo/ in
Contemporary Standard Russian, though not in all dialects); the latter survives
mainly because there are many dialects which do not have [v] (but other variations, including [g] and [ɣ] – see chapter 3 (section 2.1.4.3) for the development
of this form in Contemporary Standard Russian), the former (absence of *ë*) survives with less justification, though there are dialects in which the sequence
'soft C + /o/' occurs also in unstressed syllables (as part of the more general
non-reduction of unstressed vowels).

3   Morphology

1   Introduction

This chapter deals with 'inflectional morphology' (as opposed to 'derivational morphology', treated in chapter 5), including those morphological categories which are not formally inflected. As elsewhere, we begin the chapter with some basic concepts and terminology. While those familiar with these may pass on to section 2, this section does contain some important information on notation (section 1.1.1), as well as Russian examples of concepts and terms.

In this chapter the basic dictionary forms (Nominative Singular Masculine, Infinitive) are given in both Cyrillic and morphemic transcription (or phonemic, where appropriate) with all morphemes set off by dashes; discussion of particular forms will normally use transcription (or transliteration) only.

1.1   The 'morpheme' and related terminology

In parallel with the concept of the phoneme (chapter 2, section 1), the 'morpheme' is a theoretical, or deep structure, element. It is described in non-specialist sources as 'the smallest meaningful linguistic unit', or similar, which assumes that the phoneme is not meaningful; however, 'meaningful' here must be taken to mean 'having grammatical meaning', and not just 'semantic' or 'lexical' meaning. While many morphemes do have lexical meaning, for example, roots and most affixes, many have only relational meaning, that is, functioning logically at the syntactic level, for example 'plural', 'past', 'locative', etc.

The term 'morphology' is in principle parallel to 'phonology' in covering the whole area of the form of 'words', however we must define 'word' rather carefully. Further discussion of the concept of the 'word' will be found in chapter 5, section 1.1, but for the purposes of this chapter we emphasise the important distinction between lexically distinct words and non-lexical forms of words, the former referring to different objects, actions, qualities, etc., the latter to the same object, action, etc. In English the verbal system offers the best view of this distinction: the forms *see*, *sees*, *saw*, *seen* are casually called different 'words', but at the semantic level they all refer to the one action, 'see', and are therefore only different (morphological) forms of the one 'lexical word', used mainly to indicate different syntactic (or spatial/temporal) relationships. Other English terms which make this distinction, while trying to keep the overall term 'morphology', are 'derivational morphology' – for the separate lexical word – and 'inflectional morphology' – for the formal changes to the same word. In a language like Russian (or all but two of the Slavonic languages) this procedure is much more important, being inherent in the whole system, that is, in both the nominal and verbal parts.

Also like the phoneme, there may be several surface realisations of a given morpheme, which are called individually 'morphs', and a class of 'allomorphs' – differing by the context in which each is applied. The morpheme is conventionally written in braces, and the underlying form, as with the phoneme, may be given as the most general or unencumbered form. For example, the plural noun morpheme in English may be written {s}, since written *s* and phonetic [s] are its typical realisations, while other realisations (i.e. allomorphs) include [z], as in *dogs* and [əz], as in *buses*. Since allomorphs are phonetically distinct, it is normal to write them as such, in square brackets.

The process of generating surface forms from the underlying ones is in principle the same for both phonemic and morphemic levels, since morphemes will be described in terms of phonemes, which will be subject to the normal phonemic processes which produce the surface forms. Thus, the English plural morpheme {s} is made up of the phoneme /s/, which is realised as [z] or [əz] according to the phonetic context. There may of course be other realisations of a morpheme which are not formally (phonemically) related at all, which will normally be remnant or foreign forms, for example [rən] in *children*, or [a] in *phenomena*. For this reason it is usually better to use descriptive forms rather than phonemic ones, such as {plur}, within which one can list the occurring forms in order of frequency and ability to derive surface forms.

1.1.1 Morphophonemics and notation

In many cases we need special 'morphophonemic' rules to derive forms, rules which do not attach to every phoneme or sequence of phonemes, but only to those in certain morphological contexts ('morphophonemes'); a minor example in Russian is the sequence /d/+/t/, which, when it occurs between prefix and root (e.g. *pod–t'anut'* 'pull up' Inf), is phonetically [–tt–], but between the root and infinitive ending the /d/ typically becomes [s] on the surface (e.g. {ved}+{ti} 'lead' + {Inf} > v'est'i). (We will maintain the convention of using the plus sign as a joiner of morphemes making up a word *only* when we write the morphemes in braces, when discussing forms in abstract; for the most part, in full word examples, we will omit the braces and use dashes, thus *ved–ti*.) Several vowel phonemes require special comment; these are treated in the following.

The morphophoneme {i} may be treated in the same way as was the phoneme /i/, the same rules producing [ɨ] or [i] (see chapter 2, section 3.2.3.1): a morpheme beginning with {i} will be realised as [ɨ] after morphemes ending in hard or hard palatal consonants, as [i] after one ending in soft or soft palatal or velar consonants. However, the 'softness' often resides in the second morpheme itself, that is, it 'contains' the front vowel [i], which softens a preceding hard consonant; in this case we will mark the morph(ophon)eme {'i}. See further below on softness in morphemes.

For the morphophoneme {e}, insofar as we are dealing with inflectional and derivational morphemes, the issue of foreign sequences scarcely arises (in this case hard C + /e/), thus we may also assume that a morpheme beginning with {e} likewise causes softening of all paired preceding consonants, and so such softening will not be marked.

The case of the morphophoneme {o} when it follows a soft or palatal consonant presents some challenges to intuition, given that the orthographic shape is almost always *e* (stressed also *ë* or *o*) and frequently only one out of all forms is stressed and therefore pronounced [ɔ]; nevertheless it makes descriptive sense, given the simplicity of the phonemic rules for the phoneme /o/ in this context (stressed [ɔ], unstressed as for /e/, see chapter 2, section 3.2.3.2), to name such morphophonemes {o}. The above root 'lead' will thus be written {v'od}, since its one root-stressed form is *вёл/v'o'(d)–l–ø* Past Masc. This will suffice for most contexts, and certainly for endings; however there are cases where an (additional) alternation occurs between stressed {e} and {o}, usually within roots, which is not explicable by any phonemic rules, and for which we must therefore have morphophonemic rules. The most effective rules use {o} as the underlying morphophoneme, converted to /e/ ([ɛ]) in the following contexts:

(1) before a suffix beginning with a front vowel (which assumes softening, e.g. {'in});

(2) before a suffix marked as beginning with 'softness', e.g. {'sk}, {'n}, even though there is no other surface indication of this softening (see also chapter 5, section 3.2); a following soft consonant is actually the historical context which prevented the shift of /e/ to /o/ – see chapter 2, section 3.1);

(3) in forms marked as belonging to the Russian Church Slavonic layer, in which the sequence SC + /o/ does not occur, e.g. *крест/kr'e'st* 'cross' Russian Church Slavonic ~ *крёстный/kr'o'st–'n–ij* 'god–(father etc.)' (underlying {o}).

In order not to complicate the transcription of group (3), we will mark the {o} in native words, but leave {e} in the Russian Church Slavonic ones (rather than *kr'ost* Russian Church Slavonic). An example of rules (1) and (2) is the root morpheme (see below, section 1.2.1) {žon} 'wife, woman', which has the following surface forms:

Unstressed	*жена*/žon–a' 'wife' NS	[ʒɨna']
Stressed +HC	*жёны*/žo'n–i 'wife' NP	[ʒo'nɨ']
Stressed +{'in}	*женин*/žo'n–'in 'wife's	[ʒe'nʲin]
Stressed +{'sk}	*женский*/žo'n–'sk-ij 'feminine'	[ʒɛ'nskʲɪj]

On the historical motivations of this behaviour, see chapter 1, section 2.4.1.1 and chapter 2, section 3.1.

1.2   Russian morphemes

For Russian, as a European language, the majority of morpheme classes are familiar to English users, the most significant differences lying in the nominal inflectional system, which requires us to posit morphemes of case, and mostly with accompanying number and gender, e.g. Nominative Singular Masculine, virtually always different from Nominative Plural Masculine, as well as from Nominative Singular Feminine and Nominative Singular Neuter; where there is coincidence of forms, we talk of 'syncretism', for example Dative Plural forms are always the same for all three genders. Such a system means that one cannot, for example, posit a single {plur} morpheme, since first, the realisations will depend on the given nominal pattern (declension type) and second, the relevant case must also be referred to. The major differences between analytically structured languages like English and synthetically structured ones like Russian really belong to the syntactic (and semantic) levels, and we take up this topic in chapter 4.

Details of the morphemes will be given below in relevant sections. Here we look at the types of morpheme classes we will need.

1.2.1   Root

This is the 'basic' morpheme, found in principle in all languages insofar as it represents the lexical level of word forms, though beyond the major classes (noun, adjective, verb) the membership of this class will vary widely according to the nature and structure of the 'word'. Again, as a(n Indo-)European language, Russian shares this overall structure with the rest of the group, thus inside each 'word' there will be at least one root morpheme; this is valid even for the minor classes (preposition, particle, etc.).

Thus, typical root morphemes are:

Nominal   {golov} 'head', {ruk} 'hand', {čas} 'hour, time';
Adjectival   {dobr} 'good', {star} 'old', {zelen} 'green';
Verbal   {lʲub} 'love', {jed^1} 'go, travel', {jed^2} 'eat'.

Note that there may exist homographic – and, notionally, homophonic – root morphemes, even though no actual surface form of the two is identical.

Prepositional   {na} 'on', {pod} 'under', {čerez} 'across', {v} 'in'.

Note that morphemes in this group may be non-syllabic, unsurprising in that all are in principle proclitic.

1.2.2   Affix

Affixes belong to the word-formational aspect of words, which is treated in detail in chapter 5. Their meanings are mostly not simple, though a summary meaning can often be offered. For Russian, the relevant ones, with examples and summary meanings, are:

prefix: {na} 'on top of', {pod} 'under, from under', {ne} 'negative'. Note that many of the same *forms* may be prepositions or prefixes, as in English, e.g. *undertake*, *overtake*.

suffix

noun   {t'el'} 'agent', {k} 'diminutive';

adjective   {ovat} 'approximate' ('–ish'); {ist} 'similar' ('–like').

There is one sort of suffix which is genuinely (only) morphological: this consists of forms which have become reduced to that role from their original word-formational role, as a result of historical developments. The most common examples are the verbal suffixes {a}, {e} and {'i}, acting now as simple theme, or link, vowels between stem and ending, which in the past had functions like 'iterative', 'acquisitive', 'stative'. They do not form new lexical words, and so are simply morphological; suitable terms are 'morphological suffix' or 'theme'.

1.2.3   Ending

For a typical inflectional language like Russian, word forms indicating mainly syntactic relationships are made by altering the *ending* of the word (while other types of languages might do this by altering the root or the beginning of the word or by some other structural change). Thus it is the ending of nouns, adjectives, pronouns and numerals which indicates syntactic relationships of case (e.g. subject, object, recipient, instrument, etc.), as well as number and gender; the ending of verbs indicates number and tense, and either person or gender. The typical 'grammar' section of a textbook lists the 'paradigm' of such major classes, that is, the collection of their endings, known more traditionally as 'declension' for the nominal classes and 'conjugation' for the verbs. The 'base' forms, used in dictionaries and textbooks, are Nominative Singular for nominal and Infinitive for verbal classes.

Some typical endings are:

nouns   NSn {o}, NSf {a}, ASf {u}, GSm {a}, NPn {a}; note the multiple meanings of the same morphemes, distinguishable only within the whole paradigm, as well, of course, as within the syntax of discourse; declension type (class) is also relevant for these morphemes, for example, NSf {a} is relevant only for Class II nouns (see below, section 2.1.3);

adjectives NSm {ij}, NSf {aja}, GSm {ogo};
verbs 1ps Pres {u}, 1pp Pres {m}, Masc Sing Past {l}, Plur Past {l′i}, 2ps Imper {′i} (again, relevant for most, but not necessarily all, verbal classes).

1.2.3.1 Zero ending. Within such an inflectional system, in which all words of major classes have a full paradigm of endings, it is inappropriate to say that any one form has 'no ending', though this is frequently done in textbooks (perhaps in a futile attempt to reduce the number of learnable forms?). In those forms in which this appears to occur, that is, where the form appears to be that of the bare stem (see next section), it makes more sense to say that there is indeed an ending, and that it is 'zero'. The symbol used for this is {ø}. The most common form with this ending is the Nominative Singular of masculine nouns, as such also the base form, which may encourage the view that there is no ending. However, the zero ending occurs in many other frequent contexts, for example the Genitive Plural of feminine and neuter nouns, and must be taken to be an inherent part of the inflectional system.

Examples are:

nouns {stol} + {ø} NSm 'table', {lamp} + {ø} GPf 'lamp', {slov} + {φ} GPn 'word';

pronouns {on} + {ø} NSm Pers 'he' (cf. {on} + {a} NSf Pers 'she');

adverbs {naverx} + {ø} 'upwards' (cf. {naverx} + {u} 'up above');

verbs {n′os} + {ø} Past Masc Sing 'carry'.

1.2.4   Stem
This term is highly useful, yet in one sense vague: in order to more easily observe and discuss the structure of a word at the inflectional level, it is useful to be able to distinguish simply the parts which are not inflectional, regardless of the internal structure of those parts. Thus, in discussing the collection of endings, or morphological suffixes, of a word, we are not interested in the presence of word-formational affixes, and it follows that a single term for all that is not inflectional is useful. Moreover, at the word-formational level we are also interested in the mechanics of affixation, regardless of the whole existing form to which an affix is being attached, and for this form, too, a single term is useful. The term which serves both these purposes is 'stem'. Thus a 'stem' is any collection of morphemes to which one adds at some point another morpheme, be this a morphological or word-formational morpheme. In the current context of the morphology, we can use this to our advantage in discussing endings, since it does not matter what shape of stem we use as the base. We shall see below that the only formal issue at stake is the nature of the juncture point, at

which morphophonological alternations may be generated; in other words, this is a question of surface realisation only.

The relativity of the 'stem' is illustrated by the following derivational sequence (shown also in chapter 5, section 1.2, since some morphemes are word-formational), in which each form except the final one is a stem:

(1) {uk} 'learn': root and non-derivative stem;

(2) adding {′i} verbal morphological suffix (theme) to (1) makes a functional verbal stem, historically derivative, synchronically non-derivative (with velar mutation > *uči*–);

(3) adding an ending to (2) produces a form of this verb, e.g. + {t′} 'teach' Inf (> *uči–t′*);

(4) adding {t′el′} to (2) makes a derivative noun stem 'teacher' (*učit′el′*–);

(5) add an ending for forms of this noun, e.g. +{ø} NS (*učit′el′–ø*);

(6) adding {nic} 'female' to (4) makes the derivative noun stem 'female teacher', e.g. +{a} NS (*učit′el′nic–a*).

2   The morphology of Modern Russian

In the remainder of this chapter we concentrate on forms, the essence of 'morphology'; the syntactic or semantic function of particular forms will inevitably be mentioned, but the way in which the parts join together belongs to chapter 4.

2.1   Nominal

The nominal category includes nouns, pronouns, adjectives and numerals, which all share to one degree or another the features Case, Gender and Number. As in other European languages with grammatical gender, the adjectives and non-personal pronouns take their gender and number by agreement with their noun or referent, the numerals their gender likewise, and the personal pronouns from the natural gender of the referent. Of the last group, only the third person has grammatical gender. Where pronouns referring to persons have no formal referent, as, for example, the interrogatives, the default gender is masculine. The gender of such pronouns, of course, is relevant only at the syntactic level, where it may determine verbal agreement.

2.1.1   Historical orientation

As noted in chapter 1 (section 2.4.2), the major operative motivation for morphological change, in Russian as elsewhere, has been regularisation of pattern (by the exclusion (or conversion) of exceptional and infrequent forms). In the nominal system the most important one was the formal distinction of important syntactic forms (e.g. Subject/Object, Direct/Indirect Object), as well as strictly morphological ones (e.g. Singular/Plural).

The declension system was reorganised on the basis of gender rather than stem type, basically reducing the number of noun classes from five to two; the process of fusing the three sets of nouns referred to in chapter 1 as *o/jo-stems*, *u-stems* and Masculine *i-stems* into one 'Masculine' class (with a 'Neuter' variant) was partly assisted by phonetic changes, but in many cases the competing forms were completely dissimilar, and so there was much confusion for centuries over which of the two should be the single form, with various semantic distinctions being assigned to each; this has often led to the survival of a secondary form in some 'odd' usages, for example the secondary GS expressing 'partitive' (GS^2), or the secondary LS expressing location (LS^2) (while the primary form may express in addition other, non-locative, functions). The classes which remain 'exceptional' are those whose form did not match the one selected as typical for that gender, making levelling too difficult; the prime example of this is the small anomalous group of neuter nouns, formally *consonant (n-)stems*, ending in *–m'a* (NS), but still occurring with the extra syllable *–en–* in the oblique cases (see below, section 2.1.3, Class III).

Other features of particular classes will be treated in relevant sections.

2.1.2   Features

2.1.2.1 Case and function. In general terms (taken further in chapter 4) the cases and their functions are as follows, the majority parallel to Latin usage. The order is at this point not significant.

(1) *Nominative*: expresses the subject or unconnected, parenthetic reference, including dictionary form. This now subsumes, therefore, the function of the 'Vocative', for which Old Russian had a special form for masculine and feminine singular nouns only. Other Slavonic languages have retained these forms, some even introducing new ones.

(2) *Accusative*: expresses the direct object; in temporal contexts extent of time ('for how long'); in prepositional phrases motion and destination or goal ('to'), in temporal contexts limitation of time ('in how long', 'projected for how long').

(3) *Genitive*: expresses possession ('of'); negation, separation or absence (cf. 'none of', 'out of', 'away from'); and partitive ('some of'). In the last meaning a small number of nouns have an extra (singular) form, which we may call G(S)^2.

(4) *Dative*: expresses the indirect object ('to') or recipient ('for'); in prepositional phrases movement in a general direction ('towards').

(5) *Prepositional/Locative*: used only with prepositions, virtually all with locational meaning, but not exclusively, hence the currently preferred name of Prepositional, at least in pedagogical usage; linguists tend to prefer

Locative, as this is the more 'meaningful' name. A small number of nouns make a formal distinction between locative and non-locative, with a special (singular) locative form we may call $L(S)^2$.

(6) *Instrumental*: expresses instrument or means; in prepositional phrases accompaniment ('with') and some location ('above', 'below').

The attempt to attach distinctive features to the case system (dating essentially from Jakobson in the 1930s) has produced features such as: ±Marginal, for which Nominative, Accusative and Genitive are +, the others −; ±Quantifying, for which Genitive and Locative are +, the rest −; and ±Directional, for which Accusative and Dative are +, Nominative and Instrumental are −, and Genitive and Locative are 0. The attempt to account for the remnant case forms G^2 and L^2 has seen them opposed to G^1 and L^1 as follows: G^2 and L^2 are +Directional (G^1 and L^1 0); the last feature has been renamed Ascriptive (by Neidle 1982), allowing the elimination of 0, thus: G^1 and L^1 are +Ascriptive, G^2 and L^2 −Ascriptive.

In terms of form, any given nominal form may have twelve distinct endings, representing the six cases and singular or plural number. Reductions on this total come partly from the fact that some may have semantically only one number, but mainly from the considerable syncretism to be found throughout the system.

2.1.2.2 Gender and relation to class. There are three grammatical genders – Masculine, Feminine and Neuter. All three may have animate referents (humans and animals); the norm is correlation with natural gender, such that neuter is very rarely used for animates, but there are various exceptions (see below, section 2.1.3.1), at least if one correlates gender to class. Traditionally, the modern classification of nouns is tied to gender, such that one regularly sees descriptions like 'masculine declension', etc. (certainly more in textbooks than more formal descriptions). However, fewer anomalies need to be accounted for if one separates the two, describing a given class as having associated gender for inanimates, but able to include other natural genders for animates. The most common 'anomaly' of this sort is the continued, and increasing, use of 'feminine-type' nouns (NS in −*a*) for male persons. See further below (section 2.1.3.1).

2.1.2.3 Number. There now remain only Singular and Plural forms, since the demise of the Dual (see chapter 1, section 2.4.2). Remnants of the Dual are still around, and will be noted as appropriate. Nouns with one number only – *singularia tantum* and *pluralia tantum* – are common, normally for the expected semantic reasons (abstract, collective, etc.). As elsewhere, collectives have often given way to plural forms through loss of the perceived need for a special form (cf. Eng *children*, now plural, versus *brethren*, still collective). In Russian, this accounts for many anomalous plural forms, parallel to the anomalous Eng *children*. The more interesting aspects of number actually belong to syntax, where there are 'odd' associations of numerals and number (see chapter 4, section 3.2.2.3).

2.1.3   Nouns: classification and form

In place of the five Old Russian classes, there are now only three distinct major noun classes, one with an important variant, and a small fourth class. Allotting names is arbitrary, so we will first say simply what they are: (1) the inheritor of the OR *o/jo-*, *u-* and Masculine *i-stem* groups, containing mainly masculine gender, but with a neuter variant differing typically in three of the twelve case forms; (2) the continuation of the OR *a/ja-stem* group, mainly feminine, but including many male persons; (3) the continuation of the OR Feminine *i-stem* group, all feminine; and (4) the remnant of the OR Neuter *n-stem*. Naming systems most often call the first three respectively Declensions I, II and III, and leave (4) as an irregular set, not allotted a declension name. Other variants include the reversal of I and II, calling (4) Declension IV, and conflating (3) and (4) into Declension III. Yet another splits the masculine and neuter parts of (1) into two declensions. The first is the most common approach, including in Russian textbooks and descriptions (the main exception being the 1970 Academy Grammar (pp. 370 ff.), which conflated (1) and (2) into Declension I and (3) and (4) into Declension II, not the least of this work's radical – and heavily criticised – attempts at being different!). The 1980 Academy Grammar retains Declensions I and II as normal, but conflates (3) and (4) into Declension III (pp. 1, 491); this approach has some merits in view of the shared endings involved, even though there are very marked differences, and this is the approach that we shall follow.

Some generalisation across the classes has occurred, the most important being that of the three cases Dative, Instrumental and Locative, in the Plural, now the same (*–am*, *–am′i*, *–ax*) for all nouns. It has been suggested that these are the least important or frequent cases in the system, hence their greater susceptibility to regularisation.

In looking at the sets of endings, a further question of the order of cases in a list arises. Again, for the most part this may be an arbitrary question, however, it has been shown that there are advantages for the perceiving of patterns – notionally also related to a speaker's underlying understanding of, or intuition about, the system – in the order: Nominative, Accusative, Genitive, Locative, Dative, Instrumental ('NAGLDI', cf. Levin 1978, Chvany 1982), and we shall follow this order, even though it is not that used in textbooks or native Russian descriptions (which is most often NGDAIL). For one thing, the association between the Accusative and Genitive is important, given that for masculine animate nouns the Genitive form is that used also for Accusative

(Direct Object) (mainly a result of the phonetic fusion of the Nominative and Accusative forms, countered by the need to keep subject and object forms distinct), so it is worth listing them in adjacent positions; in the following tables 'In.' means 'inanimate' and 'An.' – 'animate'. The order of LDI or DIL is less important, but their adjacent listing is also worthwhile.

The basic sets of endings of the three classes are as follows, attached to the stem as shown in the examples. Phonotactic adjustments are assumed, e.g. stems in velars or soft palatals – as well as paired soft consonants – cause an ending-initial –*i* (the phoneme /i/) to be realised as [i], and spelt as *u* (otherwise as [ɨ], spelt usually *ы*, but *u* after hard palatals); the ending –*e* causes softening of even a hard (paired) stem.

(1) Nouns Class I
   (a) 'Hard' stems. Examples (Nominative Singular): *стол/stol–ø'* 'table'; *студент/stud'e'nt–ø* 'student'; *лето/l'e't–o* 'summer'. (On stressed –*ø* see below, section 2.1.3.3.)

	Masculine	**Neuter**
Singular		
Nominative	ø	o
Accusative	In. ø; An. a	o
Genitive	a	a
Locative	e	e
Dative	u	u
Instrumental	om	om
Plural		
Nominative	i	a
Accusative	In. i; An. ov	a
Genitive	ov	ф
Locative	ax	ax
Dative	am	am
Instrumental	am′i	am′i

   (b) 'Soft' stems. Examples (Nominative Singular): *огонь/og(o)n'–ø'* 'fire'; *гость/go'st'–ø* 'guest'; *море/mo'r'–o* 'sea'. The endings of nouns with stems ending in a soft consonant undergo the normal phonological process (see chapter 1, section 3.2.3.2), whereby unstressed /o/ is realised as (allophones of) /e/ (orthographically *e*); this applies simply to Nominative Singular Neuter (e.g. *море/mo'r'–o*) and Instrumental Singular (*гостем/go'st'–om*, *морем/mo'r'–om*); stressed /o/ remains [ɔ] (orthographically *ё*, e.g. *огнём/ogn'–o'm*); in the case of the Genitive Plural, the normal ending is –*ej* (*морей/mor'–ej*, *гостей/gost'–ej*), while the expected soft form –*ov* occurs in only a set of the palatal

subgroup (namely stems ending in *–j* and *–c*; see below). (This is an example of the selection of conflicting forms from the Old Russian declensions, *–ov* being there the *u-stem* ending, *–ej* the *i-stem*.) Otherwise the endings are as for the hard stems.

(c) 'Palatal' stems. Examples (Nominative Singular): *нож/nož–ø'* 'knife'; *месяц/m'e's'ac–ø* 'month'; *край/kra'j–ø* 'edge'; *лицо/lic–o'* 'face'.

'Palatal' in this (morphological) context means 'former palatal', that is, including also /c/. Stems ending in the unpaired palatals, whether phonetically hard (š, ž, c) or soft (č, šč, j), share the soft stem endings, that is allophones of /e/ for unstressed /o/; a spelling rule (firm for endings only) prescribes the letter *o* for stressed /o/ after all but /j/, where either *e* or *ё* is written (*ножом/nož–o'm* IS, *лицо/l'ic–o'* NS, *плечо/pl'eč–o'* NS 'shoulder', but *копьё/kop'j–o'* NS 'spear').

(2) Nouns Class II

(a) 'Hard' stems. Examples: *карта/ka'rt–a* 'map'; *жена/žon–a'* 'wife'; *слуга/slug–a'* '(male) servant'; *коллега/koll'e'g–a* 'colleague' (common gender).

	Feminine (and Masculine and Common personal)
Singular	
Nominative	a
Accusative	u
Genitive	i
Locative	e
Dative	e
Instrumental	oj
Plural	
Nominative	i
Accusative	In. i; An. ф
Genitive	ф
Locative	ax
Dative	am
Instrumental	ami

Note that Accusative Singular has a discrete form, it is not like either Nominative Singular or Genitive Singular, but Accusative Plural follows the rule of Class I Masculine.

(b) 'Soft' stems. Examples: *неделя/n'ed'e'l'–a* 'week'; *земля/z'eml'–a'* 'land'; *богиня/bogi'n'–a* 'goddess'; *дядя/d'a'd'–a* 'uncle'

/o/ > /e/ when unstressed, relevant here for IS *oj* (e.g. unstressed *неделей/ n'ed'e'l'–oj* [ɪj]; stressed *землёй/z'eml'–o'j* [ɔj]).

(c) 'Palatal' stems. Examples: *афиша/af'i'š–a* 'poster'; *госпожа/gospož–a'* 'lady'; *улица/u'l'ic–a* 'street'; *семья/s'em'j–a'* 'family'.

As for soft (e.g. unstressed IS *афишей/af'i'š–oj*, *улицей/u'l'ic–oj* (hard + [əj]), *тучей/tu'č–oj* (soft + [ɪj]); stressed IS *госпожой/gospož–o'j*, *семьёй/ s'em'j–o'j* [əj]).

(3) Nouns class III

All stems in this class are soft or palatal (not *j*). The latter are arbitrarily spelt with a soft sign in the Nominative Singular (–ø ending), this providing a useful visual indication of class, given that the palatals are unpaired, thus either they cannot be softened (š, ž, c) or their softness is automatic (č, šč).

As noted above, we are including here two subgroups which are not always so joined. Both represent classes for which no regular correlation of form and gender was available during the regrouping. All members of the main subgroup (Group 1) are feminine; the secondary subgroup (Group 2) is neuter, and is typified by having a suffix, or theme syllable, *–on'–* (> hard *–on–* in plural) between the root (all soft final) and the ending, *in the oblique cases only*. Group (2) is a remnant of the Old Russian *n-stem*, and two of Group (1) also reflect an Old Russian remnant, this time of the *r-stem*, namely *дочь/doč–ø* 'daughter' and *мать/mat'–ø* 'mother', which have the theme syllable *–er–* in the oblique cases, whose age can be seen in its parallel English form. Group (2) are all soft stems, never palatal.

Examples are

> Soft: (1) *кость/kost'–ø* 'bone'; *лань/lan'–ø* 'doe'; (2) *время/ vr'e'm'(on)–a* 'time'
>
> Palatal: (1) *ночь/noč–ø* 'night'; *мышь/myš–ø* 'mouse'; *вещь/v'ešč–ø* 'thing'; *дочь/doč (–er)–ø* 'daughter'.

	Feminine	**Neuter**	
Singular			
Nominative	ф	a	
Accusative	ф	a	
Genitive	i	on'–i	(*матери/mat'–er–i*)
Locative	i	on'–i	(*er–*, etc.)
Dative	i	on'–i	
Instrumental	ju	on'–om	

Note the spelling of ISf: *костью/ko'st'ju*; *мышью/my'šju*; *дочерью/do'čer'ju*

Plural		
Nominative	i	on–a
Accusative	i	on–a
Genitive	ej	on–ф
Locative	ax	on–ax
Dative	am	on–am
Instrumental	ami	on–ami

2.1.3.1 Variants, exceptions, anomalies

(1) Case

  (a) Endings

  (i) G(S)²: Partitive. Masculine nouns of Class I may have an alternative Genitive Singular ending *–u* (instead of *–a*) (in origin the Genitive Singular of the Old Russian *u-stem*) in the expression of the meaning 'a quantity of'. Typically this form occurs after quantitative nouns like 'a kilo', 'a cup'; to a lesser – and diminishing – extent after quantitative adverbs like 'a lot', 'a little'; to a still lesser extent in the simple partitive meaning 'some'. Thus one has regularly *чашка чаю/čašk–a čaj–u* 'a cup of tea', *кило сахару/kil–o saxar–u* 'a kilo of sugar' (versus normal GS *чая/čaj–a* and *сахара/saxar–a*); possibly *много сахару/mnogo saxar–u* 'a lot of sugar', more likely now *saxara* (this form fixed in the expression *много народу/mnogo narod–u* 'a lot of people' (versus GS *narod–a*); and virtually never now *купите сахару/kup–ˈitˈe saxar–u* 'buy some sugar'. In other words, this variant is steadily disappearing.

  (ii) L(S)²: Locative. A subgroup of the same group of nouns (Class I Masculine) may also have a variant LS ending *–uˈ*, always stressed (in origin the Locative Singular of the Old Russian *u-stem*) in the strictly locative meaning, after the prepositions *в/v* 'in' and *на/na* 'on'. In this case we are not dealing with variants, but exceptional forms, that is, a given word either does or does not have this ending. All are monosyllabic stems (except for one, *берег/bˈeˈrˈeg–ø* 'shore', actually historically monosyllabic, PS **berg–*) – the common ones are *сад/sad–ø* 'garden', *мост/most–ø* 'bridge', *лес/lˈes–ø* 'forest' (*в саду/v sad–uˈ*, *на мосту/na most–uˈ*), but by no means all such nouns have this form, cf. *в доме/v doˈm–e* 'in the house', *на столе/na stol–eˈ* 'on the table'. Insofar as the same words require the Prepositional, as opposed to the Locative, they take the regular ending, e.g. *о саде/o saˈd–e* 'concerning the garden'.

  In Class III nouns, there is a now rare variant involving only a stress shift to the ending in this locative meaning, e.g. *на двери/na dvˈerˈ–iˈ* 'on the door' (versus *о двери/o dvˈeˈrˈ–i* 'concerning the door').

  (iii) Vocative. Only two words retain a remnant Vocative form, both religious and belonging, therefore, to Russian Church Slavonic: *бог/bog–ø* 'God' has the form *боже/bož–e* 'God!' (with mutation of the /g/) and *господь/gospoˈdˈ–ø* 'Lord' the form *господи/goˈspodˈ–i* 'Lord!'

  Perhaps since ellipsis is not unexpected in vocative forms, it is not surprising that a new vocative form is appearing on affectionate names, but *in casual style only* (see also chapter 7, section 3.4.2). The typical form of such names, for both males and females, is Class II, for males usually with a softened stem (for details see chapter 4 on word-formation), e.g. *Ваня/Vaˈnˈ–a* from *Ivaˈn*, *Лена/Lˈeˈn–a* from *Jelˈeˈn–a*, or for either with a suffix, e.g. *Павлуша/Pavluˈš–a* or *Паша/Paˈš–a* from *Paˈvˈel*, *Наташа/Nataˈš–a* from *Nataˈlˈj–a*. In all of these the apparent new vocative form 'deletes' the ending – or rather the new ending is zero (–∅), thus: *Вань!/Van'–∅, Лен!/L'en–∅, Наташ!/Nata'š–∅.*

(iv) Exceptional endings within Class I

• Nominative Plural Masculine in –a   An increasing number of Class I Masculine nouns are acquiring the Nominative Plural ending –*a'* (instead of –*i*); this trend has been on the increase for many centuries, having originated as a southern dialectal feature. It appears to be popular mainly as a contributor to stress patterns, since any noun with this NP ending has end stress throughout the plural, opposed *en bloc* to the stem-stressed singular (see further below, section 2.1.3.3, on stress patterns). Well established examples are (Nominative Plural): *дома/dom–a'* 'houses', *города/gorod–a'* 'towns', and many foreign borrowings, e.g. *доктора/doktor–a'* 'doctors'; at the non-standard level many more are popular, e.g. *инженера/inžen'er–a'* 'engineers', *трактора/traktor–a'* 'tractors'.

• Nominative Plural Neuter in – *'i*   A small number of neuter nouns have the Nominative Plural ending –*'i* (instead of –*a*); some (semantically body parts) are remnants of the dual, e.g. *плечи/pl'e'č–i* 'shoulders', *уши/u'š–i* 'ears' (NS *yxo/u'x–o*). A few others have no apparent motivation, e.g. *яблоки/ja'blok–i* 'apples' (NS *яблоко/ja'blok–o*).

• Nominative Plural Masculine in –*e*   Nouns of the semantic group 'inhabitant' which have the suffix –*jan* have a couple of peculiarities: in respect of endings, their 'normal' NP has the ending –*e*, e.g. *англичане/angl'iča'n–e* 'the English'. See below on other characteristics of this group.

• Genitive Plural Masculine in –∅   The zero ending in this case (identical to the Nominative Singular) is in origin the Old Russian GP of the *o-stem*, which survived in the neuter group because the Nominative Singular did not have zero (but -*o*) (the normal GPm –*ov* being the Old Russian *u-stem* ending). There is no apparent pattern in standard words with this form, though at the non-standard level quantity words are frequently involved, e.g. standard *глаз/glaz–∅* GP/NS 'eye(s)', *солдат/solda't–∅* 'soldier(s)'; non-standard *(кило)грамм/(kilo)gra'mm–∅* '(kilo)gram(s)' (versus standard *граммов/gra'mm–ov*).

• Genitive Plural Neuter in –*ov*   This is the converse of Genitive Plural Masculine in –∅; it occurs regularly for stems ending in –*j*, e.g. *платьев/pla't'j–ov* 'dress(es)' (NS *платье/pla't'j–o*), irregularly otherwise, e.g. *личиков/l'i'čik–ov* 'face(s), diminutive' (NS *личико/l'i'čik–o*).

(v) Exceptional endings within Class II.

• Genitive Plural in –*ej*   The regular zero ending in this case occasionally gives way to the Genitive Plural ending from Class III with no apparent motivation, e.g. *тётей/t'o't'–ej* 'aunts' (NS *тётя/t'o't'–a*), *дядей/d'a'd'–ej* 'uncles' (NS *дядя/dá'd'–a*).

(vi) Exceptional endings within Class III

● Instrumental Plural in *–m'i'* A few remnant forms retain this, the Old Russian *i-stem* Instrumental Plural (versus the regular *–am'i*), e.g. *детьми/d'et'–m'i'* 'children', *людьми/l'ud'–m'i'* 'people', both *pluralia tantum* (or at least suppletive forms – see below); a couple of others have it as a (disappearing) variant, e.g. *дочер–ьми/–ями/dočer'–m'i'/–a'm'i* 'daughter(s)'.

(b) Stems. There are a few instances of stem changes between Singular and Plural, all in Class I, given below.

(i) Masculine Plural has the suffix *–j*, and the Nominative Plural ending *–a*, e.g. *братья/bra't–'j–a* 'brothers' (NS *брат/brat–∅*), *друзья/druz–'j–a'* 'friends' (NS *друг/drug–∅*, with irregular mutation of /g/; see chapter 1, section 2.2.1.8 and chapter 2, section 3.5.2.1). The Genitive Plural depends on stress: stem stress gives *–ov* (thus always realised as unstressed /e/) (*братьев/bra't–'j–ov*); end stress *–ej–∅* (*друзей/druz–'(e)j–∅'*). In origin this suffix was a collective (singular) form, similar to Eng *brethren*.

(ii) Masculine Singular has the suffix *–'in*, missing in the Plural; this is mostly again the semantic group 'inhabitant' with the suffix *–jan*, e.g. NS *англичанин/angl'ič–a'n–in* 'Englishman', NP *англичане/angl'iča'n–e*, though odd others occur, e.g. *господин/gospod–'i'n* 'gentleman', NP *господа/gospod–a'*. In origin this *–'in* suffix meant 'one, single', and was added to collective (plural) stems.

(iii) Neuter Plural has the suffix (or rather theme) *–'es*: these are remnants of the Old Russian *s-stem*, regularised at least in part by the limiting of the suffix to the Plural only, e.g. *небо/n'e'bo* 'sky, heaven', NP *небеса/n'eb–'es–a'*, *чудо/ču'do* 'miracle', NP *чудеса/čud–'es–a* GP *чудес/čud–'e's–∅'*; other former members of this class regularised the whole paradigm with or without the suffix; in the latter case the former suffix becomes a root syllable *–os*, e.g. *колесо/kol'os–o'* 'wheel', NP *колёса/kol'o's–a* (cf. Russian Church Slavonic forms which have retained the stressed {e}, e.g. *čud–'e's*).

(iv) Masculine words with the suffix *–'onok*, meaning 'young animal': in the plural the suffix's form is *–'at* and the endings are those of the neuter group, e.g. NS *телёнок/t'el–'o'nok–∅* 'calf', NP *телята/t'el–'a't–a*. This pair arose from a fusion of two suffixes with the required meaning, formerly distinguishing domestic from wild animals; the domestic one, *–'at*, belonged to the Old Russian *nt-stem*, with an irregular singular, whose removal was facilitated by the other suffix.

(c) Suppletives. There are only a few suppletive noun forms (using different roots in different morphological forms), typically related to collective (plural) forms. The two major ones are: Sing *человек/čelov'e'k–∅* 'person' ~ Plur *люди/l'u'd'–i* 'people'; *ребёнок/r'eb–'o'nok* 'child' ~*дети/d'e't'–i* 'children'.

(d) Declensions

(i) Indeclinable. Always indeclinable are:

- foreign borrowings ending in a vowel other than *o/e/a* (orthographically *o/ё/e/a/я*), e.g. *такси/taks'i'* 'taxi', *кенгуру/k'enguru'* 'kangaroo';
- borrowings ending in a consonant and referring to a female person, e.g. *мадам/mada'm* 'madame', *Браун/Brown* '(Mrs) Brown', *Горбачевич/ Gorbače'v'ič* '(Mrs) Gorbachevich (which, though Slavonic, cannot be a Russian surname, since this suffix is that of the patronymic);
- borrowings ending in *–o/–e* and referring to a (male) person, e.g. *маэстро/ mae'stro*, *конферансье/konferans'je'* 'MC', *атташе/attaše'* 'attaché';
- native proper names which are morphologically case forms, e.g. *живаго/ Živa'go* (GS, RCS), *Донских/Donski'x* (GP Adj);
- semi-native proper names, often Ukrainian or dialectal, e.g. *Евтушенко/ Jevtuše'nko* 'Yevtushenko', *Пушкино/Pu'škino* 'Puskino' (town);
- abbreviations, including acronyms, until these become perceived as words, and are written in lower case (on the model of Eng *radar, scuba*, etc.), e.g. *вуз/vuz* 'tertiary institute', from the initials *ВУЗ/VUZ* 'higher learning institute', and still sometimes seen in that form (see chapter 5, section 2.2.3.3).

Often indeclinable are:

- borrowings ending in *–o/–e*, e.g. *кофе/ko'f'e* 'coffee', *пальто/pal'to'* 'overcoat', *кино/kino* 'cinema'; these are unpredictable, cf. *вино/v'in-o'* 'wine' is fully declined as Class I Neuter;
- the first half of a compound word: here the issue is the perception of the word as compound (the parts recognised) or fused (the parts not recognised), thus the normal direction is from declension of both (or all) parts to declension only of the last part; the issue of which part is the logical head and which the modifier is not significant for declension, though it is for gender (see below); the norm is modifier + head. Examples of hesitation within the above direction are: *дизель-мотор/d'iz'el'-moto'r–ø* 'diesel engine', *вагон-ресторан/vagon-r'estora'n–ø* 'restaurant car', *диван-кровать/d'ivan-krova't'–ø* 'bed settee', in all of which declension of the first part is possible, but less and less recommended.

(ii) Irregular declension. Proper names (surnames) ending in *–ov/–'in*, e.g. *Чехов/Če'xov–ø* 'Chekhov', *Пушкин/Pu'škin–ø* 'Pushkin', and their female counterparts (*Če'xov–a, Pu'škin–a*) have a mixed declension, with some adjectival forms, reflecting their origin as possessive adjectives (cf. English surnames ending in *–s*, e.g. *Johns, Edwards*); for the Masculine form, only the Instrumental Singular has the adjectival form (*–ым/–im*) (and all the plural except the Nominative Plural), for the Feminine all the Singular except GS (and NS) has the adjectival form (all *–ой/–oj*) (no separate plural).

The noun *путь/put'* 'way' is a solitary remnant of the Old Russian Masculine *i-stems*, the rest of which have joined the soft Class I; in modern terms, this noun has the expected IS (in *–ём/–o'm*) and all the plural, but all the other cases (Genitive Singular, Dative Singular, Locative Singular) have the ending *–u/–i* of Class III. Most likely this survival is due to the high-frequency adverbial phrases *no пути/po put'–i'* '(while) on the way' DS, *на пути/na put'–i'* '(be) on the way' LS.

(iii) Semantic variation. Some words which are homonyms – usually by extension – in the singular may have a different plural; often these are Class I Masculine with the regular versus new Nominative Plural and accompanying end-stress pattern, e.g. *тон/ton–ø* (1) '(musical or mood) tone': NP *тоны/to'n–i*; (2) '(colour) tone': NP *тона/ton–a'*; but there may be more significant differences, e.g. *зуб/zub–ø* (1) 'tooth': NP *зубы/zu'b–i*; (2) 'cog': NP *зубья/zu'b–'j–a*; *колено/kol'e'n–o* (1) 'knee': NP *колени/kol'e'n–'i*; (2) 'joint': NP *коленья/kol'e'n–'j–a*; (3) 'bend (river)': NP *колена/kol'e'n–a*.

(2) Gender

(a) Exceptions to the basic correlation between class and gender. These include:

- Class II Masculine male persons, especially professions, e.g. *дядя/d'ad'–a* 'uncle', *судья/sud'j–a* 'judge', *слуга/slug–a* 'servant', *мужчина/mužčin–a* 'man'; and affectionate male names, e.g. *Коля/Kol'–a* 'Kolya (Nikolai)', *Ваня/Van'–a* 'Vanya (Ivan)'.

In this group the names of professions occupied by both sexes, e.g. *sud'ja*, tend to become common gender, as is already the norm in the next group.

- Class II Common: common personal, including professional, e.g. *коллега/koll'eg–a* 'colleague', *сирота/s'irot–a* 'orphan', *запевала/zap'eval–a* 'choir-leader', *умница/umn'ic–a* 'clever person'; and affectionate common-sex names, e.g. *Саша/Saš–a* 'Sasha (Aleksandr or Aleksandra)', *Валя/Val'–a* 'Valya (Valentin or Valentina)'.

Class I common personal nouns still remain in principle grammatically masculine, even for females, e.g. *профессор/prof'essor* 'professor', *директор/d'ir'ektor* 'principal, director', *врач/vrač* 'physician'; these, too, are beginning to become common gender – accompanying past tense verbs show agreement by natural gender, but accompanying adjectives must still be masculine (see further in chapter 4, section 3.2.2.3). Insofar as the two words for 'child' are used with unspecified sex, they are both grammatically controlled in the standard: *ребёнок/r'eb'onok–ø* is masculine (Class I) and *дитя/d'it'–a*, now archaic or high style, is neuter (Class III).

- Class I Masculine in *–o/–e*: virtually all indeclinable forms referring to male persons; all agreement is masculine; see examples above (*maestro* etc.). A native, and thus declinable, example of the same is *подмастерье/podmast'e'r'j–o* 'apprentice'; a different native example is the suffix *–'išk–o* when added to a masculine base, e.g. *городишко/gorod–'i'šk–o* 'small town'.

Indeclinable words not referring to people or animals are normally neuter; only one common exception exists in the standard: *кофе/kof'e* is officially masculine, though it is frequently treated in non-standard usage as neuter by analogy. Conversely, non-standard usage may allot other genders by association, e.g. *taksi* 'taxi' may appear as feminine by association with the common word for 'car' – *машина/maši'n–a*, or as masculine by association with the more formal word *автомобиль/avtomobi'l'–ф*. Geographical names tend to follow the gender of the class word, for example masculine for towns (*gorod–ф*), e.g. *Batu'mi*, feminine for rivers (*rek–a*), e.g. *Missisipi*, neuter for lakes (*ozer–o*).

(b) Gender in compound words and abbreviations. In principle the gender is taken from the head element, whether this comes first or last: *музей–квартира/ muz'èj-kvart'i'r–a* 'a flat functioning as a museum' is masculine because it is a *muz'ej* 'museum', *книга–справочник/kn'iga-spra'vočn'ik–ф* 'information booklet' is feminine because it is a *kn'iga* 'book' (though it has now commonly become simply *spravočn'ik* and masculine).

In the case of abbreviations the same principle applies, however this assumes that speakers know what words underlie the abbreviation, and this is less and less likely in Russian, as in other languages, as modern societies develop more complex sets of initials and acronyms (e.g. how many English speakers know what words underlie such a common acronym as *AIDS*?). Thus, while *МИД/MID* 'Ministry of Foreign Affairs' is officially neuter, since its head word is *m'in'ist'erstv–o*, and *ИТАР(ТАСС)/ITAR(TASS)* 'Russian (formerly Soviet Telegraphic) TV News Agency' is neuter because its head word is *agentstv–o*, both are likely to be treated as masculine on the basis of their shape as an acronym, namely a word ending in a consonant.

(c) Collectives. The gender of collective (singular) words is strictly grammatical. The only issue with these is the syntactic one of Singular versus Plural (see below and chapter 4, section 3.2.2.3). Thus *молодёжь/molod'o'ž–ф* 'young people' is Class III Feminine, *крестьянство/krest'a'nstv–o* 'peasantry' is Class I Neuter.

(3) Number. All *singularia tantum* words in Russian are basically as logically expected, fitting into the semantic classes of abstract (e.g. *sadness*), collective (singular) (e.g. *foliage*), uncountable mass (e.g. *milk*) or proper names (e.g. *towns*). Only the collective group is open to interpretation as plural (e.g. *старьё/star'j–o'* 'old clothes/things').

On the other hand, there are many *pluralia tantum* which are not so expected: while the collective group is represented here by expected plurals (e.g. *брюки/br'u'k–i* 'trousers', *очки/očk–i* 'spectacles'), they may produce a different view to English (e.g. *сливки/sl'i'vk–i* 'cream', *деньги/d'e'n'g–i* 'money'); another interesting group is that of games or customs (e.g. *именины/ im'en'i'n–i* 'name-day', *прятки/pr'a'tk–i* 'hide-and-seek'); and there are unclassifiable ones (e.g. *часы/čas–i* 'clock', *сумерки/su'm'erk–i* 'dusk', *ясли/ja'sl'–i* 'creche').

2.1.3.2 Morphophonology in the noun

(1) 'Inserted vowels.' There are relatively few alternations within the noun system. One, however, is a most important one, namely the $o \sim \emptyset$ and $e \sim \emptyset$ which resulted from the loss of the *jers* (see chapter 2, section 3.5.1.2). The basic synchronic rule is: /o/ and /e/ are inserted within stem-final consonant clusters when an appended suffix or ending is zero; /o/ is inserted after hard and palatal consonants, /e/ after soft or (rarely) palatal, and also where the first member of the cluster is a hard non-velar and the second soft – but there are many exceptions, in particular in respect of the choice of /o/ or /e/. The basic effect of this is seen to be the avoidance of word-final clusters, but this is not a phonological rule, as many of the clusters in question often occur in other final contexts.

The morphological notation of this feature is also problematic: one approach is to mark the inserted vowel in brackets within the morpheme (in its underlying form), however, this is intuitive only when the insertion occurs in the base form (Nominative Singular Masculine), which is certainly very common; it is less readily acceptable when it appears only in one oblique case (especially Genitive Plural); a second approach is to leave the insertion rule to the phonological stage, but the problem here is that the insertion is morphologically or lexically (in fact etymologically) motivated, so phonological rules cannot cope. The intuitive approach – which we will adopt – is thus a compromise: to mark the inserted vowel in brackets only in the zero form.

Examples are:

- $o \sim \emptyset$
  stressed [ɔ]
  /HC— *сон/s(o)n–ø'* 'sleep' NS $\sim$ *сна/sn–a'* GS;
  /SC— *лёд/l'(o)d–ø'* 'ice' NS $\sim$ *льда/l'd–a'* GS; *пёс/p'(o)s–ø'* 'dog' NS $\sim$ *пса/ps–a'* GS;
  /PC— *сверчок/sv'erč(o)k–ø'* 'cricket' NS $\sim$ *сверчка/sv'erč k–a'* GS;
  unstressed [ə]/[ʌ]
  /HC— *окно/okn–o'* 'window' NS $\sim$ *окон/o'k(o)n–ø* GP; *доска/dosk–a'* 'board' NS $\sim$ *досок/do's(o)k–ø* GP;
  /PC— *кошка/ko'šk–a* 'cat' NS $\sim$ *кошек/ko'š(e)k–ø* GP [ə];
  unstressed [ɪ]
  /PC— *кусочек/kuso'č–(o)k* 'small piece' NS $\sim$ *кусочка/kuso'č–k–a* GS;
  (Note: {–(o)k} is here the form of the suffix, thus /o/ even when not stressed.)
  /VelC—SC *кухня/ku'xn'–a* 'kitchen' NS $\sim$ *кухонь/ku'x(o)n'–ø* GP.

• *e ~ ø*

   stressed [ɛ]/[e]

     /SC—*день/d'(e)'n'–ø* 'day' NS [e] ~ *дня/dn'–a* GS; *статья/stat'j–a*
     'article' NS ~ *статей/stat'(e)j–ø'* GP;

     /HC—SC *земля/z'eml'–a* 'earth' NS ~ *земель/z'em'(e)' l–ø* GP;

     /PC—*чей/č(e)j–ø'* 'whose' NSm ~ *чья/čj–a* NSf;

   unstressed [ɪ]

     /SC— *капля/ka'pl'–a* 'drop' NS ~ *капель/ka'p'(e)l'–ø* GP [ɪ].

It will be seen that where we have a Class I Masculine noun, in which it is the Nominative Singular which has the zero ending and thus the inserted vowel, and since this is the dictionary form, we cannot predict from the orthographical shape whether the *o/e* is an inserted vowel or an inherent one; compare, for example, the NS forms *дом/dom–ø* 'house' or *лес/l'es–ø* 'forest', in which the vowel is not inserted and so does not 'disappear' (GS *dom–a, l'es–a*). In the case of Class I Neuter and Class II nouns, the zero ending is the Genitive Plural, and we can predict, at least in principle, that insertion will occur. Hence our preferred approach to notation.

(2) Consonants. The only other regular alternation is that of hard ~ soft consonants, which one can regard as always predictable on simple phonological grounds, since the cause is always the ending *–e*, with the automatic softening which occurs before the phoneme /e/ in all native words. In this case, even foreign words will undergo softening, providing only that they do decline.

   Beyond that, there are odd forms, all remnants, as follows:

     Hard (Singular) ~ Soft (Plural): a few neuter words have a hard stem
     in the singular, soft in the plural, e.g. *сосед/sos'ed–ø* 'neighbour' ~
     Plur *соседи/sos'ed'–i*, etc.; *колено/kol'en–o* 'knee' ~ Plur *колени/*
     kol'en'–i etc. (see also above, section 2.1.3.1, on anomalous
     forms).

     Velar (Singular) ~ Palatal (Plural): odd exceptional words, e.g. *ухо/*
     ux–o 'ear' ~ Plur *уши/uš–i*, etc.; *око/ok–o* 'eye' (obsolete, high) ~
     Plur *очи/oč–i*, etc.

2.1.3.3 Stress patterns in nouns.

The centre of all morphological stress patterns in Russian is the opposition between stem and ending. Only very rarely does stress shift within the stem or ending, except where particular suffixes are involved. This last group is treated in chapter 5.

   From amongst the various ways of describing patterns which have been adopted, we will adopt that which uses 'A' for stem stress and 'B' for end stress when all of the singular or plural is homogeneous; where the stress shifts within these forms, 'C' is used (and the particular mobility can be described for each

Table 10 *Model stress pattern (AB)*

Case	Singular	Plural	
Nominative	*нос/no's–ø*	*носы/nos–i'*	
Accusative	*нос/no's–ø*	*носы/nos–i'*	
Genitive	*носа/no's–a*	*носов/nos–o'v*	
Locative	*носе/no's'–e*	*носах/nos–a'x*	(LS² also: *(на) носу/nos–u'*)
Dative	*носу/no's–u*	*носам/nos–a'm*	
Instrumental	*носом/no's–om*	*носами/nos–a'm'i*	

class). Thus, we have patterns like 'AA', meaning fixed stem stress throughout, 'BB' fixed end stress, 'AB' shifting from stem in the singular to end in the plural, 'BA' the reverse, and so on. Clearly the global opposition of singular and plural is a popular pattern and one which is on the increase, hence this descriptive model is most useful. While statistics of patterns do exist (e.g. Fedjanina 1976), they have usually been based on dictionary materials and so bias the results towards formal vocabulary; counts of high-frequency vocabulary give a better picture of popular patterns. Formal counts also generally group nouns by gender, not distinguishing the two Feminine classes (II and III). Some of these statistics accompany the patterns given below: '(Fed)' means from Fedjanina 1976 (a corpus of some 33,000 words), '(HF)' stands for a count of high-frequency vocabulary done by this author (Cubberley 1987, a corpus of the first thousand nouns of a frequency list).

Allowing the zero ending to be notionally stressed permits a simplification of patterns: the assumption is that where all other endings (within singular or plural) are stressed, we may call zero stressed also; at the surface (phonetic) level the stress falls on the preceding (actual final) syllable. The disyllabic Instrumental Plural is always stressed on the first syllable (/a/). The example of a full 'AB' paradigm (of *нос/nos* 'nose') in table 10 shows how to read the patterns.

Stress patterns by gender and class

(1) Class I Masculine. For this group, 'C' applies to the Plural only, where it means stress on the stem in Nominative Plural (and Accusative Plural when these are the same), otherwise on the ending.

Pattern	Example	% of Masculine (Fed)	% of Masculine (HF)
AA	*завод/zavo'd–ø* 'factory'	85	68.4
BB	*стол/stol–ø'* 'table'	12.7	14.7
AB	*нос; дом/do'm–ø* 'house' (NP *dom–a'*)	1.9	12.9

BA	*глазок/glaz(o)k–ø'*		
	'little eye'	0.1	0.5
AC	*зуб/zu'b–ø* 'tooth'	0.3	3
	(GS *zu'b–a*, NP		
	zu'b–i, GP *zub–o'v*)		

Note the greater popularity of 'AB' and 'AC' in high-frequency words, alongside the formal dominance of 'AA'.

(2) Class II Feminine. For this group 'C' in the Plural means the same as for Class I Masculine; 'C' in the Singular means stress on the stem in Accusative Singular, on the ending elsewhere.

Pattern	Example	% of Feminine (Fed)	% of Feminine (HF)
AA	*книга/kn'i'g–a* 'book'	95.4	76.7
BB	*статья/stat'j–a'* 'article'	2.8	1.7
AB	—	0	0
BA	*сестра/s'ostr–a'* 'sister' (NP *сёстры/s'o'str–i*)	0.8	7.3
AC	*доля/do'l'–a* 'share' (NP *do'l–i*, GP *dol'–e'j*)	(included in (c) below)	
BC	*губа/gub–a'* 'lip' (AS *gub–u'*, NP *gu'b–i*, DP *gub–a'm*)	0.3	2.2
CA	*спина/sp'in–a'* 'back' (AS *sp'i'n–u*, NP *sp'i'n–i* DP *sp'i'n–am*)	0.1	2.2
CC	*рука/ruk–a'* 'hand' (AS *ru'k–u*, NP *ru'k–i*, DP *ruk–a'm*)	0.1	2

The zero Genitive Plural of 'AC' and 'CC' may look as if it has a stem-internal stress shift in words whose stem contains *–oro–* or *–olo–*, however the stressed zero rule accounts for this satisfactorily, e.g. *голова/golov–a'* 'head' is 'CC', hence NP *go'lov–i*, DP *golov–a'm*, and GP *golov–ø'*, realised as /*golo'v*/. In origin these words have monosyllabic *CoRC–* stems (e.g. PS *golv–*), in which the pitch has left its trace (see chapter 1, sections 2.2.1.6, 2.3.1.6).

(3) Class III Feminine

Pattern	Example	% of Feminine (Fed)	% of Feminine (HF)
AA	тетрадь/*t'etra'd'–ø* 'exercise-book'	(included in (b) above)	
AC	дверь/*dv'er'–ø* 'door'	0.5	7.8

(4) Class I Neuter. For this group 'C' in the plural means the same as for Class I Masc, and there is no singular 'C'.

Pattern	Example	% of Feminine (Fed)	% of Feminine (HF)
AA	правило/*pra'vil–o* 'rule'	95.4	81
BB	серебро/*s'er'ebr–o'* 'silver'	2.5	2.5
AB	слово/*slo'v–o* 'word'	0.6	8.5
BA	окно/*okn–o'* 'window'	1.4	7
AC	ухо/*u'x–o* 'ear'	0.04	0.5
BC	крыльцо/*kril'c–o'* 'porch'	0.06	0.5

Note here, too, the differences in the frequencies of 'AB' and 'BA', which are particularly popular in this group.

There is one common word with a stem-internal shift within 'AA': Sing *o'z'or–*, Plur *oz'o'r–* 'lake': NS озеро/*o'z'or–o*, NP озёра/*oz'o'r–a*.

(5) Class III Neuter

Pattern	Example	% of Neut (Fed)	% of Neut (HF)
AB	имя/*i'm'(on)–a* 'name'	(included in (d) above)	

(GS имени/*i'm'on'–i*, NP имена/*im'on–a'*, GP имён/*im'on–ø'*)

One word in this group is 'AA', but with stem-internal shift: знам–ен–/*znam'–on–* 'banner': NS знамя/*zna'm'(on)–a*, GS знамени/*zna'm'–on'–i*, NP знамёна/*znam'–o'n–a*.

2.1.4 Pronouns

Russian has essentially the 'normal' European set of pronoun types, in terms of their semantic and syntactic functions. The basic list includes (with an English example of each): personal (*I*), interrogative (*who*), demonstrative (*this*), indefinite (*someone*), negative (*nothing*), relative (*which*), possessive (*whose*), determinative (*all*), reciprocal (*each other*), correlative (*such*), reflexive (*myself*). The central issue for us at this point is the declension types used for these pronouns, and there are several: there is a special pronominal declension and a special adjectival declension, and in addition some have the normal adjectival declension, some are adverbial and/or indeclinable, one has a noun declension and one the numeral declension. Let us take these in turn.

2.1.4.1 Pronominal declension. There are two types of pronominal declension: one is specifically used for personal pronouns, as archaic and different in Russian as in any other language (cf. English's retention of (accusative) case in this group – *me*, *him*, etc.), the other for the interrogative pronouns, with derivations of these for indefinite and negative. These two types do not have the feature of gender.

(1) Personal. This special type covers the 1st and 2nd Persons Singular and Plural, and the reflexive; the parallels with English or, say, French, reflecting their Indo-European origins, are clear (see table 11). The reflexive pronoun (-*self*) has the same forms as the 2nd Person Singular, with *c–/s–* in place of *t–* (cf. French likewise: *se* and *te*), without, of course, a Nominative, thus: AG *себя/s'eb'–a'*, LD *себе/s'eb'–e'*, I *собой/sob–o'j*. This is an emphatic pronoun, and not the simple reflexive verb form, which is in origin the short enclitic form of the Accusative: *–ся/s'a*, on which see below, under verbs. The Instrumental of these two forms has a high-style variant *тобою/tob–o'ju*.

(2) Non-personal pronominal
   (a) Interrogative. The base representatives of this type are the interrogatives meaning 'who?' and 'what?' They have all cases in singular only; in origin the

Table 11 *Personal pronoun declension*

Person	Case	Singular	Plural	Compare French
1st: *I, we*	Nominative	*я/ja*	*мы/my*	*je, nous*
	Accusative	= Genitive, as always animate		
	Genitive	*меня/m'en'–a'*	*нас/n–as*	*me, nous*
	Loccative	*мне/mn'–e*	*нас/n–as*	
	Dative	*мне/mn'–e*	*нам/n–am*	
	Instrumental	*мной/mn–oj*	*нами/–na'm'i*	
2nd: *you*	Nominative	*ты/ty*	*вы/vy*	*tu, vous*
	Accusative	= Genitive, as always animate		
	Genitive	*тебя/t'eb'–a'*	*вас/v–as*	
	Locative	*тебе/t'eb'–e'*	*вас/v–as*	
	Dative	*тебе/t'eb'–e'*	*вам/v–am*	
	Instrumental	*тобой/tob–o'j*	*вами/v–a'm'i*	

Table 12 *Interrogative pronouns*

Case	*who?*	*what?*
Nominative	*кто/k–to*	*что/č–to*
Accusative	= Genitive, as animate	= Nom, as inanimate
Genitive	*кого/k–ogo*'	*чего/č–ogo*'
	(phonetic [kʌ'vɔ], [tʃɪ'vɔ]) (see below, section 2.1.4.3)	
Locative	*ком/k–om*	*чём/č–om*
Dative	*кому/k–omu*'	*чему/č–omu*'
Instrumental	*кем/k–'em*	*чем/č–em*

k– and *č*– derive from IE *k*ʷ– (as do Eng *wh*–, Lat *qu*– etc.; cf. chapter 1, section 2.1) via *k*–, the /č/ resulting from a following front *jer*, the *k*– unaffected by a following back *jer* (PS *kъ–/kь–*); when final *jers* disappeared (or, rather, were about to disappear), the identity of the Nominative Singular was preserved by the addition of the particle –*to*, not necessary in the other forms.

The basic negative and indefinite pronouns are derived from these by the addition of particles, the declension remaining identical to that above, the particles invariable.

(b) Negative. The proclitic (unstressed) particle *ни–/ni–* is attached, unhyphenated, e.g. *никто/n'i–kto*' 'no-one', G *никого/n'i–kogo*'.

(c) Indefinite. Two degrees of indefiniteness are recognised: one refers to persons or objects known (or assumed) to exist, but whose identity is not known or stated; the other to those whose existence is not certain. The particles indicating these are:

(1a) enclitic –*mo/–to*, hyphenated, e.g. *кто-то/kto'-to* 'someone', G *кого-то/kogo'-to*;

(1b) prepositive, stressed *не–/n'e'–*, unhyphenated, e.g. *некто/n'e'–kto*, G *некого/n'e'–kogo*; this form is more formal or literary;

(2a) enclitic -*нибудь/–n'ibud'*, hyphenated, e.g. *кто–нибудь/kto'-n'ibud'* 'anyone', G *кого-нибудь/kogo'-nibud'*;

(2b) enclitic –*либо/–l'ibo*, hyphenated, e.g. *кто-либо/kto'-l'ibo* 'anyone', 'someone or other', G *кого-либо/kogo'-l'ibo*; this form is more colloquial, at least in the simple meaning 'anyone'.

(d) Relative. In restricted circumstances, the same basic interrogative forms may be used as for relative pronouns (*which*), specifically, when the antecedent is a demonstrative (correlative) pronoun (e.g. *тот, кто* 'the one who', *то, что* 'that which'). Where the antecedent is a noun (phrase), this form appears only in high or poetic style.

2.1.4.2 Special adjectival declension. A second set of pronouns has a variant of the adjectival declension (see section 2.1.4.3), with Nominative and (some) Accusative having noun endings. The main ones belonging here are 3rd Person personal, demonstrative, determinative and possessive. Other than the personal pronouns, most of the pronoun forms described here and in the next group can function as adjectives as well (with no change in form). In all adjectival declensions, including this type, gender is distinguished in the singular only, so that there are potentially only four forms for any one case (Masculine/Feminine/Neuter Singular and one Plural).

(1) Personal. The 3rd person personal pronoun is a hybrid form, its Nominative deriving from an obsolete demonstrative pronoun with the stem *он–/on–*, related to Eng *yon–*. Its four Nominative forms are: Masc *он/on–ø'*, Fem *она/on–a'*, Neut *оно/on–o'*, Plur *они/on'–i'*; note the softening of the stem in the Plural, which is also typical of this whole declension type. The remaining forms of this pronoun (see table 13) are from another former demonstrative, related to Lat *is/ea/id*, reduced to personal in very early Proto-Slavonic, possibly via a definite article (in the same way as English derived *the* from a former demonstrative), since this pronoun is the one used in Slavonic to make definite adjectives (see below). From the synchronic viewpoint, if we wish to relate it to the adjectival declension, we must call its stem *j–* and the rest the adjectival endings (cf. the

Table 13 *3rd person pronoun*

Case	Masculine Singular	Feminine Singular	Neuter Singular	Plural
Nominative	*он/on–ø'*	*она/on–a'*	*оно/on–o'*	*они/on'–i'*
Accusative[a]	*его/j–ogo'*	*её/j–ojo'*	*его/j–ogo'*	*их/(j)–ix*
Genitive	*его/j–ogo'*	*её/j–ojo'*	*его/j–ogo'*	*их/(j)–ix*
Locative[b]	*нём/n'–om*	*ней/n'–ej*	*нём/n'–om*	*них/n'–ix*
D	*ему/j–omu'*	*ей/j–ej*	*ему/j–omu'*	*им/(j)–im*
I[c]	*им/(j)–im*	*ей/j–ej*	*им/(j)–im*	*ими/(j)–im'i*

[a] In this one case, the Accusative always has the form of the Genitive, that is, even for inanimate referents. The 'personal' connection has dominated the grammatical one. The plural form reflects the phonetic change whereby /ji/ has been reduced to /i/. This is only a phonetic change, which does not necessarily mean that the stem is zero, though an alternative view is to call {ø} a variant (allomorph) of {j}; we prefer to write {j} in brackets rather than use {ø}.

[b] Here we have an oddity involving the prepositional side of this case and of this whole pronoun: the rule is that when this pronoun is preceded by any preposition, in any case, it acquires a prothetic [nʲ]; in origin this /n/ belonged to several Indo-European and Proto-Slavonic prepositions (PS *vən* 'in', *sən* 'with' (cf. Gk *syn–*), and *kən* 'toward'), but could become transposed to words with an initial vowel or /j/ (cf. the reverse in Eng **a norange > an orange*). This pattern became the norm first with these prepositions, where the fused form was a palatal /n'/; then it was extended to cover all prepositions. Thus we have forms like *у него/u n'–ogo'* (G) 'by him' (> 'he has'), *с ним/s n–im* 'with him'. Since the Prepositional/Locative case does not (any longer) occur without a preposition, it cannot appear without the prothetic /n/, and so must be listed with it; the form {n'} is thus also an allomorph of {j}, this time controlled by syntactic context.

[c] Same comment for initial /i/ forms as above.

forms of *k–to* above), though this is a counter-intuitive approach, which also presents a problem in naming the plural stem (see below). As we will also see below, in considering the adjectives proper, it is appropriate to call the first vowel of the singular endings {o}, and in the case of this pronoun we can derive all but one of the forms. That one form is the D/LSf *jej*, since there is no phonological rule to cause underlying /joj/ to become [je'j], any more than there is one to cause the reverse; the rule operating here is therefore strictly morphophonemic, and is exceptional within the adjectival declension, since elsewhere the soft D/LSf ending *–ej* is never stressed, and can thus safely be called {oj} (see also chapter 2, section 3.2.3.2 on vowel allophones). The stress pattern is end (BB) and on the disyllabic singular endings it falls on the second syllable (a pattern impossible on normal adjectives).

(2) Demonstrative. The basic demonstrative pronouns have the Indo-European stem *t–* (cf. Eng *that*); the other old stem in *s–* (Eng *this*) was still there in Old Russian, but gave way to a new form derived from the *t–* one. One of the problems both of these faced was the same as with the interrogatives, that the NSm consisted of consonant +*jer*, and was thus imperilled by the loss of the weak *jers*. The *t–* form solved its problem by reduplicating the syllable *t–*, which allowed it later to treat the original *jer* as strong (thus *ъ > o*), giving the form *tot*; the other forms did not require this. The equivalent *s–* form likewise became *s'es'*, though this was soon replaced by RCS *s'ij/s'ej* (reflected in the adverb *сейчас/s'ej–ča's* '(right) now'); in all the Russian area this was in turn replaced by the forms of *tot* with a prothetic [ɛ'] added (orth. *э*). This *e–* was most likely an exclamatory form, like Eng *hey!*, this view being supported by the dialectal (and Belarusian) form [ɣɛt–], and also by the fact that this is the only native word with initial /e/ (not preceded by /j/).

The Masculine/Neuter Singular forms of *тот/t–ot* 'that' follow those of *kto* (*t–ogo'*, *t–omu'*, *t–om*, *t–'em*, etc.), including stress; the Feminine forms are Accusative *ту/t–u*, all the rest *той/t–oj*, and the vowel in the Plural is /e/ (NP *те/t–e*, G/LP *mex/t–ex*, etc.); those of *этот/e't–ot* 'this' have the same, but with /i/ for /e/ throughout (all the Plural and Instrumental Singular Masculine/Neuter: NP *эти/e't'–i*, G/LP *этих/e't'–ix*, ISm/n *этим/e't'–im*, ISf *этой/e't–oj*), and the stress pattern is 'A' (stem) (GSm *этого/e't–ogo*).

(3) Determinative. The determinative pronouns with this declension are *весь/v(e)s'–∅* 'all' and *сам/sam–∅* (emphatic) '-self' (as in 'I myself'). The first is a soft stem – *vs'–* followed by the same forms as *tot,* that is, with *–e–* in the plural and end stress (e.g. GSm *всего/vs'–ogo'*, LSm *всём/vs'–o'm*, NP *все/vs'–e*, G/LP *всех/vs'–ex*); the NS has inserted *e* before the zero ending. The NSn *всё/vs'–o* serves for 'everything', the NP *все/vs'–e* for 'everyone'.

The second (*sam*) is a hard stem, following the pattern of *etot*, i.e. with *–i–* in the plural, but with the end-stress pattern (e.g. GSm *самого/sam–ogo'*,

DSm *самому/sam–omu'*, D/L/ISf *самой/sam–o'j*); further, the plural is pattern 'C': NP on the stem, the rest on the ending (e.g. NP *сами/sa'm'–i*, GP *самих/ sam'–i'x*, IP *самими/sam'–i'm'i*). *Sam* can semantically and syntactically only be a pronoun.

(4) Possessive. Here belong primarily the 1st and 2nd Person pronouns ('mine', 'ours', 'yours') and adjectives ('my', 'our', 'your'), and also a reflexive form meaning 'one's own', that is, referring back to the subject (similar to Fr *son*); all have palatal stems, three ending in *–j–* and two in *–š–*, as follows:

1st Person Singular	2nd Person Singular	Reflexive	1st Person Plural	2nd Person Plural
мой/moj–ø'	*твой/tvoj–ø'*	*свой/svoj–ø'*	*наш/na'š–ø*	*ваш/va'š–ø*

All have *–i* in the plural; the first three (in *–j–*) have the pronominal end-stress pattern (GSm *моего/moj–ogo'*, DSm *моему/moj–omu'*, NP *мои/ mo(j)–i'*, GP *моих/mo(j)–i'x*), the last two (in *–š–*) have stem stress throughout (GSm *вашего/va'š–ogo*, DSm *вашему/va'š–omu*, NP *ваши/va'š–i* (phonetic [ʃɨ]), etc.).

Also here comes the possessive interrogative 'whose?', whose stem is *čj–*: NSm (with inserted vowel) *чей/č(e)j–ø'*, NSf *чья/čj–a*, thereafter as expected (NP *чьи/čj–i*), the stress, of course, falling on the only syllable, the ending.

The 3rd Person possessive (*his*, etc.) is an invariable form derived from the personal pronoun. See below (section 2.1.4.5).

2.1.4.3 Adjectival declension. What is called the 'normal', or 'long' adjective declension – which we discuss here rather than later, under 'adjectives' proper, because the pronouns are historically the basis of the long adjectives, thus should come first, and discussion of the forms cannot be postponed – has the endings shown in table 14, which may be attached to any sort of stem, though with alternations as expected after soft and palatal (especially *o ~ e*).

Table 14 *Normal adjectival declension*

Case	Masculine Singular	Feminine Singular	Neuter Singular	Plural
Nominative	*–ый/'–ij*; *–ой/–o'j*	*–ая/–aja*	*–ое/–oje*	*–ые/–ije*
Accusative	= N or G by ±animate	*–ую/–uju*	= N	= N or G
Genitive	*–ого/–ogo*	*–ой/–oj*	*–ого/–ogo*	*–ых/–ix*
Locative	*–ом/–om*	*–ой/–oj*	*–ом/–om*	*–ых/–ix*
Dative	*–ому/–omu*	*–ой/–oj*	*–ому/–omu*	*–ым/–im*
Instrumental	*–ым/–im*	*–ой/–oj*	*–ым/–im*	*–ыми/–im'i*

The Nominative Singular is the only form to show a segmental (phonemic) difference for stress pattern: end-stress (possible in hard or palatal stems only) is realised as *–o'j*, (versus *–ij* for unstressed ending); given that unstressed /o/ in such a (post-tonic) position is realised as [ə], the pronunciation of unstressed [ɨ] is not what we might expect, thus we must treat these as different phonemes; the historical reason for this oddity is the role of Russian Church Slavonic, since it had [ɨ] in this position, even stressed; this substitution was no doubt encouraged by the similarity of pronunciation of the two unstressed vowels ([ə] and [ɨ], the former simply a less tense version of the latter).

In soft and palatal stems, the first vowel (/o/) is realised, when unstressed, as [ɪ] (orthographic *e*) after soft consonants (e.g. *синем*/*si'n'–om* 'blue' LSm) and soft palatals (e.g. *горячем*/*gor'a'č–om* 'hot' LSm), as [ə] after hard palatals (e.g. *свежем*/*sv'e'ž–om* 'fresh' LSm); the ending is never stressed after soft consonants, but may be stressed after hard palatals ([ɔ], orth. *o*, e.g. *большом*/*bol'š–o'm* 'big' LSm); /i/ is realised as [ɨ] after hard C (orth. *ы*, see table 14) and hard palatals (orth. *u*, e.g. *большим*/*bol'š–i'm* 'big' ISm).

The GSm/n ending requires special comment: it is one of the rare examples of complete non-correspondence between orthography and pronunciation, since there is nothing in the phonetic context which allows us to predict the pronunciation [v] for written *г/g*; the phoneme involved cannot therefore be /g/, but must be /v/, in spite of the spelling. Historically, this situation appears to be the result of the confluence of dialects in Moscow during the period of its rise (see chapter 1, section 3.1), when speakers with both [g] and [ɣ] for /g/ came together, the resulting confusion producing, in this particular context only, the two new variants [ɔɔ] and [ɔvɔ]. Modern dialects still reflect both of these shapes, as well as the older [ɔɣɔ].

We find this declension in the following pronoun types, all of which are clearly more (or more often) adjectival than the previous group.

(1) Interrogative. The meanings 'of what sort' and 'which (one of)' belong here, namely (respectively): *какой*/*kak–o'j* (end-stress), *который*/*koto'r–ij* (stem-stress).

(2) Relative. The same two pronouns may be relative, in the meanings 'which' (*kotorij*) (that is, the normal relative), and 'the like of which' (*kakoj*).

(3) Correlative (Demonstrative). The correlative demonstrative *такой*/*tak–o'j* 'such', 'that sort of', matches *kakoj* in the same way as all other *k–* versus *t–* forms throughout the Indo-European group.

(4) Determinative. Here belong *каждый*/*ka'žd–ij* 'each', *любой*/*l'ub–o'j* 'any', *другой*/*drug–o'j* 'other', and *всякий*/*vs'a'k–ij* 'every (kind of)'.

(5) Negative. Only *никакой/n'i–kak–o'j* 'no (sort of)', derived from *kakoj* plus negative proclitic *n'i–*.

(6) Indefinite. Only *некоторый/n'e'–kotor–ij* 'some', derived from *kotorij* with prepositive *n'e'–*, stressed throughout.

2.1.4.4 Mixed pronoun declension. The pronoun meaning 'the (very) same' is a compound form joining the demonstrative *tot* with a full adjective form (stem-stressed) of *sam*, namely *tom самый/t–ot sa'm–ij*, to which is commonly added the intensive particle *že*: *tom же самый*, both pronoun parts being declined (e.g. GSm *t–ogo' (že) sa'm–ogo*).

2.1.4.5 Indeclinable pronouns. The most important here is the 3rd person possessive, which is formally the Genitive of the personal pronoun, namely Masc *eго/jogo'* 'his', Fem *eё/jojo'* 'her(s)', Plur *ux/ix* 'their(s)'.

Also here come those quantitative pronouns which may double as adverbs (always indeclinable), e.g. *сколько/sko'lko* 'how much/many?', *столько/sto'l'ko* 'so much/many' (note again *k–* versus *t–*), *несколько/n'e'–skol'ko* 'several'.

2.1.4.6 Pronouns with noun declension. One pronoun has a noun declension, namely the reciprocal *друг друга/drug dru'g–a* 'each other'. Its structure is like English, with the first form *drug* (originally – and still also – lexically the noun 'friend', then the adjective 'other') acting as a noun subject, thus always Nom *drug–ø*, the second indicating the syntactic relationship between the two, e.g. direct object: Acc – *drug–ø dru'g–a*, indirect object: Dat – *drug–ø dru'g–u*; this second member may be governed by a preposition, e.g. *s* + Instr – *drug–ø s dru'g–om* 'with each other', that is, 'together'.

2.1.4.7 Pronouns with numeral declension. One pronoun has a form of numeral declension, though it is an archaic one, namely *оба/o'b–a* 'both'. Its form is a remnant of the dual numeral declension, some of which survives also in the related cardinal numeral *два/dv–a* 'two'. The latter (exceptionally within the numerals, see details below, section 2.1.6.1) distinguishes gender in the Nominative only, while *oba* distinguishes it in all cases, but in the oblique cases by stem shape, not ending: Nm/n *оба/o'b–a*, Nf *обе/o'b'–e*; thereafter the Masculine/Neuter stem is *obo'–*, the Feminine stem *ob'e'–*, and to these are added the Plural adjective endings: G/L *–ix*, D *–im*, I *–im'i* (e.g. Gm/n *обоих/obo'–ix*, Gf *обеих/ob'e'–ix*).

2.1.5   Adjectives

Formally, adjectives have two forms, referred to as 'long' and 'short'. In function, the long form is used in the regular attributive position, where the short is impossible; the short form is usable in the predicative position only, where the long is also possible. Details of these functions will be dealt with in chapter 4, here we restrict ourselves to formal questions.

In origin, the Old Russian difference between the long and short forms was the feature ±Definite: the short form, with noun declension, was unmarked (−Definite), the long, initially formed by the addition of a personal (earlier demonstrative) pronoun (retained in the oblique forms of modern *on* – see above, section 2.1.4.2, which explains the coincidence of pronoun and adjective endings), was the marked form (+Definite). Between Old Russian and Modern Russian this feature was lost, the long form became the unmarked one, and a remnant of the short form survived in the predicate.

2.1.5.1 Normal (long) forms.
The long form consists of a stem and the set of endings given – with comments – in table 14, section 2.1.4.3, above. Common examples with a range of stems are (NSm):

- hard, stem-stressed: *старый/sta'r–ij* 'old';
- hard, end-stressed: *молодой/molod–o'j* 'young';
- velar (/i/ > [ɨ])
    - stem-stressed: *русский/ru's–sk–ij* 'Russian';
    - end-stressed: *морской/mor–sk–o'j* '(of the) sea';
- soft, stem-stressed only: *синий/s'i'n'–ij* '(dark) blue';
- palatal, stem-stressed
    - soft: *горячий/gor'a'č–ij* 'hot';
    - hard (/i/ > [ɨ]): *свежий/sv'e'ž–ij* 'fresh';
- palatal, end-stressed, hard only: *большой/bol'š–o'j* 'big'.

2.1.5.2 Short forms.
Since in origin the short adjectives were formally nouns, and since they have become restricted to the predicative position, all that remain are the four Nominative forms (Masculine/Feminine/Neuter Singular, and Plural), each with endings appropriate to the gender, e.g. masc *стар/star–ǿ*, fem *стара/star–a*, neut *старо/star–o*, plur *стары/star–i*. The masculine ending, being zero, has the inserted vowel – {o} – in stems ending in most clusters, e.g. *близок/bl'i'z–(o)k–ǿ* 'near', fem *близка/bl'iz–k–a* (long NSm *близкий/bl'i'z–k–ij*); *умён/um–'(o)n–ǿ* 'clever', fem *умна/um–('n–a*; *грустен/gru'st–'(o)n* 'sad', fem *грустна/grust–(')n–a*. As this inserted vowel reflects a former *jer*, it is phonologically unpredictable, since the softness of the stem-final consonant is not visible; however, in most cases a suffix is present (see examples above), and this allows prediction, e.g. before –*k* the stem is always hard (thus insert orth. *o*), before –*n* it is soft (thus orth. *e*, if stressed *ë*). In either case the morphophoneme is {o}, since the stressed realisation is [ɔ]. In the relatively rare cases where a suffix is not present or cannot be

identified, prediction is less easy, including prediction of non-insertion, but softening is the norm, e.g. *хитрый/xi'tr–ij* 'cunning': *хитёр/xit(′o)r–ø*; /l/ remains hard, e.g. *долгий/do'lg–ij* 'long': *долог/do'l(o)g–ø, полный/po'ln–ij* 'full': *полон/po'l(o)n–ø*; (cf. also *жёлтый/žo'lt–ij* 'yellow': *жёлт/žo'lt–ø* with *no* insertion).

The occurrence of short forms other than in the predicate, or declension of these forms, is restricted to (folk) poetic style or fixed phrases.

The stress patterns of these forms is rather complex: other than fixed stem-stress, which is statistically the dominant pattern, end-stress may occur on all, or only on Feminine, or on Feminine and Plural. There are conflicting pressures towards regularisation of these last two types, one towards generalising end-stress, one strengthening the Feminine-only end pattern, which is clearly very popular. As we shall see below, similar patterns and pressures are operating in the past tense of verbs.

2.1.5.3 Special adjectival declension. The special declension common in the pronouns (see above, section 2.1.4.2) appears as an exception in adjectives proper. It is now restricted to possessive adjectives (cf. Eng–*'s*), which are in any case disappearing – certainly from the colloquial level – in favour of noun phrases using Genitive (cf. Eng *of*); the suffixes with this meaning are: *–ов/–ov*, added to Class I (Masculine) stems, and *–ин/–in*, added to Class II (Feminine) stems – both mainly added to personal names, and *–j*, almost exclusively used in the semantic group of animals. The first two are very common in surnames, where their declension is a mixed one (see above, section 2.1.3.1(d)). In the possessive meaning they are really restricted to Nominative, though not necessarily predicative. Examples are: *иванов дом/iva'n–ov–ø dom–ø* 'Ivan's house' (NSm), *иванова мать/iva'n–ov–a mat'–ø* 'Ivan's mother' (NSf); *сашин дом/sa'š–in–ø dom–ø* 'Sasha's house' (NSm) – regardless of whether Sasha is male or female. The suffix may be stressed, where the base is end-stressed, e.g. *петров/petr–o'v–ø* 'Peter's' (from *Пётр/P'otr–ø'*), *ильин/il'j–i'n–ø* 'Ilya's' (from *Илья/Il'j–a'*).

The case of *–j* is parallel, though spelling makes it look much more complex than it is: the problem is that the addition of *–j* produces a cluster, and thus an inserted vowel in the NSm; but in this case the inserted vowel is, exceptionally, /i/ (orth. *и*); moreover, the preceding consonant is mutated to its palatal alternant (for a list of mutations see table 15); these forms are never end-stressed; examples are:

> from *волк/volk* 'wolf': NSm *волчий/vo'lč–(i)j–ø* 'wolf's', NSf *волчья/vo'lč–j–a*, NP *волчьи/vo'lč–j–i*, GSm *волчьего/vo'lč–j–ogo*;
> from *медведь/m'edv'e'd'* 'bear': NSm *медвежий/m'edv'e'ž–(i)j–ø* 'bear's', NSf *медвежья/m'edv'e'ž–j–a*;
> from *баран/bara'n* 'ram': NSm *бараний/bara'n–(i)j–ø* 'ram's', NSf *баранья/bara'n'–j–a* (since /n/ simply mutates to /n'/).

Only one other common adjective has this special declension, and it is also one with a –*j* suffix, but without mutation, namely the ordinal numeral *третий/tr'e't'–(i)j–ø* 'third', NSf *третья/tr'e't'–j–a*, GSm *третьего/ tr'e't'–j–ogo*, etc.

2.1.5.4 Indeclinable. Indeclinable adjectives – always foreign borrowings – are extremely rare. Failing, as they do, to fit the inflectional system, they are even more unnatural than indeclinable nouns. An indication of the problem is seen in the fact that, virtually always, such adjectives abnormally occupy the post-nominal position in a phrase. Examples of such adjectives are (in common semantic groupings):

- colour of clothes: *беж/bež* 'beige', *бордо/bordo'* ('Bordeaux'), *хаки/xa'ki* 'khaki';
- dress style:*декольте/dekol'te'* 'décolleté', *демисезон/d'em'is'ezo'n* 'spring/ autumn';
- language: *хинди/xi'nd'i* 'Hindi', *урду/urdu'* 'Urdu', *коми/ko'm'i* 'Komi'.

Only with the last group are there signs of change: they alone may occupy the normal pre-nominal position, e.g. *коми язык/kom'i jazyk–ø* '(the) Komi (language)'; while this appears to be the norm for this particular language, for most others the 'reverse' order is still the norm, e.g. *язык хинди/jazyk–ø xind'i* '(the) Hindi (language)'.

2.1.5.5 Substantivised adjectives. Many adjectives may function syntactically as nouns, sometimes as alternatives, sometimes exclusively, e.g. *больной/ bol'–n–o'j* may be the adjective 'ill' or the noun 'patient', while *ванная/ va'n–n–aja* 'bathroom' can only be a noun (unless in formal style accompanied by the noun *комната/ko'mnat–a* 'room'). A rare form distinguishes stress position in the two functions, e.g. *жаркий/ža'r–k–ij* 'hot' (of non-liquids) (NSn *ža'rkoje*) versus *жаркое/žar–k–o'je* 'roast meat'. A similar case applies to family names derived from possessive adjectives (see above, section 2.1.5.3), where the stress position may differ, e.g. *иванов/iva'n–ov–ø* 'Ivan's' versus *Иванов/Ivan–o'v–ø* 'Ivanov', possibly accompanied by automatic segmental changes, e.g. *толстый/to'lst–ij* 'fat' versus *Толстой/Tolst–o'j* 'Tolstoy'. Since formally all of these remain adjectives, this is really a purely syntactical question, and is taken up in chapter 4.

2.1.5.6 Comparative. As in English, there are two ways of forming the comparative degree of adjectives: an inflectional (synthetic) one (like Eng *x–er*) and an analytical one (like Eng *more x*). The essential difference is one of syntax, the latter being the only attributive form, the former occurring only in the predicate. In the predicate, where both types may occur, the difference is one of style, the analytical form being more formal or literary, the synthetic more colloquial. Also as in English, though less surprisingly, there is no sign that the inflectional type is losing ground, even though there are many more complications than in English.

(1) Analytical (attributive) type. The analytical form is made by adding the invariable particle *более/bo'l'eje* (in origin a synthetic comparative from the root *bol'–* 'big') to the positive (attributive, long-form) adjective; this form can therefore be fully declined and must agree with its head word, whether it occurs in the subject or predicate. For example:

> NSf *более интересная книга/bo'l'eje int'er'e'sn–aja kn'i'g–a* 'a more interesting book';
>
> ASf *более интересную книгу/bo'l'eje int'er'e'sn–uju kn'i'g–u* 'a more interesting book';
>
> LSf *о более интересной книге/o bo'l'eje int'er'e'sn–oj kn'i'g'–e* 'about a more interesting book'.

A parallel reverse comparative is formed by the use of *менее/m'en'–eje* 'less' in place of *bol'eje*.

A small group of high-frequency adjectives have inflected attributive forms with a suffix other than *bol'eje* (similar to English irregular formations like *good/better, bad/worse*), e.g.:

> *хороший/xoro'š–ij* 'good' ∼ *лучший/lu'čš–ij* 'better';
>
> *плохой/plox–o'j* 'bad' ∼ *худший/xu'd–š–ij* 'worse';
>
> *большой/bol'–š–o'j* 'big' ∼ *больший/bo'l'–š-ij* 'bigger';
>
> *маленький/ma'l'en'k–ij* 'small' ∼ *меньший/m'en'–š-ij* 'smaller';
>
> *старый/sta'r–ij* 'old' ∼ *старший/sta'r–š–ij* 'older, senior';
>
> *молодой/molod–o'j* 'young' ∼ *младший/mla'd–š–ij* 'younger, junior'

(2) Inflectional (predicative) type. The inflectional type is further complicated by the fact that it has an older and a newer form, as well as irregular forms; the older form is no longer productive, and is restricted to relatively high-frequency words. Given words have one form only – there is no choice within this type. The resulting forms are invariable, and for that reason may not occur in attributive position (though there is a colloquial, low style variant in which this form may appear attributively, see chapter 7, section 3.4.2). We will treat them in the order: newer, older regular, older irregular.

(a) Newer form. This form adds the ending *–ee/–eje* to the adjective stem. The only phonemic change involved is the automatic softening of hard stems before /e/. The stress may be on the stem – regular on polysyllabic stems, especially

literary or foreign, or on the ending – regular on monosyllabic stems, where it parallels the end–stress on the Feminine short adjective.

Some examples are:

Positive (Nominative Singular Masculine)	**Comparative (Indeclinable)**
интересный/int'er'e'sn–ij	*интереснее/int'er'e'sn–eje*
красивый/kras'i'v–ij 'beautiful'	*красивее/kras'i'v–eje*
быстрый/bi'str–ij 'fast'	*быстрее/bistr–e'je*
(Short NSf: *bistr–a'*)	
сложный/slo'žn–ij 'complex'	*сложнее/složn–e'je*
(*složn–a'*)	

A casual style variant of this form has *–ej* instead of *–eje*, but this is really more common in adverbial use (see below), e.g. *быстрей/bistr–e'j*.

(b) Older regular. This form has a single *–e*, however its origin as *–je* is reflected in the mutation of the preceding consonant. The mutated alternants of consonants (the Proto-Slavonic *Cj* results, see also chapter 2, section 3.5.2.1) are shown in table 15.

This *–e* is never stressed. Examples:

Positive (NSm)	Comparative (Indecl.)
дешёвый/d'ešov–ij 'cheap'	*дешевле/d'eše'vl'–e*

(Note: here is a case of {o} being realised as stressed /e/ before soft suffix (see above, section 1.1.1).)

Table 15 *J–mutation of consonants*

Class	Consonants	∼	(j-)mutated form
Labial	p, b, m, f, v		pl', bl', ml', fl', vl'
Dental	t		č *or* šč (RCS)
	d		ž *or* žd (RCS)
	n		n'
	s		š
	z		ž
	st		šč
Velar	k		č
	g		ž
	x		š
	sk		šč
Liquid	r, l		r', l'

богатый/boga't–ij 'rich'   богаче/boga'č–e
молодой/molod–o'j 'young'   моложе/molo'ž–e
простой/prost–o'j 'simple'   проще/pro'šč–e
дикий/d'i'k–ij 'wild'   диче/d'i'č–e (also possible
                                        d'ič–e'je)

дорогой/dorog–o'j 'dear'   дороже/doro'ž–e
тихий/t'i'x–ij 'quiet'   тише/t'i'š–e
плоский/plo'sk–ij 'flat'   площе/plo'šč–e

Note that stems ending in –k are virtually always in clusters, where the –k is a (former) suffix. This –k may behave like a normal stem ending, that is, it becomes /č/, or it may disappear in the comparative – meaning that the comparative is formed from the suffix-less stem. This may happen even if the form of the suffix is –ok (and not –(o)k). The latter are treated in the next group; examples of the former are:

громкий/gro'm–k–ij 'loud'   громче/gro'm–č–e
жаркий/ža'r–k–ij 'hot'   жарче/ža'r–č–e

(c) Older irregular.
(1) the suffix –k–/–ok– is lost

короткий/koro't–k–ij 'short'   короче/koro'č–e
редкий/r'e'd–k–ij 'rare'   реже/r'e'ž–e
близкий/bl'i'z–k–ij 'near'   ближе/bl'i'ž–e
высокий/vis–o'k–ij 'high'   выше/vi'š–e
широкий/šir–o'k–ij 'wide'   шире/ši'r'–e

(2) the suffix –še is added: the stem may be unchanged, but more often is changed in a range of ways, from softening, through loss of a suffix (–n as well as –k), to lexical change:

старый/sta'r–ij 'old'   старше/sta'r–še
ранний/ra'n–n'–ij 'early'   раньше/ra'n'–še
долгий/do'lg–ij 'long (time)'   дольше/do'l'–še
большой/bol'š–o'j 'big'   больше/bo'l'–še
     (suffix –š here too)
маленький/ma'l'–en'k–ij 'small'   меньше/m'e'n'–še

(3) other irregular forms include the addition of –že, in origin presumably a variant of –še after voiced obstruents:

поздний/po'zd–n'–ij 'late'   позже/po'z–ž–e
глубокий/glub–o'k–ij 'deep'   глубже/glu'b–že
сладкий/sla'd–k–ij 'sweet'   слаще/sla'šč–e
плохой/plox–o'j 'bad'   хуже/xu'ž–e (root xud–)
хороший/xoro'š–ij 'good'   лучше/lu'č–še

2.1.5.7 Superlative. Here, too, there are both older, suffixed, forms and newer, analytical, ones. In the case of the superlative, the basic analytical form is in practical terms the only one, apart from a few forms which may be regarded as exceptional remnants.

(1) Analytical forms. The normal form is a compound made by adding the pre-positive, fully declined adjectival form самый/sa'm–ij to the positive adjective, e.g. самая красивая дама/sa'm–aja kras'i'v–aja da'm–a 'the most beautiful lady' NSf, о самой красивой даме/o sa'm–oj kras'i'v–oj da'm–e 'about the most beautiful lady' LSf.

A second form involves instead the pre-positive invariable particle наиболее/nai-bo'l'–eje, itself derived from the comparative particle bol'eje by the addition of an even older particle nai–. This form is strictly high/bookish style.

(2) Suffixed forms. The older form involves the suffix –ш/–š, cognate with Eng –st. It occurs on some of the expected group of high-frequency words, and is added to the comparative stem, e.g.:

хороший/xoro'š–ij 'good'   лучший/lu'č–š–ij 'best'
плохой/plox–o'j 'bad'   худший/xu'd–š–ij 'worst'
старый/sta'r–ij 'old'   старший/sta'r–š–ij 'oldest'
молодой/molod–o'j 'young'   младший/mla'd–š–ij 'youngest'
высокий/vis–o'k–ij 'high'   высший/vi's–š–ij 'highest'
низкий/n'i'z–k–ij 'low'   низший/n'i'z–š–ij 'lowest'

Note that all the forms on the right can thus be either comparative or superlative, only the context indicating which. In the case of the third and fourth, this form is used only within the family group, that is, in reference to children and siblings; otherwise 'oldest' and 'youngest' are made analytically, i.e. sam–ij star–ij, etc. With the last two examples, this form is used only in technical contexts (e.g. высший сорт/viss–ij sort–∅ 'highest quality', 'superior brand') and some fixed phrases; otherwise sam–ij visok–ij, etc. are used. A possible concession may be made to the ambiguity of the first two by the addition of sam–ij to the superlative form, e.g. sam–ij lučš–ij/xudš–ij, similar to Eng the very best/worst.

Another, expanded, form of the *–š* suffix survives in a few adjectives, namely *–ейш/–ejš* (*–айш/–ajš* – after stems in a palatal, almost always, as in the comparative, a mutated velar), e.g. *ближайший/bl'iž–ajš–ij* 'nearest' (from *близкий/bl'iz–k–ij*, comparative *ближе/bl'iž–e*), *величайший/v'el'ič–a'jš–ij* 'greatest' (from *великий/v'el'i'k–ij*). The stress is usually on the suffix vowel – always in the case of monosyllabic stems. However, this form of the suffix is mostly confined to high/literary style; otherwise it is now almost exclusively used for the absolute superlative ('a most', 'a very'), e.g. *важнейший/važn–e'jš–ij* '(a) most important', *интереснейший/int'er'e'sn–ej–š–ij* '(a) most interesting', *высочайший/visoč–a'jš–ij* '(a) very high'.

Lastly, a few of the high-frequency (and irregular) adjectives may combine the particle *nai–* with the suffix *–š*, again added to the comparative stem. This form is typical of journalistic style, e.g. *наибольший/naibo'l'–š–ij* 'the greatest/largest', *наименьший/nai–m'e'n'–š–ij* 'the smallest', *наилучший/nailu'č–š–ij* 'the very best'.

2.1.6   Numerals

Apart from the cardinal and ordinal numerals, Russian has also a small set of collective numerals. Ordinals have the adjectival declension, while collectives and most cardinals have a noun declension. A few cardinals have a remnant of the former numeral declension proper, and one ('one'!) has the special adjective declension. There are complications and regularisations involved with compound numerals, both cardinal and ordinal. The structure of compound cardinal numerals is essentially like English: the teens are formed by single-word compounding based on the structure 'one on ten', e.g. *тринадцать/tr'i–na–dcat'* 'thirteen'; the tens on the structure 'two tens', e.g. *тридцать/tr'i–dcat'* 'thirty' (in each case, the form *–dcat'* is an elliptical version of *десять/d'e's'at'* 'ten'); the units are simply added as separate words, e.g. *тридцать три/tr'i-dcat' tr'i* 'thirty three'. Beyond one hundred, the style is the European and American, rather than the British, without 'and', e.g. *сто тридцать/sto tr'idcat'* 'a hundred and thirty'/'one hundred thirty'.

2.1.6.1 Cardinal numerals

(1) 'one.' Only 'one' has the special adjective declension, that is, it has three genders, and the Nominative has noun-like endings, the other cases adjectival; the stress is on the final syllable (like *tot*). The stem is *одн–/odn–*; the NSm, with the zero ending, is exceptional in having the inserted vowel /i/ rather than the expected /e/ (the reflex of the front *jer*, which this numeral does have in the West and most South Slavonic languages). In origin it is actually the /i/ which is 'correct', having been shortened to a *jer* after the Proto-Slavonic stage. The form *–in* is related to the general Indo-European root *oin–* (*one, ein, un,* etc.),

the initial *od–* (from PS *ed–*) most likely a pointing form meaning 'lo, behold, over there' (cf. Lat *ecce* and Rus *vot*).

There is also a plural form, with the meaning 'some' (versus 'others'), also used formally with *pluralia tantum* words. Some of the forms are (for the rest see above, section 2.1.4.3):

Case	Masculine	Feminine	Neuter	Plural
Nominative	один/od('i)n–ø'	одна/odn–a'	одно/odn–o'	одни/odn–'i'
Genitive	одного/ odn–ogo'	одной/ odn–o'j	одного/ odn–ogo'	одних/ odn–'i'x
Instrumental	одним/ odn–'i'm	одной/ odn–o'j	одним/odn–'i'm	одними/ odn–'i'm'i

(2) 'two', 'three', 'four'.' These three numerals have an archaic declension shape, in origin a variant of the Dual, which was the appropriate form for 'two', and has spread to the others. 'Two' is the only numeral other than 'one' to show any gender, and it does this only in the Nominative (and Accusative for inanimates) (and the forms of the pronoun *оба/oba* 'both' may usefully be compared, see above, section 2.1.4.7); the oblique cases show the ending vowel {u}; the forms are as follows:

Nominative	два/dv–a Masc/Neut две/dv–'e Fem
Accusative	= Nom (Inan.) or Gen (An.)
Genitive/Locative	двух/dv–ux
Dative	двум/dv–um
Instrumental	двумя/dv–um'a'

mpu/tr'i 'three' and *четыре/četi'r'e* 'four' have the oblique case vowel {o} (orth. *ё/e*, almost always stressed):

Nominative	три/tr'–i	четыре/četi'r'–e
Accusative	= Nom (Inan.) or Acc (An.)	
Genitive/Locative	трёх/tr'–ox	четырёх/četir'–ox
Dative	трём/tr'–om	четырём/četir'–om
Instrumental	тремя/tr'–om'a'	четырьмя/četir'–m'a'

(3) Typical forms from 'five' upwards. Simple forms from 'five' onwards are all noun declension; almost all belong to Class III Feminine, odd ones being 'forty', 'ninety', 'hundred' and 'thousand' (and 'million', etc.). All but 'seven' and 'eight' have stems in *–t'*, those two having *–m'*: семь/s'em'–ø' 'seven' and восемь/vos'(e)m'–ø' 'eight'. The remaining base forms are: пять/ p'at'–ø' 'five', шесть/šest'–ø' 'six', девять/d'ev'at'–ø' 'nine' and десять/ d'es'at'–ø' 'ten'. Most have end stress.

The majority type – regular Class III Feminine (including Accusative always = Nominative) – is illustrated by *пять/p'at'–ø'* 'five':

Nominative/Accusative	*пять/p'at'–ø'*
Genitive/Locative/Dative	*пяти/p'at'–i'*
Instrumental	*пятью/p'at'–ju'*

The variants of this type are as follows.

(a) In the tens from 'fifty' to 'eighty' the Nominative ends in a hard /t/ (orth. no ь), and both parts decline (as Class III Feminine) in parallel, reflecting their compound formation, e.g.

Nominative/Accusative	*пятьдесят/p'at'–d'es'a't–ø* 'fifty'
Genitive/Locative/Dative	*пятидесяти/p'at'–i'–d'es'at'–i*
Instrumental	*пятьюдесятью/p'at'–ju'–d'es'at'–ju*

The remaining regular tens are: *двадцать/dva'–dcat'–ø* 'twenty', *тридцать/tr'i'–dcat'–ø* 'thirty', *шестьдесят/šest'–d'es'a't–ø* 'sixty', *семьдесят/s'e'm'd'es'at–ø* 'seventy' and *восемьдесят/vo's'em'd'es'at–ø* 'eighty'.

(b) In the teens the stress is on the central element *–na–* 'on' in all except 'eleven' – *одиннадцать/od'i'n–na–dcat'–ø*, e.g. *тринадцать/tr'i–na'–dcat'–ø* 'thirteen', and the end of the first element is hardened, e.g. *пятнадцать/p'at–na'–dcat'–ø* 'fifteen'; only the final element is declined, e.g. Gen *пятнадцати/p'at–na'–dcat'–i*. In 'twelve' the base form is the Feminine: *двенадцать/dv'e–na'–dcat'–ø*.

(c) *восемь/vo's'(e)m'–ø'* 'eight' has a stem-final cluster – *vos'm'–*, the /e/ of the Nominative being an inserted vowel, e.g. Gen *восьми/vos'm'–i'*; the Instrumental is interesting in that, given the ending *–ju*, an inserted vowel is expected to break up the three-element cluster (which is the same as two elements plus zero), and indeed *восемью/vos'(e)m'–ju'* is acceptable, but so also is the newer *восьмью/vos'm'–ju'*.

(4) Others

(a) *сорок/so'rok–ø* 'forty' is a Class I Masculine noun, but with all its oblique forms reduced to a single form: *сорока/sorok–a'*; in origin this may not even be a Slavonic word, though most likely it is from an old local term of measurement (a sort of sack). The form occurs only in East Slavonic.

(b) A similar syncretism affects *девяносто/d'ev'ano'sto* 'ninety' and *сто/sto* 'hundred', both in principle Class I Neuter nouns, but with the single oblique forms *девяноста/d'ev'ano'st–a* and *ста/st–a* respectively. While these are certainly Slavonic roots, the form of *d'ev'anosto* is strange: its elements appear to be *d'ev'at'–*'nine', *no* 'but' and *sto* 'hundred', but the first is more

likely *d'ev'an–*, a hybrid form of the Indo-European root **neven–* and the initial syllable of *d'es'a–t'* 'ten' (IE **dek'–*), after which the original '–ten' (of 'ninth ten' or 'nine tens' – the form still used in West and South Slavonic) was replaced by the word for 'hundred'; a Finnish model has also been suggested, but is unlikely, since why it might be used just for this numeral remains unclear.

(c) The hundreds are compounds of units plus 'hundred', as in English, however, their form reflects a syntactic feature of the numerals which is taken up in chapter 4: 'two', 'three' and 'four' are followed by (govern) the *Genitive Singular* of a noun, 'five' to 'ten' the *Genitive Plural* (in origin this is because the latter were nouns, such that the phrase meant 'a five etc. of *x*', while 'two' was adjectival, followed by the dual number of nouns in the same case; subsequently 'three' and 'four' were grouped with 'two' and the remnant of the lost dual was associated with the Genitive Singular through closeness of form). This applies to the Nominative/Accusative forms only, while in the rest, like the tens, both parts decline independently. Note that *cmo/sto* in these forms has a full declension, not the syncretic one of the simple numeral. Thus we have the following (the Genitive Plural of *sto* here is *com/s(o)t–ø*, the /o/ being inserted before the zero ending):

Nominative/Accusative	*двести/dv'e'–sti* (old NDual) '200';
	триста/tr'i'–sta (GS) '300';
	четыреста/četi'r'e–sta (GS) '400';
	пятьсот/p'at'–s(o)'t (GP) '500', etc.
Genitive	*двухсот/dvux–s(o)'t–ø*; *пятисот/*
	p'at'–i–s(o)'t–ø (both G(P))
Locative	*двухстах/dvux–st–a'x, пятистах/*
	p'at'–i–st–a'x (both L(P)), etc.

(d) *тысяча/ti's'ač–a* 'thousand' is a regular Class II Feminine (soft) noun (with a variant Instrumental Singular of Class III: *тысячью/ti's'ač–ju*), *миллион/m'ill'io'n–ø* 'm'ill'ion' and *миллиард/m'ill'ia'rd–ø* '1,000 million' (Amer 'billion') are Class I Masculine nouns.

(e) 'Zero' is expressed by either *ноль/n'ol'–ø* – Class III Feminine, or *нуль/nul'–ø'*, Class I Masculine. The difference is largely in usage, *nol'* being more colloquial and general, *nul'* more formal (e.g. only *nol'* is used in scoring and saying telephone numbers, only *nul'* is used in the figurative sense 'worthless').

(f) An interesting extra is a numeral for 'one and a half': *полтора/pol–tor–a'* N/Am, in origin a compound meaning 'half of three'. It has a Nominative/Accusative Feminine form *полторы/pol–tor–i'*; its sole remaining form, for all cases and genders, is *полутора/pol–u'–tor–a* (*pol–u* being the oblique form of *pol* 'half–').

(5) Compound cardinal numerals. In formal standard style, all elements of compound cardinals are declined in parallel; the case of the noun in agreement when the numeral is in an oblique case (not Nominative/Accusative), e.g.: Instr: *с тремя тысячами тремястами тридцатью тремя рублями/s tr'–om'a' ti's'ač–am'i tr'–om'a–st–a'mi tr'i'–dcat'–ju tr'–om'a' rubl'–a'm'i* 'with three thousand three hundred and thirty three rubles'.

In colloquial style, however, some elements are left undeclined (in Nominative): one reduction declines only the first and last elements, not the internal ones, e.g. *с тремя тысячами триста тридцать тремя рублями/ s tr'–om'a' ti's'ač–am'i tr'i'–<u>sta</u> tr'i'–dcat'–ø tr'–om'a' rubl'–a'm'i*, while the most extreme reduction declines only the final element, e.g. *с три тысячи триста тридцать тремя рублями/ tr' <u>–i</u> ti's'ač<u>–i</u> tr'i'–<u>sta</u> tr'i'–dcat'–ø tr'– om'a rubl'–am'i*. This last is the pattern already fixed in the standard for the ordinals – see next section.

2.1.6.2 Ordinal numerals
(1) Form. All ordinals are adjectives, and all but 'third' have the normal declension. *Третий/tr'e–t'(i)j–ø* 'third' has the special declension, with the stem ending in *–t'j* and the Nominative ending in a single vowel, e.g.: NSf *третья/ tr'e'–t'j–a*, NSn *третье/tr'e'–t'j–e*, NP *третьи/tr'e'–t'j–i*, GSm *третьего/ tr'e'–t'j–ogo*.

Of the rest, those for 'first' and 'second' are, as in English, from different roots to the cardinal, respectively: *первый/p'e'rv–ij*, *второй/vtor–o'j*; 'fourth' and 'seventh' have variant forms, respectively: *четвёртый/četv'o'r–t–ij*, *седьмой/ s'ed'm–o'j*; 'eighth' is regularly formed from the cardinal stem: *восьмой/ vos'm–o'j*. For the remainder, the ordinal is normally formed with the suffix *–t*, matching the soft *–t'* ending of the cardinal, e.g. *пятый/p'a't–ij*. This pattern covers also *сотый/so't–ij* 'hundredth', from *сто/sto*.

The high numerals take rather the regular adjectival suffix *–n*, e.g. *тысячный/ ti's'ač–n–ij* 'thousandth', *миллионный/m'ill'io'n–n–ij* 'millionth'.

All but 'second', 'sixth' (*шестой/šest–o'j*), 'seventh' and 'eighth' are stressed on the stem-final syllable, regardless of the stress on the cardinal (cf. *d'e's'at'–ø* versus *d'es'a't–ij*).

(2) Compound ordinal numerals. In compound ordinals, only the final element is declined, and indeed only the final element has its ordinal shape, the rest being in the Nominative of the cardinal, e.g.: Loc: *в тысяча девятьсот девяносто девятом году/v ti's'ač–a d'ev'at's(o)'t–ø d'ev'ano'st–o d'ev'a't–om god–u'* 'in (the year) 1999'.

2.1.6.3 Collective numerals. The low numbers, from two to ten, have collective forms which signify groups of that number. They are, therefore, logically

Table 16 *Collective numerals*

Case	two, three	four–ten
Nominative	двое/dv–o'j–e	пятеро/p'a't'–or–o
Accusative	= Nominative (Inan) or Genitive (An)	
Genitive/Locative	двоих/dv–o(j)–i'x	пятерых/p'at'–or–y'x
Dative	двоим/dv–o(j)–i'm	пятерым/p'at'–or–i'm
Instrumental	двоими/dv–o(j)–i'm'i	пятерыми/p'at'–or–i'm'i

nouns meaning 'a group of *x* of'. In reality only those up to about seven are used in this sense, but there is another role which they all fulfil: to qualify *pluralia tantum*, especially important in the case of 'two', 'three' and 'four', which normally require the Genitive Singular, missing in such words.

'Two' and 'three' are formed with the suffix *–oj*, the rest with *–'or*, both typically attached to the cardinal stem (except for 'four', which uses the ordinal stem *četv–'or–* – with the same suffix), including stress position, and having the declension of neuter special adjectives; we give *dv–o'j–e* as the model for 'two' and 'three' (*troj–*), *p'a't'–or–o* 'five' as that for the rest in table 16.

Note that the fact that the second suffix is *–'or–* and not *–er–* is seen in derivation, where the suffix is stressed, e.g. *пятёрка/p'at'–o'r–k–a* 'a five (cards, marks, etc.)'.

The oblique cases are becoming more and more rare, replaced by the cardinal form in all but formal style (and common expressions, e.g. *комната на двоих/ko'mnat–a na dvo–i'x* 'a room for two'). Like the cardinals above 'five', when used in the Nominative/Accusative (Inan) they are followed by the Genitive Plural of the noun, but when used in other cases the noun agrees with the case of the numeral. Some examples of usage follow.

(1) Collective. In the standard occurs only with animate masculine nouns, and is especially common with Class II Masculine and Common, and also with substantivised adjectives, e.g.:

> Class I Masc: *трое мальчиков/tro'j–e ma'l'čik–ov* 'three boys (in a group)' (compare *три мальчика/tr'i ma'l'čik–a* 'three (individual) boys' – with GS);
>
> Class II Masc: *пятеро мужчин/юношей/p'a't'or–o mužči'n–ø/ ju'noš–ej* 'five men/youths';
>
> Class II Common: *двое сирот/dvo'j–e siro't–ø* 'two orphans'; *трое судей/tro'j–e sud'–e'j* 'three judges';
>
> Substantivised Adjective: *трое больных/tro'j–e bol'n–i'x* 'three patients'.

Usage with Class II Feminine is colloquial only, e.g. *двое женщин/dvo'j–e že'nščin–ø* 'two women', versus standard *две женщины/dv–e že'nščin–i*).

(2) Pluralia tantum. Obligatory for the numerals 'two', 'three' and 'four'; for 'five' and above, where both forms take Genitive Plural, the standard demands the collectives, while the cardinals are normal at the colloquial level, e.g. *двое часов/dvo'j–e čas–o'v* 'two clocks'; *двое ножниц/dvo'j–e no'žn'ic–ø* 'two pairs of scissors' (alongside the latter type is the more popular construction, parallel to English: *две пары ножниц/dv–e pa'r–i no'žn'ic–ø*); *пятеро/пять носилок/p'a't'or–o ~ p'at'–ø nos'i'l(o)k–ø* 'five stretchers'.

(3) The latter set is augmented by the two common suppletive plurals *дети/ d'et'–i* 'children' and *люди/l'ud'–i* 'people', where the standard requires the collectives (at least up to 'seven'), while the colloquial variant allows the cardinals, certainly with 'two', 'three' and 'four', with the singular stem (respectively *ребёнок/r'eb'o'n(o)k–ø* and *человек/čelov'e'k–ø* 'person'): *трое детей/tro'j–e d'et'–e'j* 'three children' (coll. *два ребёнка/dv-a r'eb'o'nk–a*); *трое людей/tro'j–e l'ud'–e'j* 'three people' (coll. *три человека/tr'–i čelov'e'k–a*).

Note that *čelov'e'k–ø* has a Genitive Plural form (also *čelov'e'k ø*) used in counting above 'five'; this would *ipso facto* be the counting form (of individuals) (e.g. *пять человек/p'at'–ø čelov'ek–ø*) as opposed to the group form (*пятеро людей/p'a't'or–o l'ud'–ej*).

In this last meaning, the collective may be used on its own to indicate a group of people, e.g. *Вошли трое./Voš–li' tro'j–e.* 'Three people came in.'

2.2   Verbal

2.2.1   Historical orientation

From the Old Russian verbal system (see also chapter 1, section 2.4.2), with a large number of tense forms – three simple and four compound (five including the conditional/subjunctive) – and a formally marked aspect system which to a large extent overlapped with the tenses, Modern Russian has ended up with a system in which aspect dominates over tense. The changes may be summarised as follows:

- the former simple past tenses (Imperfect, Aorist), which had effectively been Imperfective and Perfective Aspect respectively, disappeared, replaced by the former compound Past Tenses (Perfect, Pluperfect);
- the latter were simplified by the removal of the auxiliary;
- the compound Future Imperfective remained, but with a different auxiliary (and only in the Imperfective sense);
- the compound Future Perfect was replaced by the former present (of Perfective stems);
- and the Conditional/Subjunctive reduced its auxiliary to a particle (*bi*).

Moreover, the formation of the aspectual pairs continued, and still continues, to develop, shifting from the early opposition of 'basic' (= Imperfective) ~

'prefixed' (= Perfective) to, in addition, the pairing of prefixed verbs by suffixation (prefix + suffix = Imperfective); the language is still full of three-way sets in which the unaffixed 'basic' form is paralleled (often synonymously) by a form with both prefix and suffix.

2.2.2   Conjugation

The traditional classification of verbs is little different in Modern Russian as compared to Old Russian: while the latter usually identified five conjugations/ classes, three of these were in reality variants, and one was a small remnant class of high-frequency irregular verbs, so that the step to the typical modern grouping into two conjugations is a small one.

At the root of the Old Russian system was the 'theme' joining the present tense stem to the personal endings, giving the following five classes:

(1) {e} added to a consonant stem;
(2) {ne} added to a consonant stem (where the {n} was originally a suffix);
(3) {je} added to any stem, giving new stems in palatals, including {–j} itself (after an original vowel stem);
(4) {i} added to a consonant stem;
(5) {ø} added – the so-called 'athematic' ('theme-less') class, with endings joined directly to the stem.

With the rearrangement of the phonological system in terms of the relationship between hard, soft and palatal consonants, it was natural for types (1) and (3) to become perceived as simple variants; the {n} of type (2) was unstable, in that it was often absent in the past tense, and the number of verbs involved was in any case small, so the option of regarding it as an odd variant of type (1) was also simple; and the membership of type (5) was reduced from a maximum of five verbs to two by a combination of lexical and morphological processes, leaving it better treated as a set of two irregular verbs (and not a class). Paradoxically, the verb 'be' was to a large extent regularised by the effective full-scale loss of its present tense forms (see below).

Thus the normal classification of Modern Russian verbs is into two conjugations, distinguished by the theme vowels {$'$o} (= OR {e}, now phonemic /o/, orthographic *e/ë* – that is, always with at least softening, if not mutation, of the stem) (= Class I) and {i} (= Class II). (The matter of mutation belongs to the particulars of stem and theme.) We shall, however, use a version of the older classification, in order to make identification of the {je} group in both its variants clear, as follows (with model verbs in brackets):

• the {$'$o} group = Class I (e.g. *нести/n$'$es–t$'$i* 'carry'); mutation of velars only;
• the {Vjo} group = Class II (e.g. *читать/čit–a–t$'$* 'read'); included here are stems ending in /j/ (e.g. *пить/pi–t$'$* 'drink'), though formally they might be regarded as Class I;

- the {Cjo} group = Class III (e.g. *nucamь/pis–a–t'* 'write'); *j*-mutation of all;
- and the {'i} group = Class IV (e.g. *говоримь/govor–'i–t'* 'say, speak').
- The former {ne} group (now {n'o}) remains a variant of Class I, in which the /n/ behaves somewhat unpredictably (though some guidance is given in chapter 5, section 4.2.3).

2.2.3   Stems

A complication of the system, both old and new, has been the presence of two rather distinct stems for many verbs, in the extreme case lexically different, but in most cases only phonologically variant; in some cases the two are identical. At issue are the so-called 'present tense stem' (to which are added the theme vowel plus endings for the present, and suffixes for present participles) and the 'infinitive stem' (to which are added the past tense endings and suffixes for past participles); the former, as mentioned above, was the basis for classification, while the latter resulted from the shift from participial status (suffixed) within compound past tenses to past tense status (the suffixes being reinterpreted as endings). In addition, what were earlier suffixes with aspectual meaning have often become inseparable parts of the stem. At the Old Russian stage, therefore, the difference between the stems existed only in the Infinitive form, insofar as its ending was seen as an ending and not (i.e. no longer) as a suffix. Examples of the Modern Russian differences are given in table 17.

From this table one can see that the old theme classification – at least sepa-rating –*'o*– and –*jo*– – remains a useful option, allowing the present stem to be more simply stated (e.g. *pis*–, *čita*–; *sliš*–, *sluša*–); however, the real problem

Table 17 *Present ~ Infinitive/Past stems*

Lexical stem	Present	Theme	(3rd Person Singular)	Infinitive/Past	(Infinitive)
нес–/n'os– 'carry'	*n'os–*	–*'o*–	*n'os–'o'–t*	*n'os–*	*n'os–t'i'*
чит–/čit– 'read'	*čit-aj–*	–*'o*–	*čit–a'j–o–t*	*čit–a–*	*čit–a'–t'*
пис–/p'is– 'write'	*p'iš– (*sj)*	–*'o*–	*p'i'š–o–t*	*p'is–a–*	*p'is–a'–t'*
говор–/govor– 'speak'	*govor–*	–*'i*–	*govor–'i'–t*	*govor–'i–*	*govor–'i'–t'*
слуш–/sluš– 'listen'	*sluš-aj–*	–*'o*–	*slu'š–aj–o–t*	*sluš–a–*	*slu'š–a–t'*
слыш–/sliš– 'hear'	*sliš–*	–*'i*–	*sli'š–i–t*	*sliš–a–*	*sli'š–a–t'*
[б(e)р–/b(e)r– 'take' (Impf)	*b'er–*	–*'o*–	*b'er–'o'–t*	*br–a–*	*bra't'*
в(o)зя–/v(o)z'a– 'take' (Perf)	*voz'm–*	–*'o*–	*voz'm–'o'–t*	*vz'a–*	*vz'a–t'*
mреб–/tr'eb– 'demand'	*tr'eb–uj–*	–*'o*–	*tr'e'b–uj–e–t*	*tr'eb–ova–*	*tr'eb–ova–t'*
cox–/sox– 'dry'	*sox–n–*	–*'o*–	*so'x–n–'o–t*	*sox–nu–/sox–*	*so'x–nu–t'*
cma(н)–/sta(n)– 'stand'	*sta–n–*	–*'o*–	*sta'–n–'o–t*	*sta–*	*sta't'*

has been the two different stems, and the majority of describers, certainly all Russian ones, accept the necessity of stating the two as above. The desire to reduce the description to one stem for any given verb has tempted many, beginning with Jakobson (in 1948), and even pedagogical descriptions have attempted it (e.g. Townsend 1968/1975, 1974). It remains, in this writer's view, an unsuccessful exercise, as the complications seem to outweigh the advantages (though it has had many defenders, e.g. Channon 1975). The problem is that one must deal with a high degree of abstractness – often a feature of linguistic description, which is on the whole most unhelpful in pedagogy. The essence of the one-stem approach is the use of an underlying stem which is in effect an older stage of the language, stripping away, as it were, its history. Thus, the single stem of the above verbs would be stated as follows, with our comments:

> *n′os–*   not a problem, since both are still the same;
>
> *čitaj–*   a rule would then be required to delete /j/ before consonants, to give the Inf in *–at′*; but this fails in the Imperative, with the 2nd Person Singular ending *–ajt′e*;
>
> *slušaj–*   same as preceding;
>
> *pisa–*   a rule must state that stems ending in *–a* lose the vowel and take the *j*-mutation in the present, but only if the theme is *–′o–*;
>
> *govor′i–*   this incorporates the theme *–′i–*;
>
> *sliša–*   stems ending in palatal + /a/ lose the vowel and their theme is *–i–*;
>
> *voz′m–*   one can surely not hope to describe this verb other than historically (see below);
>
> *trebova–*   a simple rule converts *–ova* to *–uje–* in the present;
>
> *soxnu–*   a rule with exceptions allows *–nu–* to disappear in the past;
>
> *stan–*   a variant of the preceding rule allows *–n–* to disappear.

In other words, we do not achieve a great deal – in fact we achieve nothing – in descriptive terms: the result is at least as complicated as the one it attempts to replace.

From the pedagogical point of view, and ultimately from the linguistic one also, the fact is that there are two stems, both historically and still, and we must simply try to identify the relations between them and admit where they must simply be acknowledged and/or learnt. The dictionary form of verbs is the Infinitive, so in theory we could seek rules to allow us to derive as many of the other forms as possible from that form. In practical terms good dictionaries always offer the present stem in the entry, along with enough forms to indicate conjugation and stress pattern. Ultimately, therefore, the relationship between the two stems is best described on a diachronic basis, using effectively Proto-Slavonic forms as the underlying ones; and in some cases – basically where there are no suffixes – this does lead us to a single-stem description.

The example of the very different shapes in *vz'at'* may serve as an illustration: the root of this verb is actually *'a–* (from IE *ĭm–* via nasal *ę–*, hence the pre-vocalic softening); the initial *v(o)z–* was (and still is elsewhere) a prefix, sharing the regular *o* ~ *ø* alternation (*o* appearing when the stem begins with a consonant). The variants of the root are those of the former nasal vowels, namely Proto-Slavonic front vowel + nasal consonant. (F(V)+N) > OR *ę* > MR *'a /—C*, # (otherwise no change); in this particular case the base form F(V)+N was *ьм–/ьm–*, which remains before vowels, as in the present, where the next element is the theme *–'o–* or an ending in *–u–*; the pre-consonantal form is *я–/'a–*, as before the infinitive ending *–t'* or the past *–l–*. A modern version of this derivation would therefore state the stem as *ьm–* and add a rule corresponding to the historical process: *ьm* (and more generally F(V)+N) > *'a* before a suffix or ending beginning in C, e.g. *vz'ьm– > vz'a– /–C*; in turn the initial cluster would be stated as (the prefix) {v(o)z}, realised as *voz–* before (stem-initial) C, which in this case means the base form *–ьm*, as *vz–* before V; thus we get *v(o)z'ьm– > voz'–m–u/'o–*, etc. in the present and *v(o)z'ьm– > vz'–a–t'/l–*, etc. in the infinitive and past. Thus, morphophonological rules allow us to set up one stem. We shall pursue the question of such derivations under 'Morphophonology' below (section 2.2.10).

2.2.4   Aspect

The concept of aspect has proved a major problem in pedagogy, where the forms involved have pushed both teachers and students to perceive the whole topic as fraught with danger and often just too difficult. At the level of linguistics, the concept is not overly difficult, and it is clear that all languages have the concept, and even in English it is expressed formally in many instances (though the term 'aspect' is assumed to be a translation of the Russian term *vid* ('view', derived from the verb 'see'), cf. Lyons 1968: 313, no doubt because it was such a prominent feature of Russian (and all the Slavonic languages)). For example, the difference between *have done* and *have been doing* is precisely the same as the parallel forms in Russian, namely the first expresses and emphasises completion in the past resulting in a present state, while the second expresses and emphasises an on-going process, in this case begun in the past. Likewise the difference between *did* and *was doing* expresses a typical Russian aspectual distinction also – between a simple past statement not necessarily implying completion, and certainly not emphasising it, and a process statement. Or, finally, the difference between *did* and *used to do* distinguishes a simple past action from a habitual one. So it is not the overall concept which is a problem, but only differences of detail in usage and of formal expression.

The aspects distinguished are called Imperfective (Rus *n'e–sov'erš–e'nn–ij vid*) and Perfective (Rus *sov'erš–e'nn–ij vid*) (more literally 'incomplete(d)' and 'complete(d)' respectively). The Imperfective is the unmarked partner, used where the aspect is irrelevant (a simple statement of fact) or not being emphasised (the emphasis being elsewhere, most often on the subject) (both Eng *–ed*); in addition, forms called thus indicate process (Eng *–ing*) and repetition or habit (Eng *used to*). The Perfective form emphasises completion and, by implication, a resulting state (Eng *have –ed*); by contrast, the Imperfective may indicate the cancellation of a previous state (e.g. 'I (had) opened the window' – but I note that it is now closed). The Perfective also expresses the point of onset of an action (*start –ing*), where the resulting state is the action itself; and the singleness (*give a shout*, etc.) or instantaneousness ('suddenly') of an action.

In some cases the English form is not a guide to usage, mainly where the context is relevant, for example, a context of expectation or intention will lead to a Perfective, either positive (success, fulfilment) or negative (failure), where English need not express this differently; thus, Eng *Have you read* War and Peace? will be Perfective only if there is a context of prior discussion; as an unmotivated, general question, it is Imperfective, in spite of the English 'perfect' form. This feature allows the Imperfective to express the *attempt* itself, without expressing forms like *try to* (e.g. the English lexical set *tackle/work on* (a problem) versus *(re)solve* is a simple aspectual pair in Russian). Conversely, in the recounting of sequential action, any action clearly preceding (completed before) another will be Perfective, where English will use the simple *–ed* form (e.g. 'I had dinner and (then) watched television').

2.2.4.1 Verbs of motion. Verbs of motion (in the most general sense, including verbs of transporting, throwing, etc.) have, rather, a three-way aspectual division: the Perfective form of these means essentially 'set off' – that is, the 'start –ing' function noted above, while the Imperfective distinguishes what are most commonly called 'indeterminate' and 'determinate' motion; the former expresses multiple or uncertain direction and multiple occasions (e.g. 'go and return', 'wander', 'always/often go'), while the latter expresses only single direction ('be going') and usually single occasion – though the spatial aspect dominates over the temporal, e.g. 'I go to school by bus and walk home (come home on foot)' uses normally the 'determinate' form, in spite of the temporal frequency (though speakers do waver in this context). (Alternative names for these types, used especially in pedagogical texts, are, respectively, 'round-trip' versus 'one-way' and 'multidirectional' versus 'unidirectional'.)

2.2.4.2 Aspectual form. At the level of form, where English uses mainly auxiliary verbs to indicate both tense and aspect (e.g. *do, have, be*), Russian uses affixes for aspect and inflection for tense. The basic principle of aspect identification (in the Infinitive) is still as follows: an unaffixed (= basic) verb is

Imperfective, a basic (non-derived) stem plus prefix is Perfective, and a basic stem plus prefix *and* suffix is Imperfective. A distinction needs to be made between productive and unproductive affixes, since the majority of 'basic' verbs formally contain a suffix which we might call a 'morphological' suffix, which, while in some cases a synchronically operative one, is in most verbs a remnant of a former suffix, usually iterative (itself often referred to – though not by Russian grammarians – as an 'aspect'). This is clear from the structure of the Infinitive, since non-derived roots from Indo-European are monosyllabic, and the typical infinitive has a root plus a vowel (/a/, /e/, /i/). The modern function of such suffixes is treated in chapter 5.

Verbs occur in pairs where a logical aspectival distinction can be made. It cannot be made, for example, with verbs which imply one or other aspect, e.g. 'work' implies duration or process and cannot be perfective; at best we might add a limiter, e.g. 'work for a while', which Russian can express by a prefix, producing a perfective verb, but it is not the 'simple' partner to the imperfective verb; likewise Russian can also express 'start working' by a prefix, but this is not a simple partner either (this form has also been called 'inceptive aspect' – though not by Russian grammarians). The process of suffixation of prefixed verbs is very active, and often produces verbs which are synonymous with the unaffixed form; many of these have now disappeared from the language, but many survive, making a three-way set quite common. The normal aspectual pair of verbs will thus be: (1) basic (Imperfective) ∼ prefixed (Perfective) (table 18, columns 1 ∼ 3); or (2) prefixed + suffixed (Imperfective) ∼ prefixed (Perf) (table 18, columns 4 ∼ 3), with the three-way set also possible. Many pairs are on the surface opposed by suffix only, in which case: (1) the suffix involved will be a 'morphological' one only; and (2) there will usually be a fused prefix, identifiable at least as an apparently polysyllabic root; only a few exceptional cases of this sort have a genuine basic root. Finally, the small group of verbs of motion retain a more active remnant of the iterative suffix (especially –a–) in the non-prefixed forms known as 'indeterminate' (indicating multiple direction), opposed to the completely unaffixed – or differently suffixed (especially –i–) 'determinate' form (indicating a single direction) (see also chapter 5, section 4.2.3).

In a very small number of cases, one form may be bi-aspectual, e.g. *жениться* /žon–'i–t'–s'a 'get married', *организовать*/organ–'izova–t' 'organise'; however, this possibility is being lost – and mostly is lost already from the colloquial level – as the formation of a partner is pursued, normally by prefixation, e.g. *пожениться*/po–žon–'i–t'–s'a and *сорганизовать*/s–organ–'izova–t' as new perfectives; less popular is the formation of a new imperfective by suffixation, e.g. *организовывать*/organ–'izo'v–iva–t' (see also chapter 7, section 3.5).

In principle any prefix added to a root produces a perfective verb, the original semantics involved being that of 'limitation' of the action to the semantic sphere of the prefix (e.g. up, down, in, out, etc.). Originally the prefix always added

Table 18 *Aspectual sets*

1 **Basic unaffixed** **(Imperfective)**	2 **Basic** **+ morphological suffix** **(Imperfective)**	3 **Basic + prefix** **(Perfective)**	4 **Basic + prefix** **+ suffix** **(Imperfective)**
нести/n'os–t'i 'carry' (determinate) Class I	*носить/nos–'i'–t'* (indeterminate) Class IV	*понести/po–n'os–t'i* 'take/start carrying' Class I	
трясти/tr'as–t'i 'shake' Class I		*потрясти/po–tr'as–t'i* Class I	*потрясать/po–tr'as–a'–t'* Class II
	писать/p'is–a'–t' 'write' Class III	*написать/na–p'is–a'–t'* Class III	
		вписать/v–p'is–a'–t' 'inscribe' Class III	*вписывать/v–p'i's–iva–t'* Class II
	просить/pros–'i'–t' 'ask' Class IV	*попросить/po–pros–'i'–t'* Class IV	

Sets with purely suffixal opposition:

(1) No prefix (rare):
    кончать/konč–a'–t'   *кончить/ko'nč–i–t'*
    'finish' Impf Class II   Pf Class IV

(2) Fused prefix (common):
    ответить/ot–v'e't–'i–t'   *отвечать/ot–v'eč–a'–t'*
    'answer' Pf Class IV   Impf Class II (suffix = –ja)

its own semantic load to the verb, but as aspect developed, there occurred a semantic fusion between roots and prefixes wherever this was possible (e.g. the limitation of 'write' by 'on' was quickly perceived as 'fusable', meaning that the prefix's semantic load was 'lost' with this root, and it became 'empty', its sole function being to indicate perfective aspect. With other prefixes (on the same root) this did not happen, so that prefixes meaning, say, 'again/re–' or 'over/super–' do produce perfective verbs, but ones which retain the semantic load of the prefix, and so do not form a 'simple' pair with the unaffixed form. It is significant that by far the most common prefix to be 'empty' is по–/po–, whose basic meaning is 'limited to (a space, time, etc.)' (see chapter 5, section 4.1.2).

Table 18 gives examples of all the types of sets.

2.2.5   Infinitive

The Infinitive is an invariable (uninflected) form, whose ending is normally –t' (orth. –ть), with the variant –t'i when stressed (orth. –ти), and a few cases of –č (orth. –чь). In origin –t'i was the Old Russian form, the vowel later being lost when unstressed. The ending may be added directly to the non-derivative stem

Table 19 *Infinitive form and class*

Stem + Suffix + Ending	Class	Examples
–HC–(ø)–t'i'	I	*нести/n'os–t'i'* 'carry'
–HC–(ø)–t'	I	*лезть/l'ez–t'* 'climb'
–V–(ø)–č' (<K–(ø)–t')	I	*мочь/moč'* (< *mog–t'*) 'be able'
–V–(ø)–t'	any, usually irregular	*дать/da–t'* 'give' (V); *пить/p'i–t'* 'drink' (III)
–HC–a–t'	II	*читать/čit–a'–t'* 'read'
	III	*писать/p'is–a'–t'* 'write'
–PC–a–t'	II	*слушать/slu'š–a–t'* 'listen'
	IV	*слышать/sli'š–a–t'* 'hear'
–SC–e–t'	II	*иметь/im–'e'–t'* 'have'
	IV	*видеть/vi'd–'e–t'* 'see'
–SC–i–t'	IV	*просить/pros–'i'–t'* 'ask'

HC = hard consonant, SC = soft consonant, PC = palatal (mutated from non–palatal stem or present in stem), K = velar consonant; V = vowel.

(the root), though this is common only with Class I verbs with end stress (e.g. *нести/n'os–t'i*); verbs in –*č* reflect an underlying stem in /k/ or /g/, since /kt/ and /gt/ always gave /č/ in East Slavonic; where the stem ends in a root vowel verbs are typically irregular; most often there is a suffix, either morphological or derivational, either a single vowel or ending in a vowel. For the purposes of perceiving the correlation between the ending and the class, we might say that the first type (stem + ending) has a zero suffix, and then consider the combined 'suffix + ending' as 'ending'. The correlation is fairly good, but there are a few major problems, as seen in table 19 (using 'ending' in this expanded sense).

Thus the class of forms in –*a*– and –*e*–, or –*Vø*–, cannot be predicted from the infinitive form. Other anomalous (and unpredictable) shapes include 'hidden' suffixes, where the root is (now) non-syllabic, e.g. *брать/br–a–t'* 'take' (root *b(e)r–*, Class I), *спать/sp–a–t'* 'sleep' (root *s(o)p–*, Class IV), and the expanded roots in *oRo*, *eRe* (from PS *CoRC*, etc. see chapter 1, section 2.2.1.6), e.g. *колоть/kolo'–(ø)–t'* 'stab' (root *kol–*, Class I), *умереть/u–m'er'e'–(ø)–t'* 'die' Pf (root *m(e)r–*, Class I).

2.2.6   Tense

The importance of aspect means that tense is marked only in elementary fashion: present, past and future, with no formal indication of temporal relationships like pluperfect or future perfect, which means, for example, that there is no formal distinction between 'have done' and 'had done': each will be a perfective past form and the temporal relationship is inferred from the context (e.g. 'have/had done . . . before you arrived' implies pluperfect).

2.2.6.1 Present and Perfective Future. Only imperfective verbs have a present tense, while the former present-tense form of perfective verbs has come to signify the Perfective Future (= intention to complete). The same set of inflectional endings, but on different aspectual stems, mark three persons and two numbers. If we count the theme vowel as part of the stem, five of the six endings are identical across all regular classes, the odd one being 3rd Person Plural. The more traditional view regards the theme as part of the ending, so that only one ending is identical, namely 1st Person Singular. The common personal endings in summary are:

> 1ps: –*u*   2ps: –*š*   3ps: –*t*
> 1pp: –*m*   2pp: –*t'e*   3pp: –*ut*/–*'at*

The forms of the Present/Future are as given in table 20, in which for each combination of person and number line 1 gives the formula, line 2 the transcription and line 3 the orthography; for meanings see above; stems indicate also Infinitive suffix).

The most important alternation of this set of forms is the *j*–mutation (see above, table 15, section 2.1.5.6), which occurs in the 1st Person Singular only of Class IV, and in all forms of Class III, as opposed to the Infinitive; in each

Table 20 *Present/Future tense*

Stems	*n'os–ø–*; *mog–ø–*	*čit–a–*	*p'is–a–*	*pros–'i–*; *stoj–a–*
Person/Number	Class I	Class II	Class III	Class IV
1st Person Singular	HC–*u*, K–*u*	V–*ju*	PC–*u*	PC–*u*
	n'os–u', *mog–u'*	*čit–a'–ju*	*p'iš–u'*	*proš–u'*
	несу, могу	*читаю*	*пишу*	*прошу*
2nd Person Singular[a]	SC–*o–š*, PC–*o–š*	V–*jo–š*	PC–*o–š*	SC–*i–š*
	n'os'–o'–š, *mo'ž–o–š*	*čit–a'–jo–š*	*p'i'š–o–š*	*pro's–'i–š*
	несёшь, можешь	*читаешь*	*пишешь*	*просишь*
3rd Person Singular[b]	SC–*o–t*, PC–*o–t*	V–*jo–t*	PC–*o–t*	SC–*i–t*
	n'os'–o'–t, *mo'ž–o–t*	*čit–a'–jo–t*	*p'i'š–o–t*	*pro's–'i–t*
	несёт, может	*читает*	*пишет*	*просит*
1st Person Plural	SC–*o–m*, PC–*o–m*	V–*jo–m*	PC–*o–m*	SC–*i–m*
	n'os'–o'–m, *mo'ž–o–m*	*čit–a'–jo–m*	*p'i'š–o–m*	*pro's–'i–m*
	несём, можем	*читаем*	*пишем*	*просим*
2nd Person Plural	SC–*o–te*, PC–*o–te*	V–*jo–te*	PC–*o–te*	SC–*i–te*
	n'os'–o'–te, *mo'ž–o–te*	*čit–a'–jo–te*	*p'i'š–o–te*	*pro's–'i–te*
	несёте, можете	*читаете*	*пишете*	*просите*
3rd Person Plural	HC–*ut*, K–*u–t*	V–*jut*	PC–*ut*	SC–*at*
	n'os–u't, *mo'g–ut*	*čit–a'–jut*	*p'i'š–ut*	*pro's–'at*
	несут, могут	*читают*	*пишут*	*просят*

[a] The final soft sign has a purely visual effect, not a phonological one.
[b] The theme {o} is realised as /o/, thus = [ɔ] when stressed, orth. *ё*.

Table 21 *Present irregular*

Inf/Pres Stem	da–ø–/da(d)–	jed–ø–	xot–'e–	bi–ø–/jes–ø–
1ps	дам/da(d)–m	ем/je(d)–m	хочу/хоč–u'	—
2ps	дашь/da(d)–ø–š	ешь/je(d)–ø–š	хочешь/хо'č–o–š	—
3ps	дacт/dad–ø–t	ecт/jed–ø–t	хочет/хо'č–o–t	ecтb/jes–ø–t'
1pp	дадим/dad–'i'–m	едим/jed–'i'–m	хотим/xot–'i'–m	—
2pp	дадите/dad–'i'–te	едите/jed–'i'–te	хотите/xot–'i'–te	—
3pp	дадут/dad–u't	едят/jed'–a't	хотят/xot–'a't	—

Table 22 *Past tense*

Masculine Singular	Feminine Singular	Neuter Singular	Plural
–л/–l–ø	–лa/–l–a	–лo/–l–o	–лu/–l–'i

class, if the infinitive stem ends in a palatal, there is no alternation. Class I verbs with a velar stem only show mutation before the theme {'o}.

There are really only three irregular verbs, plus one defective: *дamь/da–ø–t'* 'give' and *ecmь/jed–ø–t'* 'eat' (/d/ > /s/ /–/t/) have a mix of irregular stems and endings (and even themes), while *хоmеmь/xot–'e–t'* 'want' has a Class III Singular and a Class IV Plural, and *быmь/bi–ø–t'* 'be' has only a 3rd Person Singular form. These are shown in table 21.

Note that the similar behaviour of the stem-final /d/ in the first two verbs (lost or dissimilated) disguises the difference in their roots – the /d/ being 'genuine' only in *jed–*, in *da(d)–* being an inserted /d/, probably by reduplication (also found in other Indo-European languages, e.g. Lat *do* ∼ *dedi*, Gr *didomi*).

Since all these forms may be either present or future, depending on the aspect of the stem, and since there are no formal future endings, it is not uncommon for textbooks to refer to them as 'non-past'.

2.2.6.2 Past. Formally the past tense has arisen from an Old Russian past participle (adjectival) which was used in the formation of various compound tenses, both past and future, and also the conditional/subjunctive mood. The auxiliary verbs which used to accompany this participle have been lost in all tense forms; the two compound past tenses (Perfect and Pluperfect) thus formally merged and the participial form became seen as the sole marker of past tense, allowing the simple past tenses (Aorist and Imperfect) to disappear. The end result is a very simple formal past tense, expressing only gender and number, since the participle was a short-form adjective.

The ending (the former suffix) is *–l–* plus one of four gender/number markers as in the special adjectives, as shown in table 22. These are added to the infinitive stem (all but the *–t'* ending); if this ends in a vowel the attachment is uncomplicated, but if it ends in a consonant there are adjustments to be made: mostly the problem lies with the Masculine Singular form, where we have potentially a final cluster ending in /l/, which is morphologically unacceptable; the normal solution is to drop the /l/, leaving the bare stem, e.g.:

Infinitive	Masculine	Feminine	Neuter	Plural
нести/*n'os–ti'*	нёс/*n'os–(l)–ɸ'*	несла/	несло/	несли/
		n'os–l–a'	*n'os–l–o'*	*n'os–l–'i'*
мочь/*mog–t'*	мог/*mog–(l)–ɸ'*	могла/	могло/	могли/
		mog–l–a'	*mog–l–o'*	*mog–l–'i'*

Included here are verbs which lose the suffix *–nu–* in the past, e.g.

Infinitive	Masculine	Feminine	Neuter	Plural
сохнуть/*so'x–nu–t'*	сох/*so'x–(l)–ɸ*	сохла/	сохло/	сохли/
'dry' (Intr)		*so'x–l–a*	*so'x–l–o*	*so'x–l–'i*

Reflecting a much older stage are stems ending in /t/ and /d/, where this consonant was lost (phonologically) before /l/ in all East and South Slavonic, e.g.:

Infinitive	Masculine	Feminine	Neuter	Plural
вести/*v'od–t'i'*	вёл/*v'o(d)–l–ɸ'*	вела/	вело/	вели/*v'o(d)*
'lead'		*v'o(d)–l–a'*	*v'o(d)–l–o'*	*–l–'i'*
есть/*je'd–t'*	ел/*je'(d)–l–ɸ*	ела/	ело/	ели/*je'(d)*
'eat'		*je'(d)–l–a*	*je'(d)–l–o*	*–l–'i*
плести/*pl'ot–t'i'*	плёл/	плела/	плело/	плели/*pl'o(t)*
'plait'	*pl'o(t)–l–ɸ'*	*pl'o(t)–l–a'*	*pl'o(t)–l–o'*	*–l–'i'*

Note that the Infinitive, too, shows an old feature: the dissimilation of /tt/ and /dt/ to /st/.

2.2.6.3 Imperfective Future. This is the one remaining compound form, based on the Imperfective Infinitive plus a (normally) pre-positive auxiliary verb; the latter is itself the one and only inflected Imperfective Future, that of the verb 'be'; its stem is *буд–/bud–* and it has the forms of Class I (1ps буду/*bu'd–u*, 3ps будет/*bu'd–'o–t*, 3pp будут/*bu'd–ut* 'will be'), e.g. буду говорить/*bu'd–u govor–'i'–t'* 'I will say' Impf.

2.2.7   Mood
Russian has only two formal moods (other than Indicative): Imperative and Conditional/Subjunctive.

2.2.7.1 Imperative. Old Russian had inflected Imperative forms for 2nd Person Singular, 2nd Person Plural and 1st Person Plural. Since then the 1st Person

Plural form has been lost, partly as a result of the phonological fusion of /ě/ (*jat'*) and /e/, but probably mainly because of the loss of a need for such a form. While the plural *endings* in Old Russian were the same as for the Indicative Present – namely 1pp –*м(ъ)/–m(ъ)*, 2pp –*me/–t'e*, and the same stem was the basis for both, the Imperative *theme* vowel for most classes was /ě/ (Cyrillic ѣ) against the indicative /e/, e.g. *несѣмъ/n'es'ě'mъ* 'let us carry' versus *несемъ/n'es'e'mъ* 'we carry'. In verbs of this class and stress pattern the latter became first *n'os'o'm*, while the former became *n'os'e'm*, so that no phonological fusion occurred; however, with stem-stressed verbs (the majority), the unstressed theme did become phonetically identical (unstressed /o/–/e/); subsequently, the theme morpheme was regularised as {'o}. The same should have happened to the 2nd Person Plural, but did not, the ending of the 2nd Person Singular (always –'*i*) being extended to this form (–'*i–te*), thus keeping the two sets separate. This supports the notion that the loss of the separate 1st Person Plural form was functionally and not phonetically based. For this, Modern Russian simply uses the Indicative form, syntactically distinguished by the omission of the 1pp pronoun, usually – though not obligatorily – present in the Indicative (e.g. *мы пойдём/my pojd–'o'm* 'we shall go' versus *пойдём/pojd–'o'm* 'let's go').

A second phonetic change affecting these forms was the loss of (syllable-) final unstressed /i/ within the verbal system (we have already noted this loss in the Infinitive ({t '*i*} > {t'}) and in the 2nd Person Singular Present ({ši} > {š}). In the Imperative such an /i/ occurred in the 2nd Person Singular (final) and 2nd Person Plural (pre-consonantal desinence) endings: –*u/–'i*, –*ume/–'it'e*, and its loss produced the main variants in Modern Russian's forms, since such a post-vocalic /i/ was reduced to /j/ (a post-consonantal one left its trace in softness only). The exception are stems ending in a cluster, where zero was not allowed, and these retained unstressed /i/. Formally, we may regard the {'i} as a theme, thus the 2nd Person Singular always has a zero ending, and in the case of unstressed endings the theme is either {j} or {'} (that is, softening of the final consonant) (the alternative, traditional view, must call the *ending* {'}). Thus we have the Modern Russian forms shown in table 23, with themes and endings attached to the Present stem.

In summary, verbs with end-stress in the 1st Person Singular Present take the stressed theme –*u–me/–'i'–t'e*, others have stressed stem plus either *C+'+ ø* or *V + j (V + i'* (Class II) does not occur); stressed stems ending in a cluster retain /i/ (as in the final example – *po'mn–'i*).

2.2.7.2 Conditional, Subjunctive, Hypothetical. Note, first, that open (non-hypothetical, present or future) conditions use the Indicative, e.g. 'if you come tonight' has the Future, 'if you think so' the Present (see chapter 4, section 4.2.5.6).

Table 23 *Imperative*

Person/ Number	Stress	Class 1	Class II	Class III	Class IV
2nd Person Singular	end	–u/–ʹi̯–ø иди/id–ʹi̯–ø 'go'	—	–u/–ʹi̯–ø пиши/piš–i̯–ø 'write'	–u/–ʹi̯–ø попроси/popros–ʹi̯–ø 'ask'
	stem	–ь/(C)–ʹ–ø будь/bud–ʹ–ø 'be'	–ŭ/(V)–j читай/čita̍–j–ø требуй/tr'e̍b–uj–ø 'demand'	–ь/–ʹ–ø плачь/pla̍k–ʹ–ø 'cry' пей/p'(e)̍j–ø 'drink'	–ь/–ʹ–ø оставь/osta̍v–ʹ–ø 'leave'
	(stem in –CC)	–u/–ʹi– погибни/pogi̍bn–i 'perish'			–u/–ʹi–ø помни/po̍mn–ʹi–ø 'remember'

2nd Person Plural Substitute *–me/–t'e* for zero in all above forms, with no other change.

Table 24 *Conditional/Subjunctive*

Masculine Singular –л бы/–l–ø bi	Feminine Singular –ла бы/–l–a bi	Neuter Singular –ло бы/–l–o bi	Plural –ли бы/–l–ʹi bi

For the hypothetical condition and for subjunctive mood, Russian has only one form to express all, in origin the Old Russian Conditional, which was formed with the same participle used for compound past tenses (with suffix –l–) (that is, the modern Past Tense) accompanied first by a special form of the verb 'be' which was the only remnant of a separate Conditional, then by the Aorist form of that verb. After the demise of the Aorist and the loss of the auxiliary verbs in the past tenses, leaving just the –l– form, the Conditional retained a single form of the original auxiliary, namely the 3ps бы/bi, as an invariable particle. This particle is separable and functions as an enclitic form, normally attached to the verb, but tending also to follow the first word of a clause, typically a conjunction, although also often a personal pronoun. The most common conjunction in this context, the conditional если/je'sl'i 'if', is virtually inseparable from it, and colloquially the standard если бы/je'sl'i–bi is normally reduced to если/б/je'sl'i–b. Thus, the formal possibilities are as for the Past, as can be seen in table 24. No tense distinction is made within this mood – e.g. it is not possible to distinguish formally 'I would do' from 'I would have done'. In hypothetical conditions one cannot distinguish between 'if I had done' and 'if I were to do'.

The most common *subjunctive* usage is the expression of a desire introduced by phrases like 'I would (not) like you to . . .': the above form is used for this too, though in slightly disguised form, in that the conjunction introducing the subordinate clause has the inseparable form *чтобы/čto–bi*, in origin simply *что/čto* 'that' plus the particle *бы/bi*, attached as with *jesl'i*, but no longer separable. This conjunction, too, is colloquially reduced to *чтоб/čto–b*. The reflection of the particle's former status is seen in the apparent past tense verb form. Thus, for example, 'I want you to speak' is *Я хочу, чтобы вы говорили/Ja xoču, čtobi vi govor'il'i*; it is not possible to use an Infinitive in such cases, as English does, since the Infinitive can refer only to the subject, but a sign of *čtobi*'s acquired independence is that it may be followed by an Infinitive when the subject of both clauses is the same, in the meaning 'in order to', and indeed is virtually compulsory in this function (e.g. 'I rang to remind you . . .' requires *čtobi* in the standard, but may lose it in the colloquial).

Any other sort of hypothetical subjunctive will also be expressed with *bi*, for example, the speaker not vouching for the truth of a claim, as in 'I didn't see him falling', which in Russian will have the Indicative if the speaker is certain that the falling took place, the Subjunctive with *bi* if he is not.

For further examples of all types, see chapter 4 (esp. sections 4.2.2, 4.2.5.6).

2.2.8   Voice
Other than active voice, expressed by transitive or intransitive verbs as in English, Russian has formal ways of expressing the Reflexive (or Middle-Reflexive) and the Passive.

2.2.8.1 Reflexive. The reflexive proper, that is, the subject acting upon itself, is formally expressed as in other European languages, by the addition of the Reflexive personal pronoun, which in Russian may be a full, separable and declinable form, corresponding to English's use of 'myself' etc., namely *себя/s'eb'a* (see above, section 2.1.4.1), e.g. *спрашивать себя/sprašivat' s'eb'a* 'to ask oneself', or it may be an enclitic, non-separable and invariable form (in origin the Old Russian enclitic Accusative), namely *–ся/–s'a*, now also written attached to the verb form, added *after* the ending (hence sometimes called a 'post-fix', rather than a suffix; Russian grammars, however, do refer to it as a 'suffix'), e.g. *мыться/mi–t'–s'a* 'to wash (oneself)', *одеваться/od'eva–t'–s'a* 'to get dressed'.

This suffix presents another example of a lost unstressed vowel: since the important element of this particle is the consonant, the vowel survives only when without it one would have a final cluster, thus the working rule for its form is that it is *–ся/s'a* only after stem-final (or rather ending-final) consonants, as in the infinitives above; if the stem (ending) ends in a vowel, the form is simply a soft /s'/: *–сь/–s'*, e.g. 1st Person Singular of the same verbs: *моюсь/mo'–ju–s'*, *одеваюсь/od'eva'–ju–s'*.

As a form, this structure has been extended to serve three other major functions – intransitive, passive and reciprocal, and also a minor one – behavioural inclination.

The *intransitive*, or *middle*, function is frequently handled in this way in European languages (e.g. Fr *la porte s'ouvre* 'the door opens'), but the Slavonic languages have made much greater use of this possibility. Thus, Russian distinguishes transitive 'begin' ('(he) begin(s) the lesson') from intransitive 'begin' ('the lesson begins') by the addition of this suffix, respectively *(он) начинает урок/(on) načina'j–ot urok–ф* versus *урок начинается/urok–ф načina'j–ot–s'a*. Included here may be verbs expressing emotional states, e.g. *сердиться/s'erd'it'–s'a* 'be/get angry'.

The *passive* function is also thus expressed in other European languages, though probably only when they are really inanimate and impersonal reflexives (e.g. Fr *ce mot s'écrit . . .* 'this word is written . . .'), rarely when there is a stated agent ('by someone'). Russian is able to do this, stating the agent in the Instrumental, the norm for any passive construction, e.g. *Эта книга читается всеми студентами/Et-a kn'i'g–a čit'aj–ot–s'a vs'-e'm'i stud'e'nt–am'i* 'This book is being read by all the students'.

The *reciprocal* function is also a general European possibility (e.g. Fr *ils s'aiment* 'they love each other') and is widely employed in Russian, e.g. *скоро увидимся/sko'ro uv'i'd–'im–s'a* 'we'll (let's) see each other soon' (cf. Fr *on se voit bientôt*). Another common verb is *встречаться/vstr'eča't'–s'a* 'to meet (each other/one another)'.

The 'behavioural inclination' function is an odd and uncommon one, used in expressions like 'this dog bites' – *эта собака кусается/e't–a soba'k–a kusa'j–ot–s'a*. The inanimate equivalent expresses an object's capacity to be acted upon, e.g. *стаканы бьются/stakan–i b'j–ut–s'a* 'glasses (will) break'.

2.2.8.2 Passive. While one way of expressing the passive has just been described, there is also a construction parallel to English (and others), based on the verb 'be' and a past passive participle. We will take up the form of this participle in the following section.

Russian has other, syntactic, ways of expressing the passive, with or without an agent. The impersonal type ('it is said that . . .') is expressed by the 3rd Person Plural of the Present, e.g. *говорят/govor–'at* 'it is said', 'people/they say'; the personal type is expressed by word order, made possible by the role of inflection in identifying parts of the sentence (see chapter 4, sections 3.2.2.4, 3.4).

2.2.9 Participles
Russian has four adjectival participles and two adverbial ones. The former fulfil mainly the Relative Clause function, whether formally post-positive like

English ('the man *sitting* in the corner') or attributive (*'the *sitting* in the corner man'). (For usage see chapter 4, section 4.2.4.) To a greater extent than in English, such participles belong to formal style, a clause introduced by a relative pronoun being the colloquial norm ('the man *who is sitting* . . . '). The adverbial participles refer mainly to temporal or concessive circumstances (*'while –ing'*, *'after having –ed'*) and may refer only to the subject of the main clause.

2.2.9.1 Adjectival participles. The four adjectival participles are full adjectives, distinguishing case, gender and number; two are active and two passive; two present and two past. Aspect is normally Imperfective for Present, Perfective for Past; however, Past Imperfective is also possible. The suffixes for the Present participles are added to the Present stem, with its 3rd Person Plural theme (Class I–III –*(j)u–*, Class IV –*'a–*) for the active, with the 'normal theme' (Class I–III –*' (j)o–*, Class IV –*'i–*) for the passive; those for the past are added to the Infinitive stem, as in table 25. Only the last of these four participles may also have a short form in the predicate, and indeed it is then obligatory. None of the others may occur in the predicate. (See further chapter 4, section 3.2.2.8. For stress patterns in these forms, see below, section 2.2.11.4.)

2.2.9.2 Adverbial participles. Being adverbs, adverbial participles are invariable forms (hence their obligatory agreement with the subject). The present ('while –ing') is imperfective only, the past ('having –ed') perfective. Both are active voice. Again, the first is based on the present stem, the second on the infinitive. The suffixes are shown in table 26.

Some prefixed verbs of motion display an unusual form – aspect/tense relationship: while the Present is formed as expected, from the Present Imperfective stem + –*'a*, e.g. *входя/v–xod–'a'* '(while) entering', the Past uses the same ending, but on the *Perfective* stem, e.g. *войдя/v(o)–jd–'a'* 'having entered'. Strictly, only a few such common (intransitive motion) verbs do this, but colloquially it is more common, for example with 'transitive motion' verbs, e.g. standard, or formal *принёсши/pri–n'o's–ši* 'having brought' ~ coll. *принеся/pri–n'os–'a'*. We may say, therefore, that the aspect of the stem determines the tense of this participle, regardless of its form (Perfective = Past, Imperfective = Present).

2.2.10 Morphophonology in the verb
In summary, the main alternations occurring in the verb system are as follows:

(1) j-mutation (see section 2.1.5.6, table 15) occurs in:
- all the Present of Class III verbs (Inf *писать/p'is–a'–t'* 'write': 1ps *пишу/p'iš–u'*, 3ps *пишет/p'i'š–o–t*, 3pp *пишут/p'i'š–ut*);
- 1st Person Singular Present only of Class IV verbs (Inf *просить/pros–'i'–t'* 'ask': 1ps *прошу/proš–u'*, 3ps *просит/pro's–'i–t*, 3pp *просят/pro's–'at*);

Table 25 *Adjectival participles*

Tense	Voice	Stem	Suffix
(1) Present[a]	Active	Pres + 3pp theme	*–щ–/–šč–*
Examples		Class II: *знающий/zn–a'j–u–šč–ij* 'know–ing'	
		Class IV: *видящий/vi'd–'a–šč–ij* 'see–ing'	
(2) Present	Passive	Pres + 1pp theme	*–м–/–m–*
Examples		Class II: *читаемый/čit–a'j–e–m–ij* 'being read'	
		Class IV: *любимый/l'ub–i'–m–ij* 'being loved'	
(3) Past[b]	Active	Infinitive	*–(в)ш–/–(v)š–*

*–vš–*is added to vowel stems, *–š–*to consonant stems.

Examples		Class II: *прочитавший/pro–čit a' – vš ij* 'having read'	
		Class I: *принёсший/pr'in'o's–š–ij* 'having brought'	
		Class IV: *увидевший/uv'i'd'–e–vš–ij* 'having seen'	
(4) Past	Passive	Inf	*–(e)нн–/–('o)nn–,*
			–m–/–t–

The three variants are added as follows:

         –nn– to a suffix vowel stem:

            Class II: *прочитанный/pro–či't–a–nn–ij* '(having been) read'

         –'onn– to:

            (1) a consonant stem (stressed = /o/):

            Class I: *принесённый/pri–n'os'–'o'nn–ij* '(having been) brought'

            (2) to Class IV, *–'o–* replacing Inf *–i–* and with *j–*mutation of stem consonant:

            Class IV: *поставленный/po–sta'vl'–onn–ij* '(having been) placed'

         –t– to:

            (1) root vowel stem (no suffix):

            Class I: *забытый/za–bi'–t–ij* 'forgotten' (from root *by–* 'be')

            (2) to suffix *–nu–*:

            Class I: *сдвинутый/s–dvi'–nu–t–ij* 'moved aside'

---

[a] Reflexive verbs with these forms exceptionally do *not* reduce the particle *–s'a* to *–s'* after the final vowel, e.g. *учашаяся/uč–a'–šč–aja–s'a* 'studying' NSf.

[b] Same comment applies as in *a*, e.g. *встретившиеся/vstr'e't–'i–vš–ije–s'a* 'having met' NP.

- the Past Participle Passive (PPP) of Class IV verbs (Inf *повесить/po–v'e's–'i–t'* 'hang': PPP stem *повешен–/po–v'e'š–on–; поставить/po–sta'v–'i–t'* 'place': *поставлен–/po–sta'vl'–on–*).

(2) Velar mutation (same results as *j*–mutation) occurs also before a theme in {*'o*}. The most common context is therefore the Present theme vowel in Class I, e.g.:

Stem	3rd Person Singular
мог–/mog– 'be able'	*может/mo'ž–o–t*
пек–/p'ok– 'bake'	*печёт/p'oč–o'–t*

Table 26 *Adverbial participles*

Tense	Stem	Suffix
(1) Pres	Pres	*–я/–'a*
Examples	Class I:	*неся/n'os–'a'* 'while carrying'
	Class II:	*читая/čit–a'j–a* 'while reading'
	Class IV:	*любя/l'ub–'a'*
(2) Past	Inf	*–в/–v, –ши/–ši*
	(a) in V:	*–в/–v*
Examples	Class II	*прочитав/pro–čit–a'–v* '(after) having read'
	Class IV	*увидев/u-vi'd–'e–v* 'having seen'
	(b) in C:	*–ши/–ši*[a]
Example	Class I	*принёсши/pr'i–n'o's–ši'* 'having brought'

[a] A high-style variant of (a) adds the syllable *–ши/–ši* of (b) to the *–v*
(as seen also in the adjectival form) (e.g. *прочитавши/pro–čit–a'–*
vši); reflexive verbs *must* add this extra syllable before the reflexive
particle (in its non-syllabic form *–s'*), e.g. Inf *научиться/na-uči t'–s'a*
'learn' – *научившись/na–uči'–vši–s'* 'having studied'.

Velar stems in Class IV show the mutation throughout, thus there is no
alternation within the verb, e.g. *кричать/kr'ič–a–t'* 'shout' (stem *kr'ik*-): 1ps
кричу/kr'ič–u' (by (1) above), 3ps *кричит/kr'ič–i'–t*, 3pp *кричат/kr'ič–a't*.

(3) Hard (other than velar) > soft occurs in any context in which the theme or
ending begins with {'o} (orth. *e/ё*) or {'i} (orth. *u*). The most common context
is therefore the Present theme vowel in Classes I and IV (II and III have either
(vowel +) *j* or a *j*-mutated stem-final element), but it also occurs before the
Class IV 3rd Person Plural ending {'at}, e.g.:

	Stem	3rd Person Singular	3rd Person Plural
Class I	*нес–/n'os–*	*несём/n'os–'o'–t*	(*несут/n'os–u't*)
	лез–/l'ez– 'climb'	*лезет/l'e'z–'o–t*	(*лезут/l'e'z–ut*)
Class IV	*прос–/pros–*	*просит/pro's–'i–t*	*просят/pro's–'at*

(4) Root-final /t/, /d/: > /s/ before Infinitive ending *–t'*; > ø before Past ending
–l, e.g.:

Root (base stem)	1st Person Singular Present	Infinitive	Past stem
плет–/pl'ot– 'plait'	*плету/pl'ot–u'*	*плести/pl'o(t)–t'i'*	*плел–/pl'o(t)–l–*
вед–/v'od– 'lead'	*веду/v'od–u'*	*вести/v'o(d)–t'i'*	*вел–/v'o(d)–l–*

(5) Root in nasal consonant (/n/, /m/): > /a/ before ending beginning in
consonant, e.g.:

Root (base stem)	1st Person Singular Present	Infinitive	Past stem
(на)чн–/(na)–č(ь)n– 'begin'	*начну/na–č(∅)n–u'*	*начать/ na–ča'(n)–t'*	*начал–/ na–ča(n)–l–*
стан–/stan– 'stand'	*стану/sta'n–u*	*стать/sta(n)–t'*	*стал–/sta(n)–l–*
жн–/ž(ь)n– 'reap'	*жну/ž(∅)n–u*	*жать/ža(n)–t'*	*жал–/ža(n)–l–*
жм–/ž(ь)m– 'squeeze'	*жму/ž(∅)m–u*	*жать/ža(m)–t'*	*жал–/ža(m)–l–*

(6) Root in /v/: > ø before ending beginning in consonant, e.g.:

Root (base stem)	1st Person Singular Present	Infinitive	Past stem
жив–/živ– 'live'	*живу/živ–u'*	*жить/ži(v)–t'*	*жил–/ži(v)–l–*
плыв–/pliv– 'sail'	*плыву/pliv–u'*	*плыть/pli(v)–t'*	*плыл–/pli(v)–l–*

(7) Root or (historical) suffix *–ov–* (from Proto-Slavonic diphthong *ou̯/eu̯*): > /u/ before ending/suffix beginning in consonant (esp. Present theme *j–*), e.g.:

Root (base stem)	1st Person Singular Present	Infinitive
ков–/kov– 'forge'	*кую/ku–j–u'*	*ковать/kov–a'–t'*
рисов–/r'is–ov– 'draw'	*рисую/r'is–u'–j–u*	*рисовать/r'is–ov–a'–t'*
плев–/pl'ov– 'spit'	*плюю/pl'u–j–u'*	*плевать/pl'–ov–a'–t'*

(8) Root-final /i/ before /j/ (Present theme or Imperative ending): [i] > /e/ stressed, ø unstressed; [ɨ] > /o/, e.g.:

Root (base stem)	Infinitive	1st Person Singular Present	Imperative stem
бри–/br'i– 'shave'	*брить/br'i–t'*	*брею/br'e'–j–u*	*брей–/br'e'–j–*
пи–/p'i– 'drink'	*пить/p'i–t'*	*пью/p'(e)–j–u'*	*пей–/p'e'–j–*
мы–/mi– 'wash'	*мыть/mi–t'*	*мою/mo'–j–u*	*мой–/mo'–j–*

2.2.11   Stress patterns in verbs

Since there is little correlation between the stress patterns of the Present and the Past, it is simplest to treat them as separate systems and then observe what useful correlations we can identify. This is of interest pedagogically in the prediction of patterns from the Infinitive, as this is the dictionary form, hence the perceived base form. The attempt to combine both forms into single patterns simply complicates the description to no useful purpose.

2.2.11.1 Present. We shall use the same descriptors as for the nouns, namely: A = fixed stem-stress; B = fixed end-stress; C = mobile stress. The theme vowel is better counted as part of the ending, if only because three of the four theme-vowel forms have non-syllabic endings (2nd Person Singular, 3rd Person Singular, 1st Person Plural), and the fourth (2nd Person Plural) cannot be stressed on its final vowel. Only one mobile pattern exists, namely: 1st Person Singular on the ending ∼ the rest on the stem (which may mean either root or suffix). According to one relatively small count (Fedjanina 1976: 196) pattern A accounts for some 50 per cent of all verbs, 62 per cent of Classes I–III and 29 per cent of Class IV; pattern B for 30 per cent of all, 29 per cent of I–III and 32 per cent of IV; and pattern C for 20 per cent of all, 9 per cent of I–III and 39 per cent of IV. Thus A is by far the most typical pattern for Classes I–III, this being assisted by the popularity of suffix stress in Class II; B is equally distributed amongst Classes I, III and IV, but virtually does not occur in Class II; and C is much more common in Class IV (it does not occur at all in Classes I–II) – indeed, a shift among these from B to C has been occurring over many centuries, and is still continuing; this is because C is particularly popular in the southern dialects, which continue to impose many of their features on the standard.

The 2nd Person Plural is the only polysyllabic ending, and its stress is always on its first syllable (–'o–t'e/–'i–t'e). Some dialects have stress on the second syllable, as did Old Russian, but this is no longer possible in the standard.

In the examples in table 27, we give the 1st Person Singular and 3rd Person Singular of all types (the latter represents the position of all other forms).

2.2.11.2 Past. The four forms of the Past (see table 28) have three patterns in common with the short adjectives (see above, section 2.1.5.2), namely A (stem – root or affix), B (ending, where the stress is on the three final vowels and the stem-final syllable in the Masculine non-vocalic ending, the latter marked as stressed zero) and C (end in Feminine only). B and C occur only on unsuffixed stems, that is, where the element before the –l is root-final, whether consonant or vowel. Class is not significant here, as that is based on the Present stem; here only the Infinitive stem is relevant.

2.2.11.3 Correlation between Present and Past stress. We can make only the following generalisations:

- suffixed verbs with stress on the root (or prefix) in the Infinitive have stress fixed on that syllable in all forms (e.g. d'el–a–t', v'id–e–t');
- verbs with Infinitive in –t'i have fixed end-stress throughout (e.g. n'os–t'i').

Beyond that, there are problems in prediction: verbs with stress on the suffix in the Infinitive may be either Class II (e.g. čit–a'–t'), III (e.g. p' is–a'–t') or IV (e.g. l'ož–a'–t'), and their stress may be fixed or mobile; monosyllabic verbs may have any stress pattern, but are more likely to have end or mobile stress in both Present and Past; as with the adjectives, there is pressure to eliminate

Table 27 *Stress patterns in Present*

		Type A	
	Infinitive	**1st Person Singular**	**3rd Person Singular**
Class I	*лезть*/l′ez–t′	*лезу*/l′e′z–u	*лезет*/l′e′z–′o–t 'climb'
(only two roots, plus perfectives with the prefix *вы-*/vi–, always stressed on prefix)			
Class II (root)	*делать*/d′e′l–a–t′	*делаю*/d′e′l–aj–u	*делаем*/d′e′l–aj–o–t 'do'
Class II (suffix)	*читать*/čit–a′–t′	*читаю*/čit–a′j–u	*читаем*/čit–a′j–o–t 'read'
Class III	*резать*/r′e′z–a–t′	*режу*/r′e′ž–u	*режет*/r′e′ž–ot 'cut'
Class IV	*видеть*/v′i′d–′e–t′	*вижу*/v′i′ž–u	*видим*/v′i′d–′i–t 'see'

		Type B	
	Infinitive	**1st Person Singular**	**3rd Person Singular**
Class I	*нести*/n′os–ti′	*несу*/n′os–u′	*несём*/n′os–′o′–t 'carry'
Class II (root)	—		
Class II (suffix)	*давать*/da–va′–t′	*даю*/da–j–u′	*даём*/da–j–o′–t 'give'
(Only three roots, could all be said to be really Class III, stem in –j)			
Class III	*слать*/sl–a–t′	*шлю*/šl′–u′	*шлём*/šl′–o′–t 'send'
(j-mutation of /s/ through /l/) (Only two roots, plus some in /j/, e.g. *смеяться*/sm′ej–a′–t′–s′a, *смеётся*/sm′ej–o′–t–s′a 'laugh')			
Class IV	*говорить*/govor–′i′–t′	*говорю*/govor′–u′	*говорит*/govor–′i′–t 'say'
	лежать/l′ož–a′–t′	*лежу*/l′ož–u′	*лежит*/l′ož–i′–t 'lie'

		Type C	
	Infinitive	**1st Person Singular**	**3rd Person Singular**
Class I	—		
Class II (root)	—		
Class II (suffix)	—		
Class III	*писать*/p′is–a′t′	*пишу*/p′iš–u′	*пишет*/p′iš–o–t 'write'
Class IV	*просить*/pros–′i′–t′	*прошу*/proš–u′	*просит*/pro′s–′i–t 'ask'

C in the Past, usually in favour of B, but C remains popular on high-frequency verbs.

2.2.11.4 Stress in participles

(1) Adjectival. In principle stress is as for the relevant stem (see above, section 2.2.9), but note the following:

(a) Present Active. Class IV Type C (mobile) may have stress on theme–′a– (this is an older type, being replaced by stem-stress, matching the 3pp, e.g. 3pp *любят*/l′u′b–′at 'love': older l′ub–′a′–šč–ij, newer l′u′b–′a–šč–ij; 3pp *учатся*/ u′č–at–s′a 'study': *учащийся*/uč–a′–šč–ij–s′a ('student').

(b) Present Passive. Class IV Type C (mobile) have stress on theme, e.g. 1pp *любим*/l′u′b–′i–m: *любимый*/l′ub–′i′–m–ij.

Table 28 *Stress patterns in Past*

	Infinitive	Type A Masculine	Feminine	Plural
Stem in root C:				
	лезть/*l'ez–t'*	лез/*l'e'z–ø*	лезла/*l'e'z–l–a*	лезли/*l'e'z–l–'i*
Stem in root V:				
	стать/*sta–t'*	стал/*sta'–l–ø*	стала/*sta'–l–a*	стали/*sta'–l–'i*
Stem in suffix (stress on either root or suffix):				
(Root)	делать/*d'e'l–a–t'*	делал/*d'e'l–a–lø*	делала/*d'e'l–a–l–a*	делали/*d'e'l–a–l–'i*
(Suffix)	читать/*čit–a'–t'*	читал/*čit–a'–ø*	читала/*čit–a'–l–a*	читали/*čit–a'–l–'i*
	Infinitive	Type B Masculine	Feminine	Plural
Stem in root C:				
	нести/*n'os–t'i'*	нёс/*n'os(–l)–ø'*	несла/*n'os–l–a'*	несли/*n'os–l–'i'*
No other types				
	Infinitive	Type C Masculine	Feminine	Plural
Stem in root C:	—			
Stem in root V:				
	жить/*ži(v)–t'*	жил/*ži'(v)–l–ø*	жила/*ži(v)–l–a'*	жили/*ži(v)'–l–'i* 'live'
	дать/*da–t'*	дал/*da'–l–ø*	дала/*da–l–a'*	дали/*da'–l–'i* 'give'

(c) Past Active. Only irregular Infinitive in *–epe–/–er'e'–* 'lose' the second vowel (in fact the root is *Cer*, expanded to *Cere* /–C, so it is the expanded vowel which is lost in spite of the following C); the stress falls on the remaining root vowel: Inf умереть/*um'er'e'–t'* 'die' (Past Masc умер/*u'm'er–(l)–ø*) ∼ умерший/*um'e'r–š–ij* 'dead'.

(d) Past Passive

stem V + *–nn–*   always stressed on preceding vowel: Inf прочитать/*pro–čit–a'–t'* ∼ прочитанный/*pro–či't–a–nn–ij*;

stem C + *–'onn–*   Class IV Type C (mobile) have stress on preceding (stem): Inf получить/*poluč–i'–t'* 'receive' ∼ полученный/*polu'č–onn–ij*;

suffix *–nu + –t–*   stressed on preceding (stem): Inf растянуть/*ras–t'a–nu'–t'* 'stretch out' ∼ растянутый/*ras–t'a'–nu–t–ij*.

(2) Adverbial

(a) Present. The stress for all verbs follows that of 1st Person Singular Present (thus stem for Type A, end for Types B and C), e.g. *čit–a'–ja, n'os'–a', l'ub–'a'*. Exceptions are some verbs of position – where this participle is effectively

an adverb, in which even Type B have stem-stress, e.g. *сидя/s'i'd–'a* 'sitting, seated', *лёжа/l'o'ž–a* 'lying down', *стоя/sto'j–a* 'standing'.
  (b) Past. The stress is always as in Infinitive.

2.3   Other categories (invariable)

Other categories, with only one form, will be referred to briefly in terms of their general shape; comments on their formation and usage are left to chapters 5 and 4 respectively. The comparison of adverbs is possibly also best treated as a formational issue, but will be treated here as parallel to that of adjectives (above, section 2.1.5.6).

2.3.1   Adverbs
The most common adverbial formation is from the adjective, but, interestingly, not by suffixation: the form in question is simply that of the neuter short form, ending in *–o* (including stress and hard/soft stem variants), e.g. *хороший/xoro'š–ij* 'good' ~ *хорошо/xoroš–o'* 'well'; *скучный/sku'č–n–ij* 'boring' ~ *скучно/sku'č–n–o* 'boringly'; *крайний/kra'j–n'–ij* 'extreme' ~ *крайне/ kra'j–n'–e* 'extremely'. In synchronic terms, since it is not necessary to talk of an ending on an invariable form (because it is not opposed to any other ending), we should rather say that the form of the adverb is word-formational ({Adj stem}+{formant *–o*}), and not morphological, as opposed to the Nominative Singular Neuter of the adjective ({stem}+{ending *–o*}).
  Adjectives with the suffix *–('e)sk–* do not have short forms, and the adverb is formed with the ending *–i*, e.g. *дружеский/dru'ž–esk–ij* 'friendly' ~ *дружески/dru'ž–esk–i* 'in friendly manner'; *воровской/vor–ov–sk–o'j* 'thieving' ~ *воровски/vor–ov–sk–i* 'thief-like'.
  Older, more 'elementary' adverbs, like many of time and quantity, have usually been formed from nouns or noun phrases long in the past, their etymology now obscure, e.g. *вчера/včera* 'yesterday' (from *вечер/v'ečer* 'evening'), *очень/očen'* 'very' (probably from *око/oko* 'eye', via 'obvious'). In this group belong the interrogative and demonstrative adverbs, made up, as in English, of the interrogative or demonstrative pronoun (Rus *k–/t–*, Eng *wh–/th–*) plus an element meaning time, place, etc., e.g. *когда/ko–gda* 'whe–n' (from older *kъ–gda*), *тогда/to–gda* 'the–n' (from *tъ–gda*), *где/g–d'e* 'whe–re' (from older *kъ–de*), *здесь/zd'es'* 'he–re' (from older *sъ–de–sъ*).
  A final set of common adverbs are derived from case forms of temporal or quantity nouns, sometimes prepositional phrases, e.g. *летом/l'e't–om* 'in summer' (Instrumental Singular of *лето/l'e't–o*), *утром/u'tr–om* 'in the morning' (Instrumental Singular of *утро/u'tr–o*), *слишком/s–lišk–om* 'too (much)'

(from the preposition *s* 'with' and root *liš–* 'excess' and Instrumental Singular ending).

At the formal level, there are also many compound adverbial phrases structured as in English types like 'to a certain extent', 'in the final analysis', etc., which are common in all European languages.

2.3.1.1 Comparative adverbs. There is no formal distinction between comparative adverbs and the predicative comparative adjectives. We noted (section 2.1.5.6) that the latter were invariable forms used only in the predicate, and the same forms may also be adverbs, identified only by context. Thus given forms will be adjectival in the predicate, adverbial when clearly modifying other adjectives or verbs, e.g.: *лучше/lu'čš–e* 'better' may be an adjective: 'This book is better than that', or an adverb: 'You draw better than me'); likewise *интереснее/int'er'e's–n'–eje* may be '(is) more interesting' or 'more interestingly'; *поближе/po–bl'i'ž–e* '(is) closer' or 'more closely'.

As with the adjective, a more formal style is available in the analytical construction with *более/bo'l'eje* 'more' (or *менее/m'e'n'eje* 'less'). This structure is the only possibility for adverbs other than those in *–o/–e*, especially those in *–ski* (e.g. only *более дружески/bol'eje družeski* 'in more friendly manner') (parallel to their missing predicative adjectival form).

Superlative adverbs may be formed by the combination of comparative plus the Genitive of the pronoun *весь/v(e)s'–ø* 'all', Singular for inanimate, Plural for animate, e.g. *лучше всего/lučše vs'–ego'* 'best of all (things)', *лучше всех/lučše vs'–ex* 'best of all (people)'. A formal-level alternative is the particle *наиболее/naibo'l'eje* 'most', as for the adjectives. Again, this is the only possibility for non-basic adverbs, e.g. *наиболее дружески/naibol'eje družeski* 'in the most friendly manner (of all)'.

2.3.2   Prepositions

The most basic prepositions are those inherited from Indo-European, though many are disguised by their phonological history. Some are regional developments (Balto-Slav); several are lexically non-syllabic, the result of their having had a weak back *jer* (*ъ*) as their vowel, which was allowed to disappear when the following syllable (the initial one of the noun, adjective, etc. to which the preposition was proclitic) had a full vowel – that is, in most cases. Where the following syllable had a weak *jer* which disappeared, the preposition showed the strong *jer* development, namely > /o/. Thus these prepositions should be stated as having variant forms with or without /o/. The three concerned are:

> *в(о)/v(o)* 'in' (< PS *vъn* < *ъn*, cf. Eng *in*, via loss of /n/ by realignment of boundary – see above, section 2.1.4.2)

c(o)/s(o) 'with' (< PS *sъn-*, cf. Gk *syn*, Lat *cum*, via loss of /n/ as above)

к(о)/k(o) 'towards' (< PS *kъ(n)*, possibly also related to Lat *cum*, Sanskrit *kam*)

The other basic prepositions have full vowels (and those ending in a consonant have inserted /o/ before certain stem-initial clusters); they include:

без/b'ez 'without' (Balto-Slav), *до/do* 'up to' (cf. Eng *to*), *за/za* 'behind' (Balto-Slav), *из/iz* 'out of' (cf. Lat *ex*), *на/na* 'on' (cf. Eng *on*), *о(б)/o(b)* 'against/around' (< PS *ob*, cf. Gk *epi*)), *om/ot* 'from' (Balto-Slav), *по/po* 'within limit/in relation to' (cf. Gk *apo*), *при/pri* 'attached to' (cf. Lat *prae*), *про/pro* 'about' (cf. Lat *pro*), *у/u* 'next to/away' (cf. Lat prefix *au–*), *через/čer'ez* 'across' (< PS *čerz*).

All but one of the above serve also as verbal prefixes, expressing primarily location or movement. The exception is *k(o)*, and there are also a few prefixes which are not also prepositions (see chapter 5, section 4.1); an interesting case is the prefixal equivalent of *čer'ez*, which is (the possibly formally related) *nepe–/p'er'e–* 'across' (cf. Lat *per*, Gk *peri*). Sometimes the prefixal meaning differs from the prepositional one, e.g. *u–* as a prefix mostly means 'away' (though see chapter 5, section 4.1.2), as a preposition 'next to, at'.

In terms of location and direction, many are flexible, since the case system also contributes to these meanings. Thus, *v(o)* and *na* mean 'in' and 'on' respectively when they govern the Locative, but 'into' and 'onto' with the Accusative; this applies also to *za*: + Locative = location behind, + Accusative = direction behind. (For discussion of the semantics of these and other prefixes see chapter 5; for the cases governed see chapter 4.)

A second group of prepositions are originally compound, but now perceived as non-derived; they are formed from some of the above basic forms plus an element *–d* meaning 'place' (the same as found in the adverbs *g–d'e*, etc., above), namely *над/na–d* 'above', *под/po–d* 'below', *перед/p'er'e–d* 'in front of'.

A third group are derived from adverbs (often themselves originally phrases), most of which may also continue to function as adverbs, e.g. *вместо/v–m'esto* 'instead (of)', *мимо/mi'mo* 'past', *против/pro't'iv* 'opposite', *вокруг/vo–kru'g* 'around'.

A fourth group are derived from nouns, verbs, etc., but also now considered non-derived, e.g. *для/dl'a* 'for (the benefit of)', *ради/ra'd'i* 'for the sake of', *кроме/kr'om'e* 'except', *между/m'e'ždu* 'between', *около/o'kolo* 'near', *благодаря/blagodar'a* 'thanks to'.

Lastly, of the basic types, there are two clearly compound (and hyphenated), self-evident forms: *из-за/iz–za* 'from behind' and *из-под/iz–pod* 'from under'.

Beyond these there are many phrasal prepositions, used mainly in the formal style, parallel to English forms like 'in the course of', 'in spite of', 'in accordance with', etc. Some common ones are: (1) noun phrases (preposition plus noun): *во время/vo vr′e′m′a* 'during' (lit. 'in the time'), *ввиду/v–v′idu′* 'in view of' (note the fused spelling, from the phrase *в виду/v vid–u′* 'in view'), *вследствие/v–sl′e′dstv′ije* 'as a result of' (also fused spelling); (2) adverb phrases (adverbs plus prepositions): *вместе с/vm′e′st′e s* 'together with', *рядом с/r′a′dom s* 'along with', *вслед за/vsl′ed za* '(following) after', *вблизи om/vbl′iz′i′ ot* 'close by' (lit. 'from').

2.3.3   Conjunctions

The structure and function of conjunctions are typical of European languages. Details of the function belong to chapter 4, and here we only summarise the types and their general structure, with a minimum of examples.

2.3.3.1 Coordinating

(1) Connective. The simple connective is *и/i* 'and' (etymology unclear, possibly cognate to Gr *ei* 'if'), which joins elements of equal value, whether words, phrases or clauses. The negative emphatic form – 'neither ... nor' – is done by the addition of the negative element /n′/: *ни... ни/n′i ... n′i*.

(2) Adversative. The strong adversative 'but' is *но/no* (etymology unclear, possibly cognate to Eng *now*), that is, implying contradiction or antithesis ('but nevertheless/in spite of that/at the same time'). A more formal variant is *однако/odna′ko* 'however'.

A weaker adversative is *a/a* (etymology unclear, possibly from Indo-European demonstrative *at*), which may appear as either 'and' or 'but' in English; it implies only contrast, and not contradiction.

A colloquial variant with an element of emphasis is *же/že*, which displays its (intensive) particle origin (see below) also in its enclitic position, e.g. *Иди, я же останусь./Idi, ja že ostanus′* 'You (can) go, (but) I'll stay/I'm staying.'

Emphasis via contrast may be done by a combination of negative *не* and *a*, 'not ... but' e.g. *Это не газета, а журнал./Eto n′e gaz′eta, a žurnal.* 'This is not a newspaper, but a magazine.'

(3) Disjunctive. The simple disjunctive 'or' is *или/i′l′i* (formally compounded from *i* + *l′i*, interrogative particle). When doubled – *или... или* – it expresses the exclusive 'either ... or' (that is, only the expressed options are possibilities), also done more colloquially by *либо... либо/l′i′bo ... l′i′bo*.

Open 'either ... or' (that is, where the expressed options are not the exclusive set, as in uncertainty about the possibilities), may be expressed by *не то ... не mo/n′e to ... n′e ... to* or *то ли ... то ли/to l′i ... to l′i* (*ли/l′i* being an interrogative particle (see below), here emphasising the element of conjecture).

Alternation in time is expressed by *mo ... mo/to ... to* 'now ... now'.

2.3.3.2 Subordinating. Beyond the basic forms, the most common compound type uses a preposition plus a neuter case form of the demonstrative *mom/tot*, followed by either *čto* 'that' or *kak* 'as'. There follows a semantically ordered list of the most common ones:

'that':

что/čto (same form as interrogative 'what?');

будто/bu'd–to implies 'allegedly' (from *bud'*('be' Imper) + *to*);

'in order to': *чтобы/čt'o–bi* (where -*bi* is the hypothetical/subjunctive particle);

'if': *если/je'sl'i* (from *jest' li* 'is it?'); hypothetical 'if' colloquially shortens and fuses the –*bi*: *если6/jesl'ib*;

'unless': *если не/jesl'i n'e* (lit. 'if . . . not');

'like/as': *как/kak* (cf. interrogative long form *kak–o'j*);

'since/because': *так как/tak kak*; *потому что/po–tomu' čto* (from *po tomu, čto*); colloquial *раз/raz* (lit. 'once', thus – 'seeing that');

'although': *хотя/xot'a* (from adverbial participle 'will–ing'); *несмотря на то, что/n'e–smotr'a' na to, čto* 'in spite of the fact that'; *будь то/bud' to* 'even if/though';

'when': *когда/kogda'* (= interrogative, as Eng);

'while': *пока/poka'*;

'until': *пока . . . не/poka' . . . n'e* (lit. 'while . . . not');

'since (the time that)': *с тех пор как/s t'ex por kak* (lit. 'from the time that');

'before': *до того как/do togo kak*; *перед тем как/p'er'ed t'em kak* ('immediately before'); *прежде чем/pr'ežd'e čem* (esp. 'in anticipation');

'after': *после того как/posl'e togo kak*;

'as if/though': *как будто (бы)/kak budto (bi)* (*bi* emphasising unlikelihood); *словно/slo'vno* (from *slovo* 'word', thus 'one might say');

'inasmuch/insofar/as long as': *поскольку/po–sko'l'ku* (from *skol'ko* 'how much?').

2.3.4 Particles

(1) Simple particles. In formal terms, the simple particles, with their basic meanings, are: *не/n'e* (negative); *бы/bi* (hypothetical); *ли/l'i, a/a* (both interrogative); *же/že, уж/už, –ка/–ka, –то/–to* (all intensifying). Here belongs *да/da* 'yes', while *нет/n'et* 'no' (from *не есть/n'e jest'* 'is not') strictly belongs in the next group.

(2) Derived particles. Derived ones which are formally perceived as simple, e.g.: *вот/vot, вон/von* (both primarily demonstrative 'lo!'); *всё/vs'o, ведь/v'ed'* (both intensifying); *разве/ra'zv'e* (interrogative); *пусть/pust', давай/dava'j*

(both imperative/exhortative 'let'); *почти/počt′i′* (approximative 'almost'); *именно/i′m′enno* (definitive 'exactly'); *только/tol′ko* (restrictive 'only'); *было/ bi′lo* (cancellation of action); *мол/mol, дескать/d′e′skat′* (both 'allegedly').

(3) Compound particles. Compound ones, mostly modal and formed from the above, e.g.: *всё же/vs′o že* (concessive), *вот уж/vot už* (emphatic), *ещё бы/ ješčo′ bi* (affirmative), *что ли/čto l′i* (interrogative), *чуть (ли) не/čut′ (l′i) n′e* (approximative), *так и/tak i* (emphatic), *лишь бы/l′iš bi* (desire).

Many of the above are clitic, either proclitic, e.g. *не, вот, пусть, почти,* or enclitic, e.g. *же, бы, ли, было* and the orthographically fused *–то, –ка.* Some are unstressed, but may be either proclitic or enclitic, e.g. *ведь, уж.*

2.3.5   Interjections
The functional range of interjections is parallel to that of the other European languages: mainly modal, expressing positive or negative emotion or desires, but also the commonalities of speech (and social) etiquette. Some are ono-matopoeic, some foreign borrowings. Examples of the main types follow.

(1) Emotion. These may be either positive or negative, or just surprise, excite-ment, etc.:
(a) onomatopoeic: *ага/aga′, ого/ogo′* (phonetic [a′ɦa], [ɔ′ɦɔ]);
(b) *боже мой/bo′že moj* 'My God', *господи/go′spod′i* '(Good) Lord', *батю-шки/ba′t′uški* 'Good Heavens' (lit. '(priestly) fathers'), *на тебе/na′ t′eb′e* and *вот тебе на/vo′t t′eb′e na* 'well I never'.
The following are mainly negative:
(a) onomatopoeic: *ай–ай–ай/aj–aj–a′j* 'oh, no' (dismay), *тьфу/t′fu* 'yuck' (disgust);
(b) *ахти/axt′i′* and *увы/uvi′* 'alas', *однако/odna′ko* 'really!', *чёрт/čort* 'hell' (lit. 'the devil'), *чёрт возьми/čort voz′m′i′* 'to hell with you/it' (lit. 'the devil take (you/it)').

(2) Desire
(a) onomatopoeic: *ау/au′, эй/ej* (both calling), *тпру/tpru* (driving animals);
(b) *брось/bros′* 'stop' (Imper 2ps), *караул/karau′l* 'help' (archaic noun 'po-lice');
(c) borrowed: *алло/allo* 'hello' (phonetic [alɔ'] or [alʲɔ']), *стоп/stop, баста/ ba′sta* both 'stop'.

(3) Etiquette
(a) regular verb forms: *прости(те)/prost′i′(te)* 'excuse me' (Imper 2p);
(b) fossilised verb forms: *здравствуй(те)/zdra′vstvuj(te)* 'good day/hello' (Imper 2p from obsolete verb 'be well'), *спасибо/spas′i′bo* 'thanks' (from 'God save');
(c) other: *привет/pr′iv′e′t* 'hi' (coll.) (from noun 'greeting').

An interesting syntactic feature of some of these, namely those expressing sudden movement or noise, which are mostly formally bare verb stems, is that they may function as the predicate, e.g. *А он хлоп ему*...*/A on xlop jomu'*... 'And he thumped him (went 'thump')...', *Я хвать его за воротник/Ja xvat' jogo' za vorotni'k–ø* 'I grabbed him by the collar'. See further chapter 4, section 3.2.2.2.

2.3.6   *Parenthetic forms*

Parenthetic forms, too, parallel normal European usage, either expressing modality (attitude to context), e.g. *может быть/možet bit'* 'perhaps' (lit. '(it) may be'), *наверно/nav'e'rno* 'probably/no doubt'; or maintaining address mode (sometimes called 'comment clauses' or 'fillers'), e.g. *знаете ли (вы)/zna'jote l'i (vi)* '(do) you know', *видите ли/v'i'd'ite l'i* '(do) you see'.

4   Syntax

1   Introduction: basic concepts and approaches

Those familiar with the basic concepts of syntax may pass on to section 2.

The transcription used in this chapter is in fact *transliteration* of the surface form (using the ISO/Slav system, see chapter 1, section 4.1, table 5 – note especially the use of *ja*, *ju*, and not *'u*, *'u*, for the letters я, ю), that is, neither phonemic nor morphophonemic, but with (only) endings separated from stems by a dash, and zero endings noted.

1.1   The sentence

The base unit of syntax is the sentence, whose constituent parts may be single words or phrases. In so-called 'phrase structure' grammar, the customary formulas for these are noun phrase (NP; for a single noun or a phrase built around a 'head' noun) and verb phrase (VP; for a single verb or a phrase built around a 'head' verb). In this approach a sentence is seen as being made up of NP + VP, though either one of these may be zero (at least on the surface). In more traditional terminology, the NP is equivalent to the subject (noun, nominal phrase or pronoun), and the VP to the predicate, made up of the verb plus its complement (or objects) and adverbial modifiers (for some the 'predicate' is strictly only the verb). In fact these two approaches should be seen as complementary, since we have to deal sometimes with the overall structure of sentences, for which the former approach is more useful, at other times with the constituent parts of phrases, for which the latter is more useful.

Both of these approaches are centred on the analysis of existing sentences, from which one is expected to draw conclusions about the available sentence types in a language. Alongside this, there is the approach of 'transformational grammar', whose explicit aim is to account for the 'generation', or formation, of acceptable sentences. This approach, too, is of use at times to make clear the relationship between sentence types, or between constituent parts and the whole. Since our aim is precisely to offer a description which makes things clear to as many readers as possible, our approach will be eclectic: any of the above will be called upon as appropriate. The overall description, however, will be based on the traditional approach, allowing us to move more freely from words (as described in chapter 5) and their morphology (chapter 3) to their behaviour in sentences.

The means by which syntactic relationships are expressed may be morphological (inflectional), lexico-morphological or positional (word order); in addition, either graphic (for the written language) or phonetic or extra-linguistic (for the spoken) features will be relevant.

The *morphological* features which are of relevance for Russian are:

(1) *number*: the subject's head noun and the verb must agree;
(2) *case*:
    (a) within the NP all Adj + N units must agree (the formal subject will be Nominative);
    (b) within the VP the case of any nominal elements (in the complement) is controlled (governed) by the verb;
(3) *gender*:
    (a) the Adj + N units of an NP must agree;
    (b) the subject and a past tense verb must agree;
(4) *person*: the subject and verb must agree (a nominal subject must have a 3rd person verb, a pronominal subject the appropriate person).

That is, all of these features are involved in the 'agreement', or 'concord', between the subject and predicate (verb) as well as within these.

The *lexico-morphological* features are the so-called 'function' words: conjunctions, prepositions, relative pronouns, particles, etc., which indicate relationships between the various parts of a sentence.

Word order is of particular significance in Russian, since, given that the inflectional morphology indicates major relationships (like subject, object), it is less important to maintain the typical (and normal) word order (Subject–Verb–Object – SVO), leaving the way clear for shifts to SOV or OVS to serve other functions.

The main *graphic* feature is punctuation; the marking of stress is another (though rare) possibility.

Phonetic features include intonation and pause placement.

Extra-linguistic features include gesture and facial expression, as well as the real context in which the utterance takes place.

Only the last of these will be excluded from our account; some contextual aspects are treated in chapter 7.

1.2   Sentence structure and analysis

Sentence types may be described in two ways:
(1) *semantically*: that is, based on the meaning of the sentence, which in turn is related to the intention of the speaker; this method produces basic types like

'statement', 'question', 'command', with extensions related to 'modality' (the speaker's attitude to the context of their utterance, e.g. doubt, desirability, necessity, etc.) and 'emotion' (pleasure, annoyance, etc.); the speaker's attitude to the *content* of their utterance adds the element of 'style' (degree of formality displayed in form). These may be summed up as 'types of utterance'.

(2) *structurally*: that is, the actual form of sentences, with types like 'simple' (with one clause/idea centred around one verb), 'compound' (with more than one clause of equal rank, said to be 'coordinated'), and 'complex' (with more than one clause, but with one dominant – the 'main' or 'principal' clause, and the rest said to be 'subordinate').

Of these, the second is by far the simpler descriptive approach, since it can cover all forms and allow the utterance types to be seen as examples of these, while the first approach would mean covering all types of structure under each of the many semantic headings. Thus, our description will follow the structural path.

(The majority of English descriptions of the 'grammar' of Russian do not separate out morphology and syntax, but combine both in one way or another, typically making the morphology the centre and including the syntactic properties of each category within the given chapter (for example Borras and Christian (1971/1977), Wade (1992); Unbegaun (1957/1962) does have a short chapter on Syntax, but most of what belongs under 'Syntax' is actually covered in the earlier chapters. There would appear to be no English description of Russian syntax alone.)

2   Nominal phrases

Since nominal phrases are the key element of all parts of the sentence, we describe first their structural possibilities in Russian. Verb phrases are treated under 'Predicate' (section 3.2.2).

The main types of freely constructed nominal phrase (that is, in which the meaning of the phrase is the sum of its parts, as opposed to the fixed phrases seen in chapter 5, section 5.2, though these, too, may function as syntactic phrases) which may appear as the parts of a sentence (subject, object, complement, adjunct) are as follows.

(1) Adjective + Noun. This is the neutral order; reversal is normally contrastive or stylistic, both in the same case, as required by their position in the sentence, here in Nominative: *старая собака/star–aja sobak–a* 'a/the old dog'. (Only foreign, indeclinable adjectives neutrally follow the noun: *платье беж/plat'–e bež* 'a beige dress'.)

Included are the pronominal adjectives (with the special adjectival declension, see chapter 3, section 2.1.4.2), e.g. possessive, demonstrative: *мой дом/moj–ø dom–ø* 'my house'; *этот дом/èt–ot dom–ø* 'this house'; and the numeral 'one' (and compound numerals ending in 'one'): *один мальчик/odin–ø mal'čik–ø* 'one boy'; *одна девочка/odn–a devočk–a* 'one girl'; *двадцать один мальчик/dvadcat'–ø odin–ø mal'čik–ø* 'twenty one boys'.

There is no lexical marker for definite/indefinite ('the/a'); this feature is expressed by word order (see below, section 3.4).

Where the adjective is a participle, it reflects an underlying adjectival (relative) clause:

опоздавшие зрители/opozdavš–ie zritel–i
be late Past Act – spectator NP   'the/those spectators who had come
                                                  late';
запрещённая книга/zapreščёnn–aja knig–a
ban Past Pass – book NS   'a banned book'.

(2) Noun + Noun$_{Gen}$. Normally in that order only, only the first noun controlled by position:

The main function of Genitive here is possessive or quantitative: *крыша дома/kryš–a dom–a* 'the roof of the house'; *бутылка молока/butylk–a molok–a* 'a bottle of milk'.

Where the first Noun is deverbal, the Genitive most often reflects the underlying object: *объяснение поступка/objasneni–e postupk–a* 'the explanation of the action'; however, it may also reflect an underlying *subject*, such that we have the same potential ambiguity seen in English 'John's defence' (of John/by John): *чтение Толстого/čteni–e Tolst–ogo* 'the reading of Tolstoy' or 'Tolstoy's (own) reading' (= by T.). The second meaning ('by') may also be (and is more often) indicated by putting the second noun into the Instrumental (see (3) below).

(3) Noun + Noun$_{Instr.}$ (in that order only). Normally the first noun is deverbal, and the Instrumental reflects the underlying subject: *утверждение Думой (закона...)/utverždeni–e Dum–oj IS (zakon–a... GS)* 'the passing by the Duma (of the law...)'.

However, in the case of underlying verbs which govern the Instrumental, it reflects the *object*: *обмен информацией/obmen–ø informaci–ej IS* 'exchange of information'.

(cf. *обменить информацией/obmenit' informaci–ej* 'to exchange information'; see below on verbs).

(4) Noun/Pronoun + Conjunction + Noun/Pronoun (same case). Nouns or pronouns may be conjoined by either a coordinating or a disjunctive conjunction: *папа и мама/pap–a i mam–a* 'Papa and Mama'; *папа или мама/pap–a ili mam–a* 'Papa or Mama'; *Виктор и я ~ я и Виктор/Viktor–ø i ja ~ ja i Viktor–ø* 'Victor and I'. Coordination may also be done in a different way: by the use of the preposition *с/s* + Instrumental ('with'), as follows:

> Noun + *s* + Noun_{Instr}: *папа с мамой/pap–a s mam–oj* 'Papa and Mama' (with no intervening verb the meaning is simply 'together' – see below for *s mam–oj* as an adverbial complement).

When a 1st person pronoun is involved, the structure used is the 1st Person Plural pronoun to cover all parties, then to specify the other person with *s* + Instrumental: *мы с Виктором/my s Viktor–om* 'Victor and I' (lit. 'we with Victor'); *мы с ним/my s n–im* 'he and I' (lit. 'we with him').

With two pronouns, as in the last example, this form is the norm, the *i* structure (*on i ja*) being much less common.

(5) Noun + Noun (same case). Usually such a group, with the two nouns in apposition, involves a classifier and a specific member of the class; as in English, the classifier can usually be omitted: *река Волга/rek–a Volg–a* 'the (River) Volga' *город Москва/gorod–ø Moskv–a* '(the city of) Moscow'.

Another type involves an explanatory element, usually a name: *этот дурак Ваня/èt–ot durak–ø Van–ja* 'that idiot (of) Vanya'. This type is popular with titles, however the reason for this is that titles are often difficult to adjust morphologically to the syntax, so that the classifier performs this function; for both reasons, the title is then not declined at all – even if it would not be difficult to do so:

> *балет 'Лебединое озеро'/balet–ø 'Lebedin–oe ozer–o'* 'the ballet "Swan Lake"' ~ *в балете 'Лебединое озеро'/v balet–e LS 'Lebedin–oe ozer–o NS'* 'in (the ballet) "Swan Lake" – where the title is complex;
> *газета 'Правда'/gazet–a 'Pravd–a'* 'the newspaper "Pravda"' ~ *в газете 'Правда'/v gazet–e LS 'Pravd–a NS'* or: *в 'Правде'/v 'Pravd–e'* *LS 'Pravd–e LS'* 'in (the newspaper) "Pravda"' – where inflection of the title is not a problem.

(6) Preposition + Noun. Most such groups are syntactically adverbial phrases (adjuncts), and these will be dealt with below as such. A few, however, are nominal phrases, most often involving numerals: *около десяти ребят/okolo desjat–i GS rebjat–ø GP* 'about ten kids/guys'; *по два яблока/po dv–a AS jablok–a GS* 'two apples each'.

(7) Noun + Preposition + Noun. The second part of these is normally attributive, often an alternative to an adjective:

> *дверь из стекла/dver'–ø iz stekl–a*
> door – out of – glass GS
> 'a glass door /door made from glass'

> *гость из Парижа/gost'–ø iz Pariž–a*
> visitor – from – Paris GS
> 'a visitor from Paris'.

(8) Cardinal numeral (+ Adjective) + Noun. Where the cardinal numeral is Nominative or Accusative, the following noun is Genitive after all but 'one' and compound forms ending in 'one' (see (1) above); 'two', 'three' and 'four' (and compounds ending in them) are followed by the Genitive Singular; the rest by Genitive Plural: GS: *два мальчика/dv–a mal'čik–a* 'two boys'; *три девочки/tr–i devoček–i* 'three girls'; GP: *пять мальчиков/девочек/pjat'–ø mal'čik–ov/devoček–ø* 'five boys/girls'. However, when the numeral is in any other case, the following noun is in that same case: *в двух километрах/v dv–ux kilometr–ax* LP 'at (a distance of) two kilometres'; *с пятью мальчиками/s pjat'–ju mal'čik–ami* IP 'with five boys'.

With the numeral in Nominative or Accusative, intervening adjectives are normally Genitive Plural, even after 'two' and 'three', and always with Masculine and Neuter nouns: *два больших дома/dv–a bol'š–ix* GP *dom–a* GS 'two big houses'; with Feminine nouns, the stress pattern is relevant: where the Genitive Singular and Nominative Plural have identical stress, the adjective is normally Nominative Plural (by 'infection'), but if they are different, it is normally Genitive Plural: *две красивые девушки/dv–e krasiv–ye de'vušk–i* GS (= NP) 'two beautiful girls'; *две сильных руки/dv–e sil'–n–yx ruk–i'* GS (NP = *ru'k–i*) 'two strong arms'.

Otherwise, only when the adjective precedes the numeral will it agree with it (when the adjective concerned is 'first' or 'last', as in English): *первые три приза/perv-ye* NP *tr–i* NP *priz–a* GS 'the first three prizes'.

3   Simple sentence

This basic type is made up of one clause, that is, with only one predicate. Its form is NP + VP, with the following possibilities:

> (1) N + V   *Собака лает./Sobak–a la–et.*
> dog NS – bark 3ps Pres
> 'The dog is barking.'

(2) NP + VP   *Старая собака страшно лает./Star–aja sobak–*
                     a strašno la–et.
               old NSf – dog NS – frighteningly Adv – bark 3ps
                 Pres
               'The old dog is barking frighteningly.'

(3) N (VP = ø)   *Тишина./Tišin–a.*
                   silence NS
                   'Silence.' (e.g. as a stage direction)

We would include Vocative forms here, e.g. *Коля!/Kol–ja!* 'Kolya!', whether spoken or in letter openings, and perhaps also (nominal) exclamations in general, although for many linguists these are not 'sentences' in the proper sense. It remains unclear what else to do with them if they are excluded. Russian grammars differentiate between, on the one hand, the *Tišina* ((3)) and vocative types, which they call the sole primary part of a 'one-member sentence' – along with the next two sets ((4) and (5)), and, on the other, the exclamation type, which they call 'unanalysable' (*nečlenimoe*), as being neither a primary nor a secondary (complement, etc.) part.

(4) V (NP — ø)   *Морозит./Moroz–it.*
                   freeze 3ps Pres 'There's a frost.'

                   Слушаю./Slušaj–u.
                   listen 1ps Pres 'Hello.' (on phone, lit. 'I am listening.')

(5) VP (V = ø)   *Холодно./Xolodn–o.*
                   ø – cold NSn
                   'It's cold.' (copula = ø, see below).

The VP in turn may include a NP:

V + N$_{Acc}$ *... купил (красивую) шубу/... kupi–l (krasiv–uju)*
                   šub–u
               buy Past Masc – (beautiful ASf) – fur coat AS
               '... bought a (beautiful) fur coat' (direct object)

V + N$_{Dat}$ *дайте мне.../daj–te mne...*
               give 2pp Imper – me DS
               'give me...' (indirect object)

V + N$_{Oblique}$ *... занимается спортом/... zanima–etsja*
                   sport–om
               engage in 3ps Pres – sport IS
               '... engages in/plays sport'

Or it may include a second, non-finite verb:

V+V$_{Inf}$ *хочу купить.../хоč–u kupi–t'...*
want 1ps Pres – buy Inf
'I want to buy' (complement)

Or it may include an adverbial modifier, which itself may be a phrase:

V+Adv$_{Time}$ *... придёт завтра/... prid–ët zavtra*
come 3ps Fut – tomorrow Adv
'... will come tomorrow'

... придёт после обеда/... prid–ët posle obed–a
come 3ps Fut – after – dinner GSm
'... will come after dinner'

Any NP or VP may be expanded by sets or alternatives (as in English, joined by 'and', 'or', 'but', etc.):

Мама, папа и бабушка.../Mam–a, pap–a i babušk–a...
Mum NS – Dad NS – and – Grandma NS
'Mum, Dad and Grandma'

... читал громко и выразительно/... čita–l gromko i vyrazitel'no
read Past Masc – loudly – and – expressively
'(he) read loudly and expressively'

And the whole sentence may be expanded by a parenthetic word or phrase, usually expressing such attitudes as (un)certainty, relief, regret, etc., e.g. Eng *of course, perhaps, probably, (un)fortunately,* or by making a tag question, e.g. Eng *isn't it?, don't you think?.*

3.1   Features of the main types of simple sentence

(1) Declarative/affirmative. Normal order is SVO; other orders have contrastive or stylistic effect. See below on word order (section 3.4). Intonation is IK-1 (see chapter 2, section 3.6), with logical stress neutrally on the final word (marked"):

Он работает в магазине./On–ø rabota–et v magazi"n–e.
he NS – work 3ps Pres – in – shop LSm
'He works in a shop.'

(2) Negative. Negation is basically done by insertion of the negative particle *не/ne* before the verb (before other parts indicates another, contrastive, centre of the negation); *ne* is not stressed, except with the verb 'be' in the past non-Feminine; logical stress is neutrally on the verb, or on the other word after *ne*. (For other forms of negation see below, section 3.2.2.9.)

Он не работает в магазине./On-∅ ne rabo"ta–et v magazin–e.
he NS – not – work 3ps Pres – in – shop LSm
'He doesn't work in a shop.'

Он работает не в магазине, а в бюро./On–∅ rabota–et ne v
   magazi"n–e, a v bjuro.
he NS – work 3ps Pres – not – in – shop LSm – but – in – office
   (LS indecl.)
'He doesn't work in a shop, but in an office.' (> 'He works in an office,
not a shop.')

Они вчера не были на уроке./On–i včera ne" by–li na urok–e
they NP – yesterday – not – be Past Plur – at – lesson LSm
'They weren't at class yesterday.'

Added negatives, e.g. adverbs or pronouns, simply emphasise the negative,
they do not 'cancel' it as in English:

Он никогда ничего не читает./On–∅ nikogda nič–ego ne čita–et.
he NS – never – nothing GSn – not – read 3ps Pres
'He never reads a thing.'

(3) Interrogative

(a) Wh-questions have normal order, with flexibility about reversing SV: wh-
VS(O) or wh- SV(O); intonation is IK-2 (see chapter 2, section 3.6), with logical
stress neutrally on the verb:

Где вы работаете?/Gde vy rabo"ta–ete?
where – you Nom – work 2pp Pres
'Where do you work?'

(b) Yes/No questions may retain normal declarative order and be identified
only phonetically – by intonation (IK-3, see chapter 2, section 3.6) – or graphically – by '?':

Он работает в магазине?/On–∅ rabota–et v magazi"n–e?
he NS – work 3ps Pres – in – shop LS
'Does he work in a shop?'

Tag questions may colloquially be appended to this type:
правда/pravda, не правда ли/ne pravda li, не так ли/ne tak li, all meaning
'isn't that right' (Fr n'est-ce pas); more colloquial still are a/a or да/da in the
same meaning.
In the literary language the particle ли/li may be used to mark the interrogative; its position is second in the clause, following the word central to the

question, which is most often the verb, leading to inversion of S–V; intonation is still IK-3, centred on the last word:

> *Работает ли он в магазине?/Rabota–et li on–ø v magazi"n–e?*
> work 3ps Pres – Question – he NS – in – shop LSm
> 'Does he work in a shop?'

(4) Imperative. Order is (S)VO, normally 2nd Person Imperative verb form (chapter 3, section 2.2.7.1), hence no subject; use of a subject is to soften the request. Intonation is IK-2 for command/order, IK-3 for request (see chapter 2, section 3.6); use of intonation makes formal markers of softening (e.g. 'please') unnecessary; their presence is considered formal:

> *Закройте окно!/Zakro"j–te okn–o!*
> close 2pp Imper – window ASn (+IK-2)
> 'Close the window!'

> *Закройте (, пожалуйста,) окно./Zakro"j–te (, požalujsta,) okn–o.*
> close 2pp Imper – (please –) window ASn (+IK-3)
> 'Please close the window.'

(5) Exclamatory/Exclamative. Most often introduced by an interrogative pronoun (cf. Eng *what (a)* + Noun, *how* + Adj), and distinguished from the question only by intonation (IK-5, see chapter 2, section 3.6):

> *Как он (хорошо) играет!/Ka"k on–ø (xorošo) igra"–et!*
> how – he NS – (well –) play 3ps Pres
> 'How well he plays!'

3.2   The parts of the sentence

3.2.1   The subject

3.2.1.1 Formal versus logical subject. Semantically, or logically, the subject of a sentence is the person, object or concept which is the centre of the information: the performer of an action (agent), possessor of a feature or state, etc., in other words the item about which something is being said. The formal ways in which this element is indicated, however, vary widely both within and across languages, so that it is not possible to say that in an analytical language like English the subject is always the first element in the sentence (consider passive sentences, where the subject is last, preceded by 'by', or the relatively uncommon English impersonal structures like 'it seems to me', where the subject is in the indirect form); or that in an inflected language like Russian the subject is always in the Nominative case. While these statements may be valid generalisations for each language-type, they are not fixed rules. (This matter is somewhat confused by the use in English linguistics of the term 'nominative' to refer to the logical subject. Certainly it is true that the Nominative *case* in Russian may not be used for any other part of the sentence.)

For Russian, then, we may state the basic (default) situation to be as follows: nominal subjects are in the Nominative; verb subjects are in the Infinitive; and the subject comes first (the neutral order is SVO). We can now look at those situations in which the form is not the default (the topic of word order is treated separately below, section 3.4).

(1) Case of subject. All the oblique cases except Locative (Prepositional) may express the logical subject:

(a) Accusative. The use of the Accusative is limited to a few expressions of ailments, where one might say that logically the 'subject' is actually the sufferer, hence in fact the 'object':

> *Меня тошнит./Men-ja tošn-it.*
> me AS – be nauseous 3ps Pres
> 'I feel sick/nauseous.'

(b) Genitive. The Genitive is used mainly in negative and partitive contexts:

(i) In negative contexts, where the notional subject is 'absent'; this is an extension of the use of the Genitive for negativised objects (see below, section 3.2.2.9):

> *Таких стран не существует./Tak–ix stran–ø ne suščestvu–et.*
> such GP – country GPf – not – exist 3ps Pres
> 'Such countries do not exist.'

> *Писем не приходило./Pisem–ø ne prixodi–lo.*
> letter GPn – not – arrive Past Neut
> 'No letters arrived.'

(ii) In (rare and optional) partitive contexts:

> *Воды убывает./Vod–y ubyva–et.*
> water GSf – decrease 3ps Pres
> 'The water is going down.'

> But: *Вода убыла./Vod–a uby–la.*
> water NSf – decrease Pf Past Fem
> 'The water has gone down.'

(iii) In addition, a most important construction involves a preposition plus Genitive, as this is the normal way of expressing possession of physical objects:

> *У меня есть карандаш./U men–ja est' karandaš–ø.*
> next to – me GS – is 3ps Pres – pencil NSm
> 'I have a pencil.'

Compare this to the verb 'have', used only with abstract objects, e.g.:

> *Я имел возможность . . ./Ja ime–l vozmožnost'–ø . . .*
> I NS – have Impf Past Masc – possibility ASf
> 'I had the opportunity . . .'

This construction is used also for ailments:

> *У меня грипп./U men–ja gripp–ø.*
> next to – me GS – influenza NSm
> 'I have the 'flu.'

> *У меня колёт в боку./U men–ja kol–ёt v bok–u.*
> next to – me GS – jab 3ps Pres – in – side LSm
> 'I have a stitch (in the side).'

The Preposition *y/u* 'physically' expresses location (e.g. *у стола/u stol–a* 'next to the table'), including, for people, the meaning 'at someone's place' (Fr *chez*); parallel locative expressions with inanimate objects clearly cannot have a possessive meaning, but the logic is the same: 'on the table is a book' does mean 'the table has a book (on it)'; however, the fact is that animate subjects do possess, so we must interpret these as true subjects, and not just locative statements.

(c) Dative. By far the most common non-Nominative subject case, through its use in so-called 'impersonal' sentences; if they are called thus on the basis of the formal subject not being Nominative, this is a circular argument; however, there is a sense in which the true subject may be some external force. The distinction which many languages make between personal and impersonal *forms* is indicative: for example, Fr *je dois* versus *il faut que je* is based (at least formally) on the notion that the second structure implies some compulsion from outside, in which the person is not *choosing* to act; English does this less, and mainly at formal levels (*I must* versus *It is necessary that I*). Russian does it much more than most other languages, using it for all sorts of physical and psychological feelings or effects impinging upon us from outside:

> *Мне надо (нужно) было . . ./Mne nado (nužno) by–lo . . .*
> me DS – necessary Indecl (or Neut Sing) – be Past Neut
> 'I had to . . .'
> (cf. *Я должен был . . ./Ja dolžen–ø by–l . . .*
> I NS – (duty-)bound Masc Sing – be Past Masc
> 'I had to/ought to have . . .')

> *Мне было холодно./Mn-e by–lo xolodn–o.*
> me DS – be Past Neut – cold Neut Sing
> 'I was cold.'
> (cf. the distance expressed by Fr *j'ai froid* lit. 'I have cold'.)

(d) Instrumental. This is the case used for the passive expression of the subject ('by'); order is reversed as in English:

> Дом был построен моим братом./*Dom–ø by–l postrojen–ø mo–im brat–om.*
> house NSm – be Past Masc – build Past Pass NSm – my ISm – brother ISm
> 'The house was built by my brother.'

An unusual extension of this occurs when the logical subject is a natural phenomenon: the order is normally that of an active sentence, but the subject is Instrumental, the verb Active and Past Neuter (Neuter being the default form for non-agreement):

> Ветром сорвало крышу./*Vetr–om sorva–lo kryš–u.*
> wind ISm – tear off Pf Past Neut – roof ASf
> 'The wind tore off the roof.'

> Дорогу занесло (снегом)./*Dorog–u zanes–lo (sneg–om).*
> road ASf – carry off Pf Past Neut – (snow ISm) (phrase: 'block up (with snow)')
> 'The road is snowed up.'
> (The order is OV(S) because 'road' is the topic – see below.)

(2) Zero subject. Other English terms used for the 'zero' concept in syntax are 'empty' (category), 'null' and 'covert'. As done for the morphology, we use 'ø' to mark this.

(a) Personal verb. 1st and 2nd person personal pronouns may be omitted with non-past verbs, when there is no emphasis on the pronoun, since the verb form makes the person clear. In fact, this means that the subject is actually expressed, but only inside the verb; it is, thus, not a zero subject in the logical sense:

> (Я) Знаю, что он прав./*(Ja) Znaj–u, čto on–ø ø prav–ø.*
> (I) know 1ps Pres – that – he NS – (be 3ps) – right NSm short
> 'I know (that) he's right.'

(The same may be said of imperative forms, where the 2nd person pronoun is omitted in principle, as in English.)

With past-tense verbs, this is in principle not possible, since they do *not* indicate person, only number and gender, e.g. *знал/zna–l* could be 1st, 2nd or 3rd person, so the pronoun should be expressed. Only colloquially, when the context is clear, may the pronoun be omitted:

> Ты об этом знал? (Я) Знал./*Ty ob èt–om zna–l? (Ja) Zna–l.*
> you 2ps – about – this LSn – know Past Masc; (I) know Past Masc
> 'Did you know about this?' 'Yes (I did).' (lit. '(I) knew')

(b) Impersonal. A true zero subject occurs essentially with natural phenomena, especially the weather; English uses the 'introductory' 'it' or 'there':

> *Светает./ø Sveta-et.*
> (weather) – get light 3ps Pres
> 'It's getting light.'

> *Холодно./ø ø Xolodn–o.*
> (weather) – (be 3ps) – cold NSn short
> 'It's cold.'

> *Пахнет луком./ø Paxn–et luk–om.*
> (something) – (emit a) smell 3ps Pres – onion ISm
> 'There's a smell of onion.'

Another type is the generalised subject, usually in Russian a 3rd Person Singular reflexive verb or a 3rd Person Plural non-reflexive:

> *Здесь хорошо работается./Zdes' xorošo ø rabota–et–sja.*
> Here – well – (work) – work 3ps Pres Refl
> 'One can work well here.'

> *Говорят, (что)... /ø Govor–jat (čto)...*
> (they) – say 3pp Pres – (that)
> 'They say (that)...'

(3) Infinitive. We noted above that the Infinitive was the normal form for a verbal subject, but it is worth viewing a few examples to see the correlation with English. While English can use the Infinitive as a simple first-element subject (e.g. 'To work is to suffer'), it generally prefers to use the introductory 'it' and formally invert the subject and complement ('To work is essential' > 'It is essential to work'); in the spoken language this is the usual form, and even formally it is often obligatory (e.g. *'To discontinue this conversation would be best' > 'It would be best to...'). For Russian the Infinitive is normal:

> *Прекратить разговор было бы самое лучшее.*
> */Prekrati–t' razgovor–ø by–lo by sam–oe lučš–ee.*
> curtail Inf – conversation ASm – be Condit Neut – very/most
>   NSn – best NSn
> 'It would be best to discontinue this conversation.'

> *Переводить этот текст без словаря трудно.*
> */Perevodi–t' èt–ot tekst–ø bez slovar–ja ø trudn–o.*
> translate Inf – this ASm – text ASm – without – dictionary GSm –
>   (be 3ps Pres) – difficult NSn
> 'It's difficult to translate this text without a dictionary.'

The Infinitive also corresponds to an English verbal noun:

> *Курить запрещено./Kuri–t'* ∅ *zaprеščen–o.*
> smoke Inf – (be 3ps) – forbid Past Pass NSn
> 'Smoking is prohibited.'

3.2.2   The Predicate

The 'Predicate' is for some simply the verb (the more traditional view); for others the verb plus its dependent object or complement and any attached adjuncts (adverbial phrases); and for others again, including most Russian grammarians, it is the verb plus a complement only. Further, for some, 'complement' means any nominal phrase dependent on the verb, for others – only those noun phrases which follow the copula (the verb 'be' in its equational sense). Since we wish to consider these last as parts of the sentence in their own right, and also since the copula in Russian is a special case, we will adopt an approach which is essentially the Russian one, that is, we shall include under 'Predicate' those complements which are 'bound up' with the copula (what Russian grammars call the 'nominal predicate') and treat the 'Object' (after other verbs) separately, along with the adverbial modifiers. Somewhat confusingly for us, the Russian term for the Object actually means 'complement', or 'supplement' (*дополнение/do–poln–eni–e*); the term for 'Predicate' is the expected *сказуемое/skaz–uje–m–oe*, lit. 'that being said'. As for 'Complement', it is called 'the nominal (or "attached-to-the-copula") part of a compound nominal predicate'; the 'copula' is called *связка/svjazk–a*, lit. 'ligament' – that is, binding the other elements.

3.2.2.1 Finite verb. The centre of most predicates is a fully formed verb, showing at least aspect, tense, mood, voice and number, plus either person (non-past forms) or gender (past forms). The forms are the business of morphology (see chapter 3), though we will comment below on some special features. For Russian descriptions, this represents the 'simple verbal predicate'. The verbs in this role are not auxiliary or modal, both of which are normally prepositively attached (and may even be proclitic) to a full verb (like Eng *want, can*); however, the central verb is formally – in Russian as in English – in the Infinitive, thus all the particular features noted above are actually seen in the auxiliary verb; hence the full predicate must include both verbs, and is termed a 'compound verbal predicate'.

3.2.2.2 Non-finite or non-agreeing forms. In some cases the main verb either fails to indicate any of the above features or indicates only a subset.

(1) Impersonal verbs. The structure, mentioned above, of an 'impersonal' verb accompanied by a subject expressed in the Dative, means that even a non-past

verb does not express person, since it is obligatorily 3rd Person Singular; the 'person' information comes from the dative subject; otherwise these are normal verbs:

> *Мне кажется (что . . .)./Mne kaž–et–sja (čto . . .)*
> me DS – seem 3ps Pres – (that Conj)
> 'It seems to me (I think) (that) . . . '

(2) Infinitive. The Infinitive appears as a main verb with three functions.
　(a) To express a formal order or instruction addressed to no one in particular:

> *Вынести его вон!/Vynes–ti e–go von!*
> take out Inf – him ASm – (to) outside
> 'Take him out(side)!'

> *Добавить три ложки сахара./Dobav–it' tr–i ložk–i saxar–a.*
> add Inf – three – teaspoon GSf – sugar GSm
> 'Add three (tea)spoons of sugar.'

　(b) to express some inevitable future action; the person who must undergo the effect is in the Dative:

> *Всем нам умереть./Vs–em n–am umere–t'.*
> all DP – us DP – die Inf
> 'We all must die.'

> *Мне ещё ужин готовить./Mn–e eščё užin–ø gotovi–t'.*
> me DS – still Adv – dinner/supper ASm – prepare Inf
> 'I still have to prepare dinner.'

A negative particle here expresses impossibility:

> *Здесь не пройти./Zdes' ne proj–ti.*
> here – not – pass through Inf
> 'You/One can't go through here.'

In a question format, it is a request (including to self) for advice on how to act:

> *С кем мне посоветоваться?/S k–em mn–e posovetova–t'–sja?*
> with – whom IS – me DS – take advice Inf
> 'Who should/can I ask for advice?'

> *Не пойти ли мне в кино?/Ne poj–ti li mne v kino?*
> not – go Inf – Interrog. Part. – me DS – to – cinema ASn
> 'Should I (Perhaps I should) go to the cinema?'

Addition of the hypothetical particle *бы /by* (see further below on mood) gives the meaning 'ought to':

Вам бы подать заявление./V–am by poda–t' zajavleni–e.
you DP (polite Sing) – Hypothet. Part. – hand in/over Inf – application
  ASn
'You ought to apply (make an application).'

(c) A stylistically limited usage appears in folk poetry, expressing the sudden
onset of an activity:

*А царица хохотать и плечами пожимать./A caric–a xoxota–t'
i pleč–ami požima–t'.*
and – tsaritsa NSf – guffaw Inf – and – shoulder IP – shrug Inf
'And the tsaritsa (suddenly) began to laugh loudly and shrug her
  shoulders.'

(3) Imperative (when mood is not in fact Imperative). This usage is strictly
colloquial. It appears with two functions.
  (a) To express a sudden past action, usually in narration:

*Мы все сидели, а вдруг она выскочи и выбеги.
/My vs–e side–li, a vdrug on–a vyskoč–i i vybeg–i.*
we NP – all NP – sit Past Plur – and – suddenly – she NS – jump up
  Imper 2ps – and – run out Imperative 2ps
'We were all sitting (there), and suddenly she jumped up and ran out.'

  (b) To express an undesirable but necessary activity:

*Он себе спит, а мать работай за него./On–ø seb–e sp–it, a
mat'–ørabota–j za ne–go.*
he NSm – self DS – sleep 3ps Pres – and – mother NSf – work Imper
  2ps – for – him ASm
'He spends all his time sleeping, while his mother has to work
  for him.'

The addition of the particle *бы/by* makes the Imperative form into a subordinate hypothetical conditional clause (see below, section 4.2.5.6).

(4) Verbal root (bare stem). Again a rare form, restricted to colourful narration;
the form is the bare verb stem, with no ending, thus visually more like a noun,
the meaning a sudden sound or movement:

Кто-то стук в дверь./Kto-to stuk–ø v dver'–ø.
someone NS – knock Vb stem – on – door ASf
'Someone banged (went 'knock') on the door.'

Собака хвать его за ногу./Sobak–a xvat'–ø e–go za nog–u.
dog NSf – grab Vb stem – him ASm – by – leg ASf
'The dog (suddenly) grabbed him by the leg.'

(5) Existential 'be'. We shall see below that the copula (equational 'be') is virtually always omitted in the present tense. Existential 'be' (mainly 'be somewhere', as opposed to 'be something') is also normally omitted in the Present:

> *В комнате старый диван./V komnat–e φ star–yj divan–φ.*
> in – room LSf – old NSm – settee NSm
> 'In the room (there) is an old settee.'

This is not the case in the Past:

> *В комнате был старый диван./V komnat–e by–l star–yj divan–φ.*
> in – room LSf – be Past Masc – old NSm – settee NSm
> 'In the room (there) is an old settee.'

The remnant 3rd Person Singular Present form *есть/est'* may be used in the sense 'exist', that is, where existence is being emphasised:

> *Есть люди, которые . . . /Est' l'ud–i, kotor–yje . . .*
> be 3ps – people NP – who NP
> 'There are people who . . . '

And this is where the odd impersonal possessive construction (mentioned above in relation to the subject) belongs, since it is precisely emphasising existence.

> *У меня есть карандаш./U men–ja est' karandaš–φ.*
> next to – me GS – be 3ps Pres – pencil NSm
> 'I have a pencil.'

This construction is especially interesting in that it does not occur in any other Slavonic language; it seems likely that it has entered Russian through Finnic contact. There is a negative version of both of these *est'* constructions, denying the existence of the given item. Examples of this will be given below (section 3.2.2.8), since it involves another case issue.

3.2.2.3 Agreement (concord) between Subject and Verb. The basic agreement between subject and verb is as expected, namely:

Non-past:

- personal pronouns require a verb in the appropriate person and number;
- nouns (and nominal phrases) require verbs in 3rd person and appropriate number;

Past:

- both personal pronouns and nouns require a verb in the appropriate gender and number; for pronouns the gender is natural (by sex), for nouns grammatical.

We comment here on cases of unexpected or exceptional agreement.

(1) Gender. Personal nouns usually have the same natural and grammatical gender – assuming that we allow Class II nouns (those with the ending *–a* in the NS) to be Masculine as well as Feminine, which accounts for the large number of affectionate male personal names (*Kol–ja*, etc.); beyond that, there are a very few native forms which are unexpected (e.g. Class II Neuter for male persons), but the exceptions are almost all foreign words, where the declension type may not match the gender expectation; for all of these, the natural gender determines the agreement.

(We should note that gender agreement between the parts of a noun phrase involving foreign roots may present more problems, e.g. Class I Common nouns must have a masculine attribute, e.g. *nov–yj direktor–ø* covers both male and female incumbents: 'the new director/headmaster/headmistress'; **nov–aja direktor–ø* is still not acceptable in the standard.)

For animals, the formal class determines the gender agreement, even where the non-sex-specific form is Class II; thus *собака/sobak–a* 'dog' and *кошка/košk–a* 'cat' are both grammatically feminine, and demand a feminine verb even though they are the general terms for these animals (in each case there is a sex-specific parallel form which is regarded as technical, similarly to Eng *bitch*). For indeclinable names of foreign animals the default gender is masculine (e.g. *кенгуру убежал/kenguru ubeža–l* 'the kangaroo ran off').

For inanimate indeclinables, the gender is that of the (or 'a') perceived class term, e.g. *сирокко/sirokko* 'the Sirocco' is masculine as a type of *ветер/veter–ø* 'wind'; *Баку/Baku* is masculine as a kind of *город/gorod–ø* 'town', etc.; if no such class term can be perceived, the default gender is neuter, e.g. *такси/taksi* 'taxi' is officially neuter, though in substandard usage it may be masculine, based on *автомобиль/avtomobil'–ø* 'automobile/car' (more formal) or feminine based on *машина/mašin–a* 'car' (less formal).

Abbreviations take their gender from the head word, at least if that is known to a speaker – which it is less and less often; if it is an acronym it may take its gender from its shape and the associated declension class (e.g. *МИД/MID* 'Ministry of Internal Affairs' is officially neuter from the head word *ministerstv–o*, but colloquially masculine from its shape as a Class I Masculine word. Speakers may guess at a class term and apply that gender rather than simply follow the form.

Similarly, with compound forms or nouns in apposition with different genders, speakers look for the most central, general class word for gender, e.g. *музей-квартира/muzej-kvartir–a* 'museum-apartment' is masculine, since it is in fact now a museum, and only a former apartment, in other words 'museum' is the semantic class, 'apartment' an attribute.

(2) Number. There are two situations where the agreement of number is not straightforward:

(a) Collective subject. As in English (and no doubt most languages with distinctive number), there is hesitation between the formal and logical expectations with collective subjects: where the subject is formally singular, speakers often feel it to be plural (e.g. Eng *the Government, the majority*):

> *Человечество идёт вперёд./Člověčestv–o id–ёt vperёd.*
> mankind NS – go 3ps̲ Pres – forward
> 'Mankind is advancing (lit. moving forward).'

– where the singular is not unexpected, given the slogan-like formality of the subject and the whole expression;

> *Большинство дыло/проголосовало «за»./Bol' šinstv–o by–lo*
> */progolosova–lo 'za'.*
> majority NSn– be/vote Past Neut Sing̲ – 'for'
> 'The majority were/voted "for".'

A plural verb here would be substandard. However, if a plural noun specifying the corpus is appended, a plural verb becomes more likely:

> *Большинство делегатов проголосовало/–ли «за».*
> */Bol' šinstv–o delegat–ov progolosova–lo/–li 'za'.*
> majority NS – delegate GP – vote Pf Past Neut Sing̲/Past Plur̲ – 'for'
> 'The majority of the delegates were/voted "for".'

(English, for the same reason, would be less likely to use the singular 'was' here).

(b) Numeral Subject. Similarly, where the subject is an unqualified cardinal numeral, the verb is singular (as in English), since the numeral is perceived as a 'digit':

> *Восемь делится на два./Vosem'–ø del–it–sja na dv–a.*
> eight NS – divide 3ps Refl. – into – two A(S)
> 'Eight is divisible by two.'

When there is a specified noun, that is, when we have a nominal phrase involving a numeral, where the noun is normally in the Genitive Plural, the verb will typically be plural if it *follows* the noun (subject), but singular if it *precedes*; in other words the nature of what precedes the verb is important, and this is determined in principle by the topic and comment operative in the sentence:

> *Пять человек стояли около входа./Pjat'–ø čelovek–ø stoja–li*
> *okolo vxod–a.*
> five N(S) – person GP – stand Impf Past Plur̲ – at/near – entrance GSm
> '(The) five people were standing at the entrance.'

*Около входа стояло пять человек./Okolo vxod–a stoja–lo
pjat'–ø čelovek–ø.*
at/near – entrance GSm – stand Impf Past Neut <u>Sing</u>– five N(S) –
person GP
'Five people were standing at the entrance.' ('There were . . . standing . . . ')

(The difference in order is produced by different topics and comments.)

This same principle adheres also with vaguer quantifying subjects (e.g.
'many', 'several' etc.):

На улице играло много детей./Na ulic–e igra–lo mnogo det–ej.
in – street LSf – play Impf Past Neut <u>Sing</u>– many Adv – children GP
'A lot of children were playing in the street.'

Прошло несколько лет./Proš–lo neskol'ko let–ø.
pass Past Neut <u>Sing</u>– several Adv – year GP
'Several years passed.'

The fact is that almost always such numerical subjects are the comment of
a sentence, thus normally come last in Russian, which means the singular is
actually the typical pattern. Where their *topic* status is emphasised, e.g. by a
demonstrative, they will normally come first and the verb be plural:

*Эти пять лет прошли очень быстро./Èt–i pjat'–ø let–ø proš–li
očen' bystro.*
this NP – five N(S) – year GP – pass Pf Past <u>Plur</u>– very – quickly
'These five years have passed very quickly.'

Even if they do not come first, but are clearly the topic, the verb will be plural:

*Выступили все пять делегатов./Vystupi–li vs–e pjat'–ø
delegat–ov.*
perform Pf Past Plur – all NP – five N(S) – delegate GP
'All five delegates spoke/gave a talk.'

(See further below, section 3.4, on topic and comment.)

3.2.2.4 Voice

(1) Reflexive/middle. Reflexive, or middle, voice is essentially a morphological
issue, since the central form is the formal 'reflexive' verb, with its suffix *–ся/-
sja* (see chapter 3, section 2.2.8.1); it is really only in contrastive or emphatic
reflexive contexts that the (full) reflexive pronoun is used:

Он себя любит./On seb–ja ljub–it.
he NS – self AS – love 3ps Pres
'He loves himself.'

Он любит других больше, чем себя./On ljub–it drug–ix bol′še,
čem seb–ja.
he NS – love 3ps Pres – other AP – more – than – self AS
'He loves others more than himself.'

The difference between the full pronoun and the suffix is best seen with a verb like *считать/sčitat′* 'count/consider': used with the pronoun, it is an active verb with an object, meaning 'consider oneself' (cf. Fr *se croire*), e.g.:

Он считает себя гением./On sčita–et seb–ja geni–em.
he NS – consider 3ps Pres – self AS – genius ISm
'He considers himself a genius.'

Used with the suffix, its meaning is Passive:

Он считается гением./On sčita–et–sja geni–em.
he NS – consider 3ps Refl/Pass – genius ISm
'He is considered a genius.'

The simple (or 'true') reflexive use of the suffix is relatively rare, occurring only in verbs like 'wash (oneself)' (*мыться/myt′–sja*) (and other verbs of bodily treatment) or 'go up/ascend' (*подниматься/podnimat′–sja*).

(2) Passive. Russian has several ways of expressing passive voice, only one of which is parallel to the common European format – the verb 'be' plus a passive participle ('be + –en'). The following passive types are roughly ordered by frequency, though stylistic questions are always relevant. The aspect of the verb is also relevant in that certain structures are usable only in one or other aspect. It should be noted that a formal view of 'passive voice' includes only those of the following which show a formal non-active marker, that is, a participle (a) or the reflexive suffix (b); some would further accept (d) and (e), but few perhaps would include word order (c); we include it on the grounds that inverted word order (OVS) is functionally the semantic equivalent to a passive – and is normally translated thus in English.

(a) Passive participles. The construction with a passive participle, parallel to English, is more typical of written style; formally the participle involved is the past passive of a perfective verb (with suffix –*n*– or –*t*–, see chapter 3, section 2.2.9.1) *in its short form* (see below, section 3.2.2.8, on the form of adjectives after the copula); the tense of the copula relates to the point of time referred to by the overall statement: the Present copula (formally ∅) refers to a present state (like a perfect tense), the Past to a past state (like a simple past tense or a pluperfect):

Этот дом построен моим братом./Èt–ot dom–∅ ∅ postro–en–∅
mo–im brat–om.

this NSm – house NSm – (be 3ps Pres) – build Past Pass Part NSm
Short – my ISm – brother ISm

'This house was built by my brother.' (lit. 'has been built' –
completion/resulting state relates to the present)

*Этот дом был построен Петром первым./Èt–ot dom–∅ by–l
postro–en–∅ Petr–om perv–ym.*

this NSm – house NSm – be 3ps Past Masc – build Past Pass Part NSm
Short – Peter ISm – first ISm

'This house was built by Peter the Great.' (completion relates to
the past)

Attributive (long) forms of these participles represent underlying attributive
passive clauses (see below, section 4.2.4(4)).

(b) Reflexive verb. The formal reflexive verb has many functions, of which
the passive is perhaps the most common; in principle only imperfective verbs
are possible here, certainly when an agent is made explicit:

*Этот дом строится моим братом./Èt–ot dom–∅ stro–it–sja
mo–im brat–om.*

this NSm – house NSm – build 3ps Pres Refl – my ISm – brother ISm

'This house is being built by my brother.'

Как пишется это слово?/Kak piš–et–sja èt–o slov–o?

how – write 3ps Pres Refl – this NSn – word NSn

'How is that word written/spelt?'

This example, in which no subject is expressed, shows rather the middle-
reflexive function; for the other main functions of the reflexive form, see
chapter 3, section 2.2.8.1.

(c) Word order. Since one effect of the passive voice is to make a logical
subject (especially an agent) into a comment, and since the natural position of
the comment is the final position, the order OVS is the logical equivalent of a
passive construction; languages like English, which have no formal markers of
S and O, are forced to mark the relationships in analytical ways (e.g. Eng *be* +
participle (*-en*) + *by*), but inflectional languages, such as most of the Slavonic
group, do not need such extra markers: the order $N_{Acc} + V_{Act} + N_{Nom}$ indicates
that the last noun is the agent and that it is the comment of the sentence (and
its form indicates that it is the subject):

*Этот дом построил мой брат./Èt–ot dom–∅ postroi–l moj–∅
brat–∅.*

this ASm – house ASm – build Pf Past Masc – my NSm – brother NSm

'This house was built by my brother.'

Either aspect is possible: *строил/stroi–l* (Impf Past Masc) gives the meaning 'was being built' (e.g. when the action was interrupted).

This construction is therefore not possible – or at least not selected – where the N_{Acc} and N_{Nom} forms are not distinctive or distinguishable, for example with inanimate Masculine nouns or Class III Feminine nouns, where the above shape must be interpreted as SVO:

> *Мать любит дочь./Mat'–ø ljub–it doč–ø.*
> mother NS (=AS) – love 3ps Pres – daughter AS (= NS)
> 'The mother loves her daughter.'

(d) 3rd Person Plural. Where the agent is unknown (or at least not made explicit), but is clearly human, the 3rd Person Plural (either aspect) may be used *without a pronoun*; this is found mainly in spoken style:

> *Этот дом строили три года./Èt–ot dom–ø stroi–li tr–i god–a.*
> this ASm – house ASm – build Impf Past Plur – three A(S) – year GS
> 'They took three years to build this house.' (lit. '...were building...
>   for three years')

> *Этот дом построили три года назад./Èto–t dom–ø postroi–li*
>   *tr–i god–a nazad.*
> this ASm – house ASm – build Pf Past Plur – three A(S) – year GS –
>   ago
> 'This house was built three years ago.'

(e) Past Neuter (Singular). Where the explicit agent is inanimate, normally a force of nature, the Past Neuter form is used (see also above, section 3.2.1.1), normally Perfective only, as relating a single action and its result:

> *Крышу сорвало ветром./Kryš–u sorva–lo vetr–om.*
> roof ASf – tear off Pf Past Neut – wind ISm
> 'The roof was torn off by the wind.'

3.2.2.5 Mood. The expression of the basic moods – Indicative and Imperative – is straightforward (with the appropriate morphological forms as seen in chapter 3). Of some syntactic interest is the expression of the Hypothetical or Subjunctive moods, in that it involves the separable clitic particle *бы/by* (a remnant of the lost Aorist tense of 'be'), along with the past tense form (formerly a participle itself used in compound verb forms). The most frequent usage of this particle is in the expression of the Hypothetical Conditional, where it appears in both halves of the conditional sentence (protasis and apodosis); we will deal with this structure below (section 4.2.5.6), as a type of complex sentence, and there, too, belong clauses introduced by verbs of wishing (e.g. 'I want you to...'), commanding (e.g. 'I told him to...'), fearing ('I'm afraid he might...') and doubting ('I doubt that he...').

Here we note only the relatively uncommon appearance of this particle in simple sentences, where it may express such subjunctive meanings as 'desirability' ('should (have)', 'ought to (have)', 'if only', etc.); its normal position is after the verb, though it may also appear as second word in the sentence (or clause) when this is central to the meaning; note that no tense is expressed in this form, since the 'past' form is obligatory (and not actually past), so that tense must, if at all, be expressed by adverbial means:

> *Я с удовольствием пошёл бы в кино./Ja s udovol'stvi–em poš–ël by v kino.*
> I NS – with – pleasure ISn – go Pf Past Masc – (Subjve) – to – cinema
> 'I would really like to go to the cinema.'

> *Вы бы написали родителям./Vy by napisa–li roditel–jam.*
> you NP/polite Sing – (Subjve) – write Pf Past Plur – parents DP
> 'You should write/have written to your parents.'

3.2.2.6 Expansions of the simple verb. Extra elements added to the verb usually have an expressive function, and are thus normally stylistically restricted to spoken or colourful literary levels. The two most used in Russian are particles and verbal reinforcers.

(1) Particles. The two most frequent particles – which are both stylistically neutral – are those used in 1st and 3rd Person Imperatives.

(a) давай(me)/davaj(–te) (formally the 2nd Person Singular (or 2nd Person Plural) Imperative of *давать/davat'* Impf 'give') is preposed before either the Infinitive or 1st Person Plural Future of an Imperfective verb or the 1st Person Plural Future of a Perfective verb, to give the 1st Person Imperative ('let us . . . '); the singular form is used when the other person is on *ty* terms with the speaker (see chapter 7, section 5.1.1), the plural when they are on *vy* terms or when more than one other person is involved:

> *Давайте играть (будем играть) в шахматы.*
> */Davaj–te igra–t' (bud–em igra–t') v šaxmat–y.*
> let (2pp Imper) – play Impf Inf (1pp Fut) – at – chess AP
> 'Let's play some chess.'

> *Давайте сыграем в шахматы./Davaj–te sygra–em v š axmat–y.*
> let (2pp Imper) – play Pf 1pp Fut – at – chess AP
> 'Let's have a game of chess.'

(b) пусть/pust' (formally a deviant form (different stress) of the 2nd Person Singular Imperative of *пустить/pustit'* Pf 'let, allow') is preposed before the subject (which may be zero if pronominal) to give the 3rd Person Imperative; a

more colloquial variant is *пускай/puskaj* (formally 2nd Person Singular Imperative of *пускать/puskat'* Impf 'let, allow'); the verb is 3rd Person Imperfective Present or Perfective Future:

> *Пусть Ваня/он сам это сделает./Pust' Van–ja/on–ø sam–ø*
> *èt–o sdela–et.*
> let – Vanya/he NS – self NSm – this ASn – do Pf 3ps Fut
> 'Let Vanya/him do it himself.'

> *Пусть (он) читает, если хочет./Pust' (on–ø) čita–et, jesli (on–ø)*
> *xoč–et.*
> let – (he NS) – read 3ps Pres – if – want 3ps Pres
> 'Let him read if he wants (to).'

A third particle is an intensifier added to the basic 2nd person forms: *смотри (те)/smotri(–te)* (formally the 2nd Person Imperative of *смотреть/smotret'* Impf 'look') is added to a negative 2nd Person Imperative to emphasise a 'warning' (cf. Eng *see that you don't*):

> *Смотри не опаздывай./Smotri ne opazdyvaj–ø.*
> look/see 2ps Imper – not – be late Impf 2ps Imper
> 'See that you're not late (ever).'

> *Смотри не упади!/Smotri ne upad–i!*
> look/see – not – fall Pf 2ps Imper
> 'Be careful not to fall!'

Two particles add a temporal dimension to an Indicative verb.

(a) бывало/byvalo (formally Past Neuter of *бывать/byvat'* 'be' Iterative) is added in parentheses either in first place in the clause (before the subject) or before the verb; the verb is Present or Past Imperfective, or Perfective Future; the meaning is always past frequentative (the Perfective implies that each action was complete, usually in a sequence – which it may do on its own in similar contexts):

> *Бывало, он сидит и смотрит на неё./Byvalo, on–ø sid–it i*
> *smotr–it na n–её.*
> (Frequentative) – he –sit 3ps Pres – and – look 3ps Pres – at – her ASf
> 'He would sit looking/gazing at her.'

> *Бывало, он звонил нам каждый день./Byvalo, on–ø zvoni–l n–am*
> *každ–yj den'–ø*
> (Frequentative) – he – ring Impf Past Masc Sing – us DP – each
> ASm – day ASm
> 'He was in the habit of ringing us every day.'

Бывало, приду после такой работы домой и даже есть не могу.
/Byvalo, prid–u posle tak–oj rabot–y domoj i daže jest' ne mog–u.
(Frequentative) – come Pf 1ps Fut – after – such GSf – work GSf –
    home Adv – and – even – eat Impf Inf – not – be able 1ps Pres
    'I would often come home after work like that and not even be able to
    eat.'

(b) было/bylo (formally Past Neuter of *быть/byt'* 'be') is added usually after
the verb, but also before; the verb is Perfective Past; the meaning is failure to
carry out or complete the action (Eng *was about to...*, *but...*), or to cancel or
reverse it immediately (Eng *had just begun to...*, *when...*):

Я было поправился, но вдруг... /Ja bylo popravi–l–sja, no vdrug...
I NS – (cancellation) – get better/recover Pf Past Masc – but – suddenly
    'I was on the point of recovery, when suddenly...'

Она запела было, но вдруг замолчала./On–a zape–la bylo, no
    vdrug zamolča–la.
she NS – begin to sing Pf Past Fem – (cancellation) – but – suddenly–
    fall silent Pf Past Fem
    'She had just started singing, but suddenly stopped.'

One particle which adds intensity and criticism by the speaker is *себе/sebe*
(formally Dative Singular of the reflexive pronoun); it is added before the verb:

Он себе спит./On–ø sebe sp–it.
he NS – (intensive) – sleep 3ps Pres
    'He's fast asleep.'

Он себе идёт вперёд./On–ø sebe id–ёt vperёd.
he NS – (intensive + neg) – go 3ps Pres – forward Adv
    'He just goes right ahead.'

(2) Reinforcing verbs. Two verbs are commonly used colloquially as intensi-
fiers/reinforcers, taking the same inflection as the main verb; one is accompanied
by conjunctions, the other not.

(a) взять да/и/да и//vzjat' da/i/ da i (lit. 'take and') (*da* is a colloquial variant
of *i* 'and') emphasises suddenness or spontaneity (cf. Eng *up and...*):

Он взял да убежал./On–ø vzja–l da ubež a–l.
he NS – (suddenly) – run away Pf Past Masc
    'He up(ped) and ran off.'

Он возьмёт и напишет обо всём отцу./On–ø voz'm–ёt i napiš–et
    obo vs–ёm otc–u
He NS – (immediately) – write Pf 3ps Fut – about – all LSn – father
    DS
    'He'll write straight away to father about all this.'

(b) *пойти/pojti* (Pf 'go'); emphasises purpose (cf. Eng *go and...*, or rather Amer Eng *go...*, since there is no 'and' in the Russian version):

> *Пойду скажу ему обо всём./Pojd–u skaž–u e–mu obo vs–ёm.*
> go Pf 1ps Fut – say/tell Pf 1ps Fut – him DS – about – all LSn
> 'I'll go (and) tell him all about it.'

> *Пойдём посмотрим новый фильм./Pojd–ёm posmotr–im nov–yj*
> *fil'm–ø.*
> go Pf 1pp Imper – look Pf 1pp Imper – new ASm – film ASm
> 'Let's go (and) see the new film.'

3.2.2.7 Compound verbal predicates (VP = V + V$_{Inf}$). Compound verbal predicates (in Russian grammatical terminology) are those verb phrases in which the main verb appears in the infinitive and is preceded by an auxiliary verb showing the necessary agreement. Such auxiliary verbs are in Russian primarily modal or phasal, since Russian has virtually no temporal (tense) auxiliaries (like Eng *have, had, was*, etc.).

(1) Modal verbs. Here belongs any auxiliary expressing the speaker's attitude towards the main verb; the principle ones are 'can', 'want' and 'must'. Russian does not have any choice in the Infinitive shape (like Eng *want/ought to* versus 'can/must *ø*'), but it does have a similar range of modal forms (including the '*be* + Adj' shape), and the shapes do not always coincide.

 (a) Finite verbs include *мочь/moč′* 'be able/can' (Fr *pouvoir*), *уметь/umet′* 'be able/can' (Fr *savoir*), *хотеть/xotet′* 'want':

> *Я очень хотел пойти в театр./Ja očen′ xote–l poj–ti v teatr–ø.*
> I NS – very much Adv – want Impf Past Masc – go Pf Inf – to – theatre
> ASm
> 'I really wanted to go to the theatre.'

> *Я не могу идти с вами./Ja ne mog–u id–ti s v–ami.*
> I NS – not – can 1ps Pres – go Impf Inf – with – you IP
> 'I can't go with you.'

> *Он не умеет плавать./On–ø ne ume–et plava–t′.*
> he NS – not – can 3ps Pres – swim Impf Inf
> 'He can't swim.'

 (b) '*be* + Adj' shapes include the short adjectival forms *должен/dolž(e)n–ø* 'must/ought/should' (Fr *devoir*) (see below on 'be'):

> *Цены должны быть гибкими./Cen–y ø dolžn–y by–t′ gibk–imi.*
> price NP – (be 3pp Pres) – ought NP – be Inf – flexible IP
> 'Prices ought to/should be flexible.'

(c) In *impersonal* constructions the logical subject is Dative, the verb 'be' and the modal an indeclinable form; these forms include *можно/možno* 'may' (cf. Eng *it is possible/permitted to*), *нельзя/nel'zja* 'may not', *надо/nado* 'must', *нужно/nužno* 'must/need to' (cf. Fr *il (me) faut*, Eng *it is necessary (for me) to*); the Dative Subject pronoun may be omitted when the logical subject is clear from the context:

> *Можно (мне) пойти с вами?/ Možno ∅ (mn–e) poj–ti s v–ami?*
> possible/permitted – (be 3ps Pres) – (I DS) – go Pf Inf – with – you IP
> 'May I go with you?'

> *Нет, нельзя./Net, nel'zja ∅.*
> no – (you DP) – not permitted – (be 3ps Pres)
> 'No, you may not.'

> *Мне надо идти./Mn–e nado ∅ id–ti.*
> me DS – necessary – (3ps Pres) – go Impf Inf
> 'I must go.'

A variant uses an invariable 3rd Person Singular finite (usually reflexive) form, e.g. *приходиться/prixod–it'–sja* 'have to', *следует/sledu–et* 'must/ought':

> *Мне придётся скоро вернуться домой./Mn–e prid–ёt–sja skoro*
> *vernu–t'–sja domoj.*
> me DS – be necessary 3ps Pf Fut – soon Adv – return Pf Inf – home
> Adv
> 'I'll have to go back home soon.'

(2) 'Semi-modal' verbs. Verbs which add a comment or qualification about the speaker's attitude towards a virtually obligatory main verb function in the same way, though they are not strictly modal, since they contain a major lexical component, and not normally classified separately; such verbs are those meaning 'intend', 'hope', 'be afraid', 'be glad', 'be ready', 'be used to' and the like; for the sake of a name, we call them 'semi-modal'. The same range of structures is available:

(a) Finite verbs, e.g. *любить/ljubit'* 'like', *надеяться/nadejat'–sja* 'hope', *стараться/starat'–sja* 'try':

> *Я очень люблю ходить по снегу./Ja očen' ljub–lju xodi–t' po*
> *sneg–u.*
> I NS – very much – like 1ps Pres – walk Impf/Indet Inf – through –
> snow DS
> 'I love walking in the snow.'

(b) '*be* + Adj', e.g. *рад/rad–∅* 'glad', *готов/gotov–∅* 'ready', *намерен/ namer(e)n–∅* 'intend':

Я очень рад познакомиться с вами./Ja očen' ф rad–ф poznakomi–
t'–sja s v–ami.
I NS – (be 1ps Pres) – very – glad/happy – meet Pf Inf – with – you IP
'I'm very happy to make your acquaintance.'

(c) Reflexive impersonal, e.g. *нравится/nrav–it–sja* 'like' (cf. Eng *it gives*
me pleasure to):

Ей не нравится танцевать./Ej ne nrav–it–sja tanceva–t'.
she DS – not – please 3ps Pres – dance Impf Inf
'She doesn't like dancing.'

Most of the above (in (1) and (2)) may function also as transitive verbs taking
a nominal object/complement (see below, section 3.2.2.9); those which may not,
which must be followed by an Infinitive, are: *moč'* (cf. also Eng *can*), *nadejat'sja*
(cf. also Eng *hope*) and all of (b) (also Eng). Some of the impersonal group in
(c) may take a logical object (cf. Eng 'need', 'like'), which will formally be
Nominative in Russian (see below, section 3.2.2.9).

(3) Phrasal. Similar 'V + V$_{\text{Inf}}$' phrases can describe some point in the action of
the main (infinitival) verb, e.g. 'begin' (*начинать/načinat'*, *стать/stat'* Pf),
'finish' (*кончать/končat'*, *переставать/perestavat'*, *бросать/brosat'*), 'continue' (*продолжать/prodolžat'*); the aspect of the Infinitive is always Imperfective, as it is seen as the action in general, with the overall aspect of the
particular event shown in the auxiliary:

Он начал (продолжал, кончил) укладываться.
/On–ф nača–l (prodolža–l, konči–l) ukladyvat'–sja.
he NS – begin Pf (continue Impf, finish Pf) (all Past Masc) – pack
   Impf Inf
'He began (continued, finished) packing.'

Of this group, all but *stat'* and *perestavat'* can take a noun object (e.g. 'begin
the lesson'); *prodolžit'* Pf is used here, while the Impf *prodolžat'* is normal with
infinitives.

3.2.2.8 Compound nominal Predicate (VP = V + NP). A distinction is normally made between verb phrases made up of 'verb plus object' – where the
object is, as it were, external to the subject, being 'acted upon' independently,
and those made up of 'verb + complement' – where the complement, as the
name should suggest, is an extension of the subject itself, another way of seeing or expressing, or adding information about, the subject. (We say 'should',
because this distinction is lost terminologically in the approach which unites
both object and complement under 'complement', or even 'complementiser'.)
In the latter case, the verb means essentially 'be', that is, it simply forms an

equational sentence joining the two views of the subject. This is the type of verb known as the 'copula'. We consider this type first, what Russian grammatical tradition calls a 'compound nominal predicate'.

(1) The copula. The simplest form of the copula is the verb 'be', as in English sentences like 'John is a student.' In sentences like 'John is at home', 'is' is 'locational', and in ones like 'There is a book on the table', it is 'existential'; neither of these cases of 'is' is 'equational'. The Russian verb *быть/byt′* serves all of these functions, as does 'be' in English, but with a small, but important, formal difference between the first two and the last. The principle may be stated thus: the Present of *byt′* is defective, and is usually zero in all forms; but in the existential sense, it has an invariable form, *jest′*. We shall consider the non-copular types below; for the moment let us concentrate on the copula.

The Past of *byt′* is formed regularly from the Infinitive stem: *был, была, было, были/by–l, by–la, by–lo, by–li*; the Future has the stem *буд–/bud–* and has the form of the Present of a Class I verb (*буду/bud–u, будешь/bud–eš′*, etc.; see chapter 3, section 2.2.6.1). Thus, for example:

> *Иван студент. Иван будет студентом. Иван был студентом.*
> */Ivan–ø ø student. Ivan–ø bud–et student–om. Ivan–ø by–l student
> –om.*
>
> Ivan NS – (be 3ps Pres) – student NS
>   – be 3ps Fut – student IS
>   – be Past Masc – student IS
> 'Ivan is (will be, was) a student.'

(See (4) below on the reasons for the use of the Instrumental; for the moment note that only the Nominative may follow the zero Present.)

There are a further two forms which may be regarded as copular forms equivalent to *byt′*.

(a) The suffixed form *бывать/by–va–t′*, with the extra meaning 'frequentative':

> *Осенью погода бывает дождливая. /Osen′–ju pogod–a by–va–et
> doždliv–aja.*
> in autumn Adv – weather NSf – be Freq 3ps Pres – rainy NSf
> 'In autumn the weather is always rainy.'

(b) The verb *являться/javljat′–sja*, used in formal written style:

> *Москва является столицей России./Moskv–a javlja–et–sja
> stolic–ej Rossi–i.*
> Moscow NS – be 3ps Pres – capital ISf – Russia GSf
> 'Moscow is the capital of Russia.'

There are various other verbs used in particular semantic contexts which are often treated as copulas (and are translatable by 'be'), however they usually have some additional content:

состоять/*sostojat′*, with the meaning of 'be a constituent', e.g. *состоять членом*/*sostojat′ člen–om* 'be a member'

доводиться/*dovodit′sja* 'be related as', e.g. *доводиться племянник-ом*/*dovodit′sja plemjannik–om* 'be a/someone's nephew'

работать/*rabotat′* 'be working as': *работать шофёром*/*rabotat′ šofër–om* 'be (employed as) a driver'

Lastly, there is a group of verbs expressing a change (or explicit non-change) of state or of appearance, e.g. 'become', 'remain', 'seem (to be)', 'be considered'; Russian grammar refers to these variously as 'copulas', 'semi-copulas' (semi-copulative verbs) or 'semi-independent verbs' (meaning 'not of full semantic value'):

Ваня хочет стать (быть) учителем./*Vanja xoč–et sta–t′ (byt′) učitel–em.* Vanya NS – want 3ps Pres – become Pf Inf – (*or* be Impf Inf) – teacher ISm
'Vanya wants to become (be) a teacher.'

(Note that *byt′* can be substituted for *stat′* in the meaning of 'become' (cf. English also).)

Он считается гением./*On–∅ sčita–et–sja geni–em.* he NS – be considered 3ps Pres – genius ISm
'He is considered a genius.'

It will be noted from all the above examples that the standard case for the complement of all copulative verbs other than *by(va)t′* is Instrumental, no matter the tense. This derives from the Instrumental's meaning of 'in the capacity of', that is, it expresses an attribute. In these cases there is no choice, but in (4) below we shall see the availability of this case to express something different from the Nominative.

(2) Locational and existential 'be'

(a) Locational. Sentences like 'The book's on the floor', where the comment is a location and the topic nominal, follow the English pattern: the copula is the verb *быть*/*byt′*, zero in the Present:

Книга на полу./*Knig–a ∅ na pol–u.* book NSf – (be 3ps Pres) – on – floor LSm
'The book is on the floor.'

However, more commonly in this type a more specific verb of position is used, in this case 'be lying' (as opposed to, say, 'be standing on a shelf'):

> *Книга лежит на полу./Knig–a lež–it na pol–u.*
> book NSf – lie 3ps Pres – on – floor LSm
> 'The book is (lying) on the floor.'

Past and future tenses have the full verb:

> *Книга была (лежала) на полу./Knig–a by–la (leža–la) na pol–u.*
> book NSf – be (lie) Impf Past Fem – on – floor LSm
> 'The book was (lying) on the floor.'

(b) Existential (есть/est'). As mentioned above (section 3.2.2.2), where the copula is itself the comment, that is, where the existence of something is being specified, the Present uses the non-zero invariable form *есть/est'*, while the Past and Future are in their normal forms (of *byt'*). Other than the impersonal construction for possession (*у меня есть x/u menja est' x* 'I have an *x*', where '*x*' is Nominative; see above, section 3.2.1.1), the most common context for this form is in sentences where the presence of something in a particular location is being specified; the topic of the sentence is thus the location phrase, the comment the '*be* + subject' phrase, with the subject primary (and bearing the logical stress); English does this with the introductory 'there (is/are)...' (as do most European languages, e.g. Fr *Il y a un livre sur la table*, Ital *C'è un libero sulla tavola*):

> *На столе есть книга./Na stol–e est' kni"g–a.*
> on – table LSm – be 3ps Pres – book NSf
> 'There's a book on the table.'

As an unprovoked statement, the verb, as in the simple locational context above, may also be a positional verb:

> *На столе лежит книга./Na stol–e lež–it kni"g–a.*
> on – table LSm – lie 3ps Pres – book NSf
> 'There's a book on the table.'

However, if the context is provoked by the question:

> *На столе есть книга?/Na stol–e e"st' knig–a?*
> on – table LSm – be 3ps Pres (logical stress) – book NSf
> 'Is there a book on the table?'

... where the positional verb is unlikely since the issue is one of existence, then the short natural response will likewise be:

> *Есть./Est'* 'Yes (, there is).'

... or, in the negative:

> *Нету./Netu.* 'No (, there's not).'

(*Netu* is derived from OR *ne e(st′) tu*; 'there is not here', used colloquially for emphatic negation and in the short answer.) The normal negative form of *est′* is *нет/net* (derived from OR *ne est′*) plus the *Genitive* of the object whose existence is denied:

> *На столе нет книги. (Книги нет(у) на столе.)*
> */Na stol–e ne″t knig–i. (Knig–i ne″t(u) na stol–e.)*
> on–table LSm–not + be 3ps Pres–book GSf
> 'There isn't a book on the table.'

An interesting extension of the use of *est′*, or rather its negative form, involves its being followed by interrogative adverbial or pronominal forms plus Infinitive to express the absence (more rarely presence) of time, place, person, etc. The former combination of *net* + Interrogative now has the shape *ne–Interrogative*, normally written as one word and forming an impersonal construction (with the logical subject, if expressed, in Dative) (the stress on *ne–* reflecting the old stucture):

> *Мне некогда разговаривать с вами./Mn–e ne′–kogda ø*
> *razgovariva–t′ s v–ami.*
> me DS – not + when – (be 3ps Pres) – converse Impf Inf – with –
> you IP
> 'I have no time to talk to you.'

> *Некуда идти./Ne′–kuda ø id–ti.*
> not + to where – (be 3ps Pres) – go Inf
> 'There's nowhere to go.'

These adverbial forms are inseparable, and perceived as adverbs with the zero verb; the past and future are expressed by non-zero forms of *byt′*:

> *Ей некогда было разговаривать./J–ej ne′–kogda by–lo*
> *razgovariva–t′.*
> she DS – not + when – be Past Neut – talk Impf Inf
> 'She had no time to talk.'

When attached to pronouns (giving the meanings 'there is no one/nothing . . .'), this *ne–* *is* separable when governed by a preposition; the pronoun declines according to its role in the clause:

> *Нечем писать./Ne′–č–em ø pisa–t′.*
> not + what IS – (3ps Pres) – write Impf Inf
> 'There is nothing to write with.'

> *Не с кем (было) разговаривать./Ne s k–em ø (by–lo)*
> *razgovariva–t′.*
> not + with + who IS – be (3ps Pres) (Past Neut) – talk Impf Inf
> 'There is (was) no one to talk to.'

Another, minor, use of the form *est'* is stylistic, namely the use of the copula in scientific definitions:

> *Движение есть форма существования материи.*
> */Dviženi–e est' form–a suščestvovani–ja materi–i.*
> movement/motion NSn – be 3ps Pres – form NSf – existence
>   GSn – matter GSf
> 'Motion is an attribute of matter.'

(3) English 'it'. We have seen several examples where English prefers to use an introductory 'it' as a way of allowing the shift of a subject comment to the end, that is, to the normal position of comment ('it's interesting that . . . '). Such an approach is also common in other European languages, but Russian does not have to do this, since its inflectional structure allows it to invert the word order without trouble (see examples in section 3.2.1.1 (3) above); further, English (and other languages, like French and German) must use 'it' to handle natural-world subjects (Eng *it is cold*; Fr *il fait froid, c'est (il est) vrai/intéressant, que* . . .), while others (e.g. Italian and Spanish), like Russian, do not (Ital *fa freddo, è vero, che* . . .). Russian has no formal equivalent of this 'it', though the Russian form is somewhat complicated by the behaviour of the copula, with its zero Present (*ø xolodno, ø interesno, čto* . . .).

One sort of 'it' for which there may be a formal equivalent is that which allows a subject comment to come first ('It's John who did it.'); this is not a structure involving a simple 'be' verb; here Russian may simply use word order:

> *Это сказал Ваня./Èt–o skaza–l Va"n–ja.*
> this ASn – say Pf Past Masc – Vanya NSm
> 'It was Vanya who said that.'

But it may also use a different *это/èto* as a marker of contrast, allowing the comment to appear first, as in English:

> *Это Ваня это сказал./Èto Va"n–ja èt–o skaza–l.*
> 'it' (NSn) – Vanya NSm – this ASn – say Pf Past Masc
> 'It was Vanya who said that.'

The latter usage is more colloquial than the former.

(4) The Complement (NP after copula). Russian grammar refers to this as the 'nominal (or post-copula) part' of a compound nominal predicate. The form may be a noun, noun phrase or any form of attributive phrase:

(a) Noun phrase. The central issue here is the case of the noun: where the simple copula is Present, the noun must be Nominative:

> *Он студент./On–ø ø student–ø.*
> he NS – (be 3ps Pres) – student NSm
> 'He is a student.'

When the verb is Past or Future, there is a choice: Nominative represents a *permanent* feature or characteristic of the subject, Instrumental a *transitory* feature:

> *Он был способный человек./On–ø by–l sposobn–yj čelovek–ø.*
> he NS – be Past Masc – capable NSm – person NSm
> 'He was a capable man.'

> *Он был (тогда) студентом./On–ø by–l (togda) student–om.*
> he NS – be Past Masc – (then) – student ISm
> '(At that time) he was a student.'

As noted above (1) all other copulative verbs *must* take Instrumental.

Where the subject and complement are nouns and the verb Pres, it is normal to write a dash for the copula:

> *Москва – столица России./Moskv–a – (ø) stolic–a Rossi–i.*
> Moscow NSf – (be 3ps Pres) – capital NSf – Russia GSf
> 'Moscow is the capital of Russia.'

A demonstrative particle may be inserted after the dash (a more colloquial variant):

> *Луна – это естественный спутник земли.*
> */Lun–a – èto estestvenn–yj sputnik–ø zeml–i.*
> moon NSf – that (invar = NSn) – natural NSm – satellite NSm – earth GSf
> 'The moon is a natural satellite of Earth.'

(b) Adjective (phrase). There are two choices to be made here: first, the same as with the noun phrase, that of Nominative or Instrumental, for the same reasons:

> *Он был маленький (человек)./On–ø by–l malen'k–ij (čelovek–ø).*
> he NS – be Past Masc – small NSm – (man NSm)
> 'He was small (a small man).'

> *Он был (тогда) маленьким./On–ø by–l (togda) malen'k–im.*
> he NS – be Past Masc – (then) – small ISm
> 'He was (still) small then.'

Secondly, there is a choice of long or short form. The criteria here are very similar, this time centring on the notion of *general* versus *particular*: the long form represents a generalised, inherent quality, the short a quality limited in its application or manifestation, the limitation normally being made explicit; examples are given first of the Present, where the only choice is long Nominative or short (Nominative only):

> *Этот доклад очень интересный./Èt–ot doklad–ɸ ɸ očen'*
>   *interesn–yj.*
> this NSm – lecture NSm – (be 3ps Pres) – very – interesting NSm long
> 'This lecture is very interesting.'

> *Этот доклад интересен только для специалистов.*
>   */Èt–ot doklad–ɸ ɸ interes(e)n–ɸ tol'ko dlja specialist–ov.*
> this NSm – lecture NSm – (be 3ps Pres) – interesting NSm short –
>   only – for – specialist GP
> 'This lecture is of interest only to specialists.'

The use of the short form in a clearly general context is stylistic: usually bookish, and especially poetic:

> *Психология личности очень сложна./Psixologi–ja ličnost–i*
>   *očen' složn–a.*
> psychology NSf – personality GSf – (be 3ps Pres) – very –
>   complex NSf short
> 'The psychology of personality is very complex.'

. . . or else expressive:

> *Он стар и слаб./On–ɸ ɸ star–ɸ i slab–ɸ.*
> he NS – be 3ps Pres – old NSm short – and – weak NSm short
> 'He is (really) old and weak.'

. . . or it occurs in a poetic or folk-style expression, e.g. sayings:

> *Любовь слепа./Ljubov'–ɸ ɸ slep–a.*
> love NSf – (be 3ps Pres) – blind NSf short
> 'Love is blind.'

The Past and Future offer both possibilities, and while it can be seen that there is a natural correlation between 'permanent/inherent' and 'general' on the one hand, and 'transitory' and 'limited/particular' on the other, the two need not be automatically associated; the simple choice of general versus limited/particular is demonstrated by the following:

> *Он был тогда уже старым./On–ɸ by–l togda uže star–ym.*
> he NSm – be Past Masc – then – already – old ISm
> 'He was already old then.'

Он был уже стар для такой работы./ On–ø by–l už e star–ø dlja tak–oj rabot–y.
he NSm – be Past Masc – already – old NSm short – for – such GSf – work GSf
'He was already (too) old for such work.'

The use of the unqualified long Nominative where the meaning is clearly *not* general is stylistically motivated, being more expressive and more colloquial as against the factual (or bookish) Instrumental:

Он был старый и слабый./On–ø by–l star–yj i slab–yj.
he NS – be Past Masc – old NSm long – and weak NSm long
'He was old and weak.'

Adjectives may be in the comparative or superlative degree, followed by a measure of comparison ('–er than', '–st of all', etc.) (on formation see chapter 3, section 2.1.5.6); the Comparative is typically an invariable adverbial form followed by the Genitive of the measure of comparison:

Ваня моложе меня./Van–ja ø molože men–ja.
Vanya NSm – (be 3ps Pres) – younger Adv – me GS
'Vanya is younger than me.'

... though the analytical form is also possible, parallel to English:

Эта книга гораздо более интересная, чем первая.
/Èt–a knig–a ø gorazdo bolee interesn–aja čem perv–aja.
this NSf – book NSf – (be 3ps Pres) – much Adv – more Invar – interesting NSf long – than – first NSf long
'This book is much more interesting than the first.'

(c) Passive participle. The Past Passive Participle is a special case of adjectival complement, expressing the passive as in English. Since it virtually always represents a qualified, or 'limited' attribute, its shape is naturally short, and this has been generalised, occurring even in apparently open, non-qualified contexts and in all tenses:

Горы были покрыты снегом./Gor–y by–li pokryt–y sneg–om.
mountain NP – be Past Plur – cover PPP Plur – snow ISm
'The mountains were covered with snow.'

Окно было открыто./Okn–o by–lo otkryt–o.
window NSn – be Past Neut – open PPP Neut
'The window was open.'

(d) Non-adjectival attributes. Here belong:

(i) Noun phrases in the Genitive of description:

> *Он был высокого роста./On–ø by–l vysok–ogo rost–a.*
> he NS – be Past Masc – high GSm – size/height GSm
> 'He was tall.'

(ii) Prepositional phrases:

> *Я из Москвы./Ja ø iz Moskv–y.*
> I NS – (be 1ps Pres) – from – Moscow GSf
> 'I'm from Moscow.'

(iii) conjunctional phrases expressing comparison ('like . . . '):

> *Всё это будто сон./Vs–ë èt–o ø budto s(o)n–ø.*
> all NSn – this NSn – (be 3ps Pres) – like/as if – dream NSm
> 'All this is like a dream.'

> *Он как зверь./On–ø ø kak zver'–ø.*
> he NS – (be 3ps Pres) – like – wild animal NSm
> 'He's like a wild animal.'

(5) Adjunct (adverbial modifier/circumstance). The range of adverbial phrases/adjuncts is again firmly in the European pattern; the main types, with common examples, are:

(a) *adverb:* *завтра/zavtra* 'tomorrow'; *здесь/zdes'* 'here'; *часто/často* 'often'; *нарочно/naročno* 'on purpose';

(b) *adverbial phrase* (fixed, no longer with straight meaning): *тому назад/tomu nazad* 'ago' (lit. 'back to that'); *спустя рукава/spustja rukava* 'carelessly' (lit. 'with sleeves rolled down');

(c) an *oblique case* of a noun or nominal phrase (and still recognisable as such): *утром/utr–om* 'in the morning' (ISn); *осенью/osen'–ju* 'in autumn' (ISf); *стрелой/strel–oj* 'like an arrow' (ISf); *весь день/ves'–ø den'–ø* 'all day (long)' (ASm);

(d) *prepositional phrase:* *после обеда/posle obed–a* 'in the afternoon' (lit. 'after lunch' GSm); *ради шутки/radi šutk–i* 'for fun/for a joke' (GSf); *при большом желании/pri bol'š–om želani–i* 'with the best will in the world' (lit. 'in spite of great desire' LSn); *на столе/na stol–e* 'on the table' (LSm);

(e) *adverbial participle* (not those representing a clause (see below)): *покраснев/pokrasnev* 'blushing' (lit. 'having gone red'); *улыбаясь/ulybajas'* 'with a smile' (lit. 'smiling'); *молча/molča* 'in silence' (lit. 'being silent');

(f) *infinitive* of purpose, used only after verbs of motion; this may be better interpreted as a purpose clause without a conjunction:

> *Я пришёл проверить работу./Ja priš–(ë)l proveri–t' rabot–u.*
> I NS – come Pf Past Masc – check Pf Inf – work ASf
> 'I've come to check the work.'

3.2.2.9 The Object

(1) Direct Object. The Direct Object (after transitive verbs) may appear in the Accusative or Genitive; further, in impersonal constructions the logical Direct Object may be in the Nominative.

(a) Accusative. The normal case is Accusative, and this is effectively the only function of the Accusative (apart from some adverbial time uses); the form of the Accusative is discrete only for Class II nouns; for Class III and Class I Neuter it is the same as the Nominative; for Class I Masculine it is the same as either the Nominative (for inanimates) or the Genitive (for animates):

> *Я читаю интересную книгу./Ja čitaj–u interesn–uju knig–u.*
> I NS – read 1ps Pres – interesting ASf – book ASf
> 'I am reading an interesting book.'

> *Я очень люблю своего учителя./Ja očen' ljubl–ju svo–ego učitel–ja.*
> I NS – very much – like 1ps Pres – own ASm (= GSm) – teacher
>   ASm (= GSm)
> 'I really like my teacher.'

(b) Genitive. The Genitive appears with three functions.

(i) To express a *partitive* object:

> *Дайте, пожалуйста, хлеба./Daj–te, požalujsta, xleb–a.*
> give 2pp Pf Imper – please – bread GSm
> 'Please pass some bread.'

(ii) To express a *negative* object, that is, a denied one; English typically uses 'any' for such objects:

> *Я не получала письма./Ja ne poluča–la pis'm–a.*
> I NS – not – receive Impf Past Fem – letter GSn
> 'I didn't receive a letter/I haven't received *any* letter.'

> *Я там не видел кошки./Ja tam ne vide–l košk–i.*
> I NS – there – not – see Impf Past Masc – cat GSf
> 'I didn't see a/*any* cat there.'

> *Не обращайте внимания на него./Ne obraščaj–te vnimani–ja*
>   *na ne–go.*
> not – turn Impf 2pp Imper – attention GSn – onto – him ASm
> 'Don't pay *any* attention to him.'

The basis of this rule is the denial of the object's existence, 'absence' being a fundamental meaning of the Genitive, so that the object of a negative verb whose existence is not in question will remain Accusative; such objects will normally be definite in English:

Я не получила письмо./Ja ne poluči–la pis′m–o.
I NS – not – receive Pf Past Fem – letter ASn
'I didn't receive *the* letter.'

Я там не видел Аню./Ja tam ne vide–l An–ju.
I NS – there – not – see Impf Past Masc – Anya ASf
'I didn't see Anya there.'

Such definite objects are in fact usually the topic of the sentence, and so are often first in Russian:

Письмо я ещё не получила./Pis′m–o ja eščё ne poluči–la.
letter ASn – I NS – still – not – receive Pf Past Fem
'I still haven't received *the* letter.'

(iii) As the object of verbs of *wishing, desiring, expecting, seeking* and the like; this possibility is also tied to the definiteness of the object: in such sentences the object is normally hypothetical, when the Genitive is possible, while definite objects must be Accusative:

Я жду от вас ответа./Ja žd–u ot v–as otvet–a.
I NS – await 1ps Pres – from – you GP – answer GSm
'I'm awaiting *an* answer from you.'

Чего вы ищете?/Č–ego vy išč –ete?
what GS – you NP – look for 2pp Pres
'What are you looking for?'

but:

Ищу свою книгу./Išč–u svo–ju knig–u.
look for 1ps Pres – own ASf – book ASf
'I'm looking for *my* book.'

(c) Logical Direct Object. In some impersonal constructions the logical object may appear in the Nominative, though one may argue that the Nominative is as much logical subject as object:

> 'need': in sentences like 'I need this book', it is not only Russian which prefers the structure 'this book is necessary for me' (cf. Eng *this book is indispensible for me*); Russian (like French – *il me faut* x, *j'ai besoin de* x)) has no personal way of expressing this (that is, with a transitive verb);
>
> 'like': similarly, in 'I like *x*', Russian is not the only language to prefer the structure '*x* pleases me' (cf. Fr *x me plait*); the transitive verb *ljubit′* (like Fr *aimer*) expresses either an inherent/generalised liking or a stronger degree ('love').

Whatever the interpretation of such sentences, the Russian approach, given its inflectional possibilities, is of interest. It uses two types of construction: for 'need' the Predicate is *be* + Adj (short), with the adjective (*нуж(е)н/nuž(e)n–ø*) agreeing (in number and gender) with the 'object' needed, which is Nominative:

Мне нужна (была) эта книга./Mn–e nužn–a ø (by–la) èt–a knig–a.

me DS – necessary NSf Short – be (3ps Pres) (Past Fem) – this NSf – book NSf

'I need (needed) this book.'

'See' and 'hear' have similar possibilities: while the personal (transitive) verbs (respectively *видеть/videt', слышать/slyšat'*) are the normal form, the impersonal adjectives *вид(е)н–/vid(e)n–* 'visible' and *слыш(е)н–/slyš(e)n–* 'audible' are also available, parallel to the English construction '*x* is visible/audible' in form and usage (indefinite personal, thus normally without a personal Dative):

Отсюда видны здания центра города./Otsjuda ø vidn–y zdani–ja centr–a gorod–a.

from here Adv – (be 3pp Pres) – visible NP Short – building NPn – centre GSm – city GSm

'From here you can see the buildings in the city centre.'

For 'like' the verb (*нравиться/nravit'sja*) is 3rd Person Reflexive, agreeing in number with the 'object' liked:

Мне нравится эта пьеса./Mn–e nrav–it–sja èt–a p'es–a.

me DS – please 3ps Pres – this NSf – play NSf

'I like this play.'

Мне очень понравился этот фильм./Mn–e očen' ponravi–l–sja èt–ot fil'm–ø.

me DS – very much – please Pf Past Masc – this NSm – film NSm

'I really liked that film.' (Pf means '. . . and still like')

Also interesting in this context is the (more colloquial) possibility of the adjective type of impersonal (*nužn–*) being used in the non-agreeing Neuter form and taking an *Accusative* of the object needed (seen, heard):

Нужно врача./Nužn–o ø vrač–a.

necessary NSn – (be 3ps Pres) – doctor ASm

'We need a doctor.' (lit. '. . . is needed')

Оттуда хорошо было видно дорогу./Ottuda xorošo by–lo vidn–o dorog–u.

from there Adv – well Adv – be Past Neut – visible NSn – road ASf

'The road could be seen (You could see the road) clearly from there.'

This structure can be seen also with 'pure' (invariable, that is, with no adjectival forms) impersonals (like *надо/nado* 'necessary', *жаль/žal'* 'sorry for/pitiable'):

>*Мне надо эту книгу/Mn–e ∅ nado èt–u knig–u.*
>me DS – necessary Invar – (be 3ps Pres) – this ASf – book ASf
>'I need this book.'

>*Мне жаль эту девушку./Mn–e žal' ∅ èt–u devušk–u.*
>me DS – sorry for/pitiable Invar – (be 3ps Pres) – this ASf – girl ASf
>'I feel sorry for that girl.'

(2) Indirect Object. Three 'straight' cases may be used for an indirect complement: Dative, Genitive and Instrumental; in addition some verbs may require a preposition with one or other case, the Locative/Prepositional obligatorily having a preposition.

(a) Dative. The Dative primarily expresses the beneficiary or recipient of the action, that is, the classic 'Indirect Object', expressed typically by Eng *to/for*:

>*Дайте книгу Ивану./Daj–te knig–u Ivan–u.*
>give 2pp Imper – book ASf – Ivan DSm
>'Give the book to Ivan.'

>*Миру мир./Mir–u mir–∅.*
>world DSm – (be 3ps Imper) – peace NSm
>'Peace (be) to the world.' (elliptical)

Many verbs also require the Dative where English may *not* use 'to', including the following.

(i) Verbs of telling, ordering, allowing etc. (cf. Eng *say to, give permission to*):

>*Он мне об этом рассказывал./On–∅ mn–e ob èt–om rasskazyva–l.*
>he NS – me DS – about –this LSn – tell Impf Past Masc
>'He told me about that.'

(ii) Verbs of believing, trusting, helping (cf. Eng *offer help to*):

>*Я вам не верю./Ja v–am ne ver–ju.*
>I NS – you DP – not – believe 1ps Pres
>'I don't believe you.'

(iii) Less obvious verbs include 'be happy (for)', 'commiserate (with)', 'cooperate (with)' (cf. Eng *offer sympathy/cooperation to*):

>*Мы радовались её успехам./My radova–li–s' eë uspex–am.*
>we NP – be happy Impf Past Plur – her GSf – success DP
>'We were delighted at her success.'

The 'be' + Adj form of 'be glad' does the same:

> *Он был рад нашему приходу./On–ϕ by–l rad–ϕ naš–emu prixod–u.*
> he NS – be Past Masc – glad NSm Short – our DSm – arrival DSm
> 'He was happy at our arrival.'

(iv) Most unusual, perhaps (at least from the English – and French – viewpoint) are the verbs 'teach' and 'study', where the Dative is used for the *subject* taught or learnt, and not for the *person* taught, for which the Accusative is used, seen as the Direct Object:

> *Она учит (обучает) их русскому языку./On–a uč–it (obuča–et) ix russk–omu jazyk–u.*
> she NS – teach 3ps Pres – them AP – Russian DSm – language DSm
> 'She's teaching them Russian.'

> *Мы учимся русскому языку./My uč–im–sja russk–omu jazyk–u.*
> we NP – study 1pp Pres – Russian DSm – language DSm
> 'We're studying Russian.'

Also interesting is the fact that the same basic verb *učit'* may be used (more colloquially) as a transitive verb for 'study', with Accusative for the subject studied:

> *Мы учим русский язык./My uč–im russk–ij jazyk–ϕ.*
> we NP – study 1pp Pres – Russian ASm – language ASm
> 'We're studying Russian.'

And, as seen above (section 3.2.1), the Dative represents the logical subject in impersonal sentences.

(b) Genitive. The Genitive is relatively rare as a marker of indirect object or complement; it appears with a small number of reflexive verbs, in what we might otherwise see as a direct object – which include verbs of fearing, e.g. *бояться/bojat'–sja* 'fear' ('be afraid *of*'), of achievement, e.g. *добиваться/dobivat'–sja* 'attain', and of deprivation, e.g. *лишаться/lišat'–sja* 'lose, be deprived *of*':

> *Я боюсь холода./Ja boj–u–s' xolod–a.*
> I NS – fear 1ps Pres – cold GSm
> 'I'm afraid of the cold.'

> *Он наконец добился хорошего места./On–ϕ nakonec dobi–l–sja xoroš–ego mest–a.*
> he NS – finally Adv – achieve Pf Past Masc – good GSn – position GSn
> 'He finally achieved a good position.'

(c) Instrumental. A group of non-reflexive verbs with the general meaning of 'control' governs the Instrumental, e.g.: *владеть/vladet'* 'master, possess', *заведовать/zavedovat'* 'manage', *командовать/komandovat'* 'be in command of', *руково дить/rukovodit'* 'guide', *управлять/upravljat'* 'govern'; these, too, might formally be treated as instances of Direct Object, but the meaning is rather one of indirect activity 'in relation to' the object, and this is precisely the reason for the Instrumental, this being one of its primary meanings.

A similar relational meaning is seen in the case of many reflexive verbs which require the Instrumental, e.g. a group meaning 'be involved in': *интересовать- ся/interesovat'–sja* 'be interested in', *заниматься/zanimat'–sja* 'be occupied with/at', *увлекаться/uvlekat'–sja* 'be infatuated with', *любоваться/ljubovat'– sja* 'admire'.

Another semantic group is that meaning 'appear' or 'change appearance', some members of which we considered under the heading of 'semicopula-tive' verbs (section 3.2.2.8), e.g.: *казаться/kazat'–sja* 'seem', *становиться/ stanovit'–sja* 'become', *делаться/delat'–sja* 'become', *претворяться/pretvo-rjat'–sja* 'pretend to be', and one non-reflexive verb – *выглядеть/vygljadet'* 'look (like)'.

Other verbs governing the Instrumental include: *гордиться/gordit'–sja* 'be proud of', *делиться/delit'–sja* 'share'.

(d) Cases with prepositions. Here we are interested in verbs (or rather predi-cates) which, as it were, have an inseparable (attached) preposition (as opposed to the use of prepositions independently of the verb to make an adverbial phrase); this is the typical English situation.

(i) Accusative. A few verbs with the prepositions *за/za* meaning 'in re-turn for', 'on behalf of', e.g. *беспокоиться/bespokoit'–sja* 'worry about', *извиняться/izvinjat'–sja* 'apologise for'; and a few with *на/na* 'onto, against', e.g. *смотреть/smotret'* 'look at' (as opposed to 'watch', when it is transitive), *сердиться/serdit'–sja* 'get angry at', *жаловаться/žalovat'–sja* 'complain of':

> Извиняюсь за опоздание./Izvinja–ju–s' za opozdani–e.
> apologise 1ps Pres – for – lateness ASn
> 'I apologise for my late arrival (being late).'

(ii) Genitive. Possibly only one, with the preposition *из/iz*, meaning 'from, out of': *состоять/sostojat'* 'consist of':

> Роман состоит из трёх частей./Roman–ø sosto–it iz tr–ëx čast–ej.
> novel NSm – consist 3ps Pres – of – three GP – part GPf
> 'The novel consists of (contains) three parts.'

(iii) Dative. The only common preposition here is *к/k*, with the basic mean-ing of 'towards', e.g. *готовиться/gotovit'–sja* 'prepare for', and its stative,

adjectival version *быть готов/byt' gotov–ø* 'be ready for'; *привыкаться/privykat'–sja* 'get used to'; *относиться/otnosit'–sja* 'relate to':

> *Мы готовимся/готовы к экзаменам./My gotov–im–sja*
> *(ø gotov–y) k èkzamen–am.*
> we NP – prepare 1pp Pres Intrans ((be 1pp Pres) + ready NP Short) –
> towards – exam DP
> 'We're preparing (ready) for the exams.'

> *Как вы относитесь к этому?/Kak vy otnos–ite–s' k èt–omu?*
> how – you NP – relate to 2pp Pres – towards – this DSn
> 'What do you think (What's your view) of that?'

The preposition *по/po* 'in respect of' is another possibility, e.g. *скучать/skučat'* 'miss' ('yearn for'):

> *Она скучает по матери./On–a skuča–et po mater–i.*
> she NS – yearn 3ps Pres – for – mother DS
> 'She misses her mother.'

(iv) Instrumental. The common preposition here is *с/s* 'with', attached to verbs with an inherent reciprocal meaning, e.g. *разговаривать/razgovarivat'* 'converse with/talk to', *знакомиться/znakomit'–sja* 'get to know, meet, become acquainted with', *здороваться/zdorovat'–sja* 'greet', *встречаться/vstrečat'–sja* 'meet (with)', *видеться/videt'–sja* 'see (someone regularly)', *разводиться/razvodit'–sja* 'divorce'. One unexpected verb is *поздравлять/pozdravljat'* 'congratulate', where the preposition governs the reason for the congratulations:

> *Поздравляю (вас) с днём рождения./Pozdravljaj–u (vas) s dn–ёm*
> *roždenij–a.*
> congratulate 1ps Pres – (you AP) – with – day ISm – birth GSn
> 'Happy Birthday!'

(v) Prepositional. Several verbs with the preposition *в/v* 'in', e.g. meaning 'accuse' or 'confess': *обвинять/obvinjat'* 'accuse of', *признаваться/priznavat'–sja* 'admit to', *упрекать/uprekat'* 'reproach'; and meaning 'convince', 'persuade': *уверять/uverjat'* 'assure', *убеждать(ся)/ubeždat'(–sja)* '(be) convince(d)'; also *сомневаться/somnevat'–sja* 'doubt':

> *Его обвинили в убийстве./E–go obvini–li v ubijstv–e.*
> him ASm – accuse Pf Past Plur – in – murder LSn
> 'He was accused of murder.' (lit. 'They accused him ...')

And a few with *на/na* 'on(to)', e.g. *жениться/ženit'–sja* 'marry (take a wife)', *настаивать/nastaivat'* 'insist on'.

(3) Double Direct Object. Where there is a second direct object, functioning as a further definition of the first, the modern structure is to put the additional one into the Instrumental (whereas in Old Russian the second was also Accusative, in apposition):

> *Его выбрали президентом клуба./E–go vybra–li prezident–*
> *om klub–a.*
> him AS – choose/elect Pf Past Plur – president ISm – club GSm
> 'He was elected President of the club.' (lit. 'They elected him...')

> *Сына мы назвали Ваней./Syn–a my nazva–li Van–ej.*
> son ASm – we NP – name/call Pf Past Plur – Vanya ISm
> 'We named (We've called) our son Vanya.'

The only exception to this concerns the same verb 'name /call' when used in the Imperfective to refer to someone's on-going name; here the name appears in the Nominative, taken, as it were, outside the syntax of the sentence, rather like the status of titles of books, etc. when accompanied by a classifier (see above, section 2(5)):

> *Его (Брата) зовут Ваня./E–go (Brat–a) zov–ut Van–ja.*
> him (brother) ASm – name/call 3pp Pres – Vanya NS
> 'His (My brother's) name is Vanya.' (lit. 'They call him...')

3.3   Incomplete/elliptical sentences

Elliptical sentences are generally a feature of colloquial style, as in most languages. Any part of the sentence may be formally omitted, its content being recognised, or 'understood', usually from the preceding context, possibly also from the extra-linguistic context. Thus it is the topic which may be omitted, while the (only or main) comment must be kept.

(1) Subject omission. We noted above (section 3.2.1.1) the possible omission of a pronominal subject; omission of 1st and 2nd person pronouns may be a feature of spoken style:

> *Понял?/ø Ponja–l?*
> (you NS Masc) – understand Pf Past Masc (IK-3)
> '(Do you) Understand?' (lit. 'Have you understood?')

The expected (positive) response to this is:

> *Понял./ø Ponja–l.*
> (I NS Masc) – understand Pf Past Masc (IK-1)
> 'Yes.' (lit. 'I have understood.')

This omission is also possible in formal, especially written, style:

> *Прошу (вас)./Proš–u (vas).*
> ask 1ps Pres – (you AP):
> 'Please . . . ' (do whatever my gesture indicates, e.g. come in,
>   go first, etc.)

> *Остаюсь Ваш./Ostaj–u–s′ Vaš.*
> remain 1ps Pres – your NS Masc
> '(I remain) Yours' (letter ending)

(2) Verb omission. In answers to *yes/no* questions Russian may use simple 'yes' or 'no' as other languages, but in fact it prefers to repeat the central element (usually the verb) of the question, as in the example in (1) above of 'understand'; thus verb omission is less frequent than in other languages. Otherwise, omission occurs mainly with motion verbs, where the motion in process is understood from the extra-linguistic context:

> *Куда ты?/Kuda ty ∅.*
> to where – you NS – (go 2ps Pres)
> 'Where are you going/off to?'

> *Я в школу./Ja ∅ v škol–u.*
> I NS – (go 1ps Pres) – to – school ASf
> 'I'm going (off, on my way) to school.'

> *Вы ко мне?/Vy ∅ ko mn–e.*
> you NP – (come 2pp Pres *or* Pf Past) – to – me DS
> 'Are you looking for me?' (lit. ' . . . coming/have come to me').

As in English, a verb repeated in a compound sentence may be deleted:

> *Нина принесла хлеб, а Виктор — молоко.*
>   */Nin–a prines–la xleb–∅, a Viktor–∅ ∅ molok–o.*
> Nina NS – bring Pf Past Fem – bread ASm – and – Viktor –
>   (bring Pf Past Masc) – milk ASn
> 'Nina brought the bread and Victor the milk.'

(3) Omission of Object or Complement. Typically the object would be understood from the extra-linguistic context, again as in the 'understand' example in (1) above, where the thing understood is also omitted; another example is:

> *Вы читали?/Vy čita–li ∅?*
> you NP – read Impf Past Plur – (this book, etc. AS)
> 'Have you read this?'

(4) Predicate omission. Only the subject – as the comment – may remain; a common context is again the answer to a question, whether *wh–* or *yes/no*:

('Who's going to do it?'): *Я./Ja ø ø.*
I NS – (do Fut) – (it AS)
'Me (I am, I will).'

('Is this your bag (*сумка/sumk–a*)?'): *Моя./ø ø Moj–a ø.*
(this NS – be 3ps Pres) – my NSf – (bag ASf)
'Yes (, it is)' (lit. 'Mine.')

Another common context is the contrastive subject, typically introduced by the conjunction *a/a* 'and, but' (see below, section 4.1.2):

('Vanya's coming tomorrow.'): *А Наташа?/A Nataš–a ø?*
and – Natasha NS – (also – come 3ps Pres)
'And (what/how about) Natasha?'

Finally, the extra-linguistic context may be sufficient, mostly with simply the copula omitted:

Ваша сумка?/ø Va"š–a sumk–a?
(be 3ps Pres – this NS) – your NSf – bag NSf (IK-3)
'Is this your bag?'

... but other verbs are possible:

Ваш билет?/ø Vaš–ø bilet–ø?
('may I see') – your ASm – ticket ASm (IK-4)
'Ticket, please.' (conductor)

(5) Exclamations and interjections. In principle these are also examples of elliptical sentences, though they may also be treated as separate full, but non-analysable sentences. Here belong greetings and other social-relationship exclamations:

Здравствуйте!/Zdra'vstvujte. 'Hello/Good Day!'
Спасибо./Spasi'bo. 'Thanks.'

... and generally modal exclamations, in response to a linguistic context:

Разве?/Ra'zve? 'Really?'
Может быть./Mo'ž–et byt'. 'Could be/Perhaps.'
Конечно!/Kone'čno! 'Of course!'

... or interjections in response to an extra-linguistic context:

Боже мой!/Bo'že moj! '(Oh,) My God!'
Стоп!/Stop! 'Halt!'

3.4   Word order

We have seen examples of word order problems at various points above. Here
we summarise the main principles at work in Russian.

The important typological factor is that inflectional languages have available
much freer word order than non-inflectional, since the inflections can provide
the necessary information about the syntactic role of each element. This freedom
is apparent even when the inflection does not in fact give sufficient information –
compare English, in which even the remnant inflections of the personal pronouns
do not allow them to move about freely (e.g. *'I can him see.'); it is only when
the Subject/Object status of two neighbouring nouns is genuinely ambiguous
that order is restricted (to SVO or SOV) – not a very common situation:

> *Мать любит дочь./Mat'–ø ljub–it doč–ø.*
> mother NS (=AS) – love 3ps Pres – daughter AS (=NS)
> 'The mother loves her daughter.'

The natural order of 'topic + comment' is able to remain undisturbed by
the problem of a subject comment, where, for example, English must resort
to structures like '*y* was V–en by *x*' for passive or 'it was *x* who V–ed *y*' for
contrast or emphasis; Russian is able simply to use the order OVS (see above,
section 3.2.2.4).

Within the topic, order is rather flexible, allowing in principle a hierarchy of
topicality, though this is not apparent in speech; personal pronouns are particularly flexible:

> *Я его встретил на улице./Ja ego vstreti–l na u"lic–e.* or:
> *Я встретил его на улице./Ja vstreti–l ego na u"lic–e.*
> I NS – [him AS ↔ meet Pf Past Masc] – in – street LSf
> 'I met him in the street.'

> *Я взял у Вани книгу./Ja vzja–l u Van–i kni"g–u.* or:
> *Я у Вани взял книгу./Ja u Van–i vzja–l kni"g–u.*
> I NS – [take Pf Past Masc ↔ at – Vanya GSm] – book ASf
> 'I borrowed a book from Vanya.'

In casual speech it is also possible to use intonation (including location
of logical stress) to identify the comment, rather than word order; the above
sentences could be said (but not written) as follows:

> *Я на улице его встретил./Ja na u"lice ego vstreti–l.*
> *Я книгу взял у Вани./Ja kni"g–u vzja–l u Van–i.*

Each has the emphatic IK-2 intonation centred on the comment; but this style
would still be interpreted as contrastive rather than declarative ('It was in the

street that ... ', 'It was a book that ... '). If written, these must mean that the comments are, repectively, 'met' and 'from Vanya' (and the topic 'book' in the second would be definite in English: 'I borrowed *the* book from Vanya.'). The neutral statement intonation with final comment is IK-1 on the final word. (See chapter 2, section 3.6).

Adverbial modifiers (adjuncts) within the topic – or at least not the central comment – normally precede the verb:

> *Мы в воскресенье отправились на экскурсию.*
> /*My v vokresen'–e otpravi–li–s' na èksku"rsi–ju.*
> we NP – on – Sunday ASn – set off Pf Past Plur – on – excursion ASf
> (IK-1)
> 'On Sunday we set/went off on a trip.'

Had the comment been 'on Sunday', that phrase would have come last or been emphasised in speech by IK-2.

4   The complex sentence

Traditional English terminology presents us with an ambiguity, in that the term 'complex sentence' may serve two functions: (1) it may be the general term for any sentence with more than one clause (verb, predicate); and (2) it may be the term for the subgroup of such sentences with one main clause and one or more subordinate clauses. Alongside this, the term 'compound sentence' is given to sentences with two or more main clauses. Within this system, ideally we should have a separate term for one of the 'complex' functions, such as is standard in Russian grammar, where the simple term meaning 'complex' is the general one (meaning (1)), while the subtypes are compound terms specifying the use of either coordination or subordination (the term for 'sentence' which would accompany these is neuter *предложение/predloženi–e*, hence the adjectives are neuter; their stems are calques from the Latin, translating 'co–' as *co–/so–* 'with', 'sub-' as *под–/pod–* 'under', and '-ordin-' as *–чин–/–čin–* 'rank, order', the suffix *–нн–/–nn–* being a past passive participle '–en'):

> *сложное/složn–oe* 'complex' in general;
> *сложносочинённое/složn–o–so–čin–ënn–oe* 'complex-coordinate';
> *сложноподчинённое/složn–o–pod–čin–ënn–oe* 'complex-
>   subordinate'.

A transformational (generative) grammar approach would allow us to avoid this terminological problem, in that all clauses are seen as simple sentences at the deep structure level, embedded in a relational way parallel to the parts of the simple sentence; however, first, this is not a generative description and, second, such a description in our view creates a lot of unnecessary complications for what are otherwise simple concepts: for example, an apparently simple sentence with a coordinate subject should be seen as a pair of coordinate sentences sharing the same verb (e.g. 'John and Peter were both reading'), or an adverbial phrase may be seen as a sentence (e.g. 'after dinner', since it equals 'after x had dined'). So, while it is certainly of interest to observe the parallels between parts of the simple sentence and parts (clauses) of a complex sentence, this may be achieved perfectly well within a fairly traditional framework. The terminological weakness noted above is really the extent of the problem. We shall therefore pursue the parts of the complex sentence using as far as possible the same terms as for the parts of the simple sentence, though in several cases the traditional terms are indeed different. For the overall types, we append the Russian terms, and will frequently offer the Russian terms as illustrative of the function of particular clauses.

The matter of surface versus underlying (deep) structure also forces us to make another decision about our description: we might start our description from the surface structure, and from there observe what the underlying relationships are (e.g. what are the various meanings of clauses beginning with conjunction x?), or we might do the reverse (e.g. what are all the surface realisations of a subordinate time clause?). We will opt for the second approach, because it is simpler and it allows us to follow the parallels in function with the simple sentence; the first approach would lead to much repetition and, potentially, confusion, as the surface forms are often not what they seem (e.g. 'It started raining and we didn't go' is on the surface a coordinating sentence, but the relationship is in fact one of subordination, meaning '. . . and so – as a result – we didn't go'). On the other hand, surface forms must sometimes be taken more seriously, for example if we compare the sentence 'Since it started raining, we didn't go', even though the meaning is effectively identical, the relationship between the two sets of clauses is different, in that the main clause is not the same in both: in the first we would say that the main verb is 'rain' and that the second clause is one of 'result', while in the second the main verb is 'go' and the first clause is one of 'cause'. Another example shows a slightly different situation: compare 'It was beginning to get dark, but we could still see the layout of the room' and 'Even though it was beginning to get dark, we could still see the layout of the room': the relationship is concessive in each case, all that is different is the relative weight of the clauses, the 'darkness' being more important, or independent, in the first, in the second more like background information. Such relationships are relatively infrequent, always related, as in these, to a coordinative surface structure; where appropriate we will note these variants, but they are not sufficient to push us towards a general surface-based description.

4.1   The compound sentence (complex-coordinate)

The three central types of coordination are *connective* (the 'and' type), *adversative* (the 'but' type) and *disjunctive* (the 'or' type), to which we might add a fourth – *specifying* ('that is'). The normal joining method is a conjunction, though an asyndetic structure is also available. For the semantic distinctions between the conjunctions, see chapter 3, section 2.3.3.1.

4.1.1   Connective (Rus so–edin–itel′n–yj 'uniting')
The main conjunction is *u/i* 'and', which is usable in most variants:

(1) Simultaneous (verbs normally Imperfective)

> По улице дефилировали спортсмены, и мы долго смотрели
>   на них. /Po ulic–e defilirova–li sportsmen–y, i my dolgo smotre–li
>   na nix.
> along – street DSf – parade Impf Past Plur – sportsman NP – and we
>   NP – for long Adv – watch Impf Past Plur – at – them AP
> 'The sportsmen paraded along the street and we watched them for a
> long time.'

Emphasis ('both . . . and') is done by doubling *i*, and placing it before the connected elements (more commonly nominal than verbal):

> Ребёнок уже и ходит, и говорит./Rebënok–ø uže i xod–it,
>   i govor–it.
> child NSm – already – and (both) – walk 3ps Pres – and – talk 3ps Pres
> 'The child is already both walking and talking.'

Other intensive sets are: *не толко . . . но и/ne tol′ko . . . no i* and *как . . . так u/kak . . . tak i*, both 'not only . . . but also' (the latter literary style, lit. 'as *x* . . . so also *y*').

The double negative ('neither . . . nor') belongs here, as logically 'not *x* and not *y*'; its form is just that in Russian: *ни . . . ни/ni . . . ni* (from *не–и/ne–i*):

> Он ни читает, ни играет./On–ø ni čita–et, ni igra–et.
> he NS – and not (neither) – read 3ps Pres – and not (nor) – play
>   3ps Pres
> 'He's neither reading nor playing./He neither reads nor plays.'

Of other conjunctions with this sense *да/da* is colloquial.
    The asyndetic structure is literary:

> Было холодно, падал мокрый снег./By–lo xolodn–o, pada–l
>   mokr–yj sneg–ø.

be Past Neut – cold NSn – fall Impf Past Masc – wet NSm –
  snow NSm
'It was cold and wet snow was falling.'

(2) Successive ('and then') (verbs normally Perfective, certainly the first)

> *Разговор прекратился, и Иван вышел из вагона.*
> */Razgovor–ø prekrati–l–sja, i Ivan–ø vyš–(e)l iz vagon–a.*
> conversation NSm – stop Intrans Pf Past Masc – and – Ivan NSm –
>   go out Pf Past Masc – from – carriage GSm
> 'The conversation ceased and Ivan left the carriage.'

Other conjunctions include *затем/zatem*, *потом/potom*, both '(and) then'.
  Again, the asyndetic structure is literary:

> *Зашло солнце, стало темнеть./Zaš–lo solnc–e, sta–lo temne–t'.*
> set Pf Past Neut – sun NSn – begin Pf Past Neut – get dark Impf Inf
> 'The sun set and it began to get dark.'

(3) Additional ('and also')

> *Вы уезжаете, и мы уезжаем сегодня./Vy uezža–ete, i my*
> *uezža–em segodnja.*
> you NP – leave 2pp Pres – and – we NP – leave 1pp Pres – today
> 'You're off, and we're leaving today (too).'

Other conjunctions are *тоже/tože*, *также/takže*, both '(and) also'.
  Where the 'additional' meaning is rather '(and) moreover/besides', the conjunctions include *кроме того/krome togo*, *к тому же/k tomu že*, *притом/*
pritom, and *not* simple *i*. These last three illustrate the structure of a large number of conjunctions, formed from a preposition plus the appropriate case-form
of the demonstrative pronoun *том/tot* (see chapter 3, section 2.1.4.2).

(4) Intensive ('and indeed/after all'). Intensive particles are used alone or with
i, e.g. *же/že* (second word), *ведь/ved'*:

> *Расскажи ей — она же твоя мать./Rasskaž–i e–j – on–a že*
> *ø tvo–ja mat'–ø.*
> tell 2ps Pf Imper – her DS – she NS – after all – (be 3ps Pres) – your
>   NSf – mother NSf
> 'Tell her, she is (after all) your mother.'

(5) Result ('and so/thus'). As noted above, this is a type which is very close to a
subordinate clause, but may be included here as connective so long as the first
clause is seen as independent and not truly subordinate. The result is usually
only implied as being connected:

Стал накрапывать дождик, и все вернулись в гостиную.
/Sta–l nakrapyva–t′ doždik–ø, i vs–e vernu–li–s′ v gostin–uju.
begin Pf Past Masc – drizzle Impf Inf – light rain NSm – and – all
    NP – return Pf Past Plur – into – living-room ASf
'It began to spit with rain and everyone went back into the living-room.'

More specific conjunctions meaning 'and so/thus' are: neutral: *поэтому/poe′tomu, итак/itak, так что/tak čto*; literary: *следовательно/sledovatel′no* 'consequently'; colloquial: *значит/značit* (lit. '(it) means').

4.1.2   Adversative *(Rus* protiv–itel′n–yj *'oppositional' or* so–postav–itel′n–yj *'contrasting')*

The two Russian terms indicate the two main subdivisions of this group: the 'adversative' type proper is that which contradicts or conflicts with the preceding statement in some way, the 'contrastive' type simply points to a difference.

(1) Oppositional ('but, however'). The primary conjunction is *но/no* 'but', which serves all the variants given below.
    (a) Limiting ('but unexpectedly/surprisingly . . . '):

Троллейбус остановился, но никто не вышел.
/Trollejbus–ø ostanovi–l–sja, no nikto ne vyš–(e)l.
trolleybus NSm – stop Intrans Pf Past Masc – but – no one NS –
    not – get off Pf Past Masc
'The trolleybus stopped, but no one got off.'

Other conjunctions are *однако/odnako* 'however', *только/tol′ko* 'only' (colloquial).
    (b) Concessive ('and yet/nevertheless') (a variant of subordinate concessive in which the first clause is independent):

Становилось темно, но он ещё хорошо видел всю комнату.
/Stanovi–lo–s′ temn–o, no on–ø ešče xorošo vide–l vs–ju komnat–u.
become Impf Past Neut – dark NSn – but – he NS – still – see Past
    Masc – all ASf – room ASF
'It was getting dark, but he could still see the whole room very well.'

Other conjunctions, usually added to *no* 'but', are *всё–таки/vsë–taki* 'all/just the same', *тем не менее/tem ne menee* 'nevertheless'.
    (c) Compensatory ('on the other hand'):

Забот прибавилось с появлением ребёнка, но/зато жить стало радостнее. /Zabot–ø pribavi–lo–s′ s pojavleni–em rebënk–a, no/ zato ži–t′ sta–lo radostn–ee.

worry GPf – add Intrans Pf Past Neut – with – appearance ISn – child
GSm – but – live Impf Inf – become Pf Past Neut – joyful Compar
Invar
'There were more worries with the arrival of the baby, but at the same
time life became more joyful.'

(d) Conditional ('or else'). This is close to a subordinate conditional, but
with emphasis on the main verb, usually an Imperative form:

>*Расскажи ей, а то я ей расскажу./Rasskaž–i e–j, a to ja e–j*
>*rasskaž–u.*
>tell 2ps Pf Imper – her DS – or else – I NS – her DS – tell 1ps Pf Fut
>'(You) Tell her, or else I will.'

Other conjunctions are *или/ili* 'or' (colloquial), *иначе/inače* and
в противном случае/v protivn–om sluča–e, both 'otherwise' (literary) (the
latter lit. 'in the opposite event').

This sense may have an asyndetic structure (colloquial), though treating it as
coordinate has rather less justification:

>*Будет время – зайду к тебе./Bud–et vrem–ja – zajd–u k teb–e.*
>be 3ps Fut – time NSn – call in 1ps Pf Fut – to – you DS
>'If I have the/some time I'll drop in (on you).'

Since the first clause here is the condition, this may also be interpreted as a
subordinate clause with ellipsis of the conjunction 'if'.

(2) Contrastive ('while, whereas'). The primary conjunction here is *a/a*, translatable as either 'but' or 'and':

>*Ваня пишет письмо, а Нина читает книгу.*
>   */Van–ja piš–et pis'm–o, a Nin–a čita–et knig–u.*
>Vanya NS – write 3ps Pres – letter ASn – and/but – Nina NS – read
>   3ps Pres – book ASf
>'Vanya is writing a letter and Nina is reading a book.'

Other conjunctions are: *тогда как/togda kak* and *в то время как/v to
vremja kak*, both 'whilst' (literary); *же/že* (second word after the contrasted
word).

Asyndetic (colloquial):

>*Он гость – я хозяин./On–∅ ∅ gost'–∅ – ja ∅ xozjain–∅.*
>he NS – (be 3ps Pres) – guest – I NS – (be 1ps Pres) – master/host
>'He's (only) a guest, (but/and) I'm the master of the house.'

An intensive variant ('whereas in fact') uses conjunctions or particles added
to *a*: *a всё же/a vsë že, a ведь/a ved'*.

4.1.3   Disjunctive (Rus raz–deli–tel′n–yj 'separating/dividing')
The primary conjunction is *или/ili* 'or', occurring singly only when the alternatives are nominal; with alternating clauses it is repeated before each. The main variations are 'exclusive' alternatives ('either ... or'), 'open' ones ('maybe/possibly ... or') and 'alternating' ones ('now ... now').

(1) Exclusive

> *Или я не понимаю, или же ты не хочешь меня понять.*
> /Ili ja ne ponimaj–u, ili že ty ne xoč–eš̌ men–ja ponja–t′.
> or (either) – I NS – not – understand 1ps Pres – or – (Intensive) – you
>   NS – not – want 2ps Pres – me AS – understand Pf Inf
> 'Either I don't understand or else (it's) you (who) don't want to
>   understand me.'

Other conjunctions are: *либо ... либо/libo ... libo* (colloquial)

(2) Open. Two sets are used here: *не то ... не то/ne to ... ne to* and *то ли ... то ли/to li ... to li*, both expressing uncertainty or indefiniteness about the possibilities:

> (Context: 'I can't remember when we last met'):
> *Не то он ко мне приходил, не то я у него был.*
> /Ne to on–ø k(o) mne prixodi–l, ne to ja u ne–go by–l.
> (possibly) – he NS – to – me DS – come Impf Past Masc – (or possibly) –
>   I NS – at – him GS – be Past Masc
> 'Maybe he came to my place or I was at his.'

These need not be the only possibilities, just the most likely.

(3) Alternating. The set used exclusively in this sense is *то ... то/to ... to*:

> *Он то вскочит, то ляжет./On–ø to vskoč–it, to ljaž–et.*
> he NS – now – jump up Pf 3ps Pres – now – lie down 3ps Pf Pres
> 'One minute he'd jump/be jumping up and the next he'd lie/be lying
>   down (again).'

While *ili* and *libo* may be used in this sense, they still imply that the choice is limited to those stated.

4.1.4   Specifying ('that is', 'or rather')
These conjunctions, adding further detail or alternative ways of saying the same as in the first clause, are virtually identical to English in form and function; they include: *то есть/to est′* 'that is', *(а) именно/(a) imenno* 'namely', *(или)*

точнее/(ili) točn–ee '(or) rather', *другими словами/drug–imi slov–ami* 'in other words' (IP phrase), *иначе говоря/inače govor–ja* 'to put it another way' (lit. 'otherwise saying' – adverbial participle).

Also as in English, a written colon represents an asyndetic structure:

> *О нём знали одно: он был моряком./O n'–om zna–li odn–o: on–ø by–l morjak–om.*
>
> about – him LS – knew Impf Past Plur – one NSn – he NS – be Past Masc – sailor ISm
>
> 'They knew only one thing about him: (namely, that) he was a sailor.'

4.2   Complex sentence (complex-subordinate)

Subordinate clauses may be introduced by conjunctions or by pronouns, or by a combination of these; they may in a few situations be asyndetic; and their surface form may be a participle. We shall follow the pattern of the parts of the simple sentence in describing the types of clause (even though this does not correspond to the relative frequency of clauses).

Both conjunctions and pronouns are frequently preceded by a form of the demonstrative *to(t)* (in its Neuter form): this is obligatory when the main verb requires a case other than Accusative or requires a preposition, since this is the only way of marking the case; when the Accusative is the case required, that is, essentially, when the verb is transitive, the use of *to* is either formal (even pedantic) or simply unacceptable (depending on the particular verb).

A formal *punctuation rule* states that a comma must precede all subordinate clauses, thus the use of the comma to distinguish types of clause (as in English attributive clauses, see below) is excluded.

4.2.1   Subject clauses

Subject clauses are rare, occurring mainly in what we have called the 'logical subject' structure, where the main predicate is an impersonal copulative verb; the normal conjunction is *что/čto* 'that', the most common pronoun *кто/kto* 'who':

> *Мне приятно, что вы пришли./Mn–e prijatn–o, čto vy priš–li.*
>
> me DS – (be 3ps Pres) – pleasant NSn – that – you NP – come Pf Past Plur
>
> 'I'm delighted/pleased that you've come.'

> *Бывает, что люди этого не понимают./Byva–et, čto ljud–i èt–ogo ne ponima–jut.*
>
> be (Freq.) 3ps Pres – that – people NP – this GSn – not – understand 3pp Pres
>
> 'It sometimes happens that people don't understand this.'

Where more specific pronouns than just *to* are used, e.g. meaning 'every-one', 'everything', 'anyone', 'anything', etc., one may call such clauses subject clauses, parallel to the use of *to*, or one may regard the pronoun itself as the subject and the following clause as attributive (qualifying the pronoun); consider the following:

(1) *(Тот,) Кто не верит, пусть скажет./(Tot,) Kto ne ver–it, pust′ skaž–et.*

(he NSm) – who NS – not – believe 3ps Pres – let (particle) – say 3ps Pf Fut

'Let him/anyone who does not believe (this) say so.'

(2) *Самое главное – (то,) что всё было во-время кончено. /Sam–oe glavn–oe (ø) (to), čto vs–ë by–lo vo–vremja končen–o.*

most NSn – main NSn – (be 3ps Pres) – (that NSn) – that Conj – be Past Neut – in time Adv – finish PPP NSn Short

'The main thing is that everything was finished in time.'

The possible omission of *to* in (1) and (2) suggests that these are best seen as subject clauses.

(3) *Каждый, кто хочет поехать в Москву, сможет записаться завтра. /Každ–yj, kto xoč–et poexa–t′ v Moskv–u, smož–et zapisa–t′–sja zavtra.*

each NSm – who NS – want 3ps Pres – go Pf Inf – to – Moscow ASf – be able 3ps Pf Fut – register Pf Inf – tomorrow

'Anyone/Those who want(s) to go to Moscow can/will be able to register tomorrow.'

(4) *Все, кому знакомо было его имя, вспомнили и случай. /Vs–e, k–omu znakom–o by–lo ego im–ja, vspomni–li i slučaj–ø.*

all NP – who DS – familiar NSn – be Past Neut – his Invar – name NSn – remember Pf Past Plur – also – event ASm

'All (those) who knew/were familiar with his name, remembered the event also.'

In (3) and (4) the pronouns *každyj* and *vse* have enough semantic content to merit being treated as the real subject, leaving the *kto* clause as a relative (attributive) one.

A similar situation arises in the case of adjectival participles when they are used as substantivised forms, e.g.:

Читающий эти слова всё поймёт./Čitajušč–ij èt–i slov–a vs–ë pojm–ët.

read Pres Adj Part NSm – this AP – word APn – all ASn – understand 3ps Pf Fut

'Anyone who reads these words will understand everything.' (lit.
'A person reading...')

On the surface this is a simple sentence with a substantivised adjectival
subject, but the verbal content of the subject – as a generative analysis would
show – means that two actions are involved and so in reality two clauses; as to
the question of what sort of clause the first is, it is semantically identical to Rus
and Eng *t–ot, kto čita–et* 'he who reads' or to *vs–e, kto čita–et* 'all who read',
and thus is open to the same choices as for those above.

On balance, we would – with most Russian grammars – prefer to make a
distinction between these bare pronominal subjects and regular subjects with
attributive clauses attached, and so we accept this type as a subject clause.

4.2.2   Object or Complement clauses
(1) Direct Object

(a) Factual/reported statement. The most common Direct Object clause type
is the reporting of speech, thought etc., for which the primary conjunction is
что/čto 'that':

> *Он сказал, что придёт./On–ø skaza–l, čto prid–ёt.*
> he NS – say Pf Past Masc – that – come 3ps Pf Fut
> 'He said (that) he would come.'

> *Я думаю, что он придёт./Ja dumaj–u, čto on–ø prid–ёt.*
> I NS – think 1ps Pres – that – he NS – come 3ps Pf Fut
> 'I think he will come.'

This conjunction may *not* be omitted in the standard; omission is definitely
substandard.

(b) Perception of process. Another conjunction, used with verbs of perception
to indicate the perception of a process, is *как/kak* (lit. 'as'):

> *Я слышал, как она поёт./Ja slyša–l, kak on–a po–ёt.*
> I NS – hear Impf Past Masc – as – she NS – sing 3ps Pres
> 'I heard her singing.'

(c) Subjunctive. Where there is any subjunctive element (e.g. wishes, requests,
commands, doubts, etc.) the conjunction used is *чтобы/čtoby*, which is a fusion
of *čto* and *by*, the subjunctive particle (see chapter 3, section 2.2.7.2), and the
verb is formally Past:

> *Она сказала (хотела), чтобы я ушёл./On–a skaza–la (xote–la),*
> *čtoby ja uš–(ё)l.*
> she NS – say Pf (want Impf) Past Fem – that (Subjve) – I NS – leave
> Pf Past Masc
> 'She told (wanted) me to leave.'

In the colloquial standard, verbs of *request* only may take an Infinitive instead of the conjunction structure:

> *Она попросила меня уйти./On–a poprosi–la men–ja uj–ti.*
> she NS – request Pf Past Fem – me AS – leave Pf Inf
> 'She asked me to leave.'

After verbs of fearing, the subjunctive is expressed not only by the addition of *by* (and the Past form), but also by the negation of the verb (as happens also, for example, in French); the conjunctions are *как бы не/kak by ne* and *чтобы не/čtoby ne* (the negative particle placed before the verb):

> *Мы боялись, чтобы Ваня не провалился./My boja–li–s′, čtoby*
> *Van–ja ne provali–l–sja.*
> we NP – fear Impf Past Plur – that (Subj) – Vanya NS – (not) – fail
> Pf Past Masc
> 'We were afraid (that) Vanya would/might fail.'

(d) Allegation. Where the object is only alleged or only thought to be true, the conjunctions used are: *будто (бы)/budto (by)* (historically 'be it'), *якобы/jakoby* (bookish, Russian Church Slavonic equivalent of *kak by*); in these cases *by* (emphasising doubt, etc.) does *not* force a Past form:

> *Он говорил, будто (бы) выборов не будет.*
> */On–∅ govori–l, budto (by) vybor–ov ne bud–et.*
> he NS – say Impf Past Masc – that (allegedly) – election GPm –
> not – be 3ps Fut
> 'He said/was saying that (he had heard) there might not be any
> election.'

(e) Repeated subject. With all Direct Object clauses, as happens with the modal auxiliaries, if the subject of the subordinate clause is the same as that of the main clause, the subordinate verb is in the Infinitive:

> *Мы боялись опоздать в театр./My boja–li–s′ opozda–t′ v teatr–∅.*
> we NP – fear Impf Past Plur – be late Pf Inf – to – theatre ASm
> 'We were afraid of being late for the theatre.'

(f) Reported questions. Reported *wh*-questions are done, as in English, directly, that is, using the interrogative pronoun as a conjunction, and adjusting the person if necessary (but not the tense; see below, section 5):

> *Я спросил, когда должен прийти поезд./Ja sprosi–l, kogda*
> *dolž–(e)n–∅ ∅ prij–ti poezd–∅.*
> I NS – ask Pf Past Masc – when Interrog – must Masc – (be 3ps Pres)
> – come Pf Inf – train NSm
> 'I asked when the train was due to arrive.'

When the original interrogative is *čto* 'what', it is differentiated from the reported statement (*čto* 'that') by stress: the *wh–* version has stressed /o/ ([ɔ]); the stress may be orthographically marked to avoid written ambiguity:

> *Она спросила, чтó мне надо./On–a sprosi–la, čtó mn–e nado.*
> she NS – ask Pf Past Fem – what – me DS – necessary Invar
> 'She asked what I wanted.' (lit. ' . . . what I needed')

Reported *yes/no* questions are done differently: the conjunction used is *ли/li* 'whether', placed second in the clause, normally after the verb (in principle after the comment), with the same adjustment of person (and again note the non-adjustment of tense):

> *Он спросил, пойду ли я в театр./On–∅ sprosi–l, pojd–u li ja*
> *v teatr–∅.*
> he NS – ask Pf Past Masc – go 1ps Pf Fut – whether – I NS –
> to – theatre ASm
> 'He asked if/whether I was/would be going to the theatre.'

(2) Indirect Object or Complement. Finite verbs which require a case other than Accusative must be followed by a form of *to* (see above, section 4.2). In the following the verb requires an Instrumental of the object of interest:

> *Я очень интересуюсь тем, что вы изучаете русский.*
> */Ja očen′ interesuj–u–s′ t–em, čto vy izuča–ete russk–ij.*
> I NS – very much – be interested 1ps Pres – (the fact ISn) – that – you
> NP – study 2pp Pres – Russian ASm
> 'I'm very interested (to know) that you're studying Russian.' (lit. 'in
> the fact that . . . ')

With non-finite forms the use of *to* is optional, omission being colloquially normal. In the following, *rad* formally requires the Dative:

> *Я очень рад (тому), что вы пришли./Ja ∅ očen′ rad–∅ (t–omu), čto*
> *vy priš–li.*
> I NS – (be 1ps Pres) – very – glad NSm – (the fact DSn) – that – you
> NP – come Pf Past Plur
> 'I'm very glad (that) you've come.'

4.2.3 Predicative clause

Infrequently a clause may occupy the place of the nominal predicate, that is, following the copula or another copulative verb. An introductory correlative pronoun is obligatory in this type, and not only where the case required is Instrumental (again, where this pronoun is not simply *to*, one might analyse it as the full nominal predicate, with what follows seen as an Attributive clause); most common are pronouns meaning 'the sort of person/thing (who/which) ...'; in the second example *stat'* requires the Instrumental.

> *Он такой, какой/кто ничего никогда не делает.*
>   /On–∅ ∅ tak–oj, kak–oj/kto nič–ego nikogda ne dela–et.
> he NS – (be 3ps Pres) – such NSm – the like of which NSm/who NS–
>   nothing GS – never – not – do 3ps Pres
> 'He's the sort of person who never does a thing.'

> *Он стал тем, кем хотел стать./On–∅ sta–l t–em, k–em*
>   *xote–l sta–t'.*
> he NS – become Pf Past Masc – that ISm – who IS – want Impf
>   Past Masc – become Pf Inf
> 'He became what he wanted to become.'

This construction is more frequent with some common introductory predicative phrases, e.g. *Дело в том, что.../Del–o ∅ v t–om, čto...* 'The fact of the matter is that...' (lit. 'The matter is in...'), *Задача состоит в том, чтобы.../Zadač–a sosto–it v t–om, čtoby...* 'The crux of the problem is that/to...' (lit. 'The problem consists in...').

4.2.4   Attributive/relative clause

Clauses which fulfil the role of attribute to a noun (or pronoun, but see above, section 4.2.1) are most often called in English 'relative'; Russian grammar uses the same term as that used for words, namely 'defining', or 'attributive' (*opredel–itel'n–yj*). They are introduced by any interrogative word (pronoun or adverb), functioning as a 'relative pronoun/adverb'.

(1) 'which'. The most common of the interrogative words used is the pronoun *который/kotor–yj* 'who/which', which is rather rare as a genuine interrogative, when it means 'which particular one out of a limited set'; the more common interrogative form with this meaning is *какой/kak–oj*, which, in turn, is more restricted in the relative function, where it has the (more etymologically correct) sense of 'the like/sort of which'. Both of these are adjectival forms which take their number and gender from the antecedent (the word they are qualifying), and their case (with or without preposition) from their role in their own clause; the following clauses might qualify a noun like *девушка/devušk–a* 'girl':

> *... которая стоит у двери/... kotor–aja sto–it u dver–i*
> which NSf – stand 3ps Pres – at – door GSf
> '... who's standing by the door'

... которую мы вчера видели/... kotor–uju my včera vide–li
which ASf – we NP – yesterday – see Impf Past Plur
'... whom we saw yesterday'

*... о которой ты мне рассказывал/... o kotor–oj ty mn–e
rasskazyva–l*
about – which LSf – you NS – me DS – tell Impf Past Masc
'... you were telling me about' (lit. '... about whom you...')

Where *kotoryj* singles out a particular person/object, *kakoj* refers to types, comparing one with others; in each case emphasis on the particular or the type may be achieved by the addition of the correlative *tot* or *takoj* respectively, e.g. *та девушка, которая/t–a devušk–a, kotor–aja* 'the (particular) girl who', *такая девушка, какая/tak–aja devušk–a, kak–aja* 'the (sort of) girl who'.

There is a parallel to the English use of 'that' in relative clauses, but it is not common, though it does not seem to have any formal stylistic connotation:

... дом, что стоит на углу/dom–ø, čto sto–it na ugl–u
house NS – that – stand 3ps Pres – on – corner LSm
'... the house that stands on the corner'

This is no doubt an extension of the regular use of *čto* after pronouns like *to* 'that' or *vsë* 'everything', or substantivised adjectives like *perv–oe* 'the first thing' or *glavn–oe* 'the main thing', which we have interpreted above (section 4.2.1) as introducing subject clauses rather than as being themselves a part of the main clause.

(2) 'whose'. The possessive 'whose' is colloquially formed by using the Genitive of *kotor–yj*, placed after the 'possessed' noun in the subordinate clause:

*... (девушка,) книгу которой я сейчас читаю/... (devušk–a,)
knig–u kotor–oj ja sejčas čitaj–u*
(girl NSf) – book ASf – which GSf – I NS – now – read 1ps Pres
'... (the girl) whose book I'm reading at the moment'

But there is also a literary (bookish, poetic) pronoun which parallels English in form, function and position, namely *чей/č(e)j–ø* 'whose' (for forms see chapter 3, section 2.1.4.2); its case matches that of the possessed noun:

*... (девушка,) чью книгу я читаю/... (devuška,) čj–u knig–u
ja čitaj–u*
whose ASf – book ASf – I NS – read 1ps Pres
'... whose book I'm reading'

(3) 'Restrictive' and 'non-restrictive' attributes. Since Russian punctuation rules require a comma before every subordinate clause, the distinction between

restrictive and non-restrictive attributes of a group (sometimes distinguished as 'relative' and 'adjectival' clauses respectively) which English achieves by the presence versus absence of a comma cannot be done by punctuation; Russian must (to avoid ambiguity) specify the restrictive type by the addition of a specifier like 'that/those', that is, a form of *tot*; for example, for Eng (1) *foreign students, who receive a grant* ... (= 'who all', non-restrictive) Russian does not need a correlative, but for (2) *foreign students who receive a grant* ... (= 'only those who', restrictive) written Russian requires *t–e ... kotor–ye*:

    (1) *иностранные студенты, которые получают стипендию*
        /inostrann–ye student–y, kotor–ye poluča–jut stipendi–ju

    (2) *те иностранные студенты, которые получают стипендию*
        /t–e inostrann–ye student–y, kotor–ye polučaj–ut stipendij–u

A less formal spoken form may rely – as in English – on stress and timing: in (2), *student–y* (like Eng *students*) would receive a weaker stress and not be followed by a pause.

(4) Participles. In literary or formal style, any of the four adjectival participles may function as the predicate of a relative clause (for forms see chapter 3, section 2.2.9); the two active ones (suffixes –*šč*– and –*vš*–) are the equivalent of an active or reflexive verb, the passive ones (suffixes –*m*– and –*nn–/–t*–) of a passive verb; the present ones must of course be imperfective aspect, the past passive is perfective only, and only the past active (–*vš*–) may be of either aspect. As adjectives, they must all agree also in case with the antecedent; this construction parallels that of the English omission of the relative pronoun and main auxiliary verb:

    ... *с девушкой, стоящей у двери/* ... *s devušk–oj, stojašč–ej u*
        dver–i
    with – girl ISf – stand Pres Part Act ISf – at – door GSf
    '... with the girl (who is) standing by the door'
    ... *с девушкой, стоявшей у двери/* ... *s devušk–oj, stojavš–ej*
        u dver–i
    with – girl ISf – stand Impf Past Part Act ISf – at – door GSf
    '... with the girl (who was) standing by the door'

While this last (Imperfective Past Active) may accompany only a past tense main verb, the present participle is also possible in such cases, since it implies simply simultaneity (or overlap) of the two events, while the Perfective Past Active implies a succession in which the subordinate action preceded the main:

... с девушкой, написавшей это письмо/... s devušk–oj,
  napisavš–ej èt–o pis′m–o
with – girl ISf – write Pf Past Part Act ISf – this ASn – letter ASn
'... with the girl who has/had written this letter' (depending on the
  tense of the main verb)

The Present Participle Passive (*–m–*), meaning 'which is being –en', is rare
(and the most literary of the four):

учебники, используемые в этом году/učebnik–i, ispol′zuem–ye
  v èt–om god–u
textbook NP – use Pres Part Pass – in – this LSm – year LSm
'the textbooks being used this year'

The Past Participle Passive is the least formal, occurring easily in colloquial
usage:

в книге, написанной моим братом/v knig–e, napisann–oj
  mo–im brat–om
in – book LSf – write Past Part Pass LSf – my ISm – brother ISm
'in the book written by my brother'/'in the book my brother wrote'

(5) Relative adverbs. Any interrogative adverb may be used as a relative form
(also as in English):

Это было то время года, когда оживает вся природа.
  /Èt–o by–lo t–o vrem–ja god–a, kogda oživa–et vs–ja prirod–a.
this NSn – be Past Neut – that ASn – time ASn – year GSm – when –
  revive 3ps Pres – all NSf – nature NSf
'It was that time of the year when all of nature comes to life.'

There may only be a correlative adverb instead of a noun:

Он уехал туда, где никто его не найдёт.
  /On–ø uexa–l tuda, gde nikto e–go ne najd–ët.
he NS – go away Pf Past Masc – to there – where – no one NS – him
  AS – not – find 3ps Pf Fut
'He's gone off/away (to) where no one will find him.'

(6) Clausal antecedent. Where the whole main clause is the antecedent of the
subordinate one, that is, where the subordinate clause describes an effect of the
main, the conjunction used is *что/čto,* in the meaning 'something which', an
elliptical form of a potential double *to, čto* in what is in reality a noun clause
(subject or object) ('that which ... is/was the fact that ... '):

Она не приходила на вечер, что нас удивило.
   /On–a ne prixodi–la na večer–ø, čto n–as udivi–lo.
she NS – not – come Impf Past Fem – to – party ASm – that (which)–
   us AP – surprise Pf Past Neut
'She didn't come to the party, which surprised us.'

4.2.5   Adverbial/adjunct clause

Adverbial clauses modify main clauses in the same way as adverbs do single words; while adverbs modify verbs, adjectives or other adverbs, adverbial clauses normally modify the whole verb-based content of the main clause. One group includes the basic adverbial notions of time, place, cause and manner (answering, as it were, the questions 'when', 'where', 'why' and 'how'), and a second covers secondary notions of accompanying circumstance: condition, concession and degree. We shall consider them in that order.

4.2.5.1 Time

(1) Simultaneous ('while'). The two primary conjunctions are *когда/kogda* 'when' (also the basic interrogative form) and *пока/poka* 'while'; where the two actions are fully simultaneous, both verbs will be Imperfective:

Когда/Пока Витя читал книгу, Володя решал задачу.
   /Kogda/Poka Vit–ja čita–l knig–u, Volod–ja reša–l zadač–u.
when/while – Vitya NS – read Impf Past Masc – book ASf – Volodya
   NS – (try to) solve Impf Past Masc – problem ASf
'While Vitya was reading a book, Volodya was working on a problem.'

Where there is only partial overlap, the main verb may be perfective:

Когда/Пока я смотрел телевизор, в комнату вошёл брат.
   /Kogda/Poka ja smotre–l televizor–ø, v komnat–u voš–(ë)l brat–ø.
when/while – I NS – watch Impf Past Masc – television ASm –
   into – room ASf – enter Pf Past Masc – brother NSm
'While I was watching television, my brother came into the room.'

Other conjunctions are based on prepositional phrases attached to forms of *to*: *между тем как/meždu t–em kak* and *в то время как/v t–o vrem–ja kak*, both 'while/during the time that', *по мере того как/po mer–e t–ogo kak* 'as' (lit. 'in measure with').

The present adverbial participle (in *–ja*, see chapter 3, section 2.2.9) has the same meaning, but is usable only when the subjects are the same (as with English '–ing'):

Смотря телевизор, я заснул./Smotr–ja televizor–ø, ja zasnu–l.
watch Pres Adv Part – television ASm – I NS – fall asleep Pf Past
   Masc

'While watching television I fell asleep./I fell asleep watching television.'

(2) Successive ('before', 'after'). In any sequence of actions, the non-final ones are normally perfective.

(a) Subordinate action occurs *after* main:

'before': all conjunctions are compound, the primary ones being *до того как/do t–ogo kak* 'generally before' (*do* is the preposition 'before') and *прежде чем/prežde č–em* and *перед тем как/pered t–em kak*, both 'immediately before' (*prežde* is the adverb 'previously' and *pered* the preposition 'just before', also 'in front of'):

> *До того как пришли гости, Нина убрала всю квартиру.*
> /Do t–ogo kak priš–li gost–i, Nin–a ubra–la vs–ju kvartir–u.
> before – arrive Pf Past Plur – guest NP – Nina NS – tidy up Pf Past
> Fem – all ASf – apartment ASf
> 'Before the guests arrived, Nina (had) tidied up the whole flat.'

Where the subjects are the same, the subordinate verb may be Infinitive:

> *Прежде чем прочитать (я прочитал) книгу, я познакомился с историей её издания.*
> /Prežde č–em pročita–t' (ja pročita–l) knig–u, ja poznakomi–l–sja s istori–ej e–ë izdani–ja.
> before – read Pf Inf (I NS – read Pf Past Masc) – book ASf – I
> NS – become acquainted Pf Past Masc – with – history ISf – its
> Fem – publication GSn
> 'Before reading the book, I familiarised myself with the history of its publication.'

(b) Subordinate action occurs (or ought to occur) *before* the main:

'after': *когда/kogda* after a perfective verb; also *после того как/posle t–ogo kak* (*posle* being the preposition 'after'):

> *Когда я открыл окно, в комнату влетела пчела.*
> /Kogda ja otkry–l okn–o, v komnat–u vlete–la pčel–a.
> when – I NS – open Pf Past Masc – window ASn – into – room ASf
> – fly in Pf Past Fem – bee NSf
> 'When I opened the window, a bee flew into the room.'

'from the moment': *с тех пор как/s t–ex por–ø kak* (*por–a* means 'time'), *с того времени как/s t–ogo vrem–eni kak* (*vrem–ja* also means 'time')

'immediately after': *как только/kak tol'ko* 'as soon as', *едва/edva* 'no sooner had'. The past adverbial participle (in –*v*), always perfective, may be used with the same subject as in the main:

Посмотрев телевизор полчаса, я лёг спать.
/*Posmotre–v televizor–ø polčasa, ja lëg–ø spa–t'.*/
watch Pf Past Adv Part – television ASm – for half an hour – I NS lay
Pf Past Masc – sleep Impf Inf:
'Having watched/After watching television for half an hour, I went to
bed.'

'until': the main action cannot take place until the subordinate has: the primary conjunction is again *poka* ('while'), but with a *negative perfective* verb; the main verb will also be negative:

Он не может уехать, пока не закончит работу.
/*On–ø ne mož–et uexa–t', poka ne zakonč–it rabot–u.*/
he NS – not – be able 3ps Pres – leave Pf Inf – while – not – finish
3ps Pf Fut – work ASf
'He can't leave until he has finished (his) work.'

A compound variant is *до тех пор пока/do t–ex por–ø poka* 'until such time as'.

As in English, the order of clauses is flexible, the second position simply giving more importance to that clause, on the principle of topic and comment.

4.2.5.2 Place. The three interrogative adverbs of place (*где/gde* 'where', *куда/kuda* 'to where', *откуда/otkuda* 'from where') function also as conjunctions, normally preceded by a correlative adverb (*там/tam* 'there', *туда/tuda* 'to there', *оттуда/ottuda* 'from there', respectively); omission of the correlative form is colloquial:

Иди (туда), куда хочешь./Id–i (tuda), kuda xoč–eš'.
go 2ps Impf Imper – (to there) – to where – want 2ps Pres
'Go where(ver) you want.'

Other place adverbs which may function as correlatives include: *везде/vezde* and *всюду/vsjudu*, both 'everywhere'; *нигде/nigde* 'nowhere'; *отовсюду/otovsjudu* 'from everywhere'.

4.2.5.3 Cause (Why₁). These are clauses which answer the question 'why?' *in retrospect*, that is, 'what is the reason?'; the main conjunctions are: *потому что/po–tomu čto* (from *po t–omu* DS) 'because' (general) (matching the basic interrogative form *почему/po–čemu* 'why?'), *оттого что/ot–togo čto* (from *ot togo*) 'because' (as a direct result) (interrogative *отчего/ot–čego*), and *так как/tak kak* 'since'; the last is the only one usable in sentence-initial position (like Eng *since*), so it serves to set the cause as the topic, while *potomu čto* must follow the main (like Eng *because*):

Так как у меня не было карандаша, я не мог оставить вам записку. /*Tak kak u men–ja ne by–lo karandaš–a, ja ne mog–ø ostavi–t′ v–am zapisk–u.*

since – at – me GS – not – be Past Neut – pencil GSm – I NS – not – be able Impf Past Masc – leave Pf Inf – you DP – note ASf

'Since I didn't have a pencil, I couldn't leave you a note.'

Я не оставил вам записку, потому что у меня не было карандаша. /*Ja ne ostavi–l v–am zapisk–u, po–tomu čto u men–ja ne by–lo karandaš–a.*

I NS – not – leave Pf Past Masc – you DP – note ASf – because, etc.

'I didn't leave you a note because I didn't have a pencil.'

Other conjunctions are: *ибо/ibo* 'for' (bookish), *раз/raz* 'seeing that/as how' (colloquial) (lit. 'once'); and a set of technical or bureaucratic ones: *ввиду того что/v–vid–u t–ogo čto* (from *vid–ø* 'view') and *в силу того что/v sil–u t–ogo čto* (from *sil–a* 'force'), both 'in view of the fact that', 'given that'; *вследствие того что/v–sledstvi–e t–ogo čto* (from *sled–* 'follow') 'in consequence of the fact that'; *благодаря тому что/blagodar–ja t–omu čto* (from *blagodar–it′* 'thank') 'thanks to the fact that'.

An asyndetic construction is possible, both literary and colloquial, marked graphically by a colon:

Пора спать: 12 часов./*Pora ø spa–t′: 12 čas–ov.*

time Invar – (be 3ps Pres) – sleep Impf Inf – twelve NS – hour GP

'It's time for bed (lit. 'to sleep'): it's 12 o'clock.'

Все замолчали: его любили слушать./*Vs–e zamolča–li: e–go ljubi–li sluša–t′.*

all NP – fall silent Pf Past Plur – him AS – like Impf Past Plur – listen to Impf Inf

'Everyone stopped talking: they liked listening to him.'

4.2.5.4 Purpose (Why₂). Purpose clauses answer the question 'why?' *prospectively*, that is, 'for what intended purpose/aim?' (Rus *зачем/za–čem* from *za č–em*). The basic conjunction is *чтобы/čto–by* 'so/in order that'; if the subjects are the same, it is followed by an Infinitive, otherwise by a Past Tense form (since the *–by* element is subjunctive):

Я хочу купить (Мне нужен) этот учебник, чтобы готовиться к экзамену.
/*Ja xoč–u kupi–t′ (Mn–e nuž(e)n–ø) èt–ot učebnik–ø, čto–by gotovi–t′–sja k èkzamen–u.*

I NS – want 1ps Pres – buy Pf Inf – (me DS – necessary NSm) – this
ASm (NSm) – textbook ASm (NSm) – so that – prepare Impf Inf Refl
– towards – exam DSm
'I want to buy (I need) this textbook to prepare for the exam.'

Папа дал мне деньги, чтобы я купил учебник.
/Pap–a da–l mn–e den'g–i, čto–by ja kupi–l učebnik–ø.
papa/father NS – give Pf Past Masc – me DS – money AP – so that –
I NS – buy Pf Past Masc – textbook ASm
'Father/Papa gave me money to buy the textbook.'

Expanded formal forms, all also meaning 'in order that', are *для того
чтобы/dlja t–ogo čto–by*, *затем чтобы /za–t–em čtoby* (from *za t–em*) and *c
тем чтобы/s t–em čto–by*.

4.2.5.5 Manner.   These answer the question 'how?', and the primary
conjunction is *как/kak* 'like, as'. Most often this is a particle governing
a nominal phrase ('like a...'), and as a conjunction it is not often used
alone:

*Он всё исполнил, как ему приказывали./On vs–ë ispolni–l,
kak e–mu prikazyvaa–li.*
he NS – all ASn – carry out Pf Past Masc – as/like – him DS – order
Impf Past Plur
'He carried out everything just as he had been ordered/told.'

More often it is preceded by the correlative *так/tak* 'thus', and also by the
intensifying particle *же/že*, giving the meaning 'just as'; in this case, there must
be a comma between *tak* and *kak*, distinguishing them from *tak kak* 'since' (see
above):

*Я сделал всё так (же), как посоветовал преподаватель.
/Ja sdela–l vs–ë tak (že), kak posovetova–l prepodavatel'–ø.*
I NS – do Pf Past Masc – all ASn –thus – (Intens) – as – advise Pf Past
Masc – teacher NSm
'I did everything (just/exactly) as the teacher advised (me to).'

A technical variant is *подобно тому как/podobno t–omu kak* 'similarly to
how'.
The meaning 'as if' is conveyed primarily by *будто/budto*, which may be
added to *kak*:

Ты ведёшь себя, (как) будто ты хозяин дома.
/Ty ved–ëš' seb–ja, (kak) budto ty ∅ xozjain–∅ dom–a.
you NS – conduct 2ps Pres – self AS – as if – you NS – (be 2ps Pres)
– master NSm – house GSm
'You're behaving as though you were the master of the house.'

Literary conjunctions include *словно/slovno, точно/točno* and *как если бы/kak esli by*, all 'as if', the last paralleling the English construction as a version of the conditional 'if' (see next).

4.2.5.6 Condition

(1) Real/open. The primary conjunction is *если/esli* 'if', used normally with a Future verb (of either aspect); the Conditional clause normally comes first as the topic, as in English:

Если вы придёте вечером, я вам покажу новые снимки.
/Esli vy prid–ëte večerom, ja v–am pokaž–u nov–ye snimk–i.
if – you NP – come 2pp Pf Fut – in the evening – I NS – you DP –
show 1ps Pf Fut – new AP – photo AP
'If you come this evening, I'll show you some new photos.'

A more generalised condition can be expressed by *когда/kogda* 'when/if ever', with imperfective verbs, cf. Eng *If/When you don't water flowers they die*; the colloquial conjunction *раз/raz*, normally meaning 'since' in the causal sense (above), may be conditional when used with a future verb, when it indicates certainty about a future event:

Раз ты придёшь, давай сыграем в шахматы.
/Raz ty prid–ëš', davaj sygra–em v šaxmat–y.
since – you NS – come 2ps Pf Fut – let (us) – play 1pp Pf Fut –
at – chess AP
'Since you're going to come, let's have a game of chess.'

Others meaning 'if' include: *ежели/eželi* (low style), *коли/koli* (archaic/poetic).

Colloquially, there may also be no conjunction, probably best interpreted as ellipsis:

Будет время – зайду к тебе./Bud–et vrem–ja – zajd–u k teb–e.
be 3ps Fut – time NSn – drop in 1ps Pf Fut – to – you DS
'If I have the/Should there be time, I'll drop in on you.'

Compare this to the standard, which would simply add *esli* at the front.

'Unless' is simply 'if...not' (*esli...ne*).

The main clause may have an emphatic particle attached (cf. Eng *if... then*); these include: *mo/to*, *тогда/togda*, both essentially temporal 'then', *так/tak* 'so', *значит/znač–it* (from the verb 'mean'), both in the consequential sense of 'so'.

(2) Hypothetical. Hypothetical conditions are expressed by the addition of the subjunctive particle *бы/by*, with the verb in the past tense form, in both clauses; note that the fixed form of the verb means that no tense can be indicated in the verb, this having to be done by other means, for example adverbs, but often simply by context. *By* is enclitic and tends towards the second position in a clause, thus it always follows *esli*, so much so that the colloquial version of the two is *eslib*, written in literary dialogue as one word – *еслиб*; in the main clause it is also drawn to the verb, which may not be the first word:

> *Если бы ты пришёл, я бы показал вам новые снимки.*
> */Esli by ty priš–(ё)l, ja by pokaza–l v–am nov–ye snimk–i.*
> if – (Subjve) – you NS – come Pf Past Masc – I NS – (Subjve) – show
>   Pf Past Masc – you DP – new AP – photo AP
> 'If you had come, I would have shown you some new photos.' *or:*
> 'If you were to come, I would show you...' (expressing an unlikely
>   future event)

Here, too, there is an asyndetic colloquial form:

> *Пришёл бы ко мне – я бы тебе всё рассказал.*
> */Priš–(ё)l by k(o) mn–e – ja by teb–e vs–ё rasskaza–l.*
> come Pf Past Masc – (Subjve) – to – me DS – I NS – (Subjve) – all
>   ASn – tell Pf Past Masc
> 'Had you come to me I would have told you everything.'

The 2nd Person Singular Imperative form may be used for conditions, most often hypothetical, rarely open; most common in this usage is the Imperative of 'be' – *будь/bud'*:

> *Будь они все вместе, им было бы легче жить.*
> */Bud' on–i vs–e vmeste, im by–lo by legč–e ži–t'.*
> be 2ps Imper – they NP – all NP – together – them DP – be Past Neut –
>   (Subjve) – easy Compar Invar – live Impf Inf
> 'Were they all together, they would find life easier.' (lit. '... it
>   would be easier for them to live')

> *Не будь меня, он бы умер./Ne bud' men–ja, on–ø by umer–ø.*
> not – be 2ps Imper – me GS – he NS – (Subjve) – die Pf Past Masc
> 'But for me, he would have died.' ('me' Genitive because of the
>   negative)

Other such Imperative forms are accompanied by the particle *by*:

> *Знай бы об этом раньше, мы бы туда не пошли.*
> /Znaj–ø by ob èt–om ran'–še, my by tuda ne poš–li./
> know 2ps Imper – (Subjve) – about – this LSn – before Adv – we
> NP – (Subjve) – to there – not – go pf Past Plur
> 'If we had known about this before, we wouldn't have gone there.'

4.2.5.7 Concession. The basic concessive conjunctions are *хотя/xotja* 'although' (from the verb 'want') and the more formal *несмотря на то что/ nesmotrja na to čto* 'in spite of the fact that' (from the verb 'look'):

> *Хотя (Несмотря на то что) я очень устал, я принялся за*
> *работу.*
> /Xotja (Nesmotrja na to čto) ja očen' usta–l, ja prinja–l–sja*
> *za rabot–u.*
> although – (in spite of the fact that) – I NS – very – get tired Pf
> Past Masc – I NS – set about Pf Past Masc – to – work ASf
> 'Even though I was very tired, I got down to work.'

The particle *пусть/pust'* (normally used for 3rd Person Imperative, in the meaning 'let', and indeed derived from the Imperative of the verb 'let' – see above, section 3.2.2.6) may have the sense 'even if, albeit', most often governing a nominal phrase, but possibly also a clause:

> *Пусть я неправ, но ты должен меня выслушать.*
> *Pust' ja ø neprav–ø, no ty dolž(e)n–ø ø men–ja vysluša–t'.*
> even if – I NS – (be 1ps Pres) – wrong NSm Short – but – you
> NS – ought NSm– (be 2ps Pres) – me AS – hear out Pf Inf
> 'Even if I'm wrong, you should still hear me out.'

The concessive type 'no matter wh–' is handled by the addition of the particle *ни/ni* to an interrogative adverb or conjunction (parallel to Eng *'wh–ever'*), placed before the verb:

> *Как он ни изменился, я сразу узнал его.*
> /Kak on–ø ni izmeni–l–sja, ja srazu uzna–l e–go./
> how – he NS – (Conc) – change Pf Past Masc Refl – I NS – immediately
> – recognise Pf Past Masc – him AS
> 'No matter (In spite of) how much he had changed, I recognised
> him immediately.'

> *Кому он ни рассказывал о своей идее, его не понимали.*
> /K–omu on–ø ni rasskazyva–l o svo–ej ide–e, e–go ne ponima–li./

who DS – he NS – (Conc) – tell Impf Past Masc – about – own
LSf – idea LSf – him GS – not – understand Impf Past Plur
'No matter who he told about his idea, no one understood him.'

A variant which emphasises the subjunctive element adds *by* and makes the verb Past (again making the actual tense ambiguous):

> *Как бы я ни старался, я не выполнил (выполню) задание в срок.*
> /Kak by ja ni stara–l–sja, ja ne vypolni–l (vypoln–ju) zadani–e
> v srok–ø.
> how – (Subjve) – I NS – (Conc) – try Impf Past Masc – I NS – not
> – carry out Pf Past Masc (1ps Pf Fut) – task ASn – in – period ASm
> 'No matter how (much/hard) I try/tried, I couldn't (won't be able to)
> carry out the task within the time allowed.'

Here the tense of the subordinate verb is seen only in the main verb.

4.2.5.8 Degree

(1) '–er than'. Comparisons of degree are done with the predicative comparative (adverbial) form (in *–e(e)*; see chapter 3, section 2.1.5.6) followed by чем/*čem* (formally the Instrumental Singular of *čto*):

> *Писатель должен знать больше, чем написал.*
> /Pisatel'–ø dolž(e)n–ø ø zna–t' bol'–še, čem napisa–l.
> writer NSm – ought NSm – (be 3ps Pres) – know Impf Inf – more
> Compar Adv – than – write Pf Past Masc
> 'A writer should know more than he has written.'

The phrase 'none other than' is expressed by *не кто иной как/ne kto in–oj–ø kak* for persons and *не что иное как/ne čto in–oe kak* for objects ('nothing other than'), *inoj–ø* meaning 'other, different'.

(2) 'the more ... the more'. The same form *čem* introduces the first comparative item, and the second is introduced by the Instrumental of *to*, namely тем/*tem*:

> *Чем выше мы поднимались в горы, тем труднее становилось
> дышать.* /Čem vyš–e my podnima–li–s' v gor–y, tem trudn–ee
> stanovi–lo–s' dyša–t'.
> by as much – high Compar Adv – we NP – go up Impf Past Plur –
> into – mountain AP – by that much – difficult Compar Adv – become
> Impf Past Neut – breathe Impf Inf
> 'The higher we climbed into the mountains, the harder it became to
> breathe.'

(3) 'so x, that'. These are structured like English, namely either 'so' + adjective/adverb + 'that', or 'so much' (+ NP) + 'that'; in the first case 'so' is *tak* before adverbs or short adjectives, *takoj* before long adjectives; in the second 'so much' is столько/*stol′ko* (the correlative form of interrogative сколько/*skol′ko* 'how much?'):

> *Песни пели так тихо, что на улице не было слышно.*
> /*Pesn–i pe–li tak tix–o, čto na ulic–e ne by–lo slyšn–o.*
> song AP – sing Impf Past Plur – so – quietly – that – on – street LSf
> – not – be Past Neut – audible NSn
> 'They were singing (the songs) so quietly that they couldn't be heard outside'. (lit. '. . . in the street')

When the concessive clause is negative ('not so much . . . that', 'too much . . . to'), the subjunctive nature of the main clause is indicated by the conjunction чтобы/*čto–by* and either a past tense verb or an infinitive (for the same subject):

> *Он не так хорошо себя чувствует, чтобы его выписали*
> *из больницы.* /*On–ø ne tak xorošo seb–ja čuvstvu–et, čto–by e–go*
> *vypisa–li iz bol′nic–y.*
> he NS – not – so – well – self – feel 3ps Pres – that (Subjve) – him
> AS – discharge Pf Past Plur – from – hospital GSf
> 'He doesn't feel so well that he could be discharged from hospital.'
> (lit. 'they might/could discharge him')

> *Я слишком устал, чтобы заниматься.*
> /*Ja sliškom usta–l, čto–by zanima–t′–sja.*
> I NS – too much – get tired Pf Past Masc – that (Subjve) – study
> Impf Inf
> 'I'm too tired to study.'

(4) 'as (much) . . . as'. The first member of this set (which may in some cases be omitted) is the same correlative form as in the 'so much' set – столько/*stol′ko*, the second the interrogative form, сколько/*skol′ko*:

> *Он дал мне столько денег, сколько я просил.*
> /*On–ø da–l mn–e stol′ko den(e)g–ø, skol′ko ja prosi–l.*
> he NS – give Pf Past Masc – me DS – as much – money GP – as –
> I NS – ask Impf Past Masc
> 'He gave me as much money as I asked for.'

A cognate conjunction is поскольку/*po–skol′ku* 'insofar/inasmuch as':

> *Поскольку вы готовы подписать, готов и я.*
> /*Poskol′ku vy ø gotov–y podpisa–t′, gotov ø i ja.*

inasmuch as – you NP – (be 2pp Pres) – ready NP – sign Pf Inf – ready
NSm – (be 1ps Pres) – also – I NS
'Inasmuch as (Since) you're ready to sign, so am I.'

5   Reported/indirect speech

5.1   Direct speech and punctuation

Written direct speech is indicated only by a long (em) dash at the onset; no
quotation marks are used (except where the direct speech is not set off into
a new paragraph). Two sorts of quotation marks have been traditionally used
in the latter case, as well as for inner monologue, quotations, titles or abnor-
mal/ironic meanings: one set – now less common – is like the English double
quotation mark, except that the front one is turned outwards from the quote
and is at line level („ ... "); the second set, now the norm, are double arrows
(« ... »; Fr '*guillemets*') enclosing the quote; both are called *кавычки/kavyčk–i*
('hooks').

5.2   Reported speech

Since syntactically reported speech usually functions as an Object clause of
the 'reporting' verb ('say', 'tell', 'ask', etc.) – as indeed does written direct
speech, since it is normally introduced by a similar verb in the 'author's speech'
('said', 'asked', etc.), we have dealt with this to a large extent above under the
'Object clause' section (4.2.2). What follows is intended to complement that,
by bringing all the procedures together in their own right as 'reported speech';
also there are some extra features which were not relevant to clause structure.

(1) Statement. Following the introductory past tense verb (basic are *сказал–/
skaza–l–* 'said', *ответил–/otveti–l–* 'answered'), the person changes as in
English (1st > 3rd), but the tense remains the same as in the direct speech – there
is *no* shift of tense as in English (and other languages); nor can the conjunction
be omitted in the standard:

> *Ваня сказал, что не любит сыр./Van–ja skaza–l, čto ne ljub–it
> syr–∅.*
> Vanya NS – say Pf Past Masc – that – not – like 3ps <u>Pres</u> –
> cheese ASm
> 'Vanya said he didn't like cheese.' (lit. 'that ... *does* not like')

> *Ваня сказал, что придёт./Van–ja skaza–l, čto prid–ёt.*
> Vanya NS – say Pf Past Masc – that – come 3ps Pf <u>Fut</u>
> 'Vanya said he would come.' (lit. 'that ... *will* come')

This is less of an issue in the Past, since Russian does not in any case distinguish between perfect and pluperfect, so that the English transformation 'I have seen' > 'said he had seen' cannot formally be done.

(Only one verb, 'promise', as in English and others, may be followed by an Infinitive where the subjects are the same; however, it is debatable whether this is actually a 'reporting' verb, in spite of the parallel structure, since the addition of 'promise' is not governed by the direct speech, only by the reporter's view.)

Semantic adjustments of temporal adverbs are as expected, for example 'yesterday' > 'the day before' ('I saw her yesterday' > '... that he had seen her the day before' – unless the day is still the same).

Reporting in the direct form is a feature only of colloquial dramatic style, usually also seen in the tense of the main verb:

> *А она говорит, я не приду./A on–a govor–it, ja ne prid–u.*
> but – she – say 3ps Pres – I NS – not – come 1ps Pf Fut
> 'But she says "I'm not coming."'

(2) Command/Request. The same verb *skazat'* 'say' can be used to report a command, when its English counterpart converts to 'tell'; this verb alone must be followed in the standard by the subjunctive conjunction *čtoby* and a past verb form (meaning that tense is not a choice):

> *Он сказал (мне), чтобы я ушёл./On skaza–l (mne), čtoby ja uš–(o)l.*
> he NS – say Pf Past Masc – (me DS) – that (Subjve) – I NS – leave Pf
>   Past Masc
> 'He told me to leave.' (lit. '... said that I should ... ');
> (cf. English *'said me to ... ')

All other verbs reporting either commands or requests (e.g. *приказать/ prikazat'* 'order', *посоветовать/posovetovat'* 'advise', *попросить/po–prosit'* 'ask/request') may take an Infinitive, the conjunction structure being more formal, though not as artificial as English 'asked that I should ...' etc.:

> *Он попросил меня (приказал мне) уйти./On–∅ poprosi–l*
> *men–ja (prikaza–l mn–e) uj–ti.*
> he NS – request Pf Past Masc – me AS – (order Pf Past Masc – me
>   DS) – leave Pf Inf
> 'He asked (ordered) me to leave.'

If the original command was 3rd person, again as in English, the conjunction format is obligatory:

> *Он попросил, чтобы никто не уходил./On–∅ poprosi–l, čto–by*
> *nikto ne uxodi–l.*

he NS – request Pf Past Masc – that (Subjve) – no one NS – not –
leave Impf Past Masc
'He asked that no one (should) leave.'

(3) Question. Here, as with statements, the tense remains that of the direct question; the basic verb is *спросить/s–prosit'* 'ask (a question)' (note the different prefix on the same root for the two meanings of 'ask'):

> *Он спросил меня, где я живу./On–ϕ sprosi–l men–ja, gde ja živ–u.*
> he NS – ask Pf Past Masc – me AS – where – I NS – live 1ps <u>Pres</u>
> 'He asked me where I lived.'

A past tense verb in the reported speech, viz. *...где я жил/... gde ja ži–l*, would thus be '...where I *had been* living', since the direct form must have been Past.

The reported *yes/no* question is similar:

> *Он спросил, женат ли я./On sprosi–l, ženat–ϕ li ϕ ja.*
> he NS – ask Pf Past Masc – married NSm Short – (Interrog) – (be 1ps
> Pres) – I NS
> 'He asked (me) if I was married.'

Again ... *был ли я женат/by–l* (be Past Masc) *li ja ženat–ϕ* would mean '... if I *had been* married'.

5   Word-formation and lexicology

1   Introduction

This chapter deals primarily with derivational morphology, but also with basic aspects of lexicology and phraseology. As in other chapters, we present first an introduction to the basic concepts, which may be passed over by those already familiar with them. The transcribed forms of the examples in this chapter (using morphophonemic transcription, as in chapter 3) are usually broken into their formational parts by a dash (en), which does not represent orthography; in the few cases of orthographically hyphenated words, the written hyphen is indicated by a long dash (em), which the Cyrillic form will confirm. Examples are given in their dictionary form: Nominative Singular for nominal forms, Infinitive for verbal.

The morphological concepts of Russian – types and nature of morphemes – which are assumed here are described in chapter 3, section 1.

1.1   Terminology, basic concepts

Where 'inflectional morphology' (or simply 'morphology') is concerned with the changes in the form of a particular word engendered by its syntactic role (cf. the Russian term *slovo–izmen–enie* lit. 'word-change'), 'derivational morphology', or 'word formation', is concerned with the formation of *new* words, by whatever means (cf. the Russian term *slovo–obraz–ov–anie* lit. 'word-formation'). A 'new word' means one which differs in its semantic content from any other, as opposed to one which differs only in grammatical content. For example, from the root *ruk–* 'hand' we have the base word *рука/ruk–a'* NS; the various case forms of this word, e.g. *руки/ruk–i'* GS or *рукu/ru'k–i* NP, still mean (lexically, or semantically) only 'hand', whereas the derived (affixed) word *ручка/ru'č–ka* 'little hand, pen' differs semantically in that either it has the added meaning of 'little' or it refers to an entirely different object; thus the suffix which has been added (*–k(a)*) is responsible for creating a new word. Words referring to distinct semantic concepts, that is, to different objects, actions, qualities, etc., are lexically distinct, and their formation belongs to the area of lexicology or word-formation, while the different *forms* of 'words' referring to the same object, action, etc., are not lexically distinct, but only morphologically distinct. (Refer to chapter 3 for further discussion of the concept of 'non-distinct word' and for a description of the parts of the word in Russian.)

There are borderline cases in which one may argue about the 'word' status of particular forms, notably the aspectual pairs of verbs, that is, where the affix may be said to be 'empty', and the pair distinguished only by aspect, or the related so-called 'procedural' forms of verbs (those indicating phases of the action, e.g. beginning, time-limited). For the purposes of this chapter, we do not need to make a decision on this question, since we are concerned more with the mechanics of word-formation; most of the affixes involved in aspect-formation are able also to form clearly distinct words, but the few whose sole role is aspect-formation will also be included.

Another borderline case is that of 'function words', like prepositions in Russian and English (or the articles in English), whose lexical content is minor; we deal with the form of these under 'Morphology' (chapter 3) and with their function under 'Syntax' (chapter 4).

Thus in this chapter we are interested primarily in the various methods of formation of new words (section 2), including by change of morphological class and change or extension of meaning, but mainly by affixation (section 4); we will also consider the morphophonological side of word-formation (alternations associated with particular affixes) (section 3).

In the second part (section 5), we will look at types of words and phrases, synonymy and polysemy, and stylistic aspects of both.

1.2   Stem

The various parts of the word are discussed in detail in chapter 3 (section 1.2), inasmuch as they are all 'morphemes'. The part of the word most relevant for this chapter is 'stem' (chapter 3, section 1.2.4), and the essential notion, which we repeat from there, is that this is a flexible concept: a 'stem' is any collection of morphemes to which one adds at some point another morpheme, be it a morphological or word-formational one. Its relativity may be illustrated by the following derivational sequence, in which each form except the final one is a stem:

(1) {uk} 'learn': root and non-derivative stem;
(2) adding {'i} verbal morphological suffix (theme) to (1) makes a functional verbal stem, historically derivative, synchronically non-derivative (with velar mutation > *uči–*);
(3) adding an ending to (2) produces a form of this verb, e.g. +{t'} 'teach' Inf (> *uči–t'*);

(4) adding {t′el′} to (2) makes a derivative noun stem 'teacher' (*učit′el′–*);

(5) add an ending for forms of this noun, e.g. + {ø} NS (*učit′el′–ø*);

(6) adding {nic} 'female' to (4) makes the derivative noun stem 'female teacher', e.g. +{a} NS (*učit′el′nic–a*).

1.3   Analysis and the role of etymology

A strictly synchronic view of this area, as indeed of all others, will not consider any information which is not readily available to contemporary speakers, in other words of the sort which requires etymological information. If, for example, a given affix, on a given word, has become inseparably fused with the stem, are we entitled to analyse that word by identifying (and 'removing', as it were) the affix? Again, we plan to avoid this question on the grounds that it is really only a problem in the case of obsolete affixes; for active affixes, the description is best based on the affix, and not on the particular word. If genuine etymology is required, that is, if the word's derivation simply cannot be recognised from its contemporary form, then we agree that the analysis does not belong to a strictly synchronic description. That said, it will be clear to those reading other sections of this book that we believe firmly in the usefulness of etymological (that is, historical) information, as a guide to both understanding and learning structure. Thus, we will not be overly concerned about referring to such information. An example is the word *omвemumь/ot–v′e′t–′i–t′* 'answer': the fact that *ot–* is a prefix is synchronically irrelevant and unprovable, since the root *v′et–* no longer occurs without it or another prefix, and with the other prefixes normally only on (deverbal) nouns, like *omвem/ot–v′et–ø* 'answer'; but is it not of interest to contrast the various prefixed noun forms, like *npuвem/pr′i–v′et–ø* 'welcome', *coвem/so–v′et–ø* 'council, soviet' or *завem/za–v′et–ø* 'testament' and realise that the connection is from the original meaning of the root, namely 'say, speak'?

A related matter is that of the productivity of particular methods, in particular of given affixes. Since our lists will perforce be selective samples, the selection will inevitably be based on productivity – that is, basically only productive ones will be listed – and so it is not intended to regularly comment on the productivity of these.

2   Sources of words and methods of word-formation

2.1   External sources

The first three methods of word-formation involving external sources are typical of those used in all languages, namely: creation, borrowing and calquing. The fourth is specific to Russian, namely that involving the role of Church Slavonic, not dissimilar from that of French and Latin in English, but more similar to that of Latin in many other European languages, that is, of a superimposed literary language which has left its mark on the contemporary standard, particularly strong in the case of Russian Church Slavonic and Russian because of the genetic proximity of the two languages (see chapter 1, section 3.2).

2.1.1   Creation

The only source for 'pure' creations is onomatopoeia, the making of words from sounds. For an inflecting language some ending at least – if not, additionally, a suffix – must be added to allow the word to function, e.g. *кукушка/kuku'–šk–a* 'cuckoo', *жужжать/žužž–a'–t'* 'to buzz', *ахать/a'x–a–t'* 'to groan (say "akh")'. Occasionally the sound of a noun fits the system, e.g. children's words like *nana/pa'p–a*, *мама/ma'm–a*, where the final sound may be perceived as an ending. Of interest is *баба/ba'b–a*, originally 'grandmother', then simply 'old woman', while 'grandmother' acquired a suffix: *бабушка/ba'b–ušk–a*.

2.1.2   Borrowing

The same problem of fitting into the system applies to borrowings. In principle nouns ending in a consonant, *–a*, *–o* or *–e* could be fitted into the regular noun classes, while those in other vowels could not. While the latter is certainly a rule, and words like *такси/taksi'* 'taxi', *эму/e'mu* 'emu' are indeclinable, many – indeed probably most – words in *–o* and *–e* have also remained indeclinable, e.g. *шоссе/šosse'* 'highway', *пальто/pal'to'* 'overcoat', *кофе/ko'f'e* 'coffee', *кафе/kafe'* 'café' (see also discussion in chapter 2, section 3.4.1 and chapter 3, section 2.1.5.4). Examples of fully integrated ones are: *парк/park–ø* 'park', *центр/centr–ø* 'centre', *музыка/mu'zik–a* 'music', *вино/v'in–o'* 'wine'.

2.1.3   Calquing

The alternative to straight borrowing is translation of the foreign word or concept into native morphemes. This is always a conscious process, usually inspired by the purist desire not to borrow, or at least not to be seen as borrowing, and so is usually applied to higher level words, like cultural and scientific terminology. Languages tend to go through periods of purism at some points in their history, often in conflict with the 'grass roots' borrowing running in parallel. Russia's highest point in such purism (and related conflict) was in the late eighteenth century, the conflict being typified in the so-called 'struggle' between the followers of the writer Karamzin (the willing borrowers) and those of the Minister for Education – and thus chief censor –Šiškov (the resisters and calquers) (see also chapter 1, section 3.3). At any rate, the literary and scientific

levels have many well established calques, e.g. *земледелие*/z*'eml'–e–d'e'l–*
'ij–e 'agriculture' (based on the roots *z'eml'*–'earth, land' – Lat *agr–* – and
d'el– 'do, work (land)' – Lat *cult–*), *рукопись*/*ru'k–o–p'is–'–ø* 'manuscript'
(based on *ruk–* 'hand' – Lat *man–* – and *p'is–* 'write' – Lat *scrib–*), *влияние*/v–
l'ij–a'n'ij–e 'influence' (based on *v–* 'in' – Lat in – and *l'ij* 'flow' – Lat *flu–*).

More importantly, this principle gave rise to a great increase in the productivity of many suffixes used as correspondences to Latin (mainly) or other
European Languages, though not necessarily one-to-one, e.g. *–ние*/*–n'ij–e*,
– ость/*–ost'–ø*, *–ство*/*–stv–o*, all serving to form abstract nouns whose originals had suffixes like (in their English forms) *–ence*, *–ity*, *–ness*. At the same
time foreign forms did – mainly during the nineteenth and twentieth centuries –
find their way into even this high level of vocabulary, including foreign suffixes,
e.g. *–ция*/*–cij–a* (Lat *–tia* via Pol), *–ёр*/*–'or* (Fr *–eur*).

The conflict has left Modern Russian with many doublets (synonyms), some
of which have undergone a perceived, or forced, semantic shift, while others are straight synonyms. A typical – and appropriate – example is 'linguistics', which has three shapes: (1) the foreign *лингвистика*/*l'ingv'i'st'ika*, preferred by 'modern' linguists; (2) *языкознание*/*jazik–o–zna'–n'ij–e*, a compound based on *jazik–* 'language' and *zna–* 'know', a more general term; and
(3) *языковедение*/*jazik–o–v'e'd–'en'ij–e*, the same, but with the obsolete root
v'ed– 'know', the highest style of the three, actually back-formed from the noun
языковед/*jazik–o–v'e'd–ø* 'linguist, language specialist', there being no such
personal noun from the second form, though the first has *лингвист*/*l'ingv'i'st*.
(For further discussion on attitudes to foreign borrowing see chapter 7,
section 2.)

2.1.4   Church Slavonic (RCS)

The nature of the relationship between Russian Church Slavonic and native
Russian over the whole period (from the tenth century) has led to fairly clearly
defined areas of activity for each, but ones which are only clear where there are
doublet forms within the same lexeme. The role of the Russian Church Slavonic
variants in these cases is the depiction of (1) abstract (versus concrete), (2)
high style (including religious) or (3) poetic style (in reality a variant of (2)).
Often there will not be doublets, in which case the distinction is a notional,
etymological one.

The most important features of the Russian Church Slavonic layer are as
follows.

(1) Word shape. The formula for word shape follows that used in chapter 1: C =
any consonant; R = one of the sonorants, /r/ or /l/; # = word boundary; lower
case letters represent actual phonemes.

	Russian	**Russian Church Slavonic**
	CoRoC	CraC
	короткий/koro'tk–ij	*краткий/kra'tk–ij*
'short'	physical, e.g. string	abstract, e.g. silence
	город/go'rod–ø	*град/grad–ø*
'town'	neutral	poetic, also in
	(cf. 'No'v-gorod' versus	compounds
	'Lenin–gra'd')	

	#RoC	#RaC
	ровный/ro'vn–ij	*равный/ra'vn–ij*
	'even, flat', e.g. ground	'equal'

	#o–	#e–
	один/od('i)'n–ø	*единый/jed'i'n–ij*
	'one'	'sole'

(2) Affix shape

	Russian	**Russian Church Slavonic**
	c(o)–/s(o)–; вз–/vz–;	*co–/so–; воз–/voz–;*
	–ск/–(')sk	*–еск/–esk*
	(for meanings see sections 4–5 below)	
	сбор/s–bor–ø	*собор/so–bo'r–ø*
	'assembly, meeting'	'cathedral' (via
		'congregation')
	всходить/vz–xod–i'–t'	*восходить/voz–xod–i'–t'*
	'ascend'	'go back in time,
		come from'
	мужской/muž–sk–o'j	*мужеский/mu'ž–esk–ij*
	'masculine'	'virile'

(3) Morphophonology

	Russian	**Russian Church Slavonic**
	t ~ č	t ~ šč
	просветить/pro–sv'et–'i'–t'	
	'pass light through'	'enlighten'
1ps	*просвечу/pro–sv'eč–u'*	*просвещу/pro–sv'ešč–u'*
	d ~ ž	d ~ žd
	посадить/po–sad–'i'–t' 'plant'	
	осадить/o–sad–'i'–t' 'beseige'	
Past Part Pass	*посажен/po–sa'ž–on*	*осаждён/o–sažd'–o'n*

Stress pattern in Class II verbs Present

	Mobile (Type C)	**End** (Type B)
3ps	*просветит/pro–sv′e′t–′i–t*	*просветит/pro–sv′et–′i′–t*
	посадит/po–sa′d–′i–t	*осадит/o–sad–′i′–t*

(4) Phonology

Russian	**Russian Church Slavonic**
ё/′o′	*e/′e′*

(Only reliable where a pair or *ё* exists, since *e′* may also be native Russian.)

нёбо/n′o′b–o	*небо/n′e′b–o*
'palate'	'sky'
надёжный/nad′o′ž–n–ij	*надежда/nad′e′žd–a*
'reliable'	'hope, reliance'

(5) Lexical

	Russian	**Russian Church Slavonic**
Prefix 'out'	*вы–/vi–*	*из–/iz–*
	вылить/vi′–l′i–t′	*излить/iz–l′i′–t′*
'pour out'	physical, e.g. water	figurative, e.g. one's blood
	выгнать/vi′–gna–t′	*изгнать/iz–gna′–t′*
	'drive out'	'exile'

Other words with poetic (and usually archaic) Russian Church Slavonic equivalents, e.g.:

	лоб/lob–ø	*чело/čel–o′*
	'forehead'	'brow'
'cheek'	*щека/šček–a′*	*ланита/lan′i′t–a*
'small'	*маленький/ma′l′–en′k–ij*	*малый/ma′l–ij*

Sometimes a semantic split has occurred, e.g.:

корм/korm–ø	*пища/pi′šč–a*

Originally both 'food', now the first is 'feed, fodder', and the second is 'food as nourishment'.

2.2   Internal sources

The main internal source of new words is by derivation – by affixation or compounding – but there are a few less common procedures which we note first.

2.2.1   Semantic change

Words may simply change their meaning, most often because of a change in referent, for example when an object or concept becomes obsolete and/or is replaced by another, typically in scientific or social contexts, e.g. *поезд/po'–jezd–ø* at first meant 'cavalcade', then 'train'; *вратарь/vrat–a'r'–ø* meant 'gatekeeper', became obsolete and was semantically replaced by *дворник/dvo'r–n'ik–ø* 'janitor' in the same way as in English, but has been resurrected in modern times to mean 'goalkeeper'!

More commonly, words expand their semantic range into new, but related areas, while keeping the original meaning, e.g. *долг/dolg–ø* expanded from simply 'debt' into 'duty'; *язык/jazik–ø* – as in many languages – from 'tongue' to (also) 'language', then further still to 'tribe'; *знатный/zna't–n–ij* from 'aristocratic' to 'distinguished' (the first meaning obsolete in Soviet times, but more acceptable now).

2.2.2   Morphosyntactic change

Words in an inflected language are in principle clearly marked morphologically – especially compared to a language like English, where there is no formal marker distinguishing nouns, adjectives, verbs, etc. Nevertheless, there are many examples of a word changing its syntactic function while retaining its previous form. This is sometimes referred to as morphosyntactic change. All categories may be affected, but the most common changes by far are substantivisation of adjectives (Adjective > Noun) (usually with retention of the adjectival function also) and the formation of adverbs from all three main categories (Noun, Adjective, Verb). Examples of the main types follow (see chapter 3 for morphological details):

(1) Adjective > Noun (mostly by suppression of an implied or common noun, reflected in the gender of the new noun):
   больной/bol'–n–o'j 'sick, ill' Masc > 'patient';
   столовая/stolo'v–aja 'table' Fem > 'dining-room';
   мороженое/moro'ž–en–oje 'frozen' Neut > 'ice cream'.

(2) Noun (non-Nominative case form) > Adverb:
   летом/l'e't–om 'summer' ISn > 'in summer';
   капельку/ka'p'el'–k–u 'drop' ASf > 'a little (quantity or time)';
   домой/dom–o'j 'house, home' former DSm (OR *dom–o'vi*) > 'homewards' (cf. *дома/do'ma* 'at home', which is considered a very ancient (Indo-European) locative case form, not an Old Russian one.)

(3) Adjective (short neuter) > Adverb: this is the typical source of adverbs (see chapter 3, section 2.3.1):
   хорошо/xoroš–o' 'nice' NSn > 'well'.

(4) Verb > Adverb:

значит/zna'č–it 'mean' 3ps > '(and) so, thus';

почти/po–čt–'i' 'consider' Imper 2ps > 'almost';

зря/zr–'a 'see' (obsolete) Pres Adv Part > 'in vain'.

(5) Verb > Preposition (often via Adverb):

благодаря/blagodar–'a' 'thank' Pres Adv Part > 'thanks to'.

(6) Verb > Conjunction:

хотя/xot–'a' 'wish' Pres Adv Part > 'although'.

Only in a few instances have the original forms been lost, possibly only where the new *form* is acceptable also for the new *function*, e.g.:

суть/sut'–ø 'essence': now only a noun (Class III), though it was originally the 3rd Person Plural Present of 'be' (and appears as such in very restricted, purposely archaic, contexts – the whole Present Tense of this verb is now lost, see chapter 3);

неделя/n'ed'e'l'–a 'week': now a Class II noun, originally either the Present Adverb Participle of the verb 'do, work' or (more likely) the Genitive Singular of the noun 'work', preceded by the negative n'e–, from which its first nominal meaning was 'Sunday', replaced in this meaning by the (more) Christian воскресение/voskr'es'e'n'ije lit. 'resurrection', and left free to shift to its new meaning – 'week beginning with Sunday' (cf. понедельник/po–n'ed'e'l'–n'ik 'Monday' meant 'the day after Sunday'). The remaining weekdays retain 'pre-Christian' forms, e.g. вторник/vto'rnik–ø 'Tuesday' means 'second day'.

2.2.3   Morphological derivation

In this section we deal with the types of derivation and their morphological implications. The form and semantic content of affixes are covered below (sections 4–5). In summary, the types are: affixation (with subheadings prefixation, suffixation and de-affixation), compounding and abbreviation, and the implications are the changes of category and some of the semantics involved.

2.2.3.1 Affixation

(1) Prefixation. Since prefixes do not impinge on the inflectional end of words, the addition of a prefix can have only semantic effect, including the 'weak' semantic areas of verbal aspect and procedural activity; the morphological category of the base is unaffected. Prefixation is common only on verbs. In the following note that *base* form means the semantically logical base from which a given form has been derived. Only occasionally is this unclear.

(a) Imperfective verb + prefix > perfective verb with new meaning:

Base	Prefix	Derived form
писать/p'is–a'–t'	*под–/pod–*	*подписать/*
'write' Impf	'under'	*pod–p'is–a'–t'*
		'sign' Pf

(b) Imperfective verb + prefix > perfective verb with same meaning:

Base	Prefix	Derived form
писать/p'is–a–t'	*на–/na–*	*написать/na–p'is–a'–t'*
'write' Impf	('on')	'write' Pf

(c) Imperfective verb + prefix > perfective verb with procedural meaning:

Base	Prefix	Derived form
говорить/govor-'i't	*за–/za–*	*заговорить/*
'speak' Impf	(start)	*za–govor–'i'–t'*
		'begin to speak' Pf
работать/rabo't–a–t'	*по–/po–*	*поработать/*
'work'	(time limit)	*po–rabo't–a–t'*
		'work for a while' Pf
сидеть/sid–'e'–t'	*про–/pro–*	*просидеть/pro–sid–'e'–t'*
'sit/be sitting' Impf	(whole period)	'sit for all of
		specified time' Pf

(d) Adjective + prefix > adjective with added meaning:

Base	Prefix	Derived form
высокий/viso'k–ij	*не–/n'e–*	*невысокий/n'e–viso'k–ij*
'tall'	'not'	'rather small'
грамотный/	*без–/b'ez–*	*безграмотный/*
gra'mot–n–ij	'without'	*b'ez–gra'mot–n–ij*
'literate'		'illiterate'

(e) Noun + prefix > noun with new or added meaning:

Base	Prefix	Derived form
внук/vnuk–ø	*пра–/pra–*	*правнук/pra'–vnuk–ø*
'grandson'	'proto–', (old)	'great grandson'
город/go'rod–ø	*при–/pri–*	*пригород/pri'–gorod–ø*
'town'	'attached'	'suburb'

(2) Suffixation. The addition of a suffix may or may not cause a change in category. Each suffix is marked for category and noun suffixes are marked for gender (or at least class). The following is a summary of the main possibilities (noun suffixes are accompanied by the Nominative Singular ending for their class).

(a) Noun + noun suffix > noun with new or added meaning (common):

Base	Suffix	Derived form
артист/artʲiˈst–∅	*–ка/–k–a*	*артистка/artʲiˈst–k–a*
'performer'	(female)	'female performer'
(male or common)		
Москва/Moskv–a'	*–ич/–ˈič–∅*	*москвич/moskv–ˈiˈč–∅*
'Moscow'	(inhabitant)	'Muscovite'

(b) Noun + adjective suffix > adjective with mainly qualitative or relative meaning (very common):

Base	Suffix	Derived form
сталь/stalʲ–∅	*–н/–n*	*стальной/stalʲ–n–oˈj*
'steel'	(qualitative)	'steel' (Adj)
Англия/Aˈnglʲij–a	*–ск/–sk*	*английский/*
'England'	(relative)	*anglʲiˈj–sk–ij*
		'English'

(c) Noun + verb suffix > verb with mainly relative meaning (not common):

Base	Suffix	Derived form
ночь/noč–∅	*–ова/–ova*	*ночевать/noč–ova'–tʲ*
'night'	(relative)	([tʃɪ'va]) 'spend the night'
завтрак/za'vtrak–∅	*–а/–a*	*завтракать/za'vtrak–a–tʲ*
'breakfast'	(relative)	'have breakfast'

(d) Adjective + noun suffix > noun with mainly qualitative meaning (common):

Base	Suffix	Derived form
глупый/glu'p–ij	*–ость/ost'–∅*	*глупость/glu'p–ost'–∅*
'stupid'	(abstract quality)	'stupidity'
старый/sta'r–ij	*–ик/–ik–∅*	*старик/star–i'k–∅*
'old'	(male person)	'old man'

(e) Adjective + adjective suffix > adjective with added meaning (not common):

Base	Suffix	Derived form
жёлтый/žolt–ij	*–оват/–ovat*	*желтоватый/žolt–*
'yellow'	(partial)	*ova't–ij* 'yellowish'
трудный/tru'd–n–ij	*–ейш/–e'jš*	*труднейший/trud–n–ˈ*
'difficult'	(superlative)	*e'jš–ij* 'most difficult'

(f) Adjective + verb suffix > verb with various meanings (common):

Base	Suffix	Derived form
белый/b′e′l–ij	– u/–′i (factitive)	белить/b′el–′i′–t′
'white'		'whiten'
белый/b′e′l–ij	– e/–e	белеть/b′el– ′e′–t′
'white'	(qualitative)	'be/appear white'
	(acquisitive)	'go/turn white'

(g) Verb + noun suffix > noun with various meanings (very common):

Base	Suffix	Derived form
работать/rabo′t–a–t′	–ник/–n′ik–ø	работник/rabo′t–n′ik–ø
'work'	(person)	'worker'
учить/uč–i–t′	–тель/–t′el′–ø	учитель/uči′–t′el′–ø
'teach'	(agent)	'teacher'

(h) Verb + adjective suffix > adjective with mainly qualitative or relative meaning (common):

Base	Suffix	Derived form
купать(ся)/	–льн/–l′n	купальный/kup–a–l′
kup–a′–t′(–s′a) 'bathe'	(relative)	n–ij '(for) bathing'
пугаться/pug–a′–t′–s′a	–лив/–l′iv	пугливый/pug–l′i′v–ij
'be frightened'	(qualitative)	'timid, fearful'

(i) Perfective verb + verb suffix > imperfective verb with same meaning (common):

Base	Suffix	Derived form
подписать/	–ыва/–iva	подписывать/
pod–p′is–a′–t′	(imperfective)	pod–p′i′s–iva–t′
'sign' Pf		'sign' Impf

(j) Imperfective verb + verb suffix > perfective verb with mainly added semelfactive meaning (rare):

Base	Suffix	Derived form
кричать/kr′ik–ja′–t′	–ну/–nu	крикнуть/kr′i′k–nu–t′
'shout' Impf	(semelfactive)	'let out a shout'

(3) Prefix + suffix added simultaneously. Synchronically there are many forms bearing both a prefix and a suffix whose derivation cannot be described in one step of prefixation or suffixation, sometimes because the penultimate

single-affix form has been lost, but most often because the derivation (of nouns and adjectives) is actually of the *phrase > word* type. Usually included here are forms with the reflexive suffix –ся/–s'a, which is, strictly speaking, a *post-fix*, since it is added after the ending, but since it is the only one in the language it is simpler to treat it along with the suffixes.

(a) Nouns. The prefix + base part is normally derived from a prepositional phrase:

Base phrase	Suffix	Derived form
без плода/b'ez plod–a'	*–ue/–'ij–e*	*бесплодие/b'ez–plo'd–ij–e*
'without fruit'	(abstract)	'infertility'
под Москвой/	*–ье/–'j–e*	*подмосковье/*
pod Moskv–o'j	(region)	*pod–mosk(o')v–'j–e*
'under (= outside)		'region outside/
Moscow'		near Moscow'

(b) Adjectives. The same:

Base phrase	Suffix	Derived form
на столе/na stol–e'	*–н/–'n*	*настольный/na–stol–'n–ij*
'on the table'	(relative)	'situated (etc.) on a table'
		(e.g. tennis)
до войны/do vojn–i'	*–н/–'n*	*довоенный/*
'before the war'	(relative)	*do–voj(e')n–(')n–ij*
		'pre-war'

If nouns from group (a) have an adjective suffix attached, the resulting forms may (logically) be derived either as suffixation from the phrase or by replacement suffixation from the noun, e.g. *подмосковный/pod–mosk(o')v–n–ij*:
(i) from *pod Moskv–oj* plus adjective suffix – *'n*; or
(ii) from *podmoskov–'je* with replacement of the noun suffix.

The first of these is preferable, since it does not involve us in the notion of 'replacement'. However, we will see in the next section (4) that replacement is sometimes the only analysis possible.

(4) 'De-affixation' or zero suffix. Russian sources tend to use the notion of de-affixation to account for the absence of a suffix in derived forms (mostly nouns, some adjectives, no verbs), on the grounds that derivation, at least that which changes category, must involve a suffix. While the latter assumption is reasonable, it seems simpler to say that what we have here is a zero suffix. Even more interestingly, and significantly, a variant of this phenomenon involves the phonological effect of the softening of a hard stem consonant, which surely means that there is a suffix causing this.

In some cases – those which encourage the view that de-affixation has occurred – a suffix has indeed been dropped from the base form. In such cases, if we wish to retain the notion of a zero suffix, we must say that suffix replacement has occurred ((a) below). These are actually very rare.

(a) A *suffixed noun* loses its suffix, which is replaced by zero (this is usually back formation of a previously spurious form, including of a borrowing by popular etymology):

Base	Suffix lost	Derived form
доярка/doja'r–ka	*(–k–a)*	*дояр/doja'r–ø*
'milkmaid'	(female)	'male milker'
зонтик/zo'nt'ik–ø	*(*–'ik–ø)*	*зонт/zont–ø*
'umbrella' (from	(diminutive)	'(large) umbrella/
Dutch *zonnedek*)		awning'

(b) Adjective + zero noun suffix with softening > Class III noun with abstract meaning:

Base	Suffix	Derived form
зелёный/z'el'o'n–ij	*– '–ø*	*зелень/z'el'en–'–ø*
'green'	(abstract)	'greenery'
сухой/sux–o'j	*– '–ø*	*сушь/suš–ø* (mutated velar)
'dry'	(abstract)	'dry spell/dry place'

(c) Adjective + zero adjective suffix: always prefixed, and thus derived from a phrase, as above:

Base phrase	Suffix	Derived form
без голоса/	*–ø*	*безголосый/b'ez–golo's–ø–ij*
b'ez go'losa	(qualitative)	'voiceless, with weak
'without a voice'		voice' (not linguistic,
		cf. *безголосный/*
		b'ez–golo's–n–ij
		'unvoiced')

This group is in fact limited to the prefix/preposition *b'ez–*. Clearly it should simply be grouped with the other de-phrasal derivations.

(d) Nouns derived from verbs via a straight zero suffix or zero plus softening; since we should work from the verb stem anyway, there is no need for the positing of de-affixation:

Base	Suffix	Derived form
входить/v–xod–'i'–t'	*–ø*	*вход/v–xod–ø*
'enter'	(object/abstract)	'entrance'
звонить/zvon–'i'–t'	*–ø*	*звон/zvon–ø*
'ring'	(abstract)	'ringing/peal'
записать/za–p'is–a'–t'	*–'–ø*	*запись/za'–p'is–'–ø*
'record'	(object)	'recording/record'

In sum, we have no need for a separate treatment of such derivations: the zero suffix is simply another suffix. On nouns the 'straight' zero may be regarded as having masculine gender, the 'soft' zero as having feminine gender; or one may use the morphological descriptors 'Class I (hard)' for the first, 'Class III' (automatically feminine and soft) for the second. In subsequent sections we shall use the first approach.

2.2.3.2 Compounding. Under 'compounding' come the following: direct joining of two roots; linked joining (by a link vowel, or *interfix*); and abbreviations of various sorts which reduce compound forms to simple(r) ones. Only nouns and adjectives may be compounded.

A special source of compound forms is the fusion of the elements of a phrase, of which the compound numerals are an example. Russian sources commonly treat these under the heading of 'lexico-syntactic' formation (meaning the formation of a word from a syntactic group (*syntagm*), without further adjustment), but structurally they do not differ from lexical compounds.

Examples of now obscured syntactic compounding mostly involve clitics: *если/je'sl'i* 'if' from OR *есть ли/jest' l'i* 'is it?'; *итак/ita'k* '(and) so' from *и так/i tak* 'and so'. Most others are clear, e.g. *пятьсот/p'at'–so't* 'five hundred' – its syntactic nature displayed in the declension of *both* parts: Gen *пятисот/p'at–'i–so't*, Dat *пятистам/p'at–'i–sta'm*.

We shall return to this issue in treating the 'proper' compounds below.

(1) Direct joining. Two degrees of fusion are indicated – rather unpredictably – by the writing or not of a hyphen. As with all European languages, to write or not to write the hyphen is always a problem, but notionally the dropping of the hyphen is a sign of permanent fusion into some single semantic whole, as opposed to a juxtaposition of two still separate units. In the case of nouns in this group hyphens are the norm, while adjectives show much more variety.

(a) Examples of fused units (adjectives only):

трёхлетний/tr'o`x–l'e't–n'–ij 'three-year-old';
двухструнный/dvu`x–stru'n–n–ij 'two-stringed';
двусторонний/dvu`–storo'n–n'–ij 'two-sided'.

Note the Genitive case of the first (numeral) element in these (and the archaic (Genitive Dual) form of the last – *dvu–* versus regular *dvux–*). This is the pattern for all numeral-based adjectival compounds.

(b) Examples of hyphenated nouns (mostly foreign roots):

дизель-мотор/di'zel'—moto'r 'diesel engine';
диван-кровать/d'ivan—krovat' 'bed settee'.

(c) Examples of syntactic fusion:

направо/na–pra'v–o 'to the right' (< *na* + AS);
наверху/na–v'erx–u' 'upstairs' (< *na* + LS);

сумасшедший/s–uma–s–še'd–š–ij 'mad' (< out-of-mind out gone = 'having gone out of one's mind');

вышеизложенный/više–izlo'ž–enn–ij 'abovementioned' (lit.).

(2) Linked joining. Much more common is the use of a link vowel, namely /o/, initially on the model of Greek (e.g. Eng *bi–o–graph–*, *hydr–o–gen*, *bar–o–met(e)r–*, etc.), but expanded to the status of an all-purpose interfix. This is attached to the stem of the first element. Being the phoneme /o/, it is realised as /e/ after soft or palatal consonants.

(a) In the basic type, the second element has its full normal form, including suffixes and the appropriate inflections. It bears the primary stress, while the first element has secondary stress, that is, it has the phonology of a primary-stressed word, but with relatively weaker stress. In native forms the link vowel is never stressed.

(i) Nouns.

Base 1	**Base 2**	**Compound form**
работ(а)/rabo't–(a) 'work'	*способность/ sposo'b–n–ost'–ø* 'capacity, capability'	*работоспособность/ rabo`t–o–sposo'b–n–ost'* 'capacity for work/efficiency'
велик(ий)/ v'el'i'k–(ij) 'great' (Lat *magn–*)	*душ(а)/duš)а) +* suff. *–ue/–'ij–o* 'soul' (Lat *anim–*)	*великодушие/ v'el'i`k–o–du'š–ij–o* 'magnanimity'
уг(о)ль/u'g(o)l'–ø 'coal'	*добыча/do–bï'č–a* 'mining'	*угледобыча/ u'gl'–e–do–bï'č–a* 'coal mining'

(ii) Adjectives may be formed from (or in parallel to) the above by suffixation, e.g. *работоспособный/rabo`t–o–sposo'b–n–ij* 'hardworking', *великодушный/v'el'i`k–o–du'š–n–ij* 'magnanimous'; but some exist without a parallel noun, e.g.:

Base 1	**Base 2**	**Compound form**
русск(ий)/rus–sk–(ij) 'Russian'	*английский/ angl'i'j–sk–ij* 'English'	*русско-английский/ ru`ssk–o—angl'i'j–sk–ij* 'Russian–English' (dictionary, etc.)
сво(й)/svoj– 'one's own/self'	*нрав–/nrav– + –n* 'temper/disposition'	*своенравный/ svo`j–e–nra'v–n–ij* 'wilful'

(b) In a secondary noun type, the second element is a zero-suffixed verb stem, usually derived from verb phrases denoting activities of people or machines

(especially vehicles). These seem to have been modelled most closely on the Greek pattern, where the final masculine element would have been a consonant ending in place of the Greek *–os*, as seen in Greek borrowings. These borrowings are the only type in which the link vowel may be (and normally is) stressed, and in all of this group the first element is unstressed (without even secondary stress), e.g. *биолог/b'i–o'–log–ø* 'biologist'; *библиограф/b'ibl'i–o'–graf–ø* 'bibliographer'; *барометр/bar–o'–m'etr–ø* 'barometer'. Native words on this model include:

Base 1	Base 2	Compound form
вин(о)/v'in–(o)	*дел(ать)/d'el–(a–t')*	*винодел/v'in–o–d'e'l–ø*
'wine'	'make'	'wine-maker'
пар/par–(ø)	*ход(ить)/xod–('i'–t')*	*пароход/par–o–xo'd–ø*
'steam'	'go'	'steamship'
язык/jazik–(ø)	*вед–/v'ed–*	*языковед/jazik–o–v'e'd–ø*
'language'	'know' (arch.)	'language specialist'
икон(a)/ikon–(a)	*пис(ать)/p'is–(a–t')*	*иконопись/*
'icon'	'draw'	*i'kon–o–p'is'–ø*
	(now 'write')	'icon painting'

Some of the second-place Greek elements are used almost as suffixes in combination with native elements, e.g. *туманограф/tuman–o'–graf–ø* 'fog meter' *советолог/sov'et–o'–log–ø* 'Sovietologist'. These in turn may be used as stems to derive nouns, e.g. for sciences, especially with the (foreign) suffix *–ия/–'ij–a*, but also with (native) *–ние/–n'ij–o*, or adjectives, e.g. *виноделие/v'in–o–d'el–'ij–o* 'wine-making', *иконописец/ikon–o–p'i's–ec–ø* 'icon painter', *иконография/ikon–o–gra'f–'ij–a* 'icon study', *языковедение/jazik–o–v'e'd–en'ij–o* 'linguistics'.

2.2.3.3 Abbreviations. All modern bureaucracies produce large numbers of complex names for organisations and procedures, and the Soviet Union was one of the most centralised and active of such bureaucracies this century. This is reflected in language in many ways, and in the area under discussion it was reflected most of all in the process of abbreviation. Apart from the common procedure of forming acronyms from initials, Soviet Russian developed a particular liking for the so-called (in English, as Russian has no special term for this type) 'stump compound', made up from bare stems (usually single syllables, but including prefixes) of one or more elements of the compound.

(1) Stump compound. There are two subtypes, depending on whether all elements or only the first are abbreviated. The normal base is an *adjectival phrase*.

(a) Only the non-final elements are abbreviated, the final retaining its full grammatical form and determining the declension of the compound; like normal compounds, the first part has secondary stress, the last primary:

Base 1	Base 2	Compound form
гор(одско́й)/gor(od–sk–oj)	сове́т/sov′e′t–∅	горсове́т/go`r–sov′e′t–∅
'town'	'council'	'town council'
полит(и́ческий)/	бюро́/b′uro′	политбюро́/poli`t–b′uro′
polit(ič–esk–ij)	'bureau/office'	'politbureau'
'political'		
спец(иа́льный)/	курс/kurs–∅	спецку́рс/sp′e`c–ku′rs–∅
sp′ec(ial–′n–ij)	'course'	'special/optional
'special'		subject'

Occasionally the base is a noun phrase which retains the case of the final element, and is thus indeclinable:

Base 1	Base 2	Compound form
зав(е́дующий)/	ка́федрой/ka′f′edr–oj	завка́федрой/
zav(′e′d–uj–ušč–ij)	'department	za`v–ka′f′edr–oj
'head/manager'	(academic)' IS	'head of department'
зам(ести́тель)/	дире́ктора/	замдире́ктора/
zam(′esti′–t′el′)	d′ir′e′ktor–a	za`m–d′ir′e′ktor–a
'deputy'	'director/	'deputy director/
	headmaster' GS	headmaster'

(b) Even the final element is abbreviated to a stem ending in a hard consonant, making the declension of the whole that of Class I Masculine; the first part is normally *un*stressed:

Base 1	Base 2	Compound form
испол(ни́тельный)/	ком(ите́т)/kom(′it′e′t)	исполко́м/
is–pol(n–′itel–′n–ij)	'committee'	ispol–ko′m–∅
'executive'		'executive committee'
универ(са́льный)/	маг(ази́н)/mag(azi′n)	универма́г/
univ′er(sal–′n–ij)	'shop'	univ′er–ma′g–∅
'universal'		'department store'

Occasionally parts of the compound are a noun phrase; here, given the abbreviation of the last element, the latter's case is lost:

Base 1	Base 2	Compound form
управ(ля́ющий)/	дом(о́м)/dom(–om)	управдо́м/uprav–do′m–∅
uprav(l′a′–ju–šč–ij)	'house' (IS)	'house manager'
'manager'		

Base 1
ком(мунистический)/
kom(mun'ist–'i'česk–ij)
'communist'

Base 2
со(юз)/so(ju'z–∅)
'union'

Base 3
мол(одёжи)/mol(od'ož–i)
'youth/young people' (GS)

Compound form
комсомол/kom–so–mo'l–∅
'Communist Youth League'

(2) Initials/acronyms. As in other languages, initials are used for organisations, where possible producing a pronounceable acronym; hybrid forms are also common (part pronounced as letters, part as syllable).

(a) Initials only (cf. Eng *BBC, USA, USSR*); stress on the final:

CCCP/S-S-S-R [ɛs–ɛs–ɛs–ɛ'r] 'USSR';

МВД/M-V-D [ɛm–vɛ–dɛ'] 'Ministry of Internal Affairs';

КГБ/K-G-B [kɛ–gɛ–bɛ'] 'KGB' (note: [kɛ] is not the name of the letter, which is [ka], the change no doubt caused by rhyming assimilation to the following letters).

(b) Acronyms (cf. Eng *UNESCO, ANZAAS*), pronounced as words, stress on the final if more than one syllable:

ТАСС/T-A-S-S 'Soviet News Agency', replaced now by:

ИТАРТАСС/I-T-A-R-T-A'-S-S 'Russian Television News Agency (incorporating TASS)';

МИД/M-I-D 'Ministry of Foreign Affairs'.

(c) A mixture of (1) and (2) (cf. Eng 'CTEC' ([si'tɛk]), 'VLAN' ([vi'lan])); stress on final vowel:

ЦДРА/C-D-R-A [tsɛ–dɛ–ra'] 'Russian Army Central HQ';

ЭРЦ/È-R-C [ɛrtsɛ'] 'electrical repair shop' (and not [ɛ–ɛr–cɛ] (initials) or [ɛrts] (acronym)).

The flexibility of the language, and perhaps the colloquial trend, is indicated by the pronunciation of *CШA/S-Š-A* 'USA', which has gone through the following, in chronological order: [ɛs–ʃa–a'] (initials), [ʃʃa] (acronym), [sɛ–ʃa'] (mixture). The last, and latest, version shows again a letter pronounced in a way that is not its regular letter-name: [sɛ] versus name [ɛs], showing that a 'convenient' pronunciation is seen as more important than formal rules.

(3) Mixture of (1) and (2). Hybrid forms including both (stump) syllables and letters; some continue to be written in capitals, while many are written in lower case, implying a change of status to normal words, like the regular stump type.

(a) Written as letters/initials:

ГОСИНТИ/GOS-I-N-T-I [gɔs-ɪnti'] 'State Institute for Scientific and Technological Information'

ГОСТ/G-O-ST 'state/national standard (measure)'.

(b) Written as a word (declinable only if ending in a consonant):

сельпо/*s'el'–p–o*' 'rural consumers' association';

гороно/*gor–o–n–o*' 'city/urban department of education';

самбо/*sam–b–o*' 'unarmed self-defence' (which – perhaps not by co-incidence – looks like an oriental martial arts term!).

(c) Mixed:

горСЭС/*gor–S–È–S* [gɔrsɛ' s] 'municipal epidemiological unit'.

And one well known one from Soviet times which varies in its spelling:

ГУЛаг/*G–U–Lag*, ГУЛАГ/*G–U–LAG*, Гулаг/*G–u–lag* or гулаг/ *g–u–la'g–ø* 'state labour camp', the first reflecting the formation (*lag–* being the first syllable of лагерь/*lag'er'–ø* 'camp').

3   Morphophonology in word-formation

All the alternations which occur at inflectional boundaries occur also at affix boundaries, since they are simply the results of older phonotactic processes. For the full list of alternations, see chapter 3, sections 2.1.3.2, 2.2.10. Here we offer a sample of the main affix-boundary ones.

3.1   Vowels

3.1.1   e ~ 'o

Since the main historical context for /o/ to derive from /e/ was a following hard consonant (chapter 1, section 2.4.1.1) (as well as stress), any suffix beginning with either a soft consonant or a front vowel would have prevented the change from occurring. The synchronic problem is that the old context is often disguised, notably where the suffix began with the front *jer* (ь), which was the case with the two most common adjectival suffixes *–sk* and *–n*. In the modern system the soft sign (ь) is written (and soft pronounced) before them only after a stem ending in /l/, otherwise the suffix looks (and now is) hard (though velar stems will have undergone mutation, see below, section 3.2.1). For example, within the noun stem жен–/*žon–* 'wife (< woman)', the vowel phoneme is /o/ to account for the plural stem жён–/*žon–* (e.g. NP жёны/*žo'ni*), the singular [ɨ] accounted for by its lack of stress and being after a palatal; but in the derived adjective [ɔ] never occurs, even though the stem is always stressed:

Stem	**Suffix**	**Joined form**
жен–/*žon–*	–ск/–'*sk*	женский/*že'n–('')sk–ij*
'woman/wife'	(relative)	'female'

Similarly:

сел–/*s'ol–* (e.g. NS село/*s'ol–o*',	сельский/*s'e'l–'sk–ij*
NP сёла/*s'o'l–a*)	'rural'
'village/country'	

One solution is to make a rule for particular affixal morphemes (here – *'sk*) which says that where the stem has the *e/ë* alternation, the realisation before them will be the *e* alternant. However, as argued in chapter 3, section 1.1.1, we opt for a description which leaves the morpheme marked as {*'o*}, realised normally as /o/, that is, as [ɔ], [ɪ], [ə], etc. depending on stress and preceding consonant, to which we must now add: (1) a *morphophonemic* rule which realises it as [ɛ] when stressed and followed by a suffix beginning with {*'*} (whether followed by the vowel /e/ or /i/, or by a consonant, as in {*'sk*}, etc.); (2) another rule which causes all but /l'/ to harden before the second (consonantal) type of suffix.

3.1.2   *o* ~ ø and *e* ~ ø

The vowel alternant occurs where the boundary of the stem and affix would otherwise have three consonants or two consonants and a pause (a word boundary):

Prefix	Stem	Joined form
c(o)–/s(o)–	*шить/ši–t'*	*сшить/s–ši–t'*
('together')	'sew' Impf Inf	'sew' Pf Inf
c(o)–/s(o)–	*шью/šj–u*	*сошью/s(o)–šj–u'*
	'sew' Impf 1ps Pres	'sew' Pf 1ps Fut

Stem	Suffix + ending	Joined form
куп–/kup–	*–(e)ц/–(e)c–ø*	*купец/kup–(e)c–ø'*
'buy'	'agent' NS	'merchant' NS
"	*–(e)ца/–(e)c–a*	*купца/kup–c–a'*
	'agent' GS	'merchant' GS

3.1.3   *[i]* ~ *[ɨ]*

Given that the context producing these two variants of the phoneme /i/ is the hard/soft nature of the preceding consonant, with [i] the independent variant (see chapter 2, section 3.5.2.2), an interesting situation arises when a stem-initial [i] is preceded by a prefix (or a preposition) ending in a consonant (always hard): in this event, the prefix (less surprisingly, also the preposition) must retain its hard consonant, and so the following vowel is changed to the back variant [ɨ]; in the case of the preposition, this is purely phonetic, not reflected in any other way; however, with the prefix it is also reflected in the orthography, even in foreign words:

Stem	Prefix	Joined form
играть/igr–a–t'	*c–/s–*	*сыграть/s–igr–a–t'* [sɨ]
'play' Impf	(aspect)	'play' Pf
искать/isk–a–t'	*раз–/raz–*	*разыскать/raz–isk–a–t'*
'seek' Impf	(aspect)	'seek out' Pf [zɨ]
история/istor'ij–a	*пред–/pr'ed–*	*предыстория/pr'ed–istor'ij–a*
'history'	'pre-'	'prehistory' [dɨ]

3.1.4   Other

Alternations which depend on a simple following vowel or consonant (see chapter 1, sections 2.3.1.4, 2.4.1.1; chapter 2, section 3.5.1.2) are straightforward:

	Stem	Suffix	Joined form
ov ~ u	*рисов–/r'is–ov–*	*–нок/–nok–ø*	*рисунок/r'is–u'–nok–ø*
	'draw'	(object)	'drawing'
n ~ 'a	*начьн–/na–čn–*	*–ло/–l–o*	*начало/na–ča'–l–o*
	'begin'	(object)	'beginning'

3.2   Consonants

3.2.1   Non-palatal ~ palatal ('Mutation'; see chapter 2, section 3.5.2.1)
(1) Velars.

Stem	Suffix	Joined form
друг–/drug–	*–ьба/–'b–a*	*дружба/druž–b–a*
'friend'	(abstract)	'friendship'

(Here, too, we can mark the suffix as having a 'soft' onset, since all stems are at least softened, and in the case of the velars, mutated, cf. *прос–/pros–* 'ask': *просьба/pro's–'b–a* 'request'.)

страх–/strax–	*– н/–'n*	*страшный/straš–n–ij*
'fear, terror'	(qualitative)	'terrible'

A rare velar alternation (dating from the Proto-Slavonic 'Second' or 'Third Palatalisation' – see chapter 1, sections 2.2.1.3, 2.2.1.8) is:

g ~ z, in which structurally (semantically) the /z/ may appear in the suffixed form:

друг/drug	*–ья/–'j–a*	*друзья/druz–'j–a*
'friend'	(collective > plural)	'friends' NP

Cf. the simple hard ~ soft alternation with dentals:

брат/brat–ø	*–ья/–'j–a*	*братья/brat–'j–a*
'brother'	(collective > plural)	'brothers' NP

Even more rarely, the /z/ may appear in the (unsuffixed) base form:

князь/kn'az'–ø	*–иня/–in'–a*	*княгиня/kn'ag–i'n'–a*
'prince'	(female)	'princess'

(2) Labials.

Stem	Suffix	Joined form
куп–/kup–	*–я/–(j)–a*	*купля/kupl'–a*
'buy'	(object/process)	'purchase'

(3) Dentals.

Stem	Suffix	Joined form
свет–/sv'et–	*–я/–(j)–a*	*свеча/sv'eč–a'*
'light'	(object)	'candle'
свет–/sv'et–	*–ение/–en'ij–o*	*просвещение/*
	(abstract/process)	*pro–sv'ešč–en'ij–o*
		'enlightenment'

Stems in /t/, /d/ display the native Russian versus Russian Church Slavonic alternants of /t/(*č* ~ *šč*) and /d/ (*ž* ~ *žd*):

род–/rod–	*–я/–(j)a*	*рожать/rož–a–t'*
'give birth'	(aspect)	'give birth (animals)' Impf
род–/rod–	*–ение/–en'ij–o*	*рождение/rožd'–en'ij–o*
	(process)	'birth'

Stems in /st/ and /sk/ provide the native source of /šč/:

пуст–/pust–	*–ение/–en'ij–o*	*отпущение/ot–pušč–en'ij–o*
'let'	(abstract/process)	'remission, forgiving'

Another remnant of the Proto-Slavonic 'Third Palatalisation' is the alternation *c* ~ *č* (both derived from /k/ by different palatalisations): *отец/ot('e)c–ø'* 'father' ~ *отечество/ot'e'č–estv–o* 'fatherland'.

3.2.2 Hard/soft

Above (section 3.1.1) we noted the problem with some suffixes, notably *–'sk* and *–'n*, that they had earlier begun with a front vowel, now lost, but reflected in the effect on preceding consonants and the *e/ë* alternation. The situation in regard to consonants has now settled into a regular pattern: before these suffixes the following alternations occur:

(1) velars mutate (see above, section 3.2.1).

(2) /l/ is always soft:

Stem	Suffix	Joined form
сталь–/stal'–	*–н/–'n*	*стальной/stal'–'n–o'j*
'steel'	(qualitative)	'steel'
стол–/stol–	*–н/–'n*	*настольный/na–sto'l–'n–ij*
'table'	(relative)	'table' (e.g. tennis)

(3) other paired consonants are always hard:

Stem	Suffix	Joined form
конь–/kon'–	*–ск/–'sk*	*конский/*
'horse, steed' (poetic)	(relative)	*ko'n(')–(')sk–ij* 'horse'
Тверь–/Tver'–	*– ск/–'sk*	*тверской/*
'Tver'' (town)	(relative)	*tver(')–(')–sk–o'j* 'Tver'' (relative)

Exceptions are the four last month names (Eng *–ber*), which retain soft /r'/:

октябрь–/okt'abr'–	*–ск/–'sk*	*октябрьский/*
'October'	(relative)	*okt'a'br'–(')sk–ij* 'October' (Adj)

Note that in the short Masculine form of adjectives (see chapter 3, section 2.1.5.2), the former softness of {'n} is reflected in the insertion of *e* (and thus softening) and not *o* before the zero ending:

Long form Masculine	Short form Masculine	Short form Feminine
грозный/gro'z–(')n–ij	*грозен/*	*грозна/groz–(')n–a'*
	gro'z–'(e)n–ø	'terrible'

In subsequent examples and affix lists, we omit the soft mark in these two suffixes other than after /l/, since we believe its insertion (especially in brackets) would simply confuse and clutter. For other suffixes, an initial ' implies softening.

3.3   Stress

For the most part, stress rules belong to particular affixes. In a few cases we can give hard and fast rules, e.g. the prefix *вы–/vi–* 'out' is always stressed when on a perfective verb, or the (foreign) suffixes *–ическ/–'ičesk* '–ical' and *–ика/ –'ik–a* '–ics' always draw the stress to the syllable preceding them (cf. also Eng *histo'rical, lingui'stic*); however, we can usually state only tendencies, as the stress pattern of the stem is also relevant. See further in the following section, in the discussion of particular affixes.

4   Affixes

In the following we offer a full list of prefixes with their basic meanings, this being a relatively small full list, but for the suffixes, being a very large list, we offer only a selection of the main meanings served and the main suffixes serving them. The order is Russian alphabetical.

The affixes are given in their base form – the most neutral, or independent of context; only Russian Church Slavonic variants are noted, others being controlled by context. Other formal issues will be noted within each section.

4.1   Prefixes

We separate the nouns and adjectives from the verbs, since the latter require much more explanation and illustration. Secondary stress is marked by ` after the vowel.

4.1.1   Noun and adjective prefixes
(1) Native.

Prefix	Meaning	English affix	Example
без/b'ez	without	dis–	беспорядок/b'ez–por'a'dok–ø 'disorder'
		–less	безрукий/b'ez–ru'k–ij 'armless'
вне/vn'e	outside	extra–	внешкольный/vn'e–škol–'n–ij 'extra-curricular'
внутри/vnutr'i	inside	intra–	внутривенный/ vnutr'i–v'e'n–n–ij 'intravenous'
до/do	before	pre–	довоенный/do–voje'n–n–ij 'pre-war'
еже/ježe	each	–ly	ежедневный/ježe–dn'e'v–n–ij 'daily'
за/za	beyond	trans–	закавказье/za–kavka'z'–j–e 'Transcaucasia'
		post–	заударный/za–uda'r–n–ij 'post-tonic'
меж/m'ež	between	inter–	межзубный/m'ež–zu'b–n–ij 'interdental'
(RCS: между)			международный/ m'еždu–naro'd–n–ij 'international'
на/na	on top of		наушник/na–uš–nik–ø 'ear-phone'
			настольный/na–stol–'n–ij 'table(-top)'
над/nad	over, above	super–	надстройка/nad–stro'j–k–a 'superstructure'
			надводный/nad–vo'd–n–ij 'above-water'

наи/nai (+š–ij)	superlative	*–st*	*наилучший/nai–lu'čš–ij* 'very best'
не/n'e	negative	*un–, non–*	*недруг/n'e'–drug–ø* 'enemy' ('non-friend') *ненаучный/n'e–nau'č–n–ij* 'unscientific'
небез/n'e–b'ez (compound)	not without		*небезопасный/* *n'eb'ez–opa's–n–ij* 'not without danger'
недо/n'e–do (compound)	insufficiently	*under–*	*недоразвитие/* *n'e–do–raz–v'i'–t'ij–o* 'underdevelopment' *недоразвитый/* *n'e–do–ra'z–v'i–t–ij* 'underdeveloped'
около/o`kolo	around	*circum–*	*околоземный/o'kolo–z'e'm–n–ij* 'circumterrestrial'
пере/p'er'e	again	*re–*	*перерасчёт/ p'er'e–raz–čot–ø* 'recalculation'
по/po	along		*Поволжье/Po–vo'lž–j–e* 'Volga region' *поволжский/po–vo'lž–sk–ij* 'Volga'
	according to		*посильный/po–si'l–'n–ij* 'within ability'
	after (archaic)	*post–*	*посмертный/po–sm'e'rt–n–ij* 'posthumous'
под/pod	under	*sub–*	*подкласс/pod–kla'ss–ø* 'subclass' *подземельный/pod–z'em'e'l–'n–ij* 'subterranean'
	near		*Подмосковье/pod–mosko'v–j–o* 'Moscow district' *подмосковный/pod–mosko'v–n–ij* 'Moscow district' (Adj)
после/po`sl'e	after	*post–*	*послевоенный/po`sl'e–voje'n–n–ij* 'post-war'
пра/pra	preceding	*great–*	*прадед/pra'–d'ed–ø* 'great-grandfather'
	original	*proto–*	*праязык/pra–jazi'k–ø* 'proto-language'
пре/pr'e	exceedingly (high)		*пресмешной/pr'e–sm'eš–n–o'j* 'most funny'
пред/pr'ed	before	*pre–*	*предыстория/pr'ed–istor–'ij–a* 'pre-history' *предударный/pr'ed–uda'r–n–ij* 'pre-tonic'

при/prʹi   adjoining   *пригород/prʹi–gorod–ø* 'suburb'
                                                       приморский/prʹi–moʹr–sk–ij
                                                       'coastal'
                        additional   *привкус/prʹi–vkus–ø* 'after-taste'
противо/   against   *anti–,*   *противовес/proˋtʹivo–vʹeʹs–ø*
  proˋtʹivo   *counter–*   'counterweight'
                                                       противотанковый/
                                                         proˋtʹivo–taʹnk–ov –ij
                                                       'anti-tank'
раз/raz   exceedingly   *раскрасавица/raz–krasaʹv–ʹic–a*
                                                       'a real beauty'
                                                       развесёлый/raz–vʹesʹoʹl–ij
                                                       'very merry'
сверх/svʹeˋrx above   *super–*   *сверхчеловек/svʹeˋrx–čelovʹeʹk–ø*
                                                       'superman'
                                                       сверхъестественный/
                                                         svʹeˋrx–jestʹeʹstvʹ–en–n–ij
                                                       'supernatural'
со/so   with   *co–, con–*   *сотрудник/so–truʹd–nʹik–ø* 'co-worker'
                                                       современный/so–vrʹemʹ–eʹn–n–ij
                                                       'contemporary'
через/čerʹez across   *trans–*   *чересседельный/čerʹez–sʹedʹeʹl–ʹn–ij*
                                                       'saddle-girth (strap)'
        (RCS *чрез/črʹez* more common)   *чрезмерный/črʹez–mʹeʹr–n–ij*
                                                       'excessive'

(2) Foreign. Normally the stems also are foreign, although this is not always
the case, so one can say that these do function as Russian prefixes.

Prefix	Meaning	English affix	Example
a/a	without	*a–*	*аморальность/a–moraʹl–ʹn–ostʹ–ø* *–ный/–n–ij* 'amoral-ity'
анти/aˋntʹi	against	*anti–*	*антимир/aˋntʹi–miʹr–ø* 'antiworld' *антинародный/aˋntʹi–naroʹd–n–ij* 'antipopulist'
архи/aˋrxʹi	exceeding	*arch–*	*архиплут/aˋrxʹi–pluʹt–ø* 'arch-scoundrel' *архиопасный/aˋrxʹi–opaʹs–n–ij* 'most dangerous'
вице–/vʹiˋce-	in place of	*vice–*	*вице-король/vʹiˋce—koroʹlʹ–ø* 'viceroy'
гипер/giˋpʹer	exceeding	*hyper–*	*гиперзвук/giˋpʹer–zvuʹk–ø* 'ultrasound'
де(з)/deˋ(z)	removal	*de–, dis–*	*дезориентация/deˋz–orient–aʹcij–a* 'disorientation'

диз/d′iz	removal	*dis–*	*дизассоциация/d′iz–associ–a′cij–a* 'disassociation'
интер/i`nter	between	*inter–*	*интернациональный/ i`nter–naci–onal–′n–ij* 'international'
контр/ko`ntr	against	*counter–*	*контратака/ko`ntr–ata′k–a* 'counterattack'
обер–/o`ber-	exceeding	*arch–, over–*	*обер-кондуктор/ o`ber—kondu′kto′r–ø* 'chief guard (train)'
про/pro`	supporting	*pro–*	*проамериканец/pro`–am′erika′– n–(e)c–ø –нский/–n–sk–ij* 'pro-American'
	in place of	*vice–*	*проректор/pro–r′e′ktor–ø* 'vice-chancellor'
псевдо/ps′e`vdo	false	*pseudo–*	*псевдонаука/ps′e`vdo–nau′k–a –чный/–č–n–ij* 'pseudo-scien–ce/–tific
ре/re`	again	*re–*	*реэвакуация/re`–evakua′–cij–a* 're-evacuation'
суб/sub	under	*sub–*	*субтропики/sub–tro′p′iki* 'subtropics'
супер/su`per	over	*super–, hyper–*	*суперобложка/su`per–oblo′ž–k–a* 'dust-cover (book)'
транс/trans	across	*trans–*	*транссибирский/trans–s′ib′i′r–sk–ij* 'trans-Siberian'
ультра/ul′tra	exceeding	*ultra–*	*ультраконсерватор/ ul′tra–kons′erva′tor–ø* 'ultra-conservative' *ультразвуковой/ul′tra–zvuk–ov–o′j* 'ultrasonic'
экс–/e`ks-	former	*ex–*	*экс-чемпион/e`ks–čempio′n–ø* 'ex-champion'
экстра/e`kstra	outside	*extra–*	*экстралингвистический/ e`kstra–l′ingv′ist–′ičesk–ij* 'extralinguistic'

4.1.2 *Verb prefixes*

Each prefix has a basic physical meaning, which is given first, with at least one example (often reflexive verbs are given in addition). This meaning is seen also in the preposition, where such a parallel form exists; in the few cases where this is not the case, this and the semantically equivalent preposition are noted. All these prefixes have to some degree or other – in several cases to a high degree – extended abstract meanings; at least the main such meanings are noted, with examples of each. All examples are perfective verbs (Infinitive form), unless marked 'Impf'. (Further details on prefixal meanings may be found in Gribble 1973: 17ff.; Townsend 1968/1975: 123ff.; van Schooneveld 1978; Janda 1986.)

Prefix (Prep)	Meaning	Examples (stem + verb)
без/*b'ez*	removal	*slav–* 'fame': *бесславить*/ *b'ez–sla'v–'i–t'* 'defame'
в/*v*	in(to)	*li(j)–* 'pour': *влить*/*v–l'i–t'* 'pour in'
		čit– 'read': *вчитаться*/ *v–čit–a'–t'–s'a* 'become engrossed in reading'
вз/*vz* (No prep)	up	*l'et–* 'fly': *взлететь*/*vz–l'et–'e'–t'* 'take off'
	agitate	*mil–* 'soap': *взмылить*/ *vz–mi'l–'i–t'* 'lather'
	sudden sound	*krik–* 'shout': *вскричать*/ *vz–krič–a'–t'* 'shout out'
RCS: воз/*voz*		*n'es–* 'carry': *вознести*/*voz–n'os–t'i'* 'raise up' (poetic)
	again	*rod–* 'give birth': *возродить*/ *voz–rod–'i'–t'* 'revive'
вы/*vi* (Prep из/*iz*)	out	*n'es–* 'carry': *вынести*/*vi'–n'os–t'i* 'carry out' (physical)
	intensive	*pr'am–* 'straight': *выпрямить*/ *vi'–pr'am–'i–t'* 'straighten out'
(Stress always on *vi–* on perfective verbs)		
до/*do*	up to	*i(d)–* 'go': *дойти*/*do–i(d)–t'i'* 'reach'
	additional	*plat–* 'pay': *доплатить*/ *do–plat–'i'–t'* 'pay extra'
	excessive	*igr–* 'play': *доиграться*/ *do–igr–a'–t'–s'a* 'become exhausted from play'
за/*za*	beyond, behind	*l'et–* 'fly': *залететь*/*za–l'et–'e'–t'* 'fly over/beyond'
	on the way elsewhere	*n'es–* 'carry': *занести*/*za–n'os–t'i'* 'drop off'
		kup– 'buy': *закупить*/*za–kup–'i'–t'* 'stock up'
	excessive	*korm–* 'feed': *закормить*/ *za–ko'rm–'i–t'* 'overfeed'
	fill up, close	*stroj–* 'build': *застроить*/ *za–stro'j–i–t'* 'build on (all of)'
	begin	*kur–* 'smoke': *закурить*/*za–kur–'i'–t'* 'light up (cigarette)'
	in exchange	*rabot–* 'work': *заработать*/ *za–rabo't–a–t'* 'earn (wages)'
из/*iz* (RCS, cf. *vi–*)	out	*g(o)n–* 'chase': *изгнать*/*iz–g(o)n–a–t'* 'exile'
	intensive	*sux–* 'dry': *иссушить*/*iz–suš–i'–t'* 'dry out'

	exhaustive	*pis–* 'write': *исписать*/*iz–p'is–a'–t'* 'cover with writing'
	excessive	*b'eg–* 'run': *избегаться*/*iz–b'e'g–a–t'–s'a* 'become exhausted from running'
на/na	on(to)	*bros–* 'throw': *набросить*/*na–bro's–'i–t'* 'throw on'
	impose	*sm'ex–* 'laugh(ter)': *насмешить*/*na–sm'eš–i'–t'* 'amuse'
	cumulative	*kup–* 'buy': *накупить*/*na–kup–'i'–t'* 'buy a lot of'
	exhaustive	*jed–* 'eat': *наесться*/*na–jes–t'–s'a* 'be full (of food)'
над/nad	over	*pis–* 'write': *надписать*/*nad–p'is–a'–t'* 'superscribe'
	superficial	*kus–* 'bite': *надкусить*/*nad–kus–'i'–t'* 'take a bite (of)'
недо/n'e–do	insufficiently	*sol'–* 'salt': *недосолить*/*n'e–do–so'l–'i–t'* 'undersalt'

  (compound based on *do–*)

о(б)/o(b)	around	*b'eg–* 'run': *обежать*/*o–b'еž–a'–t'* 'run around' (all transitive senses)
	intensive	*smotr–* 'look': *осмотреть*/*o–smotr–'e'–t'* 'examine'
	cumulative	*b'eg–* 'run': *обегать*/*o–b'e'g–a'–t'* 'run round all of'
	false (Trans = cheat)	*v'es–* 'weigh': *обвесить*/*ob–v'e's–'i–t'* 'give short weight'
	(Refl = mistake)	*p'is–* 'write': *описаться*/*o–p'is–a'–t'–s'a* 'make a slip of the pen'

  (original form was *ob–*, then /b/ lost before obstruents, but subsequently
    became possible again before them)

обез/o–b'ez	removal, loss	*s'il–*'strength': *обессилить*/*ob'ez–s'i'l–'i–t'* 'weaken' (Trans)
		–еть/–'e–t' 'lose strength, weaken' (Intr)

  (compound based on *b'ez–*, this form more common than *b'ez–*)

от/ot	away (a bit)	*i(d)–* 'go': *отойти*/*ot(o)–i(d)–t'i* 'move away'
	removal	*(n')a–* 'take': *отнять*/*ot–n'a'–t'* 'amputate'
	intensive	*rabot–* 'work': *отработать*/*ot–rabo't–a–t'* 'work off (debt)'
		s(i)p– 'sleep': *отоспаться*/*ot(o)–sp–a–t'–s'a* 'make up lost sleep'
	reversal	*uk–* 'teach': *отучить*/*ot–uč–i'–t'* 'break from habit'
пере/p'er'e	across	*da–* 'give': *передать*/*p'er'e–da'–t'* 'transmit'

(Prep:	through	*s'ek–* 'cut': *пересечь/p'er'e–s'eč*
через/čer'ez)		'intersect'
(RCS: *пре/pr'e*)		*vrat–* 'turn': *превратить/*
		pr'e–vrat–'i–t' 'transmute'
		s'ek– 'cut': *пресечь/pr'e–s'eč*
		'cut short'
	Refl: reciprocal	*p'is–* 'write': *переписываться/*
		p'er'e–p'i's–iva–t'–s'a
		Impf. 'correspond'
	repetition	*p'is–* 'write': *переписать/*
		p'er'e–p'is–a'–t' 'rewrite'
	cumulative	*p'ek–* 'bake': *перепечь/*
		p'er'e–p'eč 'bake a lot of'
	excessive	*gr'e(j)–* 'heat': *перегреть/*
		p'er'e–gr'e'–t' 'overheat'
(RCS: *пре/pr'e*)		*vis–* 'high': *превысить/*
		pr'e–vi's–'i–t' 'exceed'
	superiority	*kr'ik–* 'shout': *перекричать/*
		p'er'e–kr'ič–a'–t' 'outshout'
по/po	limitation	*čit–* 'read': *почитать/po–čit–a'–t'*
		'read a bit/for a time'
	(Impf: with breaks)	*stuk–* 'knock': *постукивать/*
		po–stu'k–iva–t'
		'do some knocking (on and off)'
	begin	*zna–* 'know': *познать/po–zna'–t'*
		'get to know'
под/pod	under	*p'is–* 'write': *подписать/*
		pod–p'is–a'–t' 'sign'
	up (from under)	*bros–* 'throw': *подбросить/*
		pod–bro's–'i–t' 'throw up'
	approach	*s'ed–* 'sit': *подсесть/pod–s'es–t'*
		'pull up a chair'
	additional	*r'isov–* 'draw': *подрисовать/*
		pod–r'isov–a'–t' 'touch up'
	underhand	*d'el–* 'make': *подделать/*
		pod–d'e'l–a–t' 'forge'
	partial (coll.)	*ž(o)g–* 'burn': *поджечь/pod–žeč*
		'burn slightly'
пред/pr'ed	before, in front	*v'id–* 'see': *предвидеть/*
		pr'ed–v'i'd'–e–t' 'foresee'
(= RCS form; Prep = R form: *перед/p'er'ed*)		
		stav– 'put': *представить/*
		pr'ed–sta'v–'i–t' 'present'
при/pr'i	attached to	*v'oz–* 'take in vehicle':
		привезти/pri–v'oz–t'i 'bring'
	additional	*kup–* 'buy': *прикупить/*
		pr'i–kup–'i'–t' 'buy more'

Impf	accompanying	*sv′ist–* 'whistle': *присвистывать/ pr′i–sv′i′st–iva–t′* 'say with a whistle'
Refl	accustom self	*ži(v)–* 'live': *прижиться/ pr′i–zi–t′–s′a* 'get used to place'
	attentively	*slux–* 'listen': *прислушаться/ pr′i–slu′š–a–t′–s′a* 'listen closely'
	partial	*ot–kri–* 'open': *приоткрыть/pr′i–otkri′–t′* 'half open'
про/pro	through	*id–* 'go': *пройти/pro–i(d)–t′i* 'go through' (+Prep *čer′ez*)
Refl	fixing up	*sp–* 'sleep': *проспаться/pro–sp–a'–t′–s′a* 'sleep (it) off'
	past	*id–* 'go': *пройти/pro–i(d)–t′i* 'go past' (+Prep *mimo*)
	let pass, miss	*slux–* 'listen': *прослушать/pro–slu'š–a–t′* 'miss words'
Refl	mistake	*sčit–* 'count': *просчитаться/ pro–sčit–a'–t′–s′a* 'miscalculate'
раз/raz (no Prep)	apart	*r′ez–* 'cut': *разрезать/raz–r′e'z–at′* 'cut in two'
		da– 'give': *раздать/raz–da'–t′* 'distribute'
	reversal	*kl′ej–* 'stick': *расклеить/raz–kl′e′j–i–t′* 'unstick'
		uk– 'teach': *разучиться/raz–uč–i'–t′–s′a* 'forget how to'
	intensive	*smotr–* 'look': *рассмотреть/ raz–smotr–'e'–t′* 'examine'
(esp. Refl)	begin	*kr′ik–* 'shout': *раскричаться/ raz–kr′ič–a'–t′–s′a* 'start shouting'
c/s (Prep *s* + Instr)	together	*kl′ej–* 'stick': *склеить/s–kl′e′j–i–t′* 'stick together'
Refl	act well together	*igr–* 'play': *сыграться/ s–igr–a'–t′–s′a* 'play well together'
motion	round trip	*xod–* 'go': *сходить/s–xod–'i'–t′* 'go and come back'
(RCS: *co/so*, which is phonetic variant in R)		*b(e)r–* 'take': *собрать/so–br–a'–t′* 'collect'
(Prep *s* + Gen)	down, off	*bros–* 'throw': *сбросить/s–bro's–'i–t′* 'throw off'
	copy	*p′is–* 'write': *списать/s–p′is–a'–t′* '(make a) copy'
	exhaustive	*gor–* 'burn': *сгореть/s–gor–'e'–t′* 'burn down'

(originally two separate prepositions fused, reflected in the different cases
used with each meaning: + Instr = 'with', + Gen = 'down from')

y/u	1. away (far)	*v'oz–* 'take (in vehicle)': *уеезти/u–v'oz–t'i'*
		'abduct'
	reduce in size	*r'ez–* 'cut': *урезать/u–r'e'z–at'*
		'shorten by cutting'
	2. exhaustive	*stav–* 'put': *уставить/u–sta'v–'i–t'*
		'fill with (items)'
	resultative: pos.	*govor–* 'speak': *уговорить/u–govor–'i'–t'*
		'persuade'
		s'ed– 'sit': *усесться/u–s'es–t'–s'a*
		'settle down'
	neg.	*bi(j)–* 'beat': *убить/u–bi'–t'* 'kill'

(originally two separate prepositions fused, hence two unrelated meanings.
The preposition *y/u* (+ Gen) means 'next to', so is closest to the second set
of meanings above. There is no parallel preposition for the first set ('away'),
that used being *ot* + Gen.)

4.2   Suffixes

We shall take noun, adjective and verb suffixes separately, and within each treat
the different bases separately. As noted above, this is only a small selection of
the most common suffixes. (A full list may be found in Cubberley 1994, smaller
ones in Gribble 1973 and Townsend 1968/1975.) 'Foreign' suffixes are offered
only where they are commonly used with native bases. The order is from most
to least common.

The gender and declension class of suffixes is indicated by the Nominative
Singular ending; those with the soft sign are assumed to be Class I Masculine
unless marked 'III' (= Class III Feminine). The 'fleeting' /o/ and /e/ are set in
brackets. 'Stress' indicates the most common pattern only, unless accompanied
by 'always'; abbreviations used are: 'base' = as on base, that is, the suffix has
no effect; 'base/end' = mobile pattern bases tend to have end-stressed suffixes;
'pre' = on syllable before suffix (that is, stem-final); 'suff' = on suffix; 'suff-1'/
'suff-2' = on first/second syllable of polysyllabic suffix; 'end' = on ending.
Under '(Base)' are given stems (plus Nominative Singular ending for nouns,
with *ø'* indicating end-stress; for adjectives only, NS *–o'j* is added to indicate
end stress). Suffixes beginning with *j–* imply that *j*- mutation of the stem-final
consonant will occur; those beginning in *e–* (including fleeting *(e)–*) that stem
softening will occur. On the morphophonology of fleeting (o) and (e) see above,
section 3.1.2.

4.2.1   Noun suffixes
(1) Nouns derived from nouns
(a) *Person* related in some way to base

(i) *Male* (or common) associated with base (e.g. member, inhabitant, patronymic)

Suffix	Stress	(Base)	Example
(e)ц/(e)c–ø	pre	Ukrai'n–a	украинец/ukrai'n–(e)c–ø 'Ukrainian'
ич/'ič–ø	end	Moskv–a'	москвич/moskv–'ič–ø 'Muscovite'
ник/n'ik–ø	base/ end	put'ø 'road'	путник/pu't–n'ik–ø 'traveller'
ач/ač–ø	end	s'i'l–a 'strength'	силач/s'il–ač–ø' 'strong man'
янин/jan–'in–ø	suff-1	Ki'jev–ø	киевлянин/kijevl'–a'n'in–ø 'Kievan'
ович/ov'ič–ø	base	Iva'n–ø	Иванович/Iva'n–ov'ič–ø 'son of Ivan'

(ii) A large subgroup of the same, with a trade as the base, meaning a *practitioner* of the trade

Suffix	Stress	(Base)	Example
чик/čik–ø	pre	buf'et–ø 'snackbar'	буфетчик/buf'e't–čik–ø 'bartender'
(щик/ščik–ø) = variant on stems in non-dental			трамвайщик/ tramva'j–ščik–ø 'tramways worker'
ак/ak–ø	end	mo'r'–e	моряк/mor'–ak–ø' 'sailor'
ник/n'ik–ø	base/end	m'a's–o 'meat'	мясник/m'as–n'ik–ø' 'butcher'
ёр/'or–ø	suff	ša'xt–a 'mine'	шахтёр/šaxt–'or–ø 'miner'
ист/'ist–ø	suff	futbo'l–ø	футболист/futbol–'i'st –ø 'footballer'

(iii) *Female*, especially wife, daughter; also gender-marked trade (becoming less common); base is most often the male form, with or without suffix.

Suffix	Stress	(Base)	Example
ка/(о)k–a	pre	vnuk–ø 'grandson'	внучка/vnu'č–k–a 'granddaughter'
			may be added to suffixed Masc: москвичка/ moskv–'ič–k–a 'Muscovite (female)'

ица/'ic–a	suff	*car'–ø'* 'tsar'	*царица/car–'i'c–a* 'wife of tsar'

(ница/n'ic–a) = variant on stem with Masc suffix *n'ik* or *t'el'* (see below, from verb)

	base	*uči't'el'–ø* 'teacher'	*учительница/ uči't'el'–nic–a* (female)
иха/'ix–a	suff	*slon–ø'* 'elephant'	*слониха/slon–'i'x–a* 'elephant (female)'
ша/š–a	base	*kass'i'r–ø* (male)	*кассирша/kass'i'r–š–a* 'cashier (female)'
		man'ik'u'r–ø (trade)	*маникюрша/ man'ik'u'r–š–a* 'manicurist'
ыня/in'–a	suff	*bog–ø* 'god'	*богиня/ bog–i'n'–a* 'goddess'
овна/ovn–a	base	*Iva'n–ø*	*Ивановна/Iva'n–ovn–a* 'daughter of Ivan'

(b) Object related to the base

(i) Relative, e.g. intended or used in relation to, like

Suffix	Stress	(Base)	Example
(o)к/(o)k–ø	end	*jazik–ø'* 'tongue'	*язычок/jazič–(o)k–ø'* 'tongue (shoe)'
ка/(o)k–a	pre	*golov–a'* 'head'	*головка/golo'v–k–a* 'head (pin)'
ко/(o)k–o	base	*u'x–o* 'ear'	*ушко/uš–k–o'* 'tag'

The above are gender variants retaining the gender of the base.

ник/n'ik–	base	*čaj–ø* 'tea'	*чайник/ča'j–n'ik* 'teapot'
ница/n'ic–a	base	*sa'xar–ø* 'sugar'	*сахарница/sa'xar–n'ic–a* 'sugar–bowl'
ище/išč–o	base	*topor–ø'* 'axe'	*топорище/topor–'i'šč–o* 'axe–handle'

(ii) Augmentative: a large version of base; often also pejorative

Suffix	Stress	(Base)	Example
ища/išč–a	suff	*ruk–a'* 'hand'	*ручища/ruč–i'šč–a* 'large hand'
ище/išč–o	suff	*go'rod–ø* 'town'	*городище/gorod–'i'šč–o* 'large town'

(These are gender variants – the first for Feminine base, the second for Masculine and Neuter)

ина/in–a (coll.)	suff	*dom–ø* 'house'	*домина/dom–'i'n–a* 'large house'

(iii) Diminutive: a small version of base, including young animals; usually also affectionate

Suffix	Stress	(Base)	Example
(o)к/(o)k–ø	end	*go'rod–ø* 'town'	*городок/gorod–(o)k–ø'* 'small town'
ка/(o)k–a	pre	*kart'i'n–a* 'picture'	*картинка/kart'i'n–k–a* 'small picture'
ко/(o)k–o	base	*o'blak–o* 'cloud'	*облачко/o'blač–k–o* 'small cloud'

The above are gender variants retaining the gender of the base.

ик/'ik–ø	pre	*dom–ø* 'house'	*домик/do'm–'ik* 'small house'

On Masculine personal names = *affectionate*: *Славик/Sla'v–'ik–ø* 'Slava'; *Павлик/Pa'vl–'ik–ø* 'Pav'el'.

ён(o)k/'on(o)k–ø	suff-1	*slon–ø'* 'elephant'	*слонёнок/slon–'o'n(o)k–ø* 'baby elephant'
очка/očk–a	base	*la'mp–a* 'lamp'	*лампочка/la'mp–očk–a* 'small lamp', also 'bulb'

On Feminine personal names = *affectionate*: *Ниночка/N'i'n–očk–a* 'Nina'; *Олечка/O'l'–ečk–a* 'Olya'.
Some may have an additional *pejorative* sense:

ечко/ečk–o	suff	*m'e'st–o* 'place'	*местечко/m'est–'e'čk–o* 'tiny town' also coll. 'cushy job'
ушка/ušk–a	suff	*izb–a'* 'hut'	*избушка/izb–u'šk–a* 'tiny hut'
ишка/'išk–a	suff	*misl'–ø* 'thought'	*мыслишка/misl–'i'šk–a* 'tiny thought'

The last four are originally compound suffixes, hence the frequent double sense of *small* plus either *affectionate* or *pejorative*.

(c) Abstract state or activity related to base (e.g. science, custom)

Suffix	Stress	(Base)	Example
ство/stv–o	base	*d'e'v–a* 'maiden'	*девство/d'e'v–stv–o* 'spinsterhood'

(d) Collective

Suffix	Stress	(Base)	Example
ьё/′j–o	end	*zv′er′–∅* 'wild animal'	*зверьё/zv′er′–j–o'* 'animals'
ва/v–a	end	*list–∅* 'leaf'	*листва/list–v–a'* 'foliage'

(2) *Nouns derived from adjectives*

   (a) Person characterised by the quality of the base

Suffix	Stress	(Base)	Example
ик/′ik–∅	end	*star–* 'old'	*старик/star–′ik–∅'* 'old man'
ец/(e)c–∅	end	*mudr–* 'wise'	*мудрец/mudr– ec–∅'* 'wise man'
ач/ač–∅	end	*l′ix–o′j* 'wild'	*лихач/l′ix–ač–∅'* 'dare-devil'
ыш/iš–∅	end	*mal–* 'small'	*малыш/mal–iš–∅'* 'child'
ка/k–a	base	*n′ež(e)n–* 'tender'	*неженка/n′e'žen–k–a* 'mollycoddle'
уха/ux–a	suff	*star–* 'old'	*старуха/star–u'x–a* 'old woman'
ушка/ušk–a	suff	*čorn–* 'black'	*чернушка/čorn–u'šk–a*
янка/′ank–a	suff	*smugl–* 'swarthy'	*смуглянка/ smugl–′a'nk–a* both last two = 'dark-skinned woman'

   (b) Object displaying the quality of the base

Suffix	Stress	(Base)	Example
ок/(o)k–∅	end	*žolt–* 'yellow'	*желток/žolt–(o)k–∅'* 'egg–yolk'
як/′ak–∅	end	*pust–o′j* 'empty'	*пустяк/pust–′ak–∅'* '(a) trifle'
ица/′ic–a	suff	*t′opl–* 'warm'	*теплица/t′opl–′i'c–a* 'hothouse'

   (c) Abstract quality

Suffix	Stress	(Base)	Example
ость/ost′–∅	base	*sm′el–* 'bold'	*смелость/sm′e'l–ost′–∅* 'boldness'

oma/ot–a	end	*ostr–* 'sharp'	*острота/ostr–ot–a'* 'sharpness'
изна/'izn–a	end	*b'el–* 'white'	*белизна/b'el–'izn–a'* 'whiteness'
ина/'in–a	end	*glub–* 'deep'	*глубина/glub–'in–a'* 'depth'
ье/'j–o	base	*zdoro'v–* 'healthy'	*здоровье/zdoro'v–'j–o* 'health'
ство/stv–o	base	*boga't–* 'rich'	*богатство/ boga't–stv–o* 'wealth'

(d) Collective

Suffix	Stress	(Base)	Example
ёжь/'ož–ø	suff	*molod–o'j* 'young'	*молодёжь/ molod–'o'ž–ø* 'young people'
ье/'j–o	end	*sir–o'j* 'raw'	*сырьё/sir–'j–o'* 'raw materials'

(e) Place

Suffix	Stress	(Base)	Example
ина/'in–a	suff	*rav(e)n–* 'even'	*равнина/ravn–'i'n–a* 'plain'

(3) Nouns derived from verbs. The Infinitive theme vowel may or may not be included in the base; likewise an aspectual suffix. These optional elements are given in brackets.

(a) Person: agent; most often profession/trade

Suffix	Stress	(Base)	Example
ок/ok–ø	end	*xod–* 'walk'	*ходок/xod–ok–ø'* 'walker'
ун/un–ø	end	*b'eg–* 'run'	*бегун/b'eg–un–ø'* 'runner'
(e)ц/(e)c–ø	end	*pro–da–(v)–* 'sell'	*продавец/ pro–dav–(e)c–ø'* 'salesman'
ник/n'ik–ø	end	*pro–vod–* 'conduct'	*проводник/ pro–vod–n'ik–ø'* 'conductor'
тель/t'el'–ø	pre	*uč–(i)–* 'teach'	*учитель/uč–i'–t'el'–ø* 'teacher'

| чик/čik–∅ | pre | l'ot– 'fly' | лётчик/l'o't–čik–∅ 'pilot' |
| арь/ar'–∅ | pre | p'ek– 'bake' | пекарь/p'e'k–ar'–∅ 'baker' |

(b) Object
(i) instrument, especially from Imperfective base

Suffix	Stress	(Base)	Example
ак/ak	end	r'ez– 'cut'	резак/r'ez–ak–∅' 'chopper'
а/∅–a	pre	p'il– 'saw'	пила/p'i'l–∅–a 'saw'
ло/l–o	pre	toč–(i)– 'sharpen'	точило/toč–i'–l–o 'grindstone'

(ii) resulting from activity, especially from perfective base (typically including prefix)

Suffix	Stress	(Base)	Example
(о)к/(o)k–∅	pre	o–kur– 'smoke'	окурок/o–ku'r–(o)k–∅ 'cigarette butt'
ыш/iš–∅	pre	v–klad– 'insert'	вкладыш/v–kla'd–iš–∅ 'bush (tech.)'
ина/'in–a	pre	cara'p– 'scratch'	царапина/cara'p–'in–a 'scratch'
я/j–a	pre	nos– 'carry'	ноша/no'š–a 'burden'
–/∅–∅	pre	v–xod– 'enter'	вход/v–xod–∅–∅ 'entrance'
ь/'–∅ III	pre	za–pis– 'record'	запись/za'–pis–'–∅ 'record(ing)'

(iii) Collective result

Suffix	Stress	(Base)	Example
нье/n'j–o	pre (theme)	v'az–(a) 'tie, knit'	вязанье/v'az–a'–n'j–o 'knitting'
тье/t'j–o	pre/end	li(j)– 'pour'	литьё/li–t'j–o '(metal) castings'
иво/'iv–o	pre	m'es– 'mix, knead'	месиво/m'e's–'iv–o 'mash'
нь/n'–∅ III	pre/suff	da– 'give'	дань/da–n'–∅ 'tribute'

(c) Abstract activity

Suffix	Stress	(Base)	Example
ка/k–a	pre	r'ez– 'cut'	резка/r'e'z–k–a 'cutting'
ота/ot–a	end/suff	dr'em– 'doze'	дремота/dr'em–o't–a 'drowsiness'
ть/t'–ø III	pre	vlad– 'control'	власть/ vlas–t'–ø (dt > st) 'authority'
ние/n'ij–o	base	vi'd–('e)– 'see'	видение/vi'd–'e–n'ij–o 'vision'
ство/stv–o	pre	b'eg– 'run'	бегство/b'e'g–stv–o 'flight'
ьба/'b–a	end	bor– 'fight'	борьба/bor–'b–a 'struggle'
–/ø–ø	pre	zvon– 'ring'	звон/zvon–ø 'ringing'
a/ø–a	pre	trat– 'spend'	трата/tra't–a 'expenditure'
ь/'–ø III	pre	drož– 'shiver'	дрожь/drož(–')–ø 'shivering'

(d) Place

Suffix	Stress	(Base)	Example
ница/n'ic–a	pre	m'el'– 'mill'	мельница/ m'e'l'–n'ic–a 'mill'
ище/'išč–o	pre	u–b'eg– 'run away'	убежище/ub'e'ž–išč–o 'refuge'
ня/n'–a	pre	pax– 'plough'	пашня/pa'š–n'–a 'ploughed field'

(< –'n'–, hence velar mutation)

льня/l'n'–a	pre	sp–(a)– 'sleep'	спальня/spa'–l'n'–a 'bedroom'

(variant where theme vowel is retained)

4.2.2   Adjective suffixes
(1) Adjectives derived from nouns
(a) Qualitative: having quality typical of base

Suffix	Stress	(Base)	Example
н/'n	base	žir–ø 'fat'	жирный/ ži'r–n–ij 'fat'

	(velar mutation)	*v'ek–ø* '(an) age'	*вечный/ v'e'č–n–ij* 'eternal'
ив/'iv	suff	*pra'vd–a* 'truth'	*правдивый/ pravd–'i'v–ij* 'truthful'
ам/at	suff	*rog–ø* 'horn'	*рогатый/ rog–a't–ij* 'horned'
альн/al'n	suff	*centr–ø* 'centre'	*центральный/ centr–a'l'n–ij* 'central'

(combination of foreign –*al* and native – *'n*; as following combines foreign –*ic* and –*n*)

ичн/'ičn	suff	*istor'ij–a* 'history'	*историчный/ istor–'i'čn–ij* 'historic'

(b) Relative: having quality related to base (e.g. intended/used for, attributive)

Suffix	Stress	(Base)	Example
н/'n	base	*čaj–ø* 'tea'	*чайный/ ča'j–n–ij* 'tea'(Adj)
ск/'sk	base	*mor'–o* 'sea'	*морской/mor–sk–o'j* 'sea, nautical'
	(velar mutation)	*čex–ø* 'a Czech'	*чешский/če'š–sk–ij* 'Czech'

While –*n* is commonly either qualitative or relative, –*'sk* is normally only relative; however, extension to a qualitative sense is possible, e.g.:

d'et– 'child(ren)'	*детский/d'e't–sk–ij*	'child's' > 'childish'

Note also combination of foreign (e.g. Eng) –*ic* and native –*'sk*:

ическ/'ičesk	suff-1	*istor'ij–a* 'history'	*исторический/ istor–'i'česk–ij* 'historical', also > 'historic'
ов/ov	base	*jazik–ø'* 'language'	*языковой/ jazik–ov–o'j* 'linguistic'
		cf. *jazik–ø'* 'tongue'	*языковый/ jazik–o'v–ij* 'lingual'

ян/'an	end	*vod–a'* 'water'	*водяной/vod–'an–o'j* 'aquatic' (cf. *водный/vo'd–n–ij* 'water/watery')

(c) Similar, partial (cf. Eng – *ish*, –*y*)

Suffix	**Stress**	**(Base)**	**Example**
ист/'ist	suff	*p'atn–o'* 'spot'	*пятнистый/ p'atn–'i'st–ij* 'spotty'
оват/ovat	suff–2	*plut–ø* 'rogue'	*плутоватый/ plut–ova't–ij* 'roguish'

(d) Augmentative (having large or a lot of base)

Suffix	**Stress**	**(Base)**	**Example**
аст/ast	suff	*zub–ø* 'tooth'	*зубастый/zub–a'st–ij* 'sharp-toothed'
овит/ov'it	suff-2	*plod–ø'* 'fruit'	*плодовитый/ plod–ov'i't–ij* 'prolific'

(e) Possessive. While all the above suffixes have assumed a long adjective with the possibility of syntactically appropriate short forms, the two main possessive suffixes reflect the older situation of short *attributive* forms. We indicate this by the sign #, meaning that there is no adjectival ending, but rather a noun ending. Both of these suffixes are increasingly rarely used in the standard as simple possessives, though they are fixed in the common surname forms. For their (irregular) declension, see chapter 3, section 2.1.5.3.

Suffix	**Stress**	**(Base)**	**Example**
ов/ov#	base	*ot(e)c–ø'* 'father'	*отцов/otc–o'v–ø* 'father's'
		I'gor'–ø 'Igor'	*игорев/i'gor'–ov–ø* 'Igor's'
	cf. surname	*čex–ø* 'Czech'	*Чехов/če'x–ov–ø* 'Chekhov'
ин/'in#	base/pre	*s'ostr–a'* 'sister'	*сестрин/s'e'str–'in–ø* 'sister's' ({'o}>/e/ before {'in})
		Sa'š–a 'Sasha'	*сашин/sa'š–in–ø* 'Sasha's'
	cf. surname	*pu'š–k–a* 'cannon'	*Пушкин/Pu'šk–in–ø* 'Pushkin'

The choice between these two suffixes is based on the class of the base: –*ov* is attached to Class I (Masculine) bases, –*'in* to Class II (either gender). A long form of the latter does also exist, used with animal bases and having meanings extended beyond possessive:

> *ин/'in*   suff   *lo'šad'–∅* 'horse' лошадиный/*lošad'–i'n–ij*
> 'horse's' > 'equine'

There is another suffix, also used mainly on animal bases, which also has the special adjectival declension (cf. chapter 3, section 2.1.5.3), with velar mutation and *j*-mutation of /t/ and /d/ only:

> *(и)й/' (i)j*   pre   *ri'b–a* 'fish'   рыбий/*ri'b–' (i)j–∅*
> 'fish('s)'
>
> (velar   *soba'k–a* 'dog'   собачий/
> mutation)   *soba'č–(i)j–∅*
> 'dog('s)'
>
> (*j*-mutation) *m'edv'e'd'* 'bear'   медвежий/
> *m'edv'e'ž–(i)j–∅*
> 'bear('s)'

(2) Adjectives derived from adjectives. Base adjectives may be non-derived or derived (suffixed) forms.

(a) Similar

Suffix	Stress	(Base)	Example
ист/'ist	suff	*šolk–ov–* 'silk'	шелковистый/ *šolk–ov–'i'st–ij* 'silky'
оват/ovat	suff-2	*s'er–* 'grey'	сероватый/*s'er–ova't–ij* 'greyish'
яв/jav	suff	*molod–o'j* 'young'	моложавый/*molož–a'v–ij* 'young-looking'

(b) Diminutive (often + affectionate)

Suffix	Stress	(Base)	Example
еньк/en'k	base	*tonk–* 'thin, slim'	тоненький/*ton–en'k–ij* 'slender'

(c) Augmentative (to a high degree)

Suffix	Stress	(Base)	Example
енн/enn	suff	*tolst–* 'fat'	толстенный/*tolst–e'nn–ij* 'very fat'
ущ/ušč	suff	*tolst–* 'fat'	толстущий/*tolst–u'šč–ij* 'very fat'

(d) Superlative

Suffix	Stress	(Base)	Example
ш/š	pre	*star–* 'old'	*старший/sta'r–š–ij* 'oldest'
ейш/ejš	suff	*nov–* 'new'	*новейший/nov–e'jš–ij* 'very latest'
(айш/(j)ajš after palatal < velar:		*v'eli'k–* 'great'	*величайший/* *v'elič–a'jš–ij* 'greatest')

(3) Adjectives derived from verbs

    (a) Characteristic (qualitative): typically performing activity of base (Imperfective)

Suffix	Stress	(Base)	Example
лив/l'iv	suff	*govor–* 'talk'	*говорливый/* *govor–l'i'v–ij* 'talkative'
ист/'ist	base (inf)	*pr'e–riv–* 'interrupt'	*прерывистый/* *pr'e–ri'v–'ist–ij* 'intermittent'
к/k	pre	*kl'ej–* 'stick'	*клейкий/kl'e'j–k–ij* 'sticky'

The two present participle active suffixes (the Old Russian and Russian Church Slavonic/Contemporary Standard Russian forms) commonly produce adjectives; the Old Russian form (–*č*) can no longer be confused with a participle, while the Russian Church Slavonic form (the modern –*šč*) can; the vowel preceding the suffix is that of the 3rd Person Plural Present (*u* for 1st conj, *'a* for 2nd):

ч/č	pre	*gor–('a)–* 'burn'	*горячий/* *gor–'a'č–ij* 'hot'
		(cf. participle	*горящий/* *gor–'a'šč–ij* 'burning')
		kol–('u)– 'prick'	*колючий/* *kol'–u'č–ij* 'prickly'
щ/šč	base (3pp) (same as participle)	*v'od–* 'lead'	*ведущий/* *v'od–u'šč–ij* 'leading/ prominent'

(b) Relative: suitable for, worthy of, etc. activity of base

Suffix	Stress	(Base)	Example
н/′n	pre	*za–m′et–* 'notice'	*заметный/* *za–m′e′t–n–ij* 'noticeable'
льн/l′n–	base/pre	*spa–* 'sleep'	*спальный/* *spa′–l′n–ij* '(for) sleeping'
ов/ov	end	*b′eg–* 'run'	*беговой/b′eg–ov–o′j* 'racing'

(c) Resultative: quality resulting; from past participle forms. Where the base is an intransitive verb, the suffix *–l* (the modern past tense suffix, but former past active participle) may be used; otherwise the passive suffixes *–n* and *–t* are used:

Suffix	Stress	(Base)	Example
л/l	base (past)	*u–sta–* 'get tired'	*усталый/* *u–sta–l–ij* 'tired'
		sp′e– 'ripen'	*спелый/sp′e′–l–ij* 'ripe'
н/n	base (inf)	*rv–(a)–* 'tear'	*рваный/rv–an–ij* 'torn, lacerated'
		var–(i)– 'cook, boil'	*варёный/var′–on–ij* 'boiled'
		(preceding vowel = *a* for Class I–III, *′o* for IV)	
m/t	base (inf)	*s–ža–* 'squeeze'	*сжатый/s–ža′–t–ij* 'compressed'
		za–p′er– 'lock'	*запертой/* *za–p′er–t–o′j* 'locked'
		(cf. participle	*запертый/* *za′–p′er–t–ij*)

(4) Adjectives derived from other categories. All are *Relative*:
   (a) From adverbs *(time and place)*

Suffix	Stress	(Base)	Example
н(ий)/n′	base	*ra′no* 'early'	*ранний/ra′n–n′–ij* 'early'
шн(ий)/šn′	base	*včera′* 'yesterday'	*вчерашний/* *včera′–šn′–ij* 'yesterday's'

inserted /o/ (*o* or *e*) after stem in consonant:

tam 'there'	тамошний/*ta'm–ošn'–ij* 'of there'	
t'ep'e'r' 'now'	теперешний/ *t'ep'e'r'–ešn'–ij* 'present'	

(b) From numerals

Suffix	Stress	(Base)	Example
н/*'n*	end	*dvoj–e* 'two'	двойной/*dvoj–n–o'j* 'double'
ичн/*'ičn*	suff	*d'e's'at'–ø* 'ten'	десятичный/ *d'es'at–'ï'čn–ij* 'decimal'
–/(hard+)ø	pre	*d'e's'at'–ø* 'ten'	десятый/*d'es'a't–ø–ij* 'tenth'
	(end)	*vos'(e)m'–ø* 'eight'	восьмой/*vos'm–ø–o'j* 'eighth'

4.2.3   Verb suffixes

Suffixes are given in their Infinitive form; where this does not make clear the conjugation, an extra marker is added to indicate the Present theme, e.g. an added *–j* means Class III.

(1) Verbs derived from nouns

(a) Stative: perform activity typical of base ('be')

Suffix	Stress	(Base)	Example
ствова/*stvova* (Pres ствуе/ *stvuj–o*)	base	*uči't'el'* 'teacher'	учительствовать/ *uči't'el'–stvova–t'* 'be a teacher' (coll.)
(stst > st)		*vlast'* 'authority'	властвовать/ *vla'–stvova–t'* 'rule'
нича/*n'iča–j* base		*brod'a'g–a* 'tramp'	бродяжничать/ *brod'a'ž–n'iča–t'* 'be a tramp'
(velar mutation)			

(b) Relative: perform activity related to base

Suffix	Stress	(Base)	Example
а/*a–j*	base	*za'vtrak* 'breakfast'	завтракать/ *za'vtrak–a–t'* 'have breakfast'

| и/ʹi | base | sos'e'd 'neighbour' | соседить/sos'e'd–ʹi–t́ 'neighbour' |
| ова/ova | suff-2 | noč 'night' | ночевать/noč–ova–t́ 'spend the night' |

(c) Acquisitive (Inchoative): acquire a state ('become')

Suffix	**Stress**	**(Base)**	**Example**
е/e–j	suff	s'irot–a' 'orphan'	сиротеть/s'irot–e'–t́ 'be orphaned'

(d) Factitive: produce a state ('cause to be') or impose a feature

Suffix	**Stress**	**(Base)**	**Example**
а/a–j	base	p'atn–o' 'stain'	пятнать/p'atn–a'–t́ 'stain'
я/ja–j	base	cep' 'chain'	цеплять /cepl'–a'–t́ 'clutch at'

(из)(ир)ова/(ʹiz)(ʹir)ova (any combination in that order; combines foreign (Germ) *–is/–ier* with *–ova*); base is normally foreign:

изова/ʹizova	suff-3	st'il' 'style'	стилизовать/ st'il–ʹizova'–t́ 'stylise'
ирова/ʹirova	suff-1	kod 'code'	кодировать/ kod–ʹi'rova–t́ 'encode'
изирова/ ʹiz'irova	suff-2	go'sp'ital 'hospital'	госпитализировать/ gosp'ital'–iz'i'rova–t́ 'hospitalise'

(2) Verbs derived from adjectives
   (a) Stative: display quality of base ('be')

Suffix	**Stress**	**(Base)**	**Example**
а/a–j	suff	xvor– 'ill'	хворать/xvor–a'–t́ 'be ill'
и/ʹi	suff	xitr– 'cunning'	хитрить/xitr–ʹi'–t́ 'be cunning'
е/e–j	suff	b'el– 'white'	белеть/b'el–e'–t́ 'be/show white'
ова/ova	suff-2	pust–o'j 'empty'	пустовать/ pust–ova'–t́ 'be empty'

ича/′iča–j	base	*nagl–* 'brazen'	*нагличать/* *na′gl–′iča–t′* 'be brazen'
(mostly from base in *–n*)		*važn–* 'important'	*важничать/* *va′žn–′iča–t′* 'put on airs'

(b) Acquisitive/Inchoative: acquire quality ('become')

Suffix	**Stress**	**(Base)**	**Example**
е/e–j	suff	*t′omn–* 'dark'	*темнеть/* *t′omn–e′–t′* 'grow dark'
я/ja–j	suff	*kr′epk–* 'strong'	*крепчать/* *kr′epč–a′–t′* 'grow strong(er)'
ну/nu	pre	*t′ix–* 'quiet'	*тихнуть/t′i′x–nu–t′* 'go quiet'

The last example shows the variant of *–nu* which normally disappears in the past (see chapter 3, section 2.2.6.2 and (3) below).

(c) Factitive: produce quality ('make')

Suffix	**Stress**	**(Base)**	**Example**
и/′i	suff	*b′el–* 'white'	*белить/b′el–′i′–t′* 'whiten'

из/ир/ова//iz/ir/ova (as above, normally on foreign base, here without suffix):

изова/′izova	suff-3	*n′ejtral′(n)–* 'neutral'	*нейтрализовать/* *n′ejtral–′izova′–t′* 'neutralise'
изирова/ *′iz′irova*	suff-2	*aktiv(n)–* 'active'	*активизировать/* *aktiv–′iz′i′rova–t′* 'activate'

(3) Verbs derived from verbs

(a) Aspectual: Perfective > Imperfective. In the modern language the marking of Imperfective aspect by suffix applies only (with very few exceptions) to prefixed verbs. Formerly suffixes on unprefixed verbs indicated iteration, and when this ceased to be an active category, all those verbs became simply Imperfective. The most common suffixes in this role were *–a* (or *–a–j*) and *–e* (or *–ja*), and they both now typically mark unprefixed Imperfectives (e.g. *писать/p′is–a′–t′* 'write', *читать/čit–a′–t′* 'read', *видеть/v′i′d–e–t′* 'see',

слышать/sliš–a–t′ < slix–ja–t′ 'hear'); a variant was –ja–j, and the other (later) common one was –va, and these are both now effectively restricted to prefixed verbs, the one notable exception being давать/da–va′–t′ 'give', Pf дать/da–t′, which is in any case irregular in both forms – the Imperfective Present stem is da–j– (Class III) while the Perfect Present/Future is a remnant of the old athematic present (1ps da–m, etc.; see chapter 3, section 2.2.6.1/table 21); and there are a few archaic remnants of the iterative meaning (see (b) below).

In a small number of cases an unprefixed aspectual pair is distinguished only by suffix, e.g.:

> a ~ ′i   ступать/stup–a′–t′ Impf ~ ступить/stup–′i′t′ Pf 'step'
> ja ~ ′i   кончать/konč–a′–t′ Impf ~ кончить/ko′nč–i–t′ Pf 'finish'
>   (root kon(′e)c– < kon–(ъ)k–);
> a ~ nu   кидать/kid–a′–t′ Impf ~ кинуть/ki(d)–nu–t′ Pf 'throw'

(The last was originally an opposition of iterative ~ semelfactive.)

In the following, prefixed Perfective verbs should be assumed to be the base; typical formations are based on the shape of the perfective stem and its conjugation.

(i)   Class I, Infinitive stem in consonant, suffix –ø adds –a–j for Imperfective:

> ø ~ a–j   заплести/za–pl′os–t′i′ (< pl′ot–t′i) Pf ~ заплетать/
>   za–pl′ot–a′–t′ 'braid'

(ii)   Class I, Inf stem in root vowel, suffix –ø adds –va:

> ø ~ va   пережить/p′er′e–ži(v)–t′ Pf ~ переживать/p′er′e–ži(v)–
>   va–t′ 'endure/survive'

(iii) Class I, Inf stem in suffix vowel –a adds –iva–j:

> a ~ iva   переписать/p′er′e–p′is–a′–t′ Pf ~ переписывать/p′er′e–
>   p′i′s–iva–t′ 'rewrite'

(iv)   Class II (Inf stem in suffix – ′i or – ′e) adds –ja or –(j)iva:

> ′i ~ ja   представить/pr′ed–sta′v–′i–t′ Pf ~ представлять/
>   pr′ed–stavl′–a′t′ 'present'
> ′i ~ jiva   уловить/u–lov–′i′–t′ Pf ~ улавливать/u–la′vl′–
>   iva–t′ 'catch'

(As a rule, root vowel {o}, always under stress before this last suffix, becomes /a/.)

See (3) below for the one case of reverse formation (Impf > Pf) by suffix (–nu).

(b) Iterative (obsolete or colloquial): do frequently. The iterative meaning proper is now obsolete as a category, leaving only a few remnants, e.g.:

$\phi \sim a\text{–}j$ жечь/žeč (< ž(e)g–t′) Impf ~ жигать/žig–a'–t′ 'burn'
                    (root (e) ~ i = old ablaut)

$\phi \sim va$ знать/zna–t′ Impf ~ знавать/zna–va'–t′ 'know'

$e \sim a\text{–}j$ видеть/vi'd–e–t′ Impf ~ видать/vid–a'–t′ 'see'

$'i \sim jiva$ ловить/lov–'i'–t′ Impf ~ лавливать/la'vl'– iva–t′ 'catch'

However, a more active remnant of this group is seen in the verbs of motion, where the unprefixed members typically have an extra Imperfective form know usually as 'indeterminate' (textbooks use other terms, e.g. 'multi-directional', 'round-trip'); they depict motion undertaken at least in more than one direction, also usually on more than one occasion, both of which clearly reflect the former iterative meaning; they are formed from the 'determinate' ('uni-directional', 'single-trip') forms (also Imperfective) by the same process as above; most commonly the Indeterminate is Class I, but not exclusively; in the following the first form is Determinate, the second Indeterminate (see also chapter 3, section 2.2.4.1):

$\phi \sim a\text{–}j$ ползти/polz–t'i' ~ ползать/po'lz–a–t′ 'crawl'

$e \sim a\text{–}j$ лететь/l'et–e'–t′ ~ летать/l'et–a'–t′ 'fly'

$ja \sim a\text{–}j$ бежать/b'ež–a–t′ (< b'eg–ja–) ~ бегать/b'e'g–a–t′ 'run'

$'i \sim a\text{–}j$ катить/kat–'i'–t′ ~ катать/kat–a'–t′ 'roll'

$\phi \sim 'i$ нести/n'os–t'i' ~ носить/nos–'i'–t′ 'carry'
                    (e/o ~ o = old ablaut)

(c) Semelfactive (Punctual): do once (or suddenly). These are a small group of Perfective verbs, with only a few high-frequency members; the base is the Imperfective stem, the suffix *–nu*; the meaning is only available in unprefixed pairs, where the Imperfective will have a simple aspectual suffix (*–a, –e, –ja*); in prefixed pairs the suffix *–nu* is simply a marker of Perfective aspect:

$a \sim nu$ резать/r'e'z–a–t′ 'cut' ~ резнуть/r'ez–nu'–t′ 'make a
                    quick cut', 'cut to the quick'

$a\text{–}j \sim nu$ ахать/a'x–a–t′ 'groan' ~ ахнуть/a'x–nu–t′ 'let out
                    a groan'

$ja \sim nu$ кричать/kr'ič–a'–t′(< kr'ik–) 'shout' ~ крикнуть/
                    kr'i'k–nu–t′ 'shout out'

A colloquial variant, often with the additional sense of 'intensively', includes the base suffix *–a* in the stem:

$a \sim anu$ резать/r'e'z–a–t′ 'cut' ~ резануть/r'ez–anu'–t′
                    'strike hard'

$a\text{–}j \sim anu$ кашлять/ka'šl'–a–t′ 'cough' ~ кашлянуть/ka'šl'–
                    anu–t′ 'give a cough'

Aspect only (prefixed):

> $a–j \sim nu$ *привыкать/pri–vik–a'–t'* Impf $\sim$
> *привыкнуть/pri–vi'k–nu–t'* Pf 'get used to'
>
> $iva \sim nu$ *повёртывать/po–v'o'rt–iva–t'* Impf $\sim$
> *повернуть/po–v'or(t) –nu'–t'* Pf 'turn round'

This last *–nu* (the aspectual one, not the semelfactive) is the one which normally does *not* disappear in the Past; for one thing it is often stressed (see examples above), in which case it never disappears; when unstressed, there is some uncertainty and frequently free variation, with the tendency being to retain it in low-frequency words. The semelfactive *–nu never* loses it. Hence we have the following standard past tense forms:

Infinitive	Past Masc	Past Fem
крикнуть/kr'i'k–nu–t'	*крикнул/kr'i'k–nu–l–ø*	*крикнула/kr'i'k–nu–l–a*
привыкнуть/	*привык/pr'i–vi'k–(l)–ø*	*привыкла/pr'i–vi'k–l–a*
pr'i–vi'k–nu–t'		
гаснуть/ga's–nu–t'	*гас/gas–(l)–ø* or	*гасла/ga's–l–a* only
'be extinguished' Impf	*гаснул/ga's–nu–l–ø*	
погаснуть/	*погас/po–ga's–(l)–ø*	*погасла/po–ga's–l–a*
po–ga's–nu–t' Pf	only	only

(d) Factitive: cause the onset of an activity/state in another (as opposed to *inceptive*, where the activity begun is one's own, done by prefixation). The suffix *–'i* is the main one involved here, as it is with non-verbal bases (see above); when it appears on an unprefixed Imperfective, this will normally be the meaning:

> *ставить/sta'v–'i–t'* 'stand (put standing)'
> *поить/po(j)–i'–t'* 'give to drink'
> *морить/mor–i'–t'* 'kill (cause to die)'

Prefixed Perfective verbs with this suffix are normally formed by prefixation from such as the above, and so do not belong here; but there are some which do not have the simple unprefixed partner, e.g.:

> *положить/po–lož–i't'* 'place (put lying)' (Impf is a different root:
> *класть/klas–t' < klad–t'*) Pf
> *воскресить/voz–kr'es–'i'–t'* 'resurrect' (Impf *воскрешать/voz–*
> *kr'eš–a'–t' < –kr'es–ja–*) Pf
> (cf. Intr *воскресать/voz–kr'es–a'–t'* Impf $\sim$ *воскреснуть/voz–kr'e's–*
> *nu–t'*)

Odd here are two verbs of position which have *–ja* in their Imperfective form, with the expected *–'i* and prefix in the Perfective:

sad– 'sit'   *сажать/saž–a'–t'* (< *sad–ja–)'* 'seat/set/sit (put
                sitting)' Impf ∼ *посадить/po–sad–'i'–t'* Pf

v'es– 'hang'   *вешать/v'e'š–a–t'* (< *v'e's–ja–)* 'hang up' Impf ∼
                повесить/po–v'e's–'i'–t' Pf

(4) Verbs derived from other categories

(a) Sounds: produce given sound. The base of these is the actual sound, that is, onomatopoeic roots; bases ending in a vowel use the second suffix below:

a/a–j   *ахать/a'x–a–t'* 'groan' (say 'akh');
          икать/ik–a'–t' 'hiccup' (say 'ik')

ка/ka–j   *мяукать/m'au'–ka–t'* 'mew' (say 'miaou');
          окать/o'–ka–t' 'pronounce unstressed /o/ as [ɔ]'

(b) Numerals. Unprefixed verbs on numeral bases with the suffix *–'i* now have the meaning 'divide by'; the base form is the collective numeral (the meaning 'multiply by' was formerly possible, but this is now done with the prefixed forms (*u–*)):

dvoj–e 'two'   *двоить/dvo(j)–i'–t'* 'divide by/into two' (*удвоить/
                u–dvo'(j)–i't'* 'double')

troj–e 'three'   *троить/tro(j)–i'–t'* 'divide by/into three' (*утроить/
                u–tro'(j)–i–t'* 'treble')

5   Lexicology (and phraseology)

In this section we offer a brief overview of the types of words and phrases used in Russian, including matters of synonymy and style.

5.1   Words: types

One may distinguish between two major types of 'word' and their 'meaning' (see also above, section 1.1 and chapter 3, section 1.1): lexical and grammatical. The former have meaning related to the real world and human activity (objects, actions, concepts, etc.), the latter are linguistic facilitators allowing us to tie together (say what we want to say about) these lexical items (conjunctions, prepositions, particles, etc.). At an earlier stage of the language, and still in the structure of many other (non-European) language types, such a division would have had a different form, the difference between the two types being essentially one of substance versus relations. Russian is firmly European in this respect, with the same general possibilities; for example, there are words which are *monosemic* (having only one discrete meaning) and others which are *polysemic* (with more than one meaning, acquired through extension of the base meaning); possibly more are monosemic in Russian than in English, since suffixes are more often added to produce figurative extensions, for example *шея/šej–a* 'neck' has only the human-body meaning, extensions like 'neck of land' or 'neck of a bottle' being affixed derivatives, not necessarily with the same semantic derivation (the former may be *перешеек/p'er'e–še'j–(e)k–ɸ*, the latter may be *шейка/še'j–k–a*); polysemic extensions are generally similar, e.g. *голова/golov–a'* 'head', as in English, has extensions such as '– of cattle', '– of a column'.

This latter group must be distinguished from *homonyms* (lexically different – in principle unrelated – words which have the same form); these are language-specific, since they are usually coincidental formal developments; in many cases they are indeed old semantic splits of a single root, often paralleled in related languages, e.g. *мир/m'ir–ɸ* 'peace', 'world', *свет/sv'et–ɸ* 'light', 'universe'; *рак/rak–ɸ* 'crab', 'cancer'; while others are true coincidences, e.g. *лук/luk–ɸ* 'onion', 'bow'; *пол/pol–ɸ* 'floor', 'sex'. Some of these are *visual homonyms*, not aural (that is, 'homographs'), e.g.: *замок/za–mo'k–ɸ* 'lock' ~ *za'–mok–ɸ* 'castle'; *метр/m'etr–ɸ* 'metre' ~ *metr–ɸ* 'master, maître'; while others are aural, but not visual (that is, 'homophones'), e.g.: *компания/kompa'n–'ij–a* 'company' ~ *кампания/kampa'n–'ij–a* 'campaign' (unstressed /o/ ~ /a/, both = [ʌ]).

The inflectional system allows many *partial homonyms*, through coincidence of particular forms; some are syntactically confusable, e.g. *лечу/l'eč–u'* 1ps Pres 'fly' and 'treat (medically)', no other form of these two verbs being identical; others are syntactically different, thus rarely likely to be confusing, e.g.: *стих/st'ix–ɸ* 'verse' NS ~ 'fall quiet' Past Masc Sing (of *стихнуть/st'i'x–nu–t'*); and homophones may also be produced in this way, e.g.: *лук/luk–ɸ* 'onion' NS ~ *луг/lug–ɸ* 'meadow' NS (devoicing of final obstruent), homophonic only in this case.

There are words which are (fully or only in some meanings) restricted to a certain syntactic context, either simply by usage, e.g. *пара/pa'r–a* 'pair, couple' ~ in nominal predicate (after negative copula) '(a) match (for)' (*Она ему не пара/On–a j–emu n'e par–a* 'She's no match for him'); or as a result of different formal syntactic rules, e.g. *равняться/ravn'–a'–t'–s'a*: (1) + *na* + Acc 'model oneself on'; (2) + *s* + Instr 'measure up to'; (3) + *po* + Dat 'dress by (right/left etc.)'; (4) + Dat '(be) equal (to)'; and there are words or their meanings which are restricted to particular phraseological contexts, e.g. *крайний/kra'j–n'–ij* 'extreme' may accompany negative nouns only, like Eng *utter* (Adj) (cf. Eng **utter beauty*, **utterly beautiful*).

5.1.1   *Synonyms and style*

As in all languages, while there are many synonymous sets of words (as one finds in a thesaurus), true synonyms – that is, ones which are fully interchangeable in every semantic and syntactic context – are relatively rare. Virtually always there is only partial interchangeability, there being most often at least a stylistic difference. In theory, if there ever is really 100 per cent interchangeability, we might expect one form to dominate and the other to disappear, unless some difference can be found, in the interests of language efficiency. However, a more important principle of human speech is that of redundancy, in this case allowing communication – especially oral – to proceed even in the event that the 'mot juste' cannot be immediately found. Lists of synonyms are published (in Russian) under titles like 'a dictionary of synonyms' – and their opposites in parallel 'dictionaries of antonyms', together matching the English 'thesaurus'. All tend to share the same shortcoming, that examples of usage are missing; for these one must pursue each word in a regular dictionary.

Synonymous sets may cover all stylistic levels or only a subset. The general levels – other than 'neutral' (which means equally available to all styles) – include: (1) type of text or utterance: 'bookish or literary' (with subtypes like 'scientific', 'journalistic', 'professional/bureaucratic') versus 'colloquial', 'vulgar', etc.; (2) age: 'old' versus 'new'; (3) provenance: 'foreign', 'dialectal', 'jargon'; and (4) expressiveness: 'emotive' (including 'intensive', 'affectionate', 'pejorative').

As none of these principles are peculiar to Russian, we shall not offer examples of all of them. A few formal generalisations – equally applicable to most other languages – may be noted: bookish words in general tend to be lexically or morphologically older (e.g. reflecting older forms of government or bureaucracy), as is particularly the case with archaic or poetic styles, however scientific and journalistic styles tend to use many foreign borrowings, even where native forms exist; low colloquial style, and especially jargon, tends to use existing words in a special sense (this is true of 'slang' in general); normal colloquial style uses a high proportion of emotive suffixes (especially diminutive); and professional usage often uses phonetic or morphological variants of standard forms.

An example of a synonymous set with the meaning 'die' will illustrate the similarity of range with English (and thus others also):

Neutral	*умереть/u–m′er′e′–t′*	'die'
Bookish	*скончаться/s–konč–a′–t′–s′a*	'pass away'
Colloquial	*сдохнуть/s–do'x–nu–t′*	'drop dead'
Low	*загнуться/za–g–nu't′–s′a* (root g('i)b–)	'snuff it'

We will offer a similar set, but of phrases, with the same meaning, in section 5.2.1 below.

5.1.2   Foreign sources of lexicon

Russian's history has left it with lexical traces mainly from the following languages/language-groups (see chapter 1, section 1 for historical background).

(1) Iranian (Scythian, Sarmatian): religious-based words, probably the most notable being: the very high-frequency adjective *хороший/xoro'š–ij* 'nice, good', possibly from the name of the Iranian sun-god *Khors* (but this is rejected by Vasmer); *бог/bog–ø* 'god'; *собака/soba'k–a* 'dog' (cf. Farsi *sabah*).

(2) Germanic, both from (a) Gothic/Old High German and later (b) Scandinavian (from the time of the Vikings), e.g. (a) *хлеб/xl'eb–ø* 'bread' (Gothic *hlaifs*) *князь/kn'az'–ø* 'prince' (Old High German *kuning–*); and Latin and Greek words in Germanic format, e.g. *церковь/ce'rk(o)v'–ø* 'church' (older *cьrky*, from Gk *kuri(a)kon*), *царь/car'–ø* 'tsar' (older *cesar'*, from Lat *Caesar*); (b) *якорь/jakor'–ø* 'anchor' (Old Swedish *ankari*); *крюк/kr'uk–ø* 'hook' (Old Swedish *króker*); and names like *Олег/Ol'eg–ø* 'Oleg' (Old Swedish *Helgi*), *Игорь/I'gor'–ø* 'Igor' (Old Swedish *Ingvarr*).

(3) Turkic, from the time of the Tatars, e.g. *деньги/d'e'n'g–i* 'money' (cf. Chuvash *täŋge*); *изюм/iz'um–ø* 'raisins' (cf. Turkish *üzüm*).

(4) Greek, via Russian Church Slavonic, from the early Christian period, e.g. *икона/iko'n–a* 'icon'; *кровать/krova't'–ø* 'bed' (Gk *kravvati–on*); and names like *Евгений/Jevg'e'nij–ø* 'Evgeny/Eugene', *Елена/Jel'e'n–a* 'Elena/Helen' (cf. also the dialectal form *Олёна/Алёна /Al'o'na).

(5) German (often in Polish guise) (a), and Dutch (b) from the seventeenth and eighteenth centuries, e.g. (a) *капитан/kapita'n–ø* 'captain', *музыка/mu'zik–a* 'music', *бухгалтер/buxga'lt'er–ø* 'book-keeper', *галстук/ga'lstuk–ø* 'tie'; (b) *крейсер/kr'e'jser–ø* 'cruiser'; *руль/rul'–ø* 'helm' > 'steering-wheel'.

(6) French, from the eighteenth and nineteenth centuries, e.g. *газета/gaz'e't–a* 'newspaper'; *журнал/žurna'l–ø* 'magazine'; *магазин/magaz'i'n–ø* 'shop'.

(7) English – like all other languages – in the twentieth century, e.g. *футбол/futbo'l–ø* 'football'; *компьютер/komp'ju'ter–ø* 'computer'.

5.2   Phrases: types

Here, even more so than in the preceding section, we can offer no more than a brief overview of the ways in which phraseological units are formed and function. The units in question are what might be called common expressions, including idioms and fixed expressions, that is, phrases in which the total meaning is more or other than the sum of its morphological and syntactic elements; they are groups of words which have fused themselves together into a special meaning.

Again, Russian does this firmly in the European manner, with the extended meanings, most often figurative or expressive, usually paralleling those in other languages. Here are some examples of such parallels with English, the meanings being, as it were, literal translations (which some may well be in origin, either from English or from a common source):

> *кожа да кости*/*kož–a da kost–′i* 'skin and bones'
> *упустить из виду*/*u–pust–′i–t′ iz v′id–u* 'to let out of (your) sight'
> *синий чулок*/*sin′–ij čul–(o)k* 'blue stocking'
> *раз и навсегда*/*raz i na–vs′egda* 'once and for all' (lit. 'always')
> *вообще говоря*/*vo–obšč–e govor–′a* 'generally speaking'
> *пройти мимо*/*pro–j–t′i m′imo* 'let (it) pass' (lit. 'pass by')

Others are close, with the same basic extension, but slightly different:

> *ни рыба ни мясо*/*n′i rib–a n′i m′as–o* 'neither fish nor fowl (lit. 'nor mcat')'
> *в чём мать родила*/*v čom mat′–ø rod′il–a* 'in your birthday suit' (lit. 'as your mother gave birth to you')
> *битый час*/*b′it–ij čas–ø* 'for a full hour' (lit. 'a struck hour')
> *спустя рукава*/*spust–′a rukav–a* 'slipshod' (lit. 'with sleeves rolled down', so the opposite of Eng 'roll your sleeves up')
> *делать из мухи слона*/*d′el–a–t′ iz mux–i slon–a* 'make a mountain out of a molehill' (lit. 'an elephant out of a fly')

Of course, there are many more which are in no way parallel, but represent the expected differences in culture:

> *как снег на голову*/*kak sn′eg–ø na golov–u* 'like a bolt from the blue' (lit. 'like snow onto your head')
> *кровь с молоком*/*krov′–ø s molok–om* 'peaches and cream' (lit. 'blood and milk')
> *пить горькую*/*p′it′ gor′k–uju* 'hit the bottle' (lit. 'drink (bitter) vodka')
> *бабье лето*/*ba′b–′j–o l′et–o* 'Indian summer' (lit. 'old woman's summer')

These include some differences in sense of humour:

> *без году неделя*/*b′ez god–u n′ed′el′–a* 'only a short time' (lit. 'a year short of a week')

положить зубы на полку/po–lož–i–t' zub–i na polk–u 'tighten your
   belt' (lit. 'put your teeth on the shelf')
мухи дохнут/mux–i dox–nu–t 'you'd die from boredom' (lit. '(even)
   the flies are dying')

5.2.1   *Synonymous phrases and style*

As with single words, there are often many synonymous ways of expressing the
same meaning, differing usually in style. Most often phrases are synonymous
with single words, where the latter will usually be stylistically neutral and
strictly informative; examples similar to English are as follows.

(1) Colloquial/low style phrases

выдумать/vi'–dum–a–t' 'think/dream up' ∼
   высосать из пальца/vi'–sos–a'–t' iz pa'l' c–a '(lit. 'suck out of your
   finger')
вмешиваться/v–m'e'š–iva–t'–s'a 'interfere' ∼
   совать нос/sov–a'–t' nos–ø 'stick one's nose in'
насквозь/na–skvo'z' 'right through' ∼
   до последней нитки/do posl' e'd–n'–ej n'i't–k–i 'to the bone/the
   last drop' (lit. 'to the last thread')
замолчать/za–molč–a'–t' 'stop talking' ∼
   заткнуть глотку/za–tk–nu'–t' glo'tk–u 'shut one's mouth' (lit.
   'gullet, throat')

(2) Bookish/high style phrases

сдаться/s–da'–t'–s'a 'surrender' ∼ *сложить оружие/s–lož–i't'
oru'ž–ij–o* 'lay down one's arms'
происходить (из)/pro–iz–xod–'i't' (iz) 'come from' ∼ *вести начало
(в)/v'es–t'i' nača'–l–o (v)* 'originate from/in' (lit. 'take one's origin
in')
старость/sta'r–ost'–ø 'old age' ∼ *вечер жизни/v'e'čer–в ži'zn'–i*
'the twilight of one's life' (lit. 'evening of')
похороны/po'–xoron–i 'funeral' ∼ *последний путь/posl'e'dn'–ij
put'–ø* 'the final journey'

As we did for words (section 5.1.1), we conclude with a synonymous set of
phrases with the meaning 'die':

Neutral	(умереть/u–m′er′e′–t′	'die')
Bookish	сложить голову/ s–lož–i′–t′ go'lov–u	'lay down one's head'
	заснуть вечным сном/ za–s–nu′t′ v′e'č–n–im sn–om	'go to one's final resting place' (lit. 'fall into everlasting sleep')
	кануть в вечность/ ka–nu′t′ v v′e'č–n–ost′–ø	'ditto' (lit. 'sink into oblivion')
	сойти в могилу/so–j–t′i v mogil–u	'go to one's grave' (lit. 'down into')
Colloquial	протянуть ноги/pro–t′a–nu′t′ no'g–i	'turn up one's toes' (lit. 'stretch out one's legs')
Low	сыграть в ящик/s–igr–a'–t′ v ja'ščik ø	'kick the bucket' (lit. 'play into the box')

6   Dialects

1   Introduction

Since the time that Russian began to model its attitude to standardisation along the lines of that of the French *Académie* (see chapter 1, section 3.2), the maintenance of local dialects has been, as in France, under threat at any level above basic local communication. At the same time, it is only with mass literacy that this attitude becomes a serious threat to the vitality of dialects, and in Russia such literacy arrived only well into the Soviet period, by which time there had appeared the first major work of linguistic geography (Atlas 1915) and the early Communist notions of local and ethnic rights ensured that dialect study remained on the linguistic agenda. Throughout the Soviet period the dialects continued to be studied, with peaks in the 1950s and 1960s (e.g. Atlas 1957, Avanesov and Orlova 1964), and in the 1980s, including the latest dialect atlas (Atlas 1986); it appears that the local features identified in such studies have continued to survive to some extent in all areas, primarily those remote from the major urban centres, in the diglossic mode typical of most European areas. France is somewhat exceptional, as there the degree of pressure from the standard form has been a major 'problem' for the dialects, but Russia, in spite of its parallel worshipping of the standard, appears not to have ended up in the same situation, presumably because of the two differences noted above (literacy and ideology), though there is certainly much less active dialectal variation than in countries like Germany, Italy or England. (Another factor may be the much greater distances involved, however the identified dialectal groups are situated within a radius no larger than that of France.)

The Modern Russian dialects are normally classified into three groups: northern, southern and central, with the divisions running roughly west-northwest to east-southeast, the southern boundary of the northern group running east-southeast from Novgorod – roughly following the Volga to Saratov and on to the Caspian Sea, and the northern boundary of the southern group running east-southeast from south of Pskov through Ryazan. The central group thus represents a rather narrow band including Pskov in the northwest, Moscow in the centre, and possibly as far as Penza in the southeast (its (south-)eastern boundary is not placed even as far as this in Russian dialect studies, which limit themselves to what they regard as 'the basic dialect grouping' (Zaxarova and Orlova 1970: 31; see map 4)).

The northern group stretches east into Siberia and southeast down to the Caspian Sea, the southern south into the northern Caucasus area. The central group is limited in the east to the west bank of the Volga. The northern group is in contact only with non-Slavonic languages (Finnic, Turkic, Baltic, etc.), while the southern is adjacent in the west to Belarusian and in the south to Ukrainian; the whole of this southern area is rather a continuum of dialects arbitrarily (i.e. geo-politically) assigned to one of the three standard languages.

In this chapter non-standard examples will be given in transcription only (ISO phonemic or IPA phonetic as appropriate).

2   Historical orientation

Within Kievan Rus' the main physical dividers were the major rivers, most of which run north–south, the exception being the upper Volga, which was then, however, effectively a northern boundary and not an internal divider; the dialects then were therefore a spectrum based on simple distance, with differences being generated or emphasised only with later political developments. This absence of major physical obstacles has perhaps also contributed to the continued low level of dialectal differentiation in Russia – compared to the likes of Germany and Italy – in addition to cultural factors of the French type. These political developments included the cutting off of the western (and north-western) part by its incorporation into Lithuania (in the fourteenth century) and of the south-western part by its incorporation into Poland (in the fourteenth to fifteenth centuries) (for further details see chapter 1, section 1.1), which led to the separate developments of the future Belarusian and Ukrainian respectively. Of the part which remained 'Russian' (or 'Great Russian' as some have called it), the rise of the north (centred at first on Vladimir-Suzdal') at the expense of the south (centred on Kiev, after its initial collapse as a centre at the hands of the Tatars), led to the differentiation between a northern type and a southern one, partly by the appearance of new northern features. It is possible that contact with Finnic speakers in the north and Turkic (Tatar) speakers in the east contributed to some of the new northern features.

From the period known as 'the rise of Moscow' (fourteenth to sixteenth centuries), Moscow – initially a member of the northern group – became the centre of all that was still politically 'Russia', and as such attracted immigrants from the south also; it became therefore an area of renewed contact between the two groups, and developed its own hybrid dialect, which gradually acquired more and more influence and ultimately became the basis for the standard language, as formed during the eighteenth century. The building of St Petersburg

4 Russian dialects

in the early eighteenth century was a factor also in the spreading of this new hybrid, and of the standard, since its population included the Tsar and his court, meaning that this form represented the educated speech of the two major cities of the country. However, the dialect area around St Petersburg is still clearly northern, and not central.

While there are subgroups within each of the three main areas, we will not dwell on these and their internal differences (their names and demarcation may be found on map 4). We will consider the main linguistic features which differ from the standard, and note any correlation between such differences and location.

3   Linguistic features

As in western Europe, the main features of the dialects are phonological and lexical ones, the other levels having been more easily influenced by the standard, though there are some interesting morphological and syntactic features also.

In phonology, again as in western Europe, the primary features concern vowel pronunciation, in particular here in relation to the word stress (both its place and its acoustic nature), but consonantal differences are also very marked, in particular those of the palatal area, and there are a few suprasegmental features.

In morphology, the noun declensions may differ from the standard, mainly as a result of phonological features, though one feature is the partial loss of a case form; the gender of suffixed forms may differ; so may the stress patterns of both nouns and verbs; and so also may some Present endings.

There are very few syntactic features, and they include: the category of 'definiteness', for which one area has an explicit marker; the case of the Direct Object; and the use of gerundial or participial forms as Indicatives.

We will not treat word-formation or lexis, where differences are relatively insignificant or local.

3.1   Phonology

3.1.1   Vowels

(1) *Akan'je*. By far the most important, as well as the most striking, feature concerns the pronunciation of unstressed vowels. We have seen that Contemporary Standard Russian has reduction of qualitative differences in this context, referred to by the general Russian term *akan'je* (including the subtype after soft consonants, known as *ikan'je*) (see chapter 2, section 3.2.3.2); this general principle is shared by all the southern group and by the southern half of the central group, as well as one central subgroup reaching up to the northern group border; all of the northern group and the northern half of the central group distinguish the quality of unstressed vowels (i.e. the phonemes /o/ and /e/ are in principle always realised as [ɔ] and [ɛ] respectively); this pronunciation type is referred to as *okan'je* (or *ekan'je* after a soft consonant) (that is, 'saying [ɔ] (or [ɛ])').

The distribution of this feature is interesting, since what we observe is the reduction occurring in a band covering the southern half of the whole area, as well as Belarusian to the west, flanked by its absence in the north and further south in Ukrainian. It seems clear that it is an innovation in its area of occurrence, but explanations vary widely as to its causes (mostly favouring the influence of non-Slavonic neighbours on both sides – from the Baltic in the northwest and from the Tatar or Finnic languages (e.g. Mordvinian) to the (south)east); some have argued, it would seem counter-intuitively, that the (con)fusion of /a/ and /o/ continues the old Proto-Slavonic situation (or even earlier, Balto-Slavonic), making rather their *distinction* the innovation (but also the extension of the fusion to /e/). For discussion of the origin of this phenomenon, see Kiparsky (1979: 142–6).

Within the *akan'je* group there are variations in the actual realisations of the fused forms: some are simply variants of phonetic value, e.g. the 'strong' type, with [a] in all unstressed positions, as well as after both hard and soft consonants; the Contemporary Standard Russian type lies in the middle of the range (with [ʌ] or [ə] after hard, [ɪ] after soft); others involve following consonants (the so-called 'moderate' type – in which a following soft consonant leads to raising); or following syllables (the so-called 'assimilative' or 'dissimilative' types, in which the nature (height) of the following stressed vowel determines the 'similar' or 'dissimilar' articulation of the pre-tonic vowel). The description of all these is complex and we will not pursue it here; some discussion may be found in Matthews 1953 (pp. 91–7), but full details will be found only in Russian sources (e.g. Zaxarova and Orlova 1970, Kuznecov 1973).

Raising, or fronting, of unstressed /a/ after soft consonants to [e] (and in some areas also of stressed /a/) before soft consonants occurs in the northern group, but is unconnected to *akan'je*, being related rather to greater cohesion between C–V–C segments than in the standard and southern types, where this occurs only on stressed vowels (cf. the raising of stressed /e/ from [ɛ] to [e] before a soft consonant or the fronting of /u/, /o/ and /a/ between two soft consonants, see chapter 2, section 3.2.3.2). Examples are:

/a/ (*pr'ad*–'spin')	Contemporary Standard Russian	North
/—Hard (*pr'a–du'* 1ps Pres)	[prʲɪdu']	[prʲadu']
/— Soft (*pr'a–d'i'* 2ps Imper)	[prʲɪdʲi']	[prʲedʲi']

Where Contemporary Standard Russian fronts stressed /a/ to [æ], this group also raises it to [e], e.g.

p'at' 'five'	[pʲætʲ]	[pʲetʲ]

(2) jat'. Dialects in both north (especially) and south have preserved the Old Russian vowel /ě/, distinct from /e/; its reflexes may be: always [i] – that is,

fused with /i/; or [i] before soft consonants only, with elsewhere either [ɛ], [e] or [i̯e], e.g.:

OR *věr–* **'faith'**

(CSR *ver–*)	**NS** *v'e'r–a*	**LS** *v'e'r'–e*
CSR	[vʲɛr–ə]	[vʲerʲ–ɪ]
NR 1	[vʲer–a]	[vʲerʲ–ɛ]
NR 2	[vʲɛr–a]	[vʲirʲ–ɛ]
NR 3	[vʲer–a]	[vʲirʲ–ɛ]
NR 4	[vʲi̯er–a]	[vʲirʲ–ɛ]

Comparing this with Ukrainian, where the reflex in the standard is also always [i], we see a similar situation to *akan'je*, with the innovation of complete fusion with /e/ occurring in the central band (again along with Belarusian).

   Typologically, both central phenomena represent a trend towards removal of qualitative vocalic variety, which logically accompanies a dynamic strengthening of stress; however, see below on stress.

(3) Vowel systems. Some of the above dialects thus have an extra vowel phoneme (/ě/ – [e]) or diphthong (/i̯e/), which is normally accompanied by a back partner (/ô/ – [o]) or /u̯o/ respectively, giving a seven-vowel system in place of Contemporary Standard Russian's five. In some cases the back partner is missing, giving a six-vowel system. In some northern dialects, where former /ě/ has merged with /i/, and stressed /e/ has become /o/ (under *okanje*), the phoneme /e/ is peripheral, giving potentially a four-vowel system.

3.1.2   Consonants
Two of the dialectal features already present in Old Russian (see chapter 1, section 2.3.1.7) survive to this day: the quality of /g/ and /v/; other features of interest are: the treatment of /f/, the reflexes of the palatals, including /c/ and the 'reinstated' soft velars, the quality of /l/, and the treatment of intervocalic /j/.

   In the first two of these, the standard forms are those also of the north; for the rest, the standard forms are those of the south; for all, the central forms are the same as the standard.

(1) /g/. The old division of [g] in the north and [ɣ] in the south persists, with the central group reflecting its former northern status; however, this would have been one of the features to cause confusion at the time of the formation of the central hybrid group, since it is not a major phonetic difference, nor would it have caused phonemic problems, since either one could form a pair with the 'safe' voiceless phonemes /k/ or /x/, either solution leaving a three-way set. No doubt this is why many modern standard speakers of southern origin continue to use [ɣ] as their only 'non-standard' feature, to the extent that it is

effectively accepted as a standard variant (though not 'officially'; see chapter 7, section 3.3). ([ɣ] is also the realisation in standard Belarusian, while standard Ukrainian has [ɦ].)

There are odd cases of [ɣ] in the north, for example in the Gdov (next to Estonia) and Lake Onega areas, however, they seem always to be controlled by position (e.g. intervocalic, and especially in the Genitive Singular Masculine pronominal ending –ogo, where this must be an innovation, due either to outside influence, or, more likely, to that particular morphological ending – see also chapter 3, section 2.1.4.3).

(2) /v/ and /f/. The same applies in principle to /v/, where the old southern sound was bilabial, the northern (and the modern standard) labio-dental; the former is reflected in Ukrainian mostly as bilabial [β] in all positions, in Belarusian and southern Russian dialects as [v] in pre-vocalic position, but as the semivowel [u̯] in closed position (pre-consonantal or pre-pausal) (e.g. *pravda* 'truth': CSR [pra'vdə], SR [pra'u̯də]. However, this latter situation occurs also in some parts of the north, where the freedom of /v/ to behave in this way is related to the development of /f/: in the north, as in the south, it was not always 'accepted' in its foreign shape, but converted to the native [x] or the cluster [xv], certainly in any words which became common, e.g. CSR *fa'rtuk* 'apron' ∼ NR [xa'rtuk, xva'rtuk]. Thus /f/ failed to become a 'native' phoneme in these areas, and /v/ was left to continue life as a sonorant. In the south, since the articulation of /v/ was not then labio-dental, it did not form a pair with /f/, even when this was accepted as a (foreign) phoneme, and only partial pairing occurred when /v/ did become allophonically labio-dental. It was really only in the (north >) central group (and the standard) that /f/ became accepted, when /v/ was devoiced to [f] in final and pre-voiceless obstruent positions (/— #, –Vc).

(3) Palatals.

(a) Affricates (cokan'je). The earliest problem in this area to face Old Russian after its syllabic restructure (see chapter 1, section 2.4) concerned the phonetic value of the two affricates /č'/ and /c'/, which was very close and in the new system in danger of leading to phonetic (con)fusion. While most areas took steps to keep them apart, by making one or both hard (e.g. CSR /c'/ > /c/, Ukr /č'/ > /č/, Br /č'/ > /č/ and /c'/ > /c/), some did not, resulting in their fusion; this occurred all over, but mainly in the north; the result of the fusion is most often /c'/ (e.g. *ča'ška* 'cup': CSR [t͡ʃʲaʃkə] ∼ NR [t͡sʲaʃka], *car'* 'tsar': CSR [t͡sarʲ] ∼ NR [t͡sʲarʲ]), less commonly /c/ ([t͡saʃka], [t͡sarʲ]) or /č'/ ([t͡ʃʲaʃka], [t͡ʃʲarʲ]). This phenomenon is referred to in Russian by the general term *cokan'je*.

In a few southern areas the affrication was lost, but the opposition retained, giving usually the sibilants /š'/ and /s'/, in one area /š'/ and /t'/ (probably with some sibilance, i.e. [t͡ˢʲ]); or the opposition was lost too, giving just /t'/.

(b) Chuintantes/Hushers. The two Old Russian phonemes /š′/ and /ž′/ have a less complex history: they became hard almost everywhere, and retained their phonemic independence. In a few areas, in the north or centre, they remained unchanged (soft); and in even fewer, they are positionally hard or soft before back or front vowels respectively, like the velars in the standard; nowhere did only one of them harden, meaning that they have always behaved as a related pair.

In the northwest area (e.g. Pskov) they have sometimes fused with the dental sibilants in an alveo-palatal sound (between soft palatal and soft dental, as occurs in Polish), namely [ɕ], [ʑ].

Examples of these are:

	Contemporary Standard Russian	**Dialects**
šu'ba 'fur coat'	[ʃu'bə]	[ʃʲubə], [ɕubə]
šil 'sew' Past Masc	[ʃɨl]	[ʃʲitʲ], [ɕitʲ]
s'i'la 'strength'	[sʲi'lə]	[ʃʲilə]
žil 'live' Past Masc	[ʒɨl]	[ʒʲil], [ʑil]
z'ima' 'winter'	[zʲima']	[ʒʲima]

(c) Long chuintantes. The former Old Russian clusters /šč′/ and /ždž′/ (derived from *st/sk* and *zd/zg*; see chapter 1, section 2.3.1.1) have become CSR /šč′/ (i.e. unchanged) or /šš′/ (preferred) and /žž′/ or /žž/ (preferred) (for discussion of their current status see chapter 2, section 3.2.1.1 and chapter 7, section 3.3). All of these variants are represented in the dialects, and in addition there occur also hard /šč/ and /ždž/, soft /ždž′/, hard /šš/ and /žž/, and also /št/ and /žd/. The retention of the occlusion in Ukrainian and Belarusian, as well as in northern Russian, supports the view that its loss was an innovation of the central area.

Examples:

	Contemporary Standard Russian	**Dialects**
ja'ščik 'box'	[jæ'ʃʲʃʲɪk], [jæ'ʃʲtʃʲɪk]	[jaʃtʃɨk], [jaʃʃɨk], [jaʃtʲɪk]
je'zžu 'go' 1ps Pres	[je'ʒʒu], [je'ʒʲʒʲu]	[jeʒdʒu], [jeʒʲdʒʲu], [jeʒdu]

(4) Velars. The development of the new soft velars of Contemporary Standard Russian – /k′/, /g′/, /x′/ – before front vowels (see chapter 1, section 2.4.1.2 and chapter 2, section 3.2.1.1) from the Old Russian /c′/, /dz′/, /s′/ by analogy within nominal paradigms, had some different results in the dialects. Most interesting is the variant /t′/ and /d′/ for the plosives; /x′/ is not affected, suggesting that this result was secondary, that is, it was a change of /k′/ to /t′/ and not of the original

/c′/ direct to /t′/. While this would have made phonetic sense, it would not make morphological sense; this is rather a confusion of the velar and palatal stops. This feature appears in northwest and east-central areas, giving forms like:

		Contemporary Standard Russian	Dialects
ruk′e′	'hand' LS	[rukʲɛ′]	[rutʲɛ′]
nog′e′	'foot' LS	[nʌgʲɛ′]	[nɔdʲɛ′]

It is reflected also in the (commonly used) regional version of the Greek-origin personal name *Avdot′ja* (standard *Evdokija*).

A second feature concerns an unusual progressive assimilation of softness, occurring sporadically throughout the whole area, where hard velars are softened after a soft consonant, e.g.: *ba′n′–ka* 'jar' > [ba′nʲkʲa], *O′l′ga* 'Olga' > [ɔ′lʲgʲa].

Southern dialects, with a fricative [ɣ] for /g/, may convert the soft version, including in assimilated forms like those above, into [j]: *g′i′b′el′* 'destruction' > [jibʲelʲ], *O′l′ga* > [ɔlʲja].

(5) /l/. The strongly labio-velarised nature of Russian /l/ makes it naturally susceptible to full(er) labialisation plus loss of tongue contact, giving a semivowel [u̯], or even consonantal [w]. In a few northern dialects it has gone the whole way, replaced completely by [w], but more often the replacement is positional, in closed syllables only. Positional replacement occurs in all areas, but most often in the south (parallel in principle to the behaviour of /v/; see above), and is the situation also in Ukrainian and Belarusian. It may be seen as a natural development, while the odd northern result would appear to be the result of outside influence, no doubt from Finnic dialects. The even more unusual incidence of a medium, 'European'-type [l] in the northeast is certainly also due to Finnic influence.
Examples:

		Contemporary Standard Russian	Dialects
byl	'be' Past Masc	[bɨɫ]	[bɨu̯], [bɨl]
byla′	'be' Past Fem	[bɨɫa′]	[bɨɫa], [bɨwa], [bɨla]

(6) Intervocalic /j/. Throughout the northern area, the loss of post-tonic intervocalic /j/ is typical; the consequences are, however, varied. In order of *chronology* they are: vowels in hiatus, assimilation of the quality of different vowels (usually to the first), contraction of the geminate pair of vowels (giving a long vowel), and reduction to single vowel length; in order of *frequency of distribution*, they are: a single vowel, different vowels in hiatus, long vowel, and geminate vowels in hiatus.

Examples (dialect types in the latter order) are:

	Contemporary Standard Russian	**Dialects**
do'broje 'good' NSn	[dɔ'brəjə], [dɔ'brəjɪ]	[dɔ'brɔ], [dɔ'brɔɛ], [dɔ'brɔ̄], –
do'braja 'good' NSf	[dɔ'brəjə]	[dɔ'bra], –, [dɔ'brā], [dɔ'braa]
zna'jet 'know' 3ps Pres	[zna'jɪt]	[znat], [zna'ɛt], [znāt], –

3.1.3 Syllable

'*Second polnoglasie*'. While the 'regular' Russian development of Proto-Slavonic syllables of the shape *CъRC/CьRC* was *CoRC/CeRC* (see chapter 1, section 2.2.1.6(c)), a small group of northwestern dialects (around Pskov and Novgorod) expanded these in the same way as the Proto-Slavonic forms *CoRC/CeRC*, namely by inserting a new vowel, matching the existing one, after the sonorant, in other words, producing in Russian the 'polnoglasie' forms *CoRoC/CeReC* (hence the name 'second polnoglasie' applied to this form), with the difference, however, that the second vowel behaves like the inserted vowel of Contemporary Standard Russian. Examples are: CSR *верх/v'erx–ɸ* 'summit' NS ~ *верха/v'erx–a* GS: dialectal *v'e'r'ex–ɸ* or *v'er'o'x–ɸ* ~ *v'erx–a*; CSR *горб/gorb–ɸ* 'hump' NS ~ *горба/gorb–a* GS: dialectal *gorob–ɸ* ~ *gorb–a*. This pattern suggests that the new vowel was indeed an inserted one, and not a genuine *polnoglasie* development, in which the new vowel should be fixed (as in, for example, CSR *город/gorod–ɸ* 'town' NS ~ *города/gorod–a* GS.

Virtually the only example of this in Contemporary Standard Russian is the form *верёвка/v'er'ovk–a* 'string', a diminutive form whose root form (no longer used) is known to be *vьrv'–*.

3.1.4 Prosody

Few Soviet works treated dialectal prosody at all; it is only those published from the late 1980s that have begun to treat it. This was not because they lacked the instrumental acoustic means to study them, since they had employed these in segmental phonetics (cf. Vysockij 1977), and were in any case always very prepared to use any method to study phonetics, so the reason must have been rather simply one of tradition or preference. The one study of prosody that I am aware of, included in Vysockij 1977, was a study of sentence intonation, by Bryzgunova (1977). Some more recent works (Kasatkin 1989, Kolesov 1990) do go into this area, and the following summarises their claims.

(1) Acoustic nature of stress. The Northern Russian stress is said (Kolesov 1990) to be more 'amplitude-based' than the south or the centre, where duration is the primary feature. As noted in chapter 2 (section 3.2.2.2), Contemporary Standard Russian is usually said to have an amplitude-based stress, with duration a concomitant feature, though there is an alternative view regarding duration as primary; the two views thus pair Contemporary Standard Russian with different dialect areas in this respect.

(2) Tone. It is similarly claimed (Kolesov) that the sphere of the feature 'tone' is different in the north, functioning within the word rather than at phrase or sentence level; if this is true, then Northern Russian is indeed different from Contemporary Standard Russian, where its realm is rather the sentence. The further claim that the nature of tonal rise within the word is different in the north – occurring on the tonic vowel – as opposed to the south and centre – where it occurs on the pre-tonic – is thus not very helpful: it is difficult to see how one can claim that the rise occurs on the pre-tonic vowel, when it will only be relevant on the stressed word of the clause/sentence, and even then its nature will depend on the sentence intonation; for example, in (Contemporary Standard Russian) statements the tone *drops* on the stressed syllable, and the highest tone is on the pre-tonic (see chapter 1, section 3.6).

(3) Word rhythm. More valid (i.e. acceptable) are the findings (of Kasatkin 1989) that the word rhythm is different in the dialects, in terms of the relative 'tonic strength', or more simply 'prominence' of its component syllables. Whereas the Contemporary Standard Russian (and typical central) pattern for, say, a four-syllable word stressed on the third syllable (chapter 2, section 3.2.2.3) is 3-2-1-3, where '1' is the most prominent, '3' the least, it is claimed that in the north, at least in the *okan'je* dialects (which is the norm in the north), the more typical patterns are: (1) 3-3-1-3, that is, with much greater relative prominence (no doubt amplitude) of the tonic – suggesting a very dynamic stress, which is surprising for the *okan'je* type; (2) 2-2-1-2, that is, with less overall spread of amplitude, and more expected; or (3) 2-3-1-3, which is effectively the typical English pattern, and which also normally accompanies a less dynamic stress. Thus, two of the three are not surprising, while one is, namely 3-3-1-3; this pattern is indeed found also in the south, where it does match the *akan'je* pattern, however it occurs mainly in dissimilative dialects, when the tonic vowel is low and the pre-tonic, therefore, high. In these dialects, when the tonic vowel is high (and the pre-tonic low), the pattern is 3-1-1-3, with apparently greater prominence given to the pre-tonic; it may be, however, simply that the low pre-tonic is inherently more prominent, and not necessarily more intense. This pattern is found also in the central dialects, primarily the Moscow one referred to as the 'Old Muscovite Norm', and it is one which is still heard in the speech

of many Muscovites, accompanying greater segmental tension in these vowels, and is particularly noticeable in pre-tonic /a/ or /o/, both realised as a lower vowel – that is, more *a*-like – than the CSR [ʌ]; again, it is the low pre-tonic which stands out, so that this may be the prominent feature, and not amplitude.

(4) Vocalic Length (Quantity). The one incidence of extra vocalic length in the dialects, that occurring in the north as a result of contraction (see above), is too rare in occurrence and limited by position (to tonic and post-tonic vowels) to have any relevance to the above questions of prosodic typology, which are mostly concerned with pre-tonic syllables. Moreover, there is no question of its being phonemic. Nonetheless, it contributes an audible rhythmic effect where it occurs, making for a clearly recognisable auditory feature.

(5) Place of stress. Place of stress in the paradigm is a morphophonological question, given that there is no phonological limitation on its freedom within the (phonetic) word. Differences in patterns are treated below.

3.2   Morphology

3.2.1   Declension

3.2.1.1 Case. Fairly radical is the loss of a difference between Instrumental Plural and Dative Plural in the north, the forms occurring being usually those of the Dative Plural, much more rarely those of the Instrumental Plural; the Singular forms are not affected, so this is not yet the loss of a case as such. Examples:

Contemporary Standard Russian	**North** (DP form only)
с пустыми вёдрами/	
s pust–i'm' i v'o'dr–am'i 'with empty buckets' IP	*s pust–im v'odr–am*
с двумя ручками/ s dv–um'a'	
ru'čk–am'i 'with two handles' IP	*s dv–um ručk–am*
	North (IP form only)
(дал) молодым девушкам/(dal)	
molodï'm d'e'v(uš)kam '(gave) to the young girls' DP	*molod–im'i d'evk–am'i*

3.2.1.2 Gender. Even more radical – though also more rare – is the loss of the Neuter as a concept in many parts of the south, replaced sometimes by feminine agreement, sometimes by masculine, and sometimes by a mixture based on number; the *forms* have changed only in accordance with phonetic rules (since these are also *akan'je* dialects), that is, a stressed neuter ending like *–o* remains phonetically unchanged, giving phrases like *ma–ja' v'adr–o'* 'my bucket' NS (Fem for CSR Neut *моё/mo–jo'*), *tak–o'j malak–o'* 'such milk' NS (Masc for CSR Neut *такое/tak–o'je*); where the ending is unstressed, it takes on the normal unstressed form for the new gender, e.g. *sv'e'ž–ej ma'sl–i* 'fresh butter' GS (Fem for CSR Neut *масла/ma'sl–a*).

3.2.1.3 Nominal endings. The Nominative Plural of Class I nouns is subject to non-standard endings in all areas, though only in limited contexts: in the south and centre neuter nouns with stem stress have the ending *–i* (∼ CSR *–a*) (e.g. *o'kn–i* 'windows'); this may well be related to the frequent loss of the whole category of Neuter in these areas, though this is not normal in the centre (see below); in the north, the old ending *–ov'ja'*, in Contemporary Standard Russian occurring only on the word *сын/sin* 'son', is extended to all masculine kinship terms (e.g. *brat–ov'ja'* 'brothers' ∼ CSR *братья/bra't–'ja*).

The Genitive Singular of hard Class II nouns has the ending *–'e* in place of CSR *–i* (e.g. *žen–'e* ∼ CSR *жены/žen–i*): this has the effect of extending the syncretism in this declension, since *–e* is also the ending of Dative Singular and Locative Singular, however, it is more likely not an innovation, but an old feature, since Old Russian had in this ending *–i*, alongside *–ě* in the soft consonants, and the process of restructuring the hard/soft relations saw the *–ě* of Dative Singular and Locative Singular extended to soft consonants also (in place of former *–i*), so its extension to Genitive Singular also is not surprising. On the other hand, the Nominative Plural set was also originally *–i* ∼ *–ě*, but it behaves here as in Contemporary Standard Russian (> *–i* ∼ *–'i*), so that the final result in the singular must have undergone some other influence, and that of the Dative Singular and Locative Singular seems most likely.

Regularisation of irregular declensions is common: for example, Class III Neuter (in *–m'a*) may either lose the extra syllable *–en–* or extend it to the Nominative/Accusative; this alone gives forms like NAS *im'–o* 'name' and GS *im'–a*, or NAS *im'en–o* and GS *im'en–a*, leaving the gender intact (a solution more common in *okan'je* dialects); but the Nominative Singular ending *–m'a* 'looks like' a Feminine form, and so another possibility is to leave the Nominative/Accusative Singular untouched (*im'–a*) and convert the declension to Class II Feminine (GS *im'–i*, etc.) – more common in *akan'je* dialects.

Similar regularisation affects the types *mat'(–er–)* 'mother' and *–'an–'in* 'inhabitant', the latter frequently extending the suffix *–in* to the plural (– *'a'n* – *'in–i* ∼ CSR *–'a'n–'e*).

The 'young animals' suffixed forms (CSR Sing *–'on(o)k–* ∼ Plur*–'at–*, see chapter 3, section 2.1.3.1 and chapter 5, section 4.2.1) are regularised in one of two ways:

(1) the Plural stem is *–'on(o)k–* (e.g. NS *cipl –'onok – ɸ* 'chick': NP *cipl–'onk–i* ∼ CSR *цыплята/cipl–'at–a*) (mainly north, also south); a 'compromise'

variant (north only) uses the new (regular) form only in counting, thus mostly only in the Genitive (e.g. *p'at' cipl–'onk-ov* 'five chicks' GP ~ non-counting GP *cipl–'at–φ*);

(2) the suffix itself is regularised, to (Class I Neuter) *–'atk(o)*, e.g. NS *cipl–'atk–o*, NP *cipl–'atk–a* (north).

On the other hand, some archaisms of this sort survive: for example, Class III Feminine in *–v–* have all been regularised in Contemporary Standard Russian, usually by the inclusion of the *–v* in the NAS (e.g. CSR NAS *свекровь/sv'ekr–o'v'–φ* 'mother-in-law', GS *свекрови/sv'ekr–o'v–i*), but had in Old Russian, and still have in many southern dialects, the pattern NAS *sv'ekr–i'*, GS *sv'ekr–o'v–i*.

3.2.1.4 Pronominal endings. The 1st Person Singular and 2nd Person Plural (and Reflexive) personal pronouns have old forms in the south: the Genitive/ Accusative have a final Old Russian *–'e* in place of CSR *–a*: *m'en–'e'*, *t'eb–'e'*, *s'eb–'e'* (~ CSR *меня/m'en–'a'*, etc.), and the Dative/Locative have the Old Russian stem vowel *–o–* in place of *–'e–*: *tob–'e'*, *sob–'e'* (~ CSR *тебе/t'eb–'e'*, etc.) (the 1st Person form has no vowel in either: *mn–'e*).

On the various forms and realisations of the Contemporary Standard Russian Genitive Singular Masculine/Neuter ending *–ogo*, see chapter 3, section 2.1.4.3.

3.2.1.5 Stress in nouns. Some analogical levelling of irregular patterns has already taken place, especially in the south: for example, the odd Accusative Singular stem stress in Class II nouns has been 'brought into line' (e.g. *ruk–u'*, *nog–u'* ~ CSR *руку/ru'k–u* 'hand', *ногу/no'g–u* 'foot') and the same for the Nominative Plural of Class II Masculine (e.g. *volk–i'*, *vor–i'* ~ CSR *волки/ vo'lk–i* 'wolves', *воры/vo'r–i* 'thieves'). (Such levelling is noted to be entering Contemporary Standard Russian too, see below and chapter 7.)

The south is also leading the way in removing the anomalous shifting of stress from a noun to a preceding preposition, still accepted in Contemporary Standard Russian at least when the phrase has an adverbial value (e.g. *na do'm* ~ CSR *na' dom* '(to) home' (e.g. work to be taken and done at home), *na go'd* ~ CSR *na' god* 'for a/the year' (e.g. go away for the year)). This feature, too, is entering Contemporary Standard Russian (see also chapter 2, section 3.2.2.1).

3.2.2   Conjugation

3.2.2.1 Endings

(1) Infinitive. The unstressed final *–i* of the Old Russian Infinitive was lost in Contemporary Standard Russian, while a stressed *–i* was not, except on velar stems (e.g. *класть/kla's–t'* 'place', *нести/n'es–t'i* 'carry', *печь/p'eč* 'bake'); the dialects show: (1) the retention of unstressed *–i* (mainly northeast,

e.g. *kla's–t'i, p'e'č–i*); (2) the loss of the stressed ending and generalisation of stem stress (everywhere except northeast, e.g. *n'es–t'*); (3) the retention of end-stress on velar stems (mainly northeast, e.g. *p'eč–i'/p'ek–či'/p'ek–t'i'*); a curiosity is the Contemporary Standard Russian verb *идти/id–t'i'* 'go', in the south expanded to *id–'it'* or *it–'i't'*.

It is of interest that the other common ending from which unstressed *–'i* was lost, the 2nd Person Singular Present, has *always* lost this vowel in Contemporary Standard Russian (*–шь/–š*); this must have begun very early, though the stress patterns of Old Russian suggest that it must have sometimes been stressed. Likewise, no dialect appears to have any vowel after the *–š*. There are some examples (in the northwest and (south-)west) of the irregular verbs 'give' and 'eat' retaining the *–'i*, but only after another archaic form, *–s–*, viz. *da'–s'i, je'–s'i* ~ CSR *дашь/da–š, ешь/je–š*.

(2) Theme vowel. The stressed Present theme vowel of Class I (*–'o*, e.g. 3ps *n'es'–o'–t*) may appear as *–e'*, typically in the southwest and southeast, neighbouring with Ukrainian, where this is the norm. However, there are dialects in which *–'o* appears in only some of the four possible forms, and not necessarily according to the phonetic context for the change of /e/ to /o/ (see chapter 1, section 2.4.1.1), meaning that analogy is also at work.

See also below, under stress, for examples of the theme vowel here appearing as *–'i*, that is, that of Class II.

(3) 3rd Person Present. Two sorts of difference from Contemporary Standard Russian are apparent here: where Contemporary Standard Russian has *–t* (in both Singular and Plural), the dialects may have soft *–t'* or no *–t* at all. Soft *–t'* is common in the south, hard in the north and centre; the absence of any *–t* is most frequent in the northwest, with sporadic examples also in the southeast; it is more frequent in the Singular than in the Plural, and in Class I than in Class II; no dialect has lost it completely. Possible forms are thus (disregarding *akan'je*, etc.):

Contemporary Standard Russian	Dialects
несём/n'es'–o't 'carry' 3ps Pres	*n'es'–o', n'es'–o't'*
несут/n'es–u't 3pp	*n'es–u', n'es–u't'*
знаем/zna'j–et 'know' 3ps Pres	*zna'j–e, zna* (with contraction), *zna'j–et'*
знают/zna'j–ut 3pp	*zna'j–u, znat* (with contraction), *zna'j–ut'*

In the 3rd Person Plural of Class II, a further analogical change has occurred in the south and central areas: the ending (Contemporary Standard Russian) *–'at* when unstressed is replaced by *–'ut*, that is, the ending of Class I, but with stem softening, e.g. *xo'd'–ut* ~ CSR *ходят/xo'd'–at* 'go'.

3.2.2.2 Stress in verbs

(1) Mobile pattern. The Present pattern which opposes end-stress in 1st Person Singular to stem-stress in all other forms (see chapter 3, section 2.2.11.1) (e.g. CSR Class I *пишу/piš–u'* ~ *пишем/pi'š–et* 'write' 1ps ~ 3ps, Class II *курю/kur'–u'* ~ *курит/ku'r–it* 'smoke'), at least in respect of Class II, was a southern feature which became a new central one, and which continues to gain in popularity within Contemporary Standard Russian (see chapter 7, section 3.4.3.1). It does not occur in the north, which thus has non-standard forms like *kur–i't* 3ps; *kur'–a't* 3pp, etc.

(2) 2nd Person Plural Present. In the northeast, an unusual stress pattern occurs in the 2nd Person Plural of end-stressed verbs, in that the stress actually falls on the last syllable of the disyllabic ending *–'ot'e*, *–'it'e*, which is not possible in Contemporary Standard Russian (though it is also possible in Belarusian and Ukrainian, though they are not adjacent), giving forms like *n'es–'e–t'e'*, *n'es–'e–t'o'*, *s'id–'i–t'e'*, *s'id–'i–t'o'* (~ CSR *несёте/n'es'–o'–t'e*, 'carry', *сидите/s'id–'i'–t'e* 'sit'); even possible are the Class I forms *n'es–'i–t'e'*, *n'es–'i–t'o'*, with the Class II theme vowel *–'i*, albeit unstressed only.

3.3   Syntax

3.3.1   Predicate

Three interesting features of the verbal predicate occur in various areas, the northwest being the most versatile.

(1) Gerund (adverbial participle) as main verb. The past adverbial participle *(–(v)ši*, see chapter 3, section 2.2.9.2), virtually only Perfective, appears as the main verb in the west, both north and south, but mainly north, e.g. *on višed–ši* (CSR *on više–l*) 'he's gone out'; the effect is of dramatic Present; in some areas a dramatic Past can be formed by adding the Past of 'be', e.g. *N'edavno od'in zajac bil pr'ib'eg–ši v d'er'evn'u.* (CSR . . . *pr'ib'ež–al . . .*) 'Recently a hare ran into the village.'

Note that this adverbial form (without *byl–*) is lacking any agreement between subject and verb.

The form of this participle in the south often shows *–m–* in place of *–v–*, e.g. *vz'a–mši* 'take' (CSR *взявши/vz'a–vši*).

(2) Neuter Past Participle Passive as Nominal Predicate. In the northwest and central west areas the neuter form of the Past Participle Passive (*–n–o, –t–o*) may appear as nominal predicate, again meaning a loss of agreement, e.g.

> *Od'in–φ soldat–φ φ poxoron'e–no zd'es'.* (CSR . . . *poxoron'e–n–φ* . . .)
>
> one NSm – soldier NSm – (be 3ps Pres) – bury PPP NSn – here (CSR: bury PPP NSm)
>
> 'There's a soldier buried here.'

(3) Neuter Past Participle Passive as impersonal Predicate. The same participial form as in (2) may be used in an impersonal sense, when it is actually the main verb, e.g.:

> *U n'ego ujexa–no* (CSR *On–ɸ ujexa–l.*)
> at – him GS – go away PPP NSn (CSR: he NS – go away Past Masc)
> 'He has left.'

> *Vs'u kartošk–u sjed'–e–no.* (CSR . . . *sje–l'i*)
> all ASf – potatoes ASf – eat PPP NSn (CSR: eat Past Plur)
> 'All the potatoes have been eaten.'

(2) and (3) would seem to be related developments, and both in the direction of non-agreement.

(4) Non-zero copula. Where Contemporary Standard Russian has a zero Present copula, the northwest dialects use *ecmь/jest'*, followed by the Instrumental in the contexts where this occurs in Contemporary Standard Russian after Past and Future copulas, e.g.:

> *Jego žena jest' s'ekr'etar'–om. (CSR . . . žena ɸ s'ekr'etar'–ɸ)*
> his – wife NS – be 3ps Pres – secretary IS (CSR: – (be 3ps Pres) –
>   secretary NS)
> 'His wife is a secretary.'

This is almost certainly an archaism, matching the retention of the non-zero form in neighbouring Slavonic areas (Polish, Ukrainian, Belarusian). In particular, Polish also uses the Instrumental after the Present in the same way. The next feature supports this view, though it has been argued (Kuznecov 1973: 196) that in the northwest it is due to external influence, especially Baltic.

(5) Compound Past. The same areas may also add *jest'* to a Past form, with no apparent difference in meaning, e.g.:

> *Vas'il'ij jest' rabotal. (CSR Vas'il'ij rabotal.)*
> Vasily NS – be 3ps Pres – work Imperf Past Masc
> 'Vasily has been working.'

The coincidence of this form and that of Old Russian, as well as the continuation of this form in the West Slavonic languages (though its shape is now quite different in neighbouring Polish), suggest that this is an archaic form, and not an innovation.

3.3.2   Direct Object
The same general western areas (of all three groups) have yet another feature indicating analyticity: the use of the Nominative form for the Direct Object.

The scope of this feature varies greatly, but in most areas is limited either to certain nouns (or noun types) or to objects following an Infinitive; overall the most common type is its occurrence with Feminine (Class II) nouns after an Infinitive, and especially after the modal *nado* 'it is necessary', e.g.:

> *Nado* φ *lodk–a kup'i–t'*. (CSR ... *lodk–u* ...)
> necessary – (be 3ps Pres) – boat NSf – buy Pf Inf (CSR boat ASf)
> 'We must buy a boat.'

In the southwest particularly (though not exclusively) Plural Animate Masculine nouns may appear in the Nominative, especially animals, but also humans, e.g.:

> *Nado* φ *kon'–i poi–t'*. (CSR ... *kon'–ej* ...)
> necessary – (be 3ps Pres) – horse NP – give to drink Impf Inf (CSR horse AP)
> 'We must give the horses a drink'

While the Nominative Singular Feminine nouns must be an innovation, since there is no former evidence of such usage, the Animate Plural forms could well be taken to be archaisms, since the Old Russian form was not the Genitive, as now, but a separate Accusative, often identical to the Nominative. Also, Ukrainian and Belarusian frequently treat animals as they do inanimates, using the Nominative form. It is thus likely that it is this latter usage which has been spread to Feminine nouns, in spite of their being the only ones with a discrete Accusative Singular.

3.3.3   Definiteness

The northern group in general is typified by the use of post-positive particles which are historically the forms of the demonstrative pronoun *t–* (see chapter 3, section 2.1.4.2); this phenomenon occurs also in the central (formerly northern) group. Two questions are of interest: what are the forms of these particles? and what is their function? – as well as the general question of whether they are archaic or innovative.

(1) Form. In the north, the forms are based on grammatical criteria, namely, the gender and number of the noun to which they are attached, e.g. *dom–ot* 'the house' Masc, *žena–ta* 'the wife' and *doč'–ta* 'the daughter' Fem, *okno–to* 'the window' Neut; the Plural has one general form, variously *–t'e*, *–t'i*, or *–ti* ([tɨ]), e.g. *stoli–t'e, stoli–t'i, stoli–ti* 'the tables'; in oblique cases the invariable (Neuter Singular) form *–to* is usually used.

In the central group, on the other hand, they are based on phonetic assimilation to the preceding sound – a sort of vowel harmony, without reference to number, gender or case, e.g. *izba–ta* 'the house' NSf, *izbu–tu* ASf, *izbi–ti* GS/NPf, *saxaru–tu* 'the sugar' GSm, *na b′er′egu–tu* 'on the bank' LSm, etc.

(2) Function. Old Russian, Old Church Slavonic, and probably Proto-Slavonic, used these demonstrative pronouns as markers of definiteness, and the post-positive position reduced their meaning to just that, as opposed to the full demonstrative sense they had when they were pre-positive. Their continuation in this role depended on whether the category of definiteness itself survived, which it typically did *not* do across the Slavonic area. It survived best in South Slavonic, where it was retained on adjectives in Serbian/Croatian and Slovenian, as well as Old Church Slavonic, and on nouns in Bulgarian and Macedonian; elsewhere it has been lost – except for these northern Russian dialects, if, that is, that is its function. The parallel between the Russian forms and those of (standard) Bulgarian and Macedonian is so striking that it is difficult not to see the same function, and so see an archaism. There is, however, the alternative view that the function served by these is rather an intensifying, emphatic one (Kuznecov 1973: 197), the same as the one parallel form existing in (colloquial) Contemporary Standard Russian namely the particle *–to*; however, this parti-cle may be attached to any part of speech, to which it adds emphasis, and not only nouns (e.g. *mn′e-to* 'to me', *včera-to* 'yesterday'), which is quite distinct from the meaning with nouns. In a Contemporary Standard Russian sentence like the following one can see that the particle includes both Definite and Intensifying/Emphatic functions, while the Definite function is irrelevant on non-nouns, since if only the second function was required, it could be better expressed by a particle like *že*, which stands in second place and thus covers the whole sentence, not just the noun.

> *Зачем ты на крышу–то полез? /Začem ti na kryšu-to pol′ez?*
> why – you NS – onto – roof AS – (Intensifier) – climb Pf Past Masc
>   Sing
> 'Why (on earth) did you climb onto the roof?'

It is thus more likely that the Contemporary Standard Russian particle is indeed a remnant of the Definite function, and that the larger range in the dialects retains both functions, possibly with the Definite one being gradually weakened; in this view, the 'phonetic'-shaped forms of the central group have travelled further along this path.

7   Sociolinguistics

1   Introduction

This chapter will consider questions of standardisation, variation, bilingualism, interference and pragmatics. In several of these areas the situation has changed somewhat over the post-Soviet years as compared to the Soviet period – which is very relevant to the role and situation of Russian vis-à-vis the languages of the former republics; and at the micro level to some aspects of the address system. In some areas changes which were under way in the late Soviet period have continued at a faster pace: this refers to the acceptance of non-standard forms and of foreign elements. The general range of diglossia or bilingualism, and of contact with other languages, are in principle unchanged, as are the essentially linguistic issues of changes to the standard. Treatment of the latter will involve essentially a summary of salient features noted in previous chapters, as will discussion of some central issues of pragmatics.

Two recent English-language books dealing with all aspects of current Russian usage are Comrie, Stone and Polinsky 1996 and Ryazanova-Clarke and Wade 1999.

The transcription in this chapter is in principle transliteration only (ISO-Phonemic), unless specific phonemic or morphophonemic issues are involved; however, endings (including zero) are set off and stress position marked.

2   Historical perspectives on standard versus non-standard usage

From the initial efforts at creating a standard Russian language in the mid-eighteenth century, both writers and theorists have concerned themselves with the two central problems facing all standardisers – dialectal (or low style in general, including slang) and foreign elements; on top of this – or rather ahead of this, as the initial primary concern – was the diglossic or stylistic question of Russian Church Slavonic and its relation to the general spoken language, whether in Moscow or St Petersburg. The first major grammar of Russian proper, as opposed to Russian Church Slavonic, that of Lomonosov (1755/1757) (see chapter 1, section 3.3) set the pattern of regarding Russian Church Slavonic elements as high style – to be used in writing the higher genres (ode, elegy, satire, etc.) – and spoken Russian (that spoken by educated city dwellers) as low(er) style, to be used for the lower genres (comedy, fable, etc.). Lomonosov's attitude towards 'uneducated' speech was not explicit, and it was only at the turn of the century, and ultimately with Pushkin (in the 1820s to 1830s), that this level was seen as a valid element of the literary language. Nevertheless, throughout the nineteenth century, the role of Russian Church Slavonic continued to concern the standardisers along with the two basic problems noted above.

2.1   Russian Church Slavonic

In the twentieth century, thus essentially in the Soviet period, not surprisingly, the status of 'ordinary' speech was assured, and anything explicitly connected with 'church' usage was spurned. However, by that time, the more objective standardisers were able to regard many of these Russian Church Slavonic features as established high-style forms (e.g. non-*polnoglasie*), and indeed most had acquired revered status through their use in early socialist-revolutionary terminology, a trend begun by the Decembrist poets of the early nineteenth century; by the Soviet period, most of these features were in any case no longer in competition with local Russian ones (e.g. the participial suffix –*šč*–); in the case of word structure, the shape had become either fixed in accordance with the semantic level of the word (abstract versus concrete), or both shapes existed through semantic separation. All of this was rightly regarded as increasing the linguistic resources available to language users and thus as valuable.

2.2   Foreign

As to the problem of foreign elements, in particular words, Russian was no different to many other languages in the struggle between those who happily embraced all borrowings and those who wished to keep them out; this struggle was particularly strong in the early nineteenth century (see chapter 1, section 3.3, on Karamzin and Šiškov) and again at the height of the Soviet period: in each case the 'purists' were obsessed by the fear of the importation of foreign ideas along with the words. In between, the use of French, and not just French words, in high society was an indication of the reality that, unless there is an effective sanction – as there was in Soviet times – speakers will use whatever appeals to them for whatever reason (reasons such as nationalism, xenophobia or purism).

In the post-Soviet period, the brakes having been released, there has been a veritable flood of foreign words into Russian, mainly, but not only, the same English-language Internet-borne terminology as has invaded virtually every other language. What bothers the purists is not the appearance of new terms for new concepts, but foreign terms, or just words, taking over from (what they see as) perfectly adequate native ones. Russian is no different from other 'sufferers' of this complaint. The recent French experience – the futile attempt in the 1990s at legislation against borrowing (see Machill 1997) – shows that the sensible approach is to allow the frenetic borrowing to run its course, after which only those words found to be really useful and essential will survive. English speakers often fail to appreciate the serious nature of this problem, partly because English is the aggressive party, but mainly because English is itself historically a most ready acceptor of others' words.

2.3   'Low' style

During the Soviet period, it was in fact low-style elements which came in for the most virulent attacks. The elements concerned were mainly jargon and slang, rather than simply dialectal or local speech. During the 1930s and again in the 1960s there were major campaigns conducted in the press and popular language journals against the apparent increases in such forms appearing in writing, and they had the desired effect, since writing of that sort could be effectively muted in the state-controlled context. Such censorship is now no longer officially possible, and the new freedom is indeed reflected in a fresh wave of slang in all public language usage (media and literature) (see Ryazanova-Clarke and Wade 1999: 113ff., 310ff.).

Most of the above relates only to the written language, and the issue of the standard in speech is more elusive. In the Soviet system, a spoken standard could also be insisted upon through the centralised education and employment systems; it was made clear that in any formal situation the standard laid down by grammars and educationists must be adhered to, at the peril of sanctions which had teeth (like loss of employment). Now, the situation is like that of most democratic countries, where the sanctions may well be there, but they are not explicit and are often very subtle. Radio and television are freer than ever before to stretch the standards of usage. Again, France has attempted a less subtle approach, and has failed; it seems clear that one cannot legislate about language usage except in a totalitarian state – and even then, some social groups (e.g. youth and radicals) will ignore or resist the legislation.

2.4   Orthography

The central issues of orthography have been: which letters are in or out of the Cyrillic alphabet, on which there has been no change since 1918; and the spelling of particular words or affixes, which is on-going. There has never been a proposal to replace Cyrillic with a Roman script (which we shall call Latinica), at least not for Russian as such: in the early Soviet days there were all sorts of shifts in the scripts used for non-Slavonic languages of the Union, including Latinica and Arabic, the latter for the Turkic languages, after which they all settled down with local versions of Cyrillic (see Kirkwood 1989). Further, a knowledge of another script (specifically Latinica) has never been an expectation (since the nineteenth-century high-society French days), however in post-Soviet Russia we are seeing the new phenomenon of the assumption of just such a knowledge, and at a general level, since more and more advertisements are appearing in Latinica without any transliteration; even if it is only the brand or company name which is thus written, it must eventually lead to at least a passing understanding of the Latin alphabet and potentially, dare one say it, to moves to use this more and more, in non-commercial contexts, and ultimately to at least parallel existence with Cyrillic. While there are linguistic problems in this, Cyrillic being well tailored to the system, there are plenty of other models around for the use of Latinica, for example, Polish and Czech (and a partial model for parallel existence may be seen in Belarusian), so such a move is by no means a practical impossibility. The resistance, however, would be strong, as it would also be cultural, since Cyrillic is seen as a marker also of religious orthodoxy.

2.5   *The 'Academy'*

As the Soviet political reins were relaxed during the 1980s, the approach of the Academy (of Sciences, Russian Language Institute) began to change: whereas they had been explicitly prescriptive in their publications (and we have in mind especially the Grammars (of 1960 and 1970) and the Pronouncing Dictionaries (of 1960–1980), they clearly shifted to a more descriptive approach (e.g. in the 1980 Grammar and the 'Orthoepic Dictionaries' from 1983 on). This shift was particularly clear in the latter dictionaries: where the most typical comments alongside a variant form in the editions of the 1960s and 1970s was '*x* is unacceptable', or '*x* is not recommended', that of the 1983 and 1989 editions was rather '*or x*' (implying free variation), or '*x* is acceptable' (still implying a hierarchy of preference, but acknowledging variation within the standard). However, even this shift may not be sufficient, since in the new regime there is the inevitable feeling that *any* rule is unnecessary; still, for the time being, such publications, and their pronouncements on the standard, parallel the procedures of large dictionaries in other cultures, notably English-speaking ones.

    The fact is that the Academy continues to maintain standing committees on various aspects of standard usage, which is still more than most cultures do, and it is likely that it will continue to exist, and still, as throughout its history, on the French model – though it would seem with somewhat more pragmatism.

3   **Variation**

3.1   *Varieties, registers*

From the stylistic point of view, the range of varieties, or registers, which may be identified in Russian is the expected three levels of 'high', 'neutral' and 'low', in which 'neutral' is essentially negatively described as not having any of the features marking the other two specifically. 'High' style includes particular written variants of the standard as well as certain obsolescent or obsolete features no longer considered acceptable in the standard; 'low' covers the colloquial spoken variant of the standard as well as many features considered unacceptably low (e.g. slang, vulgarisms), which may be relegated to a fourth level (e.g. Offord 1996: 9 – 'demotic speech', Rus *prostorečie*). We discuss these unacceptable features of 'linguistic style' below (sections 3.3–3.5).

Variation within these registers is one of what we may call 'text style': the preferred linguistic variants of particular 'functional styles', now the common Russian approach to describing this topic (see Kiselyova *et al.* n.d.). In the written language, the identified stylistic types include 'scientific/academic', 'journalistic/publicistic', 'official/business' and 'literary' (or 'belles-lettres'); in the spoken language the range is the spectrum of formality – from 'very formal', in which the language is close to (any particular) written style, to 'very informal', when it may slide into the unacceptable low level – which typifies all spoken languages.

3.2   Current developments in the standard (Contemporary Standard Russian)

As in any living language, a standard which is not an artificial construct, but one based on a real subset of the regional variations – typically of the cultural centre – will at any one time, even within one register, have a range of variants, within which there are three types: (1) one variant is making inroads, but is not yet 'accepted'; (2) two variants are in free (or hierarchical) variation; and (3) one variant is departing the scene, regarded as obsolescent or archaic. As tolerance for variation in a linguistic culture increases, as it is currently doing in Russian, we find that group (2) grows larger, especially at the expense of group (1), from which it draws more members; an increase in group (1) typifies a vibrant and democratic culture, in which regional or foreign elements are continually challenging established ones, while an increase in group (2) may either be a corollary of this, in that older elements are continually being moved into and thence out of this group, or it may indicate a more static culture, if the increase is due to the longer retention there of archaic features. The particular features moving in and out of these groups give us a general indication of possible typological changes occurring in the given language.

In the following we will look at the main features of Russian variation at the main levels; further examples may be found in the relevant chapters (as indicated). The three types are best seen in phonology, and we take them in reversed order – groups (3) – (2) – (1) – as this allows us to see the newest forms last, as an indicator of current developments. In a general sense, the archaisms are Russian Church Slavonic features and the innovations (and free variants) dialectal, however there are some dialectal features – notably Muscovite ones – which have been acceptable in the past, but which are not any longer.

3.3   Phonological

(1) Group (3): archaisms. Features now (even in late Soviet times) considered substandard are as described in the following.

(a) The pronunciation of /g/ as [ɣ], both an RCS and a southern dialectal feature (chapter 2, section 3.7.2); it is still common in the 'religious' words *богъ/bog–ø* 'God' and *господь/gospo'd´–ø* 'Lord' (esp. Voc *господи/go' spod–i*), however the recommendation even in these is [g], except in the Nominative Singular of *bog*, where the devoiced version is only [x], never [k]; in these particular words, we might expect to see a reinforcement of the 'religious' pronunciation. As a dialectal feature, [ɣ] is also very common, even amongst the intelligentsia (at least of southern origin – a notable example being Gorbachev), in spite of the recommendation; but it is nonetheless frowned upon.

(b) Related to this is the former dissimilation of the velar stops /k/ and /g/ to a following stop, when they were realised as the fricatives/spirants [x] (e.g. [xtɔ] for *кто/kto* 'who') and [ɣ]; only in the two roots *лёгк–/lëgk–* 'easy, light' and *мягк–/m'agk–* 'soft' is the dissimilation not only acceptable, but obligatory (both [–xk–]).

(c) The Old Muscovite pronunciation of /i/ after velar stems as [ɨ] is now replaced with the 'spelling' pronunciation [i] (chapter 2, section 3.7.6), which conforms to the general phonotactic rule for these, namely that [kɨ], etc. are impossible (chapter 2, section 3.2.1.1). This may be regarded as the removal of an anomaly or as an example of spelling influence, of which there are many more (below).

(d) The assimilative regressive softening of consonants in clusters of different articulatory positions (chapter 2, section 3.3.2.2) is now considered clearly substandard, as is that within clusters of the same articulatory locus, though not geminates; only within geminate clusters is assimilation the norm, and indeed it would be unusual if this were not the case, since in Russian (and no doubt elsewhere) the typical articulation of such clusters is of one long consonant, that is, without a medial explosion. This development seems clearly to be heading in the direction of greater articulatory distance between segments.

(e) The non-reduction of unstressed vowels (*okan'je* and *ekan'je*) (chapter 2, section 3.2.3.2(3)) was more common in pre-Soviet times as being both Russian Church Slavonic and northern dialect pronunciation; during the Soviet period this became unacceptable, certainly partly as an anti-religious stance, but probably also because they were not typical of either the Moscow (central) or southern pronunciation. The religious revival may now allow them to resurface

in that context, but they are unlikely to achieve wider acceptance, despite the fact that they better reflect the spelling.

(2) Group (2): free variants. Two of the most important contexts of variation are related to foreign pronunciations, and demonstrate how borrowings may affect the phonological system of a language: they are the hard ∼ soft pronunciation of consonants before /e/, and the double ∼ single pronunciation of geminate clusters.

(a) Within the native system, all paired consonants may occur freely before all vowels except /e/, when only soft consonants are possible; but in the foreign subsystem (chapter 2, sections 3.4, 3.7.7) hard consonants have always been possible. While the general trend has until now been towards the assimilation of such words into the native pattern as they have become assimilated lexically and morphologically, many common words, and many more uncommon ones, have resisted assimilation; while they have no doubt done this for purely practical reasons (high or low frequency preventing change), the phonological situation is that such a phonotactic sequence would suit the system very nicely, making the pattern (of hard/soft freedom before vowels), as it were, complete. A minimal pair like *мер/m'er–ø* 'measure' GPf ∼ *мэр/mer–ø* 'mayor' NSm is notionally most desirable for the system (in this case, even more unusually, also an orthographic pair, the letter *э* rarely occurring after a consonant). The pronunciation of particular words is mostly fixed, though unpredictable, so the issue of free variation here is not of primary importance.

(b) Within the native system, geminate consonants are always separated by a morpheme boundary, and as such are naturally pronounced as double (or long) (chapter 2, section 3.3.4.1); the only such clusters not so separated are of foreign origin, some very old and common (e.g. the name *Анна/Anna*). The pronunciation of this foreign group has been uncertain and lexically specific, sometimes double, sometimes single, no doubt depending originally on the donor language; the fact remains that in the modern language some of these may be pronounced as single, and are thus unpredictable from the spelling. It should not, therefore, be surprising that many of these have variant pronunciation. Of interest to us is the direction of any decision, and it seems to be, albeit unclearly, towards allowing more single pronunciation, contrary to the spelling; however, more likely what we see is a result of the more liberal attitude towards variation, in that while a double/long articulation was previously dictated (but may also have been common), now the single version is acknowledged – cf. the more frequent addition of 'acceptable' (in Pron. Dict. 1989, as opposed to its 1960/1965 predecessor), e.g. *кассир/kassi'r–ø* 'cashier', formerly (1965) only '[sʲsʲ]', now (1989) '[sʲsʲ]', but [sʲ] acceptable'; or *российский/rossijsk–ij* 'Russian (geographic)' – 1965: '[sʲsʲ]', but [sʲ] acceptable', 1989: '[sʲsʲ]' (only); on the other hand, *группа/grupp–a* was '[p]' only in 1965, but '[pp] or [p]'

in 1989. But even more telling is the possibility of *native* words having single pronunciation, e.g. *бессонница/bes–son–nic–a* 'insomnia': '[nʲnʲ]' in 1965, '[nʲ]' in 1989 (though the fact that it had any comment at all in 1965 indicates that the single pronunciation was common); and many nouns ending in *–n–nik–* are now given as '[nʲnʲ]', but [nʲ] acceptable'. In sum, the picture is still very unclear, but on balance the trend is against spelling.

(*c*) The remaining cases of consonantal variation all concern clusters.

(*i*) One group concerns the structurally (phonetically) geminate pairs of (1) [š] + [š] and (2) [ž] + [ž], though phonemically and/or morphophonemically they are in fact non-geminate clusters (e.g. phonemically /s/ + /š/, /z/ + /š/, /s/ + /ž/, /z/ + /ž/, or involving morphophonemic boundaries like {s} + {s} + {j}, {z} + {d} + {j}, etc.) (see chapter 2, section 3.3.3.1 and chapter 3, sections 2.1.3.2, 2.2.10). The orthographical sequences are: *щ/сщ/сч/зч/жч* for the first and *жж/зж/сж* for the second; the variation involves: (1) the *dialect-based* pronunciation of the first as either [ʃʲ] + [ʃʲ] (or long [ʃʲː]) (central and south) (with a range of 'always' (for *щ*) to 'rarely' (for *жч*), since the awareness of a morpheme boundary is highly relevant) – or [ʃtʃʲ] (north) for all; and (2) the mainly *age-based* pronunciation of the second as either [ʒʲʒʲ] (or [ʒʲː]) (older speakers) (except where the initial /s/ or /z/ is the final sound of a prefix or preposition, when pronunciation for all is hard, e.g. *разжечь/raz–žeč′*, *сжечь/s–žeč′* both 'burn' Pf Inf, both [ʒʒ]) – or [ʒʒ] (or [ʒː]) (younger speakers). The fact of the different bases for variation of (1) and (2) really means that these are (now) different phenomena in spite of their structural similarity, and their projected fates are also different: for the first, the superior influence of the central/south variant, including Moscow, is certainly winning the day, and for the second, by definition the 'old' variant may be expected to disappear with its current supporters.

(*ii*) The other group of clusters with variant pronunciation involves various assimilative or dissimilative adjustments, that is, for the most part, simplifications. There are four types, all of which in their older variant are contrary to spelling predictions, and all of which are correspondingly shifting to some extent towards greater conformity to these predictions, although high-frequency words are resisting with some ease.

● the Reflexive suffix *–ся/–s′a* (*–сь/–s′* after vowels): the Old Muscovite pronunciation always had hard [s] ([sə]/[–s]); this hard variant survives now (amongst younger speakers) only when the preceding ending terminates in /t/ or /t′/ (thus 3rd Person Singular and 3rd Person Plural Present, and Infinitive), when the realised sound is [t͡sː], that is, with both elements lengthened (chapter 2, section 3.3.3); otherwise, the realisation is [sʲə]/[sʲ].

● underlying hard consonants followed by /j/ (chapter 2, section 3.3.2.2) – only possible where the /j/ is root-initial and the consonant part of a prefix or preposition; in orthography this is the surviving function of the hard sign (e.g.

съесть/s–jest' 'eat' Pf Inf, *объявить/ob–javi't'* 'announce' Pf Inf). The older variant involved assimilative softening of the first (thus [s̪ʲjes̪ʲt̪ʲ], [ʌb̪ʲjɪvit̪ʲ]), the newer has hardened all labials (thus only [ʌbjɪvit̪ʲ]), but is still hesitant about dentals (thus [s̪ʲjes̪ʲt̪ʲ] *or* [s̪jes̪ʲt̪ʲ]); the direction is clearly towards following the spelling indicated by the 'hard sign'. (This may be seen as an extension of the loss of assimilation noted in 1(d) above.)

• the clusters /č/ + /t/ and /č/ + /n/ (chapter 2, section 3.3.4.2): the older variant dissimilated /č/ to [ʃ], certainly in high-frequency words (e.g. *что/čto* 'what', *скучно/skuč–no* 'boring' NSn); such high-frequency words continue to be so pronounced, but others are shifting in the newer version to [tʃt]/[tʃn] (e.g. *чтение/čte'nij–e* 'reading' [tʃt̪ʲ], *яичница/jai'č–nic–a* 'fried eggs' [ʃn̪ʲ] or [tʃn̪ʲ], *срочно/sroč–no* 'urgent' NSn [tʃn]]).

• three-(plus-)member clusters involving a medial dental stop (e.g. /stn/, /stl/) lost this stop in the older variant (e.g. *грустный/gru'st–n–yj* 'sad' [sn], *счастливый/sčast–li'v–yj* 'happy' [s̪ʲl̪ʲ]) (chapter 2, section 3.3.4.2), and again such high-frequency words continue thus, while others (a few only) retain the stop (e.g. *полистный/poli'st–n–yj* 'per sheet (of paper)', *костлявый/kost–l'a'v–yj* 'bony'). The cluster /vstv/ used to lose the first /v/, and this version is retained in the two high-frequency roots *čuv–* 'feel' and *zdrav–* 'greet' (e.g. *чувство/ču'v–stv–o* 'feeling' [tʃu'stvə], *здравствуйте/zdra'v–stvuj–te* 'hello' [zdra'stvujt̪ʲɪ]), but not otherwise (e.g. *девство/de'v–stv–o* 'spinsterhood, virginity' [d̪ʲɛ'fstvə]).

(d) Finally, two cases of unstressed vowels also show *age-based* variation, the older being the Old Muscovite version (chapter 2, section 3.2.3.2(3)).

• pre-tonic /a/ after /š/, /ž/, /c/ was pronounced [ɨ], unlike the [ʌ] of other contexts (e.g. *жара/žar–a'* 'heat' NSf, *шаги/šag–i'* 'pace' NPm); the newer variant has regularised [ʌ]. Only a few specific lexemes retain [ɨ] for all speakers (e.g. *жалеть/žal–e'–t'* 'pity' Inf, *лошадей/lošad–e'j* 'horse' GPf).

• the nominal endings {a} and {o} after soft paired stems often contradicted spelling (or morphological) expectations: NSn {o}(orth. *–e*) was typically pronounced [ə] (e.g. *море/mo'r–e* 'sea'), where the expectation, and the newer variant, is [ɪ]; holding out best is the NSn adjective ending *–oje*, still most often [ɔ'jə/əjə] (e.g. *старое/sta'r–oje* 'old') (which also causes the potential complication of making a homophone with the (unstressed) NSf *старая/sta'r–aja*, also [əjə]); conversely, the nominal GSn {a} (orth. *–я*) could be pronounced [ɪ] (e.g. *моря/mo'r'–a*), which matches the phonological rule that unstressed /a/ after a soft consonant > [ɪ], but not the morphophonemic expectation of unstressed ending {a} > [ə]; the variant becoming fixed is [ə], which means that in this case the morphophonemic pattern is dominating.

(3) Group (1): new variants. All of the new variants which might be said to be 'on the horizon', with the potential to enter the standard, are assignable to

'casual' or 'rapid' style: they are clearly caused by rapid speech, and so the likelihood is that they would not pass beyond the lowest (most informal) register of the standard. Two are certainly in this situation, since they involve the loss of segments which are of lexical and/or morphological significance, and as such cannot be lightly lost, and will certainly be retained in any formal register, while a third involves a particular morphological context.

(a) Lost unstressed vowels, which may be part of an ending (e.g. *проход-um/proxo'd–it* 'pass be' 3ps Pres > [prʌxɔ'dʲt]), a suffix (e.g. *писатель/pisa'–tel'–ø* 'writer' NSm > [pʲisa'tʲlʲ], *бабушка/ba'b–ušk–a* 'grandmother' NSf > [ba'bʃkə] – note the absence of devoicing in the resulting cluster), a prefix (e.g. *пошёл/po–š(o)l* 'go' Pf Past Masc > [pʃɔl]), or a root (e.g. *часов/čas–o'v* 'hour' GPm – especially in clock time > [tʃsɔf], *у меня/u men'a'* 'I have' (lit. 'at me') > [umʲnʲa']).

(b) Lost intervocalic consonants, normally voiced obstruents (e.g. *будет/bu'd–et* 'be' 3ps Pres > [bu'ɪt], *девушка/de'v–ušk–a* 'girl' NSf > [dʲɛ'uʃkə]).

(c) The third involves principally the adjective Accusative Singular Feminine ending *–ую/–uju*, in which the first /u/ may be reduced to [ə] or [ɪ] (e.g. *старую/sta'r–uju* 'old' > [sta'rəju], *синюю/si'n'–uju* 'blue' > [sʲi'nʲɪju]; a similar reduction (unrounding) occurs in the two frequent lexemes *пожалуйста/poža'lujsta* 'please' (> [pʌʒa'ləstə], and further, as above, > [pʌʒa'lstə]) and *здравствуй-(ме)/zdra'v–stvuj(–te)* 'hello' Sg/Pl (> [zdra'stvəj(tʲɪ)], and the plural further > [zdra'sʲtʲtʲɪ] > [zdrasʲtʲ])).

(4) Stress (lexical). Variation in lexical stress (in principle the whole paradigm of a word) is not very common. One list (Jakovenko 1966) gives 151 pairs, covering all categories, but many are from the same root and by far the largest group (57) are Past Passive participles of prefixed verbs; other large groups are nouns (33), adverbs (18; plus 4 adverbial participles) and long adjectives (12); there are 14 verbs, but these include 4 pairs of ±Reflexive forms. Another source (Gorbačevič 1973, reported in Gorbačevič 1978) gives larger numbers of variant forms, e.g. *c.* 250 for Class II Feminine alone, *c.* 250 for long adjectives and *c.* 300 for verbs.

For the most part the variation (shown by a double stress mark) is between stem and ending (e.g. *баржа/ba'rž̈–a'* 'barge', *ушко/u'šk–o'* 'little ear/tag', *вк-линить/vkli'n–i'–t'* 'wedge in', *запасный ~ запасной/zapa's–n–yj ~ zapas–n –o'j* 'reserve', *загруженный ~ загружённый/zagru'ž–o'nn–yj* 'load' PPP, *широко/širo'k–o'* 'widely'), but also between prefix and stem (especially the participial forms, e.g. *замерший/za'–me'r–š–ij* 'freeze' PPA); in the latter case, the prefix stress is older and usually losing ground (parallel to the Past, see below), but the variation is still active, for example Pron. Dict. 1989 has: *допитый*: *do'pit–yj* or *dopi't–yj* 'drink up' PPP; *добытый*: *doby't–yj*, also acceptable *do'byt–yj* 'acquire' PPP; and *дожитый: do'žit–yj*, also acceptable *doži't–yj* 'live (till)' PPP (where 'also acceptable' implies a less recommended form; overall this dictionary supports all the variants in this list, even if with this proviso).

3.4   Morphological

Variation in morphology is due mainly to dialectal or foreign input and to uncertainty about ambiguous forms; also operative are social issues like that of gender (the conflict between human and grammatical gender in the context of occupations), and linguistic issues like the form and status of abbreviations and compounds as morphological units and the ever-active regularisation of anomalous forms.

3.4.1   Gender

(1) Common gender. The blurring of the relationships between gender and occupation causes problems for all languages with grammatical gender, leading them either to create parallel 'other gender' forms, if possible with marked suffixes (e.g. Eng *actress* – but not **directress*; Fr *actrice, directrice*), otherwise simply applying a new gender, a process normally strongly resisted (cf. Fr *la présidente*; Ital **la presidenta*). Against this process runs the modern social resistance to marking occupations in gender terms at all, leading to the understanding of such words as being common gender, and indeed the removal of existing marked forms (e.g. Eng *actor*, Fr *acteur* as common gender); occasionally the language assists by having an (or a partly) ambiguous form (e.g. Fr *l'athlète*, but *un(e) athlète*).

For Russian the ambiguous forms are Class II nouns (NS in –*a*), which have always been available for male occupations (e.g. *vojevod–a* 'commander', *vladyk–a* 'bishop'); thus new words with this shape have easily become common gender (e.g. *kolleg–a* 'colleague'), able to be accompanied by modifiers of either gender (see chapter 3, section (2.1.3.1(2)) and chapter 4, section 3.2.2.3). Unfortunately, the vast majority of occupational terms, including foreign ones, belong to Class I (Nominative Singular in consonant + ϕ), and the language has thus far been able to accept feminine modifiers with such nouns only at the colloquial level (e.g. forms such as **новая секретарь/nov–aja sekretar'–ϕ* are acknowledged by Academy Grammar 1980 (p. 57) as 'normal' in speech and newspapers, but only in the Nominative).

In the meantime, the same trends towards removal of gender markers noted above is present also in Russian (e.g. former *aktri's–a* 'actress' being replaced by *aktë'r–ϕ*, at least in formal professional usage). Only where gender is actually relevant to the occupation, as in most sports, is the distinction still fully operative (e.g. *gimna'st–ϕ* ~ *gimna'stk–a* 'gymnast' Masc ~ Fem respectively).

(2) Variants. Variation in gender occurs only with non-human nouns, where the gender is usually purely grammatical. Alternative forms are sometimes old

and well established, and so often both are standard (e.g. *žira'f–ɸ* ~ *žira'f–a* 'giraffe', *ža'r–ɸ* ~ *žar–a'* 'heat'); more often one is substandard (e.g. *brasle't–ɸ* ~ **brasle't–a* 'bracelet', *fi'l'm–ɸ* ~ **fi'l'm–a* 'film'); but often the variation is stylistic (specialist or sociolectal) (e.g. Fem *spa'zm–a* 'spasm' is Masc *spa'zm–ɸ* in professional medical usage; similarly *špri'c–ɸ* ~ *špric–a'* 'syringe'; or *kompone'nt–ɸ* 'component' ~ *kompone'nt–a* '(mathematical) component').

More expected is hesitation over the gender of indeclinable words, especially when the final vowel is not a possible native one (e.g. *taksi'* 'taxi', *vi'ski* 'whisky'): for the standard these are always neuter, the default gender for indeclinables, but colloquially they may be allotted other genders by association with some generic form (e.g. *taksi* Masculine like *avtomobi'l'–ɸ* 'automobile' or Feminine like *maši'n–a* 'car'; *viski* Masculine like *napi'tok–ɸ* 'drink' – or more likely *spirt–ɸ* 'spirit'). Indeclinables ending in the neuter markers *–o/–e* are less likely to vary, yet often do (e.g. *dina'm–o* 'dynamo' is often feminine, no doubt through the phonetic identity of final unstressed *–o* and *–a*); conversely, in the standard the word *kofe* 'coffee' is unexpectedly masculine, but is, inevitably, frequently treated as neuter (by natives as well as learners).

Generic animal names may be of any class, the allotted (default) gender being grammatical (e.g. *soba'k–a* 'dog', *ko'šk–a* 'cat', with feminine modifiers only); in these cases there is usually a lexically different name for the other, marked, sex (e.g. *pës–ɸ'* 'male dog', *kot–ɸ'* 'tom-cat'); only foreign indeclinable names may be formally neuter (e.g. *kenguru'* 'kangaroo'), their gender common (i.e. modifiers of either gender as required), but masculine for the default gender – unless their generic class is feminine, e.g. fish (*ryb–a*), birds (*ptic–a*) (e.g. *ivasi'* 'type of sardine', *koli'bri* 'humming-bird').

(3) Abbreviations. Chapter 3, section 2.1.3.1 discusses the gender of abbreviations in some detail; of relevance here is the growing number of acronyms which will inevitably be allotted gender according to their shape (e.g. *MID* 'Ministry of Internal Affairs' > Masculine, like a Class I noun), rather than according to the standard rule that gender follows that of the underlying headword (in this case the neuter form *ministe'rstv–o* 'ministry'); with new and unfamiliar acronyms, speakers really have no alternative, and there is a fair chance that the 'rule' will be amended (cf. the completed process in the case of very familiar words, e.g. *vuz–ɸ* 'tertiary institution' Class I Masculine, from *VUZ* 'institution of advanced study/learning', where *zavedeni–e* 'institution' is neuter; *sa'mbo* 'unarmed self-defence' indeclinable neuter, from a phrase in which the headword *samozaščit–a* 'self-defence' is feminine). The question of declension is relevant here too (the declension of the acronym-word versus non-declension of the initials) – see below.

(4) Compounds. The principle of allotting gender to compounds also follows the notional headword (see chapter 3, section 2.1.3.1), which may not be the

second element, which in turn causes a conflict between official gender and the ending of the compound form (e.g. *диван-кровать/divan—krova't′–ø* 'bed-settee'). In such cases both parts of the noun are in principle declined, but as the compound (object) becomes perceived as a single concept, the first element ceases to be declined, and thus the only grammatical information resides in the second, which thus determines the overall gender. In the example of *divan—krovat′–ø*, both approaches are standard (e.g. *на удобном диване—кровати/ na udo'bn–om divan–e—krova't–i* 'on a comfortable bed-settee', with masculine modifier and declension of both, or *на удобной диван—кровати/ na udo'bn–oj divan—krova't–i*, with feminine modifier and indeclinable first part). Another current example is *кафе-столовая/kafe—stolo'v–aja* 'snack-bar', shifting from neuter (from the first element) to feminine (from the second). This will be the direction of development of such compounds.

3.4.2   Declension
(1) Indeclinable forms. So long as the vast majority of indeclinable forms are foreign, and even if their number is growing, we cannot simply extrapolate from that to say that Russian is losing its declension system, that is, becoming analytic in its nominal morphology. Nonetheless, the existence of a large corpus of such forms has the capacity to influence the native system. Native examples of the loss of declension are rare, and some of those proposed (e.g. GPm shifting from *–ov* to *–ø*, see below) are better described as a rearrangement of endings, since a zero-ending is not to be interpreted as no ending, zero being a fully fledged member of the ending category. The only area in which limitations are being put on the declension system is in the *syntactic* one of compound numerals, where the already standard practice of declining only the final element in ordinal numbers is clearly spreading to the cardinal numbers also (chapter 3, section 2.1.6.1); in the same area comes the increasing use of classifiers and/or inversion to allow cardinal numerals to remain undeclined (e.g. *в комнате номер пять/v komnat–e nomer–ø p′at′–ø* 'in Room 5', with inversion and the classifier *nom'er–ø* 'number' (so common in this particular usage that it has come on its own to mean '(hotel) room'); *на поезде семьдесят пять /na pojezd–e sem'des'at–ø p′at′–ø* 'on train no. 75', with inversion alone). The defective declensions of the numerals 'forty', 'ninety' and 'hundred' (chapter 3, section 2.1.6.1) are old and not likely to affect others.

Inversion also allows the small number of indeclinable (root only, no ending) adjectives to survive as such (e.g. *костюм беж/kost'u'm–ø bež* 'a beige suit'; see chapter 4, section 2); far from affecting other forms, these are rather being brought into line by suffixation and declension (> *бежевый костюм/be'ž–ev–yj kost'um–ø*). The even rarer examples of a non-inverted adjective of this sort (e.g. *коми язык/ko'mi jazyk–ø* '(the) Komi (language)') are certainly not in danger of affecting anything native.

Similarly, a comparative attributive adjective in the Direct Object may have – at the very informal colloquial level – its indeclinable predicate form in the inverted order, e.g.:

> *Дайте мне книгу по–интереснее./Daj–te mne knig–u po–interesn–eje.*
> give Imper 2pp – me DS – book ASf – interesting Compar Adv
> 'Give me a more interesting book.' (see chapter 3, section 2.1.5.6(2))
> for regular formation)

More likely, this should be interpreted as an elliptical relative clause in which the adjective is in fact the predicate ('a book which is more interesting').

(2) Case forms. The process of regularising old variant forms is at the centre of some of the current changes to particular case endings. This concerns the following Class I Masculine noun endings (see also chapter 3, section 2.1.3.1):

(a) GSm in *–a* ~ *–u*: the latter has all but disappeared, having survived until now in the partitive sense, including after expressions of quantity. The only non-varying usage left is the true partitive, still preferred in some words (e.g. *положите сахару/položi–te saxar–u* 'put some sugar in'), not available in others (e.g. only *хлеба/xleb–a* '(some) bread'); with quantity words, there is a choice (e.g. *чашка чая/чаю/čašk–a čaj–a/čaj–u* 'a cup of tea'). Only in the two colloquial forms *чай ку/čajk–u'* 'a (drop of) tea' and *кофей ку/kofejk–u'* 'a (drop of) coffee' is *–u* the only available form.

(b) LSm in *–e* ~ *–u'*: there is little sign that the group of masculine monosyllabic words using the latter ending in the locative sense (e.g. *на полу/na pol–u'* 'on the floor', *в саду/v sad–u'* 'in the garden'), all high frequency words, is losing this feature; one survey (Krysin 1974: 177), however, has suggested that younger speakers are more likely to choose *–e* in cases of uncertainty.

(c) NPm in *–y* ~ *–a'*: the latter ending is a southern dialectal feature which has been steadily infiltrating the standard for many centuries; currently there are cases of standard variants (e.g. *тракторы/tra'ktor–y* 'tractors' ~ *трактора/traktor–a'*) and of substandard ones (e.g. *инженеры/inžene'r–y* 'engineers' ~ **инженера/inžener–a'*), with every indication of further increase of the latter type. Part of its attraction for speakers is the stress pattern, since it allows (and indeed forces) all plural endings to be stressed, in contrast to the stem stress of the singular, an oppositional pattern clearly achieving popularity (see chapter 3, section 2.1.3.3).

(d) The other case involved in variation is the Genitive Plural, the case with the largest range of endings; in one group only, there is variation reaching into the standard.

Class I Masculine in *–ov* ~ *–ø*: a small group of nouns has only the *–ø* ending (thus = NS), for them an old form (e.g. *солдат/solda' t–ø* 'soldier', *носок/nos(o)k–ø'* 'sock'); many, like the latter example, denote pairs, and are thus most likely remnant dual forms; others, like the former, are members of types of people (cf. also the inhabitant suffix *–jan(in)–*, with GP *–ø*, e.g. *англичан/angličan–ø* 'Englishman' (NS *–anin–ø*), and also *грузин/gruzin–ø* 'Georgian' (GP = NS)). Most commonly such forms would follow a quantifier ('many', etc.), and it is in this context that the current variation occurs, both standard (e.g. *двести граммов/dvesti gramm–ov* '200 grams' ~ *грамм/ gramm–ø*) and substandard (e.g. *кило помидоров/kilo pomidor–ov* 'a kilo of tomatoes' ~ **kilo pomidor–ø*); in many cases the zero form is recognised as the 'counting' form (e.g. *200 вольт/200 vol′t–ø* '200 volts'), alongside the 'regular' one (*вольтов/vol′t–ov*), though such words would rarely occur without such a context.

In other types, any regularisation of the plethora of forms is still substandard: in the Class II Feminine Soft Genitive Plural in *–ø ~ –ej*, we have the anomalous latter ending being brought into line with the regular zero; only two words stand out – *дядя/d′ad′–a* 'uncle' and *тётя/tët′–a* 'aunt', and both are regularly, but so far in substandard usage only, given the zero endings by analogy. The Class I Neuter Soft Genitive Plural endings *–ej* (e.g. NS *поле/pol–e* ~ GP *полей/pol–ej* 'field'), *–ij* (e.g. NS *поместье/pomest′–j–e* 'estate' ~ GP *поместий/pomest– ij* – which is actually a zero ending with the inserted vowel *–i-: –(i)j–ø*), and *–ev* (e.g. NS *платьеplat′j–e* 'dress' ~ GP *платьев/plat′j–ev*) alongside the hard zero ending must cause problems, and are a potential area for regularisation – especially the last two, given their infrequency of occurrence.

(e) The last case with variation is the Instrumental Plural of Class III Feminine, where the remnant forms *–ьми/–′mi'* (e.g. *дочерьми/dočer′–mi'* 'daughter') may survive – in a very few words – alongside the newer, regular *–ями/– ′a'mi* (*дочерями/dočer′–a'mi*); only in two words is the old form still the only standard one (*детьми/det′–mi'* 'children', *людьми/l′ud′–mi'* 'people'), though the other forms do occur at the 'very substandard' level (Pron. Dict. 1989).

(3) Analyticity. Overall, therefore, we can see plenty of regularisation of declension patterns, but little evidence of the loss of declension as such, certainly within the native lexicon (the foreign lexicon being, however, an increasingly greater proportion of the whole, as also are acronyms and other abbreviations). Indeed, if we wish to regard the Vocative as a case, we could say that case forms are on the increase, in light of the colloquial forms of affectionate names (*Наташ!/Nata′š!* 'Natasha', *Коль!/Kol′!* 'Kolya') (see also chapter 3, section 2.1.3.1; chapter 4, section 3).

3.4.2.1 Stress patterns in the noun and adjective. The two motivations for change in stress pattern – and thus the interim stage of variation – are (all examples shown as '>' ('becoming') are standard variants unless otherwise noted): (1) regularisation, which tends to remove any irregular type (C) (for types, see chapter 3, section 2.1.3.3), in principle by unifying the whole of the Singular or Plural; and (2) the opposition of the Singular and Plural sets. In most cases these two tendencies are complementary, for example, the aligning of the Plural forms of Class I Masculine Type AC by adjusting the odd Nominative Plural (e.g. *воры/vo'r–y* > *vor–y'* 'thief' NP) produces just that opposition (giving a new AB pattern); the aligning of the oblique cases of Class II Feminine Type BC with the odd Nominative Plural does the same in reverse, producing a BA pattern; and the same goes for the aligning of the Singular of Class II Feminine Type CC by adjusting the odd Accusative Singular (e.g. *реку/r'e'k–u* > *r'ek–u'* 'river' AS), also giving BA.

In the four forms of the short adjective (chapter 3, section 2.1.5.2), the clearest shift is actually one of *anti*-regularisation, in that the isolated Feminine end-stress is not being shifted, but frequently being joined by the Plural (e.g. *просты/pro'st–y* > *prost–y'* 'simple', and still substandard *правы/pra'v–y* > *prav–y'* 'correct', a very high-frequency form in the structure *Вы правы./Vy (ø) prav–y.* 'You're right.'). The pattern thus produced is on the surface one of Masc + Neut (stem) ~ Fem + Plur (end); however, if we regard the Masculine as potentially end-stressed (stressed zero) – as we would in the case of a wholly end-stressed set, we would have sets of forms in which the Neuter is actually the odd one, and in many of these we find that there is a stress opposition between it and the homographic adverb (e.g. *полно/po'lno* 'fully' Adv ~ *poln–o'* 'full' Neut); in most cases, however, the two are identically stem-stressed, suggesting a direct influence of the adverbial form in maintaining the stem stress. It is most likely, therefore, that syntactic or semantic considerations are here in conflict with the notional tendency toward morphological regularisation.

3.4.3 Conjugation

Still less than in the nominal system is there any loss of synthetic type in the verbal system, at least any more than had taken place many centuries ago (simplification of the Past forms by expansion of the aspect system, see chapter 3, section 2.2.1). Again, we observe simply the removal of anomalous forms, in particular where the Infinitive and general Class are the same, as with Class II (Present theme *–aj–*, e.g. *читать/čitat'* 'read') and Class III (Present theme *–j–e–*, e.g. *писать/pisat'* 'write'): we find the less common members of the numerically smaller Class III acquiring the theme of Class II (e.g. *капать/kapat'* 'drip': 3ps Pres *каплет/ka'pl–et* > *капаем/ka'pa–j–et*), many of these being standard variants.

The influence of the Infinitive is also seen in the shift of verbs with Inf *–e–t'* from Class II (Present theme *–ej–e*) to Class IV (Present theme *–i–*) (e.g.

опротиветь/oproti'v–et' 'become repulsive': 3ps *опротиееет/oproti'v–ej–et > *oproti'v–i–t*). None of these (cf. Zaliznjak 1980) are considered standard.

Variation in the standard is seen in the Class I verbs with the suffix *–nu–*, in which some verbs officially lose the suffix in the Past while others retain it (see chapter 3, section 2.2.6.2 and chapter 5, section 4.2.3): the earlier word-formational basis for the retention ('semelfactive') or loss ('acquisitive') is being lost, and many verbs which formerly lost the suffix (in principle verbal roots) are now retaining it, since retention is more regular (e.g. *гибнуть/gi'b–nu–t'* 'perish': Past Masc *гиб/gib–ø–ø ~ гибнул/gi'b–nu–l*).

One (southern) dialectal ending which has made some inroads into the standard, but is still officially rejected, is the expansion of the 3rd Person Plural Present Class I ending *–ut* into Class IV verbs when unstressed (against the standard *–'at*, e.g. *ходят/xo'd'–at* 'go' 3pp Pres > **xo'd'–ut*). One may hear this from well educated southerners, along with the fricative [ɣ], which is equally officially substandard.

3.4.3.1 Stress patterns in the verb.

Within the Present the main area of variant stress pattern is Class IV verbs with suffix-stress in the Infinitive, where the historical movement has been one of the steady expansion of the mobile pattern at the expense of the end-stress one (Type B > Type C; see chapter 3, section 2.2.11.1); Gorbačevič (1973, 1978) lists over 300 such verbs. A verb which seems to typify the continuing resistance to this shift is *звонить/zvon–i't'* 'ring', still shown in Pron. Dict. 1989 as being end-stressed only, yet all agree that the mobile pattern is the 'norm' among the young. This source shows many verbs with the end-stress marked as 'old', though still acceptable (e.g. *дружить/druž–i't'* 'be friends with', *грузить/gruz–i't'* 'load').

In the Past, there are several areas of variation. (1) As with the short adjectives, the mobile pattern involves an odd Feminine end-stress alongside stem-stress for the other three forms (though the Masculine could, again, be treated as 'zero-end-stressed') (e.g. *жить/žit'* 'live': *ži'–lø ~ ži–la' ~ ži'–lo ~ ži'–li*). On simple verbs, this pattern is not under threat, but on prefixed verbs there is more likelihood of the Feminine coming into line, however the standard is resisting such change (as, e.g. *подобрать/pod(o)–bra–t'* 'select': Past Feminine officially *podo–bra–la'* only, like simple *bra–la'* 'take'); as yet probably none have made it into the standard. (2) Prefixed non-Feminine forms have often had prefix-stress, but this is now being replaced by stem-stress (e.g. *прожил(–о)/(–и)/pro'ži–l– > pro–ži'l–* 'live through'; *налил–/na'–li–l– > na–li'–l–* 'pour'). (3) A few Reflexive verbs had the stress on the postfix *–s'a* in the Masculine form, an odd form now being replaced by end-stress (e.g. *родился/rod–il–s'a' > rod–i'l–s'a* 'be born'). This latter form may be matched by stem-stress in all forms – *rod–i'la–s'*, etc. – while users of the former would certainly have end-stress for the rest – *rod–i–la'–s'*, etc. – such global variation between end- and stem-stress in the Past is rare.

3.5   Word-formational

The only word-formational feature we will note in the context of current developments concerns aspectual formation. Within the verbal system, aspect is still of central importance, (and will no doubt continue to be so while verb forms are relatively so few). Thus the existence of bi-aspectual verbs, in which there is no formal aspect marker (but where aspect is not predictable), the aspect being left to the syntactic context, represents a weakness in the system. Essentially such verbs are only foreign, all with the suffixes *–(iz)(ir)–ova–* (see chapter 5, section 4.2.3), and their (relatively) low frequency of occurrence is largely what allows them to survive in this form; however, any which are or have become more frequent are immediately likely to develop a formally different pair, most typically via a prefix which marks the Perfective form. Chronological examples of the process are: *редактировать/redakt–i'rova–t'* 'edit', in the early Soviet period bi-aspectual, but for some time now only Imperfective, the Perfective role taken by *отредактировать/ot–redakt–i'rova–t'*; *организовать/organiz–ova'–t'* 'organise', which has for some time had the alternative Perfective form *сорганизовать/s–organiz–ova'–t'*; and *интегрировать/integr–i'rova'–t'* 'integrate', whose prefixed form *pro–integr–i'rova'–t'* is still limited to professional/scientific style.

A less popular solution is to supply a suffix-marked Imperfective (usually *–yv–*) – less popular also at the systemic level, since non-prefixed but suffixed forms are rare (see chapter 5, section 4.2.3(3)). One example which has been in the standard for some time is *арестовывать/ar'est–o'v–yva–t'* 'arrest' (in Pron. Dict. 1960); another which has more recently made it into the standard is (paradoxically, since it has also the new prefixed form) *организовывать/organiz–o'v–yv–at'*; competing with *za–atak–ova'–t'* 'attack' is the equally substandard *atak–o'v–yv–at'* (which has now appeared in the latest Orthographic Dictionary (Orth. Dict. 1999), but not yet in any explanatory dictionary, up to Ožegov and Švedova 1999).

Within the native system, there are few examples, since there were few bi-aspectual verbs; one of interest is *жениться/žen–i't's'a* 'marry (of a man)/get married (of a couple)': in the first meaning (Singular) it has always been and still is bi-aspectual, but in the second (Plural) it has acquired the new prefixed alternative form *пожениться/po–žen–i't's'a* (not in the 1972 edition of Ožegov, but in later ones; the non-Reflexive form, meaning 'to marry (a man) off' still has no prefixed form in Ožegov and Švedova 1999, though this does appear in other dictionaries (e.g. Orth. Dict. 1984).

Beyond this feature, word-formational developments come down to the shifting popularity of particular affixes and compounding methods.

4   Contact/interference

As a strongly centralised and standardised language, Russian (Contemporary Standard Russian) is not easily open to uncontrolled outside influence. We have reviewed its attitude to foreign borrowing and to dialectal input elsewhere (chapter 1, section 4.3, chapter 6, section 2 and above, section 2). At the non-standard level, speakers living in border areas have been exposed to contact with other language groups, including non-Slavonic ones, for example Finnic in the north and northeast, Baltic in the northwest, Uralic (mostly Finno-Ugrian) in the east, Altaic (mostly Turkic) in the south and southeast, and Caucasian in the south; claims of the effects of such contact are dubious and disputed, though some of the more interesting Russian peculiarities may well be just such effects (e.g. *akan'je*, some numeral forms, esp. 'nine', the expression of possession by *u men'a jest'*).

4.1   Soviet period

During the Soviet period, the role of Russian was not only that of the prestige language and the administrative language of the Union, but in effect the compulsory first language for all public activities; and in the school system, it was Contemporary Standard Russian that was uniformly taught; as such, every effort was made to impose the standard. The extent to which this was successful is difficult to estimate, since the public speakers that one heard were well educated and indeed steeped in Russian, so the only real interference one observed was in phonetics; for less prominent speakers, one is left with subjective opinions related in the post-Soviet period, when it is claimed that as little attention was given to Russian as possible; the fact is that anyone who wished to 'get anywhere' had to be competent in Russian. The caricatures of regional accents which one heard in jokes about Armenians and Georgians no doubt reflected some realities of interference, but they are nevertheless caricatures. Nonetheless, in a multi-cultural, federal system like the USSR, where local languages were also officially used, it was natural that there should be a variety of regional variants of the national language, reflecting the distance between the national and local phonological systems; most typical features were the absence of *akan'je* (that is, *okan'je*, also a northern dialectal feature) and of soft consonants (not a dialectal feature). The presence of such features was no more a hindrance to political progress than are, say, regional accents in Britain (witness the 'success' of Georgians Stalin and Shevardnadze), though the federal context does make the situations somewhat different.

The situation of Ukrainian and Belarusian (then Belorussian) was some-what different: as Slavonic languages they were at least partially intelligible to Russians, and in turn their speakers had little trouble in learning Russian; on the other hand, this similarity encouraged the use of local forms and could make for lazy acquisition of Russian. Ukrainian, in particular, had both *okan'je* and few soft consonants, so that they easily displayed the two features most typical of the non-Slavonic group; Belarusian was phonetically much closer to Russian, with only the quality of their palatals and affricates standing out; in both cases, there were transitional dialects with the same features, so it was common for Russians to look with some contempt even on the standard languages, regard-ing them as 'corrupt' or dialectal Russian; this attitude naturally spread also to those speakers' accented Russian. At the same time, in both republican capitals, Kiev and Minsk (perhaps especially the latter), Russian was effectively the only public language.

4.2   Post-Soviet period

In the post-Soviet period, the majority of the former republics are now indepen-dent countries, in which Russian has, at best, the role of first foreign language, though reaction has usually meant that even this is no longer true, English sweeping all before it in this role. Still, as long as those in power belong to the former Soviet generation, Russian will continue to maintain a presence. As for those republics (not full ones, but various autonomous regions and the like) which have remained inside the Russian Federation, their situation has changed only slightly, in that they may opt for less centralised educational materials. Russian remains the language of the whole Federation.

As for Ukrainian and Belarusian, the former has gone its own way, formalis-ing standard Ukrainian as its national language (Constitution 1996, Art. 10; see further below, section 4.5); but the latter is very ambivalent: the President (as of 2002), Lukashenko, is, no doubt mainly for economic or political reasons, seeking close ties with Russia, and – possibly also for some more personal reason – in effect seeking to make Russian the formal language of his country. Its current Constitution (1996, Art. 17) declares both Belarusian and Russian to be the national languages, but this is seen by many as an excuse to allow the continued dominance of Russian. (For example, government resolutions and edicts are virtually exclusively issued in Russian only, see BLS/Web.) Just possibly, the practicalities of the high proportion of Russian native speak-ers (who would never have had to learn Belarusian, living in the main cities and dominating the intelligentsia) are the primary motivation (cf. the claim that only 11.2 per cent of Minsk's secondary school students were taught in Belarusian in 1998/99 – see BelaPAN 1999). Certainly, the closeness of the two languages was exaggerated in the Soviet period, with any variant forms which were closer to Russian being pushed in favour of more distant ones, but the fact is that they are probably closer than any other pair of Slavonic languages.

4.3   Diaspora

One case of diaspora use of Russian is that of the FSU, many republics of which still have large, even majority, populations of native Russian speakers; their case is that noted above. Otherwise, we are dealing almost exclusively with emigration to various western countries over the last century, and especially its second half; the majority of such emigrants live in English-speaking countries (USA, UK, Canada, Australia), where the effects of contact are rather well documented (for overview see Sussex 1982, 1993). Typically the pattern is that seen in the 'Matrix-Language Frame Model' (Myers-Scotton 1993), with (1) lexical (content) morphemes (of the 'embedded' language) the first to infiltrate the immigrants' speech, followed in the second generation by (2) system (grammatical, morphosyntactic) morphemes, at which point the immigrant language starts to become the second language. Type (1) parallels current developments in Russia, where the influx of English lexical items, especially via the Internet, is having exactly the same results, and one might see in type (2) – as it would operate in an English environment – a parallel to, possibly even a model for, the phenomenon of indeclinable nouns.

4.4   Diglossia

Diglossia ceased to be a viable possibility for Russian with the elaboration of the Russian/Russian Church Slavonic relationship during the eighteenth and nineteenth centuries, before which these two varieties did indeed offer such a relationship (see chapter 1, section 4.3 and above, section 2). Now the high status of the standard ensures that no other variety has any validity. All that is now possible are stylistic alternatives within the one system (e.g. formal/informal, including dialectal usage); or bilingualism (that is, involving two completely different language systems).

4.5   Bilingualism

Most of the recent and current situation in respect of Russian ~ Other bilingualism has been noted above in the discussion of language contact. During the Soviet period, especially in its last forty years, the occurrence of bilingualism diminished greatly, as Russian was promoted as the 'uniting' language of the Union, and the teaching of local languages in many areas virtually stopped. The result was that by 1990, at the time of the break-up, Russian was the only, or at least the only admitted, language of the majority of speakers in most republics, including ethnic non-Russians (cf. LOC/Web); this has produced the strange situation in many FSU countries (except Belarus, see above) that the declared national language is spoken by a *minority* of the population, and in many cases, is incapable of functioning in many required capacities (e.g. administrative, academic, literary). Reimmigration of ethnic emigrants and the emigration of ethnic Russians may help to some extent, but the problem is not one which will be easily or quickly solved. In the meantime, these countries are forced to acknowledge the role that Russian must be allowed to play, that of a major language of use in all public activities, and one which must be retained in schools for some time. Bilingualism will be around for some time to come in all these countries. Somewhat paradoxically, one of the long-term solutions is to persuade or compel ethnic Russians (mainly children, by compulsory schooling) to learn the local (state) language, which they have not had to do before; so the incidence of bilingualism will in fact rise before it declines. Also paradoxically, it is the view of many such ethnic Russians that they are now being discriminated against, and that this is unconstitutional and thus challengeable. Approaches to this problem have varied from the antagonistic (e.g. Kazakhstan, which has actively banned the use of Russian at any public level, and has come up against the problems noted above) to the (relatively) mild (e.g. Latvia, which has declared a phasing-out period for Russian); Ukraine tried the former (antagonistic) approach at first (1991–1993), but this allegedly led to the downfall of President Kravchuk and his replacement (1994) by Kuchma, who favoured equal status for Russian; in the end, the Ukrainian Constitution (1996, Art. 10) still declared Ukrainian the sole official language. No doubt what hurts them all particularly is the knowledge that Russian is going to be a more useful international language than their own, and that eliminating it for ideological reasons may well be counter-productive.

Within the Russian Federation, the situation is essentially the same as in the Soviet period, in spite of the noises being made about the new importance and standing of the local languages (as guaranteed in the Constitution, 1993, Art. 26). Officially the direction is thus towards increased bilingualism, at least among non-Russians. Again, the main problems are the high number of Russian first-language speakers (whether ethnic Russian or not) and the inability of the local language to serve all the necessary social functions; in principle ethnic schooling is now guaranteed, but that requires suitable teachers and textbooks which are not yet available, so again the process of activating the local languages is not a short-term one. Another drawback lies in the administrative system, within which the unit known as the *oblast'* (the largest regional division within a republic) does not necessarily correspond to a particular ethnic grouping, so that groups which are not the titular one of a republic, and who do not have their own 'autonomous region' (*okrug*) within the *oblast'*, find that they have no formal grounds on which to base their ethnic language needs. There are at least 120 ethnic groups in Russia (some say 150, e.g. Sanukov 2000), fitted into 32 'ethnically designated jurisdictions' (21 republics, 1 autonomous *oblast* and 10 *okrugs*), and in most republics the titular group forms less than half of the population, so it can be seen that satisfying the desires of all is not going to be easy.

5   Pragmatics

Many of the central (pre)occupations of pragmatics – insofar as they have distinct formal expression in Russian – are treated within other chapters, for example:

- deixis and anaphora (under 'Pronouns', chapter 3, section 2.1.4; also chapter 4, section 3.2.2.8);
- topic and comment (chapter 4, section 3.4);
- presupposition (context), as the basis for ellipsis (chapter 4, section 3.3);
- the expression of modality, including request, desire, etc. via modal words (chapter 3, sections 2.2.7, 2.3.4), verbal mood (chapter 4, section 3.2.2.5) or intonation (chapter 2, section 3.6);
- and many issues of style have also been noted, though seldom in a formal section.

Other aspects of pragmatics, such as 'implicature' (the implications which lie beneath particular utterances), are logical in nature, with no formal language-based expression.

In this section we shall concentrate on one main topic which is not treated elsewhere, that of speech etiquette, within which we shall observe various features of politeness, formality, and register.

5.1   Speech etiquette

We shall treat here (1) the address system, since it has several rather unique features, and (2) a couple of representative thematic areas (the sociative one of greetings, etc. and the directive/conative one of requests, etc.).

5.1.1   Address (system)
Three aspects of the address system are of interest here: the 2nd person pronoun form, personal name forms, and anonymous name forms.

(1) 2nd person pronouns. Formally, Russian parallels French, in having a Singular (*ты/ty*) and Plur (*вы/vy*) pronoun, the Plural one being used also as a

polite singular. The choice is described as *говорить на «ты» /«вы»/govorit′ na 'ty'/'vy'* 'use *ty* or *vy*' (Fr *tutoyer, vousvoyer*); there is also the low-style verb *тыкать/ty′–kat′* 'use *ty* inappropriately'. The functions are also parallel to French, namely:

(a) *basic:* the Singular is applied (neutrally, or naturally) to family and close friends, to acquaintances within the younger generation (e.g. fellow students), to young children, and to God; and the Plural to adult acquaintances;

(b) *as a mark of relative seniority (age or rank):* the Singular is a mark of junior status of the addressee, the Plural of equal or senior status;

(c) *as a mark of relative formality (of situation):* the Singular marks informality, the Plural formality;

(d) *the Singular may be a mark of disrespect.*

In some cases there is hesitancy, mainly as related to function (c):

• with a person who is normally *ty*, in a formal situation *vy* may be more appropriate, especially in a mixed formal group;

• a switch from *ty* to *vy* may also indicate annoyance (via greater 'distance');

• conversely, a switch from *vy* to *ty* may be (as would certainly be the immediate use of *ty* on first meeting amongst adults) an application of function (d), if it has not been arrived at naturally under function (a). The point at which this last switch occurs is itself often a matter of hesitancy, with many close friends, especially older people, never making it.

(2) Personal names.

(a) First name plus patronymic (имя и отчество/i′m′a i o′tčestvo) (e.g. *Иван Петрович/Iva′n–ø Petr–o′vič–ø, Нина Михайловна/Ni′n–a Mixa′jl–ovn–a*). A Russian feature, uncommon among European languages at least, is the patronymic (derived by suffixation from the father's name; for forms see chapter 5, section 4.2.1), which is not only a formally recognised middle name (e.g. recorded in all documents, from birth certificate on), but used along with the first name as the formal and polite form of address to all adults, on first acquaintance and in formal contexts; it is used particularly by colleagues, at least while at work, and this includes such contexts as journalists addressing the President. This form is also a mark of respect for older persons even in the private domain, for example elderly friends, neighbours, etc.

(b) First name alone, in full form (e.g. *Иван/Iva′n–ø, Олег/Ole′g–ø, Ольга/ O′l′g–a, Нина/Ni′n–a*). This form is used in informal contexts, mainly to less close acquaintances of the same age or younger. If used by a parent or teacher to a child, it is likely to indicate annoyance, since the expected form in that context is one of the following.

(c) First name, in shortened form (e.g. *Ваня/Va′n′–a* (< Ivan), *Оля/O′l′–a* (< Ol′ga)). First, it should be noted that there are some first names – a small

minority – which do not have shortened forms of this sort (e.g. *Ol'eg–ø*, *Nin–a*), meaning that the following functions are for them indistinguishable from the preceding. Others may have more than one form (e.g. *Александр/Aleksa'ndr– ø* > *Саша/Sa'š–a* or *Шура/Šu'r–a*). Some variants are generationally based, e.g. from *Павел/Pa'v(e)l–ø* 'Paul' both *Павлуша/Pavl–u'š–a* and *Павлик/Pa'vl– ik–ø* are now old-fashioned, more common now being *Паша/Pa'š–a*. Furthermore, some of these may be common gender (e.g. the forms *Sa'š–a* and *Šu'r–a* may also be from the female name *Александра/Aleksa'ndr–a*).

This form (always Class II nouns; see chapter 3, section 2.1.3, and chapter 5, section 4.2.1 for formation) is the neutral one used to close friends in informal contexts.

(d) First name affectionate and/or diminutive form (e.g. *Ванечка/Va'n–ečk– a* (< Ivan), *Ниночка/Ni'n–oček–a* (< Nina), *Серёженька/Ser'ož–en'k–a* (< Serge'j)). All names have at least one such derivative, formed from (c) where it exists; the most frequent suffixes are *–oček–a* and *–on'k–a*. They are used mainly to children, thus mainly as diminutive forms (most useful to distinguish between parents and children with the same name, even when the children are adults!), but also as affectionate forms between adults (e.g. spouses, close friends).

(e) First name, pejorative and/or diminutive form (e.g. *Ванька/Va'n'–k–a* (< Ivan), *Нинка/Ni'n–k–a* (< Nina), *Серёжка/Ser'o'ž–k–a* (< Sergej)). Also formed from (c), the suffix here is almost exclusively *–k–a*; these may be neutral, if used amongst young children, but when used by adults they are usually pejorative or indicative of annoyance.

(f) Title plus surname (e.g. *Доктор Смирнов(а)/Do'ktor–ø Smirno'v–ø/a* 'Dr Smirnov(a)'). For native Russian names, this is the only parallel to English (etc.) formal polite usage, there being no equivalent of 'Mr', 'Mrs'. Such forms are used essentially when one does not know the person's name and patronymic; for example, university students will normally know their own professor's name and patronymic and use them, and similarly patients to their own doctor; only 'outsiders' will (have to) use the title form.

For foreign names – that is, attached to foreign persons – Soviet usage continued to use the 'pre-revolutionary' titles *господин/gospodi'n–ø* 'Mr' and *госпожа/gospož–a'* 'Mrs', which were strictly not usable on Russian names. This is still used for foreign names, and there are some attempts at resurrecting it for Russian names in what would be the English context – where one does not know the name and patronymic (see further below); but Russians will normally simply ask the person for this information, then use that form.

The term *товарищ/tova'rišč–ø* 'comrade', used widely in the Soviet period, is now abandoned, at least as a title with surname; at least theoretically, it was used primarily amongst Communist Party members, hence its present unacceptability in this role.

(3) Anonymous address. The contexts in which one needs an address form with
no name attached are varied, but three types may be distinguished:
(a) seeking information, where the requirement is politeness, without any indi-
     cation of relative status, as in the street or a public office (though the latter
     may have aspects of the next);
(b) interaction where there is a discrepancy in status, e.g. shop assistant/
     customer;
(c) attracting attention, which includes giving instructions in public (e.g. by
     police).

In (a) and (c) English speakers are unlikely to use any address form, even
the notionally available *Sir* or *Madam*, since they may appear to endow the
addressee with superiority, whereas the usage of these forms is common in (b),
where relative rank is built in. Compare French, where the equivalent forms
(*Monsieur, Madame*) are widely used in both (a) and (b), as well as (c), being
regarded simply as a mark of respect or politeness. In (a) and (b) Russian
generally now uses no terms of address; in the past either *gospodi'n/gospoža* or
tovarišč were used.

It is only in (c) that some form of address is essential (or at least desirable),
and during the Soviet period, *tovarišč* 'comrade' was a possibility and, though
many resisted it, it was certainly used widely, no doubt on the (pretended)
assumption that everyone was at least a Communist Party sympathiser. A useful
approach was to use it along with an occupational term (e.g. *tova'rišč kondu'ktor*
'conductor'), where the bare term would have been impolite. The plural form is
less unacceptable in reference to a group of friends or colleagues, and even more
acceptable to a group of strangers (e.g. on public transport), but it is probably
also doomed. *Tovarišč* does still survive within the Russian army, used with
terms of rank, e.g. *tova'rišč polko'vnik* 'colonel'.

The plural *gospod–a'* (for form see chapter 3, section 2.1.3.1) – formally
'gentlemen', but in fact common gender, thus 'ladies and gentlemen' – continued to be used in the Soviet period, mainly still for foreigners, though it
found itself converted, in formal contexts, such as diplomatic circles, to *da'm–y
i gospod–a'* 'ladies and gentlemen', no doubt on the French/English model.
Another term similarly marked and restricted to official usage (e.g. by traffic
police), was *graždani'n–ø* 'citizen' (Plur *gra'ždan–e*). There is in fact a greater
variety of plural forms, such as *druz–'ja'* 'friends', *kolle'g–i* 'colleagues' or
reb–'a'ta 'guys' (lit. 'children', used by or to young people).

Alternative singulars existed, and still exist, for young people: *molod–o'j
čelovek–ø* 'young man' and *de'vušk–a* 'young lady, Miss', which were fairly
neutral, and usable for a broad age range (i.e. not just 'young', but rather
'younger' than the speaker); but for older people there was, and is still, no
neutral form: the parallel forms *mužči'n–a* 'man' and *že'nščin–a* 'woman' are
low style or coarse, lacking politeness (similarly to Eng *Mister, Missus*), as are

the age-related terms *de'dušk–a* 'grandfather', *ba'bušk–a* 'grandmother', both used by the young to address old people, and *d'a'd'–a/d'a'd–en'k–a* 'uncle', *t'ot'–a/t'ot–en'k–a* 'aunt(y)', both used by young children to adults. The current situation is still fluid, as nothing has yet filled the gap of *tovarišč* in the neutral, polite style, though efforts at resurrecting *gospodin/gospoža* are frequent (cf. Vershinsky 1998, where it appears in recommendations to the young on etiquette, but with the note that it is slightly official and must be used with a surname or higher occupation); many, especially supporters of women's rights, see its advantage in the different gender forms, unlike the common gender *tovarišč*. Children are addressed neutrally as *ma'l'čik–ø* 'boy' or *de'vočk–a* '(little) girl', in the Plural as *de't–i* or *reb'a't–a* both 'children' (for forms see chapter 3, section 2.1.3.1).

Of course, there are much more coarse forms of address, equivalent to Eng *Hey, you there/you with the beard*, etc., e.g. *Эй, борода!/Ej, borod–a'!* lit. 'Hey, beard!'

5.1.2   Thematic examples of speech etiquette

(1) Meeting. The sociative theme of 'meeting' includes the contexts of making, maintaining and breaking social contact.

Sociative themes are peopled in all languages largely by formulas, many of which are linguistically obsolete remnants, others the result of ellipsis. Examples in Russian are:

(a) Greetings.

	Stylistic level	Linguistic form
Здравствуй(те)/*/zdra'vstvuj(te)* 'hello'	neutral, not time-of-day based	2p Imper 'be well'
(on pronunciation, see chapter 2, sections 3.3.4.2, 3.7.9 and above, section 3.3; the Plural (*–te*) is used to those on a *vy* basis, see above)		
Добрый день/do'br–yj den'–ø 'good day'		
Доброе утро/do'br–oje u'tr–o 'good morning'	all neutral	N/AS (as Eng)
Добрый вечер/do'br–yj ve'čer–ø 'good evening'		
Привет/prive't–ø 'hi, g'day'	informal, esp. young	N/AS 'greeting'
Здорово/zdoro'vo 'hi'	very informal, male	Adv/Adj NSn 'well'

Приветствую/   formal   1ps Pres 'greet'
  prive'tstvuj–u 'welcome'
С приездом/s prije'zd–om   formal   prep ('with') + IS 'arrival'
  'welcome (back)'
  (ellipsis of construction with verb 'congratulate', see chapter 4, section
  3.2.2.9(2))

(b) Follow-up to greeting

	Stylistic level	**Linguistic form**
Как живёшь/живёте? /kak živ'o'š/živ'–o'te 'how are you getting on?'	neutral	2ps/p Pres 'live'
Как (идут) дела?/kak (id–u't)/(ø) del–a'? 'how are things (going)?'	informal	3pp Pres 'go'/'be' + NP 'affair'
Как жизнь?/kak (ø) žizn'–ø 'how's life?'	informal	3ps + NS 'life'
Что нового?/Čto (ø) no'v–ogo?([–əvə]) 'what's new?	informal	Adj GSn 'new'
Как поживаете? /kak poživa'j–ete 'how are you?'	formal, old	2pp Pres 'live'
Нормально/norma'l'no 'fine, pretty good'	informal	Adv 'normal'
Ничего/nič–ego' ([–ɪvɔ']) 'not bad, all right, OK'	informal	Pron GSn 'nothing'
Не жалуюсь/ne ža'luj–u–s' 'can't complain'	informal, older	1ps Pres 'complain'
Всё по-старому/vs'–o (ø) po–sta'r–omu 'nothing new'	informal	'all' + Prep + DSn 'old'
Неважно/neva'žno 'not great, not too good'	informal	Adv 'unimportant'

These are alongside more literal answers like 'good/well', 'bad(ly)', etc., and
more colourful, idiomatic comments (e.g. *Сколько лет, сколько зим!/skol'ko
let–ø, skol'ko zim–ø* 'Long time, no see!' (lit. 'how many summers (GP),
how many winters')), as well as more meaningful questions and answers (e.g.

enquiring about health when this is an actual issue). Since adverbial forms and short neuter adjective forms are usually identical (see chapter 3, section 2.1.5.2), the elliptical answers to either zero-copula structures or other verbs (like 'go') tend to look the same.

(c) Farewells.

	Stylistic level	Linguistic form
Мне пора идти/mn–e ø pora' id–ti' 'It's time I was going.'	neutral	'me' DS + ('be') + 'time' + 'go' Inf
До свидания/do svida'ni–ja ([–a'nʲjə]) 'good-bye'	neutral	Prep ('to') + GSn 'meeting' (cf. Fr *au revoir*)
Прощай(те)/prošča'j(te) 'farewell' (Fr *adieu*)	neutral	2p Imper 'forgive'
Всего доброго/vs–ego' [–ɪvɔ'] *do'br–ogo* ([–əvə]) 'all the best'	neutral	Adj GSn 'all + good'
(the Genitive comes from the understood verb 'wish' – see chapter 4, section 3.2.2.9)		

Всего/vs–ego ''bye, cheers,
    cheerio'
	informal	further ellipsis of
		    preceding

Счастливо/sčastli'vo ''bye, cheers'	informal	Adv 'happ(il)y'
Пока/poka' 'see you (soon)'	informal	Conj 'until'
(ellipsis of verb 'see (again)'; implies expectation of seeing soon (Fr *à toute à l'heure*))		

Увидимся/uvi'd–im–s'a
    'see you soon'
	informal	1pp Fut Pf 'see
		    each other'

Спокойной ночи/spoko'jn–oj
    no'č–i 'good night'
    (Genitive from 'wish').
	neutral	Adj 'peaceful'
		    + N GSf 'night'

In all of these the semantic similarity with English and other European languages is clear. The general content of these formulas is probably universal.

(2) Requests and commands. The conative theme of 'requests and commands' includes the achievement of what one wants (imposition of one's will) by anything from suggestion to abrupt order. The base form is the Imperative, with varying degrees of insistence and politeness indicated either simply by intonation, or also by aspect, or by the addition of particles or other phrases. Here are some examples in approximately decreasing order of abruptness (for intonation contours – 'IK' – see chapter 2, section 3.6):

Intonation (IK-)	Stylistic content	Form

Открывайте окно!/Otkryva'j–te okn–o'. 'Open the window!'

| | IK-2 | urgent demand | 2p Imper Impf 'open' |

Откройте окно!/Otkro'j–te okn–o'. 'Open the window!'

| | IK-2 | order | 2p Imper Pf |

Откройте окно!/Otkro'j–te okn–o'. 'Open the window!'

| | IK-3 | request | 2p Imper Pf |

The last, preceded by 'please', a phrase, or a clause, becomes more polite, e.g.:

> *Пожалуйста, .../Poža'lujsta...* 'please'
> *Будьте добры, .../Bu'd'–te dobr–y'...*
> 2p Imper 'be' + 'good' NP short
> 'Be so kind as to...'
> *Если вам не трудно, .../Jesli v–am ne ∅ tru'dn–o...*
> 'If it's not too much trouble...'
> if – you DP – not – (be) – difficult NSn

Politeness may also be indicated by *prosit'* 'ask' + Inf:

> *(Очень) прошу вас открыть окно./(O'čen') proš–u' v–as otkry'–t' okn–o'.*
> (very much) – ask 1ps Pres – you AP – open Pf Inf – window ASn
> 'I beg you to open the window.'

The addition of the particle *by* further softens a negative request (prohibition):

> *Я попросил бы вас не курить./Ja poprosi'–l_by v–as ne kuri'–t'.*
> I NS – ask Pf Past – (Subjve) – you AP – not – smoke Impf Inf
> 'Might I (I would) ask you not to smoke.'

'Want' may be added in either mood:

> *Я хочу/хотел бы вас попросить.../Ja xoč–u'/xote'–l_by v–as poprosi–t'*
> I – want/would like 1ps Pres/Subjve – you AP – ask Pf Inf
> 'I should like to ask you to...'

The same forms with the particles *ne* (Neg) and/or *li* (Interrog) may be addressed to the other person:

Вы не хотите/хотели бы... ?/Vy ne xoti'–te/xote'–li_by...
'Would(n't) you like to... ?'

Не хотите ли вы... ?/Ne xoti'–te_li vy... 'Would you mind -ing... ?'

'Can' is also available, in similar structures:

Вы можете.../Vy može–te... 'Could you... ?' (2p Pres)

Вы не можете.../vy ne može–te... 'Couldn't you... ?'

Вы не могли бы.../Vy ne mog–li'_by... 'You couldn't..., could you?'

Не могли бы вы.../Ne mog–li'_by vy... 'Could you (by any chance)... ?'

It is also available in requesting permission, all meaning 'May I... ?':

(Не) могу (ли) я.../(Ne) mog–u' (_li) ja... (1ps Pres)

Можно (ли) (мне)... ?/Možn–o (_li) (mn–e)... (Impersonal + Dat)

An informal elliptical form of this omits the main verb, whose exact nature must be divined from the physical context:

Можно книгу?/Možn–o (ø) knig–u? ('book' ASf) 'May/Can I take/ look at this book?'

Official contexts show structures like:

Просьба не курить./Pros'b–a ne kuri'–t'.
request NS – not – smoke Impf Inf
'Please do not smoke/No smoking'.

Позвольте/Разрешите мне.../Pozvol'–te/Razreši'i–te mn–e...
allow/permit 2pp Pf Imper – me DS
'Allow/Permit me to...'

Lastly, the Infinitive may be used for categorical orders, for example in school:

Не разговаривать!/Ne razgova'riva–t'! 'No talking!' (not – talk Impf Inf)

Молчать!/Molča'–t' 'Silence/Shut up!' ('be silent' Impf Inf): low style

Bibliography

Listed in part I are sources in English only, other than dictionaries and basic grammars, for which Russian sources are given also. A full Reference list is given in part II.

I FURTHER READING BY CHAPTER

INTRODUCTION

(a) General background

Auty, R. and Obolensky, D. (eds.) (1976). *An Introduction to Russian History*, Cambridge: Cambridge University Press

Comrie, B. (1981). *The Languages of the Soviet Union*, Cambridge: Cambridge University Press

Paxton, J. (1984). *Companion to Russian History*, Melbourne: Oxford University Press

Rybakov, B. (1965). *Early Centuries of Russian History* (translated from Russian), Moscow: Progress

Strakhovsky, L. I. (ed.) (1949). *A Handbook of Slavic Studies*, Cambridge, Mass: Harvard University Press

(b) Web resources and links

AATSEEL   http://clover.slavic.pitt.edu/~aatseel
Library of Congress Handbook Series/Russia   lcweb2.loc.gov/frd/cs/russia
REES-Web   http://www.ucis.pitt.edu/reesweb
Sher's Links   http://www.websher.net/inx/link.html
University of Texas   http://inic.utexas.edu/reenic.html

(c) General descriptions of Russian

English language

Auty, R. and Obolensky, D. (eds.) (1977). *An Introduction to Russian Language and Literature*, Cambridge: Cambridge University Press

Hart, David K. (1996). *Topics in the Structure of Russian*, Columbus, Ohio: Slavica

Maltzoff, N. (1965). *Russian Reference Grammar*, New York: Pitman

Offord, Derek (1996). *Using Russian*, Cambridge: Cambridge University Press

Pulkina, I. M. (n.d.). *A Short Russian Reference Grammar*, Moscow: Progress

Unbegaun, B. O. (1957). *Russian Grammar*, Oxford: Clarendon

Wade, Terence (1992). *A Comprehensive Russian Grammar*, Oxford: Blackwell (2nd rev. edn 2000)

Ward, Dennis (1965). *The Russian Language Today*, London: Hutchinson

364   Bibliography

Russian language
Academy Grammar 1960. *Grammatika russkogo jazyka* [Grammar of Russian],
Moscow: IAN (3 vols: Phonology/Morphology/Word-formation Vol. I; Syntax
Vols II–III)
Academy Grammar 1970. *Grammatika sovremennogo russkogo literaturnogo jazyka*
[Grammar of Contemporary Standard Russian], Moscow: Nauka (1 vol)
Academy Grammar 1980. *Russkaja grammatika* [Russian Grammar], Moscow: Nauka
(2 vols.: Phonology/Morphology/Word-formation Vol. I; Syntax Vol. II)

(d) Dictionaries
Bilingual English/Russian
Axmanova, O. S. and Wilson, E. (1987). *Russko-anglijskij slovar'* [Russian–English
Dictionary], 34th rev. edn, Moscow: Russkij jazyk
Falla, P. and Wheeler, M. (1994). *The Oxford Russian Dictionary*, Oxford: Oxford
University Press (1 vol., both directions)
Gal'perin, I. R. (1987–88). *Bol'šoj anglo-russkij slovar'* [Larger English–Russian
Dictionary], 4th edn, Moscow: Soviet Encyclopaedia (2 vols.)
Lubensky, Sophia (1995). *Russian–English Dictionary of Idioms*, New York: Random
House
Marder, Stephen (1992). *A Supplementary Russian–English Dictionary*, Columbus,
Ohio: Slavica
Mjuller, V. K. (1987). *Anglo-russkij slovar'* [English–Russian Dictionary], 21st rev.
edn, Moscow: GIINS
Smirnickij, A. I. (1991). *Russko-anglijskij slovar'* [Russian–English Dictionary], 16th
rev. edn, Moscow: GIINS
Wilson, Elizabeth A. M. (1982). *The Modern Russian Dictionary for English Speakers
(English–Russian)*, Oxford: Pergamon and Moscow: Russkij jazyk

Monolingual Russian (explanatory)
Ožegov, S. E. (1972). *Slovar' russkogo jazyka* [Dictionary of Russian], 4th rev. edn,
Moscow: Soveckaja Ènciklopedija (1968 edn online at http://www.slovari.ru/
lang/ru/ivoc/oj/index.html)
Ožegov, S. E. and Švedova, N. Ju. (1999). *Tolkovyj slovar' russkogo jazyka* [Explan-
atory Dictionary of Russian], 4th rev. edn, Moscow: Azbukovnik (online at
http://www.slovari.ru/lang/ru/ivoc/ojsh/index.html)

Special Russian
Ageenko, F. L. and Zarva, M. V. (1984). *Slovar' udarenij dlja rabotnikov radio i televi-
denija* [Dictionary of Stress for Radio and Television Staff], 5th rev. edn, Moscow:
Russkij jazyk
Lopatin, V. V. et al. (1999). *Russkij orfografičeskij slovar'* [Russian Orthographical
Dictionary], Moscow: Azbukovnik (online at http://www.slovari.ru/lang/ru/ivoc/
orfo/index.html
Avanesov, R. I. (1989). *Orfoèpičeskij slovar' russkogo jazyka* [Orthoepic Dictionary of
Russian] (= 5th rev. edn of Pron. Dict. 1960), Moscow: Russkij jazyk
Vasmer: Fasmer, M. (1964–73). *Etimologičeskij slovar' russkogo jazyka*, Moscow:
Progress (4 vols.)

Zaliznjak, A. A. (1980). *Grammatičeskij slovar' russkogo jazyka* [Grammatical Dictionary of Russian], Moscow: Russkij jazyk

CHAPTER 1 HISTORY

(a) Slavonic background
Bidwell, Charles E. (1963). *Slavic Historical Phonology in Tabular Form*, The Hague: Mouton
Carlton, Terence R. (1990). *Introduction to the Phonological History of the Slavic Languages*, Columbus, Ohio: Slavica
Comrie, Bernard and Corbett, Greville G. (eds.) (1993). *The Slavonic Languages*, London: Routledge
de Bray, R. G. A. (1980). *Guide to the East Slavonic Languages*, Columbus, Ohio: Slavica (Vol. III of 3 vols.)
Entwistle, W. J. and Morison, W. A. (1949). *Russian and the Slavonic Languages*, London: Faber and Faber
Gołąb, Zbigniew (1992). *The Origins of the Slavs: a Linguist's View*, Columbus, Ohio: Slavica
Jakobson, Roman (1955). *Slavic Languages: a Condensed Survey*, 2nd edn, New York: King's Crown
Picchio, R. and Goldblatt, H. (eds.) (1984). *Aspects of the Slavic Language Question*. 2 vols., New Haven: Yale CIAS and Columbus, Ohio: Slavica
Schenker, A. M. and Stankiewicz, E. (eds.) (1980). *The Slavic Literary Languages: Formation and Development*, New Haven: Yale CIAS (Russian: pp. 119–142)
Schenker, A. M. (1995). *The Dawn of Slavic: an Introduction to Slavic Philology*, New Haven: Yale University Press
Stone, Gerald and Worth, Dean (eds.) (1985). *The Formation of the Slavonic Literary Languages*, Columbus, Ohio: Slavica
Townsend, C. E. and Janda, L. A. (1996). *Common and Comparative Slavic: Phonology and Inflection*, Columbus, Ohio: Slavica
Velcheva, B. (1988). Proto-Slavic and Old Bulgarian Sound Changes, Columbus, Ohio: Slavica (translation by E. Scatton from Bulgarian of 1980)

(b) History of Russian
Kiparsky, V. (1979). *Russian Historical Grammar*, Vol. I: *The Development of the Sound System*, Ardis: Ann Arbor (translation and revision of original: *Russische historische Grammatik*, Heidelberg: Carl Winter, 1963)
Matthews, W. K. (1953). *The Structure and Development of Russian*, Cambridge: Cambridge University Press
Vlasto, A. P. (1986). *Linguistic History of Russia to the End of the Eighteenth Century*, Oxford: Clarendon
Worth, Dean (1983). *The Origins of Russian Grammar*, Columbus, Ohio: Slavica

CHAPTER 2 PHONOLOGY

Avanesov, R. I. (1964). *Modern Russian Stress* (translated from Russian), Oxford: Pergamon
Boyanus, S. (1955) (Repr. 1965). *Russian Pronunciation*. London: Lund Humphries

Hamilton, W. S. (1980). *Introduction to Russian Phonology and Word Structure.* Columbus, Ohio: Slavica
Jones, D. and Ward, D. (1969). *The Phonetics of Russian.* Cambridge: Cambridge University Press
Nicholson, J. G. (1968). *Russian Normative Stress Notation*, Montreal: McGill University Press

CHAPTER 3 MORPHOLOGY

Dessaix, R. and Travers, M. (1994). *A Practical Handbook of Russian Aspect*, Canberra: AGPS
Durst-Andersen, P. (1992). *Mental Grammar: Russian Aspect and Related Issues*, Columbus, Ohio: Slavica
Forsyth, J. (1963). *A Practical Guide to Russian Stress*, Edinburgh: Oliver and Boyd
  (1970). *A Grammar of Aspect*, Cambridge: Cambridge University Press
Levin, Maurice I. (1978). *Russian Declension and Conjugation*, Columbus, Ohio: Slavica
Muravyova, L. (n.d.). *Verbs of Motion in Russian*, Moscow: Progress
Murphy, A. B. (1965). *Aspectival Usage in Russian*, Oxford: Pergamon
Vasilenko, E. et al. (1982). *Russian Verb Aspects*, Moscow: Russkij jazyk
Vilgelminina, A. (1963). *The Russian Verb: Aspect and Voice*, Moscow: Foreign Languages Press

CHAPTER 4 SYNTAX

Bivon, R. (1971). *Element Order*, Cambridge: Cambridge University Press
Borras, F. M. and Christian, R. F. (1977). *Russian Syntax: Aspects of Modern Russian Syntax and Vocabulary*, 2nd edn, Oxford: Clarendon
Krylova, O. and Xavronina, S. (1988). *Word Order in Russian* (English version of 1976 original), 2nd edn, Moscow: Russkij jazyk

CHAPTER 5 WORD-FORMATION AND LEXICOLOGY

Bratus, B. V. (1969). *The Formation and Expressive Use of Diminutives* (Studies in the Modern Russian Language 6), Cambridge: Cambridge University Press
Cubberley, Paul (1994). *Handbook of Russian Affixes*, Columbus, Ohio: Slavica
Gribble, Charles (1973). *Russian Root List*, Cambridge, Mass.: Slavica
Kiselyova, L. A. et al. (n.d.). *A Practical Handbook of Russian Style: Words, Phrases, Derivation*, Moscow: Progress
Norbury, J. K. W. (1967). *Word Formation in the Noun and Adjective* (Studies in the Modern Russian Language 3), Cambridge: Cambridge University Press
Shanskij, N. M. (1968). *Russian Word Formation* (translated from Russian), Oxford: Pergamon
Townsend, Charles E. (1975). *Russian Word-Formation*, 2nd edn, Cambridge, Mass.: Slavica

CHAPTER 6 DIALECTS

Avanesov R. I. and Orlova, V. G. (1966). *Russian Dialectology*, Washington: JPRS (translation of 2nd edn of 1964)

Matthews, W. K. (1953). *The Structure and Development of Russian*, Cambridge: Cambridge University Press (pp. 86–106)

CHAPTER 7 SOCIOLINGUISTICS

Comrie, Bernard and Stone, Gerald (1978). *The Russian Language since the Revolution*, Oxford: Clarendon

Comrie, Bernard, Stone, Gerald and Polinsky, Maria (1996). *The Russian Language in the 20th Century*, Oxford: Clarendon (= rev. edn of Comrie and Stone 1978)

Jones, T. R. and Stupin, L. P. (1970). *Guide to Modern Russian Speech Etiquette*, Melbourne: University of Melbourne, Department of Russian

Kirkwood, Michael (ed.) (1989). *Language Planning in the Soviet Union*, London: Macmillan

Ryazanova-Clarke, Larissa and Wade, Terence (1999). *The Russian Language Today*, London/New York: Routledge

II REFERENCES

Academy Grammar (1960). *Grammatika russkogo jazyka* [Grammar of Russian], Moscow: IAN (3 vols.: Phonology/Morphology/Word-formation Vol. I; Syntax Vols. II–III.)

Academy Grammar (1970). *Grammatika sovremennogo russkogo literaturnogo jazyka* [Grammar of Contemporary Standard Russian], Moscow: Nauka

Academy Grammar (1980). *Russkaja grammatika* [Russian Grammar], Moscow: Nauka (2 vols.: Phonology/Morphology/Word-formation Vol. I; Syntax Vol. II)

Adodurov, V. E. (1738–40). Russian version of his *Anfangs-Gründe der Rußischen Sprache* (1731). Ms., Moscow

Apres'jan, Ju. D. (1973). *Principles and Methods of Contemporary Structural Linguistics*, The Hague: Mouton

  (1992). *Lexical Semantics,* Ann Arbor: Karoma

  (2000). *Syntactic Lexicography*, Oxford/New York: Oxford University Press

Atlas (1915): Šaxmatov, A. A. (ed.). *Opyt dialektologičeskoj karty russkogo jazyka v Evrope* [Tentative Dialect Map of Russian in Europe], Moscow: Mosk. Dial. Komissija

Atlas (1957): Avanesov, R. I. (ed.). *Atlas russkix narodnyx govorov central'nyx oblastej k vostoku ot Moskvy* [Atlas of the Russian Dialects of the Central Regions to the East of Moscow], Moscow: IAN (2 vols. – text and maps)

Atlas (1986): Avanesov, R. I. and Bromlej, S. V. (eds.). *Dialektologičeskij atlas russkogo jazyka: centr evropejskoj časti SSSR* [Dialect Atlas of Russian: the Centre of the European Part of the USSR], Moscow: Nauka (3 vols., 1986–89)

Avanesov R. I. and Orlova, V. G. (1964). *Russkaja dialektologija* [Russian Dialectology], Moscow: Nauka

  (1966). *Russian Dialectology*, Washington: JPRS (translation of 2nd edn of 1964)

BelaPAN (Belarusian Information Company at http://www.belapan.com) (1999). 'Only 11.2% of Minsk's secondary school students were taught in Belarusian in 1998/99', *Online news* 95, 22 June

Bivon, R. (1971). *Element Order*, Cambridge: Cambridge University Press

BLS/Web. Belarusian Language Society at http://tbm.org.by

Bondarko, L. V. (1977). *Zvukovoj stroj sovremennogo russkogo jazyka* [The Sound Structure of Modern Russian], Moscow: Prosveščenie

Borras, F. M. and Christian, R. F. (1971/1977). *Russian Syntax: Aspects of Modern Russian Syntax and Vocabulary*, 2nd edn, Oxford: Clarendon

Boyanus, S. (1955) (repr. 1965). *Russian Pronunciation*. London: Lund Humphries

Bryzgunova, E. A. (1963). *Praktičeskaja fonetika i intonacija russkogo jazyka* [Practical Phonetics and Intonation of Russian], Moscow: IMU

(1969/1977). *Zvuki i intonacija russkogo jazyka* [The Sounds and Intonation of Russian], Moscow: Russkij jazyk

(1977). 'Analiz russkoj dialektnoj intonacii' [Analysis of Russian Dialectal Intonation], in Vysockij 1977: 231–62

Catford, J. C. (1965). *A Linguistic Theory of Translation*, London: Oxford University Press

Channon, Robert (1975). 'The single-stem verb system revisited', *Slavic and East European Journal* 19, 1: 112–22

Chomsky, N. and Halle, M. (1968). *The Sound Pattern of English*, New York: Harper and Row

Chvany, Catherine V. (1982). 'Hierarchies in the Russian case system: for NAGPDI, against NGDAIP', *Russian Language Journal* 36, 125: 133–47

Comrie, B. (1981). *The Languages of the Soviet Union*, Cambridge: Cambridge University Press

Comrie, Bernard and Corbett, Greville G. (eds.) (1993). *The Slavonic Languages*, London: Routledge

Comrie, Bernard, and Stone, Gerald (1978). *The Russian Language since the Revolution*, Oxford: Clarendon

Comrie, Bernard, Stone, Gerald and Polinsky, Maria (1996) *The Russian Language in the 20th Century*, Oxford: Clarendon (= rev. edn of Comrie and Stone 1978)

Cubberley, Paul (1987). 'Stress patterns in high-frequency Russian nouns and verbs', *Russian Language Journal* 41, 138/139: 31–44

(1993). 'The phonological dynamics of foreign borrowings in Russian', *Australian Slavonic and East European Studies* 7(1): 49–74

(1994). *Handbook of Russian Affixes*, Columbus, Ohio: Slavica

Fedjanina, N. A. (1976). *Udarenie v sovremennom russkom jazyke* [Stress in Modern Russian], Moscow: Russkij jazyk

Gallant, James (1979). *Russian Verbal Prefixes and Semantic Features: an Analysis of the Prefix vz-*, Munich: Sagner

Gamkrelidze, T. V. and Ivanov, V. V. (1995). *Indo-European and the Indo-Europeans* (tr. from Russian), Berlin/New York: de Gruyter

Garde, Paul (1976). *Histoire de l'accentuation slave*, Paris: Institut des Etudes Slaves

Gladkij, A. V. (1978). *Formal Grammars and Languages*, Amsterdam/New York: North Holland

Gladkij, A. V. and Mel'chuk, I. (1983). *Elements of Mathematical Linguistics*, Berlin/New York: Mouton

Gorbačevič, K. S. (ed.) (1973). *Trudnosti slovoupotreblenija i varianty norm russkogo literaturnogo jazyka. Slovar'-spravochnik* [Problems of Lexical Usage and Variation of Norms in Standard Russian], Leningrad

(1978). *Variantnost' slova i jazykovaja norma* [Word-level Variation and the Norm in Language], Leningrad: Nauka

Gribble, Charles (1973). *Russian Root List*, Cambridge, Mass.: Slavica

Halle, Morris (1971). *The Sound Pattern of Russian: a Linguistic and Acoustical Investigation*, The Hague: Mouton

Hart, David K. (1996). *Topics in the Structure of Russian*, Columbus, Ohio: Slavica

Jakobson, R. and Halle, M. (1956). *Fundamentals of Language*, The Hague: Mouton

Jakobson, R., Fant, C. G. M. and Halle, M. (1952). *Preliminaries to Speech Analysis*, Cambridge, Mass.: MIT Press

Jakobson, Roman (1936). 'Contribution to the General Theory of Case: general meanings of Russian cases', in L. R. Waugh and M. Halle (eds.) *Roman Jakobson: Russian and Slavic Grammar*, Berlin/New York: Mouton, 1984: 59–103

(1948). 'Russian conjugation', *Word* 4: 155–67

Jakovenko, N. P. (1966). *Slovesnoe udarenie v sovremennom russkom literaturnom jazyke* [Word Stress in CSR], Kiev: IKU

James, Richard (1618–19). (Russian–English Dictionary) Ms., Oxford. Published in: *Russko-anglijskij slovar'-dnevnik Ričarda Džejmsa (1618–1619 gg.)* [The Russian–English Dictionary–Diary of Richard James (1618–1619)], Leningrad, 1959

Janda, Laura (1986). *Semantic Analysis of the Russian Verbal Prefixes: za-, pere-, do- and ot-*, Munich: Sagner

Jażdżewski, Konrad (1948). *Atlas to the Prehistory of the Slavs*, Łódź: LTN

Jones, D. and Ward, D. (1969). *The Phonetics of Russian*. Cambridge: Cambridge University Press

Kasatkin, L. L. (1989). *Russkaja dialektologija* [Russian Dialectology], 2nd rev. edn, Moscow: Prosveščenie

Keijsper, C. E. (1992). 'Recent intonation research and its implications for teaching Russian', in A.A. Barentsen et al. (eds.) *Studies in Russian Linguistics*, Amsterdam: Rodopi, pp. 151–214

Kiparsky, V. (1979). *Russian Historical Grammar*, Vol. I: *The Development of the Sound System*, Ardis: Ann Arbor (translation and revision of original: *Russische historische Grammatik*, Heidelberg: Carl Winter, 1963)

Kirkwood, Michael (ed.) (1989). *Language Planning in the Soviet Union*, London: Macmillan

Kiselyova, L. A. et al. (n.d.). *A Practical Handbook of Russian Style: Words, Phrases, Derivation*, Moscow: Progress

Kolesov, V. V. (1990). *Russkaja dialektologija* [Russian Dialectology], Moscow: Vysšaja škola

Krysin, L. P. (ed.) (1974). *Russkij jazyk po dannym massovogo issledovanija* [Russian According to the Data of Large-scale Investigation], Moscow: Nauka

Kuznecov, P. S. (1973). *Russkaja dialektologija* [Russian Dialectology], Moscow: Prosveščenie

Levin, Maurice I. (1978). *Russian Declension and Conjugation*, Columbus, Ohio: Slavica

LOC/Web. *Library of Congress Handbook Series/ Russia* at http://lcweb2.loc.gov/frd/cs/russia

Lomonosov, M. V. (1755/1757). *Rossijskaja grammatika*, Sankt-Peterburg: Akademija Nauk (published 1755, but title page has 1757)

(1757). *Predislovie o pol'ze knig cerkovnyx v rossijskom jazyke* [Preface on the Use of Church Books for Russian], Moscow: Moscow University

Ludolf, H. (1959). *Grammatica Russica (1696)*, Oxford: Clarendon

Lyons, John (1968). *Introduction to Theoretical Linguistics*, Cambridge: Cambridge University Press

Machill, M. (1997). 'Background to French language policy and the impact in the media', *European Journal of Communication* 12, 4: 479–509

Matthews, W. K. (1953). *The Structure and Development of Russian*, Cambridge: Cambridge University Press

Mazon, André (1963). *Grammaire de la langue russe*, 4th edn, Paris: IES, pp. 282–311

Myers Scotton, C. (1993). *Duelling Languages: Grammatical Structure in Codeswitching*, Oxford: Clarendon

Neidle, Carol J. (1982). 'Case agreement in Russian', in J. W. Bresnan (ed.) *The Mental Representation of Grammatical Relations*, Cambridge, Mass.: MIT Press, 391–404

Norbury, J. K. W. (1967). *Word Formation in the Noun and Adjective* (Studies in the Modern Russian Language 3), Cambridge: Cambridge University Press

Odé, C. (1989). *Russian Intonation: a Perceptual Analysis*, Amsterdam: Rodopi

Offord, Derek (1996). *Using Russian*, Cambridge: Cambridge University Press

Orth. Dict. 1984. Barxudarov, S. G. et al. *Orfografičeskij slovar' russkogo jazyka* [Orthographical Dictionary of Russian], 21st rev. edn, Moscow: Russkij jazyk

Orth. Dict. 1999. Lopatin, V. V. *Russkij orfografičeskij slovar'* [Russian Orthographical Dictionary], Moscow: Azbukovnik (online at http://www.slovari.ru/lang/ru/ivoc/orfo/index.html

Ožegov, S. E. (1972). *Slovar' russkogo jazyka* [Dictionary of Russian], 4th rev. edn, Moscow: Soveckaja Ènciklopedija

Ožegov, S. E. and Švedova, N. Ju. (1999). *Tolkovyj slovar' russkogo jazyka* [Explanatory Dictionary of Russian], 4th rev. edn, Moscow: Azbukovnik (online at http://www.slovari.ru/lang/ru/ivoc/ojsh/index.html)

Picchio, R. and Goldblatt, H. (eds.) (1984). *Aspects of the Slavic Language Question*. 2 vols., New Haven: Yale CIAS

Pron. Dict. 1960/1965. Avanesov, R. I. and Ožegov, S. I. (eds.) *Russkoe literaturnoe proiznošenie i udarenie* [Russian Standard Pronunciation and Stress], Moscow: GIINS

Pron. Dict. 1983. Avanesov, R. I. (ed.) *Orfoèpičeskij slovar' russkogo jazyka* [Orthoepic Dictionary of Russian] (= rev. edn of Pron. Dict. 1960), Moscow: Russkij jazyk

Pron. Dict. 1989. Avanesov, R. I. (ed.) *Orfoèpičeskij slovar' russkogo jazyka* [Orthoepic Dictionary of Russian] (= 5th rev. edn of Pron. Dict. 1960), Moscow: Russkij jazyk

Renfrew, Colin (1987). *Archaeology and Language: the Puzzle of Indo-European Origins*, London: Penguin

Revzin, I. I. (1966). *Models of Language*, London: Methuen

Ridley, Mark (1996). *A Dictionarie of the vulgar Russe tongue (1594–99)* ed. with Introduction by Gerald Stone, Köln: Böhlau

Ryazanova-Clarke, Larissa and Wade, Terence (1999). *The Russian Language Today*, London/New York: Routledge

Rybakov, B. (1965). *Early Centuries of Russian History* [translated from Russian], Moscow: Progress

Sanukov, X. (2000). 'Human rights problems in Russia: the situation of non-Russian peoples', online conference paper at http://www.suri.ee/kongress/sanukov.html

Sauvage, Jean (1586). *Dictionnaire Moscovite*, Ms., Paris

Schenker, A. M. (1995). *The Dawn of Slavic: an Introduction to Slavic Philology*, New Haven: Yale University Press

Shevelov, G. Y. (1964). *A Prehistory of Slavic*, Heidelberg: Carl Winter

Smotrickij, M. (1619). *Grammatiki Slavenskija pravilnoe Syntagma* [The Correct Structure of Slavonic Grammar], Evje; (1648) Moscow (same title, author not named)

Stokes, A. D. (1976). 'Kievan Russia', in R. Auty and D. Obolensky (eds.) *An Introduction to Russian History*, Cambridge: Cambridge University Press, pp. 49–77

Sussex, Roland (ed.) (1982). *The Slavic Languages in Emigre Communities*, Carbondale/Edmonton: Linguistic Research

(1993). 'Slavonic languages in emigration', in Comrie and Corbett 1993: 999–1036

Townsend, Charles E. (1968/1975). *Russian Word-Formation*, 2nd edn, Cambridge, Mass.: Slavica

(1974). *Continuing with Russian*, New York: McGraw-Hill

Unbegaun, B. O. (1957/1962). *Russian Grammar*, Oxford: Clarendon

Uspenskij, B. A. (1975). *Pervaja russkaja grammatika na rodnom jazyke* [The First Russian Grammar Written in Russian], Moscow: Nauka

van Schooneveld, C. H. (1978). *Semantic Transmutations: Prolegomena to a Calculus of Meaning*, Bloomington, Ind.: Physsardt

Vershinsky, Anatoly (1998). 'Celesoobraznost′ bolee vysokogo porjadka' [Expediency of a Higher Order], *Tekhnika-Molodëži* 5 (online at http://www.aha.ru)

Vysockij, S. S. (ed.) (1977). *Èksperimental′no-foneticeskie issledovanija v oblasti russkoj dialektologii* [Experimental Phonetic Research in Russian Dialectology], Moscow: Nauka

Wade, Terence (1992). *A Comprehensive Russian Grammar*, Oxford: Blackwell

Ward, Dennis (1965). *The Russian Language Today*, London: Hutchinson

Zaliznjak, A. A. (1980). *Grammaticeskij slovar′ russkogo jazyka* [Grammatical Dictionary of Russian], Moscow: Russkij jazyk

Zaxarova, K. F. and Orlova, V. G. (1970). *Dialektnoe clenenie russkogo jazyka* [The Dialectal Segmentation of Russian], Moscow: Prosveščenie

Index

abbreviations, 83, 84–6, 120, 194, 271–4, 343
Académie française, 46
Academy Grammars, 67, 90, 111, 335, 342
Academy of Sciences, 15, 46, 47, 48, 100, 335
acronyms, 85–6, 271, 273–4, 343
address system, 354
  2nd person, 354–5
  anonymous address, 357
  names, 355–6
  titles, 356
adjectives, 31, 42, 69, 242
  declension, 130–1
  derived from adjectives, 297
  derived from nouns, 294
  derived from other categories, 299
  derived from verbs, 298
  indeclinable, 135, 178
  normal (long) forms, 131, 133, 212
  phrases, 271
  possessive, 118, 134, 296
  predicative, 42, 133–4, 136, 170
  qualitative, 265–6, 293, 298
  relative, 265–6, 294, 299
  short forms, 133, 212
  special adjectival declension, 134
  substantivised, 135, 145, 262
adjuncts, *see* adverbs
Adodurov, 47, 100
adverbial/adjunct clauses, 242
  cause, 244–5
  concession, 249–50
  condition, 247–9
  degree, 250–2
  manner, 246–7
  place, 244
  purpose, 245–6
  result, 230
  time, 242–4
adverbs/adjuncts, 169, 214, 216
  comparative, 170

formation, 169, 262–3
  relative, 241
affixation, 263
  affix boundary, 81, 274
  affixes, 102, 106, 107, 152, 257, 260, 278–9
agreement (concord) between subject and verb, 193–6
akan'je, 41, 316–7, 323
  types, 317
Aleksandr Nevskij, 14
allegation, 236
allomorphs, 103
allophones, 53, 63, 65–6, 69–73, 76–7, 80
alphabet
  old, 46, 48–52
  modern, 95–6, 99
alternations, 26–9, 33, 41
  see also morphophonology
analogy, 29, 41, 59
analyticity, 42, 329, 346
animacy, 31, 110–12, 115–21, 128, 330
Andrej Bogoljubskij, 13
anomalous forms, 110–11, 154
  see also dialects
antecedent, 238, 240, 241
antonyms, 308
apposition, 180, 194
Askold and Dir, 12
aspect, 32, 150–1
  formation, 93, 151–3, 349
aspirated stops (IE), 17
assimilation, 59, 60, 73–80, 85, 93, 98, 321, 330
  progressive assimilation, 29, 33, 321
  regressive assimilation, 34, 60, 69, 73
asyndetic clauses, 228, 229, 231, 233, 245, 247–8
athematic verbs, 38, 147, 303
attributive/relative clauses, 161, 238
  'restrictive' and 'non-restrictive'
attributes, 239–40
Avanesov/Orlova, 313

palatals, 27, 30, 32, 33, 39, 40, 56, 60, 65,
66, 79–80, 87–8, 276, 319
plosives/stops, 55
sonorants, 23–6, 56, 74, 75; syllabic
sonorants, 17, 24, 31, 76;
velars, 17, 19, 20, 41, 56, 87, 93, 122, 276,
277, 320–1; soft velars, 41, 61–5, 77,
78, 89
word-final, 21, 60, 73–8, 82, 99, 121
see also devoicing
Constantine, 48, 49
Constantinople, 14
contact, 5, 11, 15, 332, 350–4
contextual changes, *see* phonotactics
contraction, 36
contrast, 90, 172, 225
copula, 43, 190, 193, 197, 206–8, 210–4,
237, 329
Cossack Host, 15
creation of words, 258
Croatia, 6
Croatian, 6, 23, 24, 28, 52, 74, 331
Cubberley, 83, 123, 287
current developments in CSR, 336ff.
Cyril, *see* Constantine
Cyrillic, 49–51, 53, 54, 95–6, 334, 335
Czech, 5, 6, 20, 23, 24, 54, 335

Daniil, 14
de-affixation, 267–9
see also zero suffix
Decembrist poets, 333
declension, *see* nouns: classification
deep structure, 226
definiteness, 31, 42, 133, 179, 216, 330–1
derivational morphology, 102, 255
devoicing, 40, 60, 75–6, 98, 319
dialects, 16, 17, 39–40, 313ff.
diaspora, 352
diglossia, 332, 352
diphthongs, 19, 22–6, 34, 37, 165,
318
see also monophthongisation
direct speech, 252
dissimilation, 82, 88, 156, 157, 337
distinctive features, 57–9, 64, 66, 69,
110
distributional limitations, 66, 73–83
dual, *see* number
duration, *see* vocalic quantity

Efimov, 45
ekan'je, 92, 316, 337
ellipsis, 91, 92, 94, 115, 354, 359, 360
emphasis, 90, 172, 203, 209

enclitic, *see* clitics
ending, 106, 115–17
zero ending, 107, 121, 123, 143, 158
epenthesis, 25, 34
etymology, 257
exclamations, 90–2, 224
see also sentence, types of utterance

factitive, 305, 306
Fedjanina, 123, 166
fleeting vowels, 41, 59
Fonvisin, 46
foreign sources of lexicon, 309
foreign words/elements, 60, 65, 72– 3, 81,
83–4, 94, 118, 122, 259, 319, 333
fugitive vowels, *see* fleeting vowels
function words, 256

Gamkrelidze/Ivanov, 5
Garde, 18
geminate/long consonants, 80–4, 338
geminate vowels, 321
gender, 31, 42, 95, 108–11, 119–20, 123,
156, 177, 193–4, 324, 330, 342–4
common gender, 342
generative grammar, *see* transformational
grammar
Gimbutas, 4
Glagolitic, 49, 51
glides, 70
Gorbačevič, 341, 348
Gorškov, 45
graždanskij šrift, *see* civil script
Grand Prince, 13, 14
graphics, 48, 52, 95–9, 177
see also orthography
Gribble, 282, 287

Halle, 8, 57, 58
hard sign, 79, 95, 98, 339
hard ~ soft consonants, 39, 40, 66, 77–9,
89, 93, 122, 277, 278, 338
see also palatalised consonants
Hesychasm, 14
homographs, 68, 105, 307
homonyms, 68, 119, 307
homophones, 105, 307

idioms, 359
IK (*intonacionnaja konstrukcija*), *see*
intonation, contours
ikan'je, 316
imperative, 42, 157–9, 192, 200–1, 248,
360, 361
impersonal sentences, 189, 204, 217, 218